FORENSIC MENTAL HEALTH ASSESSMENT OF CHILDREN AND ADOLESCENTS

Forensic Mental Health Assessment of Children and Adolescents

EDITED BY

Steven N. Sparta
Gerald P. Koocher

OXFORD
UNIVERSITY PRESS

2006

OXFORD
UNIVERSITY PRESS

Oxford University Press, Inc., publishes works that further
Oxford University's objective of excellence
in research, scholarship, and education.

Oxford   New York
Auckland   Cape Town   Dar es Salaam   Hong Kong   Karachi
Kuala Lumpur   Madrid   Melbourne   Mexico City   Nairobi
New Delhi   Shanghai   Taipei   Toronto

With offices in
Argentina   Austria   Brazil   Chile   Czech Republic   France   Greece
Guatemala   Hungary   Italy   Japan   Poland   Portugal   Singapore
South Korea   Switzerland   Thailand   Turkey   Ukraine   Vietnam

Copyright © 2006 by Oxford University Press, Inc.

Published by Oxford University Press, Inc.
198 Madison Avenue, New York, New York 10016

www.oup.com

Oxford is a registered trademark of Oxford University Press

Library of Congress Cataloging-in-Publication Data
Forensic mental health assessment of children and adolescents /
edited by Steven N. Sparta, Gerald P. Koocher.
     p. cm.
Includes bibliographical references.
ISBN-13 978-0-19-514584-7

1. Behavioral assessment of children.   2. Behavioral assessment
of teenagers.   3. Forensic psychology.   4. Mental illness—Diagnosis.
I. Sparta, Steven N.   II. Koocher, Gerald P.
[DNLM: 1. Forensic Psychiatry—methods—Child.   2. Forensic
Psychiatry—methods—Adolescent.   3. Personality Assessment—Child.
4. Personality Assessment—Adolescent.   5. Mental Disorders—diagnosis—Child.
6. Mental Disorders—diagnosis—Adolescent. W 740 F714245 2006]
RJ503.5.F67 2006
614'.15—dc22   2005020333

Dedicated to my favorite child, Abby Greenwald Koocher
—GPK

The editors also wish to dedicate this volume to the memory of William N. Friedrich, Ph.D., who died just prior to its publication. Bill was a person of great character, with boundless energy, always modest and unassuming, and his contributions to the study of child abuse were enormously significant. His assessment instruments and writings will doubtless have an enduring influence in the field. In the face of increasing debilitation from cancer and on entering hospice, he wrote to many friends and colleagues, "Thanks for being the friends that you have been, the type of people who do things for others that make me smile about and be pleased with the fact that we are colleagues." He had graciously responded to editorial requests for updated citations and other chapter information within days of his death, never once mentioning his illness or its seriousness. Words cannot adequately convey our respect for Bill and how his exemplary personhood and career will live on in our hearts.

Foreword

Long before there was a field of forensic psychology, or psychiatry or social work, mental health professionals performed forensic mental health assessments for juvenile courts. Soon after Chicago inaugurated the first juvenile court in 1899, a psychologist and a neurologist developed a juvenile court clinic to serve it (Napoli, 1981; Jones, 1999), and the process was repeated in city after city during the first quarter of the 20th century. Juvenile court clinicians provided their judges mental health information related largely to questions of "disposition" (how to best meet a wayward youth's psychological needs), as they still do today. But across the years, these assessment services expanded to assist in adjudicating child and family welfare issues (abuse and neglect allegations, child custody questions, termination of parental rights) and addressing clinical and due process issues in delinquency cases (risk of harm to others, transfer to criminal court for trial, and various capacities associated with definitions of legal competency of defendants).

THE NEW EMERGENCE OF CHILD FORENSIC SPECIALIZATION

During the first 50 years of these developments, there was no recognizable field of forensic psychology, psychiatry, or social work. No organizations existed for a specialty in these areas, and even forensic evaluations of adults in criminal cases were rarely performed by clinical psychologists. Forensic mental health assessment as a professional specialty came of age in the 1960s (Bartol & Bartol, 1999; Grisso, 1991). The focus of the new specialty was almost entirely on evaluations for adults in criminal and civil courts or in adult corrections. Even near the end of the 20th century, widely used handbooks on forensic psychology sometimes contained no chapters on forensic evaluations of youths (e.g., Hess & Weiner, 1999). Thus juvenile forensic mental health assessment was widely practiced for about 40 years *before* there was a recognizable field of forensic psychology with a professional identity and a significant body of literature. Yet *after* that field had crystallized, it paid far less attention to forensic evaluation of youths than it did to evaluation of adults.

Why this happened is a treatise for another day, and that analysis will need to explain the newest development as well. Forensic mental health assessment of children and adolescents has suddenly become a primary focus of organized forensic psychology and psychiatry. Among over 100 symposia at the 2005 meeting of the American Psychology-Law Society, almost 25 were devoted to forensic issues in child welfare, delinquency, and psychological aspects of due process in juvenile courts. Yet as recently as 10 years ago that society's meetings offered only one or two symposia on forensic topics pertaining to youths. Similarly, all of the child forensic evaluation handbooks that the present one joins were published only within the past 8 years (e.g., Grisso, 1998; Grisso, Vincent, & Seagrave, 2005; Ribner, 2002; Schetky & Benedek, 2002), with the exception of earlier editions of Schetky and Benedek's book for child psychiatrists.

DEFINING ASPECTS OF THE NEW SPECIALTY

The assessment of children and adolescents for courts requires some skills and knowledge that are similar for both child and adult forensic mental health assessments. But some competencies distinguish them. There are many ways to catalogue these differences, but I will highlight three of them that seem to me of greatest importance: *law, development*, and *a systemic perspective*.

Law

Forensic evaluations are called "forensic" because they are performed in order to inform a court decision. As such, the methods and data to be obtained in a forensic evaluation are shaped by laws that define what it is the court must decide (often called legal standards for the decision), as well as laws that control the process for making the decision (procedural law). Knowledge of applicable laws, therefore, is an important part of forensic evaluation in juvenile courts, and these laws often are quite different from those that apply in adult forensic evaluations (Weithorn, Chapter 1 herein).

Moreover, laws are changing much more rapidly in areas of child welfare and delinquency than in adult criminal and civil law. For example, the fundamental legal standard for competency to stand trial in criminal court has not changed in the past 45 years. In contrast, during the 1990s, virtually every state experienced massive legislative reforms in its laws pertaining to delinquency, many of them almost abandoning a rehabilitative objective for a retributive response to youths' offenses (Grisso,

1996). If my sociolegal barometer is not too far off, the nation is beginning to undergo a compensatory set of legal reforms that will bring further change. At this moment in history, forensic mental health examiners are challenged by a short shelf life of existing laws pertaining to children and adolescents, requiring continuous vigilance to changes in laws pertaining to their evaluations.

Development

"Mental health" as a modifier when referring to forensic mental health assessments of children and adolescents is a bit misleading. It promotes a mistaken presumption that the primary purpose of forensic assessments of youths is to identify youths' mental disorders or their needs associated with mental disturbance. A review of this book shows that this is clearly not the case. If a more appropriate term were sought to characterize clinicians' assessments for juvenile courts, one might nominate "forensic developmental evaluations."

Questions of growth and development are at the heart of all juvenile forensic evaluations.

> Youths' developmental status is a defining difference between evaluations in juvenile court compared to adult criminal and civil cases. Developmental changes during childhood and adolescence—biological, cognitive, and psychosocial—greatly complicate all aspects of forensic evaluations of youths, whether we are examining the consequences of their victimization, the presumed effects of a pending parental custody decision, the likelihood of their future harm to others, or the relevance of their current mental disorders for future disorders, needs, and behaviors. Youths are "moving targets," and information about them at one point in time is likely to have a short shelf life. As many chapters in this book illustrate, the implications of this for assessment strategy, potential error, and limits to forensic evaluation of youths create demands on forensic examiners that are both fascinating and frustrating. (Grisso, 2004)

Systemic Perspective

Most forensic evaluations of adults or youths require attention to their social relations and the social agencies designed to respond to their needs and behaviors. But evaluation of youths in legal contexts raises this to a different level.

For example, occasionally there have been professional debates concerning whether mental health experts can form an opinion about criminal adult defendants without interviewing them. In child forensic practice, the parallel question is whether one can form an opinion if one has *only* interviewed the youth. Youths' dependent status (and their continuous movement toward more autonomous adulthood) makes evaluations of their behavior and their life potential literally incomplete if they are not evaluated in the context of their interactions with parents, peers, and social institutions. Forensic examiners who evaluate children consider it an essential part of their role to be evaluating others in the context of their evaluation of the individual—a youth's parents, peers, teachers, therapists, and even attorneys—in an effort to understand past and future development and behavior of the child.

A systemic perspective is also essential in translating evaluation data into recommendations and actions in the youth's and society's interests. Forensic examiners of children must have extraordinarily thorough knowledge of social services, mental health services, educational and employment options, and rehabilitation services within the child welfare and mental health system in their communities. Unlike most child mental health professionals, the primary objective of forensic child mental health professionals is referral, not treatment. Their role typically is not as a therapist, but as a social engineer who designs therapeutic plans and offers potential solutions in the interests of children, the courts, and society.

In this sense, most forensic mental health assessments of children are "local." I can go to any state in the nation and competently perform an adult evaluation for competence to stand trial or criminal responsibility. But I can competently perform a disposition evaluation in a delinquency case only in the jurisdiction in which I reside. A disposition evaluation aims substantially to recommend appropriate interventions with the youth, and I cannot sustain an intimate knowledge of the available (and continuously changing) intervention services outside my own community and the justice system that serves it.

A BIFURCATED SPECIALTY

All of the core perspectives that I have described pervade the chapters that follow. Yet there is one contour of the specialty of forensic mental health assessments of youths that this book does not make clear. It does not reveal to students or to nonchild forensic professionals that the specialty includes two groups who do not always identify with each other and who often find the other's interests only marginally relevant to their own.

The bifurcation is roughly defined by what a colleague of mine (Geri Fuhrmann) has called "kids who are done to and kids who do unto others." Forensic examiners who perform evaluations for child abuse and neglect cases, termination of parental rights, and divorce custody litigation operate in a very different context than forensic examiners who perform evaluations of juveniles' potential for future violence or sexual offending, competence to stand trial, or eligibility for trial as adults. In one sense, both groups evaluate the same youths, but often at different times in the youths' lives. They work with youths who are typically of very different ages and are before the court for different reasons (broadly speaking, either protective or accusatory). As a consequence, somewhat different interviewing skills are needed, associated with the characteristics of their examinees, quite different assessment methods, and attention to very different bodies of law and judicial objectives. In fact, it is a rare child forensic assessment professional who can practice competently across the full domain of cases that these two subspecialties represent.

I believe the editors of this volume will not take offense if I note that a handbook devoted to the different needs of these two subspecialties requires compromises. For example, those who are aware of my career-long interest in legal competencies (e.g., capacity to waive Miranda rights, competence to stand trial), especially their evaluation in juvenile cases (Grisso, 1998, 2005), would find it strange if I did not note that the present volume offers no guidance regarding the assessment of legal competencies in children and adolescents. On balance, there is a bit more in this book for those who evaluate "kids who are done to" than for examiners of "kids who do unto others." Given that compromises had to be made, I believe this was a wise choice by the editors, because past literature on the child welfare side of the specialty has been far less available than information for examiners dealing with due process issues in delinquency cases.

This volume is historically significant. For almost 100 years, mental health professionals have offered assessments to serve children, families, and legal professionals in juvenile courts. Yet only recently have we begun the process of developing textbooks that identify forensic mental health assessment of youths as a specialty, establishing its standards, and exploring its strengths and limits. This volume is not the last word on the topic, because we all recognize that we have far to go. But it is among the first, its guidance is sound, and it will have a defining impact on the growth of the field.

—Thomas Grisso, University of
Massachusetts Medical School

References

Bartol, C., & Bartol, A. (1999). History of forensic psychology. In A. Hess & I Weiner (Eds.), *The handbook of forensic psychology* (2nd ed.). New York: John Wiley.

Grisso, T. (1991). A developmental history of the American Psychology-Law Society. *Law and Human Behavior, 15*, 213–231.

Grisso, T. (1996). Society's retributive response to juvenile violence: A developmental perspective. *Law and Human Behavior, 20*, 229–247.

Grisso, T. (1998). *Forensic evaluation of juveniles.* Sarasota, FL: Professional Resource Press.

Grisso, T. (2004). *Double jeopardy: Adolescent offenders with mental disorders.* Chicago: University of Chicago Press.

Grisso, T. (2005). *Evaluating juveniles' adjudicative competence: A guide for clinical practice.* Sarasota, FL: Professional Resource Press.

Grisso, T., Vincent, G., & Seagrave, D. (Eds.). (2005). *Mental health screening and assessment in juvenile justice.* New York: Guilford.

Hess, A., & Weiner, I. (Eds.). (1999). *The handbook of forensic psychology.* New York: John Wiley.

Jones, K. (1999). *Taming the troublesome child: American families, child guidance, and the limits of psychiatric authority.* Cambridge, MA: Harvard University Press.

Napoli, D. (1981). *Architects of adjustment.* Port Washington, NY: Kennikat.

Ribner, N. (Ed.). (2002). *Handbook of juvenile forensic psychology.* San Francisco: Jossey-Bass.

Schetky, D., & Benedek, L. (Eds.). (2002). *Principles and practice of child and adolescent forensic psychiatry.* Washington, DC: American Psychiatric Press.

Acknowledgments

To my wife, Mary, I thank her for her love, dedication, and support. Completing a volume of this nature was particularly long and arduous, and with all things significant in my life for the past 39 years, my wife has been my greatest friend. To my children, Jason and Christopher, thank you for enriching my life.

I owe a huge debt of gratitude to my co-editor, Gerald P. Koocher, for his exceptional generosity, skill, and wisdom. While the experience was demanding for a substantial period of time, it was also professionally rewarding in great part due to the personal and professional strengths of Dr. Koocher.

I also wish to acknowledge the support and expert legal comments from Marc R. Stein, Esquire, for reviewing selected chapters.

In unity there is strength and thus we were fortunate to have so many professional leaders in their respective fields contribute to this volume. I thank my old friends and look forward to working again with new friends and colleagues. We are thankful for their efforts and contributions to law and mental health.

To our editor Joan Bossert at Oxford University Press and staff, thank you for your great patience and continued support.

—Steven N. Sparta, Ph.D.

Contents

Contributors

Ulla Anderson
San Diego State University

Catherine Ayoub
Harvard Graduate School of Education
Massachusetts General Hospital
Harvard Medical School

Steven B. Bisbing
Huntington Beach, California

Randy Borum
Department of Mental Health Law and Policy
University of South Florida

James N. Butcher
Department of Psychology
University of Minnesota

Jeanett Castellanos
University of California, Irvine

O. Brandt Caudill, Jr.
Tustin, California

Stephen T. DeMers
Former Professor and Director of the School
    Psychology Program
University of Kentucky
Lexington, Kentucky

Jennifer E. Denton
The Children's Hospital, Boston, Child
    Protection Team
Boston Medical Center, Child Protection
    Team
Harvard Medical School

William E. Foote
University of New Mexico School of Medicine
Department of Psychiatry

William N. Friedrich
Mayo Clinic and Mayo Medical School
Rochester, Minnesota

Maria Garrido
University of Rhode Island

Michael A. Goldberg
Director of Child and Family Psychological
    Services, Inc.
Norwood, Massachusetts;
Harvard Medical School
The Children's Hospital, Boston

Alan M. Goldstein
Department of Psychology
John Jay College of Criminal Justice—CUNY

Naomi E. Goldstein
Program in Law and Psychology
Drexel University

Linda Saylor Gudas
Harvard Medical School
The Children's Hospital, Boston
Dana Group Associates, Needham,
    Massachusetts

Rachel Kalbeitzer
Drexel University

Robin J. Kimbrough-Melton
Clemson University

Robert Kinscherff
Assistant Commissioner for Forensic Mental
    Health for the Massachusetts Department of
    Mental Health
Harvard Medical School
Boston University Law School
Massachusetts School of Professional
    Psychology

Gerald P. Koocher
Simmons College

Kathryn Kuehnle
Tampa, Florida

Paula Maness
Department of Psychology
Alliant International University

Joseph T. McCann
United Health Services Hospitals
SUNY Upstate Medical Center—Clinical
    Campus
Binghamton, New York

David Medoff
Assistant Professor at Suffolk University
Co-Director of the Children and the Law
    Program, Massachusetts General Hospital

Gary B. Melton
Institute on Family and Neighborhood Life
Clemson University

Leah Nellis
Blumberg Center for Interdisciplinary Studies
    in Special Education
Indiana State University

Alice W. Newton
The Children's Hospital, Boston
Massachusetts General Hospital
Harvard Medical School

Lois Oberlander Condie
The Children's Hospital, Boston
Harvard Medical School

Kenneth S. Pope
Norwalk, Connecticut

Jerome M. Sattler
Department of Psychology
San Diego State University

Steven R. Smith
California Western School of Law

Steven N. Sparta
School of Medicine
Department of Psychiatry
University of California, San Diego
Thomas Jefferson School of Law

Philip M. Stahl
West Palm Beach, Florida

Jerry J. Sweet
Evanston Northwestern Healthcare
Evanston, Illinois
Department of Psychiatry and Behavioral
    Sciences
Northwestern University Feinberg Medical School

Amy C. Tishelman
The Children's Hospital, Boston
Harvard Medical School
Boston College

Andrea M. Vandeven
The Children's Hospital, Boston
Harvard Medical School

Roberto J. Velásquez
Department of Psychology
San Diego State University

Lois A. Weithorn
Hastings College of the Law
University of California, San Francisco

David K. Wilcox
Middlesex County Juvenile Court
Cambridge, Massachusetts
Harvard Medical School
Massachusetts School of Professional Psychology

Karen E. Wills
Department of Psychology
Children's Hospitals and Clinics
Minneapolis, Minnesota

FORENSIC MENTAL HEALTH ASSESSMENT OF CHILDREN AND ADOLESCENTS

Introduction to Forensic Assessment of Children

Conducting psychological evaluations for use within the legal system differs significantly and in many different ways from assessment work in more traditional mental health and educational contexts, and nowhere is the distinction greater than when conducting forensic assessments of minors. Mental health professionals increasingly find themselves providing to attorneys and the courts evaluation services involving minors, with potentially serious consequences to children, their families, and the evaluators themselves. Professionals require specialized education, training, and experience to appropriately perform such services.

Although no book can provide all of the necessary skills and expertise for performing appropriate forensic evaluations, this volume offers a broad range of assessment-focused chapters addressing topics of importance to the legal and mental health professions. We hope this book will assist legal professionals, who use mental health expert opinions in cases, and forensic mental health practitioners striving toward quality in their work. Grisso (2005a) noted that forensic evaluators will want to engage in continuous personal scrutiny and self-examination in their work to ensure quality, and

that doing so requires not only basic knowledge but also an advanced degree of professional excellence.

Grisso (2005b) correctly noted that method validity for forensic mental health evaluation demands consideration in specific case contexts. The methods and interpretations associated with a forensic evaluation require consideration of their validity for a particular purpose. Every psychological method has limits. In some cases, a particular method may prove highly accurate for answering a forensic question, whereas in other circumstances the same method may hold no validity whatever. This volume describes forensic applications in the specialized context of assessing minors, where some of the applications of forensic mental health principles take complex twists and turns because of developmental factors, social or familial roles, and special legal standards crafted to take such differences into account. Some outstanding resources exist regarding forensic assessment generally; however, few published compilations specifically focus on a unique or specialized understanding required when assessing minors for the courts. Understanding the content of each chapter will help resolve the reader's *Daubert* (1993) admissibility concerns. The Supreme Court ruled in *Daubert* that a scientific technique is inadmissible as evidence unless the technique has become generally accepted as reliable in the relevant scientific community. By avoiding generalized assumptions about adult forensic mental health assessment concerning minors and providing substantial detailed documentation, readers will more likely have solid preparation for forming expert opinions.

This book represents a starting point for understanding the relevant conceptual, methodological, ethical, and procedural approaches that would assist an evaluator in providing a professionally sound report in a legal proceeding. Although legal scholars might still need to access relevant statutory or case law, and mental health professionals might still wish to survey other relevant forensic literature, this book provides a comprehensive overview and offers basic starting points for any practitioner performing assessment in the areas covered.

Human beings follow varying developmental trajectories over their life spans, thus dictating the principle that psychodiagnostic assessment of children and adolescents will necessarily involve instruments, norms, approaches, and skills that differ from those used in similar work with adult clients. In addition, factors linked to their social, physical, economic, and legal dependency on adults place children and adolescents in unique positions of vulnerability with respect to the work of both psychological assessment and the workings of the legal system. In this introduction, we elaborate on these fundamental differences as a context for understanding the special topical chapters that comprise the book.

DISTINCTIONS BETWEEN TRADITIONAL PSYCHOLOGICAL PRACTICE AND FORENSIC ROLES

From the outset, those who would understand forensic assessment must fully grasp the fundamental professional and philosophical differences between psychologists and attorneys. The legal system constitutes alien territory for most non-lawyers. Mental health practitioners will encounter frequent opportunities and enticements to compromise their scientific integrity, overlook ethical obligations, or otherwise go at their own risk. Most will resist temptation, some will step onto slippery slopes, and others will wander into an ethical morass out of blissful ignorance or misguided rationalization.

The legal system contributes to ethically compromising seduction for mental health experts in many ways. First, the attorney seeks out a clinician with special skill or expertise to help the client win a civil or criminal dispute. This courtship usually takes place amid considerable praise for the clinician's skills in anticipation of certain expected outcomes, which may or may not comport with the ethical obligations of the mental health professional. Second, the clinician has a significant degree of authority, manifested in court by a recitation of education, training, and experience leading to a judicial pronouncement of expert status. Third, elicitation of expert testimony occurs under circumstances likely to tempt narcissistically borne error. All attention focuses on the expert, and both sides attempt to elicit opinions that will support their side of the dispute or refute their opponent's. All the while, the court reporter carefully chronicles the expert's words, creating a hazard for those who expound in ignorance or ineptness.

Psychologists and other mental health experts train as behavioral scientists. An individual applying rigorous experimental methods can discover significant truths within ranges of reasonable statistical probability or more reliably determine when insufficient information exists to support a forensic opinion. Lawyers, educated as advocates, believe that the search for truth is best conducted in a vigorous adversarial cross-examination of the facts. Behavioral scientists seldom give simple dichotomous answers to questions. We prefer to use probabilities, ranges, norms, and continua that reflect the complexity of human differences. Legal education teaches that the facts must be tried or weighed, leading to clear, precise, unambiguous decisions marked by bright lines and clear dichotomies.

Mental health experts believe we should empathize with our clients and show them unconditional positive regard. We learn that little progress will occur in our work with clients if we do not trust and respect each other. We constantly collect data and try to ask all the important and sensitive questions. Attorneys believe that they can (and must) at times defend people they detest. Attorneys may choose not to ask their clients certain questions (e.g., "Did you do it?") in order to defend them vigorously, because legal ethics would preclude attorneys from calling witnesses who they have reason to believe will lie under oath.

Because of the basic distinctions in professional orientation noted above, the goals of the work performed by mental health professionals and lawyers also have inherent differences. The role of the clinician conducting forensic assessment focuses on obtaining data to assist the trier of fact in addressing a legal issue (e.g., guilt or innocence, liability, negligence, or mitigating factors). These nontraditional roles require a unique combination of skills and the ability to think differently from most of our psychologically focused colleagues as well as most attorneys.

DISTINCTIONS BETWEEN CHILD AND ADULT FORENSIC PSYCHOLOGY

Another important set of distinctions involves the special competencies required for child work (e.g., knowledge of developmental psychology, family dynamics, and specialized assessment instruments, as well as the ability to establish rapport and communicate effectively with children), but not necessary when performing general clinical or forensic assessments with adults. The most common forensic assessment activities involving children do not apply or arise only rarely in adult forensic work (e.g., child custody or guardianship matters, and assessing sexual abuse in emotionally or cognitively immature persons). Apart from basic competence, a number of special ethical considerations also come into play in child forensic assessments, including particularly complex role clarifications and competing interests among family members. (See chapter 3, this volume, for a more complete discussion.)

Which professionals should be considered experts? Melton, Petrila, Poythress, and Slobogin (1997) offer a wise response, and their answer

seems particularly relevant to child and adolescent forensic work, suggesting a functional approach that goes beyond mere educational attainments or the specific professional license one holds. Perhaps more important, they indicate a need to consider the specific experience of the professional in the relevant areas and with the particular evaluation procedures used. Given the specialized knowledge and experiences necessary to adequately assess any child, the forensic expert's qualification for evaluating children becomes even more relevant. The methodology, for example, for assessing allegations of sexual abuse, determining the amenability of an adolescent for rehabilitation following a criminal or juvenile court finding, or assessing the cognitive and emotional deficits of a child exposed to lead toxicity or physical trauma, to name a few, will often vary significantly from parallel adult forensic work because of the developmental context of the child client.

A number of particularly thorny conundrums may also come into play. For example, the normal statutory obligation of mental health professionals to report suspected child abuse may not apply in some situations where the nature of the assessment undertaken falls under attorney–client privilege. Because of case-by-case contextual differences and evolving statutes (e.g., recently establishing child abuse reporting mandates for attorneys and some other categories of people, such as priests, not previously covered under such laws). The practitioner may need to obtain updated state law consultations.

Important methodological differences also exist in child assessments contrasted with those performed on adults. In any forensic evaluation, multiple sources of independent data become essential. The family members, teachers, and caretakers can provide critical information but may have significant conscious or unconscious motives to mislead because of secondary gain based on the potential outcome of the litigation. Having critical history about the child's functioning during different points in time can prove immensely useful to forensic evaluators in framing their formulations. Often, however, the child's caretaker is the only source for some types of history. Thus, the forensic child evaluator requires methodological expertise in obtaining relevant and accurate information from the child, the child's caretakers, and others who know the child in a variety of contexts (e.g., schoolteachers, neighbors, or others in the community). When considering assessment instruments for use with the child or the child's family, one typically finds that many of the assessment instruments developed for use with children are not forensically oriented. Similarly, many of the limited number of forensic instruments that are available were not developed for or standardized on minors or are of poor quality.

In court-appointed roles, no evidentiary privilege usually exists, and forensic evaluators are expected to report their findings and opinions to others. This situation stands in sharp contrast to the more common context of children and their families engaging a professional for treatment services, where the clinician must at times call attention to a privilege on behalf of the child. Forensic evaluators of minors need to make clear the absence of confidentiality to the child, the minor's parents or guardians, and other collateral sources of information who may become involved as part of obtaining informed consent for the interviews.

The forensic role is differentiated from traditional clinical roles by numerous other factors, including the purpose of the involvement and methods employed to reach conclusions. Forensic evaluators must maintain appropriate assessment protocols unique to the problem being evaluated, follow applicable court rules, remain within the original agreed-upon forensic role boundaries, and follow other recommended practices within the forensic field. However, because of the special nature of vulnerability involving children, ethical considerations differ from those that apply to work with adults. It is one thing to have an adult forensic client fend for himself or herself in difficult circumstances, but can the forensic evaluator completely ignore the ethical dilemmas if a reasonable question of potential suffering or harm exists? Questions about possible interim recommendations or legally mandated reporting arise in such circumstances, and the child forensic evaluator must often simultaneously contend with the special ethical duties toward children while maintaining acceptable forensic standards.

The range of approaches to forensic assessment of children and adolescents generally reflects less

professional consensus with respect to protocols or methods compared with some areas of adult forensics. For example, establishing legal competency of adults to stand trial follows specific statutory definitions, and a range of established assessment instruments with norms exists. From case law or statute describing the specific legal elements required for competency to testify, forensic adult evaluators have a clearer foundation on which to formulate relevant forensically sensitive assessment instruments or develop standardized protocols that mirror the legal necessities for such cases. In contrast, forensic opinions involving children are often less precise. For example, establishing what constitutes the best interests of the child can vary widely across assessors, even when the age of the child and clinical context do not vary. Forensic evaluations of minors may occur in states with different statutory criteria for defining best-interests standards; evaluators need to be careful to not substitute values that are not empirically supported. The uniqueness of every family situation makes it exceedingly difficult to develop consensual professional agreement about assessment methods or dispositional judgments.

Because children are in the process of unfolding personality and developmental functioning, one must consider a more dynamic set of variables than the more static factors usually present in adult forensic evaluation. It becomes much more difficult to form reliable forensic conclusions about past functioning; to know whether differences or deficits exist in relation to present functioning and, if so, to what degree; or to know what one might reasonably predict in specific areas of future functioning.

The following chapters describe at least the basics of the legal requirements for the area of assessment under discussion and how the forensic evaluator might clarify and remain within an appropriate forensic role, discuss common or important potential ethical issues, and describe essential concepts and methodological approaches for the subject under discussion. This volume is not intended for use in a cookbook manner. One hopes that the forensic child professional in training will find the volume a helpful starting resource and that more experienced forensic practitioners will find themselves better informed about definitions, guidelines, and recommended methods in their own or closely related subject areas.

PREVIEWS OF
SUBSEQUENT CHAPTERS

In chapter 1, Lois A. Weithorn, a psychologist and law professor, sets a context for how children are treated in the American legal system. She provides an overview of how major court decisions and case law have shaped the context within which mental health professionals may have expert evaluative roles.

In chapter 2, Gary B. Melton and Robin J. Kimbrough-Melton describe the problem of integrating forensic assessment and mental health treatment of children in the American justice system. They present an integrated discussion of complex role demands and systemic problems as well as describing new forums and possibilities.

Ethical issues in forensic assessment comprise the focus of chapter 3 by Gerald P. Koocher. Readers will find focused discussion of ethical problems related to competence, assessment techniques, and forensic roles here.

In chapter 4, William E. Foote describes a set of strategies and rules to guide mental health practitioners as they interact with attorneys in the context of expert testimony and assessment for the courts.

Chapter 5, by attorney O. Brandt Caudill, Jr., presents a detailed set of strategies for minimizing malpractice claims and licensing board complaints when agreeing to take on forensic assessments. He pays special attention to child-custody matters.

In chapter 6, law school dean Steven R. Smith provides a thoughtful analysis of the mental health expert witness role. He provides background, context, and helpful suggestions for those who seek to serve as experts for the courts.

Roberto J. Velásquez and his colleagues provide detailed information and useful examples applicable to the forensic assessment of Latino children and adolescents in chapter 7. Despite the focus on Latinos, the chapter also illustrates the complexity of forensic assessments across cultural and linguistic groups, suggesting some generalizable principles to consider.

Chapter 8 begins a number of assessment-related chapters, providing a general framework on forensic interviewing in a developmental context. Linda Sayler Gudas and Jerome M. Sattler combine their excellent advice on general clinical interviewing with the special precautions and consideration when conducting such assessments for forensic purposes.

In chapter 9, psychologists Kathryn Kuehnle and Steven N. Sparta provide detailed suggestions for framing evaluations of child sexual abuse allegations in forensic contexts. Readers will also likely want to review chapters 20, 21, and 25, addressing related topics of forensic assessment of parenting in abuse and neglect cases, evaluation of juvenile sexual offenders, and measures for evaluating child sexual abuse.

Chapter 10 by Lois Oberlander Condie effectively addresses strategies for evaluating the effects of domestic violence on children. The data and strategies suggested will help readers separate objective forensics from popular myths in this assessment context.

In chapter 11, a team of psychologists and pediatricians expert at the forensic assessment of physical abuse and neglect of children describe best current assessment practices from the medical perspective. Amy C. Tishelman, Alice W. Newton, Jennifer E. Denton, and Andrea M. Vandeven provide an invaluable interdisciplinary resource.

Chapter 12 by Randy Borum provides a valuable forensic guide for assessing violence risk among youthful offenders, an important topic that may exist within a variety of forensic referrals.

In chapter 13, Steven N. Sparta and Philip M. Stahl detail assessment strategies for addressing the complex minefield that comprises the psychological evaluation environment represented in child custody evaluations.

Stephen T. DeMers and Leah Nellis provide their expertise in chapter 14 to assist in assessing children's eligibility for special education services and the appropriateness of such services.

Chapter 15 provides Michael A. Goldberg's description of cautions and strategies when assessing children in the course of resolving personal injury claims.

Two talented neuropsychologists, Karen E. Wills and Jerry J. Sweet, discuss neuropsychological considerations in forensic child assessment in chapter 16, along with explanations for when evaluators should consider brain–behavior consequences in referrals that are not identified as being neuropsychological in nature.

Chapter 17 provides a detailed primer on litigation related to the toxic effects of lead on children by psychologist and attorney Steven B. Bisbing.

Chapter 18 by Joseph T. McCann addresses the critical and timely topic of bullying and stalking behavior by children and adolescents from the perspective of obsessional harassment.

Chapter 19 by Robert Kinscherff provides a helpful guide to the forensic assessment of amenability to rehabilitation in juvenile delinquency proceedings.

In chapter 20 Catherine Ayoub and Robert Kinscherff combine the skills of psychologist, attorney, and nurse to discuss the forensic assessment of parenting in child abuse and neglect cases.

Chapter 21 provides a thoughtful approach to the forensic evaluation of juvenile sexual offenders by David Medoff and Robert Kinscherff.

The team of Alan M. Goldstein, Naomi E. Goldstein, and Rachel Kalbeitzer provide helpful guidance in chapter 22 on assessing childhood trauma and developmental factors as mitigating variables in capital cases involving adults. This is the only chapter that does not provide an examination of direct child assessment but is included because the knowledge, training, and experience in child-forensic assessment often represent the requisite background for formulating relevant opinions in such cases.

Chapter 23 by David K. Wilcox provides a helpful framework for assessing firesetting behavior in children and adolescents, a highly specialized but more frequently encountered problem than generally believed.

Chapter 24 focuses on the well-known Minnesota Multiphasic Personality Inventory–Adolescent (MMPI-A), addressing fundamentals and uses of the MMPI-A in forensic assessment with the expertise of James N. Butcher and Kenneth S. Pope.

Chapter 25 offers an invaluable guide to measures for evaluating child sexual abuse, a very complex area of child forensic assessment. William N. Friedrich provides evaluators with a wealth of empirical data resources in a field often lacking such consideration. This chapter represents an excellent complement to chapter 9.

Chapter 26 by Joseph T. McCann addresses the measurement of adolescent personality and psychopathology with the well-known Millon Adolescent Clinical Inventory (MACI).

In summary, we hope to have provided readers with a comprehensive survey of forensic assessment issues involving children and adolescents, as well as with appropriate caveats and cautions. Mental health experts have much to say to the courts that can assist in serving both children and the justice system. We believe it critical to offer such services with high levels of fairness, scientific rigor, and clinical competence.

References

Daubert v. Merrell Dow Pharmaceuticals, Inc., 509 U.S., 579 113 S.Ct. 2786 (1993).

Grisso, T. (2005a). Quality in the practice of forensic psychology. *American Psychology-Law Society News*, Winter, 6–9.

Grisso, T. (2005b). The empirical limits of forensic mental health assessment. *Law & Human Behavior, 29*, 1–5.

Melton, G. B., Petrila, J., Poythress, N., & Slobogin, C. (1997). *Psychological evaluations for the courts: A handbook for mental health professionals and lawyers* (2nd ed.). New York: Guilford.

Part I

FORENSIC ASSESSMENT ISSUES: ETHICS, LAWYERS, COURTS, CULTURAL CONSIDERATIONS, AND PROFESSIONAL LIABILITY

1

The Legal Contexts of Forensic Assessment of Children and Families

Lois A. Weithorn

Psychologists enlisted to perform psycholegal assessments of children, adolescents, or families typically find themselves thrust into worlds that operate quite differently from the range of clinical contexts most familiar to their profession. The ground rules, goals, principles, and ethics shift when one crosses over from psychology to law. Even within the legal system, each subsystem (e.g., criminal justice system, child protection system, or juvenile justice system, family court system) is a world unto itself, despite sometimes overlapping jurisdiction. Distinct social purposes and goals—expressed via specific statutes, regulations, and judicial opinions—underlie each system. Not surprisingly, the proceedings within each system and the roles of various actors are governed by rules developed and refined with specific reference to these goals and purposes.

Depending on the legal inquiry and the particular role requested of a psychologist, his or her evaluation may focus on any of a broad array of questions about the past, present, or future psychological functioning of specific children, adolescents, adults, or families. Some questions may be framed in language familiar to a psychologist and generally within the expertise the clinician brings to the situation (e.g., "Does a comprehensive psychoeducational evaluation of a child for whom the court is considering a custodial placement reveal that the child has any special psychological or educational needs?"). By contrast, some questions may be worded in the language of the ultimate legal issue and may tempt psychologists to exceed the boundaries of our field's expertise (e.g., "Which custodial placement is in a child's 'best interests' as between two adequate, loving, available, and devoted parents?"; Mnookin, 1975; Weithorn, 1985). Other questions will be phrased in legal language that may bear no relation to the lay uses of similar terminology (e.g., "Is a particular juvenile 'amenable to treatment' within the juvenile justice system, or should the juvenile court transfer the youth to adult criminal court?").

Some psychologists engage in forensic child or family evaluation at the request of the parties on one side of an adversarial content or the other, whereas others may serve as consultants to the court itself, thus playing a more neutral role. Psychologists' participation in these contexts may be constrained by various procedural and evidentiary rules, by the ethical tenets that guide their profession, or by the interaction of these factors. Suffice to say, psycholegal assessment presents a minefield of potential challenges to psychologists unfamiliar with the legal system and with the unique ethical dilemmas that confront those venturing into the fray.

In this chapter, it is not possible to provide a complete, or even partial, inventory of the myriad of legal-context–specific variables characterizing the range of psycholegal assessment situations in which psychologists may find themselves. Instead, I seek to review briefly the legal contexts within which forensic child and family assessment inquiries occur, and to characterize these inquiries as falling within one or more of three key categories of cases: (a) *child protection* (i.e., cases focusing on the alleged victimization of a child or adolescent); (b) *private dispute resolution* (e.g., cases in which two or more private parties have mutually conflicting legal claims regarding the custody, visitation, or adoption of a child or adolescent); and (c) *social control* (i.e., cases in which a child or adolescent is an alleged offender). With this framework, I seek to underscore the primary goals of the legal system within each category and to discuss how various substantive standards, procedural rules, and roles for psychological experts relate to these goals. First, however, I begin with a more general overview of sources of law and the modern jurisprudence relating to children and families.

SOURCES OF LAW

In the United States, *law* is generated from three primary *branches* of government (i.e., the legislature, the judiciary, and the executive branches) and may also originate in any of several *levels* of government (i.e., federal, state, and local). Citizens of the United States are governed by a federal constitution, which sets forth the structure of government, including the basics of the relationships between the branches of government as well as of federal and state relationships. The federal constitution and state constitutions not only enumerate the powers of government but also articulate a range of substantive and procedural rights of persons, thus limiting governmental authority where it infringes on these rights. The law regulating children's and families' lives is unique in that it governs a class of persons who have not yet attained many of these rights (i.e., minors), a class of persons whose status grants them rights (i.e., as parents) to direct the lives of others (i.e., their children) in a way that is not replicated in any other type of legal relationship, and the relationships among these persons.

Legislatures pass *statutes*, also known as *codes*. The legislature directs administrative agencies within the executive branches of the federal government and states, administrative agencies to promulgate regulations that direct and guide those who implement the statutes. Courts *interpret* and *apply* statutes, regulations, and of course, constitutions. Law emanating from courts is referred to as *case law*. Bodies of case law that interpret the same or similar statutory, regulatory, or constitutional provisions may articulate doctrines and principles that become precedent for future decisions. Because our legal system's roots developed in England, case law has a particularly important role in our system. England relied primarily on its case law, also referred to as the *common law*, for the development and articulation of most of the basic principles of law. In other words, most key principles were developed by judges in their written opinions. Early American law likewise reflected this bent. Although certain areas of law developed almost entirely from the judge-made common law, and some continue to evolve through judicial opinion, other areas of modern American law are grounded in statutes. For example, constitutional principles require that all crimes be defined by statute (Kadish, 1999). Our legal system reflects a delicate interplay between the legislative and judicial systems, with law emanating from both branches, to different degrees for different areas of law. As one might expect, robust debate exists about what types of functions are better relegated to legislatures versus courts, or to the federal government versus the states.

AN OVERVIEW OF CHILD–PARENT–STATE JURISPRUDENCE

Legal policies governing the well-being of children seek to balance the interests of the state, the parents, and the child. In our society, parents have substantial discretion in raising their children. Over the years, the U.S. Supreme Court has repeatedly underscored that parents' rights to control the upbringing of their children is protected by the constitutional doctrine of *family privacy*, which is the starting point of any legal analysis concerning children's well-being (*Parham v. J.R.*, 1979; *Wisconsin v. Yoder*, 1972). Parental discretion in child rearing is protected by the 14th Amendment of the U.S. Constitution, as one expression of the liberty guaranteed to all of us who live in this country. Thus, the state does not have the authority to second-guess run-of-the-mill parenting decisions and, in fact, must respect parental discretion in decision making about children's health, education, discipline, welfare, religious training, and related areas. Another component of this liberty involves parental rights to the custody and companionship of their children (*Santosky v. Kramer*, 1982; *Stanley v. Illinois*, 1972; *Troxel v. Granville*, 2000). Those rights shield parents from state intrusion in the parent–child relationship and also permit parents to limit or exclude certain other persons' contact or relationships with their children. Our constitutional doctrines articulate a tolerance for, and indeed a celebration of, diversity in child-rearing styles and family values (*Pierce v. Society of Sisters*, 1925) and espouse a commitment to supporting the family unit, even in face of parental missteps and flaws (*Santosky v. Kramer*, 1982).

The U.S. Supreme Court has also made clear, however, that parental autonomy in child rearing is not absolute (*Prince v. Massachusetts*, 1944). The state has certain obligations toward children, who—by virtue of their dependence upon others, their limited capacities for self-care and self-protection, and their vulnerability—are unable to safeguard their own welfare. Our society expects parents to support, protect, and provide for their minor children. In those instances, however, when parents fail to meet these obligations, the state stands ready to intervene to ensure children's welfare, even if such intervention means limiting parental discretion. Precisely when parental missteps and flaws become serious enough to warrant state supervention of parental autonomy is not always easy to determine. Despite the relatively clear principles that emerge as one examines constitutional precedent involving families, the precise contours

of the constitutional guarantees of parental discretion are sometimes murky. Our statutes and case law have helped to identify some of the boundaries, but there remain many gray areas.

In general, however, the state's authority with respect to children typically falls into one or both of two overlapping categories: *parens patriae* power and police power. In its *parens patriae* role, the state can intervene in the lives of children (or others who are also dependent, vulnerable, or incapable of self-care and self-protection) as would a benevolent parent, seeking to protect children for the children's own benefit. Child maltreatment laws in the statute books of all states are examples of state exercise of its *parens patriae* power, in that these laws empower states to limit parental authority and contact with their children, if doing so is necessary to protect the children from harm. By contrast, the state's police power authority allows the state to intervene in the lives of children in order to promote the health, safety, and general welfare of the community at large. Thus, police power justifies state action taken to protect society from children or adolescents who engage in conduct that endangers others, just as it has this authority to intervene when adults commit criminal acts. But, the police power goes well beyond protecting society from specific harmful acts. As it relates to children, it also encompasses a range of state policies aimed at socializing children to become productive, self-sufficient, and contributing members of society. As the U.S. Supreme Court opined, in the 1944 case of *Prince v. Massachusetts* (1944), "A democratic society rests, for its continuance, upon the healthy, well-rounded growth of young people into full maturity as citizens, with all that implies" (p. 178). The states' *parens patriae* and police power goals often overlap, as in the case of compulsory education laws. That is, the state views an adequate education as beneficial both to each individual child's own personal development and future well-being and for the welfare of society at large.

In the first century in this nation's history, parents raised children as they saw fit, with negligible interference from the state, even with respect to treatment of children that would clearly constitute abuse or neglect by modern standards (Weithorn, 2001). In the 20th century, the state became increasingly involved in protecting and socializing children (Mintz & Kellogg, 1988). And, whereas parents still do retain primary autonomy, the state checks their discretion in many instances.

In the later 20th century, children's own voices were added to the mix in selected circumstances. Until the 1960s, the law presumed that the interests of children were adequately represented by parents and the state, with each perhaps providing checks and balances on the other. But, in the 1960s and 1970s, courts began to recognize that children's interests may, at times, be distinct, and perhaps even conflicting, with those of the state (*In re Gault*, 1967) or of their parents (*Bellotti v. Baird*, 1979). Thus, in certain situations, minors are granted limited rights in their contests with the state, such as to certain due process protections in delinquency hearings. In certain other situations, minors may be granted limited decision-making autonomy. Thus, for example, they may be permitted to access mental health treatment or contraception without parental consent. Whereas parental autonomy remains the starting point in determining who has authority for decision making over minors' welfare, and minors seeking legal recognition of independent interests typically do not prevail, there are exceptions. American jurisprudence does, at times, consider the independent interests of minors when balancing the competing interests of parents and the state.

CHILD PROTECTION: LEGAL RESPONSES WHEN A CHILD MAY BE A VICTIM

There exist two systems with overlapping jurisdiction with legal authority to intervene in child abuse and neglect cases: the criminal justice system and juvenile court system (Brooks, 1996; Dorne, 2002; Goldstein, 1999; Melton, Petrila, Poythress, & Slobogin, 1997).

The Criminal Justice Response to Child Maltreatment

State penal codes (i.e., criminal law statutes) empower law enforcement and court personnel to investigate cases, prosecute alleged offenders, and sentence those found guilty (Dorne, 2002). Such cases include, for example, situations in which an adult has perpetrated a physical or sexual assault of a child, has created circumstances causing the child "unjustifiable . . . mental suffering," or has inflicted "cruel or inhuman corporal punishment" (California Penal Code, 2004). Offenders may be sentenced to prison. In imposing such a sentence, the criminal justice system seeks to accomplish various goals, which may include punishment and incapacitation of the offender, and deterrence of future crimes by the offender and others in society (Bloch & McMunigal, 2005). Punishment is often calibrated to serve the social demand for retribution. Rehabilitation, although typically cited as a goal of criminal justice system intervention in the mid-20th century, is no longer regarded as central. Despite this fact, vestiges or pockets of rehabilitation-oriented programs and approaches still exist in some places. One of those pockets, interestingly, is in the area of child abuse. Despite the current preponderance of get-tough criminal justice policies and societal disinterest in psychological interpretations of and responses to criminal conduct, some instances of child abuse perpetrated by a family member trigger interventions grounded more in therapeutic, rather than punitive, principles. As such, many criminal child abuse statutes provide an option for treatment-oriented dispositions (California Penal Code, 2004). Thus, one role a forensic psychologist may play in cases involving criminal prosecution of a defendant accused of child maltreatment is the provision of a presentence evaluation of the offender, addressing that offender's appropriateness for rehabilitative intervention.

Because imprisonment entails loss of liberty, the criminal justice system provides defendants with a panoply of constitutionally guaranteed due process protections, such as rights to a jury trial, to counsel, and to confront witnesses, and rights against self-incrimination. In addition, the prosecution must meet a stiff evidentiary burden in proving every element of the crime beyond a reasonable doubt. When the prosecution seeks to prove that the defendant victimized a child, psychologists may be asked to conduct evaluations that are used to inform the court on selected issues relevant to that context. For example, criminal defendants have a constitutional right under the 6th Amendment to confront those who testify against them in open court (*Maryland v. Craig*, 1990). Yet, such testimony may be emotionally traumatic for a child, given the child's age and past experiences with the defendant. The U.S. Supreme Court has therefore permitted states to modify traditional procedures somewhat, permitting child testimony against an alleged sexual abuser via closed-circuit television rather than in open court where the prosecution made a "particularized" showing that this procedure was "necessary" to avert a risk of harm to the child who is making the allegations (*Maryland v. Craig*, 1990). Thus, psychologists may be asked to evaluate the degree to which testifying in the presence of the alleged abuser will be emotionally damaging to a particular child witness.

The use of children as witnesses in criminal trials raises a plethora of additional questions drawing on psychologists' scientific and clinical expertise. Psychologists may be called upon to testify as to the reliability of children's testimony, developmental trends in children's memory and suggestibility, the impact of particular types of questioning on children's subsequent testimony of alleged abuse, the use of anatomically correct dolls on such testimony, or how to interpret particular manifestations of inconsistency in children's reports regarding alleged abuse (Ceci & Bruck, 1995; Lanning, 2002; Saywitz, Goodman, & Lyon, 2002).

The Civil Response to Child Maltreatment

The juvenile court's *dependency* jurisdiction authorizes civil intervention in child maltreatment cases in which the dangers to children result from the actions or omissions of the children's parents or guardians. In general, most such statutes authorize juvenile court involvement in four categories of cases: those involving suspected physical abuse, sexual abuse, neglect, and emotional maltreatment (Dorne, 2002; Goldstein, 1999). The dependency system seeks to protect children from dangerous or inadequate caregivers, to provide substitute care for those children who are removed from their homes, to remediate problematic parental conduct and conditions in the home, and to reunify the children and their caregivers when and if the home situation is deemed safe enough for the children's return. Thus, although the goals of the criminal justice system in responses to child maltreatment are generally punitive, the dependency system strives to preserve the family unit and remediate the home environment, and offers various educational and treatment services to further these aims.

Given the juvenile court system's rehabilitative posture in approaching the family, evidentiary standards and due process requirements are relaxed in contrast to criminal justice proceedings. Thus, most determinations made by the juvenile court in maltreatment cases require proof by the preponderance of evidence. Termination of parental rights, which permanently severs the legal parent–child relationship, and which is arguably the most severe disposition available to the juvenile court in maltreatment cases, must be grounded in clear and convincing evidence (*Santosky v. Kramer*, 1982).

In general, the juvenile court relies on parents' desires to retain or regain custody of their children to motivate parental compliance with the court's or child protective services' directives. For example, if the court allows a child to remain in the parents' custody, such a disposition may be conditional on parental participation in one or another treatment program and on full cooperation with child protection personnel. The dependency system is unlikely to successfully effect changes in families when parents are unmotivated to retain or regain custody of their children. In addition, if the offender in question is not a legal parent but is a companion of a parent, the dependency system may be further limited in its ability to motivate compliance. The juvenile court has certain more coercive remedies at its disposal to restrain or compel certain conduct, such as the issuance of civil protective orders and contempt sanctions (Goldstein, 1999).

Psychologists may be involved in any of several phases of juvenile court involvement in suspected cases of child maltreatment. The court may request evaluations that will help it to substantiate or reject various reports of abuse or neglect. It may seek psychological assessment of children and parents, evaluation of family functioning and parent–child relationships, in order to determine service needs. Psychologists can provide essential information critical to a proper dependency system response, such as whether a parent has a substance abuse problem, whether a mother is a victim of domestic violence perpetrated by the father or male partner, or whether a parent needs basic education on child development, child-rearing strategies, and effective discipline. Psychologists can also provide assessments of the safety of the home environment or the likelihood that certain dangerous conditions or behaviors will continue. Psychologists can assess the psychological ramifications for children of separation from and return to their parent(s), as well as the impact of termination of parental rights (American Psychological Association, 1998).

Psychologists, however, should consider some important caveats prior to embarking on evaluations in the dependency system. The grounds enumerated in those statutes authorizing juvenile court jurisdiction reflect our society's judgments as to what types of conditions and conduct are harmful to children. Some of these judgments seem fairly objective (e.g., inflicting physical harm nonaccidentally, resulting in serious injury). Yet, social values and preferences affect how we view what, on their face, seem to be fairly objective issues. Thus, for example, in an attempt to balance state and parental interests, a statute may exempt the infliction of nonaccidental physical harm from liability if that infliction constitutes reasonable discipline. For example, California's statutes exempt "reasonable and age-appropriate spanking to the buttocks where there is no evidence of serious physical injury" from its physical abuse category (California Welfare & Institutions Code, 2004). Or, a statute may exclude from its definition of medical neglect certain decisions by parents to reject medically recommended treatments if the parents' decisions are grounded in religious beliefs (California Welfare & Institutions Code, 2004).

In other words, modern child protection policy seeks to protect diversity in child-rearing styles, delicately balancing parental rights to discretion in child rearing with state interests in protecting children from harm. State officials and those psychologists performing forensic evaluations must refrain from imposing a narrow view of ideal or proper parenting upon all families. Sadly, abuse and neglect statutes have functioned over the years as instruments for the expression of social disapproval of certain lifestyles, or of the way in which particular cultures raise their children. For example, a federal court held Alabama's child maltreatment statute unconstitutionally vague in a case in which the statute was used to remove a child from the custody of his Caucasian mother because she was living with an African-American man in a neigh-

borhood that was populated primarily by African Americans (*Roe v. Conn*, 1976). In another famous case, *Mississippi Band of Choctaw Indians v. Holyfield* (1989), the Supreme Court cited congressional findings revealing strikingly high percentages of Native-American children who were removed from their parents' custody in the 1960s and 1970s by child welfare authorities unfamiliar with Indian culture and child-rearing traditions. Child protection professionals' mandates strictly limit intervention in families to circumstances in which children have been, or are at substantial risk of being, harmed by their parents or guardians, or by their parents' or guardians' failures to provide adequate care, protection, or supervision.

Yet, determining whether or not a child has suffered harm may be difficult once we venture beyond observable physical harm. In recent decades, researchers have garnered evidence to support the hypothesis that the psychological repercussions of abuse and neglect generally are the most damaging of the long-term effects (Binggeli, Hart, & Brassard, 2001). And, whereas investigators have sought, in recent years, to identify those circumstances or parental behaviors that are most likely to cause psychological harm, these inquiries are in their early stages (Binggeli et al., 2001). Furthermore, even after a wealth of data are collected and analyzed, prediction of future well-being will likely continue to be fraught with problems. As Wald (1975) noted more than 25 years ago:

No national consensus exists concerning what constitutes a "healthy" adult. Even more importantly, we really know very little about how to raise a child to make him "healthy"—however "healthy" may be defined. The few longitudinal studies of child development conclude that the prediction of future behavior from observation of childrearing practices is extremely difficult.

Although our knowledge base has moved forward, these observations still hold true to a large extent, 25 years later. Given this reality, it is incumbent upon psychologists to exercise prudence and awareness of their own limitations when predicting that certain types of parental conduct have harmful consequences to children. In its *Guidelines for Psychological Evaluations in Child Protection Matters*, the American Psychological

Association (1998) asserts that psychologists should refrain from "drawing conclusions not adequately supported by the data [and that they must] interpret data from interviews or tests cautiously and conservatively, [remaining] knowledgeable about cultural norms" (p. 590).

Criminal Versus Civil Jurisdiction of Child Maltreatment Cases

In most localities, authorities exercise substantial discretion in determining whether to handle a child maltreatment case as a criminal matter, a civil matter, or both (Besharov, 1986). Police, child welfare workers, and prosecutors take part in these decisions. When a stranger or someone not in a familial relationship with the child (e.g., a teacher or coach) allegedly perpetrates child maltreatment, legal proceedings will necessarily be criminal in nature. Civil child maltreatment statutes do not apply in such situations. Dependency court involvement occurs only when the alleged perpetrator is a parent or guardian or when a parent or guardian is charged with failing to protect his or her child adequately from an alleged perpetrator. For example, if a parent's live-in companion sexually abuses a child, the companion may have criminal charges filed against him, whereas the mother's case may be referred to the civil dependency system.

Yet, even in some of these situations, parallel criminal proceedings may also commence. If the parental acts or omissions appear to be so dangerous, so heinous, or so chronic that preservation of the family unit seems neither a desirable nor a viable goal, criminal justice intervention may be an appropriate—and perhaps even an essential—response to such conduct. For example, if a parent's abuse has led to one child's death, that parent may face criminal prosecution for that death, whereas matters relating to the custody and protection of the deceased child's siblings will likely go forward in the civil child protection system. Although the criminal prosecution may be said to serve society's retributive and utilitarian goals related to the acts already committed, the civil proceedings focus on protecting the surviving children from potential future dangers and in addressing practical concerns relating to the care of the surviving children. In extreme cases, the civil process will result in termination of parental rights if the judge determines that the child cannot be safely returned to the parent or guardian in the foreseeable future.

Most recently, there has been substantial attention to an area that involves both the criminal justice and juvenile justice systems. Empirical research demonstrates that domestic violence perpetrated by one parent or caregiver against the other can have deleterious effects on children, even when children are not the direct victims of the perpetrator's physical aggression (Fantuzzo & Mohr, 1999; Jaffe, Wolfe, & Wilson, 1990; Margolin, 1998; Rossman, Rosenberg, & Hughes, 2000; Weithorn, 2001; see also chapter 10, this volume). Children in these situations remain at risk for development of a range of psychological difficulties. In addition, research reveals that domestic violence and direct child maltreatment frequently coexist (Edleson, 1999).

Traditionally, the law viewed domestic violence as a private family matter, and victims found little support from criminal justice agencies such as the police and courts (Clark, 1987; Hanna, 1996). Only recently, policy makers have focused attention to the need to treat domestic violence offenders like other violent perpetrators and have increasingly responded to assaults with arrest, prosecution, and incarceration of offenders. Despite this fairly recent shift in policy, critics charge that domestic violence perpetrators are still not held accountable for their conduct (Clark, 1987; Hanna, 1996). Even more recently, legislatures and courts have turned attention to the needs of the children in families affected by domestic violence (Weithorn, 2001). Some states highlight the impact of domestic violence on children by providing for enhanced criminal penalties for domestic violence assaults with a minor present (Weithorn, 2001). Other states have defined children's exposure to domestic violence as a form of child maltreatment under the dependency statutes (Weithorn, 2001). Still others have enacted multiple statutes, targeting domestic violence perpetrators with both civil and criminal responses (Weithorn, 2001).

Unfortunately, until very recently, the prevailing tendency of child protection agencies and personnel in cases where domestic violence and child maltreatment coexist was to blame the adult domestic violence victim (usually the mother) for the abuse suffered by her child at the hands of her partner (Becker, 1985; Dohrn, 1995; Stark & Flit-craft, 1988). This tendency extended to situations in which the child did not experience physical victimization but appeared to suffer psychologically from the exposure to the domestic violence in the household. Specifically, child protective services typically responded to these situations by filing neglect petitions against the nonabusive parent—typically the mothers—alleging that the mothers failed to protect their children from exposure to the domestic violence. Authorities frequently chanted: "Why didn't she just leave?" (Clark, 1987). In some jurisdictions, battered mothers lost custody of their children as result of a reflexive response by child protective services to blame the mother for her batterers' conduct. Such a practice was held unconstitutional in the recent case of *Nicholson v. Williams* (2002), in which New York City child welfare authorities were enjoined from continuing to remove children of battered women from their mothers without evidence that remaining in the mother's custody placed the child at risk of harm. Unnecessary separations of children from a nonabusive parent who is a domestic violence victim was determined not to serve the children's best interests and to risk compounding the emotional injuries these children endured as a result of exposure to the domestic violence.

Furthermore, many answers exist in response to the question of why some battered women do not leave their abusers. Studies have found that there is an increased risk of severe and lethal violence against battered women when they leave or try to leave an abusive partner (Weithorn, 2001). Furthermore, batterers frequently threaten victims with a range of consequences, such as loss of custody of or harm to the children, and batterers often isolate their victims from various sources of financial and emotional support. A wealth of studies examine some of the complex dynamics of domestic violence situations, a review of which is beyond the scope of this chapter. Core groups of scholars, policy makers, and practitioners have reached the conclusion that the best way to protect children exposed to domestic violence is to hold the batterer accountable using all of the tools available in the criminal and civil justice systems, removing him from the home, while keeping the mother and child together (see, e.g., Jaffe et al., 1990; Peled, Jaffe, & Edleson, 1995; Rossman et al., 2000). Fur-

thermore, these experts agree that community-based domestic violence services should be available to the mother and child to help them find and create safety in their lives and to promote their recovery from the abuse.

Comprehensive policy-oriented approaches to domestic violence, such as that of Alaska, have sought coordination of the legal system's responses to battered women and their children, aligning criminal, civil child protection, and other legal interventions with families affected by domestic violence (Weithorn, 2001). One example of this type of policy reform is reflected in state statutes governing custodial arrangements at separation and divorce. The newer statutes require courts to consider the perpetration of domestic violence by one partner against the other in awards of custody and to disfavor perpetrators of such violence (Weithorn, 2001). In response to a 1990 U.S. Congressional Resolution stating that "[i]t is the sense of Congress that, for purposes of determining child custody, credible evidence of physical abuse of a spouse should create a statutory presumption that it is detrimental to the child to be placed in the custody of the abusive spouse," several states have enacted laws creating such a presumption (Lemon, 2001). As of 2001, 20 states and the District of Columbia had adopted some version of a statutory presumption relating to domestic violence, whereas another 28 states allow or require courts to consider domestic violence when adjudicating custody between parents (Lemon, 2001). Psychologists who venture into evaluative work in this specialized area must become familiar with the complex web of interrelated legal standards pertinent to the welfare of children in families affected by domestic violence, and avail themselves of the scientific knowledge contained in the now-copious published literature.

CHILD CUSTODY AND VISITATION: WHEN THE CHILD IS THE CENTER OF A PRIVATE DISPUTE

As noted above, in child maltreatment cases, the state confronts adults, parents, or other suspected abusers, either through the criminal justice system or the civil juvenile court system, or both. The case comes to court because an adult has violated certain minimal standards set by society regarding how adults should treat children. Claims are investigated and evidence proffered to help the court to adjudicate the claims and determine the most appropriate disposition.

Child Custody Disputes in Divorce Cases

The court plays quite a different role in the run-of-the-mill child custody case brought about by parental divorce, or (with increasing frequency in recent decades) dissolution of a nonmarital relationship. These disputes must be adjudicated by the court when parents can't agree as to the roles each will play in the upbringing of their children (i.e., with whom will the child live what proportion of the time, with what schedule, and who will make which important decisions regarding the children's well-being). The court intervenes, not because of suspicion that one parent or another is abusive or inadequate (although such information could come to light during the evaluative process), but because the divorcing couple simply cannot find a way to resolve basic custodial questions without the court's assistance (Wyer, Gaylord, & Grove, 1987). To some extent, the parents invite the court into their private lives by virtue of their inability to settle matters on their own. Once there, the court's seeks to safeguard the children's best interests as it resolves this dispute.

Often a family court judge must choose between two adequate and committed parents and must determine which offers the better custodial placement for a particular child. Sometimes one parent emerges clearly as the better parent, perhaps because the other has a substance abuse problem, has a criminal record, has perpetrated domestic violence or child abuse, or won't stop smoking cigarettes in the presence of an asthmatic child. More typically, however, both parents have something to offer the child, and neither seems clearly unfit. Whereas gender-based presumptions governed until the last few decades of the 20th century, states have abrogated such precedents either by statute or by a judicial holding that gender-based preferences are unconstitutional (e.g., *Devine v. Devine*, 1981).

Today, no bright-line rules guide judges in private custody disputes, only the hopelessly subjective and indeterminate best-interests-of-the-child standard (Rohman, Sales, & Lou, 1987). Whereas some states delineate particular factors judges must consider, and others identify factors judges may consider, there remains little guidance as to how these factors should be applied in individual cases. So, judges often fall back on their personal values, as might we all, in trying to sort out what type of home life and relationships constitute the better environment for a particular child. Judges must consider whether children should live with the parent who has served as the primary caregiver. Does it matter how many hours a week the parent works, or who provides childcare in the parent's absence? How important is the potential for continued close contact with extended family members in each placement? Should religious upbringing enter the picture? How should gender of the child and parent factor into the determination? How do parental styles of discipline differ? Do younger children need to live with their mother?

Many judges must face the question of what role, if any, a parent's unconventional lifestyle should play in the custody decision. In prior decades, a mother who had sexual relationships with men outside of marriage was automatically disadvantaged in custody cases. Parents who entered into interracial relationships after the separation likewise were also faced unfavorable rulings until the U.S. Supreme Court decided the case of *Palmore v. Sidoti* (1984) and held that grounding of custody decisions on racial considerations is unconstitutional. In this landmark case, the court rejected as inappropriate the trial court's concerns about the social stigmatization a child would face if raised by her Caucasian mother and African-American stepfather. Today, gay and lesbian parents constitute the groups most likely to confront disfavor in custody cases in many jurisdictions (e.g., *Pulliam v. Smith*, 1998).

Given the challenges faced by courts, judges all too commonly defer to experts—that is, mental health professionals who offer evaluative judgments of the prospective custodians (Weithorn & Grisso, 1985). Psychological assessments can provide useful insights about each parent's and child's psychological functioning, such as the presence or absence of adjustment difficulties; the strengths, challenges, and special needs of the parties; and the interactions and relationships of family members (Weithorn & Grisso, 1985). Yet, in the face of two adequate competing parents, typically psychologists (and other mental health professionals) are no better equipped than are judges to make value-laden judgments of what is best for a particular child. Increasingly, behavioral science informs scholars and clinicians as to what types of deleterious life circumstances and influences may impair optimal development for many children, and what types of situations and contexts promote more adaptive functioning. Yet, we do not yet have the expertise to predict which of two adequate parents will indeed provide the better home (Rohman et al., 1987; Weithorn & Grisso, 1985). We can guess, and sometimes our guess is an educated one. But, much of the time, we simply do not know. Thus, psychologists and others involved in forensic evaluations in custody cases must refrain from reaching beyond their expertise (American Psychological Association, 1994; Weithorn, 1985; Weithorn & Grisso, 1985). As one commentator pointed out, "The indeterminacy [of what is in a particular child's best interests] flows from our inability to predict accurately human behavior and from a lack of social consensus about the values that should inform the decision" (Mnookin, 1975, p. 264). In our legal system, judges—not psychologists—are empowered to make the ultimate custody decision in the face of uncertainty. Psychologists can appropriately inform judges as to psychological functioning of the parties, the nature of the family relationships, and the state of pertinent scientific knowledge. Psychological evaluations can articulate informed judgments about the relative strengths and limitations of each parent and the resulting fit with respect to the child's needs, consistent with the American Psychological Association's "Guidelines for Child Custody Evaluations in Divorce Proceedings" (1994). But, psychologists must resist the temptation to take their evaluations the additional step of deciding, in those hard cases, who is the better parent (Weithorn, 1985; Weithorn & Grisso, 1985).

Various permutations of joint custody have evolved in many jurisdictions. Whereas this disposition offers the promise of reducing the number of intractable disputes between parents, allowing them to share custody, early research revealed that joint custody can be associated with its own sets of problems (Felner & Terre, 1987). Some children fared well in the face of such arrangements, and others did not. An increasingly useful data base has developed, identifying those situations in which such arrangements appear appropriate and beneficial, and in which situations children fare more poorly (see, e.g., Hetherington and Kelley, 2002; Maccoby & Mnookin, 1992). Evaluators must acquaint themselves with the empirical literature, so that their judgments reflect the most current research findings.

Nontraditional Private Disputes Concerning Custody and Visitation

Although the large proportion of private disputes about custody of and visitation with a child arise in the context of divorce, other situations also engender private custody and visitation disputes. Unmarried parents may dispute custody and visitation in much the same manner as do married parents. Unmarried biological fathers may need to demonstrate that they have functioned in a true parental role vis-à-vis the child in order to be accorded the same paternal rights as a married father. Although the U.S. Supreme Court has not fully clarified precisely what conduct on the part of an unmarried father earns him the same paternal rights as a man who married the child's mother, statutory and case law reveal that those men who provide financial support for and have regular contact with their biological children, and particularly those who have helped to raise their biological child, are more likely than those who haven't to be accorded paternal rights (Garrison, 2000).

In recent years, more gay and lesbian couples have started families, raising children as partners. Just like heterosexual couples, many of these partners ultimately choose to dissolve their relationships, and—just like heterosexual couples—many cannot agree on arrangements for custody and visitation of children when they separate. These cases raise intriguing questions for the legal system, and often trigger heart-wrenching custody disputes, as a child is torn between adults who compete for legal rights to raise or visit him or her. Frequently, partners in a lesbian couple plan for the conception of a child together, with one partner becoming inseminated artificially, and with an explicit or implicit understanding between the women that they will coparent the child. The legal system becomes involved when the partners' separation triggers a contest between the women, with the legally recognized parent (i.e., the biological mother) claiming that she is the only adult with parental rights. As such, she argues that her former partner has no legal basis on which to claim a right to a continuing relationship to the child.

Our legal system has traditionally favored and protected the rights of biological parents as against claims for custody and visitation by third parties who do not have formal parental legal status, even if such parties do have a *de facto* or functional parent-like relationship with the child. In one case, the U.S. Supreme Court rejected the claims of parental status made by foster parents, indicating that, despite the potential existence of relationships and functioning in a foster family that are much like a birth family, claims of parental rights by foster parents must fail when competing with claims by the children's biological parents, even where the latter's loss or relinquishment of custody at a prior point in time was the basis for the foster home placement (*Smith v. O.F.F.E.R.*, 1977).

Consistent with these principles and the basic constitutional imperatives addressed above, the law favors fit biological parents over nonparents. Whereas two feuding parents each have a legal right to continued contact with the child in the form of custody or visitation after divorce "unless it is shown that the visitation would be detrimental to the best interest of the child" (California Family Code, 2004), persons not in a formal parental relationship have no such rights. Certain subcategories of individuals (e.g., grandparents or step-parents) may have standing to bring a case and request custody or visitation, but those individuals do not have rights to visitation of the same force as the rights accorded legal parents. Rather, the courts apply statutorily defined criteria and exercise discretion in determining whether court-ordered visitation is in the child's best interests (Dolgin, 2002). And, particularly following the 2000 Supreme Court decision in *Troxel v. Granville*, judges accord substantial deference to a legal parent's preferences regarding such third-party visitation.

Although legal protection to parental discretion in child rearing—including parental autonomy in deciding with whom one's child associates, visits, and lives—generally coincides with our senses of what is in the best interests of children, there are those situations in which it may not be in a child's best interest to sever a relationship with a person who has functioned just like a parent. State courts have been split in adjudicating disputes between gay and lesbian partners. Some courts have recognized the functional parental relationship between a child and the biological parent's former partner (*In re Custody of H.S.H.-K.*, 1995). Other courts have been unwilling to look past the traditional deference to the legal parent (*Alison D. v. Virginia M.*, 1991). An influential and creative approach to recognizing a nonparent's relationship with a child was offered in a 1995 decision by Justice Abrahamson, writing for the Wisconsin Supreme Court in *In re Custody of H.S.H.-K.* Going beyond the state statutes, the court fashioned a four-prong test to identify what factors were necessary to constitute a legally cognizable relationship between a nonparent and a child:

> To demonstrate the existence of the petitioner's parent-like relationship with the child, the petitioner must prove four elements: (1) that the biological or adoptive parent consented to, and fostered, the petitioner's formation and establishment of a parent-like relationship with the child; (2) that the petitioner and the child lived together in the same household; (3) that the petitioner assumed obligations of parenthood by taking significant responsibility for the child's care, education and development, including contributing towards the child's support, without expectation of financial compensation; and (4) that the petitioner has been in a parental role for a length of time sufficient to have established with the child a bonded, dependent relationship parental in nature.

It is too early to know where the law governing these relationships is headed. Psychologists should remain aware that the law has evolved rapidly in the context of same-sex relationships, and substantial variability exists across jurisdictions. Most states still do not accord any formal parental rights to gay or lesbian partners of biological parents who have coparented a child in the absence of a legal adoption. Legal adoption, of course, creates a formal parent–child relationship that is equivalent to that of a biological parent–child relationship (Ellman, Kurtz, Scott, Weithorn, & Bix, 2004).

Petitions by gay and lesbian individuals to adopt their partners' children have also raised important questions for the courts and policy makers. In order for a court to grant an adoption, the child's existing legal parent(s) must consent to the adoption, which typically extinguishes the legal rights of these existing parents, in favor of the new adoptive parent–child relationship(s) (Ellman et al., 2004). States universally allow a parent to retain his or her parental rights if his or her spouse seeks to adopt the child, and there is no person other than the consenting parent with legal parental status. States have varied, however, with respect in their willingness to extend this *spousal exception* to circumstances in which it is a legal parent's same-sex partner who seeks to adopt. When courts or legislatures have permitted such adoptions, they have referred to them as *second-parent adoptions*. Some state courts, such as the Massachusetts Supreme Judicial Court, held that second-parent adoptions are consistent with the spirit of the adoption statutes, which exist to promote the best interests of the child (*In re Adoption of Tammy*, 1993). Other state courts, such as the Nebraska Supreme Court, have refused to permit such adoptions on the basis that such adoptions have not been authorized by the state legislature (*In re Adoption of Luke*, 2002). Although the Connecticut Supreme Court held that second-parent adoptions were not permissible under the Connecticut adoption statutes (see *In re Adoption of Baby Z.*, 1999), the Connecticut legislature responded the next year by passing a statute that explicitly authorized such adoptions (Connecticut General Statutes, 2004). California and Vermont explicitly permit second-parent adoption under statutes governing the formal marriage-like statuses available in those two states (i.e., domestic partnerships in California and civil unions in Vermont; Ellman et al., 2004).

A psychologist may be asked to testify as to a range of issues in cases involving gay and lesbian parents. If, in a jurisdiction that applies the Wisconsin test, psychological expertise may be needed to evaluate the nature of the relationship between the child and putative functional parent, pursuant to the fourth prong of the standard. If the court is considering a parent's refusal to allow his or her former partner to continue a relationship with a child whom they both have raised, psychologists may be asked to assess the impact on the child of termination of the relationship with the biological parent's former partner. Assuming that a state will grant a second-parent adoptions, the court needs to determine, as in any adoption, whether the adoption is in the best interests of the child. Given that no one opposes the adoption, and particularly where the prospective adoptive parent has already functioned in a parental role with the child, this finding is a relatively easy one for judges to make. But, there are instances in which a more searching psychological evaluation, examining the psychological functioning and relationships of the parties, may be helpful to the court.

To the extent that any party may challenge the parental fitness of gay or lesbian individuals on the grounds that their sexual orientation makes them a less suitable parent, psychologists should familiarize themselves with the robust data base indicating that children raised by gay and lesbian individuals do not differ from children raised by heterosexual parents on any developmental measures or indices of psychological adjustment (Chan, Brooks, Raboy, & Patterson, 1998; Patterson, 1995).

Grandparents and Other Nonparents

There has been much action in the state legislatures and courts concerning visitation by grandparents and other extended family members. Most states have statutes of some type that enable grandparents or other family members to bring a case seeking visitation (Elrod & Spector, 2002a). Often, the circumstances that trigger these cases involve the death of one parent, coupled with attempts by the deceased parent's parents to continue a relationship with the child over the objection of the child's surviving parent. This area is in flux, because there have been challenges to these statutes by parents. In a recent U.S. Supreme Court case, a Washington statute allowing nonparent visitation was permitted to stand, but the lower court was criticized for applying the statute in a manner that did not accord sufficient deference to the parent's preferences regarding the child's contact with grandparents (*Troxel v. Granville*, 2000). Following this case, the lower courts appear to be giving parental discretion greater weight, holding unconstitutional applications of these state statutes in many cases, thus narrowing the circumstances in which a court may grant nonparent visitation over parental objection (Elrod & Spector, 2002b). Psychologists may be asked to assist in these cases, informing the court of the nature of the child's relationship with those petitioning for visitation.

DELINQUENCY JURISDICTION: WHEN CHILDREN AND ADOLESCENTS ARE OFFENDERS

In order for an individual to be held responsible for committing a crime, a court must find not only that he or she performed the acts inclusive in the definition of the crime (*actus reus*), but that he or she also had a guilty mind, or *mens rea* (Bonnie, Coughlin, Jeffries, & Low, 1997). Precisely what state of mind constitutes the *mens rea* varies from crime to crime. Yet, a basic tenet in modern criminal law is that—subject to certain limited exceptions—criminal liability will not be imposed upon a defendant unless the prosecution can prove that the defendant formed the culpable state of mind required by the statute that defines the particular crime.

At common law, certain presumptions developed and guided the adjudications of minors accused of committing criminal offenses:

In general, children under the age of 7 were presumed incapable of forming *mens rea*, and thus could not be held criminally responsible. Children between the ages of 7 and 14 also were presumed incapable, but the presumption was "rebuttable," in that evidence could be admitted to demonstrate that a particular child, in fact, entertained a "guilty mind." Children age 14 and older were viewed as adults with respect to criminal capacity. (Weithorn, 1984, p. 26)

Yet, in the early 20th century, with the development of the juvenile court system, the processing of minors who allegedly violated criminal laws was shifted from the criminal justice system to the juvenile justice system. The same system with jurisdiction over dependency cases maintained jurisdiction over juveniles determined to have committed certain offenses. The juvenile court processed claims against juveniles for allegedly committing offenses that would constitute crimes if committed by adults. In addition, the juvenile

court can intervene in the lives of juveniles and their families for *status offenses*. Status offenses are types of noncriminal misconduct which can only be committed by minors, such as truancy, running away, habitual disobedience of parents, violation of curfew ordinance, and possibly also other conduct that indicates that a minor is beyond control of parents and other supervising adults (Weithorn, 2005).

Most writers cite 1899 as the date of the juvenile justice system's inception, because in that year the Juvenile Court Act in Illinois became effective, marking the first formal appearance of the juvenile court model in a state statute (Mack, 1909; Platt, 1977; Rothman, 2002). In its first 65 years, the juvenile justice system authorized substantial, and relatively unchecked, state intervention in the lives of wayward and needy children and families. Emphasizing rehabilitation through treatment, and education, the juvenile court system distinguished its motives, goals, and methods from those of the criminal justice system (Rothman, 2002). Punishment of an offender's conduct was not the system's purpose, nor ostensibly was retribution. Rather, the juvenile justice system aspired to shape and mold the characters of young persons who had come to the attention of the court whether because of misbehavior or apparent parental neglect. In an often-cited article published in the *Harvard Law Review* in 1909, Judge Julian Mack, a respected jurist and former juvenile court judge in Cook County, Illinois, set forth the juvenile court's philosophy:

Why is it not just and proper to treat these juvenile offenders, as we deal with the neglected children, as a wise and merciful father handles his own child whose errors are not discovered by the authorities? Why is it not the duty of the state, instead of asking merely whether a boy or a girl has committed a specific offense, to find out what he is, physically, mentally, morally, and then if it learns that he is treading the path that leads to criminality, to take him in charge, not so much to punish as to reform, not to degrade but to uplift, not to crush but to develop, not to make him a criminal but a worthy citizen.

And, it is this thought—the thought that the child who has begun to go wrong, who is incorrigible, who has broken a law or an ordinance, is to be taken in hand by the state, not as an enemy but as a protector, as the ultimate guardian, because either the unwillingness or the inability of the natural parents to guide it toward good citizen ship has compelled the intervention of the public authorities; it is this principle [that] was first and fully declared, in the Act under which the Juvenile Court of Cook County, Illinois was opened in Chicago on July 1, 1899. (p. 107)

As Judge Mack's essay reveals, the juvenile court sought to distinguish itself from the adversarial and retributive model characterizing adult criminal prosecution, espousing a *parens patriae* approach toward helping troubled youngsters (Weithorn, 2005). The system was to customize interventions to the needs of each youth. Thus, the court's determinations and dispositions were to focus not on the specific offense committed by an individual, or whether an offense had been committed at all, but rather the nature, course, and extent of intervention than the youth's perceived need for intervention (Feld, 1988). The juvenile court judge wielded relatively unbridled discretion in determining how a young person spent the rest of his or her minority years, whether or not the initial basis for jurisdiction was a dangerous offense, a minor misbehavior, or merely the perceived absence of adequate parental supervision. Notions of *mens rea* were less important, and often unimportant, in the juvenile court (Weithorn, 1984). Because the system's espoused goals were benevolent, and the minor was to receive treatment, not punishment, there was substantially less concern on proof of the elements of a crime in the traditional sense. Likewise, because the system was, in theory, less adversarial, due process protections were also less important. Concerns about minors' capacities to participate in the trial process, likewise, were downplayed because of the unique structure and goals of the juvenile justice system.

Many authors have observed that the creation of the juvenile justice system was grounded in several assumptions about the nature of childhood and adolescence (Ainsworth, 1991; Feld, 1999; Scott, 2000). Minors who committed illegal acts were perceived to be less deserving of blame and punishment than were adult offenders. Their youthful stage of life rendered them less responsible for their conduct; their capacities for moral judgment and self-control were not fully developed. Consistent with this, their minds, their characters, and their behavior patterns were seen as still developing, and thus more malleable than that of adults. Proper intervention in this critical phase of life, it was believed, could rescue these children, turn their lives around, and socialize them to be constructive, contributing adult citizens. Thus, the model postulated substantially different treatment for adult versus juvenile offenders.

Several shifts occurred in the latter part of the 20th century that portended dramatic changes in the process and foundations of our approach to juvenile justice. In the mid-1960s, during an era when civil rights of many disadvantaged groups gained public and legal attention, jurists and legislatures began to limit the unbridled discretion of juvenile court judges. In reality, juvenile offenders were often incarcerated, perhaps for many years, a clear deprivation of liberty, without the types of due process protection guaranteed to adults (*Kent v. United States*, 1966). Such practices had been justified by the *parens patriae* goals and purposes of the juvenile justice system. Yet, decades of experience revealed that, all too often, juveniles committed to the system faced incarceration and other deprivations rather than the customized benevolent treatment and education (Feld, 2000).

In the first U.S. Supreme Court case to examine due process in the juvenile court, *Kent v. United States* (1966), Justice Abraham Fortas wrote these now famous words: "There is evidence, in fact, that there may be grounds for concern that the child [committed to the juvenile justice system] receives the worst of both worlds: that he gets neither the protections accorded to adults, nor the solicitous care and regenerative treatment postulated for children." Beginning with *Kent*, followed by the ground-breaking *In re Gault* in 1967, and several other cases thereafter, certain due process protections were extended to juveniles processed through the system. One author refers to the shifts that began with *Gault* as the transformation of "the juvenile court from a social welfare agency to a legal institution" (Feld, 1984, p. 151).

Other phenomena occurred as well. Society became disillusioned with the rehabilitative emphasis of the juvenile justice system and the criminal justice system (Feld, 1999). Concern about rising crime rates, and juveniles' participation in serious offenses led to an increasingly dominant get tough attitude toward crime that stressed retribution and long-term incapacitation of offenders (Ainsworth, 1991; Feld, 1999). As we begin the 21st century, images of troubled juveniles as immature persons needing society's gentle care and supervision have taken the back seat to perceptions of juvenile offenders as superpredators, as persons beyond parental or adult control, as drug-abusing and weapon-carrying gang members, or as cold and calculating mass murderers who walk into schools and start shooting (Elikann, 1999). Law makers have taken society's cue. Increasingly, the focus is on the nature of the act, not the nature of the offender. In other words, if juvenile offenders who commit violent acts harm their victims as much as do adults who commit the same acts, then juveniles should be treated similarly to adults by the law, punished to the full extent that is appropriate for adults.

Consistent with this premise, one of the most dramatic shifts in legal policy has been the increase of juveniles who are processed in adult criminal court (Fagan & Zimring; 2000; Feld, 1999). Increasingly, states have passed statutes that authorize or require that juveniles be processed in adult criminal court under specific circumstances. Juvenile courts previously had greater discretion to determine whether or not to waive jurisdiction of some offenders, resulting in a transfer of the individual from juvenile court to adult criminal court (Gardner, 1997). They were often required to ground such a determination on whether a particular minor appeared to be amenable to treatment in the juvenile justice system and, in so doing, considered various factors relating to the minor (e.g., age, history of prior offenses, psychological functioning, potential for future recidivism, and danger to others) and the present offense (nature and seriousness of the crime; Gardner, 1997). Recent changes in state laws have increased the likelihood of transfer for minors of certain ages, or who are accused of committing certain acts, by creating presumptions for waiver, often abrogating the juvenile court's discretion in the matter, and placing certain juveniles and offenses exclusively within the jurisdiction of the criminal court (Gardner, 1997). And, in some jurisdictions where juvenile courts and criminal courts retain concurrent jurisdiction over certain juvenile offenders,

prosecutors retain discretion to charge the youth as a juvenile or adult (Feld, 1999).

As the juvenile court has become more like a criminal court, and as more minors are processed in adult criminal court with the increased emphases on punishment (leading to incarceration), many scholars are taking a closer look at juveniles' psychological functioning pertinent to the processing of adult defendants more generally. An extensive program of empirical research has been devoted to these topics by the MacArthur Foundation Research Network on Adolescent Development and Juvenile Justice. Psychologists may be relied upon, increasingly, to inform the court about juveniles' psychological functioning on a range of variables (Grisso & Schwartz, 2000; Melton et al., 1997; Warboys & Wilber, 1996). In addressing these, psychologists are urged to avail themselves of the increasingly rich literature examining policy issues, assessment approaches and methods, and recent data relating to the following questions (see, e.g., Grisso & Schwartz, 2000).

For example, how capable is the juvenile of understanding her *Miranda* rights and making intelligent and voluntary decisions regarding waivers of those rights (Grisso, 1981)? Is the juvenile competent to participate in the adjudicatory process (i.e., to stand trial or plea bargain) (Bonnie & Grisso, 2000)? Should the minor be waived to adult criminal court? Is the minor cognitively or emotionally mature enough to be held responsible for his or her acts? (Grisso & Schwartz, 2000). Does the minor have a mental disorder that affects his or her ability to conform to the requirements of the law, and that necessitates special responses from the juvenile justice or criminal justice system (Grisso, 2004)? What type of disposition seems most appropriate for the minor (see chapter 19, this volume)?

Pertinent to this latter question is knowledge of whether the minor has any special mental health or educational needs that can best be met by certain types of intervention (Kazdin, 2000). Researchers have noted that a significant proportion of juveniles with serious mental disorders are processed through the juvenile court and criminal justice systems (Otto, Greenstein, Johnson, & Friedman, 1992; Teplin, Abram, McClelland, Dulcan, & Mericle, 2002; Wasserman, Ko, & McReynolds, 2004; Weithorn, 2005). In addition to the natural overlap between the populations served by the mental health and juvenile justice system (Weithorn, 1988), recent policy-oriented developments may lead to increased numbers of youth with mental disorders in the juvenile justice system. For example, recent years have seen reduced availability of mental health services for emotionally disturbed children and youth in the community, the constriction of treatment-oriented services within the juvenile justice system, and a dearth of mental health interventions in the criminal justice system (Weithorn, 2005). Given these factors, it is possible that the need for psychological expertise in the evaluation of juveniles processed through the juvenile justice or criminal justice systems will increase.

CONCLUSIONS

This chapter has discussed the legal contexts of some of the more common circumstances in which psychologists are invited to participate as forensic experts in cases concerning children and families. The legal system's treatment of children and families is not static, however. Society changes, public policies change, and laws affecting children and families change. With each transformation, new issues arise, other issues gain prominence, and still others recede into the background. And thus, the questions posed to consulting psychologists change, as well. Yet, with each shift, the obligations of forensic psychologists remain the same. Abiding by the ethical principles that guide the profession (American Psychological Association, 2002), together with applicable specialized guidelines and standards (American Psychological Association, 1993, 1994; Committee on Ethical Guidelines for Forensic Psychologists, 1991), psychologists must exercise care at every step in the process of forensic evaluation. Doing so will enhance the likelihood that one's contributions will safeguard the rights of the participants, protect the welfare of children and their families, and contribute meaningfully to the legal process. Psychologists can play unique roles in informing the court of relevant aspects of the psychological functioning of children, adolescents, and their families when the questions they address are thoughtfully framed, when their assessment methods are appropriate to

the questions, when they integrate empirical data into their analysis and formulations, and when their choice of methods, analyses, and conclusions are cautious and measured, consistent with the state of knowledge in the field.

References

Ainsworth, J. E. (1991). Re-imagining childhood and reconstructing the legal order: The case for abolishing the juvenile court. *North Carolina Law Review, 69,* 1083–1133.

Alison D. v. Virginia M., 572 N.E. 2d 27 (N.Y. 1991).

American Psychological Association. (1994). Guidelines for child custody evaluations in divorce proceedings. *American Psychologist, 49,* 667–682.

American Psychological Association. (1998). Guidelines for psychological evaluations in child protection matters. *American Psychologist, 54,* 586–593.

American Psychological Association. (2002). Ethical principles of psychologists and code of conduct. *American Psychologist, 57,* 1060–1073.

Becker, M. (1995). Double binds facing mothers in abusive families: Social support systems, custody outcomes, and liability for the acts of others. *University of Chicago Law School Roundtable, 2,* 13–32.

Bellotti v. Baird, 662 U.S. 662 (1979).

Besharov, D. J. (1986). Child abuse: Arrest and prosecution decision-making. *American Criminal Law Review, 24,* 315–377.

Binggeli, N. J., Hart, S. N., & Brassard, M. R. (2001). *Psychological maltreatment of children.* Thousand Oaks, CA: Sage.

Bloch, K. E., & McMunigal, K. (2005). *Criminal law: A contemporary approach.* New York: Aspen Law & Business Publishers.

Bonnie, R. J., Coughlin, A. M., Jeffries, J. J., Jr., & Low, P. W. (1997). *Criminal law.* Westbury, NY: Foundation Press.

Bonnie, R. J., & Grisso, T. (2000). Adjudicative competence and youthful offenders. In T. Grisso & R. G. Schwartz (Eds.), *A developmental perspective on juvenile justice* (pp. 73–103). Chicago: University of Chicago Press.

Brooks, C. M. (1996). The law's response to child abuse and neglect. In B. D. Sales & D. W. Shuman, *Law, mental health, and mental disorder* (pp. 464–486). Pacific Grove, CA: Brooks/Cole.

California Family Code § 3010(a) (2004).

California Penal Code §§ 273a, 273ab, 273d, 273.1 (2004).

California Welfare & Institutions Code § 300 (2004).

Ceci, S. J., & Bruck, M. (1995). *Jeopardy in the court-room: A scientific analysis of children's testimony.* Washington, DC: American Psychological Association.

Chan, R. W., Brooks, R. C., Raboy, B., & Patterson, C. J. (1998). Division of labor among lesbian and heterosexual parents: Associations with children's adjustment. *Journal of Family Psychology, 12,* 402–419.

Clark, N. L. (1987). Crime begins at home: Let's stop punishing victims and perpetuating violence. *William & Mary Law Review, 28,* 263–293.

Committee on Ethical Guidelines for Forensic Psychologists. (1991). Specialty guidelines for forensic psychologists. *Law & Human Behavior, 15*(6), 655–665.

Connecticut General Statutes § 45a-724(a)(3) (2004).

Devine v. Devine, 398 So. 2d 646 (Ala. 1981).

Dohrn, B. (1995). Bad mothers, good mothers, and the state: Children on the margins. *University of Chicago Roundtable, 2,* 1–12.

Dolgin, J. L. (2002). The Constitution as family arbiter: A moral in a mess? *Columbia Law Review, 102,* 337–407.

Dorne, C. K. (2002). *An introduction to child maltreatment in the United States: History, public policy, and research* (3rd ed.). Monsey, NY: Criminal Justice Press.

Edleson, J. L. (1999). The overlap between child maltreatment and woman battering. *Violence Against Women, 5,* 134–154.

Elikann, P. (1999). *Superpredators: The demonization of our children by the law.* New York: Plenum.

Ellman, I. M., Kurtz, P. M., Scott, E. S., Weithorn, L. A., & Bix, B. H. (2004). *Family law: Cases, text, problems* (4th ed.). Newark, NJ: LexisNexis.

Elrod, L. D., & Spector, R. G. (2002a). A review of the year in family law: State courts react to Troxel. *Family Law Quarterly, 35,* 577–636.

Elrod, L. D., & Spector, R. G. (2002b). Family law in the fifty states 2000–2001: Case digests. *Family Law Quarterly, 35,* 637–774.

Fagan, J., & Zimring, F. E. (Eds.). (2000). *The changing borders of juvenile justice: Transfer of adolescents to the criminal court.* Chicago: University of Chicago Press.

Fantuzzo, J. W., & Mohr, W. K. (1999). Prevalence and effects of child exposure to domestic violence. *The Future of Children: Domestic Violence and Children, 9,* pp. 21, 26.

Feld, B. C. (1984). Criminalizing juvenile justice: Rules of procedure for the juvenile court. *Minnesota Law Review, 69,* 141–276.

Feld, B. C. (1988). The juvenile court meets the principle of offense: Punishment, treatment, and the difference it makes. *Boston University Law Review, 68,* 821–915.

Feld, B. C. (1999). *Bad kids: Race and the transformation of the juvenile court.* New York: Oxford University Press.

Feld, B. C. (2000). *Cases and materials on juvenile justice administration.* St. Paul, MN: West Group.

Felner, R., & Terre, L. (1987). Child custody and children's adaptation following divorce. In L. A. Weithorn (Ed.), *Psychology and child custody determinations: Knowledge, roles, and expertise* (pp. 106–153). Lincoln: University of Nebraska Press.

Gardner, M. R. (1997). *Understanding juvenile law.* New York: Matthew Bender.

Garrison, M. (2000). Law making for baby making: An interpretive approach to the determination of legal parentage. *Harvard Law Review, 113,* 835–923.

Goldstein, R. D. (1999). *Child abuse and neglect: Cases and materials.* St. Paul, MN: West Group.

Grisso, T. (1981). *Juveniles' waivers of rights: Legal and psychological competence.* New York: Plenum.

Grisso, T. (2004). *Double jeopardy: Adolescent offenders with mental disorders.* Chicago: University of Chicago Press.

Grisso, T., & Schwartz, R. G. (2000). *Youth on trial: A developmental perspective on juvenile justice.* Chicago: University of Chicago Press.

Hanna, C. (1996). No right to choose: Mandated victim participation in domestic violence prosecutions. *Harvard Law Review, 109,* 1849–1910.

Hetherington, E. M., & Kelley, J. (2002). *For better or for worse: Divorce reconsidered.* New York: W.W. Norton.

In re Adoption of Baby Z., 724 A. 2d 1035 (Conn. 1999).

In re Adoption of Luke, 640 N.W. 2d 365 (Nebr. 2002).

In re Adoption of Tammy, 619 N.E. 2d 315 (Mass. 1993).

In re Custody of H.S.H.-K., 533 N.W. 2d 419 (Wis. 1995).

In re Gault, 387 U.S. 1 (1967).

Jaffe, P., Wolfe, D. A., & Wilson, S. (1990). *Children of battered woman.* Newbury Park, CA: Sage.

Kadish, S. H. (1999). Fifty years of criminal law: An

opinionated review. *California Law Review, 87,* 943–982.

Kazdin, A. (2000). Adolescent development, mental disorders, and decisionmaking of delinquent youths. In T. Grisso & R. Schwartz (Eds.), *Youth on trial: A developmental perspective on juvenile justice* (pp. 33–65). Chicago: University of Chicago Press.

Kent v. United States, 383 U.S. 541 (1966).

Lanning, K. V. (2002). Criminal investigation of sexual victimization of children. In J. E. B. Myers, L. Berliner, J. Briere, C. T. Hendrix, C. Jenny, & T. A. Reid (Eds.), *The APSAC handbook on child maltreatment* (2nd ed., pp. 329–348). Thousand Oaks, CA: Sage.

Lemon, N. K. D. (2001). Statutes creating rebuttable presumptions against custody to batterers: How effective are they? *William Mitchell Law Review, 28,* 601–676.

MacArthur Foundation Research Network on Adolescent Development and Juvenile Justice. Retrieved September 3, 2005, from www .mac-adoldev-juvjustice.org/

Maccoby, E. E., & Mnookin, R. H. (1992). *Dividing the child: Social and legal dilemmas of custody.* Cambridge, MA: Harvard University Press.

Mack, J. (1909). The juvenile court. *Harvard Law Review, 23,* 104–122.

Margolin, G. (1998). Effects of domestic violence on children. In P. K. Trickett & C. J. Schellenbach (Eds.), *Violence against children in the family and the community* (pp. 57–102). Washington, DC: American Psychological Association.

Maryland v. Craig, 497 U.S. 836 (1990).

Melton, G. B., Petrila, J., Poythress, N. G., & Slobogin, C. (1997). *Psychological evaluations for the courts: A handbook for mental health professionals and lawyers* (2nd ed.). New York: Guilford.

Mintz, S., & Kellogg, S. (1988). *Domestic revolutions: A social history of American family life.* New York: Free Press.

Mississippi Band of Choctaw Indians v. Holyfield, 490 U.S. 30 (1989).

Mnookin, R. H. (1975). Child-custody adjudication: Judicial functions in the face of indeterminacy. *Law & Contemporary Problems, 39,* 226–293.

Nicholson v. Williams, 203 F. Supp. 2d 153 (E.D.N.Y. 2002); *affirmed sub. nom* Nicholson v. Scopetta, 344 F. 3d 153 (2nd Cir. 2003).

Otto, R. K., Greenstein, J. J., Johnson, M. K., & Friedman, R. M. (1992). Prevalence of mental disorders among youth in the juvenile justice system. In J. J. Cocozza (Ed.), *Responding to the mental health needs of youth in the juvenile jus-* tice system (pp. 7–48). Seattle, WA: National Coalition for the Mentally Ill in the Criminal Justice System.

Palmore v. Sidoti, 466 U.S. 429 (1984).

Parham v. J.R., 442 U.S. 584 (1979).

Patterson, C. J. (1995). *Lesbian and gay parenting.* American Psychological Association. Retrieved September 3, 2005, from www.apa.org/pi/ parent.html

Peled, E., Jaffe, P. G., & Edleson, J. L. (Eds.). (1995). *Ending the cycle of violence: Community responses to children of battered women.* Thousand Oaks, CA: Sage.

Pierce v. Society of Sisters, 268 U.S. 510 (1925).

Platt, A. M. (1977). *The child savers: The invention of delinquency* (2nd ed.). Chicago: University of Chicago Press.

Prince v. Massachusetts, 321 U.S. 158 (1944).

Pulliam v. Smith, 348 N.C. 616 (1998).

Roe v. Conn, 417 F. Supp. 769 (M.D. Ala. 1976).

Rohman, L. W., Sales, B. D., & Lou, M. (1987). The best interests of the child in custody disputes. In L. A. Weithorn (Ed.), *Psychology and child custody determinations: Knowledge, roles, and expertise* (pp. 106–153). Lincoln: University of Nebraska Press.

Rossman, B. B. R., Rosenberg, M. S., & Hughes, H. (2000). *Children and interparental violence.* Philadelphia: Brunner/Mazel.

Rothman, D. J. (2002). *Conscience and convenience: The asylum and its alternatives in progressive America* (Rev. ed.) Boston: Little Brown.

Santosky v. Kramer, 455 U.S. 745 (1982).

Saywitz, K., Goodman, G. S., & Lyon, T. D. (2002). Interviewing children in and out of court: Current research and practice implications. In J. E. B. Myers, L. Berliner, J. Briere, C. T. Hendrix, C. Jenny, & T. A. Reid (Eds.), *The APSAC handbook on child maltreatment* (2nd ed., pp. 349–378). Thousand Oaks, CA: Sage.

Scott, E. S. (2000). The legal construction of adolescence. *Hofstra Law Review, 29,* 547–598.

Smith v. O.F.F.E.R., 431 U.S. 816 (1977).

Stanley v. Illinois, 405 U.S. 645 (1972).

Stark, E., & Flitcraft, A. H. (1988). Women and children at risk: A feminist perspective on child abuse. *International Journal of Health Services, 18,* 97–118.

Teplin, L. A., Abram, K. M., McClelland, G. M., Dulcan, M. K., & Mericle, A. A. (2002). Psychiatric disorders in youth in juvenile detention. *Archives of General Psychiatry, 59,* 1133–1143.

Troxel v. Granville, 530 U.S. 57 (2000).

Wald, M. (1975). State intervention on behalf of

"neglected" children: A search for realistic standards. *Stanford Law Review, 27,* 985–1040.

Warboys, L., & Wilber, S. (1996). Mental health issues in juvenile justice. In B. D. Sales & D. W. Shuman (Eds.), *Law, mental health, and mental disorder* (pp. 503–521). Pacific Grove, CA: Brooks/Cole.

Wasserman, G. A., Ko, S. J., & McReynolds, L. S. (August 2004). *Assessing the mental health of youth in juvenile justice settings.* Washington DC: U.S. Department of Justice, Office of Justice Programs, Office of Juvenile Justice and Delinquency Prevention.

Weithorn, L. A. (1984). Children's capacities in legal contexts. In N. D. Reppucci, L. A. Weithorn, E. P. Mulvey, & J. Monahan (Eds.), *Children, mental health, and the law* (pp. 25–55). Beverly Hills, CA: Sage.

Weithorn, L. A. (1985). Psychological consultation in divorce custody litigation: Ethical considerations. In L. A. Weithorn (Ed.), *Psychology and child custody determinations: Knowledge, roles, and expertise* (pp. 182–209). Lincoln: University of Nebraska Press.

Weithorn, L. A. (1988). Mental hospitalization of troublesome youth: An analysis of skyrocketing admission rates. *Stanford Law Review, 40,* 733–838.

Weithorn, L. A. (2001). Protecting children from exposure to domestic violence: The use and abuse of child maltreatment statutes, *Hastings Law Journal, 53,* 1–156.

Weithorn, L. A. (2005). Envisioning second-order change in America's responses to troubled and troublesome youth. *Hofstra Law Review, 33.*

Weithorn, L. A., & Grisso, T. (1985). Psychological evaluations in divorce custody: Problems, principles, and procedures. In L. A. Weithorn (Ed.), *Psychology and child custody determinations: Knowledge, roles, and expertise* (pp. 157–181). Lincoln: University of Nebraska Press.

Wisconsin v. Yoder, 406 U.S. 205 (1972).

Wyer, M. M., Gaylord, S. J., & Grove, E. T. (1987). The legal context of child custody evaluations. In L. A. Weithorn (Ed.), *Psychology and child custody determinations: Knowledge, roles, and expertise* (pp. 3–23). Lincoln: University of Nebraska Press.

2

Integrating Assessment, Treatment, and Justice: Pipe Dream or Possibility?

Gary B. Melton
Robin J. Kimbrough-Melton

We have argued that, whenever possible, forensic assessment should be reserved for specialists in forensic practice—"mental health professionals whose work consists *primarily* or *solely* of conducting evaluations and consultation for the legal system" (Melton, Petrila, Poythress, & Slobogin, 1997, p. 95). In making that argument, we have been clear that our preference for use of forensic specialists is "not based on a belief that the skills involved are so difficult or the relevant knowledge so vast" (p. 97). Rather, we believe that "the organizational and role demands of forensic assessment are incompatible with general clinical practice" (p. 97).

Specifically, we have argued that:

(a) "Neither conventional nor optimal clinical practice is fully compatible with the forensic clinicians' proper emphasis on uncertainty. Maximum assistance to the fact finder requires adoption of a scientist's mind-set, with a skeptical view of the validity of inferences and careful scrutiny of the probabilities involved. Although there is no question that both the design and the delivery of clinical services should be informed by empirical research, continuous

self-scrutiny—in effect, self-doubt—about the validity of one's impressions and plans is likely to undermine therapeutic efficacy." (p. 96, citation and footnote omitted)

(b) "The techniques involved in forensic assessment also may be anti-therapeutic. Forensic evaluations typically must be conducted in a relatively short time, are not for the subject's own benefit, often focus on highly emotionally charged events, and commonly involve matters about which there is motivation to lie. As a result, forensic interviews often are confrontational and address traumatic memories faster than would be common in therapeutic assessment and intervention." (p. 96)

(c) Role confusion is endemic in forensic assessment, especially when a clinician acts as both evaluator and therapist for the same individual, given that the ultimate client in forensic evaluation is rarely the person who is being assessed.

(d) "Because of the exercise of authority that may be involved . . . , forensic practice may alter clinicians' perspective or reputation in ways that interfere with therapeutic evaluations and interventions with clients *without* legal-system involvement. . . . Mere association with the justice system may be enough to compromise the clinician's current and potential therapeutic relationships." (p. 96, emphasis added)

(e) Development and maintenance of effective procedures for interaction between the mental health and justice systems (broadly defined) requires a level of commitment that is probably unrealistic for clinicians for whom forensic work is a secondary task.

These are formidable challenges in any event, but they are compounded in child and family cases by the facts that the interests at stake are nearly always complex and often conflicting and that, whether by law, custom, or psychological reality, children are rarely independent actors. (For discussions of these issues, see, e.g., Melton, 1983, 1987, 1989, 1999.) A naive observer might expect, therefore, that special efforts would be made to separate child mental health services from the justice system in order to minimize conflicts of roles. One might also expect that, when the expertise of child mental health professionals is needed in the legal process, an effort would be made, as we in effect recommended, to separate forensic assessment from treatment services.

From their inception, however, child mental health services have been closely related to—even operated by—the juvenile court (Levine & Levine, 1992). Conversely, the juvenile court itself was conceived as a therapeutic instrument (Mack, 1909). Until the last third of the 20th century (*In re Gault*, 1967), juvenile courts in most jurisdictions more closely resembled mental health case conferences than criminal courts. Juvenile hearings were typically inquisitorial proceedings led by lay judges (not lawyers), who ignored the rules of evidence and who often gave no opportunity for cross-examination of prosecutorial witnesses. Although the use of lay judges in juvenile courts is a phenomenon of the past, the courts in some jurisdictions are often still inquisitorial in practice. Juveniles in those jurisdictions typically waive their right to counsel, and these waivers are accepted as competently and voluntarily made (Feld, 1993).

Nonetheless, few observers today would question that the basics of constitutional due process should apply in juvenile and family proceedings, and a trend has been in place for some time to shrink the jurisdiction of the juvenile court—in effect, not only to strengthen the court's foundation as a legal institution but also to limit its presumably benign measures to the truly deserving (Melton et al., 1997, § 14.02[e]). Thus, liberals have sought to formalize legal procedures in juvenile courts in order better to protect children's and parents' rights, and conservatives have advocated bypass of the juvenile system altogether to ensure that adult criminal conduct is punished and deterred.

Ironically, however, this continuing decline of the rehabilitative ideal in juvenile and family law has been occurring at the same time that there has been a more general effort to integrate the mental health and justice systems. Guided by the tenets of *therapeutic jurisprudence* (see, e.g., Stolle, Wexler, & Winick, 2000; Winick & Wexler, 2003), legal policy makers have been designing new types of court proceedings and establishing court-related or even court-based treatment systems that together are intended to match the legal process with therapeutic goals—in effect, to make the legal system a therapeutic instrument. Inspired by the historic therapeutic purposes of the juvenile court, adherents of therapeutic jurisprudence have given particular attention to the application of these new structures to juvenile and family cases.

Hence, for example, *drug courts* have become a "national movement" to apply "a therapeutic approach to criminal justice where offenders are required to undergo drug treatment, frequent drug testing and close monitoring, including regular court visits" (Freeman-Wilson, n.d.). Starting from the premises that "coerced treatment works" and "that we serve society best by addressing underlying challenges faced by the criminal offender," drug courts feature a new form of judicial activism in which courts systematically use their authority to build treatment plans and then to monitor defendants' treatment compliance and service providers' responsiveness. The enthusiasm of the bench, the bar, and various legislatures for this hybrid of the legal and treatment systems has been striking. The number of drug courts in the United States grew from 12 in 1994, when the National Association of Drug Court Professionals was founded, to about 1,500 that were in existence or in planning by 2003 (Freeman-Wilson, n.d.).

Given the almost religious fervor energizing this movement, it is perhaps natural that drug court advocates have sought to apply the innovation in the legal context that has the most extensive experience with a therapeutic purpose, even if many commentators and policy makers have become disillusioned about the juvenile court's capacity to implement the rehabilitative ideal (see, e.g., the commentaries on this point in Feld, 1999). Now, almost 40% of the drug courts in the United States are juvenile or family drug courts, with the proportion increasing (National Association of Drug Court Professionals, n.d.).

The forthright acknowledgment of the judge's role as director of coercive treatment in the drug court may further illuminate and thus intensify some of the points of ambivalence in the philosophy of juvenile and family law. However, juvenile and family drug courts also capitalize on those contradictions by effectively supporting the current trend not to abolish the therapeutic purpose for courts dealing with juvenile delinquency and dependency issues but instead to find the right population—those deserving of a second or third chance—for such an approach. (By contrast, many citizens are comfortable with a hard policy in the criminal justice system and offense-based—just deserts—sentencing for adult offenders virtually throughout that system.) Therefore, it can be expected that these and other specialized courts and quasi courts with a therapeutic purpose (see, e.g., on juvenile mental health courts, Arredondo et al., 2001; DiGiovanni, 2002) are apt to continue to grow at a rapid pace.

These efforts to morph courts into clinics (or vice versa) may appear to reduce the ethical quandaries and the related strategic problems of forensic assessment in cases involving young people and their families. However, they actually add a dimension to regular issues in juvenile and family forensic mental health by explicitly making clinicians adjuncts of—not just experts for—the court and often the de facto legal decision makers about disposition and, for that matter, sanctions for noncompliance with the treatment plan.

Hence, we turn now to an overview of the ordinary issues, and then we discuss their application in another context (child protection proceedings) in which mental health professionals seem almost inevitably to have multiple roles in both law and practice. We conclude by returning to a discussion of the new legal forms and offering some principles

that should guide relevant aspects of child mental health policy and practice.

GOALS AND VALUES IN THE JUSTICE AND MENTAL HEALTH SYSTEMS

Conflicts in Goals

The Consideration of Evidence

Some of the problems in integration of the legal system and the mental health system arise from conflicts in their goals. The primary purpose of the legal system is the pursuit of justice. Pursuant to that goal, American jurisprudence relies on an adversarial process for consideration of evidence. Each side in a dispute has the opportunity to put its best case forward—an approach that matches citizens' intuitive judgments of fairness, whether they are parties to the dispute or merely observers (Duquette, 1997; Lind & Tyler, 1988).

Although the legal process is sometimes described (incorrectly) as a search for the truth, it is designed to produce at least two views of reality, neither of which is an unbiased view. Facts and opinions most central to a material scientific or clinical issue may never be admitted into evidence, either because the information is perceived by the attorney(s) to whom it is known to be unhelpful to their client(s) or because it was gathered in a legally impermissible manner (Lind & Tyler, 1988).

Moreover, the opinions of experts themselves may be shaped by the process. When professionals are hired by interested parties, they may feel pressure to help their side. In posing questions for studies and analyzing findings, lawyers may encourage the experts, overtly or subtly, to give a certain slant or twist to what is known, or even to project an unjustified level of certainty (see *Daubert v. Merrell Dow Pharmaceuticals, Inc.,* 1993). Indeed, the experts know that their continued involvement in a particular case—and, therefore, their continued receipt of an hourly fee—is likely to be conditioned on their finding a way to construe their observations and expert knowledge in a manner supportive of the employing party's case. As consultants, they may properly guide their counsel in helping to choose which questions to ask, which ones to avoid, and which additional experts to employ. Even if the consultants are absolutely scrupulous in giving truthful answers, the process is designed in a manner that prevents telling the whole truth. Indeed, efforts by witnesses to provide the full picture as they believe it to be are likely to result in having answers stricken from evidence as unresponsive to the questions asked.

By contrast, mental health practice and, even more so, related research are grounded in scientific values. The processes of scientific research and clinical assessment are designed to follow the truth wherever that inquiry may lead, and scientists have an ethical duty not to suppress findings that are inconsistent with their own hypotheses or their employers' interests.

Promoting Clients' Well-Being

Although the conflict that may occur between the pursuit of justice and the search for truth may be the clash of goals that is the most likely to be addressed in discussions of law and mental health, perhaps the most fundamental clash of goals that sometimes occurs is between the pursuit of justice and the promotion of mental health. Indeed, it was this very issue that led to watering down of criminal procedure in juvenile courts, so that their rehabilitative purpose would not be thwarted. The formal adversarial process commonly used in American courts seems, on its face, to be at odds with the goal of promoting mental health.

This point was at the root of the flood of legislation in the 1980s and 1990s to reform procedures for testimony by child victims in both criminal and family law proceedings. The effort to draw a line on the use of special procedures (compare Goodman, Levine, Melton, & Ogden, 1991) illuminated the underlying problem with the approach:

> Although induction of anxiety certainly is not in itself a goal of the legal process, it may be an inevitable by-product of fulfillment of goals that the law does have. Legal proceedings have serious consequences, and legal settings must be sufficiently distinctive to symbolize their authority and dignity. Accordingly, both performance anxiety (as a result of the law's concern with the quality of testimony, given the significance of legal decisions, especially in the criminal law) and generalized anxiety (as a re-

sult of uncertainty about an unfamiliar setting) are expectable short-term effects of testimony. Demonstration that child witnesses are anxious about testimony thus proves too much. If the law permitted special procedures whenever witnesses were anxious, its legitimate goals would be frustrated. (Melton, 1992, pp. 154–155)

In essence, as this quote suggests, any involvement in the legal process may be problematic for individual children. Further, because of the perception of a clinician's cooperation in such a process, any entanglement by mental health professionals within the legal system may work against the effective functioning of the mental health system in pursuit of its central goal.

Beyond the psychological costs of involvement in the legal system per se, it is not difficult to imagine instances in which mental health professionals find themselves unwitting pawns of lawyers working toward contrary objectives. This situation is most apt to arise when clinicians (and their clients) believe that they are in a helping role but are in fact being used for forensic assessment or even criminal or child-protective investigation. Consider this troubling hypothetical case. Suppose that there is weak evidence supporting a sexual abuse allegation against a child's father. The prosecutor might decide to seek a civil (juvenile or family court) finding of child abuse with a dispositional order that the father enter psychotherapy. After a time, the prosecutor might ask the grand jury to subpoena the therapy records in the hope of finding new leads or an outright confession. The therapist who has promised a safe setting in which to explore and change pedophilic urges might then find that the therapy room at the mental health center has been transformed without the therapist's or the client's knowledge or consent into a substitute for the interrogation room at the police station.

Although the process described in this particular case is questionable not only ethically but constitutionally (Levine & Doherty, 1991), the ethical issue is present even when participation in treatment is *encouraged* but not *compelled* by state authorities and, therefore, the 5th Amendment's protection against self-incrimination probably does not apply. The ethical problem also arises, although perhaps less acutely, when there is self-referral into treatment but prosecutors seek to discover incriminating statements made in therapy sessions. Indeed, our society has institutionalized a version of this conflict by requiring clinicians to report to authorities (and thereby to initiate an investigation) each time that a client makes a reasonably believable statement in therapy that he or she has abused or neglected a child.

In short, the promise that "I'm here to help you" is not one that mental health professionals can reasonably make when they enter legal arenas. Moreover, the chances of such involvement in unwitting ways—in effect, of unplanned forensic assessment or investigation—may be especially great in child mental health practice, because child clients and often even parents who are clients are likely to be referred because of actual or threatened coercive or punitive action by a school or a social service agency or even by the court itself.

Congruence of Values

Although the significance of such conflicts between the legal and mental health systems, whether inherent or manufactured, should not be minimized, it also should not be overemphasized. Similar values underlie both the legal and the mental health systems. Both systems reject deceit and exploitive use of power; such use of power is a clear violation of both the person-to-person respect that is basic to a therapeutic relationship and the respect for personal dignity that is fundamental to Anglo-American jurisprudence.

Beneficence—the duty to promote the welfare of others—is the foremost value in the current edition of psychologists' ethical principles and code of conduct (American Psychological Association, 2002, Principle A), as it is in most of the codes of the helping professions. However, justice and respect for persons are also central values in psychologists' ethics. Psychologists are thus strongly cautioned to "respect the dignity and worth of all people" (Principle E), "respect and protect civil and human rights" (Preamble), and "ensure that their potential biases, the boundaries of their competence, and the limitations of their expertise do not lead to or condone unjust practices" (Principle D). Although these principles are aspirational in nature, their intent is to "guide and inspire psychologists toward the very highest ethical ideals of the profession" (Introduction to the General Principles).

Psychological ethics also are premised on due process: "Psychologists seek to promote accuracy, honesty, and truthfulness" (American Psychological Association, 2002, Principle C). When serving in multiple roles for judicial or administrative proceedings, they "clarify for relevant parties the roles they are performing at the outset" (Standard 3.05[c]). They avoid entering multiple relationships if the relationships could reasonably be expected to impair the psychologists' professional performance or could exploit or harm the other individual (Standard 3.05[a]).

As is true of most of the ethical standards discussed, similar, more specific provisions are present in the ethical guidelines (Committee on Ethical Guidelines for Forensic Psychologists [Committee], 1991) promulgated by the American Psychology-Law Society (Division 41 of the American Psychological Association) and the American Academy of Forensic Psychology (the association of diplomates in forensic psychology). Thus, as might be expected, forensic psychology comes even closer to sharing the core values present in the law. Thus, forensic psychologists have a duty to "*understand* the civil rights of parties in legal proceedings in which they participate, and manage their professional conduct in a manner that does not diminish or threaten those rights" (Committee, 1991, Guideline III(D), emphasis added). Note that this duty goes beyond the general obligation of psychologists to protect clients' civil rights by implicitly requiring education in the nature of those rights as they apply in various legal proceedings.

At this writing, the guidelines for forensic psychology are undergoing revision. However, revised guidelines undoubtedly will continue to emphasize forensic psychologists' "special responsibility for fairness and accuracy" (Committee, 1991, Guideline VII[B]) in presenting "findings, conclusions, evidence, or other professional products" (Guideline VII[D]) as part of legal proceedings. To that end, forensic psychologists have an affirmative obligation to present the boundaries of their competence regarding the specific matters to which they will testify and the factual basis of their testimony and conclusions (Guideline III[B]). In keeping, however, with the supreme value on justice in the legal system, forensic psychologists generally do not provide services to individuals prior to their representation by counsel (Guideline VI[D]), and they minimize reliance on information that would not otherwise be admissible in court (Guidelines VI(F) and VI[G]), presumably even if it would provide a more complete picture of relevant facts.

MENTAL HEALTH PROFESSIONALS' PARTICIPATION IN CHILD PROTECTION PROCEEDINGS

The Nature of Mental Health Professionals' Participation

The difficulties in blending assessment, treatment, and justice can be easily inferred by taking even a cursory look at the child protection system in the United States. More than a decade ago, the U.S. Advisory Board on Child Abuse and Neglect (1990) declared a national emergency in the child protection system. In presenting a proposed new national strategy, the U.S. Advisory Board on Child Abuse and Neglect (1993) subsequently lamented that the

> design of the child protection system is that investigation often seems to occur for its own sake, without any realistic hope of meaningful treatment to prevent the recurrence of maltreatment or to ameliorate its effects, even if the report of suspected maltreatment is validated. Obviously investigation cannot be removed altogether, but it should no longer be the centerpiece of child protection. (pp. 9–10)

The situation today has improved only marginally (Melton, 2002). This lack of improvement is unsurprising, given that the ineffectiveness of the system is the product of its design (Melton, 2005). In policy, practice, and public perception, child protection has been equated with reporting and investigation—determining what parents did or did not do. Although neither reporting nor investigation by itself prevents or ameliorates harm to children, this emphasis persists even after adjudication because of the perceived primary need to document whether parents have complied with court orders. The result is that caseworkers spend most of their time on investigation and the related paperwork (Weber, 1997).

This priority, in turn, detracts from the time, attention, and resources devoted to helping the child and the family. Even children who enter state care rarely receive treatment (National Research Council, 1993). Indeed, by state social service agencies' own admission, the proportion of families who are reported for suspected child maltreatment who, as a result, ever receive any service other than an investigation is minuscule (Melton, 2005). In the rare circumstances when services are provided, they are typically inexpensive, convenient to administer, and easily monitored in regard to parent compliance (e.g., parent education classes)—but ill-matched to the complex needs that brought families to the attention of public authorities.

Tragically, the current design of the child protection system may lead indirectly even to diminution of informal systems of social support and control. The message that has been well ingrained among both the general public and the professionals who work with children and families is that their duty is to report suspected child maltreatment to Child Protective Services (CPS) in the public social services agency, which will then investigate whether abuse or neglect has occurred. Many people probably believe that, having reported their suspicions, they should stay out of CPS's way. No one may perceive a duty to take further action, and no one may assume the responsibility to make everyday life in the community safer for children. Further, no systematic action may be taken to prevent further harm when maltreatment has already occurred.

Mental health professionals themselves potentially fulfill a number of roles in child protection cases that are not necessarily compatible, for example, reporter of suspected abuse or neglect; investigator; evaluator; mediator; expert witness, whether at adjudication (i.e., at a proceeding to determine whether legally cognizable maltreatment occurred), disposition, or sentencing; child therapist; parent or perpetrator therapist; or family therapist. Such a multiplicity of roles by its nature leads almost inherently to intractable conflicts that can be minimized—but not necessarily eliminated—by attempting to act only as an investigator or a helper. In the latter case, for example, a clinician might act only as evaluator for the purpose of service planning and as therapist.

Unfortunately, however, the disproportionate allocation of caseworkers' time and effort may be mirrored by psychologists' work related to child protection. If the published literature is an indicator, it seems clear that professionals in the behavioral sciences (whether researchers or clinicians), like those in the field of child protection as a whole, are more frequently involved in cases of child maltreatment as sleuths than as helpers. Forensic activities, especially those related more to adjudication than to disposition, appear to be drawing disproportionately on the time of mental health professionals in the child protection system. When clinicians do intend to be helpers, the actual or potential demand for their involvement as gatherers of evidence may loom large (Melton, 1994). Further, even research related to child maltreatment is heavily skewed to focus on legal processes (specifically, clinicians' decisions whether to report cases of suspected child maltreatment, and children's ability to fulfill the role of witness), with relatively little attention given to the design of policies and practices that would demand the safety of children (Melton et al., 1995).

Children's Advocacy Centers

The increase of mental health professionals' involvement in the steps leading to the adjudication of child protection cases has been promoted by the growth of children's advocacy centers (CACs). CACs typically integrate law enforcement, child welfare (CPS), victim assistance, and prosecutorial agencies with various forensic health and mental health services, typically at a single site. Commonly focusing largely but not exclusively on sexual abuse, the CACs are intended to facilitate interagency coordination and multidisciplinary input (especially in prosecutorial decision making), minimize the number of investigatory interviews to which children are subjected, and provide a relatively nonthreatening setting for these interviews. In part because of federal assistance for development of CACs, they have quickly become widely available, such that more than 500 had joined the National Children's Alliance by 2003 (for a list, see www .nca-online.org/members.html), up from 22 in 1992 (National Children's Alliance, 2004).

CACs often include mental health professionals on staff. Because of their presumed skill in interviewing children, the mental health profes-sionals may conduct many or all of the investigatory interviews on which CPS, police, and prosecutors rely. Even when mental health professionals in such settings do not themselves conduct the investigatory interviews, they are likely to participate as team members in prosecutorial decision making, and information that they gather in therapeutic interviews may be used in the team process. Thus, clinicians directly or indirectly participate in the gathering of evidence to determine, among other possible decisions, whether child maltreatment has occurred, a dependency petition will be filed in family court, criminal or juvenile charges will be brought against a suspect, the child will be placed into an emergency shelter or foster care, restrictions will be placed on the child's contact with parents, or both. Besides often acting directly as therapists and advocates to help to alleviate a crisis, mental health professionals become actively engaged as prosecutorial investigators and decision makers.

Although the role conflicts that result for mental health professionals are not unique to CACs, they are especially stark in such programs because of their prosecutorial linkage. Shortly after he founded the original CAC in Huntsville, Alabama, U.S. Rep. (then state district attorney) Robert Cramer noted the problems in blending treatment and investigation within CACs:

> I have seen our children's center develop components that I didn't think we would develop, particularly the mental health component. . . . In my opinion, the mental health component of this program is probably the most important component, because if we're truly to react to children and families in a therapeutic way, if we're truly to look beyond just the goal of criminal prosecution and what that might address, it is only through a properly trained and committed therapeutic staff that we are going to be able to do that. But you have all these complicated issues of how do you mix and mingle that therapeutic component with the investigative component. I am lumping CPS and the law enforcement detectives and prosecutors into that [investigative] aspect. (National Legal Resource Center on Child Sexual Abuse, 1991, appendix)

Congressman Cramer was so concerned with ensuring access to therapeutic services while also preserving the capacity for investigation that he wondered whether it made sense to put the investigative and the therapeutic staffs on different floors. Of course, physical separation only marginally mitigates the problem if functions and auspices remain integrated.

The dilemma that Congressman Cramer discussed is essentially twofold. First, if a mental health professional becomes concerned with gathering evidence and helping the prosecution to make its case (whether for conviction and incarceration of an incestuous father or a civil adjudication of abuse, placement of the child in foster care, and ultimately termination of parental rights), will the clinician's ability to function as therapist for the child or the family be compromised? Indeed, will the slippage into law enforcement activities compromise that clinician's ability—or even other clinicians' ability—to help other children and families? Second, will adoption of an explicit stance of children's advocate compromise mental health professionals' ability to act as unbiased experts?

Although these multiple roles (or a subset of them) can arise no matter what the auspice for the clinician's work, employment in a prosecution-affiliated facility makes the potential role conflicts explicit. Even if investigatory staff are physically separated from therapeutic staff as mentioned by Congressman Cramer, the problems persist of (a) possible spillover effects from proximity and contact with investigative staff on perceptions of clinicians among clients and the general public and (b) at least the appearance of bias in clinicians' judgments. The former possible effects can impede the clinicians' ability to act as effective therapists; the latter can adversely affect their objectivity as experts and clinical evaluators.

The role conflicts between investigator and therapist or even clinical evaluator are so profound that we believe that mental health professionals should avoid the investigative process altogether. The transition to investigator is even more striking than the transition to forensic evaluator. If mental health professionals are to become expert interviewers for prosecutorial agencies, then the need truly to specialize (as we suggested in regard to forensic evaluators) becomes still more pronounced.

As one well-known therapist for abused children observed:

> The tone of therapeutic work with children is acceptance, support, and advocacy. Investiga-

tive interviewers, although they may present to the child as warm, empathetic, accepting, and supportive, must remain objective, skeptical, and open to all information and alternative explanations. They must pursue details, attempt to learn from the elements of the crime, gently quiz the suspected victims, and refrain from advocacy. I submit that this is a very difficult shift for the CSA [child sexual abuse] therapist to make. (Saunders, 1993, p. 8)

Practically, the question is whether mental health professionals can act like therapists and also be effective investigators—or, more specifically, whether a confrontative style or an absence of confidentiality (at least as applied to criminal or civil prosecution of child abuse cases) tends to impede effective psychotherapy and social support or, conversely, whether involvement in treatment colors the validity of clients' testimony. Ethically, the parallel question is, even if mental health professionals can make the adjustment of roles, whether the people with whom they are working can make the necessary cognitive shift. Implicit social contracts and corollary duties of fidelity that emanate from clinicians' usual role may be violated when mental health professionals become investigators.

Indeed, the name *children's advocacy center* may be a misnomer. Typically, these centers assist the prosecutor to investigate and bring claims on behalf of the state. We do not have a system of private prosecution. When John Doe is accused of molesting Sally Doe, the case is called the *State* (or *People*) *v. John Doe*, not *Sally Doe v. John Doe*. In determining whether to bring these claims, the key question is not what would benefit the child or be in her best interest, but rather whether there is enough evidence to prove a violation of law. Although that determination can coincide with a child's interest, it does not always do so. Simply put, doing good—particularly doing good for a particular individual[1]—and doing justice are not synonymous.

We have focused on CACs because they have facilitated a refocusing of mental health professionals' involvement in child maltreatment cases in a manner that has increased the already substantial difficulty of such work and that may actually have inadvertently resulted in less availability of treatment services. However, we do not wish to leave the impression that this particular innovation is at the root of the problem. The dilemmas faced by clinicians working in CACs differ only in degree from those of child mental health professionals in general. Because of mandated reporting, a mental health professional may be required at the very first point in the process to move from the role of therapist directed by the client to that of decision maker mandated by the state to determine whether confidentiality should be violated and a legal process should be invoked involuntarily. Then the clinician may be expected to shift again to the role of neutral expert and then again to therapist for one or more parties who are involved in the case and still again to provider of information about compliance with court orders and of an opinion about potential for change. In such a complex and shifting environment, it is unsurprising that many clinicians themselves, the family members with whom they are working, and the general public become confused about the proper roles of mental health professionals, with concomitant overstepping of bounds, diminution of trust, or avoidance of work with high-need families altogether.

NEW ROLES AND NEW FORUMS

CACs are but one example of a new legal structure designed to respond to the complex psychosocial problems of people who become entangled in the justice system. Perhaps reflecting the peculiar focus of the child protection system, CACs are unusual in blending justice and treatment systems in large part for the purpose of evidence gathering.

The more common feature among new blended legal and quasi-legal forms is a focus on problem solving. Collectively, these approaches emphasize the quest for meaningful resolutions to the specific problems of defendants, such as substance abuse, mental illness, and child maltreatment. Problem-solving approaches typically stress comprehensive assessments, services tailored to the needs of the offender, and increased accountability to keep the offender in treatment. These new legal forms include a variety of specialty courts, such as adult and juvenile drug courts, mental health courts (modeled after drug courts), family drug courts, and domestic violence courts.[2] In these new models, the court moves to the center of treatment

monitoring and, to some degree, treatment delivery. The clinician becomes part of a multidisciplinary team that includes justice system representatives, mental health providers, and other sources of support.

Most problem-solving courts dispense with the traditional adversarial process and instead use a multidisciplinary, collaborative team approach in addressing the needs of the offender. Although the adversarial process is well suited to fair resolution of disputes, it is not a good means of problem solving and is viewed by many justice officials as being antithetical to obtaining appropriate services for the individual (Petrila, Poythress, McGaha, & Boothroyd, 2001). In muting the adversarial process, the judge becomes central to driving the rehabilitation of the defendant. Accordingly, substantive conversations in court are more likely to occur between the court, the individual, his or her family if present, and the treatment staff representing mental health and substance abuse treatment providers than with the lawyers. (Note that this inquisitorial process starts with an assumption of an admission of guilt by the defendant—or an acceptance of the allegations in the petition in a family [dependency] court proceeding.)

The belief of some that the authority of the court enhances the effectiveness of services, thereby increasing the likelihood that behavior change will occur, also has increased the attractiveness of drug and mental health courts to many in the legal and helping professions. By bringing to bear the full weight of the entire drug court team, the court is presumed to have the capacity to force offenders to deal with their problems or suffer the consequences (Chriss, 2002; Maxwell, 2000). On the one hand, the collaborative or team approach, where trust is established with the offender and treatment progress is encouraged, can feel more comfortable to treatment providers. On the other, in the context of the court setting, it can produce a paternalistic or coercive approach in which the offender is removed from treatment decisions, which are made in his or her best interests (Bean, 2002).

In addition to these new court forms, several quasi-legal strategies have been developed to improve service outcomes for young people in the juvenile justice system and families in the child protection system. Many of these, including family group conferences and circles of healing, blend Western norms of due process with indigenous Pacific Islander or Native-American traditions and are restorative in nature. The emphases are on enhancing and relying on the responsibility of both the individual offender and the extended family and community of which he or she is a part. These natural sources of support work in concert with court staff, mental health professionals, and others who may assist them in designing or implementing a service plan.

Initial evaluations of these new forms have generally been positive. Although selection factors complicate interpretation of evaluation results, drug courts have been associated with reduced recidivism, increased retention in treatment, better supervision and monitoring, and reduced jail costs (Belenko, 2001; Huddleston, Freeman-Wilson, & Boone, 2004; National Drug Court Institute, n.d.). Preliminary evaluations of mental health drug courts indicate that they have been effective in linking participants to treatment services, providing more treatment while involved in the mental health court than before, and structuring treatment plans to meet the specific needs of the individual (Casey & Rottman, 2003). Similarly, evaluations of the restorative approaches have shown that the level of satisfaction with the process is generally very high, except among victims (Levine, 1998).

Still, we should be cautious about such approaches. For one thing, criminal and juvenile justice systems are not the appropriate front door to access mental health and other treatment services (Bazelon Center for Mental Health Law, 2003). Specialty courts and other quasi-legal programs are largely reactions to the failure of the traditional treatment systems. However well-meaning these programs are, use of the legal system to provide help is intrusive, inefficient, and costly. Although judges should have alternatives to incarceration, it would make more sense to strengthen the voluntary system of services so that individuals do not have to offend to receive responsive services.[3] Moreover, if a strong community-based system of services is lacking, any progress that offenders may make in court-based programs is potentially threatened when they leave the court's jurisdiction to return to the community. Indeed, these programs may have the unintended effect of reducing service options for the general population and thereby leaving some in the community with even less access to services. The bottom line is that essential services and supports for individuals are critical to effective intervention, regardless of whether the individual is in the community or in the legal system.

More than a century of experience with juvenile courts gives no reason to believe that court personnel (e.g., judges, probation officers), as a group, are especially insightful in their attempts to be therapeutic. In fact, the inability of traditional juvenile courts to fulfill their rehabilitative potential has been a key factor in the growth of juvenile drug courts. Even though juvenile courts already have the authority to craft individualized and creative dispositions, judges creating drug courts have argued that they simply do not have the time to dedicate to each case. They have reasoned that, by pulling together a team under the authority of the court, juvenile drug courts could produce more comprehensive assessments; better integration of information about the juvenile and the juvenile's parents; increased coordination among the court, the treatment community, the schools, and other agencies; and improved training of professionals involved with the juvenile. Few would argue with such admirable goals. Nonetheless, juvenile drug offenders are neither more deserving of a responsive system nor better suited to a therapeutic approach by the court than are juveniles who commit other types of offenses. Ultimately, the further specialization of juvenile courts probably decreases the odds that youth who do not have the right offense history will receive the level of attention that they deserve.

Of course, using the coercive power of the court to access treatment services does not mean that treatment will be any more effective or responsive than badly designed voluntary services, but it may be very costly to relationships. As Diamond (1996) has noted, the need for coercive treatment is indicative of a failure of the relationship between the client and the treatment staff (p. 61). When coercion is introduced, the relationship moves from collaborative to controlling.

Specialty courts, including juvenile drug courts, are only nominally voluntary. When the juvenile's choice is between seeing a drug counselor and being locked up for an indefinite period in a juvenile correctional facility, not only does the dynamic of the relationship between juvenile and clinician change, but it is also questionable whether the court is doing justice, given the incentive for a quick guilty plea. In that regard, specialty courts are simply the latest in a long history of efforts to reconcile the promise of the juvenile court as a therapeutic instrument with requirements for due process and public desire for offender accountability. (Analogous issues apply in specialized courts for families facing child protective jurisdiction.)

Although mental health professionals generally have welcomed the emergence of these new legal and quasi-legal forms, the role conflicts discussed previously still apply. Indeed, they are ubiquitous. The role conflicts for clinicians may be the most pronounced in the specialty courts where treatment providers find themselves in the unusual position of acting as employees of the court (Bean, 2002)—in effect, becoming de facto probation officers. Working in the specialty courts means undertaking and completing treatment as directed by the judge, yet also offering expertise and advice (Bean, 2002). It also means monitoring the treatment progress and compliance of the offender and reporting back to the court. Where the offender does not comply, it means participating, as a member of the team, in the imposition of sanctions, which can range from more intensive treatment to incarceration. The threat not only to the immediate therapeutic relationship but also to the integrity of the mental health system is obvious.

CONCLUSIONS: FROM PIPE DREAMS TO POSSIBILITIES

Mental Health Professionals in New Legal Forums

As the general tenor of this chapter makes clear, we are skeptical about the use of the legal system as a therapeutic instrument and ironically, therefore, the transformation of mental health professionals into agents of the court. Our skepticism rests on doubt about (a) the legal system's capacity to do justice well when the professionals involved are putting therapeutic goals first, (b) the mental health system's capacity to do prevention and treatment well when it is identified by the

public as an arm of the court (more an agent of control than of help), and (c) the ethical problems resulting from possible violations of clients' reasonable expectations because of professionals' conflicts of role and interest.

We have given particular attention to ways that clinicians may act, even unwittingly, as agents of the prosecution or the court. New legal forms that place treatment in the justice system are particularly suspect because of their coercive elements. In such a context, regular clinical assessment may produce recommendations that effectively have force of law. The new forms also tend to give short shrift to the basics of due process. Doing justice gives way to promoting treatment.

Promoting Perceived Justice

Ultimately, however, the most important issue may be less the form than the feel of the proceeding. As discussed above, psychologists should "respect the dignity and worth of all people" (American Psychological Association, 2002, Principle E). Similarly, as recognized in the Convention on the Rights of the Child (1989), the legal system should treat every child within it "in a manner consistent with the child's sense of dignity and worth, which reinforces the child's respect for the human rights and fundamental freedoms of others and which takes into account the child's age and the desirability of promoting the child's reintegration and the child's assuming a constructive role in society" (Article 40, § 1).[4]

Thus, the most important goal in these new court forms and, for that matter, in traditional settings may be to create processes in which children and parents have a say and in which they feel that they are treated fairly and taken seriously by the justice and mental health professionals. Research has shown that perceptions of coercion in the mental health system are based less on objective voluntariness than on the opportunity to tell one's story and the experience of being treated with respect and without deception, even when the ultimate decision was negative (Diamond, 1996). Studies of perceived procedural justice in the courts have produced similar results (Lind & Tyler, 1988). Further, preliminary evaluations have shown that problem-solving approaches generally have been regarded more highly than traditional court proceedings on the dimensions of respect, neutrality, voice, and trustworthiness (Casey & Rottman, 2003).

Whether in the new or the old justice system, mental health professionals thus may be helpful consultants or family advocates in enabling the affected parties to optimize their use of the legal system (compare Melton et al., 1997, § 6.07[a]) and thus to feel that they are being taken seriously (for an extensive proposal for creation of a role of *family associates* to aid families in navigating the juvenile justice system, see Melton, Frick, Lyons, & Vazzana, 2002). This role is especially significant in the light of evidence that even young people with extensive experience as respondents or witnesses often have basic misunderstandings of the legal process, discomfort in relying on professionals, or both (Grisso, 1981; Melton & Limber, 1992), that many youth in the system have significant levels of emotional disturbance (Grisso, 2004; Melton et al., 1998), and that family members are often kept in the dark about what is happening in the legal process (Melton et al., 2002).

Such a role does clearly offer a means of using psychological expertise to facilitate protection of civil rights and assertion of some level of personal control. As such, it offers a coherent, unconflicted blend of the pursuit of justice (foremost) and mental health.

QUESTIONS FOR ASSESSMENT

The development that we find most troubling is the trend toward increasing involvement of mental health professionals in developing evidence as part of the case in chief, whether in a criminal proceeding, juvenile court, or a dependency proceeding. Such a role brings mental health professionals' credibility as both experts and helpers into question. Further, when clinicians not only gather evidence but also render opinions about its meaning (regarding, e.g., whether a child was abused), they almost inevitably go beyond the bounds of specialized knowledge. By diverting mental health professionals to law enforcement tasks, such work also makes the shortage of help available to troubled children and their families even more acute.

The most useful role of mental health professionals in juvenile and family cases is apt instead

to be the most traditional: *dispositional assessment.* Whether the specific context is delinquency, status offense, child abuse and neglect, or child custody in divorce, forensic issues in juvenile and family courts typically are dispositional. Even in preadjudication contexts (e.g., consideration of transfer to criminal court), the questions (e.g., amenability to treatment) are typically dispositional in content.

In such contexts, mental health professionals can be helpful to juvenile courts in conducting assessments that preserve justice goals while improving interventions for youth and families. If done well, such assessments differ from conventional clinical assessment in two ways. First, the scope is apt to be much broader. Juvenile and family courts typically have very broad jurisdiction, sometimes including agency oversight. The potential range of conditions of probation in juvenile court or of custody and visitation in family court is virtually infinite. Hence, treatment in concept includes not only conventional mental health interventions but also educational, vocational, and both formal and informal social support for the family as a whole or as individuals. Therefore, the clinician who adopts a broad, ecological perspective can be helpful to the court in its crafting of dispositions that are more closely tailored not only to the case facts but also to the huge body of research showing complex social, economic, and psychological causation to juvenile delinquency, child maltreatment, and children's adjustment to divorce (as relevant).

On the one hand, the clinician who attempts to assess the level of a juvenile's amenability to particular treatments based on a thorough investigation of the juvenile's behavior at home, at school, and in the neighborhood and who is knowledgeable about services that exist in the community can be instrumental in assisting in the development of comprehensive services that are responsive to the specific needs of the child and the family. On the other hand, a clinician who provides the seemingly ubiquitous recommendation for a structured treatment program is not helping the court. Such a recommendation is practically worthless to a court trying to make a transfer or dispositional decision (Melton et al., 1997, § 14.05).

Mental health professionals also should be cognizant that even in dispositional planning, there may be challenging differences of perspective in trying to accommodate objectives of both personal accountability and therapeutic change. For example, analysis of the circumstances under which a particular young person breaks the law in combination with knowledge of the causes and correlates of delinquency may lead to the conclusion that neighborhood change is apt to be a critical part of an intervention plan. Even if the court has express statutory authority to address community conditions for young people, it is apt, however, to find thinking and acting in such terms —maybe even thinking and acting in terms of family change—to be a foreign endeavor (Davidson & Saul, 1982).

This point leads to the second key difference between dispositional assessment and ordinary clinical assessment. Although the client is theoretically the ultimate decision maker about treatment options, clinicians are accustomed—even expected— to give opinions about the course of treatment that should be followed and often even to act accordingly unless there is an explicit objection.

When the same sort of assessment is taken into a court, where it may be ordered involuntarily, the question at hand is a legal/moral matter that is properly reserved for the judge. Mental health professionals possess no particular moral insight that should enable them to render opinions in such a context about whether a juvenile should be subjected to a particular involuntary treatment, a child should be placed in foster care, or a particular parent should have custody of children in a divorce. As a matter of ethics, such opinions should not be offered. As a matter of law, they should not be admitted.

In the same vein, clinicians should take special care to provide information about the scientific foundation for their predictions, including the risk of error, about the likely effects of various interventions. Obfuscating or ignoring such points may make for clearer, more confident testimony, but it does not result in wiser or fairer decisions.

It is important to remember that a court—or a problem-solving, quasi-legal substitute for a court —that does not fulfill the purpose of justice, whatever its prowess in organizing treatment services, fails in the end. At the same time, therapeutic beneficence is pursued in the service of respect for human dignity. Accordingly, whether a parent, a child, an extended-family member, or a community observer, one should be able to expect that he or she will be treated politely and kept honestly informed and free of unwanted and unjustified intrusions. In that regard, the sometimes striking differences in purposes and methods between the mental health and legal systems are ultimately overcome by the commonality of values that are at their core.

Notes

Portions of this chapter were drawn in revised form from Melton (1994), which was originally published in *The Future of Children*, a publication of the Center for the Future of Children, The David and Lucille Packard Foundation.

1. An additional problem with the name *children's advocacy center* is that the fact that the interests of a particular child are served does not mean that the interests of children as a class are advanced. A ubiquitous problem in child policy is the usually erroneous assumption that children are a unitary class (Melton, 1987; Mnookin, 1985)—in effect, that child advocates can presume that the interests of children are congruent, regardless of their social class, ethnicity, religion, and so forth. Perhaps more subtly, the well-being of particular children and of children in general may be conflicting. In the aggregate, for example, children might be safer if the child protection system were fully voluntary and, therefore, the community assumed broad responsibility. However, such a policy would result in our knowingly subjecting some children to egregious situations. To bring that point to the case level, the interests of a particular victim and those of children in general may clash in the decision whether to file a legal action.

2. The list of types of problem-solving courts is lengthy. Other examples include DWI/drug courts, reentry drug courts, tribal healing-to-wellness courts, campus drug courts, community courts, teen courts, prostitution courts, parole violation courts, homeless courts, truancy courts, and child support courts (Huddleston et al., 2004).

3. In that sense, status offense jurisdiction provides a simple version of current issues regarding specialty courts. Status offenses have long provided a safety valve of sort that provided a means for moving children between the mental health and the juvenile justice systems as the door to one or the other became more difficult to enter (see Melton, Spaulding, & Lyons, 1998). Indeed, mental health

and social service personnel sometimes use the label children in need of services literally and accordingly rely on status offense jurisdiction to obtain treatment for children and families (Melton et al., 1997, § 14.08).

Although this practice often is benevolently motivated, it is problematic. In addition to the fact that the courts are not structured to do crisis intervention or to deliver mental health services, invocation of court jurisdiction is not a guarantee that the treatment provided will meet the specific needs of the family. Moreover, use of the court transforms any services that are provided into coercive services and subjects the recipient to the stigma of the label of delinquent.

4. The United States is one of two countries that are signatory but not party to the Convention on the Rights of the Child (CRC). Nonetheless, the CRC provides a statement of global consensus about the requisites for treatment of children with due respect for their dignity. In that regard, the American Psychological Association supports use of the CRC as a framework to guide psychologists' work with children (Levant, 2002).

References

American Psychological Association. (2002). Ethical principles of psychologists and code of conduct. *American Psychologist, 57,* 1060–1073.

Arredondo, D. E., Kumli, K., Soto, L., Colin, E., Ornellas, J., Davilla, R. J., Jr., et al. (2001, Fall). Juvenile mental health court: Rationale and protocols. *Juvenile & Family Court Journal, 52,* 1–19.

Bazelon Center for Mental Health Law. (2003). *Criminalization of people with mental illness: The role of mental health courts in prison reform.* Retrieved September 15, 2004, from www.bazelon.org/issues/criminalization/publications/mentalhealthcourts/index.htm

Bean, P. (2002). Drug courts, the judge, and the rehabilitative ideal. In J. L. Nolan, Jr. (Ed.), *Drug courts in theory and in practice* (pp. 235–255). New York: Aldine de Gruyter.

Belenko, S. (2001, June). *Research on drug courts: A critical review. 2001 update.* New York: Columbia University, National Center on Addiction and Substance Abuse.

Casey, P. M., & Rottman, D. B. (2003, July). *Problem-solving courts: Models and trends.* Paper presented at a conference on Problem-Solving Courts: An International Perspective, Edinburgh, Scotland. Retrieved September 18, 2004, from www.ncsconline.org/D_Research/Problem-Solving.html

Chriss, J. J. (2002). The drug court movement: An analysis of tacit assumptions. In J. L. Nolan, Jr. (Ed.), *Drug courts in theory and in practice* (pp. 189–213). New York: Aldine de Gruyter.

Committee on Ethical Guidelines for Forensic Psychologists. (1991). Specialty guidelines for forensic psychologists. *Law & Human Behavior, 15,* 655–665.

Convention on the Rights of the Child, G.A. Res. 44/25, U.N. GAOR Supp. 49 at 165, U.N. Doc. A/44 736 (1989).

Daubert v. Merrell Dow Pharmaceuticals, Inc., 509 U.S., 579 113 S.Ct. 2786 (1993).

Davidson, W. S., II, & Saul, J. A. (1982). Youth advocacy in the juvenile court: A clash of paradigms. In G. B. Melton (Ed.), *Legal reforms affecting child and youth services* (pp. 29–42). New York: Haworth.

Diamond, R. J. (1996). Coercion and tenacious treatment in the community: Applications to the real world. In D. L. Dennis & J. Monahan (Eds.), *Coercion and aggressive community treatment: A new frontier in mental health law* (pp. 53–72). New York: Plenum.

DiGiovanni, A. (2002). The Los Angeles County juvenile mental health court: An innovative approach to crime, violence, and delinquency among our youth. *Journal of Juvenile Law, 23,* 1–14.

Duquette, D. N. (1997). Lawyers' roles in child protection. In M. E. Helfer, R. S. Kempe, & R. D. Krugman (Eds.), *The battered child* (5th ed., pp. 460–481). Chicago: University of Chicago Press.

Feld, B. C. (1993). *Justice for children: The right to counsel and the juvenile court.* Boston: Northeastern University Press.

Feld, B. C. (Ed.). (1999). *Readings in juvenile justice administration.* New York: Oxford University Press.

Freeman-Wilson, K. (n.d.). *Letter From the President.* Retrieved March 5, 2005, from www.nadcp.org/about

Goodman, G. S., Levine, M., Melton, G. B., & Ogden, D. W. (1991). Child witnesses and the confrontation clause: The American Psychological Association brief in *Maryland v Craig. Law & Human Behavior, 15,* 13–29.

Grisso, T. (1981). *Juveniles' waiver of rights: Legal and psychological competence.* New York: Plenum.

Grisso, T. (2004). *Double jeopardy: Adolescent offenders with mental disorders.* Chicago: University of Chicago Press.

Huddleston, C. W., III, Freeman-Wilson, K., & Boone, D. L. (2004, May). *Painting the current picture: A national report card on drug courts and other problem solving court programs in the United States* (Vol. 1, No. 1). Alexandria, VA: National Drug Court Institute.

In re Gault, 387 U.S. 1 (1967).

Levant, R. F. (2002). Proceedings of the American Psychological Association, Incorporated, for the legislative year 2001. *American Psychologist, 57*, 531–595.

Levine, M. (1998). Empowering families and communities: The New Zealand family group conference. *Family Futures, 2*(3), 40–43.

Levine, M., & Doherty, E. (1991). The Fifth Amendment and therapeutic requirements to admit abuse. *Criminal Justice & Behavior, 18*, 98–112.

Levine, M., & Levine, A. (1992). *Helping children: A social history.* New York: Oxford University Press.

Lind, E. A., & Tyler, T. R. (1988). *The social psychology of procedural justice.* New York: Plenum.

Mack, J. W. (1909). The juvenile court. *Harvard Law Review, 23*, 104–122.

Maxwell, S. R. (2000). Sanction threats in court-ordered programs: Examining their effects on offenders mandated into drug treatment. *Crime & Delinquency, 46*, 542–563.

Melton, G. B. (1983). *Child advocacy: Psychological issues and interventions.* New York: Plenum.

Melton, G. B. (1987). Children, politics, and morality: The ethics of child advocacy. *Journal of Clinical Child Psychology, 16*, 357–367.

Melton, G. B. (1989). Are adolescents people? Problems of liberty, entitlement, and responsibility. In J. Worell & F. Danner (Eds.), *The adolescent as decision-maker: Applications to development and education* (pp. 281–306). San Diego: Academic Press.

Melton, G. B. (1992). Children as partners for justice: Next steps for developmentalists. *Monographs of the Society for Research in Child Development, 57*(5), 153–159.

Melton, G. B. (1994). Doing justice and doing good: Conflicts for mental health professionals. *Future of Children, 4*(2), 102–118.

Melton, G. B. (1999). Parents *and* children: Legal reform to facilitate children's participation. *American Psychologist, 54*, 941–951.

Melton, G. B. (2002). Chronic neglect of family violence: More than a decade of reports to guide U.S. policy. *Child Abuse & Neglect, 26*, 569–586.

Melton, G. B. (2005). Mandated reporting: A policy without reason. *Child Abuse & Neglect, 29*, 9–18.

Melton, G. B., Frick, P. J., Lyons, P. M., Jr., & Vazzana, A. D. (2002). *Supporting families of serious and habitual offenders: Family Associates manual.* Miami: Juvenile Assessment Center.

Melton, G. B., Goodman, G. S., Kalichman, S. C., Levine, M., Saywitz, K. J., & Koocher, G. P. (1995). Empirical research on child maltreatment and the law. (Report of the American Psychological Association Working Group on Legal Issues Related to Child Abuse and Neglect). *Journal of Clinical Child Psychology, 24*(Suppl.), 47–77.

Melton, G. B., & Limber, S. P. (1992). What rights mean to children: Children's own views. In M. Freeman & P. Veerman (Eds.), *Ideologies of children's rights* (pp. 167–187). Dordrecht, Netherlands: Martinus Nijhoff.

Melton, G. B., Petrila, J., Poythress, N. G., & Slobogin, C. (1997). *Psychological evaluations for the courts: A handbook for mental health professionals and lawyers* (2nd ed.). New York: Guilford.

Melton, G. B., Spaulding, W. J., & Lyons, P. M., Jr. (1998). *No place to go: Civil commitment of minors.* Lincoln: University of Nebraska Press.

Mnookin, R. H. (Ed.). (1985). *In the interest of children: Advocacy, law reform, and public policy.* San Francisco: W. H. Freeman.

National Association of Drug Court Professionals. (n.d.). *What Is a Drug Court?* Retrieved March 5, 2005, from www.nadcp.org/whatis

National Children's Alliance. (2004). *Joining Hands to Protect Children: 2003 Annual Report.* Retrieved March 7, 2005, from www.nca-online.org/files/2003 Annual Report.pdf

National Drug Court Institute. (n.d.). *Drug Court Facts.* Retrieved March 8, 2005, from www.ndci.org/courtfacts.htm

National Legal Resource Center on Child Sexual Abuse. (1991). *A coordinated community response to child sexual abuse: Assessing a model.* Huntsville, AL: Author.

National Research Council. (1993). *Understanding child abuse and neglect.* Washington, DC: National Academy Press.

Petrila, J., Poythress, N. G., McGaha, A., & Boothroyd, R. A. (2001). Preliminary observations from an evaluation of the Broward County mental health court. *Court Review, 37*(4), 14–22.

Saunders, B. (1993, July). Mental health professionals and the investigation of child sexual abuse allegations. *Violence Update, 6*, 5–6, 8.

Stolle, D. P., Wexler, D. P., & Winick, B. J. (Eds.). (2000). *Practicing therapeutic jurisprudence: Law as a helping profession.* Durham, NC: Carolina Academic Press.

U.S. Advisory Board on Child Abuse and Neglect. (1990). *Responding to a national emergency: Critical first steps toward a national strategy on child abuse and neglect.* Washington, DC: U.S. Government Printing Office.

U.S. Advisory Board on Child Abuse and Neglect. (1993). *Neighbors helping neighbors: A new national strategy for the protection of children.* Washington, DC: U.S. Government Printing Office.

Weber, M. W. (1997). The assessment of child abuse: A primary function of child protective services. In M. E. Helfer, R. S. Kempe, & R. D. Krugman (Eds.), *The battered child* (5th ed., pp. 120–149). Chicago: University of Chicago Press.

Winick, B. J., & Wexler, D. B. (Eds.). (2003). *Judging in a therapeutic key: Therapeutic jurisprudence and the courts.* Durham, NC: Carolina Academic Press.

3

Ethical Issues in Forensic Assessment of Children and Adolescents

Gerald P. Koocher

Conducting psychological assessments of children and adolescents in situations likely to involve legal proceedings presents the greatest ethical challenge most professional psychologists will encounter. Unlike the practice of psychotherapy, where clients may seek help for themselves or their children, forensic-psychological evaluations seldom result solely from the request of a single individual. Almost always, others want to know the results or to consider the data in making an important decision. In the context of the legal system, the stakes are especially high. The assessment may guide life-altering decisions such as those related to child custody, termination of parental rights, adoption, or the transfer of juvenile defendants to adult courts.

The referring parties seek answers to their questions, with varying degrees of specificity. Many such questions cannot reasonably be addressed with scientific certainty via the analysis of psychometric data. Nonetheless, many members of the public believe that quantification of human behavior or the opinions of behavioral science experts constitute important factors to guide legal decisions. No matter how competent or ethically sensitive the examiner, the results of the forensic psychological evaluation can be profoundly helpful or harmful. People subjected to psychological assessment may benefit (e.g., obtain remedial educational assistance, collect monetary damages, or gain a job offer) or suffer (e.g., lose disability benefits, lose custody of a child, or face imprisonment and even the death penalty) as a consequence of the assessment.

Psychological assessment based on a scientific foundation permits us to translate human behavior, characteristics, and abilities into numbers or other formats that lend themselves to description and comparison across individuals and groups of people. Professionally and scientifically informed evaluations can help the court make more informed decisions. However, professionals need to always be cognizant that assessments can be misleading, as well. Many behaviors studied during a psychological evaluation may appear easily comprehensible to the lay person unfamiliar with test development and psychometrics (e.g., perform mental arithmetic, repeat digits, or copy geometric shapes), thereby implying that conclusions based on the observed responses must have an inherently clear meaning (i.e., *face* validity) for some purpose. Even those psychological assessment tasks striking most people as novel (e.g., "Put this unusual puzzle together quickly." "What does this inkblot look like to you?" "What do you think of when you hear the word 'fungus'?") may be viewed by the general public as having some hidden valuable meaning discernable by the skilled examiner. After all, someone in authority suggested that the evaluation take place, and the person conducting the assessment holds a license and presumed expert status.

When forensic evaluations focus on children, the ethical requirement to provide reliable and valid assessment is more difficult to achieve. Matters become more complicated for a variety of reasons, including but not limited to developmental differences across different stages of development, individual variation, and children's status as legal minors, combined with the fact that legal concepts often have no direct equivalence to psychological constructs involving children or adolescents. For example, a preadolescent functioning at what Piaget termed the *concrete operational* level of cognitive development would seem unlikely to completely understand or anticipate long-term consequences, causing doubts about the child's ability to cooperate meaningfully in their defense at a criminal trial. A minor should have the competence to realistically appraise the charges, comprehend associated likely outcomes, grasp the sequence of the trial process, understand the consequences of plea bargaining, and weigh legal defense options in a realistic manner. Must we therefore assume that all children at this stage of development are incompetent to stand trial per se? To help answer important legal questions, best professional practice and ethical standards always require an individual objective analysis of the evaluation results, recognizing that research data concerning group averages may not accurately reflect the functioning of the specific person being evaluated.

Unfortunately, the statistical and scientific underpinnings of the best psychological assessments are far more sophisticated than most lay persons, and more than a few psychologists, truly understand. When confronted with an array of numbers or a computer-generated test profile, some people (including some psychologists) are willing to uncritically accept these data as simple answers to incredibly complex questions. A core ethical challenge for the forensic evaluator includes how we can make appropriate use of psychological science to guide critical legal decisions with full recognition of our limitations and the legal rights of the people whose lives are influenced. When we undertake assessing children or adolescents for forensic purposes, the ethical challenges become significantly more complex.

When considering the myriad issues that challenge psychologists undertaking forensic assessments with children and adolescents in the most ethically appropriate manner, one can conceptualize the process in phases: the preparation phase, the actual conduct of the evaluation, and the interpretation of the data collected (i.e., translation into legal meanings, including testimony). Some ethical considerations are best addressed before beginning the assessment, others come into play during the data collection and analysis, and still other ethical issues crop up after completion of the assessment. This chapter addresses these issues in sequence.

THE PREPARATION PHASE

Begin by contemplating the questions asked by the referral and whether psychological assessment can reasonably address these. Next, consider how the answers to the previous question will affect the child or adolescent. Part of this process involves understanding the different levels of client status and the use that each hopes to make of the data. Often, when we evaluate children or adolescents, multiple layers of people are involved, having a range of differing types of interests in the outcome (e.g., an agency or institution such as a school or legal system, a set of parents, or opposing counsel in civil litigation). The problem of parsing out the duties owed to each party follows later in the chapter. Other ethical considerations may include the qualifications of the proposed evaluator to administer the necessary instruments, to interpret the data obtained, and ultimately to offer any forensic testimony. Assuring the adequacy of the assessment by selection of strategies and instruments most appropriate for use in the particular situation also involves careful advance planning.

As one prepares to undertake the actual evaluation, other ethical issues come to the fore. Have the children and their representatives received adequate information and given consent or assent regarding both the nature and intended uses of the evaluation? Obtaining consent implies the discussion of several additional issues. Do the parties understand and agree who will pay for the evaluation, what is included, and who will have access to the raw data and report? What obligations do clinicians have with respect to optimizing the participants' performance, assuring validity, supervising any assistants used to collect data, and thoroughly documenting the process? After completing data collection, what obligations does the examiner have with respect to scoring, interpreting, reporting, and explaining the data collected? How can the psychologist deal most effectively with refusals, resistance, and mixed messages that arise during the consent process (e.g., as in cases of contested custody in divorce situations or allegations of parental abuse)? Also, thinking ahead at the start of the evaluation, the psychologist should plan prospectively about follow-through. After the data are collected and interpreted, what ongoing ethical responsibilities does the psychologist have with respect to maintaining records, allowing access to the data, and providing feedback or follow-up services? What constitutes appropriate conduct when one psychologist agrees to review and critique assessment work undertaken by another? How should one respond upon discovery of apparent errors or incompetence of a colleague in the conduct of a now completed evaluation? Even though some of these points reach beyond completion of the actual evaluation, they should have the psychologist's attention during the contracting and planning stages of the evaluation process.

Accepting the Referral: Who Is the Client?

Remember that the primary functions of the legal system often focus on either settling disputes or adjudicating alleged criminal acts. In the case of children and adolescents, the party seeking forensic evaluation may or may not have the child's best interests in mind. At times, the psychologist may act as a court-appointed evaluator designated to serve the best interests of the child or of justice. At other times, parents, guardians, government agencies, or opposing litigants may seek an evalu-

ation in the hope of collecting evidence to support their case. In some circumstances, the evaluator's identity and role will be public knowledge, or at least disclosed to all sides in the case. When this happens, the results of the evaluation may become public, subject to disclosure at deposition, or otherwise discoverable and subject to cross-examination under oath. At other times, an evaluator's work and opinions may never come to light, either because the findings do not support the case that legal counsel hopes to present or because attorneys sought the opinion as part of a legal strategy. For example, clinicians well known as expert in a given field might find themselves retained by counsel to intentionally preempt opposing counsel from consulting them. Similarly, psychologists may occasional find themselves invited by attorneys to study the work of other colleagues and advise counsel on points of vulnerability to stress during cross-examination. In all forensic roles, professionals always strive for honest, scientifically informed and objective involvement.

In forensic cases, psychologists may owe professional duties to a range of parties with differing interests with varying degrees of congruence. The evaluator should pause to consider what rights each client is owed, and consider what response is appropriate if the person to be assessed is compelled to cooperate with the evaluation; the right of access to test data and results; and the right to dictate components of the evaluation or the manner in which to conduct it. Sometimes all parties will uniformly agree with no conflicts of interest. In other circumstances, the examinee may have little choice in the matter or may wish to reserve the right to limit access to results of the evaluation. In still other instances, direct conflicts will exist among different parties about the objectives of evaluation. The duty to identify, clarify, and obtain consent regarding these relationships from all parties in advance of the evaluation rests with the forensic evaluator.

Consider the following forensic examples: two feuding parents each of whom seek designation as sole legal custodian of their child; defendants whose legal counsel hope that testing will support insanity defenses; plaintiffs who hope that test data will support claims of psychological damages or disability; or job applicants who hope that test scores will prove that they qualify for hiring. In each instance, the psychologist conducting the assessment must strive for the highest level of personal integrity, while clarifying the assessment role and the reasonably foreseeable implications for all parties to whom a professional duty is owed. Third parties (e.g., potential employers, the courts, and health insurers) become involved in many psychological assessment contexts. When the psychologist works as an independent practitioner or consultant, the third party's interest may involve making use of the assessment in some sort of decision (e.g., hiring or school placement), whereas in other cases the interest may simply involve contract fulfillment (e.g., an insurance company may require that a written report be prepared as a condition of the assessment procedure). In still other situations, the psychologist conducting the evaluation may work as a full-time employee of a company or agency with a financial interest in the outcome of the evaluation (e.g., an employer hoping to avoid a disability claim or a school system that wishes to avoid expensive special education placements or services). In all of the foregoing circumstances, clear conceptualization and accurate representation of the evaluator's obligations to all parties become essential.

When the nature of the evaluation and obligations of the evaluator are carefully delineated at the outset, the risk for ethical problems is greatly reduced. Examinees may not be happy about the prospect of evaluation, but they (or their surrogate decision maker) must understand and agree to the assessment and associated risks. Just as surgery can result in unforeseen side effects, clinicians should also remain mindful of the fact that legal proceedings have organic characteristics in the sense that changing legal circumstances can create conflicting or contradictory obligations for the evaluator. For example, suppose that at the outset of a child custody evaluation, both parents with joint legal custody of their child agree to share access to reports and records. Then suppose that the parental rights of one party are terminated or the judge orders records sealed. Such events do happen and can alter the initial agreements in place at the time the evaluator's role began. The safest ethical course, when the legal authority terrain changes, would call for reliance on court orders around release of materials when claim and counterclaim abound and to explain to the participants the legal

obligation for the evaluator to comply. The evaluator may have valuable input regarding the hazards of specific releases of information and can provide that information to the court, but ultimately it is the court that has the authority to evaluate or sort out the interests of the competing parties.

Additional issues of consent in the context of developmental challenges to competence come into play when a psychologist undertakes evaluation of a child. When beginning such an evaluation primarily as a service to the child client (e.g., as part of treatment planning), risks usually remain minimal. However, if the data might ultimately find use in legal proceedings (e.g., a custody hearing), or in any way that might have significant potentially adverse future consequences that the client cannot competently evaluate, a surrogate consent process should occur. One cannot always predict when assessment data collected for a nonforensic purpose will be sought for a forensic application. In such instances, a parent or legal guardian ought to be involved in granting permission for the evaluation. Obtaining such permission helps to address and respect the vulnerabilities and attendant obligations owed to persons with reduced decision-making capacities.

Informed Consent

As a foundation for understanding informed consents involving forensic child evaluations in general, it may be helpful to review the current revision of the *Ethical Principles of Psychologists and Code of Conduct* (American Psychological Association [APA], 2002) standard that refers specifically to obtaining informed consent for psychological assessment. The most relevant excerpt states, in part:

9.03 Informed Consent in Assessments

(a) Psychologists obtain informed consent for assessments, evaluations, or diagnostic services . . . except when (1) testing is mandated by law or governmental regulations; (2) informed consent is implied because testing is conducted as a routine educational, institutional, or organizational activity (e.g., when participants voluntarily agree to assessment when applying for a job); or (3) one purpose of the testing is to evaluate decisional capacity. Informed consent includes an explanation of the nature and purpose of the assessment, fees, involvement of third parties, and limits of confidentiality and sufficient opportunity for the client/patient to ask questions and receive answers.

(b) Psychologists inform persons with questionable capacity to consent or for whom testing is mandated by law or governmental regulations about the nature and purpose of the proposed assessment services, using language that is reasonably understandable to the person being assessed.

The issue of consent is also discussed extensively in the professional literature in areas of consent to treatment (Fundudis, 2003; Grisso & Appelbaum, 1998; Kagehiro & Laufer, 1992; Koocher & DeMaso, 1990) and consent for research participation (Nelson, 1998; Sieber, 1992; Sterling & Walco, 2003), but references to consent in the area of psychological assessment had been quite limited. Johnson-Greene, Hardy-Morais, Adams, Hardy, and Bergloff (1997) review this issue and propose a set of recommendations for providing informed consent to clients. These authors also propose that written documentation of informed consent be obtained; the APA (2002) *Code of Conduct* encourages but does not require this step. Thoughtful psychologists will establish consistent routines and document all discussions with clients related to obtaining consent, explaining procedures, and describing confidentiality and privacy issues. It is particularly wise to obtain written informed consent in situations that may have forensic implications such as personal injury law suits and child custody litigation.

Clients reasonably expect psychologists to explain the nature of the evaluation, clarify the referral questions, and discuss the goals of the assessment in language they can readily understand. One should also discuss any limitations of the assessment procedures with the client. To the extent possible, the psychologist should also remain mindful of the clients' goals, clarify misunderstandings, and correct unrealistic expectations. For example, a parent may seek a psychological evalu-

ation with the expectation that the results will ensure that their child will qualify to enter an educational program for the gifted, accident victims may anticipate that the evaluation will document their entitlement to monetary damages, and job candidates may hope to become employed or qualify for advancement. These hopes and expectations may come to pass, but one cannot reasonably comment on the outcome before valid data are in hand.

Ex Parte Communications

The legal term *ex parte* comes from Latin and means on behalf of or the application of one party. As used here, the term refers to having communications with one party, but not the other, in situations where the psychologist has equal obligations to both. For example, in conducting a child custody evaluation, one should generally not give information to or collect information regarding one party without sharing it equally with the other. In general, this doctrine will apply chiefly in situations where the psychologist acts in a court-appointed role or jointly accepted as an impartial evaluator by both parties, as opposed to civil law suits in which the clinician serves as an expert for one side.

Ideally, one avoids *ex parte* communication problems by communicating at the same time and place with all concerned. However, such scheduling may not always work out. As a result, one must take care to provide equal information in written form or by recording communications with one party and allowing the other to review it. When approached by one party directly in such case contexts, the psychologist needs not refuse contact, but should make it clear that the actual contact and information exchanged will be shared with the other party.

Special Twists Related to Consent

Not uncommonly, psychologists will encounter refusals, resistance of various sorts (e.g., partial compliance, passive aggressive withholding, etc.), or conflicting messages during or following the consent process, even when a court has ordered the evaluation. The best practice in such cases includes clarity, consistency, firmness, and patience. The clinician should clearly articulate expectations as part of the consent process for the child, parents, or guardians and any attorneys involved. Resistance should be met with consistent restatement of the expectations and patient, but firm limit setting. An explanation to the parties and their counsel that the final report will contain descriptions of incomplete cooperation or compliance failures sometimes enhances cooperation. One must be mindful of a client's right to remain mute and not take personal offense. At the same time, when lack of full cooperation hinders the evaluation, such behavior becomes part of the assessment process for reporting purposes.

Under the provisions of amendments to the Internal Revenue Code, designated Public Law 104-191, or the Health Insurance Portability and Accountability Act of 1996 (HIPAA) statute, authorizations to release protected health information must specify a limited time duration. Although forensic evaluations may or may not be considered *health information* under HIPAA, the practice of limiting duration of signed releases is a good one. In addition, one can always revoke a signed release. Such revocations obviously do not require retrieval of material sent out while the valid authorization was in force, and may have consequences of their own. For example, suppose a school system sends a child for an independent special education evaluation and the parent signs a document releasing the results to the system, but develops second thoughts regarding the wisdom of doing so after hearing some of the results from the psychologist. The parent does have the right to rescind the authorization signed previously; however, that may result in the system's refusal to pay for the evaluation.

In court-ordered evaluations, a consent form agreeing to the evaluation may be legally unnecessary; however, many wise forensic clinicians use them in every case to demonstrate that full information about the nature and intended use of the evaluation was discussed. In such cases, the person evaluated cannot usually block court access to the results, should a change of heart occur. For this reason, some attorneys choose to have clients evaluated privately, without court order, so that they have no obligation to share the results. Functioning under court order usually confers to the psychologist a degree of immunity from suit by unhappy litigants, although such appointments do not preclude the filing of licensing board complaints. For all of these reasons, one must pay critical attention to information provided in consent forms and the conditions under which one accepts referrals.

Another interesting twist sometimes occurs in civil litigation, where one side of the legal dispute has hired a psychologist as an expert evaluator. In many cases, attorneys set up the arrangements with the clinician and believe that the evaluator becomes an extension of the legal work product. Such beliefs had important implications, because the ethical obligations of lawyers and mental health experts differ significantly. For example, psychologists are mandated reporters of suspected child abuse in all United States and Canadian jurisdictions, but attorneys do not always have similar obligations. Suppose that a psychologist agrees to conduct an evaluation of a young child whose family has sued a neighbor over a bite the child received from the dog next door. The parents' attorney expects that the clinician will document the trauma experienced by the child during and subsequent to the dog attack. What happens if, in the course of the evaluation, the clinician begins to suspect that one or both parents have physically abused the child apart from any dog bite trauma. The clinician informs the parents' lawyer, who then orders the evaluator not to file a child abuse report, under the doctrine of attorney–client privilege. The attorney asserts that because he or she contracted for the psychologist's services, the psychologist's findings fall technically under the protective penumbra of the lawyer's relationship to the client, and notes that attorneys are not mandated reporters in the state at hand.

The best solution to such problems is prevention. State reporting mandates are exceptions to general confidentiality obligations and, under both the 2002 APA *Code of Conduct* and 1996 federal HIPAA rules (Public Law 104-191, 1996), should be addressed in discussions on the limits of confidentiality at the outset of the professional relationship, before the actual assessment begins. Psychologists who cannot reach a clear understanding with counsel on such matters prior to initiating assessment should not accept the referral. For those who neglected to think preventively, consultation with one's colleagues, a personal attorney, and an anonymous call to the state's child abuse reporting hot line may provide useful objective data with which to assess the validity of the assertion of attorney–client privilege.

Test User Competence

Before agreeing to undertake a particular forensic evaluation, clinicians should assure that they have the competence necessary to provide the particular service. However, evaluating such competence varies with the eye of the beholder. Psychologists are ethically bound not to promote the use of psychological assessment techniques by unqualified persons, except when such use is conducted for training purposes with appropriate supervision. Ascertaining what constitutes competence or qualifications in the area of psychological assessment becomes difficult when considering the complex nature of particular assessment questions, the diverse settings and contexts in which psychological testing takes place, and the differences in background and training of individuals providing psychological assessment services. Does such work require a doctoral degree in clinical, counseling, or school psychology? How about testing conducted by licensed counselors or by individuals with master's degrees in psychology? What tasks can a psychometrist or technician perform with or without the supervision of a licensed psychologist? Can some physicians reasonably use psychological tests? After all, Hermann Rorschach was a psychiatrist, as was J. Charnley McKinley, one of the two originators of the Minnesota Multiphasic Personality Inventory. Henry Murray, a nonpsychiatric physician, co-invented the Thematic Apperception Test with his paramour, Christiana Morgan, who had no formal training in psychology. Can psychologists trained to assess adults competently test children and adolescents?

Historically, the APA addressed this issue only in a very general manner in the *Ethical Principles of Psychologists and Code of Conduct* (2002). The earliest versions of the *Ethical Standards of Psychologists* (APA, 1953), suggested limiting distribution and sale of psychological tests to unspecified qualified persons. A system of categorization of tests and concordant qualifications that entailed three levels of tests and expertise was subsequently developed. Vocational guidance tools, for example,

fell at the low end in terms of presumed required expertise. At the high end of required competence, the guide listed tests designed for clinical assessment and diagnoses such as intelligence and personality assessment instruments. The rationale involved in this scheme originated in the belief that one must understand statistics, psychopathology, and psychometrics in order to accurately draw clinical inference or make actuarial predictions based on test data. Many test publishers adopted it and continue to use variations on the original theme. When attempting to place orders for psychological test materials, would-be purchasers must often list their credentials, cite a professional license number, or give some other indication of presumed competence. Decisions about the actual sale, however, generally rely on decisions made by a clerk processing the order, who has little understanding of the issues and considerable incentive to help the test publisher make the sale.

Further efforts to delineate test user qualifications included the lengthy efforts of the Test User Qualifications Working Group formed in 1996, sponsored by an interdisciplinary group, the Joint Committee on Testing Practices, convened and funded by the APA. This group attempted to quantify and describe factors associated with appropriate test use by using a data gathering, as opposed to a specification of qualifications approach, to study competence problems (Eyde, Moreland, Robertson, Primoff, & Most, 1988; Eyde et al., 1993; Moreland, Eyde, Robertson, Primoff, & Most, 1995). Members of the task force represent the various settings and areas of expertise in psychological assessment and include specialists in clinical, industrial/organizational, school, counseling, educational, forensic, and neuropsychology. Instead of focusing on qualifications in terms of professional degrees or licenses, the task force elected to delineate a core set of competencies in psychological assessment and then describe more specifically the knowledge and skills expected of test users in specific contexts. The core competencies included not only knowledge of psychometric and measurement principles and appropriate test administration procedures, but also appreciation of the factors affecting tests selection and interpretation in different contexts and across diverse individuals. Other essential competencies listed by the task force included familiarity with relevant legal standards and regulations relevant to test use including civil rights laws, Public Law 104-191, the Americans With Disabilities Act (Public Law 101-336, 1990), and the Individuals With Disabilities Education Act, originally enacted by Congress as Public Law 94-142 and called the Education for All Handicapped Children Act of 1975. The task force delineated the purposes for which tests are typically used (e.g., classification, description, prediction, intervention planning, and tracking) and described the competencies and skills required in specific settings (e.g., employment, education, career/vocational counseling, health care, and forensic). The aspirational guidelines produced by the task force describe the range of knowledge and skills for optimal test use in various contexts and were approved by the APA Council of Representatives in August of 2000 (APA, 2000).

The chief ethical problems in this arena involve matters of how to objectively determine one's own competence and how to deal with the perceived lack of competence in others whose work is encountered in the course of professional practice. The key to the answer lies in peer consultation. Discussion with colleagues, teachers, and clinical supervisors is the best way to assess one's own developing competence in assessment and focus on additional training needs. Following graduation and licensing, continuing professional education and peer consultation are the most effective strategies for assessing and maintaining one's own competence. When in doubt, a useful strategy would include presenting samples of one's work to a respected senior colleague for review and critique.

Dealing with the less than adequate work of others poses a different set of ethical concerns. At times, psychologists may become aware of inadequate assessment work or misuse of psychological tests by colleagues or individuals from other professions (e.g., physicians or nonpsychologist counselors). Such individuals may lack awareness of appropriate testing standards or may claim that they disagree with or have no obligation to follow them. Similarly, some psychologists may attempt to use assessment tools for which they lack qualifications to administer or interpret. The context in which such problems come to light becomes

critical in determining the most appropriate course of action. In the ideal circumstance, the presumed malefactor will be amenable to correcting the problem as a result of an informal conversation, assuming that you have the consent of the party who has consulted you to initiate such a dialogue. Ideally, a professional who is the recipient of an informal contact expressing concern about matters of assessment or test interpretation will be receptive to and interested in remedying the situation. When this is not the case, the client who has been improperly evaluated should be advised about potential remedies available through legal and regulatory channels.

If asked to consult as a potential expert witness in matters involving alleged assessment errors or inadequacies, there is no obligation to attempt informal consultation with the professional who rendered the report in question. In most cases, such contact would be ethically inappropriate, because the client of the consulting expert is not the person who conducted the assessment. In such circumstances, the people seeking an expert opinion will most likely be attorneys intent on challenging or discrediting a report deemed adverse to their clients. The especially complex issues of how to handle questions that arise in challenging a clinician's competence in the area of neuropsychological assessment are effectively discussed by Grote, Lewin, Sweet, and van Gorp (2000).

Planning the Evaluation

As an essential part of accepting the referral, the psychologist should clarify the questions to be answered in an interactive process that refines the goals of the evaluation in the context of basic assessment science and the limitations of available techniques. This becomes especially important when the referral originates with nonpsychologists or others who may lack awareness of the limitations of testing or may have unrealistic expectations regarding what they may learn from the test data. Part of the planning should also focus on the legal standards and questions that we hope the data will illuminate. Other critical plans include collection of contextual data (e.g., a developmental history, review of police reports, and data from school records), decisions about the sequence of test administration, and consideration of the data collection conditions. (E.g., should data collection take place in a single long session or several shorter ones? If the examinee takes psychoactive medications, should testing take place while the person is taking medication, after a medically supervised hiatus, or both?)

Selection of Instruments

The APA *Code of Conduct* (2002) requires psychologists to base their assessments, recommendations, reports, opinions, and diagnostic or evaluative statements on information and techniques sufficient to substantiate their findings. The psychologist should have a sound knowledge of the available instruments for assessing the particular constructs related to the assessment questions and forensic standards. This knowledge should include an understanding of the psychometric properties of the instruments selected (e.g., their validity, reliability, and normative base) as well as an appreciation of how to apply the instrument in different contexts or with different individuals across age levels, cultures, languages, and other such variables. One must also consider a particular instrument's strengths and weaknesses as an appropriate and valid measure for the intended purpose. For example, floor and ceiling constraints can have special implications for certain age groups. As an illustration, the fourth edition of the Stanford-Binet test has limited ability to discriminate among children with significant impairments at the youngest age levels (Flanagan & Alfonso, 1995). In evaluating such children, the use of other instruments with lower floor capabilities would be more appropriate.

Adequacy of Instruments

From an ethical perspective, psychologists develop, administer, score, interpret, or use assessment techniques, interviews, tests, or instruments only in a manner and for purposes that qualify as appropriate in light of the research on or evidence of the usefulness and proper application of the techniques in question. We expect psychologists who develop and conduct research with tests and other assessment techniques to use appropriate psychometric procedures and current scientific or professional knowledge in test design, standardiza-

tion, validation, reduction or elimination of bias, and making recommendations for use of the instruments. Psychologists must bear the ethical responsibility for justifying the appropriateness of the particular instruments they select. Although a test publisher has some related obligations, the APA *Code of Conduct* applies only to individuals holding APA membership, as opposed to corporations. The reputations of test publishers will invariably rise or fall based on the quality of the tools they develop and distribute. When preparing new assessment techniques for publication, the preparation of a test manual that includes the data necessary for psychologists to evaluate the appropriateness of the tool for their work becomes critically important. The psychologist in turn must have the clinical and scientific skill needed to evaluate the data provided by the publisher.

Appropriate Assessment in a Multicultural Society

In countries with a citizenry as diverse as that of the United States, psychologists will invariably confront the challenge of assessing people who by reason of race, culture, language, or other factors are not well represented in the normative base of frequently used assessment tools. Such circumstances demand consideration of a multiplicity of issues. When working with diverse populations, we expect psychologists to use assessment instruments whose validity and reliability have been established for that particular population. When such instruments are not available, we expect the psychologist to take care to interpret test results cautiously, with regard to the potential bias and potential misuses of such results. When appropriate tests for a particular population do not exist, psychologists who use existing standardized tests may ethically adapt the administration and interpretation procedures only if the adaptations have a sound basis in the scientific and experiential foundation of the discipline. Psychologists have an ethical responsibility to document any such adaptations and clarify their probable impact on the findings. We expect psychologists to use assessment methods in a manner appropriate to an individual's language preference, competence, and cultural background, unless the use of an alternative language is relevant to the purpose of the assessment.

Getting Around Language Barriers

Some psychologists incorrectly assume that the use of an interpreter will compensate for a lack of fluency in the language of the person being assessed. Aside from the obvious nuances involved in vocabulary, the meaning of specific instructions can vary widely. For example, some interpreters may tend to simplify instructions or responses, rather than give precise linguistic renditions. At other times, the relative rarity of the language may tempt an examiner to use family or community members when professional interpreters are not readily available. Such individuals may have personal motives that could lead to alterations in the meaning of what was actually said, or compromise the privacy of the person being assessed. Using family members as interpreters in forensic contexts is particularly fraught with potential problems. Psychologists using the services of an interpreter must assure themselves of the adequately of the interpreter's training, obtain the informed consent of the client to use that particular interpreter, and ensure that interpreter will respect the confidentiality of test results and test security. In addition, the psychologist must discuss any limitations on the data obtained via the use of an interpreter when presenting the results of the evaluation.

Some psychologists mistakenly assume that they can compensate for language or educational barriers by using measures that do not require verbal instructions or responses. When assessing individuals of diverse cultural and linguistic backgrounds, one cannot reasonably rely solely on non-verbal procedures and assume validity for the resulting interpretations. Many human behaviors ranging from the nature of eye contact; speed, spontaneity, and elaborateness of response; and persistence on challenging tasks may connect to social or cultural factors independent of language or semantics. For example, performance on non-verbal tests can vary significantly based on both cultural background (Ardila & Moreno, 2001) and educational level (Ostrosky, Ardila, Rosselli, López-Arango, & Uriel-Mendoza, 1998).

What's in a Norm?

Psychologists must have knowledge of the applicability of the instrument's normative basis to the client. Are the norms up-to-date or based on people compatible with the client? If the normative data do not match the client, the psychologist must discuss such limitations when making interpretations. In selecting tests for specific populations, it is important that the scores be corrected not only with respect to age but also with respect to educational level (Heaton, Grant, & Matthews, 1991; Vanderploeg, Axelrod, Sherer, Scott, & Adams, 1997). For example, the assessment of reading ability in a 10-year-old child who has had no formal education would demand very different normative considerations than simple age-equivalent scores based on children of similar age who have attended school for several years.

Psychologists should select and interpret tests with a solid understanding of how specific tests and the procedures they entail interact with the specific individual undergoing evaluation. Several tests purporting to evaluate the same construct (e.g., general cognitive ability) put variable demands on the client and can place different levels of emphasis on specific abilities. For example, some tests used with young children have different expectations for the amount of language used in the instructions and required of the child in a response. A child with a specific language impairment may demonstrate widely discrepant scores on different tests of intelligence as a function of the language load of the instrument, as some tests can place a premium on verbal skills (Kamphaus, Dresden, & Kaufman, 1993). The foregoing can have significant ethical implications; for example, a forensic evaluator would need to understand such assessment issues before mistakenly attributing low test scores to acquired deficits related to a contested legal issue.

Clinicians must remember that they cannot base their assessment, intervention decisions, or recommendations on outdated data or test results. Similarly, psychologists do not base such decisions or recommendations on obsolete test instruments and measures. Expensive testing kits may tempt more than a few psychologists to rationalize that they have no need to invest in a newly revised instrument, when they already own a perfectly serviceable set of materials from the previous edition. In some instances, a psychologist may reasonably use an older version of a standardized instrument but must have an appropriate and valid rationale to justify the practice. For example, a psychologist may wish to assess whether a deterioration in a client's condition has occurred and may elect to readminister the same instrument used in prior assessments, such as the Wechsler Intelligence Scale for Children-III, even if a newer improved version of the test is available.

Bases for Assessments

Section 9.01 of APA *Code of Conduct* (2002) holds that psychologists typically provide opinions on the psychological characteristics of individuals based "on information and techniques sufficient to substantiate their findings." At times, this means that forensic clinicians may rely on data that they have not personally collected (e.g., when a psychologist serving as an expert witness is asked to offer hypothetical opinions regarding data sets collected by others). Another example would occur when a psychologist is retained to provide confidential assistance to an attorney. Lawyers often seek such consultation to explore the accuracy of a report obtained by the other side of a case or to help frame potential cross-examination questions to ask the other side's expert. In such situations, psychologists document the data they relied on and clarify the potential impact of their limited information on the reliability and validity of their opinions. The ability to ethically offer an opinion with limitations, absent a direct assessment of the client, also becomes relevant when considering requests for the release of raw test data, as discussed below.

CONDUCTING THE EVALUATION

Optimizing Performance and Validity

In conducting their assessments, psychologists strive to create appropriate rapport with child or adolescent clients by helping them to feel physically comfortable and emotionally at ease. An evaluation climate conducive to naturalistic responses is critical for forensic child evaluations. The psychologist should prepare well, striving to create the most suitable testing environment possible. Most psychological test developers assume that the test takers have generally positive attitudes

and motivations. For example, attempting to collect test data in a noisy distracting environment or asking a young child to attempt a lengthy test battery without interruption generally violates the assumptions made in designing the individual instruments and establishing their norms.

The psychologist will also need to consider and appreciate the attitudes of the client and address any issues raised in this regard. Children and adolescents may experience and fail to report many feelings (e.g., anger, anxiety, apathy, depression) or physical states (e.g., hunger, tiredness, discomfort) that could retard their performance. In forensic cases, there are many potential explanations for a child's failure to report relevant psychological experiences, including adults attempting to coach children or otherwise seek to influence or bias the information communicated during a psychological assessment, or children traumatized by an event that is legally significant may not be able to emotionally process the questioning at the time of the forensic evaluation. If questions occur regarding a test taker's motivation, ability to sustain adequate concentration, or problems with the context of the assessment, the psychologist should attempt to resolve these issues and to discuss how these circumstances ultimately affect test data interpretations in any reports that result from the evaluation. Similarly, in circumstances where it seems that subtle or obvious attempts to bias a child's responses have occurred, the clinician should make note of these and consider additional instruments or techniques useful in resolving any ambiguities.

Another factor that can affect the test-taking environment is the presence of a parent or other third-party observer during the interview and testing procedures. In forensic evaluations, psychologists sometimes face requests from attorneys to observe evaluations. Having such observers present can compromise the ability of the psychologist to follow standardized procedures and can affect the validity and reliability of the data collection (McCaffrey, Fisher, Gold, & Lynch, 1996; McSweeney et al., 1998). The National Academy of Neuropsychology (2000b) has taken a position that clinicians should generally exclude third-party observers from evaluations. A reasonable alternative that has evolved in sexual abuse assessment interviewing, where overly suggestive interviewing by unskilled clinicians or the police has become a frequently noted problem, is to include video recording or remote monitoring of the process, assuming that appropriate consent occurs. Such recording can have a mixed effect: it can prove very useful in demonstrating that a competent evaluation took place, but it can also provide a strong record for discrediting poor-quality work.

Data Collection and Report Preparation

Psychologists must conduct assessments with explicit knowledge of the procedures required and adherence to the standardized test administration procedures prescribed in the test manuals. In some contexts, particularly in neuropsychological assessment where clinicians often use a significant number and wide range of instruments, technicians are sometimes employed to administer and score tests, as well as to record behaviors during the assessment. In such situations, the licensed psychologist remains responsible for assuring adequacy of the training of the technician, selecting test instruments, and interpreting findings (see National Academy of Neuropsychology 2000a). Even in the case of less sophisticated evaluations (e.g., administration of common IQ or achievement testing in public school settings), psychologists charged with signing official reports hold responsibility for assuring the accuracy and adequacy of data collection, including the training and competence of other personnel engaged in test administration. This becomes especially relevant in circumstances where classroom teachers or other nonpsychologists serve as proctors for group-administered tests.

A completed psychological assessment includes preparation of a report. This fact sometimes leads to disputes when the party responsible for payment refuses or delays doing so. A psychologist cannot ethically withhold a completed report needed for critical decision making in the welfare of a client. Many state laws and the 1996 federal HIPAA require the release of health records to adult clients and the parents or guardians of minors. Some have argued that reports created for a legal purpose do not fall under the penumbra of HIPAA (Connell & Koocher, 2003). Despite requirements regarding record release, psychologists need not prepare a report if payment is refused. Many practitioners require advance payment or a retainer as a prerequisite for undertaking a lengthy evaluation. In some instances, practitioners who

have received partial payment that covers the time involved in record review and data collection will pause prior to preparing the actual report, awaiting additional payment before writing the report. Such strategies are not unethical per se but should be carefully spelled out and agreed to as part of the consent process before beginning the evaluation as part of the consent process. Ideally, such agreements should exist in clear written form to avoid subsequent misunderstandings.

Automated Test Scoring and Interpretation

The psychologist who signs the report retains responsibility for the contents of the report, including the accuracy of the data scoring and validity of the interpretation. When interpreting assessment results, including automated interpretations, psychologists must take into account the purpose of the assessment as well as the various test factors, test-taking abilities, and other characteristics of the person being assessed, such as situational, personal, linguistic, and cultural differences, that might affect psychologists' judgments or reduce the accuracy of their interpretations. If allowing specific accommodations in the assessment (e.g., extra time, use of a reader, or availability of special appliances), these must be described. Automated testing services cannot take account of such factors. Although mechanical scoring of objective test data will often yield greater accuracy than hand scoring, machines can and do make errors. The psychologist who makes use of an automated scoring system should check the mechanically generated results carefully.

Psychologists must also indicate in the body of their reports any significant reservations they have regarding the accuracy or limitations of their interpretations. This includes any cautions with respect to automated interpretative reports that may become a part of the case file. For example, psychologists who obtain computer-generated interpretive reports of MMPI-A protocols may choose to use some or all of the information so obtained in their personally prepared reports. The individually prepared report of the psychologist should indicate if a computer-assisted or interpretive report was used and explain any modified interpretations made or confirm the validity of the computerized findings, as appropriate. A summary of criteria helpful in evaluating psychological assessment reports (Koocher, 2005a) is presented in Table 3.1.

After the Evaluation

Following completion of their evaluations and reports, psychologists often receive requests for additional clarification, feedback, release of data, or other information and materials related to the evaluation. Rules focusing on the release of confidential client information receive considerable attention in the APA *Code of Conduct* (2002) and under many state and federal laws, but many other issues particular to psychological assessment may arise. As noted above, forensic assessment can avoid ethical controversy by explaining at the outset what information can be disclosed and under what conditions.

Feedback Requests

We expect psychologists to provide explanatory feedback to the people they assess, unless the nature of the client relationship precludes such an explanation of results. Examples of relationships where a psychologist might not owe feedback to the person assessed would include some organizational consulting, preemployment or security screening, and some forensic evaluations. In every case, clarification regarding the nature of feedback anticipated, and any limitations thereon, must precede the assessment with clear explanation to the person or their legal guardian. Ideally, any such limitations are provided in both written and oral form at the outset of the professional relationship. In normal circumstances, people undergoing assessment can reasonably expect receiving in a timely manner an interpretation of the test results and answers to questions they may have. Applicable law in some states may require release of actual test reports upon request of the person assessed.

Requests for Modification of Reports

On some occasions, people who have been evaluated, their guardians, or their legal counsel may request modification to a psychologist's assessment report. One valid reason for altering or revising a report allows for the correction of factual errors. Another appropriate reason might involve release of information on a need-to-know basis for the protection of the client. For example, suppose that, in the course of conducting a psychological evaluation of a child victim of sexual abuse, a significant verbal learning disability becomes evident. Assume that the psychologist fully described the disability in the evaluation report. Also imagine that in an effort to secure special education services for the learning problem, the parents of the child ask the psychologist to tailor a report for the school focusing only on matters relevant to the child's educational needs. That is to say, the parents would prefer to have information on the child's sexual abuse omitted from the report sent to the school's learning disability assessment team. One can quite reasonably tailor a report or omit certain information gleaned during an evaluation to appropriately honor such requests, as long as doing so does not tend to mislead or misrepresent the relevant findings.

Psychologists must also remain mindful of their professional integrity and obligation to fairly and accurately represent relevant findings. Imagine a situation in which a case management firm approaches a psychologist with a request to perform an independent examination, asking to review a draft of the report in order to suggest editorial changes. Such a request raises serious ethical considerations, particularly in forensic contexts. Psychologists retain ethical responsibility for the content of all reports issued over their signature. One can always listen to requests or suggestions, but professional integrity and oversight of one's work cannot be delegated to another. Attempts to alter the actual data, conceal crucial information, mislead recipients, commit fraud, or otherwise falsely represent findings of a psychological evaluation constitute serious ethical misconduct. The psychologist has no obligation to modify a valid report at the insistence of a client if the ultimate result would misinform the intended recipient.

Release of Data

Who should have access to the raw or scored data on which psychologists predicate their assessments? This issue comes into focus most dramatically when the conclusions or recommendations

Table 3.1 Assessing the quality of a forensic psychological assessment report

Item to be included	Comments in report should address
Referral information	Who referred the person? What is the purpose of the evaluation, and what questions are to be addressed? If the evaluation is court ordered, cite the name of the official signing the order or the date it was filed. If the evaluation is related to a pending case, state the case name, court, and docket number (if known).
Applicable standards or laws	What legal standards or major case law apply? Use precise citations.
Documents or materials reviewed	List each document reviewed in sufficient detail to identify it, and indicate who provided each.
Collateral contacts	List and categorize each contact, including dates.
Informed consent	Was the person (or parent/guardian) advised about the nature and purpose of the evaluation, as well as who is responsible for payment, what charges are anticipated, who will have access to the data, and what feedback will be provided? Does the person granting consent have any rights to retract consent?
Contextual issues	What is the relevant psychosocial ecology (e.g., school failure, pending divorce, criminal charges, etc.)?
Third-party involvement	Does the report include a statement about any third-party obligations or entitlements (e.g., responsibility for payment or access to findings), along with notation regarding signed and dated consent or permission?
Current status observations	What behaviors were observed during the interview (e.g., mood, rapport, concentration, language barriers, physical handicaps, etc.)?
Deviations from standard practice	Were any deviations from standard practice in test administration needed to accommodate the client? If so, is the rationale explained? Were any observers present? Was the evaluation recorded?
Listing of instruments used	Is a complete list of the tests administered provided? Does the list specify the full names of the instruments and version or form used? Does the report provide descriptive information or references for any unusual instruments or techniques used? If more than one set of norms exist, are the norms used in evaluating the particular client reported on specified?
Reliability and validity	Do comments indicate whether the test results obtained are deemed reliable and valid, or should they be considered in light of any mediating factors?
Data presentation	Are scores for each instrument administered presented and explained? Are the meanings of the data discussed in the context of the referral questions? Is homogeneity, variability, or scatter in patterns of scores discussed? Are technical terms and jargon avoided?
Summary	If a summary is provided, does it err by mentioning material not addressed in the body of the report?
Recommendations	If recommendations are made, is it evident how these flow from the data? Do recommendations relate cogently to the referral questions? Does the report adequately and appropriately address the legal issues or forensic questions posed?
Diagnosis	If a diagnosis is requested or if differential diagnosis was a referral question, does the report address this using standard nomenclature and the American Psychiatric Association's multiaxial system, if appropriate? Does the examiner know when not to provide a *DSM* diagnosis, recognizing that in some forensic applications doing so may mislead the intended readers of the report?
Authentication	Is the report signed by the person who conducted the evaluation? Are the degree(s) and title of the person signing provided? If the signer is unlicensed or a trainee, has a licensed supervisor countersigned the report?

resulting from an assessment are challenged. In such disputes, the opposing parties often seek review of the raw data by experts not involved in the original collection and analyses. The purpose of the review might include actually rescoring raw data or reviewing interpretations of scored data. In this context, test data may refer to any test protocols, transcripts of responses, record forms, scores, and notes regarding an individual's responses to test items in any media (APA, 2002). Under longstanding accepted ethical practices, psychologists may release test data to a psychologist or another qualified professional once authorized by a valid client release or court order. APA ethical codes prior to 2002 advised psychologists to generally refrain from releasing test data to persons not deemed qualified to use such information. More recently (APA, 2002), it has become clear that psychologists may refrain from releasing test data to protect a client from harm or to protect test security (Editorial, 1999), except (a) as required by law or court order, (b) to an attorney or court based on a client's valid release, or (c) to the client as appropriate under legal mandates.

In recent years, psychologists had increasingly worried about exactly how far their responsibility went in upholding the standard of attempting to limit release of raw data only to another qualified professional. Expressing reservations about releasing raw data does not carry much weight when contending with the legal system. For example, if a psychologist receives a valid release from the client to provide the data to another professional, must the sending psychologist feel obligated to determine the specific competence of the intended recipient? Can one reasonably assume that any other psychologist qualifies as competent to evaluate all psychological test data? If psychologists asked to release data feel worried about possible harm or test security, must they retain legal counsel at their own expense to vigorously resist releasing the data?

The intent of the APA ethical standards focuses on minimizing harm and misuse of test data (Koocher & Keith-Spiegel, 1998). The authors of APA's *Code of Conduct* never intended requiring psychologists to screen the credentials of potential data recipients, to become litigants, or to incur significant legal expenses in defense of the ethics code. In addition, many attorneys do not want the names of their potential experts released to the other side until required to do so under discovery rules. Some attorneys may wish to show test data to a number of potential experts and choose to use only the expert(s) most supportive of their case. In such situations, the attorney seeing the file may legitimately prefer not to provide the transmitting psychologist with the name of the intended recipient. Although such strategies seem alien to many psychologists trained to think as scientific investigators, they apply quite commonly and ethically in the practice of law. Expressing reasonable professional concern to receiving clinicians or attorneys regarding the use of practitioners qualified to interpret the data will ethically suffice for the transmitting clinician, assuming that the actual release is properly authorized. Ethical responsibility in such circumstances shifts to receiving experts in justifying their own competence and the foundation of their own expert opinions, if a question arises subsequently. The bottom line is that, although psychologists should seek appropriate confidentiality and competence assurances, they cannot use the ethics code as a shield to bar the release of their complete test data file.

Test Security

The current APA *Code of Conduct* (2002) requires that psychologists make reasonable efforts to maintain the integrity and security of copyright protected tests and other assessment techniques consistent with law, and their contractual obligations. Most test publishers also elicit such a pledge from those seeking to purchase test materials. Production of well-standardized test instruments represents a significant financial investment to the publisher. Breaches of such security can compromise the publisher's proprietary rights and vitiate the utility of the test to the clinician by enabling coaching or otherwise inappropriate preparation by test takers (Lees-Haley & Courtney, 2000a, 2000b; National Academy of Neuropsychology, 2000c; Shapiro, 2000). Victor and Abeles (2004) describe the parameters of this problem well, with reference to both the ethical issues involved and the availability of considerable heretofore relatively secure information via the World Wide Web.

What constitutes a reasonable effort as envisioned by the authors of the ethics code? Close reading of the code indicates that psychologists may rely on other sections addressing testing materials in maintaining test security. In that context, psychologists have no intrinsic professional obligation to contest valid court orders or to resist appropriate requests for disclosure of test materials. That is to say, the psychologist has no obligation to litigate in support of a test publisher or to protect the security of an instrument at significant personal cost. When in doubt, a psychologist always has the option of contacting the test publisher. If publishers, who sold the tests to the psychologist eliciting a promise to uphold test security, wish to object to requested or court-ordered disclosure, they should expected to use their own financial and legal resources to defend their own copyright-protected property.

Psychologists must also pay attention to the laws that apply in their own practice jurisdiction(s). For example, Minnesota has a specific statute that prohibits a psychologist from releasing psychological test materials to individuals who are unqualified or if the psychologist has reason to believe that releasing such material would compromise the integrity of the testing process. Such laws can provide additional but illusory protective leverage, because materials available via the Internet easily cross state lines unregulated by these statutes.

Automated Testing Services

Automated testing services and software constitute a major boon to psychologists' practices and significantly enhance the accuracy and sophistication of diagnostic decision making, but important caveats apply. The APA *Code of Conduct* (2002) states that psychologists who offer assessment or scoring services to other professionals should accurately describe the purpose, norms, validity, reliability, and applications of the procedures and any special qualifications applicable to their use (Koocher & Keith-Spiegel, 1998). Psychologists who use such scoring and interpretation services (including automated services) should select them based on evidence of the validity of the program and analytic procedures. In every case, ethical psychologists retain responsibility for the appropriate application, interpretation, and use of assessment instruments, whether they score and interpret such tests themselves or use automated or other services.

One key difficulty in the use of automated testing involves the aura of validity conveyed by the adjective computerized and its synonyms. Aside from the longstanding debate within psychology about the merits of actuarial versus clinical prediction, one often finds a kind of magical faith that numbers and graphs generated by a computer program somehow equate to increased validity predictive of some sort. Too often, skilled clinicians do not fully educate themselves about the underpinnings of various analytic algorithms. Even when a clinician has the inclination to carefully study the computer model, the copyright holders of the analytic program may have significant reluctance about sharing too much information, lest they compromise their property rights.

In the end, the most reasonable approach to using automated scoring and interpretive services involves considering those data as only one component of an evaluation, and carefully seeking out and probing any apparently discrepant findings. This suggestion will not come as a surprise to most competent psychologists, but unfortunately not all users of these tools fall in that category. Many users of such tests are nonpsychologists with little understanding of the interpretive subtleties. Some will take the any computer-generated report as valid on its face, without considering individual important factors that make their client unique. A few users simply seek a quick-and-dirty source of data to help them make a decision in the absence of clinical acumen. Other users inflate the actual cost of the tests and scoring services to enhance their billing rate. When making use of such tools, psychologists should have a well-reasoned strategy for incorporating them in the assessment, and interpret them with well-informed caution (Koocher & Keith-Spiegel, 1998).

Recommendations

1. Candidates for forensic assessment (or their parents or legal guardians) must be given full informed consent about the purpose of the evaluation, payment for services, access to results, and other relevant data prior to initiating the evaluation.
2. Psychologists conducting forensic assessments should be aware of and adhere to published professional standards and guidelines relevant to the nature of the particular type of assessment they are conducting.

3. Different types of technical data on tests exist, including reliability and validity data, and psychologists should be sufficiently familiar with these for any instrument they use in order to justify and explain the appropriateness of the selection.

4. Those administering psychological tests are responsible for assuring that administration and scoring follow standardized instructions.

5. Test users should note potential test bias or client characteristics that might reduce the validity of the instrument for that client and context and specifically address these issues in their reports.

6. No psychologist is competent to administer and interpret all psychological tests or assess all potential clients. It is important to be cautiously self-critical and to agree to undertake only those evaluations that fall within one's training and sphere of competence.

7. The validity and confidence of test results rely to some degree on test security. Psychologists should use reasonable caution in protecting the security of test items and materials, and not participate in or collaborate with others who engage in coaching people for the purpose of distorting the true nature of the examinee's status.

8. Automated testing services create a hazard to the extent that they may generate data that are inaccurate for certain clients or that are misinterpreted by improperly trained individuals. Psychologists operating or making use of such services should take steps to minimize such risks.

9. Clients normally have a right to feedback and a right to have confidentiality of data protected. In forensic cases, these rights vary greatly, and clarification of reasonably foreseeable issues must occur at the outset of the evaluation or in connection with any subsequent authorized releases.

References

American Psychological Association. (1953). *Ethical standards of psychologists*. Washington, DC: Author.

American Psychological Association. (2000). *Report of the task force on test user qualifications*. Washington, DC: Author. Available at www.apa.org/science/tuq.pdf

American Psychological Association. (2002). *Ethical principles of psychologists and code of conduct*. Washington, DC: Author.

Ardila, A., & Moreno, S. (2001). Neuropsychological test performance in Aruaco Indians: An exploratory study. *Neuropsychology, 7*, 510–515.

Connell, M., & Koocher, G. P. (2003). Expert opinion: HIPAA and forensic practice. *American Psychology Law Society News, 13*(2), 16–19.

Editorial. (1999). Test security: Protecting the integrity of tests. *American Psychologist, 54*, 1078–1078.

Eyde, L. E., Moreland, K. L., Robertson, G. J., Primoff, E. S., & Most, R. B. (1988). *Test user qualifications: A data-based approach to promoting good test use, issues in scientific psychology* (Report of the Test User Qualifications Working Group of the Joint Committee on Testing Practices). Washington, DC: American Psychological Association.

Eyde, L. E., Robertson, G. J., Krug, S. E., Moreland, K. L., Robertson, A. G., Shewan, C. M., et al. (1993). *Responsible test use: Case studies for assessing human behavior*. Washington, DC: American Psychological Association.

Flanagan, D. P., & Alfonso, V. C. (1995). A critical review of the technical characteristics of new and recently revised intelligence tests for preschool children. *Journal of Psychoeducational Assessment, 13*, 66–90.

Fundudis, T. (2003). Consent issues in medicolegal procedures: How competent are children to make their own decisions. *Child & Adolescent Mental Health, 8*, 18–22.

Grisso, T., & Appelbaum, P. S. (1998). *Assessing competence to consent to treatment: A guide for physicians and other health professionals*. New York: Oxford University Press.

Grote, C. L., Lewin, J. L., Sweet, J. J., & van Gorp, W. G. (2000). Courting the clinician. responses to perceived unethical practices in clinical neuropsychology: Ethical and legal considerations. *Clinical Neuropsychologist, 14*, 119–134.

Heaton, R. K., Grant, I., & Matthews, C. G. (1991). *Comprehensive norms for an expanded Halstead-Reitan Battery: Demographic corrections, research findings, and clinical applications*. Odessa, FL: Psychological Assessment Resources.

Johnson-Greene, D., Hardy-Morais, C., Adams, K., Hardy, C., & Bergloff, P. (1997). Informed consent and neuropsychological assessment: Ethical considerations and proposed guidelines. *Clinical Neuropsychologist, 11*, 454–460.

Kagehiro, D. K., & Laufer, W. S. (Eds.). (1992). *Handbook of psychology and law*. New York: Springer-Verlag.

Kamphaus, R. W., Dresden, J., & Kaufman, A. S. (1993). Clinical and psychometric considerations in the cognitive assessment of preschool children. In J. Culbertson & D. Willis (Eds.), *Testing young children: A reference guide for developmental, psychoeducational, and psychosocial assessments* (pp. 55–72). Austin, TX: Pro-Ed.

Koocher, G. P. (2005). Assessing the quality of a psychological testing report. In G. P. Koocher, J. C. Norcross, & S. S. Hill (Eds.), *PsyDR: Psychologist's desk reference* (2nd ed., pp. 117–118). New York: Oxford University Press.

Koocher, G. P., & DeMaso, D. R. (1990). Children's competence to consent to medical procedures. *Pediatrician, 17,* 68–73.

Koocher, G. P., & Keith-Spiegel, P. C. (1998). *Ethics in psychology: Professional standards and cases* (2nd ed.). New York: Oxford University Press.

Lees-Haley, P. R., & Courtney, J. C. (2000a). Disclosure of tests and raw test data to the courts: A need for reform. *Neuropsychology Review, 10,* 169–174.

Lees-Haley, P. R., & Courtney, J. C. (2000b). Reply to the commentary on: A disclosure of tests and raw test data to the courts. *Neuropsychology Review, 10,* 181–182.

McCaffrey, R. J., Fisher, J. M., Gold, B. A., & Lynch, J. K. (1996). Presence of third parties during neuropsychological evaluations: Who is evaluating whom? *Clinical Neuropsychologist, 10,* 435–449.

McSweeney, A. J., Becker, B. C., Naugle, R. I., Snow, W. G., Binder, L. M., & Thompson, L. L. (1998). Ethical issues related to third party observers in clinical neuropsychological evaluations. *Clinical Neuropsychologist, 12,* 552–559.

Moreland, K. L., Eyde, L. D., Robertson, G. J., Primoff, E. S., & Most, R. B. (1995). Assessment of test user qualifications: a research-based measurement procedure. *American Psychologist, 50,* 14–23.

National Academy of Neuropsychology. (2000a). The use of neuropsychology test technicians in clinical practice. *Archives of Clinical Neuropsychology, 15,* 381–382.

National Academy of Neuropsychology. (2000b). Presence of third party observers during neuropsychological testing. *Archives of Clinical Neuropsychology, 15,* 379–380.

National Academy of Neuropsychology. (2000c). Test security. *Archives of Clinical Neuropsychology, 15,* 381–382.

Nelson, R. M. (1998). Children as research subjects. In J. P. Kahn, A. C. Mastroianni, & J. Sugarman (Eds.), *Beyond consent: Seeking justice in research* (pp. 47–66). New York: Oxford University Press.

Ostrosky, F. Ardila, A., Rosselli, M. López-Arango, G., & Uriel-Mendoza, V. (1998). Neuropsychological test performance in illiterates. *Archives of Clinical Neuropsychology, 13,* 645–660.

Public Law 94–142. Education for all handicapped children act of 1975 (November 19, 1975).

Public Law 101–336. Americans with disabilities act of 1990 (January 23, 1990).

Public Law 104–191. Health insurance portability and accountability act of 1991 (August 21, 1996).

Shapiro, D. L. (2000). Commentary on disclosure of tests and raw test data to the courts. *Neuropsychology Review, 10,* 175–176.

Sieber, J. E. (1992). *Planning ethically responsible research: A guide for students and internal review boards.* Thousand Oaks, CA: Sage.

Sterling, C. M., & Walco, G. A. (2003). Protection of children's rights to self-determination in research. *Ethics & Behavior, 13,* 237–247.

Vanderploeg, R. D., Axelrod, B. N., Sherer, M., Scott, J., & Adams, R. (1997). The importance of demographic adjustments on neuropsychological test performance: A response to Reitan and Wolfson (1995). *Clinical Neuropsychologist, 11,* 210–217.

Victor, T. L., & Abeles, N. (2004). Coaching clients to take psychological and neuropsychological tests: A clash of ethical obligations. *Professional Psychology: Research & Practice, 35,* 373–379.

4

Ten Rules: How to Get Along Better With Lawyers and the Legal System

William E. Foote

Over the second half of the last century, lawyers and judges have increasingly called upon psychologists to bring knowledge of the science and practice of psychology into the courtroom (Bartall & Bartall, 1987; Ogloff, Beavers, & DeLeon, 1999). For some psychologists, the experience has become a focus of practice in the specialty of forensic psychology. For others, especially psychotherapists asked to testify about their patients, a subpoena to appear in court generates suspicion and fear bordering on panic (Greenberg & Shuman, 1997; Shuman, Greenberg, Heilbrun, & Foote, 1998). Still others have expressed concern that psychologists have become "whores of the court," selling their opinions to the highest bidders (Hagan, 1997). For all the occasions they desire the testimony and consultation of psychologists to assist them in furthering the interests of their clients, even lawyers sometimes harbor resentment about the mysteries that seem to undergird much of what psychologists do, and some express concern that this seemingly arcane science of the mind will somehow supplant the judgment of judges and juries (Melton, Petrila, Poythress, & Slobogin, 1997; Williger, 1995).

Barton and Sandborn (1978), in an early contribution to the psychology-law literature, recognized that psychology and law differ in important respects. These differences give rise to conflict between professionals from the two disciplines. More recently, Melton et al. (1997) discussed paradigm conflicts that affect the interactions between lawyers and psychologists. For example, psychologists and lawyers differ in their emphasis on the individual's free will versus a perspective in which the person's behavior is predetermined by existing factor. In this conflict, psychologists will more likely hold the view that determination of behavior flows from environmental and genetic factors, whereas the law emphasizes free will and an individual's ability to make free choices. The professions also differ on the preferred manner of determining facts. In psychology, the emphasis falls on the use of the scientific method to determine truth. On the other hand, the law relies upon an adversarial process in which both sides present their case to an impartial finder or trier of fact, (e.g., a judge, jury, or administrative panel) who weighs the information and renders a decision. Melton et al. (1997) also note that the professions differ in how they define a fact. For psychologists, facts score as more or less probable, depending on relevant factors. Psychologists may say it is improbable, moderately probable, or highly probable that a particular fact is true. The law, on the other hand, prefers to rely on certainties. In court, a decision about who is at fault and who is not at fault is usually binary. A criminal defendant usually can be found only guilty or not guilty. A jury in a personal injury tort case must arrive at a dollar verdict, an eminently quantifiable outcome.

Thus, it should come as no surprise that, over the years, psychology and the law have encountered fundamental conflicts that persist despite goodwill and attempts to solve problems on the part of both professions. This goodwill has become evident in efforts by lawyers and psychologists to establish working relationships to benefit their mutual clients. These attempts have occurred at several levels. State psychology associations have worked with lawyers to put together interdisciplinary agreements. Among the first such effort was one concluded through joint efforts of the New Mexico Psychological Association and the New Mexico Bar Association in 1986 (Foote, 1994; Pope, Butcher, & Seelen, 1993). This agreement allowed for psychologists and lawyers to interact more effectively on the basis of agreed-upon principles of interaction. The New Mexico Interdisciplinary Agreement defines how the professions' respective concepts of patient and client differ and affirms that both professions hold paramount the best interests of the client. Later sections include a delineation of lawyers' and psychologists' responsibilities. The document concludes with a grievance resolution procedure.

Following the New Mexico effort, similar documents have been issued in other states, such as Colorado. The American Psychological Association has recently undertaken to formulate a similar draft document that would serve as a model for nationwide cooperation. The model interdisciplinary agreement has won approval by the American Psychological Association Council of Representatives in 1999 and is currently working through a process within the governance of the American Bar Association (ABA) for that group's review and approval. If passed by the ABA, this document should serve as a model for similar documents that may issue in local jurisdictions, including urban regions and states around the country.

However, much of the psychology-law interaction occurs at an individual level, between individual psychologists and individual lawyers. At that level, problems with friction at the interface seem more likely to affect the work of a psychologist in a particular case. This chapter's focus constitutes an attempt to provide some oil at that interface in the form of specific suggestions about how psychologists may improve their individual interactions with lawyers as they work together in both clinical and legal arenas. These suggestions follow in the form of 10 rules that reflect either good practice or hard realities. Although some rules arise in a spirit of good humor, all reflect an aspect of this most complex of professional interactions.

LEARN THE LAWYER'S RULES

The law is a rule-bound profession (Daley, 1996; Williger, 1995). Some of the rules appear in codified form as statutes that become interpreted through case law and come into force in courts governed by of rules of evidence (Federal Rules of Evidence, 2004) or rules of criminal or civil procedure (Federal Rules of Civil Procedure, 2005). Courts also operate in the context of local rules that reflect how things actually occur in different communities. Local rules may exist in written form or may be informally understood as practices known by the lawyers and the judges in particular communities.

The rules of the court determine the sequence of events in a case. For example, the usual course of events in a criminal matter may proceed as follows: The criminal suspect comes under arrest, undergoes an investigation, becomes indicted, and then, as a defendant, experiences pretrial proceedings, stands trial, and, if convicted, faces sentencing and may put forward a case for postconviction relief (i.e., appeal) once he or she faces incarceration. In a civil matter, the case begins with a civil complaint followed by written discovery, pleadings, and a trial.

The rules may also govern how a psychologist presents testimony in court. Court proceedings are formal, and lawyers occasionally utilize stilted and artificial, yet traditional language (e.g., *If it pleases the court*), which allows for dignified and orderly proceedings (Daley, 1996). Anyone who has had involvement in legal proceedings recognizes that many of these formalities originated by design to provide a civilized basis for individuals to resolve conflict that might otherwise become heated and personal.

The psychologist needs to know these rules so as not to run afoul of them and to offer assistance in a way that makes sense in the context of the legal system. It does a psychologist no good to work many hours to develop testimony that will not be admitted and presented to the jury because of evidentiary rules. Likewise, it makes no sense for a lawyer to present a case marred by statements or actions that draw objections from counsel and admonitions from the court.

DON'T PRACTICE THE LAW

Although psychologists should know the rules of the court, unless one actually attends law school, receives a law degree, and follows the procedures for gaining admitted to the local bar, psychologists cannot practice the law. Although psychologists who practice in legal settings must have some knowledge of the fundamentals of the legal system and the basic rules of the court, they may well remain ignorant of many aspects of the law or have an oversimplified idea of what the law says. Additionally, in the context of a particular case, psychologists will rarely have a grasp of the full breadth of the case as might the well-prepared lawyer.

For example, psychologists may believe that they have an understanding of the legal nuances of the phrase *best interests of the child*. However, many have argued that not even lawyers have a clear grasp of the concept, much less how it plays out in child custody litigation (Batt, 1992; Krauss & Sales, 1999; Mnookin & Kornhauser, 1979). At best, the psychologist may focus on how that legal concept becomes operationalized and assessed through the means at the psychologist's disposal: interview, record review, and testing (B. K. Clark, 1995). Psychologists should stick to what they know—the clinical or forensic topic that undergirds court testimony. This can become a sufficiently formidable task in most cases (Krauss & Sales, 2000).

REMEMBER THAT LAW]YERS MAKE THE RULES

At first blush, this may appear obvious. The legal system and court procedures evolved to make the jobs of lawyers and judges easier, even if it makes the exercise of other people's responsibilities more difficult. For example, Federal Rule of Civil Procedure 26A (Federal Rules of Civil Procedure, 2003) was designed to speed up civil litigation. The rule imposes deadlines for evaluations and disclosures concerning the evaluations (Shuman, 2000). Unfortunately, these deadlines may push the psychologist to rush an evaluation or produce an opinion before gathering all the relevant evidence. Such pressures can put the psychologist in a bind of both ethical and professional proportions (American Psychological Association, 2002; Committee on Ethical Guidelines for Forensic Psychologists, 1991).

One should also remain aware that lawyers have virtually all the power in the situations in which psychologists and lawyers interact (Daley, 1996). In forensic contexts, the psychologist's power is limited. Psychologists have only their personal integrity and the clinical and office procedures conducted directly by them or under their supervision. On the other hand, lawyers and courts have available to them legal powers occasionally used to require psychologists to behave in particular ways. The most commonly used is the subpoena, with which the lawyer can seek to require a psychologist to disclose almost any fact concerning relevant professional work or, for that matter, the psychologist's own personal history (compare *Cheatham v. Rogers*, 1992).

In contrast, a court order is issued by the judge, usually upon a motion from one of the parties in a case. Through court orders, the judge may use contempt powers to enforce the court's will, because a failure or refusal to comply with a court order may result in a contempt citation and penalties, including fines and incarceration (Slovenko, 1987). Court orders include orders for release of information, to make documents available, or to compel psychologists to present court testimony. These powers are not trivial. A psychologist may go before the court to explain why the psychologist is not obeying the court order, and probably should do so if it is necessary to assert privilege (the legally afforded right of the client to instruct the psychologist not to disclose protected communications) on behalf of a client. However, a judge can hold a psychologist in contempt of court if the psychologist fails to comply with a lawful court order.

BUT PSYCHOLOGISTS HAVE THE INFORMATION

The legal system is fueled by facts. In the case of expert testimony, these facts become linked to each other by way of expert opinions (Goodman-Delahunty & Foote, 1995). Psychologists have the training, education, and experience to deal with the arcane aspects of mental health, psychopathology, interpersonal relationships, and psychological testing. At times, lawyers need that information in order to satisfy legal requirements in a case. For example, in a child custody matter, the lawyer may have to prove that custody with one parent is more in the best interests of the child than is custody with the other parent (Krauss & Sales, 2000). Psychologists would logically constitute a major source of information for that determination on the basis of a thorough evaluation. Such an evaluation would include interviews of all the parties (B. K. Clark, 1995), appropriate psychological testing (Brodzinsky, 1993; Otto & Butcher, 1995), and collateral interviews (Heilbrun, Rosenfeld, Warren, & Collins, 1994) as described in detail elsewhere in this volume. In the absence of such information, the court may make decisions ultimately harmful to the child's emotional condition.

Thus, psychologists have information necessary for the system to function properly. Psychologists may constitute a necessary evil from a lawyer's perspective, but especially in family law cases, the psychologist's testimony has become a critical part of the matrimonial law system in America (Association of Family and Conciliation Courts, 1994).

GET PAID OUT FRONT

Psychologists often do not like to deal with the reality that they are being paid for their services (Sitkowski & Herron, 1991; Trachtman, 1999). Many psychologists have entered the field for altruistic reasons (Eber & Kunz, 1984) and seek primarily to assist people in resolving problems and improving their lives. Thus, when they charge money for their services, psychologists seem prone to experiencing some conflict.

In contrast, most competent attorneys consider the issue of money almost continuously through the process of accepting and developing a case

(Williger, 1995). Of course many lawyers do their work from an altruistic and helping perspective, and in fact have an ethical duty to provide pro bono services. However, lawyers' training focuses on dealing with money much more effectively than does psychologists' training. Most lawyers employ trust accounts to manage the costs of a case, and some lawyers have encountered severe disciplinary penalties for trust account mismanagement. In the same way that most lawyers deal with financial arrangements in a fair and business-like manner, it becomes critical for psychologists to deal effectively with fees (Fitch, Petrilla, & Wallace, 1987).

The forensic guidelines (Committee on Ethical Guidelines for Forensic Psychologists, 1991) require that forensic psychologists work out the fees from the beginning of the case. Some argue that psychologists should make secure financial arrangements, preferably in writing (Pope et al., 1993). These financial arrangements are best done in writing and best prepared by the psychologist's lawyer so that the contract may actually bind the retaining lawyer to pay the fees.

Such agreements ensure that the psychologist may function in a situation in which he or she works free of financial pressures and without the appearance of money-motivated bias. All this is recognized in the specialty guidelines (Committee on Ethical Guidelines for Forensic Psychologists, 1991), which specifically ban the employment of a psychologist as an expert on the basis of contingency fees. Legal ethics contain a similar provision (Fitch et al., 1987).

At times, psychologists employed in the legal system express concern that their fee will remain unpaid if the case results in a verdict contrary to the interests of those who hire the expert. Responding to those pressures at the expense of balance and scientific accuracy not only violates the American Psychological Association's ethical principles and code of conduct (American Psychological Association, 2002), but also threatens the role of the expert in legal proceedings.

Payment in advance constitutes a way to relieve some of this pressure. Not only does advance payment quiet concern about undue influence arising from the financial arrangements, but it also constitutes a sound business practice. Of course, the psychologist must have procedures for returning unused fees and may reasonably enter into agreements that place a ceiling upon the fees that the psychologist may bill. These concerns become small compared to the other ethical and professional issues raised above.

ALWAYS RETURN PHONE CALLS

Although this rule sounds very simple, it reflects not only common courtesy but a basic element of professionalism. A call from a lawyer may feel unwelcome for two reasons. First, it may involve a case for which the psychologist feels unqualified to render a professional opinion (Hess, 1998). Bound by ethical standards not to practice outside of the parameters of competence (American Psychological Association, 2002), psychologists should accept referrals only for cases that fall within their education, training, and experience.

However, even if the psychologist has no intent to work with that counsel, it will always prove a good idea to touch base with the lawyer and speak to him or her personally. In this way, the psychologist may develop a reputation as a community resource. By helping the lawyer define what kind of expert he or she does need (e.g., a neuropsychologist vs. a family therapist), the psychologist may enlarge the range of competent professionals available to the lawyer. Such assistance will establish a line of communication and respect, so that the next time that lawyer has a case that matches the psychologist's skills, the helpful psychologist would rank high on his list.

The psychologist should observe one caution, however. When making referrals, do not recommend unknown professionals as referrals. Although it has always been the case that we become known by the company we keep, it is also true that we are known by the professionals we recommend to others.

A second reason psychologists may not want to return the lawyer's calls may result from the past history or reputation of the calling lawyer. The psychologist may simply not want to work with this particular attorney because of the lawyer's personality, professional style, or reputation for questionable professional practices. In such cases, it remains preferable to return the call, even if to tell the lawyer that the psychologist lacks the time to work on that case.

However, it will prove important for psychologists involved in preliminary discussions with potential employers to remain alert to creating potential conflicts, especially in small communities or in legal arenas with few well-known experts. Occasionally, lawyers will utilize a referral conversation to poison the well. That is, a lawyer wishing to eliminate a particular expert from a case may call the expert and discuss confidential aspects of the case with that expert as part of a referral call. The lawyer may never intend to follow through with the actual referral. However, by going through this process, the lawyer has placed the psychologist in an ethical position where he or she cannot agree to work with another party in the matter because of the prior exposure to confidential, attorney work product information.

For that reason, some experts make it clear at the beginning of a referral conversation that they do not want the referring lawyer to discuss any confidential aspects of the case with them until after the expert has formally agreed to assist and has accepted a retention fee. Although psychologists differ on details of this policy, it would appear appropriate for a psychologist to exercise caution about referral calls that come from unlikely sources.

READ YOUR JOB DESCRIPTION

Lawyers generally seek psychologists to perform specific tasks in a case (Hess, 1998; Williger, 1995). For example, in a child custody situation, counsel may ask the psychologist to conduct an evaluation of the relevant adults and children to provide information to the court concerning most effective custody arrangements. Even in situations for which the psychologist performs a well-accustomed role, it will always prove a good idea to receive a written referral letter from the lawyer. This letter would explicate the particular tasks agreed to or information slated for inclusion in the psychologist's final report or testimony.

In some cases, as part of the referral discussion, it is appropriate for the referring lawyer and psychologist to discuss what the psychologist can and cannot do. For example, one will generally not find an ethical psychologist willing to provide testimony concerning custody following the evaluation of only one of the parents (American Psychological Association, 1994). A lawyer seeking only that type of opinion should quickly learn from his potential expert that psychologists cannot ethically render an opinion based upon such a narrow foundation. It is through this interaction between the psychologist and lawyer that the lawyer may learn about the capabilities and policies of the psychologist.

In some cases, the questions that the psychologist can answer may fall in a very narrow range indeed. For example, the lawyer may desire the psychologist to provide testimony only about the scientific research in a particular area. This scientific framework testimony (Goodman & Croyle, 1989) serves as background for the finder of fact to arrive at a legal determination without necessarily focusing on the particular aspects or individuals in the case.

In any role, clarity of purpose is a prerequisite to the psychologist functioning effectively both for the retaining lawyer and the finder of fact. The expert whose role and task remain vague may become viewed by the court as one on a fishing expedition or, at least, as one who is unprofessional.

THE PSYCHOLOGIST AND THE LAWYER DO NOT HAVE THE SAME CLIENT

Strictly speaking, in child custody cases, the lawyers, the judge, and the psychologist expert must all act in the best interest of the child (American Psychological Association, 1994). Nevertheless, the fact remains that the psychologist and the lawyer are hired by different people. The psychologist's direct client is the lawyer or the court. That is, the court becomes the ultimate consumer of psychological services, and a psychologist acting as an expert has a duty to the court to provide services that reflect accurate information and unbiased opinions (American Psychological Association, 1994; Committee on Ethical Guidelines for Forensic Psychologists, 1991). However, as noted above, the lawyer will typically retain the psychologist's services and define the scope of tasks for the psychologist to perform. As such, the lawyer stands as the direct client and consumer of the psychologist's services. The lawyer pays the psychologist and expects to get some benefit from those services.

On the other hand, the lawyer's client is usually one party in the litigation, or several parties that have congruent interests. In this situation, the lawyer is generally required by ethical canons to provide the strongest appropriate representation for the client (Fitch et al., 1987). In tort cases or criminal matters, in service of zealous representation, the lawyer may push the psychologist to produce a result supportive of that lawyer's client. In child custody cases, especially in high-conflict cases, the desires of the parents may differ significantly from outcomes that would constitute the best interests of the child (Garrity & Baris, 1994). Some lawyers interpret this requirement to mean that they must push the retained psychologist to provide testimony most favorable to their client's case.

The result is that some psychologists find themselves in a bind between a duty to the ultimate consumers of the services (e.g., the court and, indirectly, the child) and to the person paying the bills (Glassman, 1998). This problem of agency has proven a difficult one for psychologists in all legal settings (Brodsky, 1991; Rogers, 1987) and differs from the fee problem noted above because it has more to do with direct or indirect pressure from the lawyer upon the psychologist to arrive at a specific opinion. When faced with such pressure, the psychologist should remember that the court and the child are the ultimate consumers of the psychologist's services.

Many jurisdictions have laws or court rules that mandate or permit the judge to appoint the psychologist to serve as a court-ordered expert. In this case, the judge determines who the expert is and lays out the job description. Other jurisdictions allow for the parties to stipulate to the appointment of a single expert. In both these cases, the pressure associated with agency decreases significantly because the duty is owed to the hiring party, that is, the court. Court appointment may also provide additional protection for the expert in that most jurisdictions provide for testimonial immunity for court-ordered experts (Shuman & Greenberg, 2003).

IF IT FEELS IFFY, DON'T DO IT

Ethical standards for forensic work and for psychotherapy work have some overlap but differ in significant respects. Clinicians stepping into this unfamiliar territory may feel concerned that the tasks demanded of psychologists in forensic settings, sometimes with limited time and limited access to information, somehow waive the rules normally associated with psychological practice.

For example, a colleague conducting forensic ethics workshops was once asked by a participating psychologist if it was all right to have a sexual relationship with a person seen in a forensic context. The workshop leader immediately informed the questioner that such relationships were no more ethical for a forensic examiner than is a psychotherapist having sex with a patient.

In reality, the ethical and professional standards required of psychologists in forensic settings are actually higher than those for professionals in a consulting or psychotherapy setting. However, because the territory remains new and partially uncharted, psychologists may find themselves in ethical conflicts (Glassman, 1998). These arise from two main sources: the lawyer and the most beneficent motives of the psychologist.

A corollary to who is the client (Monahan, 1980) appears when a lawyer asks the psychologist to engage in activities that would constitute ethically acceptable conduct for a lawyer but ethically inappropriate conduct for psychologists. For example, a lawyer may ask the psychologist to enter into a dual relationship, that is, to provide psychological services for someone with whom the psychologist already has a personal relationship. Or, as part of trial strategy, the lawyer may ask the psychologist to engage in a personal attack on the expert hired by the other party. Although a lawyer may be allowed under legal ethical canons to do these things, for a psychologist, to have a dual relationship or to publicly attack a colleague would constitute a violation of not only professionalism but also professional ethical standards (American Psychological Association, 2002).

Psychologists may find themselves confronting information that would lead to opinions contrary to the lawyers' goals for the case (Slovenko, 1987). Again, psychologists have a responsibility to present unbiased and fair testimony and to not conceal findings adverse to the hiring party. Psychologists find themselves asked to stretch the scientific data to fit the arguments of the hiring lawyer. The duty to fidelity and accuracy that all psychologists have stands contrary to this demand.

Psychologists want to do the right thing (C. R. Clark, 1993) and will many times feel the desire to do good in a way that places the psychologist in ethical quicksand. For example, imagine a psychologist acting as a psychotherapist and aware that a patient does not want a history of child sexual abuse to become public. Now, imagine the patient has become a plaintiff in a sexual harassment claim and seeks damages based upon her emotional reactions to the alleged workplace events. Upon receipt of a subpoena, the psychotherapist, in an attempt to protect the client's privacy, removes the portions of her psychotherapy notes that reflect the sex abuse history. This spoliation of the record places the psychologist in jeopardy not only of ethical and licensing actions but also of potential perjury charges if the psychologist testifies that the records presented are the original ones or lies about the patient's history.

In the course of training and experience, psychologists gain a sense of what constitutes ethical behavior and what does not. In my experience of providing ethics consultations to colleagues, I have become impressed that the events that raised the ethical issues for the psychologist usually should have. That is, most well-trained psychologists have good ethical instincts that tell them when they fall or feel tempted to fall off an ethical track. Most cases in which psychologists find themselves before ethics committees or licensing boards consist of those in which the psychologist overrode those ethical instincts for what seemed like a good reason at the time. In forensic practice, it is a difficult task to be too ethical. If a decision seems to be a questionable decision, it probably is.

SOMETIMES YOU GET THE BEAR, SOMETIMES THE BEAR GETS YOU

In the practice of psychotherapy, the psychologist's success can sometimes be measured by improvements in the patient's relationships with family members, by the patient's increased job performance, or by decreases in substance abuse. Other times, the results of treatment remain less clear, but both the therapist and the patient agree that the work has resulted in improvement of the patient's lot.

However, for the psychologist working in forensic settings, the measures of success almost always remain unclear. Although, as noted above, the results of cases usually yield binary decisions (e.g., someone wins and someone loses), the verdict in a case may depend upon factors that have nothing to do with the performance of the expert. In most cases, the expert psychological testimony constitutes only a small part of what the jury evaluates in arriving at a decision (Cooper & Hall, 2000; Greene, Downey, & Goodman-Delahunty, 1999). Lay testimony, physical evidence, and other expert testimony often play a larger role in forming the foundation of the jury's decision (Poulson, Brondino, Brown, & Braithwaite 1998).

Jury verdicts may also rely upon the skills of the lawyers. The ability to conduct legal research, to properly prepare witnesses, and to argue a case eloquently before a jury varies among lawyers (Slovenko, 1987). These skills count for something, especially if one views the range of monetary damages garnered by top-flight lawyers compared to those less gifted.

In many cases, the credibility of the parties becomes the critical issue. Although psychologists (as most other professionals) are incapable of reliably determining credibility (Ekman & O'Sullivan, 1991), judges and juries must often choose among differing accounts of events. A party who has demonstrably distorted those events may lose the case based upon that showing alone.

At times, however, a psychologist steps down from the witness box with a profound realization that his or her work did not measure up to personal or professional standards. Such reactions occur with even the most seasoned experts and may reflect errors in evaluation, analysis, or presentation of information. However, these bad days teach psychologists the best, though hardest, lessons. Using this information, the psychologist can modify evaluation practices, office procedures, or testimony presentation so that the same mistake will not be made twice.

Whatever the outcome, the psychologist's job remains the same: to provide accurate information so that the finder of fact may reach more informed decisions (Mark, 1999). This information should have support by good science that ensures the accuracy of the psychologist's opinions. Psychologists should offer those opinions in a way that rings clear to all who listen to them. An opinion couched in jargon not only remains unhelpful to the finder of fact but also may lead to inappropriate conclusions (Daley, 1996; Hess, 1998). Psychologists should offer only opinions that they can willingly defend against cross-examination. The opinion must come well considered, taking full account of contrary data and with enough strength of conviction so as to stand up against serious scrutiny (Brodsky, 1991).

Testimony provided in this manner will not only assist the trier of fact but also can actually positively serve justice (Zacharias, 1999). At the end of the day, psychologists should ask not who won the case, but whether the psychologist's testimony assisted in the resolution of the matter (Mark, 1999). To offer clear assistance provides the best service we can.

References

American Psychological Association. (2002). *Ethical principles of psychologists and code of conduct.* Washington, DC: Author.

American Psychological Association. (1994). Guidelines for child custody evaluations in divorce proceedings. *American Psychologist, 49,* 677–680.

Association of Family and Conciliation Courts. (1994). *Model standards of practice for child custody evaluations.* Milwaukee, WI: Author.

Bartall, C. R., & Bartall, A. M. (1987). History of forensic psychology. In I. B. Weiner & A. K. Hess (Eds.), *Handbook of forensic psychology* (pp. 3–23). New York: John Wiley.

Barton, W. E., & Sandborn, C. J. (1978). Friction at the interface. In W. E. Barton & C. J. Sandborn (Eds.), *Law and the mental health professions: Friction at the interface* (pp. 311–320). New York: International Universities Press.

Batt, J. (1992). Child custody disputes and beyond the best interest standard. *Nova Law Review, 16,* 621–640.

Brodsky, S. (1991). *Testifying in court: Guidelines and maxims for the expert witness.* Washington, DC: American Psychological Association.

Brodzinsky, D. M. (1993). On the use and misuse of psychological testing in child custody evaluations. *Professional Psychology: Research & Practice, 24,* 213–219.

Cheatham v. Rogers, 231. S.W. 2d. 824 (Tex. Ct. App. 1992).

Clark, B. K. (1995). Handle with care: Interviewing children in child custody situations [Special issue]. *Michigan Family Law Journal, 29,* 28–31.

Clark, C. R. (1993). Social responsibility ethics: Doing right, doing good, doing well. *Ethics & Behavior, 3,* 303–327.

Committee on Ethical Guidelines for Forensic Psychologists. (1991). Specialty guidelines for forensic psychologists. *Law & Human Behavior, 15,* 655–665.

Cooper, J., & Hall, J. (2000). Reactions of mock jurors to testimony of a court appointed expert. *Behavioral Sciences & the Law, 18,* 719–729.

Daley, T. T. (1996). Pretrial preparations can improve a physician's value as an expert witness. *Canadian Medical Association Journal, 154,* 573.

Eber, M., & Kunz, L. B. (1984). The desire to help others. *Bulletin of the Menninger Clinic, 48,* 125–140.

Ekman, P., & O'Sullivan, M. (1991). Who can catch a liar? *American Psychologist, 46*(9), 913–920.

Federal Rules of Civil Procedure. (2003). Retrieved September 23, 2005, from www.law.cornell.edu/rules/frcp/

Federal Rules of Criminal Procedure. (2005). Retrieved September 23, 2005, from www.law.cornell.edu/rules/frcrmp/

Federal Rules of Evidence. (2004). Retrieved September 23, 2005, from www.law.cornell.edu/rules/fre/

Fitch, W. L., Petrilla, R. C., & Wallace, J. (1987). Legal ethics and the use of mental health experts in criminal cases. *Behavioral Sciences & the Law, 5,* 105–118.

Foote, W. E. (1994). An interdisciplinary agreement for psychologists and lawyers. In L. Vandecreek, S. Knapp, & T. L. Jackson (Eds.), *Innovations in clinical practice* (pp. 255–262). Sarasota, FL: Professional Resource Press.

Garrity, C. B., & Baris, M. A. (1994). *Caught in the middle: Protecting the children of high-conflict divorce.* New York: Lexington.

Glassman, J. B. (1998). Preventing and managing board complaints: The downside risk of custody evaluation. *Professional Psychology: Research & Practice, 29,* 121–124.

Goodman, J., & Croyle, R. T. (1989). Social framework testimony in employment discrimination cases. *Behavioral Sciences & the Law, 7,* 227–241.

Goodman-Delahunty, J., & Foote, W. E. (1996). Compensation for pain, suffering and other psychological injuries: The impact of *Daubert* on employment discrimination claims. *Behavioral Sciences & the Law, 13,* 183–206.

Greenberg, S. A., & Shuman, D. W. (1997). Irreconcilable conflict between therapeutic and forensic roles. *Professional Psychology: Research & Practice, 50,* 28–39.

Greene, E., Downey, C., & Goodman-Delahunty, J. (1999). Juror decisions about damages in employment discrimination cases. *Behavioral Sciences & the Law, 17,* 107–121.

Hagan, M. A. (1997). *Whores of the court.* New York: HarperCollins.

Heilbrun, K., Rosenfeld, B., Warren, J. I., & Collins, S. (1994). The use of third-party information in forensic assessments: A two state comparison. *Bulletin of the American Academy of Psychiatry & Law, 22,* 399–406.

Hess, A. K. (1998). Accepting forensic case referrals: Ethical and professional considerations. *Professional Psychology: Research & Practice, 29,* 109–114.

Krauss, D. A., & Sales, B. D. (1999). The problem of helpfulness in applying Daubert to expert testimony: Child custody determinations in family law as an exemplar. *Psychology, Public Policy, & Law, 5,* 78–99.

Krauss, D. A., & Sales, B. D. (2000). Legal standards, expertise, and experts in the resolution of contested child custody cases. *Psychology, Public Policy, & Law, 6,* 843–879.

Mark, M. M. (1999). Social science evidence in the courtroom: Daubert and beyond. *Psychology, Public Policy, & Law, 5,* 175–193.

Melton, G. B., Petrila, J., Poythress, N. G., & Slobogin, C. (1997). *Psychological evaluations for the courts: A handbook for mental health professionals and lawyers* (2nd ed.). New York: Guilford.

Mnookin, R., & Kornhauser, K. A. (1979). Bargaining in the shadows of law: The case of divorce. *Yale Law Journal, 88,* 950.

Monahan, J. (1980). *Who is the client? The ethics of psychological intervention in the criminal justice system.* Washington, DC: American Psychological Association.

Ogloff, J. R. P., Beavers, D. J., & DeLeon, P. H. (1999). Psychology and the law: A shared vision for the 21st century. *Professional Psychology Research & Practice, 39*(4), 331–332.

Otto, R. K., & Butcher, J. N. (1995). Computer assisted psychological assessment in child custody evaluations. *Family Law Quarterly, 29,* 79–96.

Pope, K. S., Butcher, J. N., & Seelen, J. (1993). Appendix D: Statement of principles relating to the responsibilities of attorneys and psychologists in their interprofessional relations: An interdisciplinary agreement between the

New Mexico Bar Association and the New Mexico Psychological Association. In K. S. Pope, J. N. Butcher, & J. Seelen (Eds.), *The MMPI, MMPI-2, and MMPI-A in court: A practical guide for expert witnesses and attorneys* (pp. 211–213). Washington, DC: American Psychological Association.

Poulson, R. L., Brondino, M. J., Brown, H., & Braithwaite, R. L. (1998). Relations among mock jurors' attitudes, trial evidence, and their selections of an insanity defense verdict: A path analytic approach. *Psychological Reports, 82,* 3–16.

Rogers, R. (1987). Ethical dilemmas in forensic evaluations. *Behavioral Sciences & the Law, 5,* 149–160.

Shuman, D. W. (2000). *Psychiatric and psychological evidence* (2nd ed.). St. Paul, MN: West Publishing.

Shuman, D. W., & Greenberg, S. A. (2003). The expert witness, the adversary system, and the voice of reason: Reconciling impartiality and advocacy. *Professional Psychology: Research & Practice, 34,* 219–224.

Shuman, D. W., Greenberg, S., Heilbrun, K., & Foote, W. E. (1998). An immodest proposal: Should treating mental health professionals be barred from testifying about their patients? *Behavioral Sciences & the Law, 16,* 509–523.

Sitkowski, S., & Herron, W. G. (1991). Attitudes of therapists and their patients toward money. *Psychotherapy in Private Practice, 8,* 27–37.

Slovenko, R. (1987). The lawyer and the forensic expert: Boundaries of ethical practice. *Behavioral Sciences & the Law, 5,* 119–148.

Trachtman, R. (1999). The money taboo: Its effects in everyday life and in the practice of psychotherapy. *Clinical Social Work Journal, 27,* 275–288.

Williger, S. D. (1995). A trial lawyer's perspective on mental health professionals as expert witnesses. *Consulting Psychology Journal: Practice & Research, 47,* 141–149.

Zacharias, F. C. (1999). Professional responsibility, therapeutic jurisprudence, and preventive law. *Psychology, Public Policy, & Law, 5,* 909–920.

5

Avoiding Malpractice in Child
Forensic Assessment

O. Brandt Caudill, Jr.

Child forensic mental health assessment poses certain types of professional liability risks. Consider child custody evaluations. The past several years have seen child custody evaluators come under unprecedented attack. The number of administrative and civil suits filed against child custody evaluators has expanded dramatically. The most active board in the country appears to be the California Board of Psychology. In a recent year, the California Board of Psychology reported that of 600 complaints against licensed psychologists, 300 involved child custody cases. It appears that less than 5% led to charges against an evaluator. Although I know of no national statistics on the frequency of licensing board discipline based on custody cases, there are appellate decisions in Oregon and Pennsylvania arising from such discipline. In addition to complaints filed with a state licensing board, suits against child custody evaluators have become frequent occurrences, even in states where some statutory immunity exists. Another growing trend involves experts sniping at each other about child custody evaluations. In many jurisdictions, some mental health professionals have acquired a reputation, rightly or wrongly, as willing to function as

a hired gun to attack another evaluator's opinion for the side disadvantaged by the opinion.

Against this backdrop, forensic evaluators must remain conscious both of the legitimate areas of criticism and of the use of civil and administrative complaints as a weapon to intimidate. This chapter provides an overview of the current status of such problems and what steps clinicians can take to minimize the risk of civil or administrative litigation.

ADMINISTRATIVE COMPLAINTS

The requirements to serve as a child custody evaluator vary from state to state. Some states have no requirements and leave the qualifications of the custody evaluator up to the court. Other states, such as California, have very specific and detailed requirements for someone to serve qualified as a custody evaluator. Recently, the California legislature adopted a set of very precise standards setting up the criteria for appointment as a custody evaluator (California Rules of Court, 2003). Psychiatrists must have a license as physician by the state in which they practice. Psychologists, with a few exceptions, must also hold a license. The licensing laws with regard to marriage and family therapists or other nondoctoral licensed professions vary a bit more. No clear statistics exist regarding what percentage of custody evaluators are psychiatrists, psychologists, or marriage and family therapists, but the author's experience in the legal defense of mental health professionals suggests that psychologists comprise a substantial number of custody evaluators.

In those states requiring a professional license, the existence of state licensing boards offers a disgruntled custody litigant an inexpensive, easily accessible avenue of attack. Such complaints can cause significant grief to the evaluator and have the possibility of creating an arguable bias. Most professionals find contact from the licensing board regarding a complaint, meritorious or not, most distressing. Although some professional liability insurance policies provide between $5,000 and $50,000 worth of coverage for defense in licensing board complaints, many mental health professionals do not have such coverage. Thus, some clinicians faced with a licensing board complaint will incur significant financial costs defending against this type of attacks. In addition, after filing such complaints, an attempt to bring the fact of filing a complaint into the public record in the court proceeding often follows before any type of investigation or resolution has taken place. Such actions seem particularly unfair because in many states unproven complaints to the licensing agency do not ordinarily become public. Also in many states, only complaints resulting in adjudicated disciplinary action or formal accusations by the state attorney general's office become public.

Complaints to licensing boards about custody evaluators have typically alleged, among other things: (a) incompetence; (b) bias; (c) racial discrimination; (d) discrimination based on national origin; (e) gender or sexual preference discrimination; (f) improper psychological test administration, interpretations, or scoring; (g) use of idiosyncratic and unaccepted psychological tests; (h) using outdated psychological tests; (i) becoming aligned with one side, having a personal relationship with one party or their counsel, or both; (j) inadequate record keeping and destruction of evidence; and (k) fabrication of evidence.

Given the frequency of the use of licensing complaints as a weapon, evaluators should understand the legal differences between a licensing board investigation and a civil law suit. Generally, civil suits involve matters heard either by a trial judge or by a jury, and the process requires proof established by a *preponderance of the evidence*. This standard equates to a 51% standard. By contrast, the standard of proof in a criminal case, termed *beyond a reasonable doubt*, equates to a standard of 90–95% in weight of the evidence in order for a party to prevail. Administrative law cases, such as licensing board actions, tend to fall in the middle of these two standards. In California, for example, the standard necessary to prove the charges stands as *clear and convincing* proof to a reasonable certainty (*Ettinger v. Board of Medical Quality Assurance*, 1982). In other states, the standard of proof may fall at the lower preponderance of the evidence level. In addition, licensees generally can generally face discipline only for gross negligence, defined as an extreme departure from the standard of care (*Franz v. Board of Medical Quality Assurance*, 1982).

Because a simple mistake or error in judgment by definition does not constitute negligence, a custody evaluator generally would not face significant risk for actual discipline, unless some extraordinary facts exist. On the other hand, noncustody evaluators such as treating therapists may face significant risk for licensing board action if they find themselves drawn into forensic roles as discussed more fully below. The administrative process becomes all the more unnerving for custody evaluators accused of violating ethical standards because of the limited discovery available. The administrative law system generally lacks the ability to take depositions or send interrogatories, the primary discovery tools used in civil suits. California administrative law does not allow depositions, except in extraordinary circumstances, such as preserving the testimony of a witness with a life-threatening illness or obtaining testimony from an out-of-state resident. Colorado, by contrast, allows limited discovery in licensing board cases. Thus, although licensing board complaints can become part of a scheme to intimidate, the actual risk remains reduced if evaluators do their best in providing the court with their best judgment and solid expertise.

CIVIL SUITS

The last decade has seen an unusually high number of suits against forensic evaluators, which have in turn spawned a number of cases at the appellate level. Many states have a statutory litigation privilege that provides immunity to witnesses for their testimony in court. California, for example, has Civil Code section 47(b), which provides an absolute privilege, meaning that the witness remains immune from suit for testimony given, even if the witness had conscious ill will toward the plaintiff and engaged in perjury. The rationale for such absolute immunity is that to allow suits over what witnesses say in court would open the floodgates to litigation. The accuracy of this perception is underscored by the number of lawsuits brought in states despite the fact that statutory litigation privilege clearly bars such claims. In California, the litigation privilege has been applied to every legal theory except abuse of process and malicious prosecution (*Silberg v. Anderson*, 1990). The privilege has applied to expert-witness preparations for testimony outside the courtroom and actions such as compiling a report for court (*Block v. Sacramento Clinical Labs*, 1982). The privilege also applies to interviews intended to resolve in court testimony (*Gootee v. Lightner*, 1990). At the federal level, witnesses have immunity under liberal common law as articulated by the U.S. Supreme Court in *Briscoe v. Lahue* (1983). Other cases holding court-appointed evaluators immune include *Muller v. McKnelly* (1985), *Ressis v. Mactye* (1985), and *Doe v. Hennepin County* (1985).

In addition to the immunity provided by statute and by federal common law, where applicable, in certain states custody evaluators have quasi-judicial immunity (*Howard v. Drapkin*, 1990). Quasi-judicial immunity, a function-based immunity, covers those individuals who perform an essential function for the courts and for policy reasons hold immunity similar to judges or other court officers. This immunity has typically accrued to mediators, child custody evaluators, and other child forensic evaluators. In order to assure quasi-judicial immunity or statutory immunity based on function, an actual court order appointing the clinician as an evaluator becomes essential. The absence of a court order may deprive the evaluator

of the immunity necessary to avoid litigation. The fact of a court appointment provides evidence of the evaluator's function for the purpose of triggering quasi-judicial immunity.

In *Cutter v. Brownbridge* (1986), a California Appellate Court held that a licensed clinical social worker who had provided marital counseling to a couple could be sued by the husband for invasion of privacy for communicating adverse opinions about him, at his wife's request, to a court hearing the couple's divorce and custody action. The court held that California's statutory litigation privilege, which would typically provide immunity for such communications, was overridden by the California Constitution's right of privacy.

In stark contrast, consider the Supreme Court of Kansas decision in *Werner v. Kliewer* (1985). In that case, Mrs. Werner, embroiled in a custody battle and having suicidal feelings, voluntarily admitted herself to the hospital where a psychiatrist interviewed her. Prior to the hospitalization, Mrs. Werner had difficulty getting her children ready for school, and her behavior frightened them. Mrs. Werner left the hospital against medical advice after a few days. At her husband's request, the psychiatrist wrote a letter to the judge hearing the custody matter, expressing his concern that Mrs. Werner might pose a risk to herself and should be evaluated further. He discussed the issue of Mrs. Werner's behavior frightening her children and her suicidal threats. The judge shared the letter with the parties' attorneys and a court services officer. Mrs. Werner sued, a trial court dismissed the case on summary judgment, and the Kansas Supreme Court upheld the dismissal of all claims including invasion of privacy. In so doing, the court held that the state's legitimate concern for the best interests and welfare of Mrs. Werner's children outweighed and overrode other concerns. The court focused in part on Mrs. Werner's reported testimony of alleged suicidal attempts, and the possibility that she posed a risk to the children.

In *Dolan v. Von Zweck* (1985), a Massachusetts Appellate Court upheld a summary judgment based on the litigation privilege in favor of a psychiatrist who had only treated Mrs. Dolan and the Dolan children. Despite never having met Mr. Dolan, the psychiatrist wrote a letter for use by a maternal aunt who sought custody of the children.

The letter contained statements interpretable as defamatory to Mr. Dolan and was criticized by his psychiatric expert. The appellate court held that the litigation immunity applied, and noted that the immunity should be applied to "permit utmost freedom or testimony in two important child custody disputes" (p. 201).

Where litigation immunity exists, it extends not only to the evaluator's interviews of the parties, but also to contacts with collateral sources. The California court stressed this in *Obos v. Scripps Psychological Associates, Inc.* (1997), where a collateral source sued the evaluator, alleging defamation and arguing that the litigation privilege did not apply because the collateral source was not a party to the litigation. Realizing the havoc that might affect custody evaluators if the privilege were limited, the Court of Appeal held that contacts with collaterals came squarely within the privilege.

Typically, the allegations found in a civil suit against a custody evaluator might include incompetence, invasion of privacy, bias, racial or sexual discrimination, and defamation. Although these theories are rarely succeed and almost never result in trial, custody evaluators might find themselves vulnerable to defending such claims at a preliminary stage of the case, if the requisite appointment order is unclear or unavailable. No evaluator should accept verbal representations as to the court's order. Only a documented order of the court or a written stipulation by the parties constitutes evidence of an appointment.

A relatively recent issue involves the extent to which forensic experts can be sued for malpractice by the side that retained them. A California decision, *Brousseau v. Jarrett* (1977) suggests that an expert cannot be sued for punitive damages on such a theory. The U.S. 5th Circuit Court of Appeal considered this point in the context of Louisiana law in *Marrogi v. Howard* (2001). Among the states that allow forensic experts to be sued by their clients are Pennsylvania (*LLMD c/Michigan Inc. v. Jackson-Cross Co.*, 1999), California (*Mattco Forge, Inc. v. Arthur Young* & Co., 1992), New Jersey (*Levine v. Wiss* & Co., 1984), and Missouri (*Murphy v. Mathews*, 1992). The courts remain split about the extent to which immunity protects forensic experts from suit. Numerous cases around the country have seen psychotherapists of all licensure status sued for communicating opinions about individuals they have assessed or treated in a custody matter. Generally, around the country, evaluators have immunity for their reports and the testimony that they give (*Ressis v. Mactye*, 1985; *Doyle v. Shlensky*, 1983). The immunity generally extends to those acts engaged in outside of court, preparatory to testifying, or as part of preparing a report (*Gootee v. Lightner*, 1990).

In some instances, the immunity extends only to individuals named in a court order. Where a state so limits the immunity, an evaluator should not proceed with an evaluation without having an actual court order of appointment. In some instances, evaluators may find themselves induced to begin evaluations prior to issuance of a court order that actually materializes. In California, the fact that the parties have stipulated to a mediator, or evaluator may give the evaluator some degree of protection under a doctrine called quasi-judicial immunity (*Howard v. Drapkin*, 1990); however, the wise clinician will not begin without having the court appointment in hand.

California has developed an interesting response to the problem of false child abuse allegations in custody proceedings. California Family Code, Section 3027 (2004), provides that if a court determines that an accusation of child abuse or neglect made during a child custody proceeding is false, and that person making the accusation knew it to be false at the time the accusation was made, the court may impose monetary sanctions against the person who made the accusation and in favor of the accused person. This section can specifically be applied to any witness, in addition to the parties. Claims have been made against mental health professionals where this statute was sought to be used as a basis for part of the claim. It is unclear to what extent other states will adopt similar measures to deal with false abuse allegations.

Forensic Multiple Relationships

One of the more complex areas of modern mental health practice involves the area of dual or multiple relationships. In fact, the American Psychological Association (APA, 2002) implicitly recognized this in its most recent ethics code, where *multiple* replaced *dual* and significant efforts to clarify appropriateness occurred. In Section 3.05(a), the current APA ethics code specifies the following:

A multiple relationship occurs when a psychologist is in a professional role with a person and (1) at the same time is in another role with the same person, (2) at the same time is in a relationship with a person closely associated with or related to the person with whom the psychologist has the professional relationship, or (3) promises to enter into another relationship in the future with the person or a person closely associated with or related to the person.

A psychologist refrains from entering into a multiple relationship if the multiple relationship could reasonably be expected to impair the psychologist's objectivity, competence, or effectiveness in performing his or her functions as a psychologist, or otherwise risks exploitation or harm to the person with whom the professional relationship exists.

Multiple relationships that would not reasonably be expected to cause impairment or risk exploitation or harm are not unethical.

The ambiguity of the term *dual relationships* has still persisted in usage by experts, psychologists, and licensing boards over the last few decades (Leslie, 1989; Younggren & Skorka, 1992). One of the first attempts to address these issues in forensic cases, Melton and Limber (1989), concerning psychologists' involvement in the assessment and treatment of child sexual abuse, also explicitly recognized the impropriety of using syndrome evidence. The article also contained warnings regarding role conflicts in forensic settings. The three primary areas of forensic multiple role relationships discussed below include (a) when a treating therapist testifies as an expert, (b) when experts occupy conflicting roles in litigation, and (c) when witnesses have an affiliation with a particular advocacy group.

TREATERS TESTIFYING AS EXPERTS

The clearest area of potential forensic multiple relationships occurs when a treating therapist for an individual takes on a secondary role of testifying as an expert about issues beyond those directly involved with treating the patient. Section 3.05 of the 2002 APA ethics code states: "When psychologists are required by law, institutional policy, or extraordinary circumstances to serve in more than one role in judicial or administrative proceedings, at the outset they clarify role expectations and the extent feasible, and thereafter as changes occur."

The cases reported at an appellate level and the cases that the author has seen involving alleged or established forensic dual roles involve several different types of situations, but the most common include (a) a treating therapist trying to testify about a defendant failing to comply with the standard of care, (b) a treating therapist trying to testify that an individual other than his or her patient met the criteria of a child abuser or pedophile, and (c) a treating therapist trying to go beyond his or her treatment knowledge and state that the cause of the patient's distress or psychological condition flows from the actions of a defendant in litigation.

A variety of articles, including those by Strasburger, Gutheil, and Brofsky (1997) and Greenberg and Shuman (1997), describe differences between the role of a treating therapist and the role of an expert in litigation. As these articles note, clear differences exist between the role as a treater and the role as a forensic expert, which include the following: (a) Patients may presume that confidentiality applies to their interactions with treating therapists, whereas interactions with the person in the capacity of forensic expert will presumptively disclose findings to a court. (b) The statements a patient makes to a treating therapist are presumed intended for the purpose of ameliorating the emotional condition leading to therapy, whereas statements to a forensic expert may be used for the purpose of enhancing a position in litigation or for purposes of rendering an objective conclusion regarding a psycholegal issue. (c) A treating therapist's primary obligation is to the patient he or she treats, whereas a forensic expert may owe a duty to the court and to other parties.

Some of the more clear-cut examples of improper forensic dual relationships have occurred in cases involving the assessment and treatment of child sexual abuse. Unfortunately, a fair number of appellate decisions address situations where treating therapists went beyond the role of treater and not only adversely affected the rights of other persons but also created significant legal liability for themselves. *Montoya v. Bebensee* (1988) provides one of the first examples of such a case. The defendant served as an intern under the supervision of a licensed psychologist. The intern treated a child and determined, through the use of nonverbal play therapy, that the child had been sexually abused by her father. Apparently, the child did not actually state that her father had sexually abused her, and no physical evidence existed to corroborate the assertion that sexual abuse had occurred. At one point the intern referred the child to a psychologist for psychological testing. The psychologist allegedly developed serious doubts as to the credibility of the child's alleged abuse. Even though the intern referred the child to the psychologist, she disregarded the consulting psychologist's report and held firmly to her own view that the child had been sexually molested. The multiple role aspect of her situation arose when the intern testified that, without a doubt, the father had sexually molested his daughter. Ultimately, the court appointed an independent expert, who concluded that the child did not know the difference between reality and fantasy, that the intern showed bias, and that her opinion about the abused was not supported by any competent evidence. The father then sued the intern and her supervisor. The Colorado Appellate Court allowed the suit to stand, even though there was no patient relationship between the intern and the father, and the court allowed the father to maintain claims for punitive damages against both the intern and her supervisor.

If this case were the only example of such conduct, one could easily dismiss it as an anomaly. However, similar cases can be found in other jurisdictions with therapists of all licensure statuses. One of the more compelling examples is *Wilkinson v. Balsam* (1996), a federal case arising out of Vermont that involved a psychiatrist as the defendant. The facts of the case appear very convoluted, involving a hotly contested child custody battle between a father and a mother over two sons. After meeting with the boys for one session, the psychiatrist allegedly diagnosed the children as suffering from sexual abuse, possibly satanic in nature. He made a child abuse report and subsequently took an active role in supporting the claims of the mother. At one point, the police interviewed the boys and asked if the charges were true, and one of the boys said that the allegations were made up with the mother's coaching. The police still pursued the matter. At one point, the mother allegedly took the children to another jurisdiction to avoid unfavorable custody rulings. The maternal grandmother reported to the psychiatrist her belief that her daughter had acted in a sexually inappropriate manner with the boys. Despite the apparent reliability of this source and despite having made a child abuse report about the father, the psychiatrist made no report about the information from the maternal grandmother and did not disclose the alleged molestations by the mother to any law enforcement agency or child abuse investigating agency. Ultimately, a court-appointed independent expert concluded that no evidence of child sexual abuse existed. The independent expert opined that the psychiatrist had blurred boundaries and had a dual role compounded by bias. The federal court found that the psychiatrist had no immunity for his actions and that the father could sue him.

We should note that currently a split in jurisdictions exists over the extent to which therapists owe duties to the family members of patients, reflected in the following states and cases: California (*Trear v. Sills*, 1999); Texas (*Bird v. W.C. W*, 1994); Connecticut (*Zarmstein v. Marvasti*, 1997); Pennsylvania (*Althaus v. Cohen*, 2000), holding that no such duty can be asserted; Wisconsin (*Anneatra v. Midlefort*, 1999); Vermont (*Wilkinson v. Balsam*, 1996); Colorado (*Montoya v. Bebensee*, 1988); New York (*Caryl S. v. Child and Adolescent Treatment Services, Inc.*, 1994); New Hampshire (*Hungerford v. Jones*, 1999), holding that therapists may owe a duty to a patient's family members when false allegations of child sexual abuse are made; and Illinois (*Doe v. McKay*, 1998). One factor that some courts have considered in determining whether to allow a family member to assert a claim of negligence against a treating therapist seems the extent to which the treating therapist has interjected him or herself into legal proceedings, particularly where the testimony has led to either impairment or curtailment of visitation rights or to criminal consequences for the accused parent.

A slightly different role conflict arises if the therapist becomes an arm of the police investigation. In *James W. v. Superior Court* (1993), the California Appellate Court (prior to the 1999 *Trear v. Sills* decision) held that, if a therapist went beyond the role of treater and beyond the role of reporting child sexual abuse to the role of determining who an alleged perpetrator of molestation was and allegedly forcing a child to identify her father as the molester, then the therapist could be sued by the father. The therapist in this case had denied the allegations. The general principle one can glean from these cases indicates that, if the therapist goes beyond treatment to becoming an investigator, potential legal exposure may.

The Specialty Guidelines for Forensic Psychologists (APA, 1991) are intended to guide forensic psychologists in their functions. Subsection IV(D) specifically addresses potential dual relationships and states in pertinent part as follows:

> Forensic psychologists recognize potential conflicts of interest in dual relationships with parties to a legal proceeding, and they seek to minimize their effects.
>
> 1. Forensic psychologists avoid providing professional services to parties in the legal proceeding with whom they have personal or professional relationships that are inconsistent with the anticipated relationship.
>
> 2. When it is necessary to provide both evaluation and treatment services to a party in a legal proceeding (as may be the case in small forensic hospital settings or small communities), the forensic psychologist takes reasonable steps to minimize the potential negative effects of these circumstances on the rights of the party, confidentiality, and the process of treatment and evaluation.

A significant risk of professional liability exists when mental health professionals function as forensic experts without having seen the specialty guidelines governing forensic psychologists and acquiring the education, training, and experience necessary for that area of forensic practice. Forensic evaluators must take care not to exceed the limits of their professional data about sexual abuse in cases that include disputed allegations and where no court has made an adjudicated finding. One of the more common mistakes that treating therapists make in attempting to become forensic experts involves a failure to recognize the distinction between testifying that a patient reported having been sexually abused and that the reported symptoms can be consistent with sexual abuse, as opposed to stating affirmatively that sexual abuse has occurred or opining as to the identity of the perpetrator. Naive treating therapists who have not had a great deal of experience with the legal process can occasionally be persuaded by attorneys to plunge into secondary roles exceeding their legitimate role or competence. As a general rule, treating therapists should remain treating therapists and, if called on to testify, provide testimony only as to their treatment and the issues their patient has identified. Forensic evaluators also need to take care not to perform additional roles not originally agreed upon or to reach beyond the limits of their data to answer other forensic questions.

EXPERTS IN CONFLICTING ROLES

Professionals involved in an initial forensic role should take care to avoid assuming a secondary or conflicting role. In one case the author defended, the California Board of Psychology took the position that a treating psychologist acted inappropriately for responding to a hypothetical deposition question about what diagnosis he would apply to his patients' parents. Doing so may violate the ethical standard not to provide evaluative opinions about those persons not evaluated, not to exceed the limits of professional data necessary to support an opinion, or both.

A common way that this situation arises happens when an expert, engaged to perform a limited professional function, is then asked to expand on that function or role. Consider, as an example, a custody matter where issues of child sexual abuse occur, and a forensic evaluation has followed. Should the court ask a different professional to render a second opinion, this new professional must take care to recognize that the court has essentially asked for a second evaluation opinion. This can create conflicts, if the second professional had already engaged in a therapeutic role. The broader role of custody evaluator is very different from a therapeutic role, requiring different duties, competence, and methods than those of the psychotherapist (see chapter 13, this volume).

A problematic situation occurs when the forensic evaluator considers a switch in professional roles, as when one or both parties ask a custody evaluator to provide psychotherapy to a parent, a child, or both. This situation seems slightly less problematic because it appears that one could resolve the potential for confusion of roles by having all parties agree that the evaluator could not assume a subsequent forensic role after becoming a treater. However, the extent of enforceability for such an agreement and the extent to which a court would decline to force a custody evaluator turned treater to testify subsequent to a role shift remain unclear and at least potentially problematic.

A more subtle problem, and one not much discussed in case law, involves situations where an expert has testified frequently and has taken irreconcilable positions on key issues in different litigation. The author knows of cases where an expert has adopted a position on whether a particular situation represents a breach of confidentiality and, in a different case, expressed the diametric opposite opinion under extremely similar conditions. Although in this instance the experts' roles do not conflict, an expert must remain mindful of the extent to which he or she has taken inconsistent positions and should disclose that to the retaining attorney. Further, the APA ethical principles impose on forensic psychologists and their forensic testimony and report a duty to testify truthfully and candidly.

Not uncommonly, experts work with the same lawyers or law firms on numerous occasions or agree to serve as experts for someone they know. Under the APA ethical principles, a prior professional relationship with a party does not preclude psychologists from testifying as fact witnesses or testifying to their services to the extent allowed by law, with the caveat that they must take into account the ways in which the prior relationships might affect their opinions.

In light of the number of ethics complaints and lawsuits that have arisen from child custody matters, particularly custody cases involving allegations of child sexual abuse, it remains important for forensic evaluators to become familiar with the relevant professional literature. One starting point is the "Guidelines for Child Custody Evaluations in Divorce Proceedings" (APA, 1994). Note that these guidelines do not carry the force of the "Ethical Principles of Psychologists [i.e., aspirational] and Code of Conduct [i.e., enforceable]." Guidance also appears in Specialty Guidelines for Forensic Psychologists (APA, 1991) and local court rules that can set criteria for child custody evaluations.

The 1994 APA guidelines for child custody evaluations, the Specialty Guidelines for Forensic Psychologists, and the California Rules of Court (Rule 5.220 [2003]) all emphasize the importance of approaching the assessment in a balanced and impartial manner, regardless of who retains the practitioner for the assignment. Reflecting the importance of impartiality for forensic evaluations, psychologists who become aware that they cannot be impartial must attempt to withdraw from the case. Psychologists should also remain alert any actual or potential biases they may have regarding age, gender, race, ethnicity, national origin, religion, sexual orientation, disability, language, culture, and socioeconomic status and strive to overcome those biases or decline cases involving such clients. In order to prevent such problems, forensic evaluators should undergo a process of self-examination regarding these issues before undertaking forensic work.

Forensic evaluators should take care to consistently apply the principles of published guidelines that may exist for those respective areas of their forensic practice. For example, the 1994 APA guidelines for child custody evaluations state, "Psychopathology may be relevant to such an assessment, insofar as it has impact on the child or the ability to parent, but is not the primary focus" (p. 678). This sentence has particular importance because many times in ethics complaints or legal suits a question arises about whether the psychopathology of a parent had adequate consideration, or whether the evaluator improperly pathologized behavior that did not truly rise to a pathological level.

These guidelines also state that a comprehensive evaluation includes an assessment of all parents or guardians and children, as well as observations of interactions between them. One may limit the function and scope of the assessment, but the conclusions should likewise have limits drawn accordingly to fit the available data. Examples of limited functions might include evaluating the parental capacity of a single parent without attempting to make any comparisons between the parents or to make ultimate recommendations about a child-sharing plan, evaluating the child, critiquing the assessment of another mental health professional, and functioning as an expert witness in the area of child development without relating the testimony specifically to the parties involved in a particular case. The guidelines also encourage the use of multiple methods of data gathering and state that important facts and opinions should have documented corroboration by at least two sources wherever their reliability is questionable. Where significant information obtained from third parties forms a basis for the psychologist's conclusion, psychologists should attempt to corroborate it by at least one other source where possible and document this in their report.

Three areas of the APA guidelines for child custody hold relevance for most forensic evaluations involving parents or their children. Licensing board complaints and civil suits have occurred with respect to the following situations. Section III-12 of the guidelines (APA, 1994) states that psychologists must not overinterpret or inappropriately interpret clinical or assessment data and must not draw conclusions unsupported by the data. Assertions that an evaluator either overstated data or inappropriately interpreted the assessment data occur very commonly. A typical scenario would involve asserting that a particular parent or child suffered from severe pathology when data supporting the diagnosis do not appear in psychological testing reports. Another area that has led to multiple complaints involves rendering opinions regarding the psychological functioning of individuals not evaluated (see *Dolan v. Von Zweck*, 1985). Similar cautionary statements in the specialty guidelines (APA 1991, Section VII-H) and 2002 APA ethical code note that one should not make statements about the mental condition of a person not evaluated. The 1994 APA guidelines for child custody evaluations specifically note that a psychologist may report what an evaluated individual has said about a third party, or respond to theoretical or hypothetical questions, as long as they note the limited source of their information. This can, however, prove a somewhat dangerous practice. The author defended a case in which the California Board of Psychology charged a psychologist with gross negligence for rendering an opinion as to the diagnosis of a patient's parents in a deposition when responding to what was clearly a hypothetical question.

Numerous complaints have also occurred regarding multiple relationships issues. Section II-7

of the 1994 APA guidelines for child custody evaluations states that psychologists should avoid conducting evaluations in cases where the psychologist served in a therapeutic role for the child or the family or had other involvement that might impair his or her objectivity. This guideline also states that psychologists do not begin therapeutic relationships with persons under evaluation, and following determination of the evaluation enter into therapy with such people only with considerable caution. This rule also states that psychologists who serve as fact witnesses should refrain from rendering opinions on custody and visitation unless ordered to do so by the court. A similar warning is found in the 2002 APA ethics code. The California Rules of Court 5.220 (2003) governing child custody evaluations attempts to set standards for evaluators, including the area of bias and the contents of evaluations. The California Rules of Court lists 11 ethical criteria for custody evaluations, including, among others, maintaining objectives, providing balanced information, protecting the confidentiality of the parties, not pressuring children to state a custodial preference, not disclosing recommendations prior to having gathered the information to support them, and operating within the evaluator's training and experience.

SYNDROME AND PROFILE EVIDENCE

In terms of the actual assessment and testimony of children and adolescents, a recurrent problem involves the use of improper syndrome testimony. Generally, the rule properly specifies that psychotherapists may not cite syndromes in court unless the current version of the *Diagnostic and Statistical Manual of Mental Disorders* (*DSM*) lists the syndrome. Cloaking of a set of symptoms in the language of a syndrome inappropriately imputes to it a level of validity and reliability, which may not have scientifically support. Cautions against the inappropriate use of syndrome evidence in forensic matters appeared in print as early as 1989, when Melton and Limber identified several areas of concern that have since formed a basis for many ethics complaints, licensing board complaints, and civil suits. The first involves the reliance on syndromes not recognized in the *DSM*, particularly the so-called child sexual abuse accommodation syndrome, as articulated by Dr. Roland Summit in his article "The Child Sexual Abuse Accommodation Syndrome" (Summit, 1983). Melton and Limber (1989, pp. 1230–1231) also caution against asserting that a particular profile for child abusers exists or that a particular set of behaviors constitute diagnostic indicia of child sexual abuse.

With regard to syndrome evidence, Melton and Limber (1989) cautioned as follows:

> As already noted, theory and clinical impressions regarding syndromes may provide a useful starting point for development of hypotheses relevant to treatment planning in a particular case. However, when the clinician enters the courtroom, he or she should don a scientist's hat. Presentation of greater certainty that is scientifically warranted does not assist the fact finder. Rather, it misleads the fact finder and, in so doing, undermines the pursuit of justice and the exercise of legitimate legal authority. (p. 1230)

The courts have generally held that the question of a child witness's credibility regarding allegations of sexual abuse remains an issue for the judge or jury, not the forensic evaluator, and expert testimony that seeks to reinforce the veracity of the child is impermissible (*Commonwealth v. Seese* 1986). This issue has become particularly concerning because of the proliferation of syndromes asserted to exist in forensic cases, many of which do not appear in the *DSM*. On the other hand, some syndromes have gained a degree of acceptance apart from the *DSM*, such as battered woman syndrome, codified in the California Evidence Code (1997), and in some other states as well, as well as rape trauma syndrome. Assertions about child sexual abuse accommodation syndrome have led to conflicting decisions around the country regarding its degree of acceptance as evidence. As with rape trauma syndrome, the case law seems to suggest that experts may testify about the syndrome to explain behavior of an alleged victim that otherwise appears inconsistent with common experience or expectations, but experts may not use the syndrome to say that an act of abuse did in fact occur or that a particular individual committed abuse.

In recent years, this author has encountered a number of syndromes cited in forensic testimony, including parental alienation syndrome, malicious mother syndrome, child abuse backfire syndrome, false memory syndrome, and litigation response syndrome (Lees-Haley, 1988). Of these syndromes, the two most discussed and probably most controversial are parental alienation syndrome and false memory syndrome. Parental alienation syndrome, first articulated by Richard Gardner (1992), has a number of proponents as well as number of detractors, who assert that it lacks a scientific foundation and has sexist elements. Parental alienation syndrome has not made its way into many appellate court decisions. One of the few decisions discussing it, *Wiederholt v. Fischer* (1992), involves an evaluator who asserted that children had experienced parental alienation syndrome to such an extent that they should have no further contact with their mother. The court characterized this recommendation as an experimental and controversial remedy that had no indication of likely success.

A distinction exists between diagnosing someone with parental alienation syndrome and commenting on the dynamic of behavior contributing to alienation. Discussing a situation in terms of the psychological dynamics does not usually pose a problem, assuming the clinical evidence supports the conclusions. One should also avoid impenetrable jargon in favor of clear explanations in understandable terms. When labeling results a *syndrome*, the evaluator risks providing a false aura of scientific validity that can tend to mislead lay people or the court.

No syndrome has generated more articles, references, and court decisions than false memory syndrome. The term was coined in 1992 with the establishment of the False Memory Syndrome Foundation. An in-depth account of the battle that still rages over whether such a syndrome truly exists or has any scientific validity falls well beyond the scope of this chapter. Forensic evaluators should make themselves aware of these issues and exercise great caution before using such concepts or terms when writing reports or providing testimony. Contrasting references regarding false memory syndrome include John Kihlstrom's *False Memory Syndrome* (1996) and Kenneth S. Pope and Laura S. Brown's *Recovered Memories of Abuse Assessment Therapy, Forensics* (1996).

The general premise of false memory syndrome holds that many individuals, particularly adults or adolescents, can develop false memories generally as a result of a variety of factors, including deliberate or inadvertent implantation or critical reinforcement by treating therapists. Generally, false memory syndrome has not come up for discussion outside the context of cases where an individual has accused someone of misconduct based on recovered memories. Some court decisions have used the term *repressed memory syndrome*, but that term does not seem widely used.

At this point, the *DSM* does not list false memory syndrome; thus, it would come under the same criticisms and cautions as any other such syndrome that is not officially recognized in *DSM* nomenclature. In fact, using any syndrome not included in the *DSM* makes the testimony subject to exclusion on a motion *in limine* by an opposing attorney. Generally, motions *in limine* represent an attempt by one side intended to preclude mention of certain evidence or terminology because of the potential that it might inflame or prejudice a jury. Motions *in limine* have come forth in cases to exclude testimony based on repressed memories (*Ramona v. Ramona*, 1997) and in cases where assertions claimed that false memory syndrome had occurred. Clinicians should think carefully and consult with both colleagues and the scientific literature before attempting to present syndrome-based testimony.

As noted in Melton and Limber (1989), no single type or profile of individuals designates those likely to engage in child sexual abuse, other than a history of such prior acts. Typically, these assertions that such profiles exist come forward in the context of criminal cases where a prosecutor wants to argue that a criminal defendant fits a particular profile and therefore is likely to have committed the crime in question. Most courts would show justifiable reluctance to allow such testimony absent some greater demonstration of a profile's scientific reliability.

BIAS

One of the most frequent areas of attack on forensic evaluators is the assertion that the evaluator is biased. Lawyers have considerable training to fo-

cus bias on when dealing with expert witnesses (McCandless and Schilfmar, 1989). Bias can manifest itself in both subtle and obvious forms. It does not necessarily suggest that the experts involved have conscious awareness of their own biases. As noted above, the guidelines for child custody evaluations and divorce proceedings list 11 different types of variables that might trigger biases: age, gender, race, ethnicity, national origin, religion, sexual orientation, disability, language, culture, and socioeconomic status. In addition, an expert may have ideological or financial biases.

A financial bias generally occurs where professionals have economic relationships with parties or the parties' attorney that would skew their objectivity. In a number of cases around the country, parties have obtained discovery of the amount of fees paid to an expert by the opposing side or the opposing side's attorney (*Stonybrook I Homeowners Associates v. S Ct.*, 2000) to explore this potential. In one case, an expert unsuccessfully sued, alleging that he was libeled by an article asserting that he billed at a rate of $5,000 per day, whereas other experts in the same case earned $1,000 per day. The plaintiff expert contended that the article falsely implied his testimony was for sale (*McBride v. Merrell Dow Pharmaceuticals Inc.*, 1986).

Financial bias allegations may also occur if an expert has links to advocacy groups with interests in a case, or if the group has served as a source of referrals to the evaluator. For example, if an evaluator has an association with a fathers' rights group or a mothers' rights group that appears to constitute a potential source of business, an allegation of some type of financial bias may follow. Not uncommonly in custody proceedings, counsel for the less wealthy party may allege biased in favor of the wealthier person. Ideological bias allegations may also come forward, if an individual has an association with the particular theory or syndrome, such as parental alienation syndrome, and tends to find that syndrome or theory occurring in a disproportionate number of cases.

USE OF NONSTANDARDIZED OR OBSOLETE TESTS

The use of outdated or idiosyncratic assessment techniques developed by the evaluator pose significant problems in forensic assessment, particularly when these have not gained general acceptance in the professional community. This has occasionally posed a problem to some degree with the advent of the Minnesota Multiphasic Personality Inventory (MMPI-2), because some evaluators prefer to use the original MMPI or feel more comfortable with it. Given the rationales for revising the original MMPI, including efforts to eliminate claims of cultural biases, using the original version probably falls below the standard of care in personality assessment today. Furthermore, forensic evaluators should be aware of the specific forensic scoring protocols available for the MMPI-2. The use of idiosyncratic tests developed by a particular evaluator will almost always prove inappropriate in a forensic evaluation. Only tests that are well accepted in the professional community should become part of the data used for forensic testimony. Typically, evaluators should only use tests that have substantial research data demonstrating their reliability and validity for the purposes of the evaluation. For an extensive discussion of these issues in the context of the MMPI-2, see Pope, Butcher, and Seelen (1993).

In assessing children and adolescents, evaluators must take care to use the appropriate instrument designed for particular age ranges. For example, using the MMPI-2 instead of the Minnesota Multiphasic Personality Inventory–Adolescent (MMPI-A) for a young adolescent would subject a clinician to attack. Also, the manner of test administration can also raise questions about the validity of the results and lead to potentially successful attacks on the evaluator's conclusions. For example, Pope, Tabachnek, and Spiegel (1987) completed a study of behaviors of psychologists that indicated that more than 50% had at least rarely allowed clients to take the MMPI or other tests at home instead of in the office. Generally, supervision of test administration occurs in supervised office settings, absent extraordinary circumstances. Allowing people under evaluation to take test materials home or outside the control of the examiner calls the validity of the assessment into question. Evaluators should also establish the degree of familiarity a particular individual may have with psychological testing or whether the person has been tested previously in order to assess for possible practice effects or efforts to conscientiously influence the results.

PREPARING FOR TESTIMONY

Having conducted the evaluation, evaluators must anticipate possible cross-examination and what limits to observe in expressing testimony. A number of books offer specific cross-examination questions for attorneys to use with mental health professionals, including Pope, Butcher, and Seelen (1993) and Ziskin (1995). A number of attorneys have attempted to apply Ziskin's argument about the subjectivity of diagnosis and the differences of theoretical orientations among professionals about a particular diagnosis (e.g., see *People v. Rosenkranz*, 1988; *People v. Lucero*, 2000). It is helpful for forensic evaluators to read the cross-examination questions from these cases. For a suggested response to a Ziskin-based attack, see Brodsky (1991). Psychologists who plan to testify in forensic cases should have a thorough familiarity with the relevant literature related to the opinion. It can prove particularly embarrassing if a supposed expert seems unaware of the requirements of his or her professional association and has not read those standards that govern his or her professional work.

Assume that, if you have had involvement in any type of litigation in the past, including divorce litigation, the person cross-examining will know of it. Rather than being defensive, prepare to discuss any litigation that may lead to cross-examination. For example, if the psychotherapist has had a divorce where restraining orders came into force, that issue will almost certainly come up in testimony if pertinent to the issues being discussed. Assume also that, if you have written any readily obtainable professional articles, the attorney questioning you will have also read them. You should educate the attorney who retained your services about any statements you have made in publications that may seem inconsistent with the position you will take in court. If your professional association has any policy statements regarding the content of the case, you should become familiar with it before testifying.

Strive for complete accuracy in your statement of your qualifications. Nothing can destroy expert witnesses faster than claiming credentials that they do not have. Remember that in most states licensing records are generally publicly available, and the opposing side may have reviewed yours. Never overstate the facts, and do not hesitate to say so when you cannot answer a question because of the manner in which it is worded or because you do not know the answer. Avoid absolutes. Pay particular attention to the opposing views of qualified mental health professionals. You need not adopt them or accept them, but you must have a reasoned assessment of them and the ability to explain why you do not agree with them. For an example of how not to handle such a situation, see *Montoya v. Bebensee* (1988). Always acknowledge that reasonable minds can differ on most issues; otherwise, you appear unreasonable. If the issue involves a matter about which little or no legitimate dispute exists (i.e., child sexual abuse is bad or sex with a patient is unethical), one can take a position that most reasonable minds would not differ on those propositions.

Understand that a goal of an opposing attorney may involve attempting to provoke you to intemperate remarks; thus, maintain calm at all times, no matter how offensive the questioning.

Expect to be asked to what extent your opinions would change if presented with evidence that a person you were testifying about had lied to you, misled you, or omitted key facts. A common and appropriate answer would be that if you were presented with such evidence, you would need to take it into account and it might affect your opinion. Generally, this will not arise unless the attorney has reason to believe that you have been either lied to, misled, or not given key facts. Except in extraordinary circumstances, do not express an opinion on the mental state of someone you have not personally evaluated. Such behavior may not be ethical and, as a practical matter, subjects you to potentially devastating cross-examination.

References

Althaus v. Cohen, 562 Pa. 547, 756 P. 2d 1166 (2000).

American Psychological Association, Division of Psychology and Law. (1991). Specialty guidelines for forensic psychologists. *Law and Human Behavior, 15,* 655–665.

American Psychological Association. (1994). Guidelines for child custody evaluations in divorce proceedings. *American Psychologist, 49,* 671.

American Psychological Association. (2002). Ethical principles of psychologists and code of conduct. *American Psychologist, 57,* 1060–1073.

Anneatra v. Midlefort, 227 Wis. 2d 124 494 N.W. 2d 423 (1999).

Bird v. WC. W, 868 S.W. 2d 767 (1994).

Block v. Sacramento Clinical Labs, 131 Cal. App. 3d 386 (1982).

Briscoe v. Lahue, 460 U.S. 325 (1983).

Brodsky, S. (1991). *Testifying in court guidelines and maxims for the expert witness.* Washington, DC: American Psychological Association.

Brousseau v. Jarrett, 73 Cal. App. 3d 864 (1977).

California Evidence Code (1997).

California Family Code § 3027. (2004).

California Rules of Court. (2003). Rule 5.220: Uniform standards for practice for court-ordered child custody evaluations. Retrieved September 5, 2005, from www.courtinfo.ca.gov/rules/titlefive/title5-1-284.htm#TopOfPage

Caryl S. v. Child and Adolescent Treatment Services, Inc., 161 Misc. 2d 563, 614 N.Y.S. 2d 661 (1994).

Commonwealth v. Seese, 512 Pa. 439, 517 A. 2d 920 (1986).

Cutter v. Brownbridge, 183 Cal. App. 3D 836 (1986).

Doe v. Hennepin County, 623 E. Supp. 982 (D. Minn. 1985).

Doe v. McKay, 183 Ill. 2d 272, 700 N.E. 2d 1018 (1998).

Dolan v. Von Zweck, 19 Mass App. Ct. 1032, 477 N.E. 2d 200 (1985).

Doyle v. Shlensky, 120 Ill. App. 3d 807 458 N.E. 2nd 120 (1983).

Ettinger v. Board of Medical Quality Assurance, 135 Cal. App. 3d 853 (1982).

Franz v. Board of Medical Quality Assurance, 32 Cal. 3d 24 (1982).

Gardner, R. (1992). *The parental alienation syndrome: A guide for mental health and legal professionals.* Cresskill, NJ: Creative Therapeutics.

Gootee v. Lightner, 224 Cal. App. 3d 587 (1990).

Greenberg, S. A., & Shuman, D. W. (1997). Irreconcilable conflict between therapeutic and forensic roles. *Professional Psychology: Research & Practice, 28,* 50–87.

Howard v. Drapkin, 222 Cal. App. 3d 843 (1990).

Hungerford v. Jones, 143 N.H. 208, 722 App. 2d 478 (1999).

James W. v. Superior Court, 17 Cal. App. 4th 246 (1993).

Kihlstrom, J. (1996). *False memory syndrome.* Philadelphia: EMS Foundation.

Lees-Haley, H. P. (1988). Litigation response syndrome. *American Journal of Forensic Psychology,* 6(1), 3–12.

Leslie, R. (1989, September/October). Dual relationships: The legal view. *California Therapist,* 9–13.

Levine v. Wiss & Co., 478 A. 2d 397 (N.J. 1984).

LLMD c/Michigan Inc. v. Jackson-Cross Co., 740 A. 2d 186 (1999).

Marrogi v. Howard, 248 F. 3d 382 (5th Cir. April 12, 2001).

Mattco Forge, Inc. v. Arthur Young & Co., 5 Cal. App. 4th 392 (1992).

McBride v. Merrell Dow Pharmaceuticals Inc., 255 U.S. App. D.C. 183,000 F. 2d 1208 (D.C. Cir. 1986).

McCandless, S. R., & Schilfmar, M. I. (1989, Spring). In sexual harassment cases: Examining the psychotherapist at trial. *Brief,* 41–47.

Melton, G., & Limber, S. (1989). Psychologists involvement in assessment and treatment of child sexual abuse. *American Psychologist, 44,* 1225.

Montoya v. Bebensee, 761 P. 2d 285 (Colo. App., 1988).

Muller v. McKnelly, 639 S.W. 2d 837 (Mo. Cal. App. 1985).

Murphy v. Matthews, 841 S.W. 2d 671 (Mo. 1992).

Obos v. Scripps Psychological Associates, Inc., 59 Cal. App. 4th 103 (1997).

People v. Lucero, 44 Cal. 3d 1006 (2000).

People v. Rosenkranz, 198 Cal. App. 3d 1187 (1988).

Pope, K. S., & Brown, L. S. (1996). *Recovered memories of abuse assessment therapy, forensics.* Washington, DC: American Psychological Association.

Pope, K. S., Butcher, J. N., & Seelen, J. (1993). *The MMPI, MMPI-2 and MMPI-A: A practical guide for expert witnesses and attorneys.* Washington, DC: American Psychological Association.

Pope, K. S., Tabachnek, B. C., & Keith-Spiegel, P. (1987). Ethics of practice: The beliefs and behaviors of psychologists as therapists. *American Psychologist, 42,* 993–995.

Ramona v. Ramona, 57 Cal. App. 4th 107 (1997).

Ressis v. Mactye, 485 N.Y.S. 2d 132 (1985).

Silberg v. Anderson, 50 Cal. 3d 205 (1990).

Stonybrook I Homeowners Associates v. S. Ct., 84 Cal. App. 4th 691 (2000).

Strasburger, L. H., Gutheil. T. G., & Brofsky, A. (1997). On wearing two hats: Role conflict in serving as both psychotherapist and expert witness. *American Journal of Psychiatry, 154,* 448–456.

Summit, R. (1983). The child sexual abuse accommodation syndrome. *Child Abuse & Neglect, 7,* 177–193.

Trear v. Sills, 69 Cal. App. 4th 134 (1999).

Werner v. Kliewer, 289 Kan. 285, 710 P. 2d 1250 (1985).

Wiederholt v. Fischer, 169 Wis. 2d 524, 45 N.W. 2d 4421 (1992).

Wilkinson v. Balsam, 885 F. Supp. 651 (D. Vt. 1996).

Younggren, J., & Skorka, D. (1992). The non-therapeutic psychotherapy relationship. *Law & Psychology Review, 16,* 13–18.

Zarmstein v. Marvasti, 240 Conn. 549 (1997).

Ziskin, J. (1995). *Coping with psychiatric and psychological testimony.* Los Angeles, CA: Law and Psychology Press.

6

Working With Courts, Judges, and Lawyers: What Forensic Mental Health Professionals Should Know About Being Expert Witnesses

Steven R. Smith

Knowing mental health principles is not enough. To be effective forensic experts, mental health professionals must understand the nature of legal proceedings, the role and limitations of expert witnesses, and the relevant legal principles. This is particularly true for child and adolescent forensic cases, as such matters may arise in many different legal settings. This chapter considers the law of expert witnesses, the nature of expertise, and the role of mental health experts in the legal system. It also considers inappropriate roles that mental health experts sometimes assume in child forensic assessment and makes suggestions for comporting professional practices with recognized legal standards.

The thesis of this chapter is that mental health professionals have enormous contributions to make to child forensic assessment. At the same time, by assuming inappropriate roles, mental health professionals not only threaten their own professional standing but also reduce their value to the legal system and clients. A basic understanding of the rules of evidence and the workings of the legal system is necessary to avoid inappropriate roles and compromising the quality of professional opinions.

THE LAW OF EXPERT WITNESSES

For several reasons, no single law of expert witnesses exists. First, each state has its own rules regarding expert witnesses in state courts. Second, there are numerous sources of the rules governing expert witnesses. Third, the rules regarding expert witnesses have been a matter of considerable change in recent years. After reviewing these matters, we then consider general principles regarding expert witnesses that are reasonably universal within the United States. Each state has its own rules of evidence, and these rules vary somewhat from state to state. In addition, the *Federal Rules of Evidence* (2004) apply to federal courts. Forensic mental health experts must clearly understand the rules of the jurisdiction in which they work.

The *Federal Rules of Evidence* have received most of the attention in the forensic mental health literature. However, for most forensic mental health experts, the state rules of evidence hold much more relevant concern. Although some child assessment issues reach federal courts, the vast majority of relevant cases fall almost exclusively in the domain of state courts. Divorce and marriage dissolution, child custody, child abuse and neglect, and juvenile delinquency and disposition all fall under the almost exclusive jurisdiction of state courts. This does not mean that child-oriented mental health professionals never appear in federal courts. Cases brought under the Individuals With Disabilities Education Act (2000), Americans With Disabilities Act (2000), and civil rights cases, for example, commonly apply federal law and will most likely arise in federal courts.

The review of the *Federal Rules of Evidence* (2004) presented here has utility as a general outline of the law of evidence and expert witnesses. The *Federal Rules of Evidence*, however, apply only to cases in federal courts. Thus, states can, and do, have state evidence rule provisions inconsistent with or in conflict with the federal rules. Certain federal laws must be enforced by the state, for example, the constitutional guarantee against self-incrimination, but that is much different than suggesting that the *Federal Rules of Evidence* in any way limit what states can do in adopting their own rules of evidence. The mental health expert should understand the state and local rules when appearing in state court. As a practical matter, the appropriate way of doing this is generally to discuss the matter with the attorneys with whom the mental health professional is working as an expert and asking for copies of the relevant law or rules.

Another reason that there is not a single law of expert witnesses is that within any jurisdiction there are multiple sources of the rules affecting expert witnesses. The federal courts and virtually every state have written sets of rules of evidence. These are the primary codification of the rules, but they are not complete. The constitution contains rules of evidence (e.g., the privilege against self-incrimination), as do statutes, and special rules regarding privileges may be scattered in a number of statutory provisions (e.g., rape shield laws, privileges, and child abuse reporting statutes), case law, and local rules.

Beyond the formal rules, as discussed in this chapter, trial judges in many jurisdictions are given enormous latitude in applying the rules of evidence. Thus, the attitude of a trial judge constitutes another important element in the actual application of the law of expert witnesses. In addition, in many jurisdictions family and juvenile courts maintain somewhat informal rules that may not carefully follow all of the formal rules of evidence. Thus, it is especially important to pay attention to the local family court rules and the circumstances for how they are applied. The forensic expert in child or adolescent matters navigates his or her practice consistent with the appropriate rules or laws, while at the same time maintaining the necessary standards for professional conduct.

The rules regarding expert witnesses are in a state of flux. The place of expert witnesses in court has been a matter of considerable discussion, public debate, and controversy. This controversy is leading to changes in the role of experts. Some of these changes may be subtle, but real nonetheless. In the federal system, for example, a series of court decisions, and amendments to *Federal Rules of Evidence* (2004), have changed the legal focus concerning expert witnesses in federal courts. Any mental health professional undertaking child forensic assessment should stay abreast of the changes in the rules in the jurisdiction in which the case is being considered. It is likely that state rules of evidence regarding expert witnesses will continue to change during the next decade as some states accept the approach of the federal rules and others modify or reject it.

Although the rules concerning expert witnesses vary from place to place, there are many common principles and trends throughout the United States. The remainder of the chapter focuses on those common features.

THE NATURE OF EXPERT WITNESSES

We are in the Age of the Expert in court. Expert witnesses are used in a large range and number of cases. The use of experts has increased so dramatically for several reasons. Many cases require expertise because the issues have become so technical. The level of scientific and specialty knowledge has increased significantly in ways that are relevant to cases that find their way to court. Finally, during the 20th century there was a substantial loosening of the qualifications required to make someone an expert, increasing substantially the number of experts available.

Fact Witnesses and Expert Witnesses

Ordinary witnesses must testify regarding their perceptions, usually what they heard or saw. (In very limited circumstances, they can testify as to the inference from their own perceptions.) Expert witnesses, on the other hand, may testify by giving opinions. They may even testify to hypothetical questions concerning their opinions. It is not their perception of facts that allows them to testify, but their expertise in an area that will assist the judge or jury.

Experts are essential in many cases because the dispute involves technical matters that are beyond the everyday competence of judges and juries. Mental health professionals bring a special understanding of emotional dynamics, interpersonal interactions, or group dynamics and of the nature and course of a variety of mental disorders. The testimony of mental health experts may therefore provide a judge or jury with additional information to resolve difficult issues that involve mental health questions, including but not limited to what is in the best psychological interests of a child, understanding the psychological needs of a child who has been the victim of abuse or neglect, or whether the observed psychological symptoms of a child are likely proximally caused by a particular event.

Expert witnesses have special roles to play, but they are still witnesses, usually presented by one party or another. As witnesses, they are subject to cross-examination as is any other witness. The cross-examination may challenge not only their professional opinions but also their credentials and the possibility that they have a bias or made a mistake for some other reason. Cross-examination is also considered in other chapters in this volume.

Admissibility and Weight

Most of this chapter discusses whether testimony by an expert witness is admissible, that is, whether it can be received or heard at all by the trier of fact (judge or jury). If a judge rules evidence inadmissible, it will not be available at all to the trier of fact.

A separate question is the weight accorded to testimony. That is, how convincing the testimony is to the trier of fact. Even evidence that is admissible may not be given much credence by a judge or jury. For that reason, attorneys spend some time considering ways to make their experts more impressive and believable and ways to make opposing experts seem less so. Mental health experts must balance the goal of effective testimony with the ethical requirement not to exceed the limits of the available data.

Trends in the Use of Expert Witnesses: From Qualifications to Reliability

A very important recent trend has been a shift in the focus of the qualifications of experts to the reliability of their testimony. For many years, our courts fairly narrowly limited the experts who were permitted to testify in court. For example, many states precluded anyone other than medical doctors testifying to physical and mental health issues. A great reform of the post–World War II period was the expansion of the definition of a qualified expert. Psychologists, for example, universally gained the authority to testify as experts on some mental health matters. From a focus on a narrow professional discipline, the courts came to accept that an expert could be qualified by "knowledge, skill, experience, training or education" (*Federal Rules of Evidence*, 2004, Rule 702).

The fairly loose rules of qualifications and the increase in the number of experts willing to testify helped create an explosion of expert testimony, some of which escaped the bounds of ordinary scientific reliability. Because good science and bad science may look about the same to a judge or jury, increasing concern has developed about the presentation of junk science in court.

In the federal system, the U.S. Supreme Court decision in *Daubert v. Merrell Dow Pharmaceuticals* (1993) heralded a shift in emphasis that continues. Subsequent cases and revisions to the *Federal Rules of Evidence* have modified the federal court rules announced in *Frye v. United States* (1923). The new emphasis removes a focus from the qualifications of the expert and refocuses it on whether the experts' testimony is reliable. Thus, even an expert with impeccable professional and scientific qualifications may not be permitted to testify unless the trial court finds that the testimony is valid and reliable.

This change, discussed in greater detail below, is of enormous importance to experts. It requires that an expert establish a professional or scientific justification that demonstrates reliability and validity of the testimony presented in a specific case.

Although these changes occurred in the federal system, they are important for the states as well. Changes in the federal rules often persuade states to make changes in the state rules as well. Indeed, the *Uniform Rules of Evidence* (National Conference of Commissioners on Uniform State Laws, 1999), the suggested rules of evidence for states, have made changes similar to those in the federal rules.

Experts and Fees

It is perfectly appropriate for mental health professionals who serve as expert witnesses to charge a professional fee for their time and special expertise. It is important to remember, however, that the payment is for professional services, not for reaching a specific conclusion. The mental health professional should reach an agreement with the party involved concerning professional fees at the very beginning of the service. The fee arrangement should be in writing and should be specific. It should include a clear statement of how the fees will be determined, when and how they will be paid, and how disagreements concerning the fees will be resolved.

It is not appropriate for an expert witness to accept a contingency fee for serving as an expert witness. Forensic experts strive to maintain objectivity when offering professional opinions and the "Specialty Guidelines for Forensic Psychologists" (Committee on Ethical Guidelines for Forensic Psychologists, 1991) specifically forbid accepting forensic cases on a fee-contingency basis. Although hired by one party, the expert serves as someone to assist the judge and jury and should not have a financial interest in the outcome of a case.

When an expert is cross-examined, the expert should be prepared to reveal the fee arrangement and the fact that the fee is for services, not for a specific statement or result.

Some Practical Suggestions

Offering a full review of practical suggestions for the mental health professional serving as an expert is beyond the scope of this chapter. There are a number of excellent sources for providing such information. Several are cited in this book. One list of recommendations can be found in Smith and Meyer (1987, pp. 363–373).

THE *FEDERAL RULES OF EVIDENCE*

This section briefly reviews the most significant aspects of the *Federal Rules of Evidence* (2004) regarding expert witnesses.

Under the federal rules, an expert is someone who has special "scientific, technical, or other specialized knowledge" (Rule 702). That knowledge may result from special education, training, experience, or skill. This determines who can be an expert.

The next question under the federal rules is what testimony the expert can present, which has two requirements. The first requirement is that the proposed testimony will assist the judge or jury to "understand the evidence or determine a fact in issue" (Rule 702). The second requirement provides that the evidence of an expert is admissible only if "(1) the testimony is based upon sufficient facts or data, (2) the testimony is the product of reliable principles and methods, and (3) the witness has applied the principles and methods reliably to the facts of the case" (Rule 702).

Rule 702 thus provides three criteria for federal trial judges to use in deciding to admit expert testimony:

- The first criterion requires "sufficient facts or data." This is a quantitative issue of whether the expert has sufficient information to support the testimony or opinion the expert offers.
- The second criterion requires that the opinion be the "product of reliable principles and methods." It is a more qualitative element, requiring "reliable" bases of scientific or technical legitimacy or dependability.
- The third criterion connects the other two by requiring that the expert "reliably" apply the

"reliable principles and methods" (the second criterion) to the facts of this case (the first criterion).

The advisory committee notes that accompany the federal rules make it clear that the third criterion does not preclude calling an expert to explain general principles to the jury without directly applying those principles to the case being tried. The note states that as long as the testimony is relevant and reliable, the expert may testify (Rule 702).

The opinions of the U.S. Supreme Court emphasize that, under the *Federal Rules of Evidence*, trial judges perform the function of gatekeepers in determining whether to admit expert testimony. Although there are general guidelines, federal judges have considerable discretion in deciding whether or not to admit supped expert testimony.

Rule 703 describes the bases of expert opinion. Experts are not limited to testifying about things they have seen themselves. Rather, they can offer opinions. Those opinions can be based on a wide range of information the expert did not personally gather, but received from other sources. Notably, experts could use hearsay in reaching a conclusion. In many places, experts can testify not only about their opinions but also about the bases of those opinions. By describing the bases, however, they were presenting hearsay testimony that could not have been otherwise introduced to the jury or judge.

The fact that experts can testify regarding the information on which their opinions are based thus gave attorneys a way of introducing inadmissible hearsay. Indeed, it became common practice to use the direct questioning of experts about the basis of their opinions as a way of having the experts repeat hearsay and other evidence that could not be admitted directly.

A change in Rule 703 was intended to close this loophole by making it more difficult to disclose inadmissible facts to the jury on direct examination. Rule 705 fits nicely with this approach by allowing experts to give opinions without first describing the underlying facts, unless the court or opposing party requires it.

For many years, there has been a substantial debate about whether expert witnesses can testify to ultimate issues in a case. Ultimate issues are essentially the basic conclusions upon which the

outcome of a case depends. Federal Rule 704 makes it clear that experts may testify on ultimate issues. The one exception in the federal rules relates to mental health professionals. An expert may not testify whether a defendant in a criminal case did or did not have the mental state necessary for the commission of a crime (Rule 704[b]).

The debate over ultimate issues has been complex, sometimes contentious, and has clouded a much more critical issue. Opinions on ultimate legal issues often have legal standards embedded in them. An expert testifying as to an ultimate issue, for example, whether someone should have custody of a child over the objections of the other parent, must understand the legal standards as well as the mental health issues in order to give precise and accurate conclusions or whether to decline providing an opinion. This is troubling in the mental health area because there appears to be considerable confusion about the legal tests, even among testifying mental health experts. Any mental health professional testifying as to ultimate legal issues should ask the attorneys or judges involved in cases to clearly identify the legal definitions and standards to be used in reaching a conclusion on an ultimate issue.

The federal rules also provide an interesting process for establishing court-appointed experts (Rule 706). Many states provide similar mechanisms for court-appointed experts, and they are commonly appointed in family and juvenile matters. Unfortunately, they have been too infrequently used in other areas of the law.

The special status of a court-appointed expert imposes a special obligation on the expert. Such experts are generally subject to cross-examination by the parties. Nevertheless, it is likely that the judge and jury will pay special attention to the opinion of a court-appointed expert. It therefore becomes especially important that the expert maintain impartiality and clearly recognize and adhere to the limits of scientific and professional knowledge in offering expert opinions.

This section has described the law in the books. In fact, the legal system often looks to experts to provide, in a formal or informal way, roles other than those officially described in the rules. In some cases the legal system may push experts to exceed the bounds of their professional roles. In the next two sections, we consider the roles experts may be asked to play and some of the consequences of exceeding professional authority.

THE ROLES OF MENTAL HEALTH EXPERTS IN THE LEGAL SYSTEM

Teacher

The appropriate role of a mental health expert is that of teacher. The expert is teaching the judge or jury about mental health subjects and suggesting the proper application of mental health principles.

As a teacher, an expert is not an advocate for one party or another. Reasonable advocacy for position or conclusion is appropriate, but that is distinctly in contrast to being the representative of a particular party. Even though the mental health expert may be called by one part to litigation, the expert's role is not to become an advocate for that side.

This is an area where the interests of the parties to litigation and their attorneys (who by definition are advocates) may be in conflict with the mental health expert. The attorneys are likely to push mental health experts to reach conclusions that are most advantageous to the attorney's presentation of a case. Mental health experts may be involved in cases where the child has suffered tremendous injury, and an attorney is attempting to influence the expert for a more favorable opinion that is believed to help the child. Mental health professionals, however, appropriately resist such efforts and limit themselves to conclusions with a sound scientific and professional basis.

This is not to say that the mental health expert should not consult and discuss the case in detail with the attorney. It is, however, the mental health expert who determines the legitimate professional conclusions, not the attorney.

Decision Maker

In many instances, courts in effect turn decision-making authority over to mental health experts. This is common, for example, in guardianship or custody decisions where the conclusions and recommendations of the mental health professionals are overwhelmingly adopted by courts.

Mental health professionals cannot and should not try to dissuade courts from relying on their expertise. It is, however, important that mental health experts clearly identify the limits of their expertise, areas of uncertainty in conclusions, and the like. This is especially critical where an expert is court appointed.

Psychic and Magician

Mental health experts are sometimes expected to foretell the future. Predicting dangerousness, a notoriously difficult and inaccurate process, is an example. Predicting whether, based on dangerousness, someone should be subject to involuntary civil commitment or the death penalty, whether someone will be a good parent based on fitness, or whether a juvenile convicted of a crime will reoffend are really efforts by the courts to have mental health professionals foretell the future. It is interesting that despite the difficulties, this is a role that mental health professionals have fairly readily assumed.

In another way, mental health professionals are sometimes expected to perform the role of magicians. The referral by courts of criminals (e.g., exhibitionists or antisocial personality types) to treatment in lieu of punishment suggests the somewhat unrealistic expectation of a magical transformation. Similarly, the role of magician may arise in child custody cases where abusive or difficult parents are ordered to undertake therapy as a condition of maintaining custody.

Priest

Mental health experts are, of course, asked to take confession. Beyond that, however, they may provide a kind of absolution by explaining why someone did a bad thing or, in the case of the insanity defense, whether the person was capable of being morally blameworthy. Confession in the context of forensic evaluation is uncommon because of heightened defensiveness against admitting psychological fault but can exist when subjects attempt to portray themselves as sympathetic.

Smoke Screen and Scapegoat

Mental health experts are sometimes used as cover in the legal system for doing things that would be otherwise impermissible. As noted above, for example, mental health experts may testify to otherwise inadmissible hearsay as an expert, although this has been reduced under recent changes in the *Federal Rules of Evidence.* The very conclusory nature of some mental health testimony allows mental health conclusions to be used as a smoke screen for another purpose. For example, in civil commitment cases mental health experts may testify that a person is dangerous and should be committed, although the conclusion is addressing a different issue that the patient needs treatment rather than that the patient is dangerous.

In a related way, mental health experts may serve as scapegoats when things go wrong. For example, if a civilly committed person is released and thereafter commits a serious crime, the judges who are responsible for the decision may say that they were simply following the advice of mental health professionals in releasing the person.

Advocate

Many attorneys who engage mental health experts as expert witnesses seek to have them become advocates for the position of the attorneys' client. One reason that mental health professionals and other experts may not work on a contingency fee basis is that their role is not one of advocacy. Becoming an advocate for one party is among the greatest risks mental health professionals run as forensic experts.

Over a period of months, it may be difficult for a mental health professional to resist the temptation slowly to become an advocate. Such advocacy is, however, sanctioned neither by professional ethics nor by the legal system.

Advisor

Mental health professionals commonly act as informal advisors to the participants in legal proceedings. A well-known example is the advice on jury selection or the use of shadow juries. In a child forensic context, an attorney may wish to have an expert review mental health records of a parent or child prior to initiating a court action. In these circumstances, the mental health professional is clearly acting as a partisan. This is certainly an appropriate role, but it cannot be mixed with such other roles as testifying in the case about individuals or taking referrals for evaluation or treatment of any of the other parties in the case.

An entirely different matter of informal advice occurs when a judge or other decision maker asks a mental health professional for thoughts or informal advice about a pending case. Such informal advice is fraught with problems, regardless of how well intended it may be. For example, a judge may ask a psychologist at a social event, "How reliable is the testimony of a 5-year-old regarding child abuse?" If the judge is hearing a case regarding such testimony, the psychologist may well have become an informal participant in the case. Such discussion is inappropriate because it has the net effect of providing evidence outside of court, without the normal protections afforded through cross-examination. It raises ethical questions both for the judge and the mental health professional and is best avoided.

Treating Clients Involved in Litigation

Mental health professionals may be treating clients who are, or may become, involved in litigation. The stress of litigation, or of the events underlying litigation (divorce, personal injury, sexual harassment, etc.) often make psychotherapy advisable. Similarly, mental health professionals may be seeing children who are the subject of custody disputes.

Although professionals may not see their roles as expert witnesses in such cases, they may nevertheless be called on as witnesses, usually fact witnesses, involuntarily. The professional may then be asked about the client's therapy, what the patient said relevant to the case, and the like. In some circumstances, these therapist–client communications may be protected by a psychotherapist–patient privilege. There are many exceptions to the privilege, however, that might apply to those involved in litigation.

The mental health professional should be aware of this risk to confidential communication and of the possibility of becoming a witness. The professional may also find it necessary to inform clients of this possibility. The forensic mental health evaluator recognizes that this role is distinct from that of treatment and informs the participants at the outset of the absence of confidentiality within the scope of the legal proceeding.

There are obviously a number of inappropriate roles into which mental health professionals can slip, whether the professional enters the case as an evaluator or therapist. Because many cases continue over a period of weeks or months, there may be a slow, almost imperceptible, move toward an inappropriate role during the course of a case. Mental health professionals need to be on guard about slipping into roles they do not wish to assume. The next section suggests ways of dealing with these conflicts.

AVOIDING INAPPROPRIATE ROLES

Mental health professionals are constrained by codes of ethics. The codes of major organizations, including the American Psychological Association (2002), contain specific rules regarding and limitations on the kind of forensic advice and assessment that a mental health professional can provide. The various statements of ethics that are part of the licensing code of virtually every state commonly cover forensic testimony directly or indirectly.

The confidentiality issues with juvenile clients are especially complicated because parents may later claim the right to information revealed in therapy. Thus, the juvenile's expectation of confidentiality and privacy deserve special attention and discussion. It is no excuse to an ethical violation that an attorney or even a court pushed a mental health professional to give expert advice or engage in conduct that is unethical. Forensic evaluations are different, and the absence of confidentiality should be made explicit as part of an adequate informed consent. Chapter 3 in this volume addresses ethical issues, including when an attorney asks a professional to offer an opinion on the mental state of someone not examined. The mental health professional should just say no, and keep saying no, to the repeated requests that may well follow. The mental health professional must also guard against slowly assuming an inappropriate role in small steps over the course of time.

The mental health professional should explain carefully to the court when a request includes some professional conduct that would be considered unethical or inappropriate. It would be an unusual court that would nonetheless order the mental health professional to undertake such conduct in any way. Should an inappropriate request occur, the mental health professional must seek the assistance of an attorney to have the court order reviewed and modified.

Confidentiality and Informed Consent

The issues of confidentiality and psychotherapist–patient and attorney–client privilege are complicated and difficult. It is important that all of the parties understand what the expectations of confidentiality are. It is also important that mental health professionals raise with attorneys the issue of how discoverable the results of the examination may be at a later time. The U.S. Supreme Court, for example, has permitted in a death sentence hearing the use of a psychiatric report made years earlier for a much different purpose. The results of this case suggest that, years after an evaluation, a mental health professional's offhand and irrelevant comments in a report may latter harm a client.

The issues of confidentiality and privilege are sufficiently complex that a discussion with attorneys involved in a case will be necessary to fully appreciate and resolve the issues of confidentiality and privilege arising from a case. In any event, it is important that the mental health professional recognize the obligation to inform clients about the limits of confidentiality as part of an informed client consent process. This would include forensic evaluations of children that could require the professional to make mandated reports of suspected child maltreatment consistent with the applicable statutes for that state.

Lawyers and judges are often unfamiliar with the ethical obligations of mental health professionals and have a natural inclination to demand as much information as possible and as strongly formulated conclusions as possible.

Multiple Roles

Mental health professionals are naturally quite cognizant of dual relationships in most of their professional service. It is the wariness of dual relationships or multiple roles that should also be present when a mental health professional is undertaking forensic work.

Simultaneously treating and evaluating the same person in a case, treating multiple parties with opposing interests, and serving as a court-appointed expert while maintaining any relationship with one of the parties are all fraught with danger. They should be undertaken only for compelling reasons after full consultation with professional colleagues and the parties involved. It is also ordinarily inappropriate to assume two roles, such as consultant and witness, in the same case.

THE ROLE OF THE MENTAL HEALTH PROFESSIONAL IN OTHER LEGAL PROCESSES

Mental health professionals make significant contributions to the law and public policy other than as experts in trial courts. Professional organizations, for example, have been very active and helpful in *amicus curia* for appellate courts. An amicus curiae, "friend of the court," is a brief filed by an organization or person with an interest in a case, but who is not a party to the case. Mental health professionals have also been active in Congress and state legislative bodies in helping fashion laws that reflect the best understanding of the behavioral sciences. Mental health professionals may help in the rule-making process before regulatory agencies or may participate in individual cases before regulatory bodies. Those with an interest in the assessment of children have an opportunity to play especially important roles in shaping public policy through the regulatory and legislative processes.

In participating in these nonjudicial bodies, it is important to remember that the rules of the game are different than they are in court. In legislative bodies or rule making, it is appropriate to offer informal advice, to contact lawmakers outside of the hearing of the opposing side, and to act as advocates. At the same time, the obligation to stay within professional and scientific knowledge remains true regardless of the public policy setting. Our society and lawmaking will be improved with the continued, active participation of mental health professionals.

CONCLUSIONS

The legal system is fortunate to have the assistance of mental health experts in making difficult decisions regarding children and adolescents. The expertise of mental health professionals will be enhanced if those professionals take seriously their obligation not only to be fully prepared in terms of mental health knowledge and experience, but also to be familiar with the legal aspects of the case. Professionals need to be prepared to participate in the legal system. This preparation requires an understanding of the relevant rules of evidence concerning expert witnesses, discussions with the attorneys or judges involved with the case, strict adherence to professional ethical requirements and guidelines, an understanding of the appropriate and limited role of expert witnesses, and appreciation of the rights of the parties involved in litigation. When mental health professionals and lawyers work together to create the conditions where the expertise of mental health professionals can be used fully and wisely, they serve the interests of their clients and our judicial system.

References

American Psychological Association. (2002). Ethical principles of psychologists and code of conduct. *American Psychologist, 57,* 1060–1073.

Americans With Disabilities Act. 42 U.S.C. 12101–12213 (2000).

Committee on Ethical Guidelines for Forensic Psychologists. (1991). Specialty guidelines for forensic psychologists. *Law & Human Behavior, 15,* 655–665.

Daubert v. Merrell Dow Pharmaceuticals, Inc., 509 U.S., 579 113 S.Ct. 2786 (1993).

Federal Rules of Evidence (2004). Retrieved September 3, 2005, from http://judiciary.house.gov/media/pdfs/printers/108th/evid2004.pdf

Frye v. United States, 293 F. 1013 D.C. Cir. (1923).

Individuals With Disabilities Education Act. 20 U.S.C. Section 1400 (2000).

National Conference of Commissioners on Uniform State Laws, Uniform Rule of Evidence (1999).

Smith, S. R., & Meyer, R. G. (1987). *Law, behavior, and mental health: Policy and practice.* New York: New York University Press.

7

Interpreting Forensic Interview and Test Data of Latino Children: Recommendations for Culturally Competent Evaluations

Roberto J. Velásquez
Jeanett Castellanos
Maria Garrido
Paula Maness
Ulla Anderson

As a psychologist who is striving for cultural competence and who cares about conducting the best and most valid psychological evaluations across cultures, imagine reading the following (genuine) assessment report on a 13-year-old female Latino client. The evaluation was conducted in 1979 by a psychologist.

PSYCHOLOGICAL ASSESSMENT

Name: Sandra XXXXX

Age: 13 years

Date of Assessment: June 20, 1979

Place of Assessment: Adolescent Day Program

Examiner: XXXXXXXXXXX, Psychologist

Referral: Speech therapist at the XXXXXX School District referred for speech anxiety and "limited social interaction."

Instruments administered: Interview; Piers-Harris Children's Self-Concept scale; Thematic Apperception Test; House-Tree-Person Test; Bender Gestalt

---

Results of test battery:

Piers-Harris Scale: Score 35–13%

TAT: Unwilling to interpret cards without much encouragement and then generally limited to description of card. Frequently had to ask, "What do you see there?" #BM—sees as boy; trouble with expressing overt aggressive tendencies; 3GF—scared, sex conflict; much conflict with female figures, 9GF—ladies being chased and running away from people who don't like them; 11—running; 13G—no affect; generally no expression of violence or anger; passive perception of situations.

House-Tree-Person: Drew opposite sex figure; forced congeniality; some schizoid tendencies in drawings; evasiveness and guilt; affective and material deprivation as background for psychopathological adjustment; clinging to family; breaks in lines tend to be pathological; house placement at bottom; poor contact with environment; reluctance to permit access; "stay away attitude"; tree, large root area tendency

97

to be demanding, not getting needs met; self-ruminating tendencies; scars on tree, traumas in past; poverty of details, placement of drawings. Poor proportion and bad judgment, agitation, and bizarreness present, whirling tendencies in foliage in tree tends to be psychotic in children; house womb-like suggests regression.

Bender Gestalt: Angulation changes, insecurity, immaturity, maladjustment; curvature; Circle A—schizoid association; immaturity and confusion, regression and emotional disturbance; poor sexual contact concept; oppositional tendencies; dots changed to circles —regression, possible organicity; possible hysterical nature; exaggerated curvature, impulsivity and poor emotional controls, over-responsiveness emotionally; oppositional tendencies; overlapping and crossing difficulties, emotional disturbance and neurosis; possible organicity; condensation, dots, circles, arrow—organicity indicated; severe personality disturbance, including schizophrenia, immature emotional development, neurosis; reduction—withdrawal tendencies; feelings of inadequacy; inhibited, constricted depression.

Test behavior and observations: Sandra was able to talk in the softest tones, and only with encouragement. She is a Mexican-American adolescent female with long, straight, black hair. She wears glasses and is thin and of medium height and stature. Most of the interview she sat looking down and had difficulty at first in handing the cards back to the examiner. She frequently sat on her hands, or flicked her fingers as she looked at the TAT cards.

Summary of results and recommendations: Sandra seems to be experiencing what may be a psychotic depression. Although she has been undergoing speech therapy, the problem seems to be more one of withdrawal and inability to express the feelings she holds, particularly for her mother or for female figures of import in her life.

It would seem imperative to have an immediate mental status taken by a psychiatrist, and

psychotherapy of a supportive nature to be undertaken as soon as possible.

XXXXXXXXXX, Ph.D.
Psychologist

After reading this report, and perhaps waking up after fainting, what are your conclusions? Does this report reflect cultural competence or incompetence? Are the tests that were selected by the psychologist the most appropriate given the referral question? Is the referral question even appropriate or clear? Are the interpretations of the test results clear, valid, or reflective of culturally based patterns or trends? What does a score of 35 or 13% mean on the Piers-Harris Self-Concept Scale? Are these interpretations empirically supported by the literature, especially for the Thematic Apperception Test (TAT), House-Tree-Person Test, and Bender Gestalt? Is the report lacking key sociodemographic information? And, are the conclusions regarding treatment appropriate?

More important, what has happened to this real client, Sandra, who should be in her mid-30s at this point in her life? What type of treatment was eventually administered to her, and did the treatment help at all? As a result of the psychologist's conclusions, did Sandra ever complete her education or was her academic career interrupted? Was Sandra hospitalized or placed on medications as a result of the findings? What is Sandra doing now? What is her quality of life? And, is she working and feeling good about herself, or the opposite? In addition, how would you feel about this psychological evaluation if you were the parent of Sandra? How would you handle the news that Sandra may be severely psychologically impaired in light of opposing evidence? And, if you were a Latino parent who had no knowledge of the role of testing, might you be inclined to accept these findings or might you be take on an assertive stance and challenge the validity of these findings?

In many ways, our need to present this case immediately (at the beginning of this chapter) underscores our collective and ongoing concerns about the status of the psychological assessment of culturally, ethnically, and linguistically diverse children in the United States. To us, psychological testing can serve as a critical gatekeeping function, especially in the era of managed care, which can either open or close doors to treatment for children, irrespective of their ethnicity or race. If the assessment is poorly done, then the chances of effectively treating the child are significantly lessened, especially if the child comes from a low socioeconomic status, which is the case for many Latino children (Garcia-Coll & Vasquez, 1995).

Over the years, we have confronted many situations similar to the case of Sandra. In fact, we have seen countless Sandras over the years, boys and girls from different ethnic or cultural backgrounds who were evaluated, and in the process wronged, by psychologists who were well meaning in their intentions. In many situations, it was too late for us to do anything to correct such an injustice, and we had to live with the fact that a child's life may have been negatively affected forever. Although we do subscribe to the idea of always maintaining objectivity in our evaluations of Latino children, we also believe in the idea that we must always attempt to see the evaluation results from a cultural context.

The primary purpose of this chapter is to educate psychologists who are involved in the assessment of culturally, ethnically, and linguistically diverse children, especially in forensic settings or environments. These might include evaluations conducted for the courts, correctional facilities, and the departments of child protective services. From the onset, it is important to note five important points. First, we have chosen to focus on Latino children because we have worked with this population the most, and because we would be doing a grave injustice to other groups, including African Americans, American Indians, Asian Americans, and other emerging groups (e.g., Iranian Americans, Filipinos, etc.), by providing the brief description necessary to fit all into one chapter. Second, we believe that many of our comments, observations, and recommendations can be applied in the assessment of these other populations. Third, we have included many of our clinical insights throughout this chapter given our many years of experience and literally thousands of Latino clients. Fourth, our focus for this chapter is on the psychological assessment of Latino children, and not on intellectual assessment that has been discussed by other researchers (see

Puente, Sol Mora, & Munoz-Cespedes, 1997; Thomas-Presswood, Sasso, & Gin, 1997).

Finally, it is important to note that there is no perfect method for evaluating Latino children. Instead, there exist many perspectives on what is the most important in the culturally valid assessment of Latino children (see G. Canino & Guarnaccia, 1997; I. A. Canino & Spurlock, 1994a, 1994b; Cohen & Kasen, 1999; Dana, 2000; Gopaul-McNicol & Thomas-Presswood, 1998; Quintana, Castillo, & Zamarripa, 2000). In this chapter, we present our approach, which is largely composed of asking and answering many key questions prior to and during the evaluation of the child. Also, although we allude to the measures that we most frequently apply to Latino children, we do invite the reader to seek further consultation in the literature (e.g., Constantino & Malgady, 1999).

This is chapter is divided into the following five interrelated sections. The first section presents a discussion on the key challenges to the assessment of Latino children. The second section presents a discussion on the initial elements of the evaluation. This includes educating the child and child's parents about the evaluation.

The third section presents a discussion of the prototypic interview that we conduct with Latino children. In particular, we discuss several dimensions that must be evaluated and that are more likely to strengthen the validity of the assessment report. The fourth section presents some practical recommendations for assessing Latino children.

The final section presents a series of case studies, with an emphasis on the measures that we have found to be useful when evaluating Latino children. For example, we have found the Minnesota Multiphasic Personality Inventory–Adolescent Version (MMPI-A), in either English or Spanish, to be valuable in understanding the issues of Latino adolescents.

KEY CHALLENGES IN THE ASSESSMENT OF LATINO CHILDREN

The psychological assessment of children remains one of the most challenging of all activities performed by the clinical psychologist. For example, psychologists must ask themselves a series of questions prior to conducting the evaluation: Who is the referral source? Is it family or juvenile court, school, or the department of social services? Is it a judge, lawyer, physician, therapist, or social worker? What problems, domains, or issues must be evaluated? Where, or with whom, is the child living at this time? With biological parents, foster parents, or extended family? Has the child been sexually, emotionally, or physically abused? Is the child functioning within the normative range of intelligence? Does the child have a psychiatric disorder or condition such as major depressive disorder, posttraumatic stress disorder, or conduct disorder? Is the child suicidal or homicidal? Is the child currently taking psychotropic medication? Is the child mature, expressive, insightful, or some combination of these? What treatment interventions might be most effective for this child? How should this child be evaluated? Should the child be evaluated through a comprehensive diagnostic interview, behavioral observations, projective drawings, a Wechsler Intelligence Scale for Children-III (WISC-III), or MMPI-A?

This process becomes even more complicated when the child to be assessed is from a particular American cultural, racial, or linguistic group (e.g., Latino, African American, Vietnamese, American Indian, etc.). In addition to posing the above standard questions, the psychologist must ask other key questions: What is the child's ethnic or cultural background? Is the child's primary language English? Is the child bilingual, and if so, what is the most appropriate language for the evaluation? Was the child born in this country? If not how long has the child resided in this country? Is the child undergoing acculturative stress in adjusting to his or her community or school? What is the ethnic identity of the child, and has the identity served as a buffer against psychological problems? Are there unique risk factors (e.g., poverty, broken home, inconsistent education, high mobility, absence of parents, undocumented status, etc.) that have contributed to the child's problems or issues? What instrument(s) is (are) most appropriate for the evaluation? Have instruments been adapted, translated, or normed with particular ethnic or cultural groups? Are linguistic test norms available should translated versions be applied? And, what are the barriers to the valid or culturally competent interpretation of test results?

Finally, psychologists must ask themselves whether they are the best candidate to conduct this evaluation: What is my past experience in evaluating and treating children from this particular cultural group? Do I speak the language of the child (e.g., Spanish, Tagalog, or Vietnamese)? What has been my level of contact with this cultural or ethnic group, beyond my professional experience? Am I aware and knowledgeable of certain belief systems, values, or attitudes that may be detected through the evaluation? And, are there unique response patterns, which have cultural roots, that I should look out for in the test performance of this child? For example, has the child been raised in a culture that emphasizes minimal self-disclosure to others in order to avoid shaming or embarrassing the family? In turn, will this affect the MMPI-A performance of the child to the extent that the Lie scale is highly elevated?

PSYCHOLOGICAL ASSESSMENT OF LATINO CHILDREN: INITIAL ELEMENTS

1. A Latino child is more likely to be open toward an evaluation if a trusting relationship is developed between the psychologist, child, and parent(s) or caretaker(s), and the child is recruited to serve as an ally in the evaluation. One of the most difficult elements of the evaluation is right at the very beginning, when the child is brought to the evaluation with no knowledge about the purpose of the evaluation. In these types of situations, the child is often very guarded, defensive, scared, and unwilling to participate. We believe that it is very important to educate the child's parent(s) or caretaker(s) prior to the evaluation so that they can then inform their child about the assessment. We have found that in most situations, Latino parents, whether they are the biological parents, foster parents, or caretakers, are not likely to understand the purpose of the evaluation because they have never had to deal with the mental health or legal system in this country or their country of origin. Oftentimes, Latino parents, especially those who are immigrants, are likely to view the evaluation as being similar to a medical examination, when in fact it is not. Thus, it is tantamount that the psychologist take the time to

educate parents and caretakers so that they can then educate the client.

2. A Latino child is more likely to be responsive in an evaluation if the child understands that the psychologist is not just for *locos* or crazy people. We have observed many Latino children, especially adolescents, to not be fully responsive or trusting of the psychologist because they have already concluded that the psychologist is only for crazy people and therefore they must be crazy because they are being seen by a psychologist. Too often, these perceptions come directly from the parents or caretakers, who themselves were raised to believe that a psychologist only works with persons who are *chiflados*, *locotes*, or mentally ill. For example, a 16-year-old Mexican-American male client was once seen by the first author for an evaluation. He came into the office with his father, both laughing at the idea that he was going to be evaluated by a *loquero*. It was observed that he did not respond to any of the interview questions in an honest manner and, instead, appeared to make fun of the complete process. Thus, we discourage parents from referring to stereotypic perceptions so as to not create a negative mind-set with their child.

3. Latino children are more likely to be responsive if they see a benefit for themselves in the evaluation.

INTERVIEWING LATINO CHILDREN: SOME KEY QUESTIONS

The key to the successful treatment of Latino children in a variety of clinical or forensic settings lies in the effective, accurate, and valid assessment of emotional, behavioral, or psychological problems (E. L. Chavez & Gonzales-Singh, 1980; Malgady, Rogler, & Constantino, 1987; Velásquez & Callahan, 1992). In our collective experience, we have found that the most useful psychological evaluation reports on individuals of culturally diverse backgrounds are those that reflect a strong desire on the part of the psychologist to answer culturally based questions or hypotheses that have not been posed before, or that have been misinterpreted by other practitioners. Hays (1996) noted that "effective intervention depends on an accurate assessment, and an accurate assessment requires both an awareness and knowledge of specific cultural influences on both clients and psychologists" (p. 193).

The assessment or evaluation, whether conducted in English or Spanish, or in both languages, serves as the sociocultural context for the understanding and appreciation of a Latino child's unique problems, issues, or concerns. In addition, the evaluation, if conducted from a culturally competent perspective, can be a potent first step in the culturally responsive treatment of the Latino child (Cervantes & Acosta, 1992; Velásquez, Ayala, & Mendoza, 1998). As a result, the psychological assessment of a Latino child should lead the practitioner to well-informed decisions that are anchored in this child's experience, language, culture, and worldview (Guarnaccia & Rodriguez, 1996; Velásquez, 1995; Velásquez & Callahan, 1992). At the same time, such an evaluation assists the practitioner in making sound and practical decisions about this client's treatment (e.g., identify and describe dysfunctional behavior, assist in diagnostic decision making, aid in treatment planning and selection, and evaluate treatment outcome).

Malgady et al. (1987), in discussing the need to validly assess Latinos, including children, observed that a Latino client's "early contacts with a mental health agency are likely to be diagnostic in nature, whether the assessment performed is formal or informal, brief or intensive" (p. 228). They also noted that

> the procedure might include a mental status examination . . . psychological tests might be administered . . . and then a social history is taken to place test and interview data in proper [sociocultural] context. At the end of this process, a diagnosis is formulated, a disposition is rendered, and a treatment plan is developed. (pp. 228–229)

In interviewing Latino children, we always pose a series of questions (or hypotheses) that will allow us to design an evaluation that reflects an anchoring in culture or ethnicity. Although we routinely ask questions related to psychosocial history (including nationality, family composition, discrimination experiences, etc.), mental health status, signs and symptoms of a particular problem or disorder, history of previous treatment, and family functioning, we also pose these additional questions as a way of supporting the cultural validity of our evaluation. Some of the questions that we pose include the following:

1. In what developmental period is the Latino/a child? Developmental milestones are very important in Latino culture. For example, a female who turns 15 years of age is typically given a quinceañera, which is a celebration of an important rite of passage in which she is considered and expected to be mature and responsible. Prior to this age, a young Latina is considered to be a child and not ready to participate as a young adult within the family system and community. Once she is beyond 15 years of age, she is given many additional responsibilities, including contributing in typical adult conversations and family decisions. With development also comes recognition and acceptance of the familial hierarchy and role of the extended family. This is taught and reinforced on a continuous basis by parents and other agents of socialization, including grandparents and *padrinos* or godparents. *Familism* is a concept with its own special meaning within Latino culture, and even varies from Latino subgroup to subgroup (Cortes, 1995; Planos, Zayas, & Busch-Rossnagel, 1995; Rodriguez & Kosloski, 1998). This term essentially defines the extent to which the family is to play a role in the life of the child, and the extent to which the child is to be embedded within the family.

2. What is the birth order of the child? The place of the child within the family constellation is very important and, to a large extent, influences the rest of the Latino child's life. For example, oldest children are given significant responsibility for younger siblings and are expected to serve as parental figures under crisis situations. The first author recalls that as early as age 7, his parents told him that if they died, he would be responsible for caring for the family for the rest of his life. Obviously, this message was overwhelming and scary, yet these messages reflect values of the culture. In this case, the meta-message was, "No one can take care of our children but our oldest child."

3. Has the child served as a cultural broker or translator for the rest of the family? That is, has the child become parentified, out of practical necessity or survival, because he or she is the most proficient in the English language or has studied in this country? This phenomenon is very common among immigrant Latino families, where the burden of translating not only language but many aspects of American culture falls upon the Latino child (Buriel, Perez, DeMent, Chavez, & Moran, 1998; Tse, 1995). In evaluating adult clients who are also immigrants, it is not usual for them to bring a child (sometimes as young as 6 years) to serve as a translator or interpreter. We have witnessed the pressure that comes along with serving such an important role, and also pseudoparental responsibility given to the child. Perhaps in some way, this is also another way of reinforcing in the Latino child the need to take care of his or her parents later in life.

4. What is the ethnic identity of the child? How do they define themselves? Are they, for instance, Chicano, Mexicano, Cubano, Dominicano, or Puerto Rican? This is very important because a strong and crystallized ethnic identity has been linked to better mental health functioning and greater feelings of self-efficacy (see Niemann, Romero, Arredondo, & Rodriguez, 1999; Quintana & Vera, 1999). Also, a strong sense of ethnic identity has been viewed as part of a Latino child's resilience in the face of external or social stressors (Gordon, 1996). We view identity as the mechanism for displaying pride and love toward one's culture or, if not crystallized, confusion, alienation, or disconnectedness toward one's culture, family, and community.

5. What is the emotional language of the child? Does the child feel more comfortable discussing his or her emotions or problems in English, in Spanish, or in both languages? Past research on bilingualism and the expression of psychopathology suggests that Latinos proficient in Spanish and English express their problems differently depending on which language they are being interviewed, and their attributions of how they became ill or disabled, and how they might become healthy, again, are different as a result of language (Bamford, 1991; Bradford & Munoz, 1993; Marcos, Alpert, Urcuyo, & Kesselman, 1973; Price & Cuellar, 1981). Also, language appears to regulate the extent to which emotions will or will not be expressed, or what types of nonverbal cues will be elicited by the child. This has also been observed in the performance bilingual Latinos on such tests as the Minnesota Multiphasic Personality Inventory-2 (MMPI-2) and its adolescent counterpart, the MMPI-A (see Velásquez et al., 1997, 2000). We have observed numerous situations where bi-

lingual children perform very differently on clinical measures as a function of language and when dealing with emotional issues or problems.

6. What are the idioms of distress, in either English or Spanish (or even in Spanglish), that the Latino child uses to describe his or her emotional or psychological problems? For example, it is not unusual for Latino children to use *triste* (sad) or *enojado* (angry) to describe depression. In many ways, these idioms, grounded in Latino culture including spirituality, religion, and cultural subgroup, are better indicators of distress than is traditional psychiatric jargon (see Aviera, 1996; Guarnaccia, Rivera, Franco, & Neighbors, 1996; Owen, 1998; Rogler, Cortes, & Malgady, 1994). For example, the term *deprimido*, which means depression, has very little meaning in many Latino groups and does not communicate severity or intensity the way words like *falta de fe* (lack of faith), *perdida de dignidad* (loss of dignity), or *encabronado* (very, very angry) do. In one case, the senior author worked with a Chicano youth from a barrio in San Diego, California. The youth, in the evaluation, kept saying that he was *locote*, or very crazy. Upon further inquiry, the client defined the word as descriptive of his lack of personal control, cultural alienation, and feelings of marginality. More important, he used this term to refer to his condition of schizophrenia.

7. Does the child come from a traditional or nontraditional family background? Most Latino families, despite acculturation toward mainstream culture, continue to hold on to traditional values that are largely defined by the community and religion. This traditionalism is seen in many aspects of family life including the adherence to sex roles, expression of emotions, morals and values, articulation of sexual themes, and the extent to which persons disclose their problems to persons outside of the household (see Flores, Eyre, & Millstein, 1998). Thus, it is often difficult to assess Latino youth because they are taught from the beginning that talking about problems outside of the home is not acceptable or can bring shame or embarrassment to the family (Santiago-Rivera, 1995).

8. What are the Latino child's beliefs about how persons become mentally ill, problematic, or dysfunctional? This question is critical because health beliefs have been found to affect compliance to treatment and prognosis in both health and mental health settings for Latinos. Tied to this question are additional issues including locus of control, fatalism, and beliefs in spiritual intervention. Obviously, when one is evaluating a child, it is very important to meet with the parent(s) or parental figure(s) to examine many issues related to the child's evaluation, including the role of mental health beliefs (Guinn, 1998; Talavera, Elder, & Velásquez, 1997).

9. What is the diagnostic history of this Latino child? In our work with Latino children, and children from other cultural groups, we are constantly frustrated with the problematic diagnostic histories of many children who have been in and out of a particular mental health care system. For example, it is very common to find that a Latino child has numerous diagnoses and that the majority are incorrect or inaccurate (Flaskerud, 1986; Johnson, 1993; Velásquez, Johnson, & Brown-Cheatham, 1993). In one recent instance, the second author was asked to consult on a case in a public school in which a Latino child was so heavily medicated that he would constantly fall asleep in class. Upon a review of the child's assessment history, she found that the child had been evaluated seven times and that each evaluation yielded a different diagnosis, ranging from dysthymia to schizophrenia. In the end, and after having the child examined by a physician, it was determined that the child's behavior was largely affected by a rare diabetic condition that had never been identified. The psychiatric diagnosis of culturally diverse children, including Latinos, continues to be a major source of discussion in the profession (I. A. Canino, 1982; E. L. Chavez & Gonzales-Singh, 1980; Cuellar, 1982; Cuellar, Martinez, Jimenez, & Gonzalez, 1983).

10. What risk factors contribute to the psychological or emotional vulnerability of Latino children? Are any of the following problems found in the child's life, now or in the past: poverty, parental absence, poor diet, a history of migration, gang affiliation, substance abuse, immigration, refugee status, medical illness, and so forth? We have found that once risk factors are identified by the psychologist, assessment can become much more direct or relevant because for the targeting of interventions (see Yin, Zapata, & Katims, 1995).

11. To what extent is the child, family, or both affected by acculturative stress, or the stress to

assimilate to mainstream culture? Acculturative stress has been found to affect many aspects of Latinos' functioning, including risk for emotional and health illness (Hovey, 2000; Saldana, 1994). There now exist many measures that are designed to evaluate some aspect of stress on Latino children and its impact on coping mechanisms, ethnic identity, and resilience (see Barona & Miller, 1994; D. V. Chavez, Moran, Reid, & Lopez, 1997; Colomba, Santiago, & Rossello, 1999; Cuellar, Arnold, & Maldonado, 1995; Norris, Ford, & Bova, 1996).

12. What factors contribute to the resilience of this child despite a multitude of stressors or risk factors? In other words, what are the buffers that serve to protect the Latino child from literally falling apart emotionally? Resilience can consist of such factors as a strong family, caring and loving grandparents or *abuelitos*, strong *compadres*, religious or spiritual beliefs, *respeto* for others, and the ability to *improvisar* or improvise in daily life situations that require problem solving. Other factors that contribute to resilience include a strong ethnic identity, maintenance of the Spanish language, familism, and *integridad cultural* (cultural integrity).

PRACTICAL RECOMMENDATIONS FOR ASSESSING LATINO CHILDREN

The following practical recommendations, based on our experiences, are suggested for practitioners who assess Latino children on a routine basis and who are striving for valid cultural formulations.

1. Practitioners must recognize that the psychological assessment or evaluation of Latino children does not occur in a vacuum or independent of the client's sociohistorical background. Too often, well-intentioned practitioners fail by not acknowledging the client's unique experiences that define his or her worldview. These experiences include sex roles, socialization processes, acculturative stress, language barriers, immigration, and traumatic experiences of prejudice and discrimination. For example, the experiences of a third-generation U.S.-born Cuban raised in an urban neighborhood outside of Miami are quite different from those of a Cuban who recently arrived

from his or her country. From the outset, practitioners must recognize that such important background variables do make a difference and need to be used in the interpretation of test data.

2. Psychologists must recognize that the psychological assessment of Latino children occurs within the context of a helping relationship. That is, practitioners are more likely to establish credibility, trust, and openness (i.e., self-disclosure) if the assessment relationship is viewed as comparable to a therapeutic relationship. Thus, a Latino client and his or her parents are more likely to participate or cooperate fully in the assessment process if they feel that the assessment is based on trust and mutual respect and that the potential for a positive outcome exists. Also, practitioners should not be surprised or uncomfortable if Latino clients and their families test the practitioner because this can be part of the process of trust building.

3. Practitioners must recognize that the assessment of Latino children is not a simple process that is mechanical or linear or based on a specific formula (e.g., conduct a mental status examination, obtain a social history, administer a series of tests, and reach a diagnostic conclusion). Instead, the process is complex and requires that the practitioner to be flexible, patient, and sensitive to alternative modes of assessment that are anchored in Latino culture. This includes assessing the belief systems that Latino children are socialized in regarding the origin and resolution of mental illness.

4. Practitioners must recognize that the assessment of Latino children should have an educational component that allows the client to feel that he or she can benefit from the ultimate goal of assessment, which is treatment. This is especially critical in Latino clients who have had limited or negative experiences in psychotherapy. Too often, practitioners present the evaluation process to Latino children in a rather secretive manner that implies an adversarial relationship between the psychologist and child. It is important to note that many children, and their families, may already have bad memories of previous evaluations or of having to fight the system.

5. Practitioners must recognize the diversity or heterogeneity among Latino children. The long-standing image that all Latino children are recent immigrants, monolingual, and of low socioeco-

nomic status is not true. Too often, practitioners depend on such a stereotype to make diagnostic and treatment decisions concerning Latino clients. Other stereotypes that are often voiced by practitioners include the belief that Latino children are not interested in treatment, that they are best treated with psychotropic medications rather than psychotherapy, or that they are not motivated to change their behaviors. Practitioners must recognize that many Latino clients have had negative experiences with prior assessment or testing. For example, it is common to work with parents who feel vulnerable or fearful about the assessment process because they were once misdiagnosed in academic settings. For these clients, it is important that the practitioner be open to discussing any reservations held by the client before the assessment or evaluation.

7. Practitioners must always recognize the role of sociocultural or moderator variables in the assessment of Latino children. These include age, gender, language, nationality, acculturation, socioeconomic status sex roles, folk beliefs, community standards, and ecological environment. For example, language or dialect is a powerful factor in defining and understanding the phenomenology of a Latino client's problems or concerns. Malgady et al. (1987) observed that "when . . . bilingualism and language . . . [are] acknowledged, the following questions arise: In which language, English or Spanish, do bilinguals express greater psychopathology? And, of course, which language conveys the true nature and extent of pathology?" (p. 231).

CASE STUDIES

Case 1: Francisco S.

Francisco is a 13-year-old Latino male who identified himself as Chicano. He was born in San Diego, California, and noted that he was very proud to consider himself Chicano. He is currently living with his cousin, Manuel Sanchez, and his wife Alma. The Sanchezes have three children of their own. Francisco was taken away from his mother by Child Protective Services because of her drug and alcohol problems. She is currently in a court-ordered rehabilitation program and cannot have custody of Francisco. He indicated that he would

be willing to go back to his mother as long as she does not "start up on drugs like crack cocaine."

One of his early recollections, when he was about 9 years of age, is "waking up in the morning, with a baseball bat in my hands, with my little brother next to me. My mom had drug dealing friends in the house." He indicated that he never met his father, that he was very close to his mother, and that he would take care of her someday when he was working. He also noted that despite his mother's problems, she had taught him and his brother to put their best face on when interacting with others. He recalled her telling him that "in our culture, you should never make your parents out to be bad, uneducated, or problematic, and instead, you should let the world know that you are strong." Francisco stated that "putting on such a face has often times caused me problems to the point of getting into fights with others."

Francisco was administered a variety of measures in English, because this was his primary language, including the MMPI-A, Wide Range Achievement Test–3, Draw-A-Family Test, and the Incomplete Sentences Blank–High School Form. Of special note is Francisco's performance on the MMPI-A and Draw-A-Person Test (see Figures 7.1, 7.2, 7.3).

His performance on the MMPI-A not only indicates depression, unusual thoughts or beliefs, alienation, and social withdrawal or isolation, but also suggests a person who is likely to be more masculine and traditional with regard to attitudes about the opposite sex and be careful to not fully disclose himself to others including the psychologist. This is especially noted in his performance on the Masculinity–Femininity (Mf) scale, which is very low, and his high performance on the Lie (L) scale. Also, his Draw-A-Person figure (Figure 7.3), which is a drawing of himself, is an extremely masculine male who is bare-chested, with muscles on his chest, arms, and stomach. Thus, despite experiencing some psychological turmoil, he also attempted to present himself as strong and possibly virtuous. Overall, this performance appeared to be consistent with Francisco's overall world-view, including his attitudes about men and women.

Case 2: Maritza G.

Maritza is a 17-year-old Puerto Rican female who is currently being held at juvenile hall because she

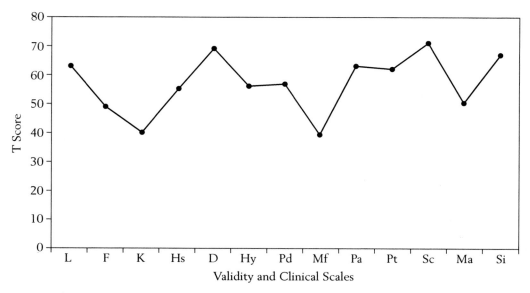

Figure 7.1 MMPI-A performance of Francisco S. on the Validity and Clinical scales

ran away from her foster parents' home. She was referred for an evaluation by her social worker, who wanted to make a determination about whether she should be reunified with her father. Maritza's mother died when Maritza was only 6 years old. She is the youngest of six children whom her father has had to raise on his own. Her

father described Maritza as being very bright, perhaps the brightest of all of his children, yet the one who did not talk about her mother's death. In fact, she appeared to "put up a good front" with everyone in her life.

Maritza was administered the WISC-III as well as other measures, including the Incomplete Sen-

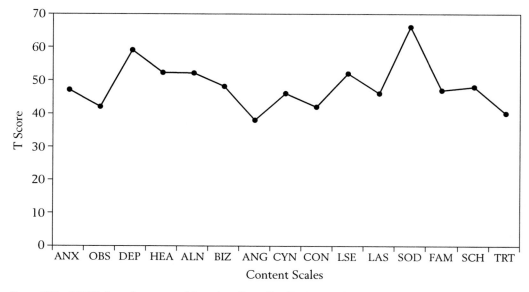

Figure 7.2 MMPI-A performance of Francisco S. on the Content scales

Figure 7.3 Draw-A-Person by Francisco S.

4. At home I clean.
6. At bedtime I sleep.
16. Sports are fun.
32. I am very smart.

Yet, there were also some revealing items, including these:

13. My greatest fear is losing control.
29. What pains me is what I can't change.
33. The only trouble is my mouth.
34. I wish to change people for good.

Her performance on the MMPI-A is very much reflective of her tendency to minimize her problems, bottle up her emotions, and appear to others as if all is right for her. This is especially evident by the validity scale pattern, which suggests an approach toward wanting to appear good and free of problems. This is also evidenced by the fact that all clinical scales are extremely low, with the exception of the Mf scale (Figure 7.4).

tences Blank–High School Form and MMPI-A. She performed within the average range on the WISC-III. She was very bright, articulate, and insightful. On the Incomplete Sentences Blank, she responded in a rather simplistic and concrete manner:

Case 3: Julio M.

Julio is a 7-year-old male who was referred by his mother's probation officer for a psychological evaluation after his mother complained about him being very aggressive, angry, disrespectful, impul-

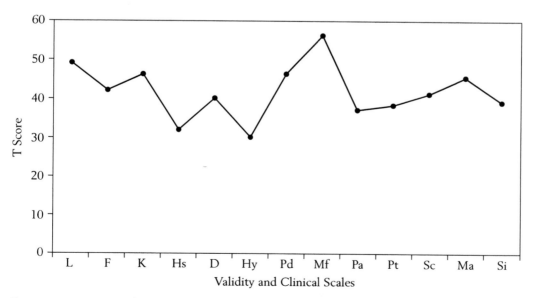

Figure 7.4 MMPI-A performance of Maritza G. on the Validity and Clinical scales

sive, and not trusting. She indicated that Julio was in foster care for about 2 years, from 3 to 4 years of age, and then raised by a grandmother until the mother got out of jail about one year ago. She noted that his father is currently serving a 10-year term in prison for attempted murder. Julio's mother stated that Julio has seen violence from the very beginning of his life, when his father would hit her in front of him and two older siblings. She also indicated that Julio was obsessed with guns and that his father's friend once allowed him to hold a real gun in his hands. She stated that "every time that we go into a toy store, he immediately runs to the section of the store that has guns and wants me to buy one for him."

He was administered a variety of measures including the WISC-III to determine his general intellectual functioning and the Draw-A-Person Test. Although performing within the normative range on the WISC-III, his performance on the Draw-A-Person is of special note. His drawing (Figure 7.5), which includes two animal-like figures, portrays them as holding, aiming, and shooting guns at each other. In addition, each of the figures has a cap on their head, one with a C and the other with a B. When asked what the letters meant, he stated that the C stood for chicanos and

the B for Blacks and "that the kid with the C wanted to kill the kid with the B." In this case, the query related to the letters on the caps was very important because what Julio was communicating was an attraction not only for guns but also for possible gang violence.

Case 4: Maria D.

Maria is a 10-year-old Colombian-American female who was referred by her mother's lawyer for a psychological evaluation. The primary concern for the lawyer was the extent to which Maria had suffered psychological damage from having been sexually and physically abused by her biological father. Her mother reported that Maria was very defiant toward authority, aggressive toward others, moody, and feeling mistreated by everyone. She also indicated that she has called her teacher a "bitch" on several occasions. Her mother also noted that Maria oftentimes says "I'm stupid" and starts to hit herself on the head and mutilate herself. She appears to touch herself in a manner suggestive of masturbation. She has also observed Maria talking to herself, as if she was hearing voices on several occasions. Maria performed within the low range of intelligence on the WISC-III and be-

Figure 7.5 Draw-A-Person by Julio M.

low grade level on the Wide Range Achievement Test-3. Her Draw-A-Person was of special significance because she drew a figure with no face (Figure 7.6). When asked why she left out the face, she responded by saying that "I don't have any emotions, I am sad, and I want to kill myself." She also stated that "nobody loves me anymore including my *padrinos* (godparents)."

CONCLUSION

The clinical or psychological assessment of culturally diverse or minority children is a very complicated process that oftentimes requires more time and effort. It is also a process that is akin to psychotherapy in many ways including the need to reach a level of intimacy that allows for trust and self-disclosure. It is a process that requires the psychologist to be aware of his or her beliefs about a particular cultural group and to walk the thin line between hypothesis testing versus simply depending on cultural stereotypes or caricatures. In many ways, a practitioner never reaches full competence in the assessment of culturally diverse persons because our world continues to become more and more diverse with respect to culture, language, and worldviews.

Figure 7.6 Draw-A-Person by Maria D.

In this chapter, we have attempted to present our perspective on the assessment of children of Latino descent. We have touched only the tip of the iceberg by sharing with you our philosophy about what needs to be considered in the culturally competent assessment of Latino children. As we noted above, and as we have learned in the process of writing this chapter, culture is anything but static and continues to evolve in ways that we cannot yet envision. Although our hope is not to overwhelm the reader, we must acknowledge the fact that we probably have. Yet, our dream continues to be that someday practitioners will find methodologies for attending to the role of culture in the manifestation of problems across and within cultures. Perhaps in the end, this is just one tiny contribution to this dream that we hope is shared by others.

References

Aviera, A. (1996). "Dichos" therapy group: A therapeutic use of Spanish language proverbs with hospitalized Spanish-speaking psychiatric patients. *Cultural Diversity & Mental Health, 2,* 73–87.

Bamford, K. W. (1991). Bilingual issues in mental health assessment and treatment. *Hispanic Journal of Behavioral Sciences, 13,* 377–390.

Barona, A., & Miller, J. A. (1994). Short acculturation scale for Hispanic youth (SASH-Y): A preliminary report. *Hispanic Journal of Behavioral Sciences, 16,* 155–162.

Bradford, D. T., & Munoz, A. (1993). Translation in bilingual psychotherapy. *Professional Psychology: Research & Practice, 24,* 52–61.

Buriel, R., Perez, W., DeMent, T. L., Chavez, D. V., & Moran, V. R. (1998). The relationship of language brokering to academic performance, biculturalism, and self-efficacy among Latino adolescents. *Hispanic Journal of Behavioral Sciences, 20,* 283–297.

Canino, G. (1982). The Latino woman: Sociocultural influences on diagnoses and treatment. In R. M. Becerra, M. Karno, & J. I. Escobar (Eds.), *Mental health and Latino Americans: Clinical perspectives* (pp. 117–138). New York: Grune & Stratton.

Canino, G., & Guarnaccia, P. (1997). Methodological challenges in the assessment of Hispanic children and adolescents. *Applied Developmental Science, 1,* 124–134.

Canino, I. A., & Spurlock, J. (1994a). Assessment strategies. In I. A. Canino & J. Spurlock, *Culturally diverse children and adolescents: Assessment, diagnosis, and treatment* (pp. 77–86). New York: Guilford.

Canino, I. A., & Spurlock, J. (1994b). Diagnostic categories. In I. A. Canino & J. Spurlock, *Culturally diverse children and adolescents: Assessment, diagnosis, and treatment* (pp. 87–124). New York: Guilford.

Cervantes, R. C., & Acosta, F. X. (1992). Psychological testing for Latino Americans. *Applied & Preventive Psychology, 1,* 209–219.

Chavez, D. V., Moran, V. R., Reid, S. L., & Lopez, M. (1997). Acculturative stress in children: A modification of the SAFE scale. *Hispanic Journal of Behavioral Sciences, 19,* 34–44.

Chavez, E. L., & Gonzales-Singh, E. (1980). Latino assessment: A case study. *Professional Psychology: Research & Practice, 11,* 163–168.

Cohen, P., & Kasen, S. (1999). The context of assessment: Culture, race, and socioeconomic status as influences on the assessment of children. In D. Shaffer, C. P. Lucas, & J. E. Richters (Eds.), *Diagnostic assessment in child and adolescent psychopathology* (pp. 299–318). New York: Guilford.

Colomba, M. V., Santiago, E. S., & Rossello, J. (1999). Coping strategies and depression in Puerto Rican adolescents: An exploratory study. *Cultural Diversity & Ethnic Minority Psychology, 5,* 65–75.

Constantino, G., & Malgady, R. G. (1999). The Tell-Me-A-Story Test: A multicultural offspring of the Thematic Apperception Test. In L. Geiser & M. I. Stein, *Evocative images: The Thematic Apperception Test and the art of projection* (pp. 191–206). Washington, DC: American Psychological Association.

Cortes, D. E. (1995). Variations in familism in two generations of Puerto Ricans. *Hispanic Journal of Behavioral Sciences, 17,* 249–255.

Cuellar, I. (1982). The diagnosis and evaluation of schizophrenic disorders among Mexican Americans. In R. M. Becerra, M. Karno, & J. I. Escobar (Eds.), *Mental health and Latino Americans: Clinical perspectives* (pp. 61–81). San Diego: Grune & Stratton.

Cuellar, I., Arnold., B., & Maldonado, R. (1995). Acculturation rating scale for Mexican Americans—II: A revision of the original ARSMA scale. *Hispanic Journal of Behavioral Sciences, 17,* 275–304.

Cuellar, I., Martinez, C., Jimenez, R., & Gonzalez, R. (1983). Clinical psychiatric case presentation: Culturally responsive diagnostic formulation and treatment in an Hispanic client. *Hispanic Journal of Behavioral Sciences, 5,* 93–103.

Dana, R. H. (2000). Multicultural assessment of child and adolescent personality and psychopathology. In A. L. Comunian & U. W. Gielen (Eds.), *International perspectives on human development* (pp. 233–258). Lengerich, Germany: Pabst Science Publishers.

Flaskerud, J. H. (1986). Diagnostic and treatment differences among five ethnic groups. *Psychological Reports, 58,* 219–235.

Flores, E., Eyre, S. L., & Millstein, S. G. (1998). Sociocultural beliefs related to sex among Mexican American adolescents. *Hispanic Journal of Behavioral Sciences, 20,* 60–82.

Garcia-Coll, C., & Vazquez, G. H. A. (1995). Hispanic children and their families: Research, health, and policy issues. In H. E. Fitzgerald, B. M. Lester, & B. Zuckerman (Eds.), *Children of poverty: Research, health, and policy issues* (pp. 57–83). New York: Garland.

Gopaul-McNicol, S., & Thomas-Presswood, T. (1998). Issues in working with culturally and linguistically diverse children and families. In S. Gopaul-McNicol & T. Thomas-Presswood, *Working with linguistically and culturally different children: Innovative clinical and educational approaches* (pp. 44–57). Needham Heights, MA: Allyn & Bacon.

Gordon, K. A. (1996). Resilient Hispanic youth's self-concept and motivational patterns. *Hispanic Journal of Behavioral Sciences, 18,* 63–73.

Guarnaccia, P. J., Rivera, M., Franco, F., & Neighbors, C. (1996). The experiences of ataques de nervios: Towards an anthropology of emotions in Puerto Rico. *Culture, Medicine, & Psychiatry, 20,* 343–367.

Guarnaccia, P. J., & Rodriguez, O. (1996). Concepts of culture and their role in the development of culturally competent mental health services. *Hispanic Journal of Behavioral Sciences, 18,* 419–433.

Guinn, B. (1998). Acculturation and health locus of control among Mexican American adolescents. *Hispanic Journal of Behavioral Sciences, 20,* 492–499.

Hays, P. A. (1996). Culturally responsive assessment with diverse older adults. *Professional Psychology: Research & Practice, 27,* 188–193.

Hovey, J. D. (2000). Acculturative stress, depression, and suicidal ideation in Mexican immigrants. *Cultural Diversity & Ethnic Minority Psychology, 6,* 134–151.

Johnson, R. (1993). Clinical issues in the use of the DSM-III-R with African American children: A diagnostic paradigm. *Journal of Black Psychology, 19*, 447–460.

Malgady, R. G. (1996). The question of cultural bias in assessment and diagnosis of ethnic minority clients: Let's reject the null hypothesis. *Professional Psychology: Research & Practice, 27*, 73–77.

Malgady, R. G., Rogler, L. H., & Constantino, G. (1987). Ethnocultural and linguistic bias in mental health evaluation of Hispanics. *American Psychologist, 42*, 228–234.

Marcos, L. R., Alpert, M.., Urcuyo, L., & Kesselman, M. (1973). The effect of interview language on the evaluation of psychopathology in Spanish-American schizophrenic patients. *American Journal of Psychiatry, 130*, 549–553.

Niemann, Y. F., Romero, A. J., Arredondo, J., & Rodriguez, V. (1999). What does it mean to be "Mexican"? Social construction of an ethnic identity. *Hispanic Journal of Behavioral Sciences, 21*, 47–60.

Norris, A. E., Ford, K., & Bova, C. A. (1996). Psychometrics of a brief acculturation scale for Hispanics in a probability sample of urban Hispanic adolescents and young adults. *Hispanic Journal of Behavioral Sciences, 18*, 29–38.

Owen, P. R. (1998). Fears of Hispanic and Anglo children: Real-world fears in the 1990s. *Hispanic Journal of Behavioral Sciences, 20*, 483–491.

Planos, R., Zayas, L. H., & Busch-Rossnagel, N. A. (1995). Acculturation and teaching behaviors of Dominican and Puerto Rican mothers. *Hispanic Journal of Behavioral Sciences, 17*, 225–236.

Price, C. S., & Cuellar, I. (1981). Effects of language and related variables on the expression of psychopathology in Mexican American psychiatric patients. *Hispanic Journal of Behavioral Sciences, 3*, 145–160.

Puente, A. E., Sol Mora, M., & Munoz-Cespedes, J. M. (1997). Neuropsychological assessment of Spanish-speaking children. In C. R. Reynolds & E. Fletcher-Janzen (Eds.), *Handbook of clinical child neuropsychology* (2nd ed., pp. 371–383). New York: Plenum.

Quintana, S. M., Castillo, E. M., & Zamarripa, M. X. (2000). Assessment of ethnic and linguistic minority children. In E. S. Shapiro & T. R. Kratochwill (Eds.), *Behavioral assessment in schools: Theory, research, and clinical foundations* (pp. 435–463). New York: Guilford.

Quintana, S. M., & Vera, E. M. (1999). Mexican American children's ethnic identity, understanding of ethnic prejudice, and parental ethnic socialization. *Hispanic Journal of Behavioral Sciences, 21*, 387–404.

Rodriguez, J. M., & Kosloski, K. (1998). The impact of acculturation on attitudinal familism in a community of Puerto Rican Americans. *Hispanic Journal of Behavioral Sciences, 20*, 375–390.

Rogler, L. H., Cortes, D. E., & Malgady, R. G. (1994). The mental health relevance of idioms of distress: Anger and perceptions of injustice among New York Puerto Ricans. *Journal of Nervous & Mental Disease, 182*, 327–331.

Saldana, D. H. (1994). Minority status and distress. *Hispanic Journal of Behavioral Sciences, 16*, 116–128.

Santiago-Rivera, A. L. (1995). Developing a culturally sensitive treatment modality for bilingual Spanish-speaking clients: Incorporating language and culture in counseling. *Journal of Counseling & Development, 74*, 12–17.

Talavera, G. A., Elder, J. P., & Velásquez, R. J. (1997). Latino health beliefs and locus of control: Implications for primary care and public health practitioners. *American Journal of Preventive Medicine, 13*, 408–410.

Thomas-Presswood, T. N., Sasso, J., & Gin, G. (1997). Cultural issues in the intellectual assessment of children from diverse cultural backgrounds. *Journal of Social Distress & Homelessness, 6*, 113–127.

Tse, L. (1995). Language brokering among Latino adolescents: Prevalence, attitudes, and school performance. *Hispanic Journal of Behavioral Sciences, 17*, 180–193.

Velásquez, R. J. (1995). Personality assessment of Hispanic clients. In J. N. Butcher (Ed.), *Clinical personality assessment: Practical approaches* (pp. 120–139). New York: Oxford University Press.

Velásquez, R. J., Ayala, G. X., & Mendoza, S. (1998). *Psychodiagnostic assessment of U.S. Latinos: MMPI, MMPI-2, and MMPI-A results: A comprehensive manual.* East Lansing: Julian Samora Research Institute, Michigan State University.

Velásquez, R. J., & Callahan, W. J. (1992). Psychological testing of Latino Americans in clinical settings: Overview and issues. In K. Geisinger (Ed.), *Psychological testing of Hispanics* (pp. 253–265). Washington, DC: American Psychological Association.

Velásquez, R. J., Chavira, D. A., Karle, H. R., Callahan, W. J., Garcia, J. A., & Castellanos,

J. (2000). Assessing bilingual and monolingual Latino students with translations of the MMPI-2: Initial data. *Cultural Diversity & Ethnic Minority Psychology, 6,* 65–72.

Velásquez, R. J., Gonzales, M., Butcher, J. N., Castillo-Canez, I., Apodaca, J. X., & Chavira, D. (1997). Use of the MMPI-2 with Chicanos: Strategies for counselors. *Journal of Multicultural Counseling & Development, 25,* 107–120.

Velásquez, R. J., Johnson, R., & Brown-Cheatham, M. (1993). Teaching counselors to use the DSM-III-R with ethnic minority clients: A paradigm. *Counselor Education & Supervision, 32,* 323–331.

Yin, Z., Zapata, J. T., & Katims, D. S. (1995). Risk factors for substance use among Mexican American school-age youth. *Hispanic Journal of Behavioral Sciences, 17,* 61–76.

Part II

FORENSIC MENTAL HEALTH APPLICATIONS

8

Forensic Interviewing of Children and Adolescents

Linda Sayler Gudas
Jerome M. Sattler

The accuracy and veracity of children's statements and testimony in the legal arena have historically been challenged. Much of the skepticism of children's statements stemmed from child sexual abuse interviews that questioned existing pretrial and trial procedures used to obtain and evaluate the testimony of young children (Bruck, Ceci, & Hembrooke, 1998). Mental health clinicians became acutely aware of their limitations in forensic situations. Tests, techniques, and psychotherapeutic strategies developed and used in general clinical settings were found to be inadequate in answering legal questions or in meeting criminogenic or traumatic needs for treatment (Borum & Otto, 2000). The ongoing development of forensic psychology, formal training programs focusing on children and the law, and research on psycholegal issues and children have all assisted in offering more sound assessments of children. Forensic interviewing of children and adolescents is now considered a task for clinicians with specialized training in child mental health and forensics, clinical supervision, and extensive knowledge of child development. This chapter is an attempt to fur-

ther clinicians' awareness of the uniqueness of forensic interviewing of children and adolescents.

PURPOSE OF THE INTERVIEW

Definition

The purpose of forensic interviewing of children and adolescents involves evaluating children's functioning in order to help the criminal and juvenile courts take appropriate actions and/or make appropriate placements. Such interviews should provide an objective, neutral opinion to the referral source. As Greenberg and Shuman (1997) state: "A forensic evaluator advocates for the findings of the evaluation, whatever those findings turn out to be" (p. 54). The forensic evaluation may apply to criminal cases (e.g., allegations of sexual abuse or physical maltreatment) or civil suits (e.g., personal injury, psychological damages, medical malpractice, child custody, competency to stand trial, potential for rehabilitation, or litigation related to in-patient psychiatric hospitalization).

The tasks of the forensic interviewer involve obtaining from children and their parents objective, truthful, and relevant information that will assist a court of law in reaching an appropriate and just decision. The interviewer should gather information to determine a preincident baseline of functioning and, when possible, describe the incident(s) or actions alleged, evaluate the child for emotional disorders and consider other possible explanations for the child's symptoms or behavior, address other relevant psychosocial questions posed by the court, demonstrate awareness of developmental issues, avoid biasing the outcome with the evaluator's own preconceptions, and keep an accurate record for possible use in future court proceedings (Bernet, 1997; Greenberg & Shuman, 1997).

> Working as a forensic evaluator, the practitioner may evaluate children in a private practice for a forensic purpose, evaluate children and collaborate with other mental health professionals in a government agency such as a protective service, or work with an interdisciplinary team at a pediatric medical center. He or she may assist the court in determining what happened to the child, make recommendations regarding placement or treatment, or offer an opinion on the termination of parental rights. A forensic evaluation may involve critiquing the work that was previously done by another mental health professional or by a protective service investigator. (Bernet, 1997, p. 423)

Essential Differences Between Forensic and General Clinical Interviews

"Forensic assessment differs substantially from traditional clinical assessment in a number of dimensions, including the goals, scope, and product of the evaluation, the role of the examiner, and the nature of the relationship between the examiner and examinee" (Nicholson & Norwood, 2000, p. 10). Bernet (1997) stresses the importance of interviewers understanding their role in the case. The prime distinction concerns whether the interview focuses on the needs of the legal system or will constitute a clinical assessment for treatment purposes.

The attorney, the court, or a third party retains the forensic specialist (Greenberg & Shuman, 1997), although the parents or child may also stand as the primary client. In the case of clinical interviews and treatment, the child's family or, in some cases, the child's school or health care provider retains the therapist for treatment. Clinicians must clarify who has hired them and to whom they owe a professional duty (Bernet, 1997). Sattler (1998) stresses, however, that "you should always represent the best interests of the child, no matter who is paying for your services" (p. 463).

Concerns of confidentiality and privacy also become relevant. Communications between a forensic evaluator and a litigant do not generally fall under a psychologist–client privilege, as would normally apply in general clinical interviews and treatment (Greenberg & Shuman, 1997).

When the evaluation has a forensic context, the evaluator should approach the assessment in a neutral, objective, and detached manner (Greenberg & Shuman, 1997). When the interview has a clinical focus (i.e., a diagnostic or an assessment for treatment), the clinician's role as a care provider usually involves adopting a supportive, accepting, and empathic stance. Placing the evaluator clearly in a court-appointed or retained role helps maintain neutrality (Nicholson & Norwood, 2000).

Forensic Interviewer Contrasted With Psychotherapist Roles

"Forensic assessment by a patient's therapist does not generally provide a reliable basis for a forensic assessment and therefore should be avoided by the ethical psychologist and viewed skeptically by the courts" (Greenberg & Shuman, 1997, p. 55). Psycholegal issues raise problems of judgment, foundation, and historical truth that become problematic within a therapeutic relationship (e.g., the relationship of diagnosis or mental status to legally defined standards of capacity). In addition, therapists who testify run the risk of disrupting their therapeutic alliance, if the testimony does not comport with the client's views or wishes. When asked to testify, a child's therapist must carefully strive to clarify his or her role. The mental health clinician must avoid agreeing to perform both clinical and forensic roles, for such duality runs contrary to both good patient care and existing clinical and forensic practice guidelines (Greenberg & Shuman, 1997).

DEVELOPMENTAL CONSIDERATIONS

Developmental factors clearly influence the capacity of children and adolescents performing tasks relevant to a forensic assessment. Marked disagreement exists as to the age at which most children can become competent and capable of accurate recall of events, with estimates ranging from 3–6 to 14–15 years (Cashmere & Bussey, 1996; Lamb, Sternberg, & Esplin, 1995; Nightingale, 1993). Despite such disagreement, one can obtain valuable and truthful information from children and evaluate the credibility of such testimony. Doing so, however, requires careful investigative procedures, as well as a realistic awareness of the capacities and tendencies of children (Lamb et al., 1995).

Infancy

Although the examiner cannot verbally interview an infant child, one can observe and evaluate him or her. The interviewer can comment on activity level, the nature of interaction and relationships with other people, affect and state regulation, general mood, and involvement in play. Parental reports of infant behavior, such as eating and sleeping patterns and general temperament, can prove useful in assessment. Observing parent–child interactions also provides valuable information, especially in evaluating cases involving child custody or potential termination of parental rights. Assessment with infant development scales may provide the clinician with an indication of how the infant functions in relation to peers.

Preschool

Preschool children have the greatest vulnerability from a forensic accuracy perspective. Such children usually show high levels of suggestibility and social compliance with adults' requests (Bruck et al., 1998). Cognition during this age period consists of prelogical, magical, and egocentric thinking, and such wishful thinking can become confused with factual events. Preschool children construct reality on their observable world, with immediate, direct cues dominating life events. Preschool children tend to think in absolute terms

(i.e., people dichotomized as good or bad). Neither conservation of affect nor perception remains well established, as exemplified in the child's rapid changes of emotional states. Lamb et al. (1995) state that although no convincing evidence exists that a child younger than 3 years could be presumed competent, extensive variability in ability exists between ages 3 and 5 years. With appropriate interviewing techniques, Ceci and Bruck (1993) believe that "even very young children are capable of recalling much that is forensically relevant" (p. 403).

Preschool children can converse about their concerns and feelings and give truthful account of events. Language skills in normal children develop rapidly during the preschool years. By 5 years of age, the typical English-speaking child handles negation, compares adjectives, uses possessives, and manipulates verb forms (Walker, 1993). Children learning English as a second language require especially careful assessment of their comprehension skills. Young children tend to provide brief accounts of their experiences, and these reports tend toward sparse detail (Bruck et al., 1998). Such reporting occurs not only because of limited experience or immature memory, but also because preschoolers have more limited vocabularies and may not have as much motivation to reveal information as do older children (Lamb et al., 1995). In addition, the egocentricity typical of this developmental period may lead some young children to assume that others must know what they mean, obviating the need for elaboration unless requested with a socially and linguistically appropriate form of inquiry. Walker (1993) stresses three chief sources of communication mischief in questioning young children: (a) lack of age-appropriate vocabulary, (b) complex syntax, and (c) general ambiguity. Preschoolers often respond best to short, concrete, probing questions designed to help them expand on and clarify their ideas.

School Age

When answering questions, the child between the ages of 6 and 12 years has the capacity to perform various mental tasks and can think more planfully than the younger child. However, the school-age child tends to think in terms of factual rather than logical relationships and cannot yet reflect upon all possible outcomes. Thinking remains concrete, rigid, and literal, and the child's reasoning seems bound by rules. One major forensic consideration involves recognition that the child understands cause-and-effect relationships. Socially, the child comprehends inconsistencies in behavior (e.g., a policeman can do something bad). The child's developing social consciousness, coupled with rule-bound beliefs, however, often compel him or her to voice strong opinions (e.g., "He wasn't fair!" "She can't do that!"). Extended discussion with adults about abstract issues, such as feelings and attitudes, tend to be limited; such children seem more concrete in their conversations. They also show vulnerability to negative feedback and misleading questions, especially in the early school years (Warren, Hulse-Trotter, & Tubbs, 1991). Engaging the child in specific age-related activities, such as board games or other structured interaction, may help establish initial rapport.

Adolescence

Variation within the adolescent age group may exceed the difference that occurs between adolescents and adults (Scott, Reppucci, & Woolard, 1995). However, ample evidence exists that children do not reach adult levels of resistance to erroneous suggestions prior to early adolescence (Bruck et al., 1998). Despite individual differences, the teenager gradually loses factual, concrete thinking and becomes capable of systematically analyzing information by thinking of logical alternatives in situations and generating hypotheses. He or she can think deductively and symbolically. However, with increased independence and capacity for abstract reasoning comes an attitude of invincibility and risk taking. Additionally, adolescents have a great inclination to respond to peer influence and thus become prone to make poor choices (Marxsen, Yuille, & Nisbet, 1995; Scott et al., 1995). Marxsen et al. (1995) suggest that assessment of adolescents in forensic settings should involve the use of personality instruments that assess the capacity for independence and decision making. Such testing may help to identify the child's susceptibility to external influences.

The adolescent can accurately report symptoms, events, and experiences with a proper sense of time and setting. The interviewer should let adolescents know that their opinions and statements have importance and value. Teenagers will have concerns regarding privacy, and it becomes important to review confidentiality limitations carefully. If the adolescent shows resistance or negativity, the interviewer might focus on obtaining neutral information, saving more sensitive material until later in the evaluation.

COMPONENTS OF THE INTERVIEWING PROCESS

A comprehensive forensic interviewing process involves more than just the assessment of the child. In most cases, the interview involves multiple steps.

Collect Third-Party Information

Forensic interviewers should prepare themselves by collecting as much information as possible about the questions to be answered, allegations, the child's capacities and propensities, and any possible motivations toward honesty, deceptiveness, or prevarication (Lamb et al., 1995). Collecting third-party information becomes a hallmark characteristic of forensic assessment that distinguishes such interviewing from traditional therapeutic assessment (Nicholson & Norwood, 2000). During this data collection phase, interviewers have the opportunity to define and clarify their role, determine the purpose of the evaluation, and discuss payment issues prior to performing the evaluation (Bernet, 1997). Three components of this phase are described below.

Review the Referral Question and Information

The legal questions will help determine the interview format and focus. Clarifying ambiguous or vague information with other involved parties and careful consideration of what the referral source's expectations are become critically important.

Obtain and Review Previous Evaluations and Records

Such prior evaluations may include school testing, police reports, psychological or psychiatric evaluation, medical records (including records of any hospitalizations), or psychotherapist notes. If the interview request is for a second opinion, the initial report may remain unavailable. If the initial report is available, the interviewer may prefer not to read it, choosing instead to do the assessment blind to the initial opinion. Such a decision should ideally fall to the interviewer's discretion. The interviewer should ask about previous forensic interviews of the child, as exposure to repeated questioning can affect the child's responses (Bruck et al., 1998).

Interview the Parents and/or Other Relevant Adults

The interviewer should obtain family history, developmental and medical history, information about the child's coping skills, and a report of what the child has been told about the interview. This information "includes the parents' perceptions and attitudes toward the child and the child's role in the family" (Bernet, 1997, p. 429). With formal written permission, the interviewer may also obtain relevant information from others, including teachers, child care providers, extended family members, or health care providers. These interviews allow an opportunity to learn about the child's behavior across settings, as well as cultural values, ethnic identification, or religious views that may relate to the child's symptoms or the child's capacities.

Interview the Child

The type of interview conducted with the child will vary, depending on the referral questions. For example, a sexual abuse evaluation would differ from a child custody/visitation assessment not involving allegations of such abuse. However, several parts of the interview remain independent of the presenting concern.

Rapport Building

Spending time getting to know the child at the beginning of the interview will assist the child in settling in and feeling more comfortable. Ricci, Beal, and Dekle (1996) determined that young children seemed measurably more relaxed 3 minutes after the start of the interview than at the beginning. Montoya (1995) also stresses the importance of a rapport-building phase for children in court situations, when all counsel have the opportunity to meet and speak briefly with the child witnesses. When children are listened to and valued, such interactions also teach them the importance of voicing their comprehension (Carter, Bottoms, & Levine, 1996). Lamb et al. (1995) suggest encouraging children, early in an interview, to recall and describe everything remembered about a recent meaningful event. Such an exercise helps evaluate many components of the child's development. Spending time with the child will also provide the interviewer with a baseline of the child's functioning, before discussing more emotionally charged information.

Explain the Interview

The questions "Why are you here today?" or "What did your Mom or Dad tell you about coming here today?" are good ways for the interviewer to assess what the child has been told and to introduce any topic of concern. A discussion of the nature and purpose of the interview, including how the interview will proceed, should follow. Bernet (1997) suggests reaching an agreement with the child that, in this interview, only the truth, not pretend or imagination, will be discussed. The interviewer may also explore the child's definition of a truth versus a lie (Haugaard, 1993), because "knowing that a child is speaking the truth is only meaningful once the child's definition of the truth is known" (Haugaard, Reppucci, Laird, & Nauful, 1991, p. 225). The interviewer might also determine if the child believes that telling the truth about the incident would result in punishment (e.g., "Uncle John will be mad, if I tell about the accident"; Haugaard, 1993).

Discuss Confidentiality

Address the questions of "Who will have access to the information?" and "What is or is not private?" The interviewer has a duty to inform the child (and parents) of the potential lack of confidentiality and privilege (Greenberg & Shuman, 1997). Discussing confidentiality becomes especially important for a child who has been in psychotherapy, as the child may assume that his or her conversation in this setting remains as confidential as discussions with the therapist.

Evaluate Mental Status

Clinicians should conduct a thorough mental status examination and carefully note any changes in status during the course of the evaluation, documenting these objectively. An example might include a dramatic change in mood, affect, or orientation when discussing a particular incident or topic.

Observe the Child at Home, School, or Other Relevant Setting, If Indicated

Such observations may prove helpful in providing further information about the child's functioning across settings. Although not always possible to accomplish, such observations can offer a broad picture of the child's abilities in various environments and with various groups of people. This part of the interviewing process also allows the evaluator to view and better understand the child's community, home, and cultural identity.

Formulate Hypotheses and Recommendations

All relevant sources of information about the child (e.g., behavioral observations, interview data, and case history) should help to generate hypotheses, formulate interpretations, and arrive at recommendations. If the interviewer believes further data are needed before formulating a diagnosis or treatment plan, the nature of the data and rationale should be clearly reported. Hypotheses and recommendations should describe realistic, developmentally appropriate, and practical strategies and goals, designed with sensitivity to the child's family and culture, whenever possible.

Write a Report

Consider the interview complete only after synthesizing, integrating, and organizing the information obtained. The traditional medium for presenting such information is a written report. Although evaluators may occasionally employ other formal

or informal methods of providing feedback, clear written documentation forms the foundation of any forensic evaluation. Reports provide accurate assessment-related information to the referral source and other concerned parties; serve as a source of information for testing clinical hypotheses, developing appropriate treatment recommendations, and conducting program evaluation and research; serve as a record of historical, observational, and other information gathered in the interview and recommended interventions; and offer legal documentation.

Bernet (1997) describes 13 components of the report: (a) identifying information, (b) referral information, (c) procedure for evaluation (evaluator's role, meetings and sessions held, testing used, outside information used), (d) current situation (i.e., symptoms of child), (e) past history related to the issue, (f) family history, (g) developmental history, (h) medical history, (i) mental status, (j) psychological testing (if done), (k) diagnosis, (l) conclusions, and (m) realistic recommendations. Although reports may vary in their composition, we strongly recommend inclusion of all 13 components in any comprehensive evaluation.

Clear and supporting data must buttress all generalizations and conclusions. Clinicians must describe the clinical facts and reasoning underlying their opinions (Nicholson & Norwood, 2000). Bernet (1997) suggests, "Indicate in detail the reasons for the conclusions in the written report, so the court will fully understand the basis for the opinion" (p. 432). The interviewer should cite the source(s) of information, with appropriate attribution and qualifiers (e.g. "according to John's mother," "Jane alleged," "Ralph reported").

Clinicians should always evaluate their findings in relation to the psycholegal questions posed, keeping in mind the reason for referral and presenting concerns. Marxsen et al. (1995) comment on the importance of having knowledge of questions that tend to arise when investigators examine children's statements (e.g. "How did the child learn of those details?"). Such information can assist in writing a logical, concise, and relevant report. Nicholson and Norwood (2000) additionally emphasize the need for a clear rationale for selection and administration of any psychological testing, for often the relationship between test findings and legal issues is not articulated.

Provide Feedback

Depending on the clinician's role, meetings with attorneys, parents, the child, or other involved parties may be indicated at the conclusion of the assessment process. Such feedback can allow for clarification of any questions and discussion of the proposed treatment plan and recommendations. However, forensic clinicians must always clarify their role to all parties at the outset of the evaluation process. This includes addressing who will have access to the data, opinions, and reports that result. In some instances, the parties under evaluation may have no right of access to the data or report. All do have the right, however, to know this in advance. Providing such information remains the responsibility of the professional conducting the evaluation.

Follow Up on Recommendations

The clinician conducting the clinical interview may, at times, have the duty of monitoring implementation of recommendations. Such follow-up may occur formally (e.g., via a meeting) or less formally (e.g., via a telephone or conference call). If the recommendations made proved effective, the interviewer has data to support his or her findings. If the interventions proved inadequate or ineffective, further review, assessment, or revision of the intervention plan is indicated. In some cases, the clinician's role will end with submission of a report. In any case, the clinician should clarify the role and scope of the evaluation to all parties at the outset and communicate any changes made subsequently, obtaining appropriate consent from the proper authority.

THE USE OF PSYCHOLOGICAL TESTING IN FORENSIC INTERVIEWING

"The appropriate role of psychological testing in forensic assessment remains unclear" (Nicholson & Norwood, 2000, p. 11), in part because of the absence of normative test data in psycholegal contexts (Heilbrun, 1992). In deciding whether to use psychological tests, interviewers must prepare to explain their decisions (Nicholson & Norwood, 2000), including defending the rationale for test selection.

A battery of tests could help answer questions regarding a child's developmental immaturity; mental, emotional, or learning disorders; or cognitive impairment (Heilbrun, Hawk, & Tate, 1996). In considering which tests to use, Heilbrun (1992) provides seven recommendations: (a) commercial availability and adequate documentation, (b) reliability and validity data, (c) relevance to the legal referral question, (d) administration in a standard manner, (e) applicability to the representative population, (f) assessment of the child's response style, and (g) appropriateness of outcome data and formulation potential.

When using psychological testing, the findings must be carefully integrated with information obtained in other components of the assessment. "Impressions from psychological testing in the forensic context should most appropriately be treated as hypotheses subject to verification through history, medical tests, and third-party observations" (Heilbrun, 1992, p. 263). Although psychological testing may shed light on issues such as a child's propensity to exaggerate, Bernet (1997) warns that testing does not, by itself, prove veracity.

CONDUCTING THE INTERVIEW

Techniques in Interviewing Children in Forensic Settings

A cardinal rule in forensic interviewing of children requires that the clinician always consider the child's age, experiences, level of linguistic and conceptual development, and the extensiveness of any emotional disturbance. The structure of the interview environment should help the child speak openly and honestly. The child's spontaneous remarks become particularly important. Studies show that children interviewed in a warm, supportive, reinforcing manner demonstrate improved memory recall and accuracy of information, increased resistance to misleading questions about events, and decreased suggestibility in response to leading questions compared to children interviewed in an intimidating or authoritative style (Carter et al., 1996; Goodman, Levine, Melton, & Ogden, 1991; Ricci et al, 1996).

Body language conveys meaning to a child, and the interviewer should maintain a relaxed and comfortable posture. Monitoring and avoiding distractions, including unusual facial expressions (e.g., frowning, grimacing, or tics), head nodding, constant or avoidant eye contact, foot tapping, hair twirling, or twisting paper clips, becomes quite important. Such nonverbal cues from the evaluator can bias the interview (Marxsen et al., 1995).

Clinicians should also maintain awareness of the influence of their verbal mannerisms on the child, using a pleasant, nonjudgmental tone of voice whenever possible. State questions clearly, confidently, and positively. Tone and mannerism can influence the child in two major ways. First, the child might not feel permission to say "I don't know" or "I don't remember," to disagree with the examiner, or to voice confusion regarding the conversation, if the interviewer's tone seems too brisk or authoritative. Second, anticipation of a positive or negative consequence as a result of an examiner's statements could influence the child's answer. Examples include giving or implying praise or approval (e.g., "You must be very smart!") or criticizing or disagreeing with the child (e.g., "Looks like you are not going to help me"). Such social influence and reinforcement can become powerful determinants of children's answers (Garven, Wood, Malpass, & Shaw, 1998).

The wording of statements and vocabulary usage by the interviewer profoundly influence the course and outcome of interviews (Lamb et al., 1995). Carter et al. (1996) interviewed 60 children between the ages of 5 and 7 years about a standard play event, varying the complexity of the questions. The children became significantly less accurate in reporting the event when questioned with complex, developmentally inappropriate questions than when asked simple questions. Most interestingly, however, the children rarely voiced their comprehension failures, indicating that they did not feel they could verbalize confusion. Warren et al. (1991) suggest that warning children of possible question difficulty and giving them instructions to answer only what they remembered can prove effective methods for reducing memory distortions and inducing resistance to suggestibility.

Formulating Questions

Questions asked during an interview vary as to degree of openness and focus. The format used can substantially influence a child's response (Peterson, Dowden, & Tobin, 1999). One end of the continuum includes open-ended or nonspecific questions (e.g., "Tell me about why you are here today"). "Ideally, information in forensic interviews is elicited by means of open-ended questions; such questions are neither leading nor suggestive" (Peterson et al., 1999, p. 551). This type of question will often prove most helpful at the beginning of the interview, as the child then has the opportunity to describe events in his or her own words. One risk of asking open-ended questions involves the tendency of children, especially younger ones, to offer more limited or less elaborate responses. However, the accuracy of replies given to open-ended questions, in comparison to closed-ended questions or specific prompts, has been well documented (Bruck et al., 1998; Lamb et al., 1995; Peterson et al., 1999).

Toward the middle of the continuum one could craft moderately focused questions, centering on a specific topic, but allowing some latitude to the child (e.g., "What is it like at your school?" or "Tell me everything you remember about that trip to grandma's house"). Such questions formulated in response to the child's answers to open-ended questions and may prove useful to clarify a response. Peterson et al. (1999) refer to the *wh-format* in these moderately focused questions, where the child is asked to specify a particular detail (e.g., "Who was there?" "Where were you?" "What did the man wear?"). According to these authors, when such wh-format is given in a neutral, unbiased context, children will generally show more willingness to answer spontaneously "I don't know" or "I don't remember" rather than give an inaccurate response.

At the other end of the continuum one finds highly focused or closed-ended questions. Such specific questions may require a yes or no answer (e.g., "Was your mother home when you came home from school?") or selection of one of two alternatives presented (e.g., "Do you like visiting Grandma or do you not like visiting her?"). Such questions elicit brief answers, often without explanation.

However, forced answers to such prompts can easily lead to falsified or inaccurate responses. For an extended discussion of the benefits and limitations of question format, see Sattler (1998, pp. 64–79).

Problematic Questions

Several major forms of questioning should be avoided or used with caution.

Yes/No Questions

Such questions, also referred to as recognition questions, have several potential pitfalls with children. The purpose of such a question tends to affirm or deny the truth of the statement queried (e.g., "Did the man wear a red shirt?"). Peterson et al. (1999) warn that the child must understand the underlying assumption of a yes/no question, specifically, that the truth of the stated proposition must constitute the sole determiner of the child's response. Warren et al. (1991) also describe the tendency of a child to give an affirmative answer regardless of the content of the question. Such a tendency may relate to issues of compliance, social desirability, and coping with anxiety. Yes/no questions may also prove restrictive, leading, and require additional queries. Unless asking about a specific fact (e.g., "How old are you?"), the interviewer should use other strategies that will help the child describe a situation as accurately and fully as possible (e.g., "Tell me what you do when you get the headaches" should provide more constructive information than "Are your headaches really bad?").

Double-Barreled or Compound Questions

Such questions simultaneously confront the child with two questions, often unrelated, that may require separate answers (e.g., "How do you feel about your mother and father?" "What are the advantages and disadvantages of your parents' separation?" "Did you go to the park with Uncle John and what did you do when you got there?"). Potential confusion of the child and chance for error or misinterpretation of the response seem obvious. Often, simply breaking up the question into parts will provide clarity of response.

Long, Multiple-Sectioned Questions

Avoid asking questions with multiple phrases or several parts (e.g., "Tell me about your parents and brothers and sisters"). Children may answer part of this type of question and avoid the rest or become distracted and answer incompletely. Haugaard et al. (1991) also stress the chance a child may misunderstand such questions. Rather than hearing a question as asked (e.g. "When the girl told the policeman that the neighbor had hit her, was she telling the truth?"), Haugaard et al. (1991) note that the child might easily hear and answer a completely different question (e.g., "Is it the truth that the girl told the policeman that the neighbor had hit her?").

Leading Questions

Leading or suggestive questions are formulated to direct or control a response and can be dangerous in forensic interviews. Examples of leading questions include the following:

- Hinting at the expected response: "Uncle Joe touched your bottom, didn't he?"
- Identifying the response you expect: "Don't you think your Mom is a good mother?"
- Telling the child that the interviewer has already received information from another person regarding the event or topic—this type of leading question creates pressure to conform (Garven et al., 1998): "Your sister said she went to the zoo with you that day. What do you say happened?"
- Persuading the child to agree: "You wouldn't want Mr. Jones to go to jail if he didn't hurt you, would you?"
- Assuming details not provided by the child: "That was scary, wasn't it?" "You were left alone in the car other times, right?" Garven et al. (1998) mention how introducing new information into the interview when the child has not already provided that information was a major downfall in the McMartin trial because doing so helped to contaminate the interview data.

Random Questions

Sattler (1998) compares random probing to "throwing lots of bait in a stream and hoping you will catch one fish" (p. 68). For example, if a child says she really enjoys visitation with her father, the interviewer says, "There must be something you don't like. Maybe playtime, or how your dad cooks, or when he has work to do?" Such questioning should be avoided.

Coercive Questions

This type of questioning has two potential negative outcomes in forensic interviewing. The first outcome forces the child to doubt an answer he or she has previously provided. Garven et al. (1998) refer to this questioning as the *asked and answered* technique. Children may interpret such questions as an assumption that their initial answer may have been incorrect and thus they should produce a different one (Ricci et al., 1996; e.g., "Are you sure?" and "Can't remember? Think about it and it may come back"). The second potential outcome of this questioning forces the child to take the interviewer's perspective (e.g., "Don't you agree that Mrs. Jones is a nice teacher?").

Embarrassing, Offensive, or Sharp Questions

Never word questions offensively or put the child on the defensive. Although the interviewer may have to ask about highly sensitive and personal information, ask such questions carefully and in a manner intended to minimize embarrassment (e.g., "What school subjects have been difficult for you?" is more thoughtfully phrased than "What subjects did you fail?" or "You received 10 warning slips last year, is that correct?").

Why Questions

Why questions can prove helpful and diagnostic when asked carefully (e.g., "Why do you think Daddy said that?"), but try to avoid them when they might cause children to feel defensive or guilty about their actions or behavior (e.g., "Why do you drink alcohol?" or "Why did you go to Jane's house when your Mom said no?"). Children have great sensitivity to such questions; parents ask them all the time to account for actions (e.g., "Why didn't you tell me?" "Why didn't you let me

know?" "Why do you do that?"). Often one can elicit the desired information through other forms of questioning (e.g., "When do you drink alcohol?" or "How did you end up at Jane's house that day after school?").

Speculative Questions

Questions that invite speculation ask the child to offer opinions or speculations about past events or frame the child's task during the interview as using imagination or solving a mystery. Bruck et al. (1998) refer to this technique as guided imagery or memory work. The danger of such questions involves their tendency to elicit false allegations (Garven et al., 1998; e.g., "Can we pretend what might have happened?" or "Where shall we begin to figure out what happened?").

Structuring Statements

Structuring statements guide the child and provide boundaries or limits regarding the direction of the interview. Ideally, statements take a nonsuggestive form and help in focusing the child's attention.

Early in an interview, structuring statements can provide a time limit, focus on the perceptions of the child, and acknowledge that the child can help by providing information (e.g., "I would like to talk with you for about an hour. Perhaps we could start with your telling me the reason you have come to see me today?"). During an interview, the following statements provide a focus on time, place, and/or situation and may elicit information not previously mentioned: "You said that your Mom was really mean to you. Could you tell me more about how she was mean?" At the end of an interview, structuring statements can provide an opportunity for the child to express any further thoughts or information (e.g., "We have about 5 minutes left together. Is there anything else you would like to talk about?").

Effective Use of Prompts and Probes

The interviewer may find that using only open-ended questions may provide incomplete, poorly organized, ambiguous, inadequate, inconsistent, or limited responses from the child. In these circumstances, effective probing can prove the key to a successful interview (Sattler, 1998). Lamb et al. (1995) warn, "Whenever it is necessary to use questions that focus the child's attention on certain events, people, or places, however, they should be followed by ('paired with') open-ended questions designed to elicit free narratives about the topic" (p. 442). For example, "Did anything happen when you were waiting for the school bus?" can be followed by "Tell me everything that happened there." Lamb et al. (1995) stress that such an approach decreases the children's reliance on recognition memory (and thus decreases errors of commission) and emphasizes free recall memory (and thus emphasizes errors of omission), making credible children less subject to facing subsequent impeachment of their testimony.

Elaboration

This probe helps to elicit additional information. Lamb et al. (1995) encourage reference to salient components of the child's statements (e.g., "Earlier you said Johnny told you he had a gun. Tell me everything you remember about what he told you"). Similarly, Walker (1993) emphasizes avoiding ambiguous referential expressions (e.g., "Do you remember that?" or "Is that all?"). Instead, Walker advises using more specific statements.

Clarification

This type of probe can help when the child's response seems confusing or puzzling (e.g., the interviewer might repeat a word used by the child: "Horrible? Tell me about how she is horrible"). When asking the child to clarify a fact, Walker (1993) warns of presenting more than one preposition but asking for only one answer. For example, if the child answers "Yes" to the probe: "You said you saw Jim with your sister, is that right?" Walker (1993) wonders if the child's "Yes" means, "Yes, that's what I said," "Yes, that's what I saw," or both. When clarifying number or frequency of events, often important in sexual abuse cases, the interviewer should avoid a yes/no answer. Lamb et al. (1995) suggest not asking "How many times?" but "Did X happen one time or more than one time?" and then probe by using location cues or references to the first time or the last time.

Repetition

Repetition will prove useful when the child has not answered the question. The interviewer can restate the question in the same words or with slight modification. Bernet (1997) states that repeating back the child's account helps determine consistency. Ricci et al. (1996) and Warren et al. (1991), however, suggest using this prompting carefully; children are prone to change more of their answers upon the second questioning, and the amount of correct information recalled does not always increase. A less threatening approach should help the child answer more clearly. For example, if the interviewer asks, "What games do you like to play with Peggy?" and the child responds, "I like lots of games," the interviewer may repeat, "What are the names of some of the games you like to play with Peggy?"

Challenging

Challenging questions help to clarify incongruent statements. By tactfully exploring inconsistencies, contradictions, or omissions, the interviewer may elicit more complete information, obtain additional facts, or give the child the opportunity to elaborate and clarify statements. For example, "Before you said you were at the park with Jane; now you stated you were in the kitchen. Can you help me understand?" Lamb et al. (1995) suggest feigning confusion as a technique: "I'm confused. You said you hated to visit your Dad, but then you said you wanted to live with him. Would you tell me more?" Never use challenging statements to chastise, judge, or threaten the child.

Silence

Silence may allow the child time to reflect or think and expresses that the interviewer has an interest in waiting for the child's thoughts. A child's pause may mean that the child has finished giving information, needs time to reflect or recall, senses he or she has been misunderstood, recognizes the interviewer has touched on a sensitive area, or doesn't know what else to say. A potential pitfall of silence might include increasing the child's anxiety, especially if resistance to speaking about the topic at hand exists. Statements that might help the child include "Do you want to sit and think for a moment?" "Can you help me understand why school is so difficult to talk about?" "I wonder what you are feeling now?" "Should we talk about Uncle Jack now or come back to him later?"

Neutral Phrases

Neutral statements may help to encourage the child to talk or to let the child know that it is all right to continue. An example of a verbal interchange using this technique would be:

> Child: "Sometimes I get so mad."
> Interviewer: "Uh huh."
> Child: "I get so mad I want to tell."
> Interviewer: "I see."
> Child: "But I don't know if I should."
> Interviewer: "Should? Go on. . . ."

Neutral phrases should be spoken in a supportive, gentle tone and never be coercive in manner. The interviewer's body language, as well as words, should remain neutral. He or she should appear calm and relaxed and should not physically encroach upon the child.

Reflective Statements

Reflection and paraphrasing provide feedback, let the child know you understand, and assist the child to verbalize more clearly. For example:

> Child: "It was just too scary. And, like, it didn't make sense. Everybody said she was real nice, and my parents like her. It was just me and her. They'd think I was lying and made it up 'cause I told them before I didn't want to go."
> Interviewer: "So you felt no one would believe you."

Although reflective statements can paraphrase or echo the child's utterances, restatements (as in the above example) can also use the interviewer's own words. Reflection can also summarize nonverbal behavior, such as "You clench your fists when you talk about the accident." or "You just started to cry." The interviewer should use reflection carefully and not so frequently that the child feels mimicked or the flow of conversation interrupted.

Periodic Summaries

Summarization assists the interviewer in several ways, but it is primarily used as a means to check accuracy and to sum up a topic. Lamb et al. (1995) also point out that summaries can help refocus attention on topics or events mentioned previously in the interview (e.g., "Let me see if I understand correctly what you saw when the car crashed into the tree"). Summaries can also help check the child's comprehension of what the interviewer is conveying (e.g., "Can you tell me what I just said about your school work?").

CHILDREN'S SUGGESTIBILITY

The issue of suggestibility holds great concern for the forensic interviewer. The emphasis in the courtroom will focus on the veracity and reliability of the child's statements and, concurrently, on the credibility of the interviewer. "The literature's overemphasis on suggestibility can give the mistaken impression that children are inherently unreliable" (Marxsen et al., 1995, p. 451). Children seem particularly vulnerable to lying or having false memories in the case of what Marxsen et al. (1995) refer to as latticed allegations, where multiple victims, perpetrators, and/or interviews exist. Children may also have increased susceptibility when there are multiple episodes or events to recall.

Suggestive statements or questions do not necessarily render the child's entire recall invalid. However, suggestion will be minimized if (a) the interviewer waits until the end of the interview, (b) the suggestion is limited (i.e., "Did anything ever happen to your pee-pee?" versus "Did Grandpa ever put anything in your pee-pee?"), and (c) a positive response to a suggestive prompt is followed by pairing it with an open-ended prompt (Lamb et al., 1995).

Ceci and Bruck (1993) warn that young children can provide much information of forensic relevance, if one knows "the circumstances under which the initial report of concern was made, how many times the child was questioned, the hypotheses of the interviewers who questioned the child, the kinds of questions the child was asked, and the consistency of the child's report over a period of time" (p. 433).

One should generally avoid certain techniques with a child in an interview that has any psycholegal implications. These techniques include hypnosis, Amytal interviews, facilitated communication, guided imagery to enhance memory, and rewards or negative reinforcement (Bernet, 1997).

CONCLUSION

The legal system has challenged mental health professionals to justify the reliability and validity of children's statements and beliefs. Such professionals have a responsibility to educate others and participate in research on developmental issues regarding children's abilities and competence in forensic contexts. "We cannot continue holding children to a higher standard than adult witnesses" (Lamb et al., 1995, p. 445).

Effective forensic or investigative interviewing of children requires skill and care but is not impossible (Marxsen et al., 1995). The interviewer who seeks appropriate training and supervision; conducts a sensitive, developmentally oriented interview; and documents findings and conclusions in a logical, realistic manner will provide a great service to those children participating in forensic assessment.

References

Bernet, W. (1997). Practice parameters for the forensic evaluation of children and adolescents who may have been sexually abused. *Journal of the American Academy of Child & Adolescent Psychiatry, 36,* 423–442.

Borum, R., & Otto, R. (2000). Advances in forensic assessment and treatment: An overview and introduction to the special issue. *Law & Human Behavior, 24,* 1–7.

Bruck, M., Ceci, S. J., & Hembrooke, H. (1998). Reliability and credibility of young children's reports: From research to policy and practices. *American Psychologist, 53,* 136–151.

Carter, C. A., Bottoms, B. L., & Levine, M. (1996). Linguistic and socioemotional influences on the accuracy of children's reports. *Law & Human Behavior, 20,* 335–358.

Cashmere, J., & Bussey, K. (1996). Judicial perceptions of child witness competence. *Law & Human Behavior, 20,* 313–334.

Ceci, S. J., & Bruck, M. (1993). Suggestibility of the child witness: A historical review and synthesis. *Psychological Bulletin, 113,* 403–439.

Garven, S., Wood, J. M., Malpass, R. S., & Shaw, J. S. (1998). More than suggestion: The effect of interviewing techniques fro the McMartin preschool case. *Journal of Applied Psychology, 83,* 347–359.

Goodman, G. S., Levine, M., Melton, G. B., & Ogden, D. W. (1991). Child witnesses and the confrontation clause. *Law & Human Behavior, 15,* 13–29.

Greenberg, S. A., & Shuman, D. W. (1997). Irreconcilable conflict between therapeutic and forensic roles. *Professional Psychology: Research & Practice, 28,* 50–57.

Haugaard, J. L. (1993). Young children's classification of the corroboration of a false statement as the truth or a lie. *Law & Human Behavior, 17,* 645–659.

Haugaard, J. L., Reppucci, N. D., Laird, J., & Nauful, T. (1991). Children's definitions of the truth and their competency as witnesses in legal proceedings. *Law & Human Behavior, 15,* 253–271.

Heilbrun, K. (1992). The role of psychological testing in forensic assessment. *Law & Human Behavior, 16,* 257–272.

Heilbrun, K., Hawk, G., & Tate, D. C. (1996). Juvenile competence to stand trial: Research issues in practice. *Law & Human Behavior, 20,* 573–578.

Lamb, M. E., Sternberg, K. J., & Esplin, P. W. (1995). Making children into competent witnesses: Reactions to the amicus brief in re Michaels. *Psychology, Public Policy, & Law, 1,* 438–449.

Marxsen, D., Yuille, J. C., & Nisbet, M. (1995). The complexities of eliciting and assessing children's statements. *Psychology, Public Policy, & Law, 1,* 450–460.

Montoya, J. (1995). Lessons from Akiki and Michaels on shielding child witnesses. *Psychology, Public Policy, & Law, 1,* 340–369.

Nicholson, R. A., & Norwood, S. (2000). The quality of forensic psychological assessment, reports, and testimony: Acknowledging the gap between promise and practice. *Law & Human Behavior, 24,* 9–44.

Nightingale, N. N. (1993). Juror reactions to child victim witnesses. *Law & Human Behavior, 17,* 679–694.

Peterson, C., Dowden, C., & Tobin, J. (1999). Interviewing preschoolers: Comparisons of yes/ no and wh-questions. *Law & Human Behavior, 23,* 539–555.

Ricci, C. M., Beal, C. R., & Dekle, D. J. (1996). The effect of parent versus unfamiliar interviewers on children's eyewitness memory and identification accuracy. *Law & Human Behavior, 20,* 483–499.

Sattler, J. M. (1998). *Clinical and forensic interviewing of children and families.* San Diego: Author.

Scott, E. S., Reppucci, N. D., & Woolard, J. L. (1995). Evaluating adolescent decision making in legal contexts. *Law & Human Behavior, 19,* 221–244.

Walker, A. G. (1993). Questioning young children in court. *Law & Human Behavior, 17,* 59–81.

Warren, A., Hulse-Trotter, K., & Tubbs, E. C. (1991). Inducing resistance to suggestibility in children. *Law & Human Behavior, 15,* 273–285.

9

Assessing Child Sexual Abuse Allegations in a Legal Context

Kathryn Kuehnle
Steven N. Sparta

Because child sexual abuse allegations occur in a variety of psycholegal contexts, considering each case according to the appropriate legal standards for the respective jurisdiction becomes critically important. Mental health opinion may arise in many different psycholegal contexts, including but not limited to child custody evaluations in a family court, child protection proceedings in a family or juvenile court, personal injury cases in civil proceedings, and criminal prosecution or defense. Few areas of psychological evaluation involve such a variety of complex evaluation issues and potentially serious consequences for error. This chapter reviews issues critical to the assessment of alleged child sexual abuse victims and, when possible, offers empirically supported procedures rather than subjective opinions.

Evaluators should never assume cause-and-effect associations between a single aspect of behavior and the occurrence or nonoccurrence of sexual abuse, or rely on subjective assessment of the child's credibility. Equally concerning are situations when evaluators offer opinions about whether abuse did or did not occur based on the

presence or absence of a constellation of behaviors or syndrome believed to indicate sexual abuse has occurred. Melton and Limber (1989) cautioned professionals against misapplication of presumed syndrome evidence as a basis for making ultimate conclusions of abuse by specific individuals. They also advised professionals to carefully distinguish postadjudication assessments from those when court has not yet determined the standing of an allegation.

Courts have increasingly sought out mental health consultations when contradictory data involving an allegation exist and no judicial determination has yet issued. The evaluator's findings can potentially have great influence upon the legal outcome. Professional practice and ethical standards require that evaluators not exceed the limits of their expertise and form opinions based on proven methods that meet general acceptance in the scientific community. Fisher and Whiting (1998) note the need to limit conclusions in legal proceedings when the questions exceed what one can reasonably answer. In the context of child sexual abuse allegations, highly publicized convictions have faced reversal by state supreme courts based on the failure of psychological expert testimony to meet standards (e.g., *Bussey v. Commonwealth*, 1984; *State of New Jersey v. Margaret Kelly Michaels*, 1993).

The approach of the mental health professional should model objectivity and impartiality, ever mindful of the seriousness of the issues potentially affecting the child's welfare, but never abandoning the ethical requirement that he or she not exceed the limits of what the available data can reasonably support. Kuehnle (1998) proposed a scientist–practitioner model to provide evaluators a framework for utilizing empirically derived information, including base rates of behavior for understanding differences between abused and non-sexually abused children. Selection of sound psychometric or other assessment techniques is necessary, but alone insufficient, to adequately assess child sexual abuse allegations.

DEFINITIONS AND TERMINOLOGY

Definitions of child sexual abuse differ within and between state statutes and the professional literature; however, both typically address factors of intent and age differential between perpetrator and victim.

Legal and Psychological Definitions

Illegal sexual interactions, for which children do not have the maturity to provide consent, include activities of contact and noncontact, such as fondling of genital areas, oral sex, intercourse, exposure to indecent acts, sexual rituals, or involvement in child pornography. The laws of all states designate children as incompetent to consent to sexual activity with an adult, with most states defining the age of majority at 18 years (Myers, 1997). Some states have specific child sexual abuse statutes, whereas others address the issue through already existing penal code sections dealing with rape, incest, and sexual battery. Whereas the professional literature recognizes the possibility of child sexual abuse as sex forced by one child on another or when the children differ in age by at least 3 years,

the majority of states do not address child-on-child sexual abuse through specific child sexual abuse statutes.

Terminology and the Incidence of Child Sexual Abuse

Some confusion surrounds the terminology (e.g., allegations vs. reports vs. founded or substantiated reports vs. unfounded or unsubstantiated reports) used by child welfare agencies and researchers. For example, allegations constitute accusations that may or may not come to the attention of state authorities, and fall into categories along a continuum of true and false claims. Thoennes and Tjaden (1990) conducted the largest study (N = 9,000) of sexual abuse allegations in contested child custody cases and found 2% involved sexual abuse allegations. Of the 129 cases for which a determination of the veracity of the allegation was available, 58% were substantiated as involving child sexual abuse, 33% were unsubstantiated and closed with no finding of sexual abuse, and 17% remained undetermined.

Reports of unsubstantiated sexual abuse do not equate to false allegations, and estimates of the latter are difficult to determine precisely. Some research findings estimate the rate of false allegations ranges from 6% to 8% (Faller, 1991; D. Jones & McGraw, 1987), whereas other experts suggest such estimates to fall misleadingly low (Ceci & Bruck, 1995). When criteria for false allegations are broadened to include not only intentional lying but also suggestive questioning, estimates range from 23% to 35% (Poole & Lindsay, 1997).

In contrast to allegations, reports constitute the actual number of cases reported to state child welfare agencies; multiple reports may occur regarding the same child. Annually, authorities receive over three million reports of child maltreatment (i.e., sexual, physical, emotional abuse, and neglect) in the United States. Approximately one million of these reports ultimately become substantiated, and 12% of these substantiated reports involve child sexual abuse (U.S. Department of Health and Human Services, 2000; Wang & Harding, 1999). As with all crime, these annual incidence reports underrepresent the actual numbers of children who experience sexual abuse.

DOWNWARD TREND OF CHILD SEXUAL ABUSE INCIDENCE FIGURES

An analysis of maltreatment cases from the 1991 to 1998 national incidence data reflect a 26% decline in child sexual abuse reports and a 31% decline in substantiated child sexual abuse (L. Jones & Finkelhor, 2001). From 1992 to 2000, the number of substantiated child sexual abuse cases declined 40% (Finkelhor & Jones, 2004). Although not universal, this 8-year decline has occurred in a majority of states. Debate has not resolved whether the statistics reflect, among other factors, an actual decline, a change in reporters' behavior, a change in investigators' behavior, or policy and program changes in child protection agencies.

National incidence data indicate that multiple factors may contribute to this downward trend and that one of these factors involves a true decline in the occurrence in child sexual abuse. Finkelhor and Jones (2004) noted that a decline in sexual abuse would reasonably precede and exceed a decline in other forms of child maltreatment, because for the past two decades greater attention has been focused on child sexual abuse compared to other forms of maltreatment. However, the U.S. Department of Health and Human Services (2000) incidence figures, which show that only 12% of the one million substantiated cases reported to child protection services involved child sexual abuse, appear to underestimate child sexual abuse by comparison to the prevalence estimates based on retrospective research (Finkelhor, 1994). These statistics suggest that although the occurrence of child sexual abuse may be declining, it remains underreported to child welfare agencies.

Deliberations for the Evaluator

Whether the base rate for substantiated or unsubstantiated child sexual abuse is high or low, such figures prove nothing relevant to an individual case before the evaluator. The objective evaluators must consider multiple hypotheses, frequently challenging their tentative conclusions until a reasonably supported opinion is justified.

EXAMINING CHILD SEXUAL ABUSE ALLEGATIONS

Violence, substance abuse, poverty, and single-parent status comprise some of the risk factors associated with a child's vulnerability for sexual abuse (Sedlak & Broadhurst, 1996). Vulnerability for sexual abuse can include early sexual maturation in girls (Fergusson & Mullen, 1999) and emotional and physical disabilities (Sobsey, Randall, & Parrila, 1997; Sullivan & Knutson, 1998). Several studies report greater incidence of physical abuse, sexual abuse, or both in families where spouse abuse exists (Rumm, Cummings, Krause, Bell, & Rivara, 2000; Straus, Gelles, & Steinmetz, 1980). The studies of associated risk factors illustrate the importance for conducting multimodal objective assessments open to considering various hypotheses, such as those listed below (Kuehnle, 1996):

Actions and Cognitions Associated With Inaccurate and Accurate Allegations

INACCURATE
- The child is credible but has misperceived an innocent interaction
- The parent has misperceived an innocent interaction
- The child has been unintentionally contaminated by an authority figure or caretaker's belief or perception
- The child has been intentionally manipulated into believing he or she has been abused
- The child has been pressured by an authority figure into making a false allegation of abuse
- The child makes a false allegation for reasons of self-aggrandizement or revenge

ACCURATE
- The child is credible and accurate
- The child does not have the verbal skills to provide a credible description of the abuse
- Due to fear, the child will not disclose the abuse
- Due to misguided loyalty, the child will not disclose the abuse

Legal Aspects

As stated in the introduction to this chapter, child sexual abuse litigation can begin in a variety of venues, each with different standards of proof and rules of court. The criminal court exists to punish the guilty and requires the highest standard (i.e., beyond reasonable doubt). Civil courts' purposes vary (e.g., best interests, protection, damages) and generally require a lesser burden of proof. Depending on the type of proceeding, some states require evaluators to comport with explicit rules for how the evaluation is conducted. Forensic evaluators must maintain current awareness of these state requirements, which vary across legal venues. For example, when conducting a child custody evaluation involving child sexual abuse allegations in California, the evaluator must comply with California Rule of Court 5.220 (2005) and California Family Code, Section 3118 (2004), which address, among other criteria, ethical, methodological, and procedural requirements.

Over the past decade, research on the relationship between child development and children's reliability in child sexual abuse cases has been driven by issues raised in a number of legal cases receiving high media attention (e.g., *State v. Buckey*, 1990; the McMartin preschool case in Garven, Wood, Malpass, & Shaw, 1998). Several appellate courts have overturned the convictions of persons convicted of child sexual abuse, because evidence came largely from the testimony of children whose reliability was deemed compromised by suggestive interview techniques and improper expert testimony admitted at trial (e.g., *State v. Michaels*, 1993). Such cases reversed by appellate court ruling highlight the need for forensic evaluators to remain within the boundaries of their competence and to reject the role of evaluator in child sexual abuse cases unless this area falls within the purview of their expertise.

Deliberations for the Evaluator

Court-ordered evaluations or stipulated agreements (by attorneys) for evaluation often pose referral questions in a dichotomous fashion (e.g., "Is the mother or the father telling the truth regarding their contradictory allegations?"). Separate from the question of whether the psychological evaluation alone can answer such a question, multiple relevant findings may provide partial support for different elements of each parent's perceptions,

which the evaluator must articulate for the court (see Drozd & Olesen, 2004). Evaluation results should clarify the nature and the meaning of the allegation and provide data addressing the veracity of the allegation. However, the evaluator should not answer the dichotomous ultimate legal question of whether an event(s) of child sexual abuse occurred.

LINKS OF PSYCHOLOGICAL SYMPTOMS AND SEXUALIZED BEHAVIORS WITH CHILD SEXUAL ABUSE

Child sexual abuse is not a diagnosis, but rather a life event or series of events that may result in a broad array of behaviors. Such abuse will affect each child in a very different way, and many individual or situational factors aggravate or moderate the effects of the abuse on the child. Some children show more resilience than others, and all process the meaning of the experience differently. External variables can influence the child's reaction, as well, including the family's response, the response of authorities, the identity of the perpetrator, and the characteristics of the sexual abuse.

Psychological Symptoms and the Link to Child Sexual Abuse

Children who experience sexual abuse may meet the threshold criteria for a variety of possible diagnoses listed in the *Diagnostic and Statistical Manual of Mental Disorders*, including mood disorders, anxiety disorders, and dissociative disorders. Because sexual abuse does not produce a single consistent set of symptoms, forensic evaluators should never assume that abuse did or did not occur based solely on a comparison of observed symptoms. When one examines base rates of presumably non-sexually abused children's problem behaviors, high percentages of preschool and school-age children from the general population demonstrate problem behaviors, including nightmares, sudden changes of mood, poor concentration, fearfulness, disobedience, and temper tantrums (Achenbach, 1991). Such behaviors, at times, have inappropriately led some clinicians to inappropriate conclusions regarding whether a specific child has experienced sexual abuse.

Children's immediate and long-term responses to sexual abuse range from neutral to very negative (Feliti, 1991; Feliti et al., 2001; Freidrich, Urquiza, & Beilke, 1986; Mannarino & Cohen, 1996). Kendall-Tackett, Williams, and Finkelhor (1993) reviewed 45 studies of child sexual abuse and found that the percentage of asymptomatic sexually abused children ranged from 21% to 49%. In the same review of studies, no single symptom was displayed by the majority of sexually abused children, and abused children showed no more symptoms than children receiving mental health services for problems unrelated to sexual abuse. However, many sexually abused children share a variety of characteristics with traumatized children, including dissociative disorders. The incidence of posttraumatic stress disorder among sexually abused children approximates the rates shown by children admitted for psychiatric hospitalization or encountering physical abuse (Deblinger, McLeer, Atkins, Ralphe, & Foa, 1989). When children experience multiple forms of maltreatment, they have an increased risk of long-term psychological problems (Shipman, Rossman, & West, 1999). Evaluators should not assume that sexual abuse by other children is benign, as some research shows children sexually abused by other children exhibit emotional and behavioral problems similar to the symptoms of children abused by adults (Shaw, Lewis, Loeb, Rosado, & Rodriguez, 2000).

Sexualized Behaviors and the Link to Child Sexual Abuse

Unusually high levels of sexualized behavior in children are associated with more intrusive sexual abuse, force of threats of harm, and a greater number of abusers (Freidrich et al., 1992). Sexual arousal during children's sexual abuse, the perpetrator's use of sadism during the abuse, and a history of physical or emotional abuse also have been found to be associated with children's initiation of developmentally abnormal sexual acts with others (Hall, Mathews, & Pearce, 1998).

Sexualized behavior problems are not specific to children who have experienced sexual abuse. Such problems can be learned in contexts other than through exploitation, including observation of sexual behaviors within the home. Friedrich

(1998) collected normative data regarding the sexualized behavior for more than 2,000 children. He found that sexual abuse was the most frequently associated factor with children's sexual acting out, sexually precocious behavior, or both. His research further showed that family sexuality, including repeated visual exposure to sexual material and activity, constituted the second most frequently associated factor.

Although sexually abused or exposed children may demonstrate developmentally aberrant sexual behaviors (e.g., performing fellatio, cunnilingus), some children with behavior problems or disorders (e.g., oppositional defiant and conduct disorders) also may demonstrate developmentally aberrant sexual behaviors (Friedrich, Grambsch, Broughton, Kuiper, & Beilke, 1991). Although sexual and other behavioral problems are not specific to children's sexual abuse, such problems could reflect psychological disruptions of a sexually abused child.

Regarding developmentally typical sexual behaviors in children, sexual play may begin as early as age 2 but typically begins between 4 and 7 years of age (Kelly and Byrne, 1992). The majority of preschool teachers observe children in their classrooms to occasionally masturbate and engage in sexual games (Gunderson, Melas, & Skar, 1981). Sexual behaviors commonly observed by preschool teachers include limited looking at and touching by preschoolers of each other's genitals, simulated sexual intercourse, and drawing genitalia. However, rarely do such teachers observe the insertion of anything into another child or engaging in oral–genital contact (Davies, Glaser, & Kossoff, 2000).

Deliberations for the Evaluator

One common error of evaluators involves confusing correlation with causation. In such cases, the evaluator may observe psychological symptoms during the examination and conclude that such symptoms necessarily reflect a causal relationship to a contested psycholegal event. For example, the examined child who exhibits anxiety in the context of a civil personal injury case is presumed to be symptomatic because of a prior legally contested event (e.g., automobile accident, dog bite, or sexual victimization). The examiner must consider whether such anxiety may have existed prior to the psycholegal event (e.g., the child was the victim of prior physical abuse), whether the anxiety arises as the result of a different concurrent situation (e.g., the parents involvement in a violent divorce coinciding with the evaluation), or whether the child could have developed symptoms of anxiety independent of the contested event. Similarly, evaluators assessing allegations of child sexual abuse must consider whether some behavior problems constitute a part of normal children's development independent of abuse or that identified psychological conditions may result from causes other than abuse. Some sexually abused children may exhibit acute, chronic, or delayed-onset symptoms of psychological trauma, of different intensity or frequency (Sparta, 2003).

One of the most important findings from research addressing the effects of child sexual abuse is that no single sign or symptom characterizes the majority of abused children, a finding well supported from the past 20 years of research (Hagen, 2003). Additionally, a significant percentage of children who experience sexual abuse will not exhibit any symptoms.

Evaluation of children demands sensitive and patient interviewing, proceeding according to the child's psychological ability to divulge potentially difficult material. The evaluator should remain aware of the possible existence of overt threats or more subtle forms of emotional coercion by a perpetrator. Scheduling a sufficient period of time will permit the child to relate potentially distressing experiences at a psychologically appropriate pace. Evaluators should inquire about exposure of sexualized material within the home, including unmonitored access to cable television, printed materials, pornographic Web sites, and sexual behavior of older siblings or parents and their companions. Children may experience shame or embarrassment, and evaluators need to balance ethical considerations of doing no harm with the need to evaluate important issues potentially affecting the child's life. Grantz and Orsillo (2003) reviewed the extant literature on child sexual abuse and concluded that no accurate and ethical way exists to testify that sexual abuse has occurred given a child's postabuse functioning. Evaluations should incorporate knowledge of these findings to avoid misleading the court, avoid treating unjustly those falsely accused, and prevent risk to future victims by causing premature termination of a case on account of invalid testimony.

CHILDREN'S MEMORY AND LEGAL COMPETENCY

Allegations of sexual abuse often involve questions about the accuracy of the alleged victim's memory for the events of interest. Alleged perpetrators who call the accusations false may cite distortion in children's reports due to presumed developmental incompetence or, as described in the next section, contamination by any number of suggestive interview techniques. Those advocating for protection of a child may argue that the child's accurate accounts face undermining by selective borrowing from the psychological literature, a prejudicial discounting of the child's allegations, or both, simply because they came from a child.

Development of Memory

Often, parents, attorneys and the court may erroneously regard memory retrieval as similar to the process of playing back audio-recorded information. The psychological and neuroscience literature describes memory processes as much more complex, subject to a variety of potential influences. Although some form of immature memory can exist in utero, such as the sound of a mother's voice (DeCasper, Lecanuet, Busnel, Granier-Deferre, & Maugeais, 1994), little scientific support suggests that memories in utero or from the first 2 years of life can be consciously recollected later in childhood or adulthood as experiences that happened to oneself. However, some causally organized event sequences can be remembered by 11- and 12-month-old infants for up to 3 months (Howe & Courage, 1997). Unique, distinctive, and personally consequential experiences, occurring during the early preschool years, which could include sexual abuse experiences, can be remembered for periods of up to 6 years during childhood (Conway, 1996; Fivush & Schwartzmueller, 1998). When not influenced by inaccurate pre- and postevent suggestions, preschool-age (i.e., 3–6 years) and school-age (i.e., 7–12 years) children's recall of past events generally proves accurate. When compared to school-age children, preschool-age children may be less consistent, although not less accurate, in what they report when questioned about specific events. Authorities disagree about whether processing of memories for traumatic events occurs in a substantially different way than for nontraumatic events (Alpert, 1995; Hembrooke & Ceci, 1995). Some researchers hypothesize that unintegrated traumatic memories become compartmentalized, consisting mainly of sensory perceptions and affective states (Van der Kolk & Fisler, 1995).

Legal Definition of the Child's Competence to Testify

Professional judgments about a child's memory not only become relevant for interpretation of evaluation data, but also prove helpful in terms of informing the legal decision maker about the child's competence to provide reliable information. Many states have adopted Rule 601 of the *Federal Rules of Evidence* (2004), which accords to children the same presumptive competence to testify as other witnesses. Proper understanding, rather than age, forms the basis of competency in a number of cases, beginning with the case of *Wheeler v. United States* (1895). In this case, the U.S. Supreme Court held that a child of any age has the competence to testify providing he or she can appreciate the difference between truth and falsehoods, understand the obligation to tell the truth, accurately perceive and recall the events witnessed, and relate facts accurately (Myers, 1997).

Deliberations for the Evaluator

Evaluators need to carefully consider variable reporting by children within a developmental context before drawing conclusions about the accuracy or inaccuracy of a child's report. Furthermore, evaluators should have knowledge of the trauma literature in order to facilitate appropriate assessment techniques and interpretations. When confronted with trauma-related questioning, children who have experienced sexual abuse may find themselves unable to process the information and may employ defense mechanisms (e.g., dissociation), which make their reporting and evaluation more difficult.

CHILDREN'S SUGGESTIBILITY AND VULNERABILITY TO MANIPULATION

All child sexual abuse evaluations should consider the possibility of various contamination factors in accounting for children's reports. One notable source of possible error concerns suggestibility, particularly in preschool-age children. Suggestibility generally refers to errors that arise when children are exposed to false information or to social pressures that encourage particular types of answers (Ceci & Bruck, 1993).

Internal Factors Associated With Children's Suggestibility

Suggestibility increases in children younger than 5 years when the characteristics of the interviewer seem intimidating and coercive and the content of the interviews feels accusatory (e.g., referring to the suspect as a bad person and or that the suspect did bad things). Individual children's characteristics may create variability in their vulnerability to suggestibility due to a variety of reasons, including temperament, the nature and quality of secure attachment, emotional factors such as self-confidence, and language factors (Bruck, Ceci, & Melnyk, 1997; Eisen, Goodman, Qin, & Davis, 1998). Children's self-confidence relates inversely to their suggestibility (Vrij & Bush, 1998).

External Factors Associated With Children's Suggestibility

Studies show repeated presentations of misinformation about events that have never occurred can affect child's reports about allegations of mistreatment. Leichtman and Ceci (1995) reported that misleading or stereotyping information contributed to 46% of 3- to 4-year-old children giving false information after four misleading interviews over a 10-week period. However, that study did not involve a child's physical touch by an adult. In studies involving physical touch, repeated presentation of misinformation of events involving physical examination by an adult resulted in significant findings. In one study (Bruck, Ceci, Francouer, & Barr, 1995), 5-year-old children's visits to the doctor's office involved getting an injection: Following three misleading interviews, 32% of children provided misleading information about who gave them the shot. Three- to six-year-old children in a different study were interviewed immediately after a pediatric exam and at 1 week and 3 weeks postexam. The younger the children, the higher the number of omissions for factual details to open-ended questions and the poorer their resistance to misleading questions after a short time delay (Baker-Ward, Gordon, Ornstein, Larus, & Clubb, 1993). Still more relevant to alleged sexual abuse, some studies have examined misinformation effects involving genital exams. Eisen et al. (1998) examined different age groups of hospitalized children involving genital examination, where the youngest age group (i.e., 3–5 years) had the greatest number of errors (20%) associated with abuse-related questions. This chapter does not reflect the comprehensiveness of the subject, but other findings relevant to assessing allegations of sexual abuse show that multiple suggestive techniques can affect children's reports, including peer pressure, selective reinforcement, repeated questions, and stereotypes (Clarke-Stewart, Thompson, & Lepore, 1989; Scullin & Ceci, 2001). Source misattribution constitutes a form of memory contamination and occurs when children become confused in distinguishing whether they performed an activity, heard about it, or imagined performing the activity (Leichtman & Ceci, 1995). For example, if a young child repeatedly hears questions and suggestions regarding whether he or she experienced a hurtful event (e.g., getting one's finger caught in a mousetrap), the child may develop a memory of physically experiencing the event when in reality the child has only heard and thought about experiencing the target event. The form of questioning can also compromise children's reports. For example, repeated reliance on closed-ended questions (Poole & White, 1993) or limiting interviews to yes/no questions followed by a request to describe only what was elicited from the original yes/no inquiry (Peterson & Briggs, 1997) may elicit inaccurate disclosures. Furthermore, an interview style that puts pressure on children for specific answers may produce inaccurate information.

Deliberations for the Evaluator

Evaluators should consider a variety of hypotheses to account for data in cases of alleged child sexual abuse, particularly when forensic cases involve highly contested allegations not yet adjudicated. Evaluators should gather data on the number of interviews the alleged child victim has experienced and the skill level of the individuals who conducted the prior interviews. Repeated interviews, the emotional tone of the interviewer, and potential confirmatory bias whereby the interviewer influences the process to obtain data to confirm already-held beliefs include only a few of the possible sources of contamination for accurate formulations. Evaluators and interviewers who do not have in-depth training in the area of child sexual abuse should have carefully supervised experience. Evaluators should review all available data, assertively ask for more information, check dates and facts, state alternative hypotheses, and examine the evidence for each.

REASONS SEXUALLY ABUSED CHILDREN FAIL TO REPORT ABUSE

In forensic cases involving disputed allegations among different parties, the evaluator should remain alert to possible influence of the child by any or all of the adult litigants. The evaluator should at least consider the competing motives of the different parties. Evaluators should take care not to reach conclusions prematurely, should maintain an objective and flexible approach, and should take guidance as much as possible from the weight of relevant and objective data. High-risk situations include those where the child has an established psychological attachment to both parents, and the child perceives serious detrimental consequences to some or all of the family as a result of disclosure.

Protection of the Family and Parent

Evaluation referrals can involve intrafamily allegations where authorities have ordered one parent removed from the home and the nonoffending parent resists believing the sexual abuse allegation. Children with supportive nonoffending caretakers will more likely disclose their abuse than children with unsupportive caretakers (Elliot & Briere, 1994). When the child becomes the sole focus of information and the consequences of the child's report will have significant impact on the entire family, the child may suffer a significant burden of responsibility. Children may feel psychological pressure to unite a divided family, reduce stress to the nonoffending parent, and otherwise act in a manner the child perceives as reducing the risk of conflict within the family.

Self-Protection and Developmental Capacity

Abused children may simply fail to disclose abuse for self-protective reasons. This may especially occur during an initial interview when the child has the least familiarity with the interviewer (Lawson & Chaffin, 1992). Other factors may influence children's reporting for social–emotional reasons. If an adult asks the child to conceal an occurrence, the child may lie about adult transactions (Bussey, 1990), with both younger and older children less likely to give accurate information if actually threatened by an adult. The evaluator should also consider the threats to other family members, not only to the child. Children with cognitive handicaps may not provide narratives judged as credible compared to children without such handicap (Elliot & Briere, 1994). Cultural factors and English learned as a second language may constitute another hindrance to the child's ability to report. When present, one should always consider such factors before prematurely rejecting the allegation.

Deliberations for the Evaluator

Evaluators should always carefully consider the children's developmental stage of functioning and the ability of the child to understand questions and temporal events and to relate past experiences in sufficient detail or accuracy. Additionally, the relationship of the child with the alleged perpetrator pre- and postallegation should be considered by the evaluator related to the child protecting the family him- or herself, or both through denying a true allegation.

SAMPLE COURT ORDERS

Mental health evaluations have use in court to the extent that they help guide decision making and address the welfare of the child. Court orders often include questions about the likelihood of whether sexual abuse has occurred and, if so, about the identity of the likely perpetrator. The evaluator can address this issue by deferring to the court on ultimate legal conclusions while providing relevant data and appropriately supported hypotheses in the report. It may assist the court if the evaluator presents a range of data that offers information toward the strength (e.g., child spontaneously discloses to a cousin) and weakness (e.g., parent has made numerous unfounded allegations regarding child maltreatment) of the allegation. Although the evaluation may assist the court in answering the ultimate issue, the evaluation may also assist the court in addressing the psychological needs of the child and how these psychological needs are best met.

Deliberations for the Evaluator

When appointed by the court, the court order should identify the mental health evaluator by formal name and specify the questions the court wants addressed in written behavioral terms. To provide the most useful information to the court, the evaluator must fully understand the court's order. Lacking the above-noted criteria, an evaluator should return the court order with a request for clarification. Evaluators should confirm that the court order has contemplated the relevant psychological issues planned for inclusion in the forensic report. A quasi-judicial immunity from lawsuits, although not from ethics or licensing board complaints, may emanate when evaluators remain within the parameters of the court's order.

BEGINNING THE EVALUATION: STRUCTURING THE FORENSIC INTERVIEW

Following a standardized evaluation procedure based upon currently accepted knowledge and practices has many advantages. Doing so minimizes the chances of omitting certain evaluation criteria from assessment. Following a protocol also permits the evaluator to make comparative judgments among different family members in the same case or across different cases. Minimal preliminary considerations include having adequate and specific training to perform the evaluation functions as specified in the referral, securing the appointment by the court or other neutral party, preserving an accurate record of the evaluation, and requesting access to other parties in addition to the alleged victim (Greenberg, Martindale, Gould, & Gould-Saltman, 2004; Jenkins & Howell, 1994). Evaluators should make requests for records or to have access to parties other than the evaluation subject, if they lack such information. When interviewing others, the evaluator should obtain an informed consent about the nature and purpose of the contact, including the limitations of confidentiality.

Most research-based guidelines and recommendations for interviewing allegedly sexually abused children form a consensus for the structure and sequence of interview components (e.g., American Professional Society on the Abuse of Children, 1997; Kuehnle, 1996). Evaluators may wish to consider the following points in conducting an evaluation of alleged child sexual abuse:

- Documenting the interview
- Developing rapport
- Assessing cognitive and language abilities: determining the ability to provide details relevant to child sexual abuse
- Assessing competence including the child's understanding of the oath to tell the truth
- Responding to inconsistency during the interview

Documenting the Interview

Evaluators may use handwritten notes, audio taping, or videotaping to preserve a record of the interview. Forensic evaluators create a record with an anticipation that it must contain sufficient detail to provide authorized others or the court with an accurate representation of what transpired during the evaluation. Handwritten notes may not allow the interviewer to fully devote attention to the child while questioning. When possible, evaluators should include verbatim quotes of the interview questions and child's responses, particularly at critical points during the sequence of verbal exchanges. Audio and video recording can provide more complete records, permit the interviewer greater attention to the child, reduce evidentiary challenges, and hold interviewers more accountable for their professional work. Ceci (2002) reported potential errors from recollections from notes as including reversals of voice, substitutions of words, and errors for the gist of the content reported.

Interviews with child caretakers represent an important source of complementary evaluation information, including reports of the child's behavior in different settings, descriptions of the child's emotions, or alterations of the child's emotional or behavioral functioning compared to baseline levels of functioning. Further, evaluators must critically evaluate various forms of convergent data, including collateral data, to support alleged verbal statements made by the target child to others. For example, research regarding a reconstructed conversation by mothers of mother–child interviews indicated that when mothers reconstructed conversations, they often proved incomplete in their disclosure of events, omitting many important details and failing to differentiate their questions from the child's responses (Bruck, Ceci, & Francouer, 1999).

Warren, Woodall, Hunt, and Perry (1996) underscore the need for interviewers to exercise extreme care. They found that experienced interviewers with an average of 16 years of experience made significant errors, including making 80% of their questions specific and 16% of their questions leading when they believed they asked primarily open-ended questions. Five minutes after the interview, they had forgotten 25% of the gist of the child's reports.

Developing Rapport

Children evaluated for sexual abuse allegations frequently show vulnerability to a number of potential influences that can compromise the accuracy or extent of their reporting. It is important for evaluators to recognize the essential element of rapport so that children can properly answer questions and provide details. Children may perceive evaluators as authority figures, increasing the risk of vulnerability to suggestion by children. Effects of authority figures include producing a differential effect on children's report of events they have experienced (Geiselman, Saywitz, & Bornstein, 1991).

It will often prove helpful to establish baseline interview data with the child by explaining ground rules for the interview and to practice on non-abuse-related questions. When introducing sexual abuse topics, the evaluator should begin with open-ended questions. Interviewers should take care not to stereotype or accuse individuals, (e.g., "Tell me about the bad man"), and one should avoid both intimidation and coercion (e.g., "You can go to the bathroom after you answer one more question"). Embedding statements in terms of expectations from psychological attachment can influence and coerce children (e.g., "Your parents believe something happened and so do I"). Similarly, pressuring a child for a different response after he or she answers the interviewer with a denial (e.g., "Think real hard about what might have happened") constitutes undue pressure. Instructing children to say "I don't know" or "I can't remember," rather than guessing, and to inform the interviewer if they don't understand or are confused by the question, will yield the most accurate data.

Assessing Cognitive and Language Abilities: Determining the Ability to Provide Details Relevant to Child Sexual Abuse

Evaluators should screen for possible developmental delay, assess for communication or language disorders, assure that interviewing occurs in the appropriate language, and approach the child, the child's family, or both in a culturally sensitive manner. Intelligence testing will not necessarily become component of every evaluation but should occur when questions about the child's ability to comprehend questions or formulate responses exist.

Children should be assessed for their ability to provide details on time, place, number of times, and intentions (Saywitz, 1995). Before 6–7 years of age, children generally cannot count abstract events and do not have discrete boundaries. Young children can have difficulty determining the sequence of events. Children can have difficulty taking another person's perspective and cannot answer questions of intention. Prior to 8 years, children can have difficulty placing things in chronological order, misinterpret legal terms, assume a familiar definition of a word is the only definition, or confuse unfamiliar words to mean something associated with a similar sounding word.

When children are asked questions difficult for their developmental capability, they may try to answer anyway, respond to a portion of the question that they think they understood, and often do not recognize their own lack of comprehension. Cross-validation of portions of reported information with established facts helps to establish validity. The interviewer can also cross-reference the child's reports with his or her own responses when asked in different ways during different times of the interview. However, the evaluator should avoid cross-referencing by repeating a question using the same language, because the children may believe, if a question is repeated, that they answered the question incorrectly the first time and then change their response.

Evaluators have a need to know details about the timing, frequency, and location of alleged events, along with precise identification of those persons discussed. To begin with, the evaluator should determine a baseline ability for the child's developmental competence to answer who, what, where, and how questions before interpreting reports by the child connected to alleged sexual abuse. The interviewer during the rapport-building stage can sample the child's baseline ability by discussing areas of interests, favored activities, friendships, or everyday routines. Saywitz (1995) developed a narrative response set called the Narrative Elaboration Technique, where children learn from the interviewer that their narrative account should include details of participants, setting, actions, conversations, and affective state.

Assessing Competence, Including the Child's Understanding of the Nature and Obligation to Tell the Truth

To assess the knowledge of truth and lies, an evaluator can ask the child to define each term and to explain the difference. To test such understandings, the evaluator can state different examples of truthful and false statements and document the child's accuracy in making correct differentiations. General competence is established by the child's ability to communicate, and the law generally recognizes a relatively easy threshold for qualification. Issues of whether the child's reports reflect coercion or suggestion constitute matters of credibility that are ultimately determined by the trier of fact (i.e., the court or jury).

Responding to Inconsistencies During the Interview

Because children show difference to adult authority figures and feel vulnerable to perceived disapproval, when the child reports inconsistent details, the evaluator should take care not to act with confrontation or displeasure. Instead, the interviewer should simply verbalize confusion and request clarification. At times, a child's experience has validity but his or her communication about it contains flaws. Should the interviewer react with confrontation or disapproval to an incorrect communication about an actual event, the child could easily interpret the interviewer's reaction as disapproval for revealing an actual act of abuse. This can contaminate all subsequent reporting despite the subsequent care of the interviewer.

Asking Forensic Questions

The initial part of the interview should rely upon open-ended questions. However, some research shows that, when asked only open-ended, non-directive questions, most young children do not disclose information about any form of touching (Keary & Fitzpatrick, 1994). Directive questions about facts elicited by the child should be constructed with care, avoiding coercion or suggestion. Suggestive and coercive questioning can occur by preceding questions with *do you remember* statements. Always use clear and developmentally appropriate language. Instead of using pronouns (e.g., him, she, we), the evaluator can minimize potential confusion by using specific names of persons and places.

Boat and Everson (1996) described a four-level conceptual framework for interviewing children. The first level involves questions about critical events or times in the child's life when the sexual abuse allegedly occurred. The second level involves questions about the suspected perpetrator. Questions about sexual activities are avoided. The third level involves general questions about different types of abuse, but without mentioning the alleged perpetrator. The fourth level involves direct questions about the alleged perpetrator, but asked with extreme caution, recognizing that these types of questions can contaminate the child's reports. It will often prove helpful to follow whatever the child volunteered independent of the interviewer's directives with "tell me more about that."

Helpful forensic questions should reflect helpful evaluation values. Berliner and Loftus (1992) caution against professional polarization because of conflicting roles and beliefs, and staying focused on the truth of what really happened. These authors also remind all evaluators to concede the possibility that in a specific case the truth of what happened may never become completely known.

Practical suggestions exist in the practice parameters of the American Academy of Child and Adolescent Psychiatry (1997), which include starting with general questions when introducing the topic of concern, proceeding as appropriate to more specific questions, and after introducing the topic of abuse, allowing the child to provide a free narrative at the child's own pace. However, none of these suggestions will prove useful if the evaluator must prematurely terminate the appointment because of insufficient time. The authors recommend that evaluators always schedule considerably longer appointment times than the 1-hour time period customarily reserved for therapy appointments, because children may require considerably more time to develop rapport or reach the stage where they feel comfortable in disclosing relevant and important data.

INDIVIDUAL EVALUATION OF THE CHILD AND FAMILY PSYCHODYNAMICS

Sometimes referral of children for individual psychological evaluation in association with forensic matters involves allegations in the context of intrafamily sexual abuse. Child custody evaluations and intrafamily incest cases comprise two common examples. Performing the evaluation without involvement of all relevant parties or at least careful attention to family psychodynamics can lead to significant distortion in the obtained data and misleading conclusions.

The Family System

Evaluators must consider the family system because the motives underlying allegations can include appropriate protection, manipulative hostility on the part of the parent or caretaker, or even the child's attempts to protect the family or injure one party. Compared to extrafamilial child sexual abuse, there can be significant overlap in symptoms exhibited by children in high-conflict child custody cases and children who have been sexually abused (McGleughlin, Meyer, & Baker, 1999). Mental health professionals assessing only the child brought by one parent must consider the potential influences upon the child prior to presenting for the interview. The child may fall under the influence of the parent waiting outside the examining room, particularly in a high-conflict divorce matter. In the matter of possible incest, the presence of the alleged perpetrator can have a significantly coercive influence upon the child.

Forensic Interviewer Versus Forensic Evaluator

Everson (1997a) proposed a distinction between the terms *forensic interviewer* and *forensic evaluator*. According to Everson, the forensic interviewer merely collects data, albeit with stringent guidelines, whereas the evaluator analyzes and integrates data from a variety of sources. According to this formulation, it becomes even more important for professionals to acknowledge the limitations of their data when interviewing a child who arrives accompanied by only one parent. In some situations, the evaluator should carefully consider whether involving the person suspected of abusing the child might cause psychologically detriment to the child. However, a multimodal and comprehensive assessment demands that evaluation of others should be at least considered. The practice guidelines of the American Professional Society on the Abuse of Children (1997) state that if an accused parent seeks to participate and no contraindications exist (e.g., a criminal investigation), then interviewing of the suspected parent should be given strong consideration.

Bow, Quinnell, Zaroff, and Assemany (2002) recommended that evaluators follow structured formats for assessing child sexual abuse, particularly in child custody disputes where only the American Psychological Association (1994) guidelines for child custody evaluations may seem to apply. These authors suggest carefully reviewing the nature, sequence, and circumstances of the allegation; interviewing the parties multiple times; collecting a thorough psychosocial history from all parties; following a comprehensive interview protocol for children; and considering different types of psychological testing with adults or children.

Fantastic, Bizarre, and Improbable Accounts of Abuse

It is especially important for forensic evaluators to strive toward careful and objective approaches toward assessing allegations of sexual abuse. Dalenberg (1996) examined disclosures of sexual abuse in children 3–17 years of age, including half the group documented as highly certainly abused (e.g., the perpetrator confessed). An overall base rate of approximately 2% of the cases of highly certain abused children provided either grossly exaggerated highly implausible or impossible events. Everson (1997b) proposed 24 explanations for fantastic elements in children's accounts, including perpetrator manipulation, traumagenic misperception or memory distortion, mastery fantasies as a coping mechanism, deceptions by the child representing a variety of needs, and external sources of confusion such as cultural factors. Kirkpatrick (1997) endorsed using the 24 explanations by Everson in cases where considerable question existed about the validity of the abuse accusation along with commentary for integrating data within a forensic context.

Assessment Tools

The variability in the temporal, relational, and behavioral aspects of child sexual abuse would make it difficult to apply a single assessment standard to the evaluation of alleged victims (Fisher & Whiting, 1998). Sequelae of sexual abuse vary by the level of cognitive and social development, the reaction of family members, and individual personality traits, making it difficult to determine a standardized assessment battery for all ages and types of alleged victims.

Sexual History Inventories, Plethysmograph, and Polygraph

Bow et al. (2002) note several challenges in assessing alleged sexual abuse, including the high degree of denial by offenders, the lack of reliable offender profiles, and the fact that many inventories that explore sexual feelings and behavior have obvious face validity. Assessment of the suspected offender may consist of sexual history or offender characteristics. Although potentially useful for other purposes, no inventory has achieved validity for proving or disproving a contested allegation of child sexual abuse. The manual of the Multiphasic Sex Inventory (Nichols & Molinder, 1990) provides this qualification. Schultz (1995) reported that Richard Gardner's Sexual Abuse Legitimacy Scale exemplified the inappropriate use of indicators to distinguish truth from fantasy in sexual abuse allegations.

The quest for alternative methods has also proven difficult with research reflecting controversy in the use of the penile plethysmograph and polygraph (Haralambie, 1999). The development of assessment guidelines becomes further complicated by their development with known sexual offenders or their focus on presentencing or treatment issues. Discussions of frequently encountered assessment tools and some of the limitations associated with their use follow.

Anatomically Detailed Dolls

The American Psychological Association (1991) adopted a formal statement on the use of anatomically detailed dolls, noting that such use may help children better communicate, especially those children who have difficulty expressing themselves verbally on sexual topics. Koocher et al. (1995) reviewed the available literature and distinguished how a clinical interview by a skilled clinician does not equate with play, and that any type of doll play alone cannot substitute for an appropriate evaluation. Evaluators should remain aware of the developmental context for children using anatomically detailed dolls, including that when most children are presented with such dolls, they explore the genitals, anuses, and breasts (Boat & Everson, 1986, 1994). The same authors reported empirical data that did not confirm that anatomically correct dolls

elicit fantasizing or sexual acting out in children. Results derived from the use of anatomical dolls should never constitute the sole basis for assessing sexual abuse. Their use represents an interview tool. No matter how explicit the sexual behavior, the use of the dolls alone cannot provide a proof of sexual abuse. Furthermore, some studies have found that assessment props such as anatomical dolls can reduce the accuracy of the children's reports (see Bruck, Ceci, Francoeur, & Renick, 1995).

Drawings

Drawings used as projective tools cannot identify sexually abused children based only on sexual symbolism. No clinical or empirical consensus exists regarding that features in drawings represent exclusive markers of sexual abuse. Attempts to standardize drawings as a projective instrument have failed to satisfy the standards required of psychometric tests (Weiner & Kuehnle, 1998). However, focused drawings may have utility as a demonstration aid. Gross and Hayne (1998) found that children who had recently experienced an event narrated significantly more information when drawing compared with peers who did not draw.

Projective Techniques

Although some forensic evaluators maintain that projective techniques have utility for detecting child sexual abuse (Oberlander, 1995), the validity of these techniques for distinguishing sexually abused from non-sexually abused children remains unestablished (Lilienfeld, Wood, & Garb, 2000).

Checklists

Standardized observation systems rather than subjective clinical observation may prove useful in collecting objective data involving parent–child interactions. Standardized behavior rating scales can provide information from family members and individuals outside the family, which can then be compared with other evaluation information. Behavior rating scales cannot be used to classify a child as sexually or not sexually abused. Furthermore, because checklist items have face validity, respondents can deny or exaggerate the presence of behaviors. This problem can occur in contested child custody conflicts involving child sexual abuse allegations.

Specialized Instruments

Two instruments particularly relevant to examining the functioning of children in alleged child sexual abuse cases include the Child Sexual Behavior Inventory and the Trauma Symptom Checklist for Children.

The Child Sexual Behavior Inventory (Friedrich, 1998), a standardized instrument normed on more than 1,000 children 2–12 years of age, includes 35 items completed by the parent or caretaker. It yields three primary scores: total score, developmentally related sexual behaviors, and sexual abuse specific items. the total score assess nine domains of sexual behavior: boundary problems, exhibitionism, gender role behavior, self-stimulation, sexual anxiety, sexual interest, sexual intrusiveness, sexual knowledge, and voyeuristic behavior. The developmentally related sexual behavior score represents sexual behaviors more common at certain ages; these sexual behaviors are viewed as more normative. Items specific to sexual abuse are associated with sexual abuse or exposure to sexual materials. Although results may reflect sexually abused children exhibiting excessive masturbation and aberrant sexual acts, such results are not specific to only sexual abuse experiences.

The Trauma Symptom Checklist for Children (Briere, 1996), a standardized instrument normed on 3,000 children 8–17 years of age, includes 54 items for completion by the child. It yields two validity scales (underresponse and hyperresponse); six clinical scales (Anxiety, Depression, Anger, Posttraumatic Stress, Dissociation); a Sexual Concerns scale; and eight critical items.

PROVIDING YOUR CONCLUSIONS TO THE COURT

The court will consider a variety of different sources of information when making ultimate legal conclusions involving child sexual abuse. Forensic mental health evaluators should not exceed the limits of reasonably supportable conclusions and should exercise caution when addressing ques-

tions about alleged abuse by specific individuals. Evaluators should reference the applicable child sexual abuse literature to support conclusions. The evaluator should maintain an objective stance and remain faithful to the available data rather than an advocate for winning a case.

Terminology

Evaluators should use terms such as *the data support* when addressing certain opinions rather than to provide definitive conclusions within their reports. The strengths and weaknesses of the data that address the allegation should be clearly delineated for the court.

Examples of report language that reflect the above include the following:

- The child has demonstrated developmentally atypical sexual behavior for a 4-year-old child. His engaging another male child at preschool in fellatio is a behavior more commonly found with preschool children who have had some exposure to sexual experience (Friedrich, 1998).
- The father's arrest for his involvement in Internet child pornography suggests a risk to the child.
- The child does not appear fearful of his father and enjoys being in his presence, despite allegations that the child has been sodomized and forced to eat feces.
- Research suggests a link between children's secure attachment (Elicker, Egland, & Sroufe, 1992) and good parent–child communication (Clarke-Stewart et al., 1989) with resistance to suggestibility.

Sbraga and O'Donohue (2003) recommend that a mental health expert refrain from providing opinions on whether or not sexual abuse did or did not occur, because the post-hoc reasoning required to reasonably substantiate such opinions does not have adequate support in the current data collection system for these evaluations. These authors further opine that valuable forensic contributions can include explaining mental health facts in an understandable way to the court, clarifying assessment data, and indicating the presence or absence of psychiatric symptoms in alleged victims. Wolfe and Legate (2003) suggest that mental health experts can potentially offer sound scientific and clinical opinion on the consistency or inconsistency of symptoms, complaints, and behavior patterns relating to child sexual abuse in order to inform the court.

Prediction or Description?

Forensic child sexual abuse evaluations often follow court orders to help determine whether a particular child was sexually abused in the past by a specific individual or whether an individual believed to have acted inappropriately with a child will reoffend in the future. As described above, the current state of knowledge may not permit the level of certainty as would ideally be helpful to the court. In a contested child custody matter where one parent has accused the other of sexually abusing their child, the court or the parents may expect the psychological evaluation to prove who is lying. Evaluators may have some ability to help the court without answering the ultimate legal question, for example, by reliably describing each person's general or specific functioning. Weiner (2003) notes that adequately interpreted information from combined evaluation sources can provide reliable and useful descriptions of the nature of people and the limitations of the data. Evaluation information about a child can include perceptions of each parent, emotional reactions to different persons in different contexts, expressed preferences, reported psychological problems, and recommendations for amelioration. Some cases may call for safeguards that minimize abuse risk to the child while avoiding unfairly stigmatizing individuals in predispositional status.

Fisher and Whiting (1998) note that several highly publicized child sexual abuse convictions were overturned by various state supreme courts on the basis of the failure of psychological expert testimony to meet legal standards for the admissibility of scientific evidence. These authors provide a variety of examples of how psychological testimony can fail to meet proven reliable methods that have received general acceptance in the scientific community (*Frye v. United States*, 1923), including the misapplication of the diagnosis of posttraumatic stress disorder as an indication of sexual abuse.

References

Achenbach, T. M. (1991). *Manual for the Child Behavior Checklist/4–18 and 1991 Profile*. Burlington: University of Vermont, Department of Psychiatry.

Alpert, J. L. (1995). Trauma, dissociation, and clinical study as a responsible beginning. *Consciousness & Cognition, 4,* 125–129.

American Academy of Child and Adolescent Psychiatry. (1997). Practice parameters for the forensic evaluation of children and adolescents who may have been physically or sexually abused. *Journal of the American Academy of Child & Adolescent Psychiatry, 36,* 423–442.

American Professional Society on the Abuse of Children. (1997). *Practice guidelines: Psychosocial evaluation of suspected child sexual abuse in children* (2nd ed.). Chicago: Author.

American Psychological Association. (1991). Minutes of the council of representatives. *American Psychologists, 46,* 722.

American Psychological Association. (1994). *Guidelines for child custody evaluations in divorce proceedings*. Washington, DC: Author.

Baker-Ward, L., Gordon, B., Ornstein, P. A., Larus, D., & Clubb, P. (1993). Young children's long term retention of a pediatric examination. *Child Development, 64,* 1519–1533.

Berliner, L., & Loftus, E. (1992). Sexual abuse accusations, desperately seeking reconciliation. *Journal of Interpersonal Violence, 7,* 570–578.

Boat, B. W., & Everson, M. D. (1986). *Using anatomically correct dolls: Guidelines for interviewing young children in sexual abuse investigations*. Chapel Hill: University of North Carolina at Chapel Hill, Department of Psychiatry.

Boat, B. W., & Everson, M. D. (1994). Exploration of anatomically correct dolls by nonreferred preschool-aged children: Comparisons by age, gender, race, and socioeconomic status. *Child Abuse & Neglect, 18*(2), 139–152.

Boat, B. W., & Everson, M. D. (1996). Concerning practices of interviewers when using anatomical dolls in child protective services investigations. *Child Maltreatment, 1,* 96–104.

Bow, J. N., Quinnell, F. A., Zaroff, M., & Assemany, A. (2002). Assessment of sexual abuse in child custody cases. *Professional Psychology: Research & Practice, 33,* 566–575.

Briere, J. (1996). *The Trauma Symptom Checklist for Children (TSCC) professional manual*. Odessa, FL: Psychological Assessment Resource.

Bruck, M., Ceci, S. J., & Francoeur, E. (1999). The

accuracy of mothers' memories of conversations with their preschool children. *Journal of Experimental Psychology, 5,* 89–106.

Bruck, M., Ceci, S. J., Francoeur, E., & Barr, R. (1995). "I hardly cried when I got my shot?" Influencing children's reports about a visit to their pediatrician. *Child Development, 66,* 193–208.

Bruck, M., Ceci, S. J., Francoeur, E., & Renick, A. (1995). Anatomically detailed dolls do not facilitate preschoolers' reports of a pediatric examination involving genital touching. *Journal of Experimental Psychology: Applied, 1,* 95–109.

Bruck, M., Ceci, S. J., & Melnyk, L. (1997). External and internal sources of variation in the creation of false reports in children. *Learning & Individual Differences, 9,* 289–316.

Bussey v. Commonwealth, 697 S.W. 2d 139 (K.Y. 1984).

Bussey, K. (1990, March). *Adult influence on children's eyewitness reporting.* Paper presented at the biennial meeting of the American Psychology and Law Society, Williamsburg, VA.

California Family Code § 3118.(2004). Retrieved September 6, 2005, from www.courtinfo.ca.gov

California Rule of Court. (2005). *Rule 5.220: Uniform Standards for Practice for Court-Ordered Child Custody Evaluations.* Retrieved September 6, 2005, from www.courtinfo.ca.gov/rules/titlefive/1180–1280.15.doc

Ceci, S. J. (2002). The development of real-world knowledge and reasoning in real-world contexts. *Developmental Review, 22,* 520–554.

Ceci, S. J., & Bruck, M. (1993). Suggestibility of the child witness: A historical review and synthesis. *Psychological Bulletin, 113*(3), 403–439.

Ceci, S. J., & Bruck, M. (1995). *Jeopardy in the courtroom: A scientific analysis of children's testimony.* Washington, DC: American Psychological Association.

Clarke-Stewart, A., Thompson, J., & Lepore, S. (1989, April). Manipulating children's interpretations through interrogation. In G. Goodman (Chair), *Can children provide accurate eyewitness reports?* Symposium presented at Society for Research in Child Development Meetings, Kansas City, MO.

Conway, M. A. (1996). Autobiographical knowledge and autobiographical memory. In D. Rubin (Ed.), *Remembering our past: Studies in autobiographical memory* (pp. 67–93). New York: Cambridge University Press.

Dalenberg, C. J. (1996). Fantastic elements in child disclosures of abuse. *APSAC Advisor, 9*(2), 1–10.

Davies, S., Glaser, D., & Kossoff, R. (2000). Children's sexual play and behavior in preschool settings: Staff's perceptions, reports and responses. *Child Abuse & Neglect, 24,* 1329–1343.

Deblinger, E., McLeer, S. V., Atkins, M. S., Ralph, D., & Foa, E. (1989). Post-traumatic stress in sexually abused, physically abused and non abused children. *Child Abuse & Neglect, 13,* 403–408.

DeCasper, A., Lecanuet, J., Busnel, M., Granier-Deferre, C., & Maugeais, R. (1994). Fetal reactions to recurrent maternal speech. *Infant Behavior & Development, 17,* 159–164.

Drozd, L., & Olesen, N. (2004). Is it abuse, alienation and/or estrangement? A decision tree. *Journal of Child Custody, 1*(3), 65–106.

Eisen, M. L., Goodman, G. S., Qin, J., & Davis, S. (1998). Memory and suggestibility in maltreated children: New research relevant to evaluating allegations of sexual abuse. In S. L. Lynn & K. McConkey (Eds.), *Trauma and Memory* (pp. 163–189). New York: Guilford.

Elicker, J., Egland, B., & Sroufe, L. A. (1992). Predicting peer competence and peer relationships in childhood from early parent-child relationships. In R. Parke & G. Ladd (Eds.), *Family-peer relations: Modes of linkage* (pp. 77–106). Hillsdale, NJ: Lawrence Erlbaum.

Elliot, D., & Briere, J. (1994). Forensic sexual abuse evaluations of older children: Disclosures and symptomatology. *Behavioral Science & the Law, 12,* 261–277.

Everson, M. D. (1997a). Response to Kirkpatrick. *Child Maltreatment, 2,* 309–310.

Everson, M. D. (1997b). Understanding bizarre, improbable and fantastic elements in children's accounts of abuse. *Child Maltreatment, 2,* 134–149.

Faller, K. (1991). Possible explanations for child sexual abuse allegations in divorce. *American Journal of Orthopsychiatry, 61,* 86–91.

Federal Rules of Evidence. (2004). Rule 601. General Rule of Competency. Retrieved September 3, 2005, from judiciary.house.gov/media/pdfs/printers/108th/evid2004.pdf

Feliti, V. J. (1991). Long-term medical consequences of incest, rape, and molestation. *Southern Medical Journal, 84,* 328–331.

Feliti, V. J., Anda, R. F., Nordenber, D., Williamson, D. F., Spitz, A. M., Edwards, V., et al. (2001). Relationship of childhood abuse and household dysfunction to many of the leading causes of deaths in adults. In K. Franey, R. Geffner, & R. Falconer (Eds.), *The cost of child maltreatment: Who pays? We all do* (pp. 53–69). San Diego, CA: Family Violence and Sexual Assault Institute.

Fergusson, D. M., & Mullen, P. E. (1999). *Child sexual abuse: An evidence based perspective.* Newbury Park, CA: Sage.

Finkelhor, D. (1994). Current information on the scope and nature of child sexual abuse. *Future of Children, 4,* 31–53.

Finkelhor, D., & Jones, L. M. (2004). *Explanations for the decline in child sexual abuse* (Juvenile Justice Bulletin-NCJ199–298. Washington, DC: U.S. Government Printing Office.

Fisher, C. B., & Whiting, K. A. (1998). How valid are child sexual abuse validations? In S. J. Ceci & H. Hembrooke (Eds.), *Expert witnesses in child abuse cases: What can and should be said in court* (pp. 159–184). Washington, DC: American Psychological Association.

Fivush, R., & Schwartzmueller, A. (1998). Children remember childhood: Implications for childhood amnesia. *Applied Cognitive Psychology, 12,* 555–580.

Friedrich, W. N. (1998). *Child sexual behavior inventory manual.* Odessa, FL: Psychological Assessment Resources.

Friedrich, W. N., Grambsch, P., Broughton, D., Kuiper, J., & Beilke, R. L. (1991). Normative sexual behavior in children. *Pediatrics, 88,* 456–464.

Friedrich, W. N., Grambsch, P., Damon, L., Hewitt, S. K., Koverola, C., Lang, R. A., et al. (1992). Child sexual behavior inventory: Normative and clinical contrasts. *Psychological Assessment, 4,* 303–311.

Friedrich, W. N., Urquiza, A. J., & Beilke, R. L. (1986). Behavior problems in sexually abused young children. *Journal of Pediatric Psychology, 11,* 47–57.

Frye v. United States, 293 F. 1023 (1923).

Garven, S., Wood, J. M., Malpass, R. S., & Shaw, J. S. (1998). More than suggestion: A historical review and synthesis. *Journal of Applied Psychology, 83,* 347–359.

Geiselman, R. E., Saywitz, K. J., & Bornstein, G. K. (1991). *Effects of cognitive interviewing, practice and interviewing style on children's recall performance* (Rep. No. NI-IJ-CX-003). Washington, DC: National Institute of Justice.

Grantz, K. L., & Orsillo, S. M. (2003). Scientific expert testimony in child sexual abuse cases: Legal, ethical, and scientific considerations.

Clinical Psychology: Research & Practice, 10, 358–363.

Greenberg, L. R., Martindale, D. A., Gould, J. W., & Gould-Saltman, D. J. (2004). Ethical issues in child custody and dependency cases: Enduring principles and emerging challenges. *Journal of Child Custody, 1,* 7–30.

Gross, J., & Hayne, H. (1998). Drawing facilitates children's verbal reports of emotionally laden events. *Journal of Experimental Psychology: Applied, 4,* 163–179.

Gunderson, B. H., Melas, P. S., & Skar, J. E. (1981). Sexual behaviors of preschool children: Teacher's observations. In L. L. Constantine & F. L. Martinson (Eds.), *Children and sex: New findings, new perspectives* (pp. 45–62). Boston: Little Brown.

Hagen, M. A. (2003). Faith in the model and resistance to research. *Clinical Psychology: Research & Practice, 10,* 344–348.

Hall, D. K., Mathews, F., & Pearce, J. (1998). Factors associated with sexual behavior problems in young sexually abused children. *Child Abuse & Neglect, 22,* 1045–1063.

Haralambie, A. M. (1999). *Child sexual abuse in civil cases: A guide to custody and tort action.* Chicago: American Bar Association.

Hembrooke, H., & Ceci, S. J. (1995). Traumatic memories: Do we need to invoke special mechanisms? *Consciousness & Cognition, 4,* 75–82.

Howe, M., & Courage, M. L. (1997). The emergence and early development of autobiographical memory. *Psychological Review, 104,* 499–523.

Jenkins, P. H., & Howell, R. J. (1994). Child sexual abuse examinations: Proposed guidelines for a standard of care. *Bulletin of the American Academy Psychiatry & Law, 22,* 5–17.

Jones, D., & McGraw, J. M. (1987). Reliable and fictitious accounts of sexual abuse in children. *Journal of Interpersonal Violence, 2,* 27–45.

Jones, L., & Finkelhor, D. (2001). *The decline in child sexual abuse cases.* Washington, DC: Office of Juvenile Justice and Delinquency Prevention, U.S. Department of Justice.

Keary, K., & Fitzpatrick, C. (1994). Children's disclosure of sexual abuse during formal investigation. *Child Abuse & Neglect, 18*(7), 543–548.

Kelly, K., & Byrne, D. (1992). *Exploring human sexuality.* Englewood Cliffs, NJ: Prentice-Hall.

Kendall-Tackett, K. A., Williams, L. M., & Finkelhor, D. (1993). Impact of sexual abuse on children: A review and synthesis of recent empirical studies, *Psychological Bulletin, 113,* 164–180.

Kirkpatrick, H. D. (1997). Commentary: A response to Everson's "Understanding bizarre, improbable, and fantastic elements in children's accounts of abuse." *Child Maltreatment, 2,* 307–310.

Koocher, G. P., Goodman, G. S., White, C. S., Friedrich, W. N., Sivan, A. B., & Reynolds, C. R. (1995). Psychological science and the use of anatomically-correct dolls in child sexual-abuse assessments. *Psychological Bulletin, 118,* 199–222.

Kuehnle, K. (1996). *Assessing allegations of child sexual abuse.* Sarasota, FL: Professional Resource Press.

Kuehnle, K. (1998). Child sexual abuse evaluations: The scientist-practitioner model. *Behavioral Sciences & Law, 16,* 5–20.

Lawson, L., & Chaffin, M. (1992). False negatives in sexual abuse disclosure interviews. *Journal of Interpersonal Violence, 7,* 532–542.

Leichtman, M. D., & Ceci, S. J. (1995). The effects of stereotypes and suggestions on preschoolers reports. *Developmental Psychology, 31,* 568–578.

Lilienfeld, S. O., Wood, J. M., & Garb, H.N. (2000). The scientific status of projective techniques. *Psychological Science, 1,* 27–66.

Mannarino, A. P., & Cohen, J. A. (1996). A follow-up study of factors that mediate the development of psychological symptomatology in sexually abused girls. *Child Maltreatment, 1,* 246–260.

McGleughlin, J., Meyer, S., & Baker, J. (1999). Assessing child sexual abuse allegations in divorce custody and visitation disputes. In R. M. Galatzer-Levy & L. Kraus (Eds.), *The scientific basis of child custody decisions* (pp. 357–388). New York: Wiley.

Melton, G. B., & Limber, S. (1989). Psychologists' involvement in cases of child maltreatment: Limits of role and expertise. *American Psychologist, 44,* 1225–1233.

Myers, J. E. B. (1997). *Evidence in child abuse and neglect cases* (Vol. 1, 3rd ed.). New York: Wiley.

Nichols, H., & Molinder, I. (1990). Multiphasic Sex Inventory manual. (Available from the authors, 437 Bowes Dr., Tacoma, WA, 98466).

Oberlander, L. (1995). Psychological issues in child sexual abuse evaluation: A survey of forensic mental health professionals. *Child Abuse & Neglect, 19,* 475–490.

Peterson, C., & Briggs, M. (1997). Interviewing children and trauma: Problems with "specific" questions. *Journal of Traumatic Stress, 10,* 279–290.

Poole, D. A., & Lindsay, D. S. (1997). Misinformation from parents and children's source monitoring: Implications for testimony. In K. P. Roberts (Chair), *Children's source monitoring and eye witness testimony.* Symposium conducted at the meeting of the Society for Research in Child Development, Washington, DC.

Poole, D. A., & White, L. T. (1993). Two years later: Effects of question repetition interval on the eye witness testimony of children and adults. *Developmental Psychology, 29,* 844–853.

Rumm, P. D., Cummings, P., Krause, M. R., Bell, M. A., & Rivara, F. P. (2000). Identified spouse abuse as a risk factor for child abuse. *Child Abuse & Neglect, 24,* 1375–1381.

Saywitz, K. J. (1995). Improving children's testimony: The question, the answer, and the environment. In M. Zaragoza, J. Graham, G. Hall, R. Hirschman, & Y. Ben-Porath (Eds.), *Memory and testimony in the child abuse witness* (pp. 113–140). Thousand Oaks, CA: Sage.

Sbraga, T. P., & O'Donohue, W. (2003). Post hoc reasoning in possible cases of child sexual abuse: Symptoms of inconclusive origin. *Clinical Psychology: Research & Practice, 10,* 320–334.

Schultz, R. (1995). Evaluating the expert witness: The mental health expert in child sexual abuse cases. *American Journal of Family Law, 9,* 1–9.

Scullin, M. H., & Ceci, S. J. (2001). A suggestibility scale for children. *Personality & Individual Differences, 30,* 843–856.

Sedlak, A. J., & Broadhurst, D. D. (1996). *The third national incidence study of child abuse and neglect.* Washington, DC: U.S. Department of Health and Human Services.

Shaw, J. A., Lewis, J. E., Loeb, A, Rosado, J., & Rodriguez, M. (2000). Child on child sexual abuse: Conceptual implications. *Child Maltreatment, 4,* 1591–1600.

Shipman, K. L., Rossman, B. B. R., & West, J. C. (1999). Co-occurrence of spousal violence and child abuse: Conceptual implications. *Child Maltreatment, 4,* 93–102.

Sobsey, D., Randall, W., & Parrila, R. K. (1997). Gender differences in abused children with and without disabilities. *Child Abuse & Neglect, 21,* 707–720.

Sparta, S. N. (2003). Assessment of childhood trauma. In A. M. Goldstein (Ed.), *Handbook of psychology, Vol. 11: Forensic psychology* (pp. 209–231). New York: Wiley.

State v. Buckey, Sup. Ct., L.A. Co., Cal. No. a750900 (1990).

State v. Michaels, 264 N.J. Sup. 579, 642A, 2d 489 (N.J. Sup. Ad. 1993).

State of New Jersey v. Margaret Kelly Michaels, 264 N.J. Sup. Ct., 579 (1993).

Straus, M. A., Gelles, R. J., & Steinmetz, S. K. (1980). *Behind closed doors: Violence in the American family*. Garden City, NY: Doubleday.

Sullivan, P. M., & Knutson, J. F. (1998). The association between child maltreatment and disabilities in a hospital-based epidemiological study. *Child Abuse & Neglect, 22,* 271–288.

Thoennes N., & Tjaden, P. (1990). The extent, nature, & validity of sexual abuse allegations in custody/visitation disputes. *Child Abuse & Neglect, 14,* 151–163.

U.S. Department of Health and Human Services, National Center on Child Abuse and Neglect. (2000). *Child maltreatment 1998: Reports from the states to the national child abuse and neglect data system*. Washington, DC: U.S. Government Printing Office.

Van der Kolk, B. A., & Fisler, R. E. (1995). Dissociation and the fragmentary nature of traumatic memories: Overview and exploration study. *Journal of Traumatic Stress, 8,* 505–525.

Vrij, A., & Bush, N. (1998, April). *Differences in suggestibility between 5–6 and 10–11 year olds: A matter of differences in self confidence?* Paper presented at the meeting of American Psychology-Law Society, Redondo Beach, CA.

Wang, C. T., & Harding, K. (1999). *Current trends in child abuse reporting and fatalities: The results of the 1998 annual fifty state survey*. Chicago: Prevent Child Abuse America.

Warren, A. R., Woodall, C. E., Hunt, J. S., & Perry, N. W. (1996). "It sounds good in theory, but . . .": Do investigative interviews follow guidelines based on memory research? *Child Maltreatment, 1,* 231–245.

Weiner, I. B. (2003). Prediction and post diction in clinical decision making. *Clinical Psychology: Research & Practice, 10,* 335–338.

Weiner, I., & Kuehnle, K. (1998). Projective assessment of children and adolescents. In M. Hersen & A. Bellak (Eds.), *Comprehensive clinical psychology* (Vol. 3, pp. 431–458). Tarrytown, NY: Elsevier Science.

Wheeler v. United States, 159 U.S. 523 (1895).

Wolfe, D. A., & Legate, B. L. (2003). Expert opinion on child sexual abuse: Separating myths from reality. *Clinical Psychology: Research & Practice, 10,* 339–343.

10

Evaluating the Effects of Domestic Violence on Children

Lois Oberlander Condie

The term *domestic violence* most often includes acts of violence between marital partners, cohabiting partners, non-cohabiting dating partners, and former partners. Domestic violence typically is contrasted with the broader term of *family violence*. Family violence encompasses a broad set of familial relationships. It includes intimate partner abuse, but it also describes other intrafamilial maltreatment, such as child maltreatment, violence between siblings, and elder abuse (American Psychological Association, 1998). Domestic violence includes a behavior or a set of behaviors arising from multiple causal mechanisms. These behaviors follow different patterns in different families. No single syndrome or single underlying mechanism effectively encapsulates domestic violence (Carter, Weithorn, & Behrman, 1999). The impact of domestic violence on parent–child relationships and child functioning varies with different patterns of violence. The impact on the child is a function of many factors, including but not limited to the developmental and individual characteristics of each involved child. Researchers are just beginning to study how child variables (e.g., age, gender, level of development, external resources, internal resilience) influ-

ence children's reactions. Researchers are investigating the impact of different forms of domestic violence, and how the impact changes with the severity and chronicity of domestic violence (Sternberg & Lamb, 1999).

Researchers of domestic violence traditionally focused on male perpetrators of violence toward female victims. There has been a recent broadening of inquiry to include the study of female perpetrators of domestic violence and domestic violence in gay and lesbian partnerships. Survey data suggest that although more women are physically injured during domestic violence episodes (Kurz, 1993; McNeely, Cook, & Torres, 2001; Straus, 1993), both men and women are victimized (Straus & Gelles, 1990). Some researchers express concern that female involvement sometimes is mischaracterized as domestic violence rather than self-defense (American Psychological Association, 1998). Regardless of perpetrator gender, domestic violence has become a pervasive phenomenon. The U.S. Department of Justice National Crime Victimization Survey (Bachman & Saltzman, 1995) showed 29% of simple and aggravated assaults were committed by intimate partners, with nonmarried (ex-spouses or dating partners) individuals committing a higher proportion of assaults than spouses (Bachman & Saltzman, 1995).

A large proportion of reported domestic violence occurs subsequent to a separation between intimate partners (Bachman & Saltzman, 1995). One study found that 75% of emergency room visits by female domestic violence victims occurred after separation (Stark and Flitcraft, 1988). In another study, almost 75% of emergency calls for law enforcement assistance in domestic violence cases took place after separation (Langen & Innes, 1986). Half of homicides by men involving female spouses or partners occurred after separation or divorce (Bernard, Vera, Vera, & Newman, 1982). Many stalking crimes involve violent former spouses, cohabiting partners, or dating partners. As with other forms of domestic violence, postseparation stalking behavior is found in both genders (Logan, Leukefeld, & Walker, 2000). More than 20% of adult women sustain at least one physical assault by a partner during adulthood (Tjaden & Thoennes, 1996). Depending on methodology and operational definitions, estimates of spouse abuse in U.S. families range from 10% to 30% (Geffner & Pagelow, 1990), with 6% of reported assaults involved serious violence such as choking, biting, kicking, or punching (Straus & Gelles, 1986). Domestic violence sometimes includes sexual assault or battering rape (National Victim Center, 1992). Based on conservative estimates, almost 1 million women are victimized by domestic violence each year. In 1993, roughly 1,300 women in the United States were murdered by partners or former partners. Thirty percent of female murders resulted from intimate partner violence. The rate may constitute an underestimate because the relationship between victim and perpetrator often remains unidentified in murder statistics (Bureau of Justice Statistics, 1998).

The American Psychological Association's *Resolution on Male Violence Against Women* (American Psychological Association, 1996b) concluded that violence against women constitutes a major source of reduced quality of life, distress, injury, and death for women. It results in acute and chronic mental health and physical health consequences (increased visits to physicians and emergency health services), along with increased risk of negative health behaviors such as excessive alcohol consumption and cigarette smoking (Browne, 1993; Koss, Koss, & Woodruff, 1991). It has secondary effects on families, communities, and the economy (American Psychological Association, 1998). Intergenerational transmission constitutes another cost of domestic violence. Although exceptions do occur, a link exists, both for men and for women, between childhood or adolescent exposure to domestic violence and later mental disorders, substance abuse, and involvement in abusive relationships. Direct victimization in childhood raises risk of adulthood perpetration of domestic violence and other forms of maltreatment, but it remains insufficient as a sole contributing factor to explain risk or desistance of risk (Belsky, 1993).

The nature of domestic violence and society's response has a basis, in part, in gender inequities (legal, economic, and physical), cultural norms and expectations, and impoverishment (Alexander, Moore, & Alexander, 1991). Impoverished women have a high risk of all types of severe and life-threatening assaults (Browne & Bassuk, 1997). Similarly, women with disabilities face higher rates of domestic violence than do women in the general population. Women with disabilities experience forms of domestic violence specific to their disability for prolonged periods of time and from multiple perpetrators (Hassouneh-Phillips & Curry, 2002). Researchers who study gay and lesbian relationships that involve domestic violence have expressed concern that societal attitudes toward same-sex relationships make it difficult for victims to seek help (Lie & Gentlewarrier, 1991). Researchers who study ethnicity and domestic violence have identified similar correlates of domestic violence across ethnic groups (Huang & Gunn, 2001). Acculturation adds an important variable that predicts domestic violence (Yick, 2000), but without clear specificity to any ethnic group. Some ethnic minority groups have much greater risk of victimization and revictimization when their minority status combines with a low socioeconomic status (Mears, Carlson, Holden, & Harris, 2001). Limits of existing research on ethnic variations make it premature to conclude that ethnicity influences particular rates or manifestations of domestic violence. Clearly, domestic violence occurs across age groups, types of couples, ethnic and cultural groups, socioeconomic groups, and religious groups (American Psychological Association,

1998). Despite two decades of emphasis on increased awareness and protective legislation, rates of assaults and lethal domestic violence remain high. Domestic violence remains a major economic, criminal justice, mental health, and public health issue (American Psychological Association, 1996b).

THEORETICAL PERSPECTIVES ON DOMESTIC VIOLENCE

Sociobiology

Explanations of domestic violence draw on many different theoretical perspectives. Comparative theories describe conflict related to survival as the central mechanism that explains violence (R. L. Burgess, 1994). Evolutionary theory emphasizes survival of the species and the reproductive interests of individuals. When the provision of sensitive and nurturing care contributes nothing to or even undermines reproductive fitness, conflict occurs that might engender violence (Belsky, 1993). Conflict and violence arise from complex transactions between individuals and environments. Conditions of conflict include scarce resources, impoverishment, duration of poverty status, and instability or unpredictability of resources (Belsky, 1993). Some advocates worry that biological explanations of violence imply a degree of inevitability and that perpetrators may have less culpability for their behavior. Research is strengthened, however, with the inclusion of multiple variables and multiple perspectives of domestic violence (Soler, Vinayak, & Quadagno, 2000). Sociobiological theorists hypothesize that awareness of the conditions that amplify biological conflicts of interest promote the development of methods to reduce conflict (Belsky, 1993; R. L. Burgess, 1994).

Attachment Theory

Researchers have turned to the robust results of attachment theory to explain mediating processes in domestic violence. Attachment theory explains how security, adaptive emotional regulation, and internal organization promote harmonious relationships. Although insecure and disorganized attachment classifications have a somewhat greater association with domestic violence than do other classifications, no single attachment classification or attachment disorder subtype provides a potent predictor of perpetration or impact of domestic violence (West & George, 1999). Subtype effects are not robust when attachment is considered in isolation from other variables (Levendosky, Huth-Bocks, Semel, & Shapiro, 2002). Nonetheless, empirical studies have illustrated a correlation between attachment problems in childhood and later attachment problems in adulthood, with males tending to externalize or act out their attachment problems more than females (Mauricio & Gormley, 2001). Intergenerational transmission theories developed in the latter third of the 20th century, spawning research on the link between perpetration of violence and childhood histories of domestic violence exposure or victimization. Researchers hypothesized that attachment theory might explain the intergenerational transmission of intrafamilial violence. Researchers have made consistent findings of an intergenerational link, but caution is urged because of methodological limitations and because the notion of intergenerational transmission sometimes focuses attention away from interpersonal processes in relationships (Alexander et al., 1991; Sternberg & Lamb, 1999; Weinfield, Sroufe, & Egeland, 2000). Attachment studies have identified variables associated with lawful discontinuity of intergenerational transmission, or the capacity of some individuals to transition to healthy intimate attachments in adulthood (Weinfield et al., 2000).

Developmental and Personality Theories

Psychoanalytic theories of personality variables associated with domestic violence describe intrapsychic conflict as the most necessary and basic aspect of violence toward partners. The central question for intrapsychic psychoanalytic theories of domestic violence asks why some partners become violent whereas other partners in similar circumstances do not. Other individual theories emphasize personality styles associated with domestic violence, and social interaction patterns between partners. Indeed, some individuals who engage in domestic violence show characteristic symptoms of mental illnesses or character disorders, and others do not (Holtzworth-Munroe, Meehan, Herron, Rehman, & Stuart, 2000). Many perpetrators of domestic violence show behaviors associated with narcissistic personality disorder, antisocial personality disorder, or borderline personality disorder. However, many individuals with these diagnoses do not engage in domestic violence (McBurnett et al., 2001).

Researchers have examined perpetrator variables such as history of abuse in early life, lack of partner empathy, excessively high expectations of the partner, impaired intimate attachment, difficulty internally reconciling a wish for toughness with a wish for intimacy, dissatisfaction with the self, immature coping resources, shallow and exploitative approaches to relationships, self-centered behavior, disinhibition of aggression, low levels of remorse or guilt, and a poorly integrated sense of identity (Tjaden & Thoennes, 1996; Watson & Clark, 1992). Personality variables consistent with seduction, intimidation, and control have been examined (Olson & Stalans, 2001). A correlation exists between individual characteristics associated with domestic violence toward partners and the tendency to use control strategies, threats, or physical discipline or to engage in physical abuse toward children (Gelles & Maynard, 1987; Jouriles & LeCompte, 1991). Studies of individuals who engage in domestic violence have shown considerable heterogeneity across offenders, but some differences in premeditated versus opportunistic offenders may exist (A. W. Burgess, Harner, Baker, Hartman, & Lole, 2001).

Some variables discriminate between those who engage in stalking behavior and those who engage in other forms of domestic violence after the relationship has ended. The stalking group shows predatory features in their personalities and behavior. The Predatory Contact Pattern (A. W. Burgess et al., 2001) has associations with behavior such as hang-up telephone calls, entering the female ex-partner's home without permission, predatory thoughts about the ex-partner, stalking behaviors, and predatory fantasies. Perpetrator character traits of emotional volatility, attachment dysfunction, primitive defenses, boundary violations (arranging proximity to the victim), weak ego strength, jealousy, and reacting with rage to perceived or actual rejection have been identified in stalking offenders (Douglas & Dutton, 2001). By contrast, the Ambivalent Contact Pattern (A.W. Burgess et al., 2001) is associated with behaviors toward ex-partners such as sending gifts and letters, watching the ex-partner without his or her knowledge, and the co-occurrence of conflicting feelings of love and hate. Classification schemes that attempt to differentiate stalkers from nonstalkers help researchers in their identification of personality correlates. However, forensic psychologists need more robust theories for clinical applications (Dutton & Kropp, 2000).

Cognitive and Socioemotional Theories

Researchers focusing on the cognitive and emotional characteristics of domestic violence have emphasized the importance of negative reactivity and an external attributional style of little personal control (Andrews & Brewin, 1990; Belsky, 1993). Researchers also have examined authoritarian attitudes in combination with negative affect in individuals who engage in domestic violence (Margolin, John, Ghosh, & Gordis, 1997). Individuals who engage in domestic violence are more physiologically reactive to distressing events. They report less sympathy and greater irritation and annoyance in response to distressing events. Hyperreactivity to aversive stimuli is explained by early learning, exposure to childhood maltreatment, biological variables, and mental health processes. Researchers have linked hyperreactivity to depression (Belsky, 1993; Watson & Clark, 1992). Although negative reactivity or hyperreactivity to aversive stimuli may be a necessary precursor to domestic violence, it is not sufficient to turn a conflicted interaction into a violent one.

Most researchers agree that people learn domestic violence, as a set of behaviors, in childhood and express them in adulthood in intrafamilial roles (American Psychological Association, 1996a). Contributory processes to learning domestic violence include modeling, direct reinforcement, coercion training, and inconsistency training. Coercion training and inconsistency training explain why behavior that feels unpleasant or emotionally harmful nonetheless becomes incorporated into a behavioral repertoire. Violent behavior unfortunately becomes increasingly more predictable in the context of an otherwise random dispensation of rewards and punishment (Belsky, 1993; Emery,

1989). Learning also may account for discontinuities or desistance of violence in adulthood. Partners with histories of exposure to domestic violence who refrain from domestic violence tend to have good social support networks, a childhood history of a close and nonviolent relationship with at least one caretaker or substitute caretaker, open anger at the domestic violence exposure, and a better capacity to describe and appreciate their histories of victimization (McBurnett et al., 2001).

COMORBIDITY WITH MENTAL ILLNESS AND SUBSTANCE ABUSE

A modest causal link exists between mental illness and domestic violence, but mental illness does not constitute a necessary condition for domestic violence, nor does violence necessarily abate following successful treatment of mental illness. Many domestic violence perpetrators have no mental illness and many partners with such conditions do not engage in domestic violence. Although many admitted perpetrators of domestic violence report that they have a diagnosable mental illness, they also report other risk factors associated with domestic violence (Carter et al., 1999; Watson & Clark, 1992). The relative weight of mental illness in comparison to other risk factors is unknown. Clusters of symptoms related to negative emotional experiences and distrust are inconsistent in their impact on the form of violent behavior toward partners (Emery, 1989; Kurz, 1993; Watson & Clark, 1992).

A modest correlation also exists between substance abuse and domestic violence (Galen, Brower, Gillespie, & Zucker, 2000; Olson & Stalans, 2001). The impact of substance abuse on domestic violence remains controversial because of the myth that the violence will abate following successful substance abuse treatment. Many negative patterns of behavior related to substance abuse remain present even after the individual has been clean or sober for a period of time. Examples include negative statements, negative affect, coercive and negative verbal exchanges, difficulty terminating negative exchanges, and escalation from mildly aversive requests to strong demands with increased negative affect (Galen et al., 2000). Although a link does exist between substance abuse and vio-

lence, with drug or alcohol intoxication lessening inhibitions, most researchers have begun to explore domestic violence as an independent process that requires treatment specific to aggression in intimate relationships. Based on a sample of probationers in several jurisdictions in one state, rates of recidivism for domestic violence are similar to rates of recidivism for other violent probationers (Olson & Stalans, 2001).

A CAVEAT ON VICTIM REACTIONS TO DOMESTIC VIOLENCE

The word *victim* carries its own set of controversies because of the tendency to reify it as a stable personality variable without due attention to individual circumstances or situational variables. In reality, individuals who are exposed to or directly victimized by domestic violence show a variety of emotional reactions, physical reactions, personality characteristics, and behavior patterns. The most common question posed about victims of domestic violence asks why they remain in violent intimate relationships. The underlying assumption is that leaving the relationship causes the violence to abate. The above statistics illustrate that domestic violence often persists, and may in fact worsen, after the termination of the relationship. Many battered individuals feel terrified of repercussions to themselves or to their children (American Psychological Association, 1996c). Another myth follows from the human tendency to classify individuals as violent or nonviolent (Sternberg & Lamb, 1999). Although positive or affable characteristics in perpetrators sometimes appear transient or unstable, many violent individuals have corresponding positive characteristics and interludes of nonviolence. They disengage from violence for periods of time or under certain sets of circumstances. Many battered individuals feel barraged by their partner's promises never to engage in violence again. Such promises may accompany control strategies that fuel the terror that victims feel even during interludes of nonviolence (America Psychological Association, 1996c). In jurisdictions without adequate education or statutory provisions, some victims might remain in domestic violence relationships because they fear they might lose custody of their children to child protective services or to their partner (Matthews, 1999). Many reasons account for why battered individuals do not leave their intimate partners, including limited or no social support, no financial resources, nowhere to go, emotional immobilization, and awareness that leaving may not stop the violence and may even make it worse (American Psychological Association, 1996c).

THE IMPACT OF DOMESTIC VIOLENCE ON CHILDREN

It was not until the late 1980s that researchers began to inquire systematically about the presence or proximity of children during episodes of domestic violence. Although estimates vary widely, data have accumulated suggesting that children frequently overhear, directly witness, or otherwise become aware of domestic violence whether or not the adults in their lives are aware of their distress (Sternberg & Lamb, 1999). One study found that children are either in the same or an adjacent room to the assault 90% of the time (Hughes, Parkinson, & Vargo, 1989). Children's exposure to domestic violence often begins in early childhood, with a substantial number of children exposed in utero. In a public prenatal health clinic study in two urban cities (McFarlane, Parker, & Soeken, 1995), researchers found that 16% of pregnant women reported victimization by domestic assault during pregnancy. Of that 16%, over half of the women reported multiple episodes of violence during pregnancy. Women victimized by domestic violence during pregnancy delayed prenatal care until the third trimester of pregnancy twice as often as did nonvictims. They showed twice the likelihood of delivering babies with low birth weight compared to other women in the public health sample. When the effects of age were controlled, pregnant women did not have greater risk of being victimized by intimate partners than did comparison women; however, pregnancy did not insulate women from the high rates of violence experienced by young women, especially women younger than 25 (Gelles, 1988). Young children carry a greater level of risk for exposure to domestic violence than do older children. In an examination of 2,400 substantiated

reports of domestic violence in five major U.S. cities (Fantuzzo, Boruch, Beriama, Atkins, & Marcus, 1997), children were disproportionately represented in households where domestic violence against women occurred. Children younger than 5 were more likely than older children to be exposed to multiple episodes of domestic violence. Other researchers found that 25% of children 8- to 11 years old witnessed spousal violence at least once in their lives (O'Brien, John, Margolin, & Erel, 1994).

Many problems common to applied research beset investigations and reports describing the impact of domestic violence exposure. A majority of relevant studies have given inadequate attention to the age and developmental level of the child participants. Most studies have not considered confounding factors. To date, there have been no studies using a longitudinal research design to study the impact of exposure to domestic violence across time (Fantuzzo & Mohr, 1999). Most studies have not described the theoretical framework that influenced which variables to include. Some studies controlled for the child's gender, and family socioeconomic status. Few studies controlled for marital status, family size, or parental age (Fantuzzo & Mohr, 1999; Margolin et al., 1997). Even fewer studies controlled for ethnicity, child health, or family stress. Many studies neglected to consider the number of participants needed to detect significant between-group differences. The field lacks objective standardized measures for assessing the impact of domestic violence exposure on children (Fantuzzo & Mohr, 1999; Sternberg & Lamb, 1999).

Variations in research results may be explained by individual differences in stress responses, variations in the form and context of domestic violence, differences in children's reactions based on their age or developmental status, variations in the severity and chronicity of violence, and methodological differences among studies (Jaffe, Wolfe, Wilson, & Zak, 1986; D. A. Wolfe, Zak, Wilson, & Jaffe, 1986). Researchers have hypothesized that chronic domestic violence has a greater impact on children than does nonchronic violence. Similarly, a severe episode of domestic violence probably has a greater impact than does less severe domestic violence (Sternberg & Lamb, 1999). Researchers are just beginning to examine the differential impact of other variables, such as coincidence with other forms of family violence (Margolin, 1998).

THE IMPACT OF EXPOSURE TO DOMESTIC VIOLENCE

Researchers traditionally made no distinction between exposure to domestic violence and awareness of domestic violence without direct exposure to it. Earlier terms included child *witnesses* or *observers* of violence. In the 1990s, *exposure* replaced those terms, as a more inclusive concept that makes no assumptions about the specific nature of children's understanding of or experience with domestic violence. Exposure includes watching violent events, hearing violent events, hearing others talk about the domestic violence, direct involvement in the form of attempts to intervene or call or help, viewing police or social service responses to domestic violence, awareness or viewing of arrests for domestic violence or violations of a restraining order, discussions of the meaning and purpose of a restraining order, and viewing the physical or emotional aftermath in the victim (Condie, 2003; Fantuzzo & Mohr, 1999). Researchers have begun to examine the effects of children's awareness of domestic violence in the household, even when they have not had direct exposure to it (Osofsky, 1999; Sternberg & Lamb, 1999). Preliminary data suggest that awareness of domestic violence significantly contributes to the level of emotional distress of children (Ayoub, Deutsch, & Maraganore, 1999).

Despite the methodological limitations of applied research, sufficient evidence exists to suggest that domestic violence exposure has adverse effects. Children who live in households with domestic violence are at greater risk of emotional and behavior problems compared to children who do not (Fantuzzo & Mohr, 1999). Specific effects vary with the presence of other risk factors in children's lives. Common effects include aggressive conduct, emotional problems such as depression or anxiety, poor social competence, compromised intellectual functioning, and poor academic functioning (Huth-Bocks, Levendosky, & Semel, 2002). Children who overhear or witness domestic violence tend to have heightened levels of fear and anger toward the vio-

lent parent, the victim, or both. They might feel responsible for the violence, particularly if the violence follows a disagreement over child rearing. Sometimes children find themselves drawn into domestic violence. Their involvement might take the form of either mimicking the actions of the perpetrator or desperate attempts to defend or protect the victim (MacKenzie-Keating & McDonald, 1997).

Several comprehensive reviews of research on the effects of domestic violence exist (Fantuzzo & Lindquist, 1989; Kolbo, Blakely, & Engleman, 1996; Margolin, 1998). The reviews included studies that compared children exposed to domestic violence with children from nonviolent homes. Areas of functioning examined included (a) externalizing behaviors, (b) internalizing behaviors, (c) intellectual functioning and academic achievement, (d) social competence with peers and adults, and (e) physical health. The reviews demonstrated that children who are exposed to domestic violence display more externalizing and internalizing symptoms and behaviors relative to comparison samples (Fantuzzo & Lindquist, 1989; Kolbo et al., 1996). Externalizing behavior included temper tantrums and fights. Internalizing behaviors included anxiety, depression, suicidal ideation and gestures, fears, phobias, poor self-esteem, tics, and nighttime enuresis.

Effects on intellectual functioning and academic achievement also became evident in variables such as capacity for attention and concentration, completion of school work in class and at home, and lower scores on intellectual and achievement measures of verbal functioning, motor functioning, and visuospatial functioning (Fantuzzo & Lindquist, 1989; Kolbo et al., 1996). The reviews revealed inconsistent results on measures of social competence (Fantuzzo & Mohr, 1999). Some studies showed that boys and girls exposed to domestic violence had lower levels of social competence than did comparison groups. Other studies revealed no statistically significant differences in levels of social competence (Fantuzzo & Lindquist, 1989; Kolbo et al., 1996). Both of the initial reviews uncovered no significant effects on children's physical health and development (Fantuzzo & Lindquist, 1989; Fantuzzo & Mohr, 1999; Kolbo et al., 1996). A review by Margolin (1998) confirmed the conclusions of the previous reviews but revealed that the results were complicated by coexisting risk factors.

Developmental Differences in Children's Reactions to Domestic Violence Exposure

Based on studies of children's exposure to all forms of violence, one could reasonably hypothesize that developmental differences would occur in children's responses to domestic violence exposure (Osofsky, 1999). Researchers have found links between exposure to violence and negative outcomes in children across all age groups (Levendosky, Huth-Bocks, Semel, & Shapiro, 2002; Thornberry, Ireland, & Smith, 2001). The level of the child's development influences the stability of the child's temperament, attachment status, internal organization, organization of play, pursuit of social support and activities as methods of coping, and concept of the future. Traumatic events can produce complex interactions between neurobiological systems, behavior, and development. Early damage to neurodevelopment can have a significant impact on behavior and mood regulation (Sparta, 2003). Researchers examining the effects of violence exposure on infants and toddlers have found that exposure correlated with excessive irritability, sleep disturbances, excessive anxiety, emotional distress, fear of being alone, reexperiencing trauma, avoidant behavior in the form of limited play, emotional numbing of responsiveness, increased arousal, and regression in toileting and language (Jaffe, Wolfe, & Wilson, 1990; Levendosky, Huth-Bocks, Semel, & Shapiro, 2002; Osofsky, 1999).

Several studies have found a link between violence exposure and anxiety, depression, and aggressive behavior in school-age children. School-age children develop sleep disturbances, and they limit their exploration and free play in the environment. They develop attention and concentration problems secondary to distraction by intrusive thoughts. Because they have some understanding of the intentional quality of violence, they worry about what they might have done to prevent or stop the violence. They sometimes show prototypical symptoms and behaviors associated with posttraumatic stress disorder (PTSD), for example, nightmares,

fear of leaving their homes, anxiety, emotional numbing, feeling jumpy or scared, and worrying about remaining safe. The symptoms and behaviors are more likely to appear in cases of exposure to chronic levels of violence (Osofsky, 1999). As children grow into preadolescence, they have increased risk of school behavior and academic problems, emotional problems, conduct problems, juvenile justice system involvement, sexual problems, and substance use or abuse (Osofsky, 1999).

Adolescents exposed to violence show high levels of aggression and other conduct problems, anxiety, behavior disorders, academic problems, attachment problems, truancy, revenge seeking, and symptoms of depression that include loss of hope and a low expectation that they will survive into early adulthood. Adolescents may show substantial numbing of emotions, restricted emotional development, and attachment to youth with conduct problems or gang involvement (Jonson-Reid, 1998; Levendosky et al., 2002; Osofsky, 1999). They have a greater likelihood than comparison adolescents to become victims of crime (Mitchell & Finkelhor, 2001). Symptoms and behaviors associated with PTSD increase with the number of violent acts witnessed or experienced (Osofsky, 1999). Although considerable heterogeneity exists among preadolescent and adolescent children who murder, a high percentage of them come from homes characterized by physical abuse, neglect, domestic violence, and general instability (Shumaker & Prinz, 2000).

Children who show resilience to the impact of violence exposure consistently identify a small number of crucial protective factors: a caring adult, a community safe haven (schools, community centers, religious centers), and a child's own internal resources. If the caring adult is a parent, the protective effects have an even more potent influence (Osofsky, 1999). Average to above-average intellectual abilities, good attention skills, and good interpersonal skills constitute individual variables in children correlated with resilience (McGlois & Widom, 2001; Osofsky, 1999). Less potent individual variables include good self-esteem and self-efficacy, physical and personality attractiveness, individual talents, religious affiliations, avoidance of conduct problems, low vulnerability to mental illness or substance abuse, socioeconomic advantage, good school and employment opportunities, and contact with positive role models or environments (McGlois & Widom, 2001; Osofsky, 1999). The child's ability to take advantage of individual resources is linked to the support of a caring adult or a community safe haven (Osofsky, 1999). Positive functioning at the time of the evaluation may reflect recovery from significant symptoms at an earlier time. It is important to consider resilience variables in an historical context.

Co-occurrence With Other Forms of Intrafamilial Violence

Different types of family violence tend to co-occur (Straus & Gelles, 1990; Straus, Gelles, & Steinmenz, 1980), with domestic violence between spouses leading to increases in physical violence by both parents toward their children (Tajima, 2000). Both male and female victims of spousal domestic violence were about one and one half times more likely to physically abuse their children than are parents who had not been victimized by their spouses (Straus & Gelles, 1990). To date, no population studies have provided estimates of the coincidence of child abuse and domestic violence between spouses (Sternberg & Lamb, 1999). The 1985 National Family Violence Survey suggested that domestic violence in the home constituted a consistent and significant specific risk factor for all forms of violence against children (Tajima, 2000).

In a comprehensive review of empirical studies of the impact of domestic violence, Margolin (1998) found that between 45% and 70% of children exposed to domestic violence were also victims of physical abuse. Children exposed to domestic violence also had a greater risk for sexual abuse than did children in nonviolent households (Bowen, 2000; Margolin, 1998). Margolin (1998) concluded that negative emotional and behavioral outcomes seemed more likely for children exposed to domestic violence and victimized by child maltreatment, compared to children who experienced either one form of violence or no violence. It seems likely that the co-occurrence of multiple risk factors constitutes a more potent and robust predictor of negative outcomes than the presence of any single risk factor (Fantuzzo & Mohr, 1999; Margolin, 1998). The legal system has begun to show awareness of the co-occurrence of domestic violence and other forms of family violence (Goldstein, 1999).

THE LEGAL CONTEXT OF CHILD EVALUATIONS OF DOMESTIC VIOLENCE EXPOSURE

The Legal Landscape

Features of Federal Statutes

Congress enacted the Family Violence Prevention and Services Act in 1984, the first major congressional effort to address domestic violence. The legislative intent included promoting state efforts to increase public awareness of the negative impact of family violence and providing shelters and other types of victim assistance. It made provisions for technical assistance, resource centers, grants, and training to states and to nonprofit agencies for the development of domestic violence services and youth education programs concerning domestic violence. The Violence Against Women Act of 1994Violence Against Women Act of 1994, P. L. 103-322, 108 Stat. 1796, 1994 reflected growing national recognition of the seriousness of domestic violence. It contained provisions to improve law enforcement, criminal justice responses, and state court system responses to domestic violence. It promoted increases in the number of primary, secondary, and tertiary services devoted to domestic violence services. It protected battered immigrant women from deportation.

Although these congressional acts improved national approaches to the social problems of domestic violence, criticisms focused on their narrow approach to the problem, possible constitutional infringements, and the failure to fund or reauthorize funding for many of the provisions (Matthews, 1999). The Violence Against Women Act of 2000 reauthorized funding for shelters and safe havens for children, transitional housing assistance, a national domestic violence hotline, services for domestic violence victims and their children, grants for model programs, education and training for judges, improvement of prevention approaches, and improvement of prosecution of domestic violence in rural areas. It contained new provisions to fund supervised visitation centers for children in families affected by domestic violence, access to legal services for domestic violence victims, monitoring of the impact of domestic violence on employment, and programs that target services to special populations.

Features of State Statutes

States have responded to the social problem of domestic violence in legislation and procedures for obtaining restraining orders issued by a judge. Orders compel the violent person to stay a specified distance away from the victim, his or her home, and his or her place of employment. To obtain an order, the victim must file a written petition in civil court and attend a petition hearing (Matthews, 1999). States have adopted similar criteria that qualify individuals for petitions, but some important differences exist. Statutes vary in the duration and breadth of civil protection orders, processes for renewing orders, provisions of exclusion from a shared residence, reimbursement of expenses caused by domestic violence, and mandated treatment for perpetrators (Henderson Gist et al., 2001). Some states allow child custody, visitation, and child support to be resolved in the context of restraining order hearings. Other states require the victim to file a separate legal action for these matters (Matthews, 1999). Statutes governing civil protection orders remain somewhat controversial because of concern over barriers to obtaining protective orders, the relevancy of qualifying criteria, and the effectiveness of protective orders. A number of issues that limit the effectiveness of civil protective orders, including financial barriers such as filing fees and access to attorneys, poor enforcement of orders, and victim fearfulness of reporting order violations (Henderson Gist et al., 2001; Matthews, 1999).

In care and protection matters, victims of domestic violence sometimes are held accountable for failure to protect children. States have adopted criminal statutes relevant to failure to protect. All but 12 states have enacted legislation that criminalizes omissions in parental protection of children victimized by family violence. Punishable omissions include being present when violence occurs while failing to intervene in a protective manner, leaving the child alone with a known perpetrator, and

failing to seek reasonably prompt medical attention for an injured child. Exposure to domestic violence has been interpreted by criminal courts as a punishable omission (Goldstein, 1999; Murphy, 1998). Some states have raised concern that codification of failure to protect in criminal statutes places impoverished domestic violence victims in a double bind due to limited resources to take steps to protect themselves and their children (Matthews, 1999).

Cases in the Legal System

Although the legal system historically gave only a minimal level recognition to the plight of children exposed to domestic violence, there has been increasing awareness across the past two to three decades. Courts have shown increased examination of the effects of domestic violence on children in child custody and visitation matters, hearings on restraining orders, criminal failure to protect a child from harm, and care and protection matters such as termination of parental rights (Goldstein, 1999; Lemon, 1999). The impact of domestic violence has been examined in criminal cases, juvenile delinquency cases, and civil tort actions (Goldstein, 1999).

Child Custody and Visitation

Legal disputes over child custody and visitation arise when parents cannot reach an agreement through mediation or other less formal approaches. Courts make child custody and visitation determinations based on the best-interest-of-the-child standard, a standard that has been adopted by all 50 states (Oberlander, 1995). Many state statutes specify factors that the court should consider, such as the relationship between each parent and the child, parenting abilities, mental health, and substance abuse. As of 1997, 44 states and the District of Columbia adopted statutes requiring courts to consider domestic violence in child custody determinations (National Council of Juvenile and Family Court Judges, 1995). Several states have adopted statutes that contain a presumption against awarding custody to individuals who have engaged in domestic violence (Lemon, 1999; National Council of Juvenile and Family Court Judges, 1995). Many states have altered procedures so that evidence of domestic violence and its impact negates *friendly parent* statutes (found in 28 states) that give custody preference to the parent most likely to encourage parent–child contact with the other parent (Lemon, 1999).

Written judicial decisions, even in jurisdictions where consideration of domestic violence is not mandatory, have begun to contain findings of the impact of children's exposure to domestic violence. Increasingly, the presence of domestic violence is cited as a factor in judicial determinations (Lemon, 1999). At the appellate level, court decisions have been reversed due to judicial neglect to include specific written findings of fact regarding domestic violence (*In re Custody of Vaughn*, 1996). Judicial decisions have contained concern about false allegations of domestic violence, using it as one of the rationale to award custody to the other parent (e.g., *Farrell v. Farrell*, 1991). Cases have been reversed on appeal when the presumption against custody by a batterer was overlooked (e.g., *Bruner v. Jaeger*, 1995; *McDermott v. McDermott*, 1997).

A review of appellate cases showed a marked trend toward ordering supervised visitation for batterers (Lemon, 1999). Unfortunately, identifying appropriate supervisors frequently is a difficult undertaking. Visitation centers are becoming more and more common, but they are not available in all jurisdictions, and many are underfunded. Even when the other party sufficiently proves the presence of past domestic violence, courts have been reluctant to issue no-visitation orders; therefore, the problem of identifying appropriate supervisors arises frequently (McGill, Deutsch, & Zibbell, 1999). Parents victimized by domestic violence sometimes file *removal* petitions in postdivorce custody matters, seeking permission to relocate the children out of state. Removal cases sometimes are granted because of safety issues. However, there have been no clear trends across jurisdictions in the granting of removal petitions to custodial parents whose children were affected by domestic violence (Lemon, 1999).

Failure to Protect Children

When a child is harmed by the domestic violence of a parent, the other parent may face criminal charges of failure to protect the child from harm.

The parent also might face child protective services involvement on similar grounds (e.g., *Whitcomb v. Jefferson County Department of Social Services*, 1987). Even when there has been no corresponding supported neglect petition, the mere possibility that a domestic violence perpetrator may return to the home has been used as justification for child protective services removal and jurisdiction over a child (e.g., *In re Nicole B.*, 1979). A review of appellate cases (Lemon, 1999) yielded several court decisions in cases involving criminal charges of failure to protect. Findings of maternal guilt for failure to protect hinged on whether the mother knew or should have known the child would be harmed. The review yielded no appellate cases in which the mother's argument of duress (fear of greater injury or death to herself if she had tried to stop the abuse) was persuasive to the court.

Once a care and protection petition has been filed alleging that a child has been maltreated, the juvenile or family court judge rules on the issue of child protective services custody. If the child is removed from the home, the parents are offered services (except in the most egregious cases) that they must complete prior to resuming custody (Condie, 2003). In states that separate the functions of juvenile and family courts in addressing child protection and child custody matters respectively, family courts may still consider the ability of a parent to protect the child. The child's removal from the home usually would be referred to the court that has care and protection oversight. State statutes define what might constitute grounds for permanent removal. If sufficient grounds, the child protective services department may petition for termination of parental rights. Parents who engage in domestic violence risk termination of their parental rights, even when there is no direct physical abuse of the child (e.g., *In re Sylvia R.*, 1997). Battered parents might face termination of parental rights for failure to protect their children from exposure to domestic violence. Appellate courts sometimes reverse such orders (Lemon, 1999). In one appellate case, the trial court's decision was reversed because the mother left the father and relocated with the children to another city (*In re Nina A.M.*, 1993). Victims of domestic violence who face possible termination of parental rights may be negatively affected by the Adoption and Safe Families Act of 1997, because of the time that it takes to ensure family safety, relocate, seek a restraining order, recover from trauma, establish a new home, and find a new job (Lemon, 1999; Matthews, 1999). The Adoption and Safe Families Act of 1997 is a federal statute that rewards states for incorporating fast-track care and protection legislation that limits the amount of time children are in foster placement prior to the filing of a termination petition. Exceptions have been incorporated in many jurisdictions, making it possible that a parent actively seeking safety might be exempted from a termination petition, even if the process of seeking safety were slow (Condie, 2003).

Some courts have held that the murder of one parent by the child's other parent is not, in and of itself, sufficient grounds to terminate parental rights (*In re Mark V.*, 1986; *In re H.L.T.*, 1982). The cases tend to hinge on how long the murdering parent will face incarceration (which is linked to degree of culpability or the brutality of the murder) and therefore be unavailable to parent. Other considerations include the suitability of alternative placements for the child and the rehabilitation of the convicted parent. In other jurisdictions, courts have held that the act itself, and the resulting imprisonment of the child's only surviving parent, deprives the child of both parents and therefore is sufficient grounds for termination. Courts have made mixed rulings on whether murdering the parent in front of the children is grounds for termination (Lemon, 1999).

Domestic Violence Queries in Forensic Interview Protocols

The impact of domestic violence is relevant in many different types of forensic referrals. The forensic evaluator needs the requisite education, training and experience in domestic violence matters, and knowledge of special rules and legal requirements in the jurisdiction where the forensic evaluator practices. This section includes some examples of how the issue of domestic violence might arise and examples of how and when to inquire about it in the context of a forensic evaluation.

Sometimes the existence of domestic violence is central to a case, as seen in direct requests for an assessment of the child to determine the impact of trauma, a divorce custody proceeding involving allegations of domestic violence, or a juvenile justice case involving a child that allegedly attacked one parent in an attempt to defend the other parent. Diagnostic, treatment, and dispositional concerns are common in care and protection matters to gather information that would help child protective service workers make informed recommendations to the court concerning a child's service plan and a child's capacity to function in the family home or in a foster care setting. Child protective service workers may request information relevant to their decisions about whether a residential or intensive mental health setting is indicated for a child. Questions about the impact of domestic violence might arise in civil tort actions, either as a proximate cause for alleged injury or as a preexisting or coexisting factor independent of the alleged tort. The existence of domestic violence by one or both parents in the same family and the impact of domestic violence on the child might be central in determining the child's best psychological interests in divorce custody cases, probate court petitions for relocation or removal of the child to another state, and visitation disputes. In all of the foregoing legal applications, theories, and research on domestic violence can provide a useful evaluation and interpretive framework for the forensic evaluation. Recommendations are more informed when they are based on the literature as well as the clinical and forensic context.

In a variety of forensic evaluation referrals, questions concerning domestic violence and its impact are indicated when any form of family violence is in question. Because of the co-occurrence of many forms of violence, it is important to ask questions relevant to domestic violence when other forms of violence have been questioned or documented. Because of the significance of the potential impact on the child, forensic child evaluations should screen for the existence of domestic violence factors in all cases, regardless of the referral question. Although the role of the evaluator typically does not parallel that of investigator, some law enforcement agencies and child protective service agencies might employ forensic evaluators to conduct or assist with the investigative phase. As with any type of investigative interview, the final judicial determination over whether a child was exposed to domestic violence is a legal matter. The forensic evaluator's expertise is used to frame questions in a developmentally suitable manner for the child and to address the relevant forms of impact described in the research literature. In a similar vein, mental health commitment procedures might include a request for forensic expertise on the impact of domestic violence on a child's mental health functioning or diagnostic status. The evaluator would provide important information on the significance of trauma to the child's current mental health status. Often evaluators identify and clarify the importance of historical, situational, and individual variables that explain and contribute to diagnostic comorbidity in complicated diagnostic cases. Records provide important information on the progression of mental health concerns. The evaluator provides meaningful data and interpretations, and the magistrate is the final arbiter of whether the child meets commitment criteria.

In care and protection cases, questions might arise concerning the child's safety in the domestic violence victim parent's home, the child's perceptions of the safety of the home environment, the child's comprehension of what has occurred and his or her level of self-blame for the domestic violence, a child's capacity to tolerate foster home placement, a child's safety during supervised or unsupervised visitation with each parent, and the child's treatment and placement needs. In termination of parental rights cases, questions might arise about the child's safety and parenting needs, the impact of exposure to repeated or severe forms of domestic violence, the child's reaction to a series of orders of protection or police responses to the home, the impact upon the child of his or her attempts to protect the victim(s) of domestic violence in the household, vicarious or overt injury to the child in the context of a domestic violence dispute, and the child's adaptation to a foster or preadoptive placement. Questions might include the nature and extent of trauma to the child, the length of the expected course of recovery, the child's sense of safety or comfort in the presence of either parent, and the impact of the violence on the parent–child relationship. Questions also might include what factors might facilitate the child's adaptation to long-term substitute caretakers.

In juvenile delinquency matters, the impact of domestic violence sometimes is directly relevant to the child's expressed rationale for a crime. For example, some preadolescent and adolescent children commit crimes toward dating partners or toward parents (threats to parents, assaults of parents, murder of parents) as a response to domestic violence. Although serious crimes usually have other complicating factors, exposure to domestic violence might be a relevant consideration in a criminal responsibility defense, in a diminished capacity defense, in a duress defense, or as a mitigating factor at the sentencing phase (see chapters 12 and 19, this volume).

After the adolescent is sentenced, a forensic evaluator might be asked by the juvenile justice system to make treatment recommendations related to the youth's trauma reaction, the youth's view of male–female relationships, the youth's risk of future harm, or the youth's risk of repeating the actions of the battering parent. Even in cases where the crime was unrelated to the direct impact of domestic violence, adolescents might need treatment for the impact of domestic violence exposure. Adolescents in the juvenile justice system should be asked about their exposure to or direct victimization by all forms of family violence, including domestic violence. Questions should not be limited to parent-to-parent abuse.

EVALUATION METHODOLOGY

Establishing Rapport

Procedures

It is commonly accepted that a moderate amount of rapport-building conversation or activities facilitates the interview process. Poor rapport can cause children to become mute, silly, fussy, hyperkinetic, or otherwise uncooperative, and overly sympathetic involvement in rapport building can compromise the interview process. Adequate professional attention to rapport helps a child overcome reluctance due to fear, shame, or mistrust. It might also produce disclosure of an adult's attempts to coach the child or threats to the child against disclosure. Rapport sometimes helps children to resist misleading or suggestive questions because of reduced fear of the interviewer and less focus on the interviewer as an authority figure. It facilitates assertiveness in children so that they can vocalize any confusion or distress over question content.

Evaluators must strike a balance, however, being careful not to convey an assumption that the child was exposed to or traumatized by domestic violence (Saywitz & Camparo, 1998).

Rapport-building procedures should not inadvertently set the stage for an expectation that the child must disclose maltreatment. Examples of statements that might produce such expectations include introducing yourself as someone who talks to children to whom bad things have happened, or reminding the child that he or she previously told others certain information. It is better to give the child permission to tell you something different and to only say what is real (Condie, 2003). Although it is important to set the child at ease in forensic evaluations, a neutral stance sometimes is preferable to warmth and supportiveness so that the evaluation process is not tainted by a child's efforts to please the evaluator (Thompson, Clarke-Stewart, & Lepore, 1997).

Rapport is difficult to define, but it contains elements of trust, empathy, positive regard, understanding, harmony, and accord. Three main goals in the rapport-building process with a child are to set the child at ease, to develop an understanding of the child's language abilities, and to provide a notification of the limits of confidentiality that is suitable to the child's comprehension. It is helpful to begin with innocuous questions, but the questions should not be so peripheral or disjointed that they have a detrimental effect on the child's comprehension of the purpose of the evaluation. It is helpful to avoid questions with the potential to heighten children's anxiety over loyalty bonds with parents (Stahl, 1994).

The following suggestions have been made to facilitate rapport. Establish a child-centered office environment with chairs and tables of the appropriate height for children. Colorful decor helps children feel at home, but too much color can be distracting to preschool children. There should be enough child-centered objects in the office to make it appear interesting, but not so many that the child is distracted. Allow the child time to get accustomed to the evaluator and to the context. Extra time may be needed for children with shy temperaments, emotional withdrawal, attention problems, or hyperactivity. In some cases of possible exposure to domestic violence, it might be useful to model safe and appropriate interactions between adults in order to set the child at ease. Be attentive to issues of personal space and boundaries. Allow the child to ask questions (Oberlander, 1995; Saywitz & Camparo, 1998).

Appropriate care should be used in the choice of rapport-building strategies because of concerns about gathering trustworthy interview data. For example, it usually is inadvisable to have an adult in the room, but some young children cannot tolerate separation. Children younger than 7 years often experience separation anxiety in unfamiliar situations. Maltreated children may be less equipped to separate from adults than other children. Sometimes it helps to ask caretakers in advance to encourage the child to go alone. The evaluator can show the child where the caretaker will wait, allowing the child to check periodically on the caretaker. Often, the problem can be resolved simply by allowing extra time for the child to feel sufficiently safe before separation from the person accompanying the child to the interview. If all the foregoing strategies fail, arrangements can be made for a suitable support figure to be present, such as a familiar and preferred child care worker. Any adult who sits in on the evaluation should be seated behind the child and instructed not to intervene. A conversation about discretion and confidentiality would be in order before the adult was allowed to sit in (Lamb, Sternberg, & Esplin, 1998; Saywitz & Camparo, 1998).

Distressed children sometimes present as silent, resistant, depressed, and avoidant. Empathy is a common clinical tool for conveying comfort without suggesting the child should respond to questions in a particular way. Children also benefit from a description of what will take place in the interview. Children sometimes have unrealistic expectations of what might take place in the interview, using fantasy to fill in the gaps in their experience base. When children do not comprehend the role of an adult, they usually rely upon roles they know, such as teacher or parent, to try to understand the role of a new adult (Condie, 2003). Obtaining background information about the child facilitates rapport development. It facilitates the use of interview content that is of high interest to the child, and the use of language that is appropriate to the child's level of linguistic development. Speaking in the language of children seems simple, but it takes training and practice.

The structure and content of questions appropriate for children should be practiced and mastered prior to engaging in clinical interviews of children, especially very young children (Condie, 2003; Saywitz & Camparo, 1998).

Developmental Factors

Questions must be designed so that the child can understand and respond to them. Children often answer questions that they do not comprehend. Depending on their response, their miscomprehension might not always be apparent. Precautions should be taken to minimize unintentional suggestions, leading questions, or complex questions. Responses should be interpreted from a developmental perspective (Saywitz & Camparo, 1998). The form, content, pace, and structure of an interview should be tailored to the child's language skills and capacity to cope. For example, one- and two-syllable words are preferable to more advanced words. Children who cannot tell the difference between a week and a month should not be asked to estimate when something happened. Young children who can count may not be able to make reliable determinations about the frequency or quantity of certain acts. Simple sentence structure using the active voice is preferable to the passive voice. Terms such as *domestic violence* are incomprehensible to many children. It is preferable to use words such as *hit, kick,* or *punch* (Saywitz & Camparo, 1998; Walker, 1999).

The pace of the interview should be tailored to the child's attention span. For example, younger children usually require shorter interview sessions and more breaks (Condie, 2003). Asking questions that require children to take perspective or to reason from cause to effect may be inappropriate for developmental reasons. For example, a young child probably would not be able to describe how her mother felt about being hit, or why the child reacted in a particular way to domestic violence (Saywitz & Camparo, 1998). Children at the same level of development might show differences in temperament, attachment, or coping resources. Individual differences should be considered, making adjustments in the interview pace and following the child's lead as indicated. The child's current mental health functioning also might influence the approach to the interview. For example, a 12-year-old boy who is depressed might cope with the interview quite differently than a 12-year-old boy in similar circumstances who has developed conduct problems (Orbach & Lamb, 2000).

A number of approaches might facilitate the child's ability to provide relevant responses to the referral question. For example, it is helpful to caution the child to listen carefully to questions and not to guess. Instructing children that it is permissible to say "I don't know" makes it easier for the child to do so. The skill should be rehearsed to determine if they indeed would respond appropriately to questions to which they do not know the answer. The child should be given the option of skipping questions that make him or her feel uncomfortable. Giving the child this option helps the interviewer detect the difference between a child's discomfort and a child's lack of knowledge of the answer to a question. Without this preinterview step, the child might act out, withdraw, or respond, "I don't know," rather than conveying discomfort. Warning the child in advance that he or she might not understand all of the questions gives the child permission to report when he or she is confused. For young children who have difficulty understanding differences in perspective, it is useful to tell them the interviewer was not present in the family home. It is useful to construct a scenario or to ask questions about a preferred children's activity (e.g., a birthday party) to gather a baseline on the child's capacity to provide a narrative, to response to open-ended questions, to respond to follow-up questions, and to resist incorporating suggestions. Experimenting with question form will help the evaluator to determine whether young children comprehend *who, what, when, where,* and *why* questions, and whether they comprehend pronouns and kinship terms (Condie, 2003; Orbach & Lamb, 2000; Saywitz & Camparo, 1998).

The Clinical Interview

Interviewing Children About Recollections of Domestic Violence

Although there is no perfect method for gathering interview data from children that is reliable and valid, in all evaluations it is important to try to minimize influences that might be detrimental to the process (Sternberg & Lamb, 1999). Many experts advise using open-ended questions when possible because information that is elicited spontaneously has the lowest margin of error. However, if that approach does not yield relevant responses, it usually is necessary to introduce the topic of interest. This can be done using direct questions, but not leading questions. Unfortunately, the effect of introducing the topic of interest is unclear. Empirical research offers little guidance, especially when it is unclear that violence took place, or when the details of the violence are poorly documented (Lamb et al., 1998; Orbach & Lamb, 2000). When asking children to discuss their experiences with exposure to or awareness of domestic violence, it is important to minimize any effects that might be related to identification with the aggressor or fear of violating family loyalty.

Some children who have been exposed to domestic violence have only limited experience with safe relationships with adults. Because child victims often have little comparative experience, children may not understand domestic violence is unusual or even violent. By extension, they might report domestic violence in a nonchalant fashion, they might laugh or show other inappropriate affect when describing domestic violence, or they might not understand what they are being asked to discuss or report. Depending on their developmental status, they might not comprehend notions such as safety and security in family life, even when those concepts are explained or contrasted with danger. When asking children to report their family experiences, the evaluator must enter their linguistic and phenomenological worlds to learn idiosyncratic words used to describe family experiences, the details of those experiences, and factors that lead up to and followed episodes of domestic violence. Even though they might not comprehend or characterize the perpetrator's behavior as violent or wrong, children might nonetheless use their own terms to describe domestic violence (Condie, 2003).

Children who have been exposed to domestic violence might be able to describe a somewhat predictable cyclical quality for their experience. If they have trouble sequencing, it is useful to say "Tell me everything about that," "Tell me more about that," or "Don't leave anything out" (Orbach & Lamb, 1999) and to ask follow-up questions about the beginning, middle, and end of what took place. Children might also be aware of perpetrator promises or transient guilt after an episode. Asking them to report details that precede and follow episodes of domestic violence provides knowledge of the progression of behavioral and affective aspects of danger in their day-to-day family experiences. Even though children have trouble reporting quantity, they might be able to describe whether something occurred a lot or a little (although one should try to determine whether their meaning of *a lot* is consistent with an adult meaning of it), and they might be able to describe their worst or most frightening recollection of domestic violence. It is useful to inquire about the details of any attempts by children to resist exposure to or avoid awareness of domestic violence (Condie, 2003).

Children's Reports of Their Reactions to Domestic Violence Awareness and Exposure

Common approaches to interviewing children include using appropriate vocal intonation, asking for examples, being open to what children say, rephrasing children's responses for confirmation, avoiding selective reinforcement for certain topics or responses, setting a tempo and interview length that is appropriate for the child's level of development, using simple questions, and using concrete referents when needed. It is helpful to avoid yes/no questions, compound questions, questions with compound elements such as two persons or situations, suggestions, leading questions, and contamination by asking leading questions with specific diagnostic criteria. Interview questions relevant to children's reactions to trauma should focus on symptoms and behaviors relevant to empirically based descriptions and diagnostic criteria for child behavior disorders and trauma reactions, but it is important to avoid suggesting those symptoms and behaviors to the child. Children may have their own way of describing their symptoms, so they should be given the opportunity to use words that are meaningful to them.

Because young children often do not understand the link between historical events and current symptoms and behaviors, it is important to avoid asking them to reason from cause to effect or to make comparisons of their reactions to one episode of domestic violence to their reactions to a later or different episode. Comparative questions can be useful, however, in helping adolescents to clarify the nature and severity of their reactions. Adolescents often compare themselves to their peers, so this process is a useful guidepost for asking them to describe the intensity of their feelings (Condie, 2003).

Although it is important not to lead the child, it also is important to include sufficient breadth in questions in order to capture the extent of the child's phenomenological experience of domestic violence exposure. Sometimes questions that seemingly are irrelevant to violence will lead to a child's description of his or her reactions. A child might provide indicators of his or her reaction in the context of a description of the routine of a typical family day, a family dinner, or a family outing. A question about whether a child once had a bruise or needed a bandage might lead to a full description of one parent's attempt to harm the other parent and then inadvertently physically injuring the child. Asking a child when his or her favorite stuffed animal needed to go to the hospital might lead to an account of an emergency department visit following an episode of domestic violence. It is important to create a context in which children have the opportunity to spontaneously report their own experiences in their own words and at their own pace (Sparta, 2003). Direct observation and caretaker observations are effective complements to interview data.

Children's statements must be understood in the context of their developmental competence to accurately report their experience, accurately describe events in a sequential fashion, and resist the effects of either intentional or unintentional suggestions from a variety of preinterview sources such as caregivers, teachers, mental health professionals, and investigators. Reports of other involved professionals can help to establish the consistency of children's statements and behaviors across settings and across time. Competence of children's recollections includes their capacity to perceive acts with accuracy, their capacity to recall, their capacity to distinguish truth from falsehood, and their capacity to communicate personal information. One must recognize the potential complications of children's recollections. Accurate recall by children represents a complicated process that may

be affected by their experience, ongoing reports by family members, shifting developmental interpretations for the original experience, learning from others about the traumatic event and their reactions to it, and internalizing a belief at variance with the actual event. Accurate recall may be complicated by suggestibility (associated with personality variables, interactional processes, and age), the length of time delay between the traumatic event and the interview, the child's desire to reach closure, and other factors associated with the child's adaptation to the traumatic event (Condie, 2003; Sparta, 2003).

Measures and Clinical Tools

Specific Assessment Measures

Trauma reactions vary with developmental and individual factors, and they vary in frequency, intensity, and duration of symptoms. Assessment strategies should be informed by empirical research about trauma reactions in children. When assessment instruments are used, the evaluator should remain open to the broadest range of possible effects. Rating scales vary in their format and the type of information revealed. Symptom and behavior checklists and structured interviews, although they may have limited content, are useful when there is a need to differentiate among classes of symptoms, and the link, if any, to trauma or to other causal factors in the individual's history (Sparta, 2003).

When child diagnosis is part of the referral question, relevant parent and teacher report forms may be used, along with individual self-report and symptom checklist measures that are appropriate for the child's level of development. Care should be taken to consider the child's developmental level rather than his or her age when choosing whether or not to use rating scales. It is useful to practice the rating scale with innocuous questions to make sure that the child has the capacity to differentiate among the qualitative dimensions of rating scales. For example, on three-point scales, young children sometimes will respond only at the extremes (Condie, 2003).

Because of conflicting data about the validity and reliability of projective measures, they should be used and interpreted cautiously. As with all assessments, multimodal approaches are the most optimal. As an adjunct to clinical measures, many evaluators find it helpful to base questions on semistructured and standardized diagnostic assessment instruments. Use of a semistructured and standardized approach should not preclude spontaneous reports from children or others. Children should be given the opportunity to describe the details of their reactions to determine if any idiosyncratic or unexpected reactions exist. Idiographic descriptions of behaviors, symptoms, and experiences have relevance and significance (Kolbo et al., 1996; Margolin, 1998). Cultural differences should be taken into account when asking children to describe or endorse symptoms and behaviors. When indicated, questions should be designed to compensate for children's special needs, bilingual status, disability status, or language delays (Condie, 2003).

There are many measures that have utility in the assessment of childhood trauma. In this section, examples of those measures are listed and briefly summarized (a more complete summary is contained in Sparta, 2003). The examples do not represent an exhaustive list, nor does their inclusion represent an endorsement of the measures across evaluations. The evaluator should carefully choose measures and clinical tools based on the referral question and the context and based on empirical support for their use with specific populations and for specific questions. Examples include structured interviews, self-report symptom and behavior checklists, and other clinical tools.

The Diagnostic Interview Schedule for Children, Version IV, PTSD Subscale (Shaffer, Fisher, Lucas, Dulcan, & Schwab-Stone, 2000), is a structured interview for children ages 6 to 12, and for adolescents ages 13 to 17. It is a guide for questions relevant to the nature of the traumatic experience, and relevant to the American Psychiatric Association's *Diagnostic and Statistical Manual of Mental Disorders* (*DSM*) symptoms and behaviors. The mental status examination enables the evaluator to focus on areas of functioning relevant to a broad range of mental health variables. It is useful in describing the range of the child's symptoms and behaviors.

The Children's Depression Inventory, for children between 7 and 17 years of age, quantifies a range of symptoms of depression (Kovacs, 1992).

Draw-A-Person, Kinetic Family Drawing techniques, sentence completion techniques, and apperception tests, although weak in their empirical validation, can facilitate communication and hypotheses about the child's experience, and they can provide an opportunity for elaboration of trauma reactions (Bellack, 1993; Pihl & Nimrod, 1976). Self-report ratings scales (compare Youth Self-Report Form, Achenbach, 1992; Behavior Assessment Rating scale for Children, Reynolds & Kamphaus, 1992) can be used with children who are old enough to describe their experiences; parallel parent and teacher forms can be used for comparison and contrast of responses.

The Trauma Symptom Checklist for Children (Briere, 1996) is a self-report measure of posttraumatic stress and related psychological symptoms for use with children between 8 and 16 years of age. It includes two validity scales and can serve as a basis for further posttest interview questions for children and for collaterals. The Clinician-Administered PTSD scale for Children (Nader, Kriegler, Blake, & Pynoos, 1994) provides data about the frequency and intensity of symptoms of posttraumatic stress, as well as the impact upon social functioning. The Child Dissociative Checklist (Putnam, 1990; Putnam & Peterson, 1994) is completed by someone familiar with the child's functioning in the past 12 months, and the Adolescent Dissociative Experiences scale (Armstrong, Putnam, & Carlson, 1994) provides children 10–21 years of age with an opportunity to endorse relevant symptoms of dissociation.

The Child PTSD Reaction Index (Frederick, Pynoos, & Nader, 1992) and the Child's Reaction to Traumatic Events scale (Jones, 1994) include items that correspond to some of the *DSM* diagnostic criteria for PTSD. The Children's Impact of Traumatic Events scale (V. V. Wolfe, Wolfe, Gentile, & Larose, 1986) captures a broad range of traumatic experiences and reactions, including noninterpersonal and interpersonal trauma. The Child Rating scales of Exposure to Interpersonal Abuse (Praver, 1994) assess the frequency of severity of children's exposure to interpersonal abuse, for children 6–11 years of age. It is available in a cartoon form known as the Angie/Andy Child Rating scale (Praver, Pelcovitz, & DiGuseppe, 1994). Fletcher (1991) designed the When Bad Things

Happen scale, for children 8 or more years of age, to assess a broad variety of traumatic events and children's symptoms. It structures the child's report of a number of traumatic events, and it helps the child reveal dynamic variables such as whether he or she feels stigmatized by the experiences.

Collateral Interviews and Records

The child's interview and assessment data should be supplemented with data from collateral contacts and records. Records of relevance include documentation of the child's self-report of exposure to domestic violence (usually contained in child protective services investigation records, but sometimes also found in pediatric records, mental health records, or police investigation records), records of the child's functioning and adaptation to placement, records of the child's relationship with caregivers and substitute caregivers, educational records, and any other relevant records. The evaluators should review data relevant to the child's family history, educational background, socialization at home and at school, neighborhood environment, birth history, early childhood development, physical health, mental health, and any history of accidents or injuries (Condie, 2003). It is useful to ask about the impact of the traumatic event on other family members, preexisting and coexisting sources of trauma, alcohol and drug abuse in the child's environment, divorce or other relationship conflicts, and dislocations of home and school environments (Sparta, 2003). Behavior rating scales can be completed by teachers and caregivers, providing data that complements collateral interviews (Condie, 2003).

The Effects of Vicarious Exposure on the Evaluation Process

The forensic interview process usually contains at least some aspects that potentially might produce a personal reaction in the evaluator, particularly when addressing domestic or family violence impacts in children. Evaluators should strive to maintain objectivity in offering forensic opinions. Many personal reactions, if dealt with appropriately, do not affect objectivity. Proper ethical conduct obligates the evaluator to maintain self-awareness of the types of cases that would compromise objectivity. Based on data from the American Psychological Association's ad hoc Committee on Legal and Ethical Issues in the Treatment of Interpersonal Violence (2002), compromises to objectivity can lead to contamination of interviews.

Possible risks of interview contamination include blending the roles of evaluator and treatment provider, framing suggestive or leading questions, and disbelieving traumatic memories of domestic violence exposure can be forgotten. The loss of balance in an interview can lead to subtle or overt cues that encourage the client to engage in embellishment or minimization. Contamination risks also occur because of inexperience or inadequate training that leads to a failure to anticipate the difficulty of formulating questions appropriate to a child's level of development, linguistic capacity, defensive avoidance, and level of anxiety. Other risks of contamination include rendering expert opinions without sufficient training or expertise in child development or the impact of domestic violence, insufficient sensitivity to the dynamics of victimization and trauma, predicting harm without conducting an appropriate evaluation or without considering the limitations in predictions of future harm, and insufficient attention to the dynamics of victim blame.

Because the rate of false allegations of domestic violence (and other forms of intrafamilial violence) may be higher in custody and visitation cases compared to other forensic evaluation cases, there is a risk of overestimating the level of false allegations in those cases and an obverse risk of dismissing true allegations. The problem of false allegations is linked to another possible compromise in custody cases. Custody evaluators often face pressure by the court or by the referring parties to determine the truth or falseness of allegations. It is more appropriate to provide descriptive data to the court, with appropriate caveats that no profession can discern whether individuals are truthful. It is optimal if evaluators have sufficient recognition of boundary issues, sufficient awareness of the vulnerability of victims of domestic violence exposure, and a broad understanding of the many ways children are affected by domestic violence (American Psychological Association, 1996c, 2002a, 2002b).

The Interpretation Process

The interpretation of assessment data involves a thought process of hypothesis testing and rejection. It is important to consider supporting data and contradictory data, to consider hypotheses and alternatives, and to recheck results and interpretations prior to finalizing the report. Children show variable reactions to trauma. Trauma is an overwhelming experience that leads to a continuum of posttraumatic adaptations, some of which make children symptomatic. Functional impairments are as relevant as formal diagnosis when understanding children's reactions to trauma. Interpretation is both a scientific and a literary process whereby empirically and logically derived findings are cogently communicated to an intended audience.

Describing the Effects of Domestic Violence Exposure in a Clinical Context

Although diagnosis is important as a mechanism of communication among professionals, evaluation of childhood trauma need not be limited to traditional diagnostic nomenclature. Even within diagnostic manuals, there are caveats that the experiences of children sometimes are qualitatively different than the symptoms and behaviors that adults manifest in response to trauma. Posttraumatic reactions can occur at any age, and symptoms typically appear within 3 months after a traumatic event. Occasionally symptoms do not appear until years later. The duration of responses varies, with complete recovery occurring within 3 months in approximately half of all cases (American Psychiatric Association, 2000; Condie, 2003; Sparta, 2003). Children can experience posttraumatic stress both directly, when they are victimized, and indirectly, when they perceive major threat to their security base, as in the victimization of their parents (Jaffe et al., 1990).

Although not all children react to trauma in the same manner, a common approach to understanding children's reactions is to use a diagnostic framework. Relevant *DSM* diagnoses include, but are not limited to, PTSD, acute stress disorder, anxiety disorders, disorders of depression, and adjustment disorders. PTSD has received the most attention as a potential diagnostic outcome. As described in the 4th edition and 4th revised edition of the *DSM*

(American Psychiatric Association, 1994, 2000), diagnostic criteria for PTSD include the precursor of a traumatic event involving actual or threatened death or serious injury, or a threat to the physical integrity of the self or others. PTSD might arise from exposure to domestic violence against a parent. To meet diagnostic criteria, a specified number of symptoms or behaviors must follow the event. The duration of time between the event and symptom onset ranges from within the first 3 months after the trauma to a delay of months or years. The individual's response to the trauma must involve horror, helplessness, or intense fear.

In children, behavioral expressions of disorganization or agitation may occur. Young children usually do not relive or reexperience the trauma as vividly as do adults. Their distressing dreams or nightmares might consist of monsters, rescuing others, or threats to self or others. Reenactments might appear as themes in repetitive play. Symptoms include persistent reexperiencing of the event, persistent avoidance of reminders, numbing of responsiveness, and persistent hyperarousal. Symptom duration must persist beyond 1 month. The symptoms must cause distress or impairment in social, occupational, or other spheres of functioning. The response is classified as acute, chronic, or delayed onset. Associated features typically seen in children might include impaired affect modulation; self-destructive and impulsive behavior; symptoms of dissociation; somatic complaints; feelings of ineffectiveness, shame, despair, hopelessness, or hostility; feeling permanently damaged; feeling constantly threatened; loss of previously sustained beliefs; social withdrawal; impaired relationships; or personality changes (American Psychiatric Association, 1994, 2000).

Other diagnostic outcomes of trauma may include reactive attachment disorder, panic disorder, dissociative disorder, agoraphobia, obsessive-compulsive disorder, social phobia, specific phobia, somatization disorder, and substance-related disorders (American Psychiatric Association, 1994, 2000). Sometimes children show reactions to trauma that do not mirror diagnostic entities. With repeated exposure to trauma, children may show gradual inability to benefit from moderating variables of internal resilience, positive coping resources, and social support (Sparta, 2003). The acute, chronic, and delayed-onset phases of trauma reactions may produce different symptoms of different quality, intensity, or frequency. The early stages are remarkable for nightmares, hypervigilance, sleep disturbance, generalized anxiety, and an exaggerated startle response, among other symptoms. The chronic stage is notable for detachment, restricted affect, sadness, dissociation, estrangement from others, and a future expectation of a difficult life (Famularo, Kinscherff, & Fenton, 1990; Sparta, 2003). Reactions vary with the level of stress, the nature of the traumatic event, the individual's coping resources, the individual's biological predisposition for autonomic arousal, personality variables, the level of constructive support available from caretakers following the trauma, and premorbidity and comorbidity with other conditions (Sparta, 2003).

Children's manifestation of symptoms may be different at different developmental stages. Some children may appear asymptomatic despite significant psychological harm. In addition to evaluating the types of potential impacts reported in the research literature, it is useful to determine whether children show resilience characteristics or other potentially attenuating characteristics, and whether they report protective factors such as a relationship with a caring and nonviolent adult (Condie, 2003).

Communicating the Impact of Domestic Violence and Domestic Violence Exposure Upon Children

After determining the significance of the data to the referral question, and after carefully entertaining competing hypotheses, the interpretation should include a clear and cogent response to the referral question, a brief analysis and summary of supporting data, and qualifications and inferences when relevant. The tone should be respectful of the child's experience, and focus should be upon the intended audience of readers. Consider the data in the context of the child's level of development (which might be different from the child's chronological level of development), and in the context of the child's world. Identify the practical and theoretical implications of the findings in a manner that is accessible to the reader. Describe the results in an unambiguous fashion but do not overstate the results. Consider how the report might be received by a scope of readers. Wording should be phrased artfully, in an unbiased fashion, and in a professional tone. The beginning of wisdom in report writing is to make conclusions with the integrity of the child, the family, and the profession in mind.

SUMMARY

Concerns about domestic violence underscore the need for accurate assessment of children's reactions to trauma. The ultimate practical usefulness of a report is its communication of findings relevant to the referral question. A useful report directly samples and measures data relevant to the referral question, and it anticipates the applications that follow from the referral question. It gives due consideration to the complicated nature and dynamics of questioning children about their experiences, it describes the child's unique experience, it places the child's experience within developmental and situational frameworks, it provides diagnostic conclusions if indicated, and it provides a venue for the child to communicate his or her experience.

Domestic violence affects children in many ways. Many children and adolescents witness horrific acts of violence against their parents or other caregivers. Some children might not witness the violence, but they still feel considerable tension in the home, they overhear the violence, and they view the injuries sustained during the violence. Children or adolescents might sustain their own injuries if they try to intervene to stop the violence. Some perpetrators or victims might ask children to engage in acts of complicity by convincing them to call the police and report false information, or to keep family secrets should the police or other officials intervene.

Children show a variety of reactions to domestic violence exposure. Siblings within the same home may respond differently to domestic violence exposure. Some children might mimic the violence and show other conduct problems, whereas others might withdraw or attempt to behave perfectly. Parental substance abuse or mental illness, although not responsible for the domestic violence, can complicate children's reactions to domestic violence. Children who are exposed to domestic violence sometimes are described as invisible victims because of neglect by adults to consider the short-term and long-term implications of their exposure. Exposure to violence can lead to recapitulations of violence, high-risk behaviors, and problems trusting and relating to others. Although diagnostic outcomes are important, professionals should be aware of the broader impact upon children in their development, their social and intimate relationships, their cognitive and academic functioning, their emotional well-being, and their sense of self.

References

Achenbach, T. (1992). *Manual for the Child Behavior Checklist/2–3 and 1992 profile.* Burlington, VT: University of Vermont, Department of Psychiatry.

Adoption and Safe Families Act of 1997, Pub. L. No. 96-272, 94 Stat. 500 (1997).

Alexander, P. C., Moore, S., & Alexander, E. R., III. (1991). What is transmitted in the intergenerational transmission of violence? *Journal of Marriage & the Family, 53,* 657–668.

American Psychiatric Association. (1994). *Diagnostic and statistical manual of mental disorders* (4th ed.). Washington, DC: Author.

American Psychiatric Association. (2000). *Diagnostic and statistical manual of mental disorders* (4th ed., rev.). Washington, DC: Author.

American Psychological Association. (2002a). *Ethical principles of psychologists and code of conduct.* Washington, DC: Author.

American Psychological Association, Committee on Legal and Ethical Issues in the Treatment of Interpersonal Violence. (2002b). *Professional, ethical, and legal issues concerning interpersonal violence, maltreatment, and related trauma.* Washington, DC: Author.

American Psychological Association Presidential Task Force on Violence and the Family. (1998). *Violence and the family.* Washington, DC: Author.

American Psychological Association, Public Interest Initiative. (1996a). *Issues and dilemmas in family violence.* Washington, DC: Author.

American Psychological Association, Public Interest Initiative. (1996b). *Resolution on male violence against women.* Washington, DC: Author.

American Psychological Association, Public Interest Initiative. (1996c). *Potential problems for psychologists working with the area of interpersonal violence.* Washington, DC: Author.

Andrews, B., & Brewin, C. R. (1990). Attributions of blame for marital violence: A study of antecedents and consequences. *Journal of Marriage & the Family, 52,* 757–767.

Armstrong, J., Putnam, F., & Carlson, E. (1994). *Adolescent Dissociative Experiences scale.* Towson, MD: Sidran Institute.

Ayoub, C. C., Deutsch, R. M., & Maraganore, A. (1999). Emotional distress in children of high-conflict divorce: The impact of marital conflict and violence. *Family & Conciliation Courts Review, 37,* 297–314.

Bachman, R., & Saltzman, L. E. (1995). *Violence against women: Estimates from the redesigned survey* (Special Rep. No. NCJ-154348). Washington, DC: Bureau of Justice Statistics.

Bellack, L. (1993). *The T.A.T., & C.A.T., & S.A.T. in clinical use* (5th ed.). Needham Heights, MA: Allyn & Bacon.

Belsky, J. (1993). Etiology of child maltreatment: A developmental-ecological analysis. *Psychological Bulletin, 114,* 413–434.

Bernard, G. W., Vera, H., Vera, M. I., & Newman, G. (1982). Till death do us part: A study of spouse murder. *Bulletin of the American Academy of Psychiatry & the Law, 10,* 271–280.

Bowen, K. (2000). Child abuse and domestic violence in families of children seen for suspected sexual abuse. *Clinical Pediatrics, 39,* 33–40.

Briere, J. (1996). *Trauma symptom checklist for children: Professional manual.* Odessa, FL: Psychological Assessment Resources.

Browne, A. (1993). Violence against women by male partners: Prevalence, outcomes, and policy implications. *American Psychologist, 48,* 1077–1087.

Browne, A., & Bassuk, S. S. (1997). Intimate violence in the lives of homeless and poor housed women: Prevalence and patterns in an ethnically diverse sample. *American Journal of Orthopsychiatry, 67,* 261–278.

Bruner v. Jaeger, 534 N.W. 2d 825 (N.D. 1995).

Bureau of Justice Statistics. (1998, March). *Violence by intimates* (No. NCJ167237). Washington, DC: U.S. Department of Justice.

Burgess, A. W., Harner, H., Baker, T., Hartman, C. R., & Lole, C. (2001). Batterers stalking patterns. *Journal of Family Violence, 16,* 309–321.

Burgess, R. L. (1994). The family in a changing world: A prolegomenon to an evolutionary analysis. *Human Nature, 5,* 203–221.

Carter, L. S., Weithorn, L. A., & Behrman, M. D. (1999). Domestic violence and children: Analysis and recommendations. *Future of Children (Domestic Violence & Children), 9,* 4–20.

Condie, L. B. (2003). *Parenting evaluations for the court.* New York: Kluwer-Plenum.

Douglas, K. S., & Dutton, D. G. (2001). Assessing the link between stalking and domestic violence. *Aggression & Violent Behavior, 6*, 519–546.

Dutton, D. G., & Kropp, P. R. (2000). A review of domestic violence risk instruments. *Trauma Violence & Abuse, 1*, 171–181.

Emery, R. E. (1989). Family violence. *American Psychologist, 44*, 321–328.

Family Violence Prevention and Services Act of 1984, 42 U.S.C. §§ 10401 *et seq.* (1992).

Famularo, R. A., Kinscherff, R. T., & Fenton, T. (1990). Symptom differences in acute and chronic presentation of childhood posttraumatic stress disorder. *Child Abuse & Neglect, 14*, 439–444.

Fantuzzo, J., Boruch, R., Beriama, A., Atkins, S., & Marcus, S. (1997). Domestic violence and children: Prevalence and risk in five major U.S. cities. *Journal of the American Academy of Child & Adolescent Psychiatry, 36*, 116–122.

Fantuzzo, J., & Lindquist, C. (1989). The effects of observing conjugal violence on children: A review and analysis of research methodology. *Journal of Family Violence, 4*, 77–94.

Fantuzzo, J. W., & Mohr, W. K. (1999). Prevalence and effects of child exposure to domestic violence. *Future of Children (Domestic Violence & Children), 9*, 21–32.

Farrell v. Farrell, 319 P. 2d 896 (Alaska 1991).

Fletcher, K. (1991). *When Bad Things Happen scale.* (Available from the author, University of Massachusetts Medical Center, Department of Psychiatry, 55 Lake Avenue North, Worcester, Massachusetts, 01655)

Frederick, C., Pynoos, R., & Nader, K. (1992). *Child PTSD reaction index.* (Available from C. Frederick and R. Pynoos, 760 Westwood Plaza, Los Angeles, CA 90024)

Galen, L. W., Brower, K. J., Gillespie, B. W., & Zucker, R. A. (2000). Sociopathy, gender, and treatment outcome among outpatient substance abusers. *Drug & Alcohol Dependence, 61*, 23–33.

Geffner, R., & Pagelow, M. D. (1990). Victims of spouse abuse. In R. T. Ammerman & M. Hersch (Eds.), *Treatment of family violence* (pp. 113–135). New York: Wiley.

Gelles, R. J. (1988). Violence and pregnancy: Are pregnant women at greater risk of abuse? *Journal of Marriage & the Family, 50*, 841–847.

Gelles, R. J., & Maynard, P. E. (1987). A structural family systems approach to intervention in cases of family violence. *Family Relations: Journal of Applied Family & Child Studies, 36*, 270–275.

Goldstein, R. D. (1999). *Child abuse and neglect: Cases and materials.* St. Paul, MN: West.

Hassouneh-Phillips, D., & Curry, M. A. (2002). Abuse of women with disabilities: State of the science. *Rehabilitation Counseling Bulletin, 45*, 96–104.

Henderson Gist, J., McFarlane, J., Malecha, A., Fredland, N., Schultz, P., & Willson, P. (2001). Women in danger: Intimate partner violence experienced by women who qualify and do not qualify for a protective order. *Behavioral Sciences & the Law, 19*, 637–647.

Holtzworth-Munroe, A., Meehan, J. C., Herron, K., Rehman, U., & Stuart, G. L. (2000). Testing the Holtzworth-Munroe and Stuart (1991) batterer typology. *Journal of Consulting & Clinical Psychology, 68*, 1000–1019.

Huang, C. J., & Gunn, T. (2001). An examination of domestic violence in an African American community in North Carolina: Causes and consequences. *Journal of Black Studies, 31*, 790–811.

Hughes, H. M., Parkinson, D. L., & Vargo, M. C. (1989). Witnessing spouse abuse and experiencing physical abuse: A "double whammy"? *Journal of Family Violence, 4*, 197–209.

Huth-Bocks, A. C., Levendosky, A. A., & Semel, M. A. (2001). The direct and indirect effects of domestic violence on young children's intellectual functioning. *Journal of Family Violence, 16*, 269–290.

In re Custody of Vaughn, 664 N.E. 2d 434 (Mass. 1996).

In re H.L.T., 298 S.E. 2d 33 (Ga. App. 1982).

In re Mark V., 177 Cal. App. 3d 754 (1986).

In re Nicole B., 93 Cal. App. 3d 874, 878–882, 155 Cal. Rptr. 916, 918–920 (1979).

In re Nina A.M., 593 N.Y.S. 2d 89 (1993).

In re Sylvia R., 55 Cal. App. 4th 559 (1997).

Jaffe, P. G., Wolfe, D. A., & Wilson, S. K. (1990). *Children of battered women.* Newbury Park, CA: Sage.

Jaffe, P., Wolfe, D. A., Wilson, S. K., & Zak, L. (1986). Family violence and child adjustment: A comparative analysis of girls' and boys' behavioral symptoms. *American Journal of Psychiatry, 143*, 74–77.

Jones, R. T. (1994). *Child's Reaction to Traumatic Events scale (CRTES): A self-report traumatic stress measure.* (Available from the author, Department of Psychology, Virginia Polytechnic Institute and State University, 4102 Derring Hall, Blacksburg, VA, 24060)

Jonson-Reid, M. (1998). Youth violence and exposure to violence in childhood: An ecological review. *Aggression & Violent Behavior, 3,* 159–179.

Jouriles, E. N., & LeCompte, S. H. (1991). Husbands' aggression toward wives and mothers' and fathers' aggression toward children: Moderating effects of child gender. *Journal of Consulting & Clinical Psychology, 59,* 190–192.

Kolbo, J. R., Blakely, E. H., & Engleman, D. (1996). Children who witness domestic violence: A review of empirical literature. *Journal of Interpersonal Violence, 11,* 281–293.

Koss, M. P., Koss, P., & Woodruff, W. (1991). Deleterious effects of criminal victimization on women's health and medical utilization. *Archives of Internal Medicine, 151,* 342–357.

Kovacs, M. (1992). *Children's Depression Inventory.* New York: Multi-Health Systems.

Kurz, D. (1993). Physical assaults by husbands: A major social problem. In R. J. Gelles & D. R. Loseke (Eds.), *Current controversies on family violence* (pp. 88–103). Newbury Park, CA: Sage.

Lamb, M. E., Sternberg, K. J., & Esplin, P. W. (1998). Conducting investigative interviews of alleged sexual abuse victims. *Child Abuse & Neglect, 22,* 813–823.

Langen, P. A., & Innes, C. A. (1986). *Preventing domestic violence against women.* Bureau of Justice Statistics Special Reports. Washington, DC: Department of Justice.

Lemon, N. K. D. (1999). The legal system's response to children exposed to domestic violence. *Future of Children (Domestic Violence & Children), 9,* 67–83.

Levendosky, A. A., Huth-Bocks, A. C., & Semel, M. A. (2002). Adolescent peer relationships and mental health functioning in families with domestic violence. *Journal of Clinical Child Psychology, 31,* 206–218.

Levendosky, A. A., Huth-Bocks, A. C., Semel, M. A., & Shapiro, D. L. (2002). Trauma symptoms in preschool-age children exposed to domestic violence. *Journal of Interpersonal Violence, 17,* 150–164.

Lie, G., & Gentlewarrier, S. (1991). Intimate violence in lesbian relationships: Discussion of survey findings and practice implications. *Journal of Social Service Research, 15,* 41–59.

Logan, T. K., Leukefeld, C., & Walker, B. (2000). Stalking as a variant of intimate violence: Implications from a young adult sample. *Violence & Victims, 15,* 91–111.

MacKenzie-Keating, S. E., & McDonald, L. (1997).

The abusive effects of marital violence on children. *Early Child Development & Care, 139,* 99–106.

Margolin, G. (1998). Effects of domestic violence on children. In P. K. Trickett & C. J. Schellenbach (Eds.), *Violence against children in the family and community* (pp. 57–101). Washington, DC: American Psychological Association.

Margolin, G., John, S. J., Ghosh, C. M., & Gordis, E. B. (1997). Family interaction process: An essential tool for exploring abusive relations. In D. D. Cahn & S. A. Lloyd (Eds.), *Family abuse: A communication perspective* (pp. 37–58). Thousand Oaks, CA: Sage.

Matthews, M. A. (1999). The impact of federal and state laws on children exposed to domestic violence. *Future of Children (Domestic Violence & Children, 9,* 50–66.

Mauricio, A. M., & Gormley, B. (2001). Male perpetration of physical violence against female partners. *Journal of Interpersonal Violence, 16,* 1066–1081.

McBurnett, K., Kerckhoff, C., Capasso, L., Pfiffner, L. J., Rathauz, P. J., McCord, M., et al. (2001). Antisocial personality, substance abuse, and exposure to parental violence in males referred for domestic violence. *Violence & Victims, 16,* 491–506.

McDermott v. McDermott, 946 P. 2d 177 (Nev. 1997).

McFarlane, J., Parker, B., & Soeken, K. (1995). Abuse during pregnancy: Frequency, severity, perpetrator, and risk factors of homicide. *Public Health Nursing, 12,* 284–289.

McGill, J. C., Deutsch, R. M., & Zibbell, R. A. (1999). Visitation and domestic violence: A clinical model of family assessment and access planning. *Family & Conciliation Courts Review, 37,* 315–334.

McGlois, J. M., & Widom, C. S. (2001). Resilience among abused and neglected children grown up. *Development & Psychopathology, 13,* 1021–1038.

McNeely, R. L., Cook, P. W., & Torres, J. B. (2001). Is domestic violence a gender issues, or a human issue? *Journal of Human Behavior in the Social Environment, 4,* 227–251.

Mears, D. P., Carlson, M. J., Holden, G. W., & Harris, S. D. (2001). Reducing domestic violence revictimization: The effects of individual and contextual factors and type of legal intervention. *Journal of Interpersonal Violence, 16,* 1260–1283.

Mitchell, K. J., & Finkelhor, D. (2001). Risk of crime

victimization among youth exposed to domestic violence. *Journal of Interpersonal Violence,* 16, 944–964.

Murphy, J. C. (1998). Legal images of motherhood: Conflicting definitions from welfare "reform," family, and criminal law. *Cornell Law Review,* 83, 688–766.

Nader, K. O., Kriegler, J. A., Blake, D. D., & Pynoos, R. S. (1994). *Clinician Administered PTSD scale: Child and Adolescent Version (CAPS-C).* White River Junction, VT: National Center for PTSD.

National Council of Juvenile and Family Court Judges. (1995). Family violence in child custody statutes: An analysis of state codes and legal practice. *Family Law Quarterly, 29,*197–225.

National Victim Center. (1992). *Rape in America: A report to the nation.* Arlington, VA: Author.

Oberlander, L. B. (1995). Ethical responsibilities in child custody evaluations: Implications for evaluation methodology. *Ethics & Behavior, 3,* 311–332.

O'Brien, M., John, R. S., Margolin, G., & Erel, O. (1994). Reliability and diagnostic efficacy of parents' reports regarding children's exposure to marital aggression. *Violence & Victims, 9,* 45–62.

Olson, D. E., & Stalans, L. J. (2001). Violent offenders on probation: Profile, sentence, and outcome differences among domestic violence and other violent probationers. *Violence Against Women, 7,* 1164–1185.

Orbach, Y., & Lamb, M. E. (2000). Enhancing children's narratives in investigative interviews. *Child Abuse & Neglect, 24,* 1631–1648.

Osofsky, J. D. (1999). The impact of violence on children. *Future of Children (Domestic Violence & Children), 9,* 33–49.

Pihl, R., & Nimrod, G. (1976). The reliability and validity of the draw-a-person test in IQ and personality assessment. *Journal of Clinical Psychology, 32,* 470–472.

Praver, F. (1994). *Child rating scales: Exposure in interpersonal abuse.* Unpublished copyrighted material. (Available from the author, 5 Marseilles Dr., Locust Valley, NY, 11560)

Praver, F., Pelcovitz, D., & DiGuseppe, R. (1994). *The Angie/Andy Child Rating scales.* (Available from F. Praver, 5 Marseilles Dr., Locust Valley, NY, 11560)

Putnam, F. W. (1990). *Child Dissociative Checklist (version 3.0–2/90).* Bethesda, MD: National Institute of Mental Health, Laboratory of Developmental Psychology.

Putnam, F. W., & Peterson, G. (1994). Further validation of the Child Dissociative Checklist. *Dissociation, 7,* 204–211.

Saywitz, K., & Camparo, L. (1998). Interviewing child witnesses: A developmental perspective. *Child Abuse & Neglect, 22,* 825–843.

Shaffer, D., Fisher, P., Lucas, C., Dulcan, M., & Schwab-Stone, M. (2000). NIMH Diagnostic Interview Schedule for Children, Version IV (NIMH DISC-IV): Description, differences from previous versions, and reliability of some common diagnoses. *Journal of the American Academy of Child & Adolescent Psychiatry, 39,* 28–38.

Shumaker, D. M., & Prinz, R. J. (2000). Children who murder: A review. *Clinical Child & Family Psychology Review, 3,* 97–115.

Soler, H., Vinayak, P., & Quadagno, D. (2000). Biosocial aspects of domestic violence. *Psychoneuroendocrinology, 25,* 721–739.

Sparta, S. (2003). Assessment of childhood trauma. In A. M. Goldstein (Ed.), *Handbook of psychology: Vol. 11. Forensic psychology* (pp. 209–231). New York: John Wiley.

Stahl, P. M. (1994). *Conducting child custody evaluations: A comprehensive guide.* Thousand Oaks, CA: Sage.

Stark, E., & Flitcraft, A. (1988). Women and children at risk: A feminist perspective on child abuse. *International Journal of Health Services, 18,* 97–118.

Sternberg, K. J., & Lamb, M. E. (1999). In M. E. Lamb (Ed.), *Parenting and child development in "nontraditional" families* (pp. 305–325). Mahwah, NJ: Lawrence Erlbaum.

Straus, M. A. (1993). Physical assaults by wives: A major social problem. In R. J. Gelles & D. R. Loseke (Eds.), *Current controversies on family violence* (pp. 67–87). Newbury Park, CA: Sage.

Straus, M. A., & Gelles, R. J. (1986). Societal change and change in family violence from 1975 to 1985 as revealed by two national surveys. *Journal of Marriage & the Family, 48,* 465–479.

Straus, M. A., & Gelles, R. J. (1990). How violent are American families? Estimates from the national family violence resurvey and other studies. In M. A. Straus & R. J. Gelles (Eds.), *Physical violence in American families* (pp. 95–108). New Brunswick, NJ: Transaction Books.

Straus, M. A., Gelles, R. J., & Steinmetz, S. (1980). *Behind closed doors: Violence in the American family.* New York: Doubleday/Anchor.

Tajima, E. A. (2000). The relative importance of wife abuse as a risk factor for violence against children. *Child Abuse & Neglect, 24,* 1383–1398.

Thompson, W. C., Clarke-Stewart, K. A., & Lepore, S. J. (1997). What did the janitor do? Suggestive interviewing and the accuracy of children's accounts. *Law & Human Behavior, 21*, 405–426.

Thornberry, T. P., Ireland, T. O., & Smith, C. A. (2001). The importance of timing: The varying impact of childhood and adolescent maltreatment on multiple problem outcomes. *Development & Psychopathology, 13*, 957–979.

Tjaden, P., & Thoennes, N. (1996). *Violence against women: Preliminary findings from the Violence and Threats Against Women in America Survey.* Denver: Center for Policy Research.

Violence Against Women Act of 1994, Pub. L. No. 103-322, 108 Stat. 1796 (1994).

Violence Against Women Act of 2000, Pub. L. No. 106-386 (2000).

Walker, A. G. (1999). *Handbook on questioning children: A linguistic perspective* (2nd ed.). Washington, DC: American Bar Association.

Watson, D., & Clark, L. (1992). On traits and temperament: General and specific factors of emotional experience and their relation to the five-factor-model. *Journal of Personality, 60*, 441–476.

Weinfield, N. S., Sroufe, L. A., & Egeland, B. (2000). Attachment from infancy to early adulthood in a high-risk sample: Continuity, discontinuity, and their correlates. *Child Development, 71*, 695–702.

West, M., & George, C. (1999). Abuse and violence in intimate adult relationships: New perspectives from attachment theory. *Attachment & Human Development, 1*, 137–156.

Whitcomb v. Jefferson County Department of Social Services, 685 F. Supp. 745, 645 (D. Colo. 1987).

Wolfe, D. A., Zak, L., Wilson, S. K., & Jaffe, P. (1986). Child witnesses to violence between parents: Critical issues in behavioral and social adjustment. *Journal of Abnormal Child Psychology, 14*, 95–104.

Wolfe, V. V., Wolfe, D. A., Gentile, C., & Larose, L. (1986). *Children's Impact of Traumatic Events scale.* (Available from V. Wolfe, Department of Psychology, London Health Sciences Center, 800 Commissioners Rd. East, London, ON, Canada, N6A4G5)

Yick, A. G. (2000). Predictors of physical spousal intimate violence in Chinese American families. *Journal of Family Violence, 15*, 249–267.

11

Child Physical Abuse and Neglect: Medical and Other Considerations in Forensic Psychological Assessment

Amy C. Tishelman
Alice W. Newton
Jennifer E. Denton
Andrea M. Vandeven

Child physical abuse and child neglect pose complex problems, with ramifications for the immediate and enduring physical and emotional welfare of children. Neither child physical abuse nor child neglect stands as a unitary concept. Instead, each term encompasses a broad range of maltreatment, not necessarily linked by etiology, interventions, or specific effects but resulting in serious infractions in the caretaking of children. Legal issues arise through a variety of paths, including adult and child criminal prosecutions, and questions related to custody, placement and visitation concerns. This chapter provides a brief overview of the concepts of child physical abuse and neglect and the parameters of these problems, and describes medical considerations as part of a comprehensive forensic assessment strategy.

SCOPE OF CHILD ABUSE AND NEGLECT

National statistics published in 2004 documented state responses to the 2002 National Child Abuse and Neglect Data System (U.S. Department of Health and Human Services, 2004). According to these data, nearly 900,000 children across the United States were considered by child protection agencies to be maltreated in 2002. These statistics are based on reports to local child protective service (CPS) agencies. Professionals were responsible for more than half of the reports accepted for investigation or assessment, and approximately 30% of investigated reports were substantiated. Child neglect ranked as the most frequently reported problem, with more than 60% of children experiencing some form of neglect and approximately one fifth of children suffering physical abuse. The data indicated that maltreated children commonly suffer in a multitude of ways, suggesting that a unifying dimension links the risk factors for seemingly diverse types of maltreatment, at least for a significant group of those children ultimately identified as maltreated.

Children in the youngest age group (0–3 years) seem to be at the highest risk for maltreatment with rates diminishing inversely with age. Child fatalities also occurred more frequently in the youngest age group, with boys younger than 12 months accounting for the highest rate of fatalities and approximately 75% of child fatalities occurring in children younger than 4. The national statistics identified parents as the most common perpetrators of child maltreatment, with approximately 40% of children maltreated by mothers. These statistics also portray maltreated children as being at high risk for repeated victimization.

Until recently, child maltreatment reports had increased significantly since 1989 (Wang & Harding, 1999). Whether these statistics reflected a rising awareness of the problem of child maltreatment, and an increased propensity to report, or an actual increase in violence directed toward children has become an important and debatable question. Kaplan, Pelkovitz, and Labruna (1999) suggest that the actual incidence of child maltreatment had escalated, based on estimates that the severity of injuries to children had increased. Wang and Harding (1999) noted that although some states experienced diminished numbers of child maltreatment reports in 1998, others reported increased incidences. A number of state CPS administrators cited changes in reporting systems and procedures as a factor in the decreased number of child maltreatment reports (Wang & Harding, 1999), an indicator of the significance of data collection processes to the understanding of trends in child protective concerns.

These statistics portray child maltreatment, sadly, as a common problem that no doubt has massive and diffuse societal effects. Unfortunately, a full understanding of the scope of these problems becomes elusive, especially as epidemiological data may be unreliable and confusing. Wang and Harding (1999) observed that estimates of the incidence of child abuse and neglect may reflect many sources of error, such as interstate inconsistencies in the methodology for tracking reports, and variable sources and methods for data compilation. Some states, for instance, report by incident, meaning that if a single child had been maltreated more than once in a given year, that child would count more than once in the overall statistics. In addition, they warn that some states provide data reflecting all reports of suspected child maltreatment, whereas other states reported only substantiated reports of maltreatment. Statistical inaccuracies not only reflect discrepancies in data collection methodologies, but also are enhanced by other difficulties endemic to the particularities of child abuse

and neglect research. For instance, as observed by Kaplan et al. (1999, p. 1216), "limited information from state child protection agencies, unreliable subject self-reports, and the frequent co-occurrence of different forms of physical and emotional abuse and neglect" hamper child maltreatment research in general. In addition, because child abuse and neglect represent an array of many types of problems, statistics documenting the general extent of child physical abuse and neglect run the risk of obscuring important distinctions between forms of child maltreatment.

A full comprehension of the scope of child maltreatment is obstructed by effective perpetrator efforts to conceal their behaviors. At any given time, one must assume that an undetermined number of cases of child physical abuse and neglect remain undocumented. Of these, it seems likely that some will eventually come to light, whereas others will perpetually elude official report and documentation. Further statistical obfuscation can arise because an uncertain number of allegations of child abuse and neglect constitute mistaken suspicions, mistaken substantiations of maltreatment, or both. Another source of error involves the category of deliberately false accusations of child maltreatment, made in bad faith, for retributive reasons or otherwise. These constitute an indefinite number of abuse and neglect reports received by child protection agencies.

Research in the area of child physical abuse and child neglect falls prey to many of the same difficulties that impinge upon statistical representations of child maltreatment. Ammerman (1998) observed that in 1993 the National Research Council considered the top priority in the field of child maltreatment research to be the development of a consensus on research definitions, whereas the second priority focused on the development of psychometrically sound research and clinical instruments. Ammerman (1998) concluded, "What is most striking about this list of priorities is the emphasis on fundamental aspects of conducting research in this area. . . . It is evident that a firm foundation in the field has yet to form" (p. 110). He outlines a number of areas in which research in child maltreatment suffered, including variability in the settings from which research recruitment occurs and other methodological inadequacies. For example, researchers may rely on subject populations most conveniently enlisted (e.g., college students), not necessarily most representative of the population of interest. In addition, research has often relied on retrospective data, maternal reports, and nonstandardized measures, all of which can lead to unreliable and invalid data of limited generalizability (Ammerman, 1998).

Despite these difficulties, the past decade has seen a critical mass of literature disseminated directly addressing problems of forensic evaluation in child physical abuse and neglect. Data related to children's memory and suggestibility have proven invaluable in informing practitioners of appropriate clinical techniques (e.g., Ceci & Bruck, 1995). Other literature related to indices of trauma and the roles of psychologists in forensic evaluations has also provided much appreciated assistance to practitioners. As a result of the increased attention to standards of practice, several associations have published guidelines to inform the mental health clinician. These include the American Psychological Association's *Guidelines for Psychological Evaluations in Child Protection Matters* (1998), the American Professional Society on the Abuse of Children's (APSAC) *Psychosocial Evaluation of Suspected Psychological Maltreatment in Children and Adolescents* (1995), and the American Academy of Child and Adolescent Psychiatry's "Practice Parameters for the Forensic Evaluation of Children and Adolescents Who May Have Been Physically or Sexually Abused" (1997). Several exemplary books, chapters, and journal articles have been published, including the Melton, Petrila, Poythress, and Slobogin (1997) volume and articles by Kuehnle, Coulter, and Firestone (2000) and Barnum (1997).

CULTURAL AND RELIGIOUS CONSIDERATIONS

The challenge of finding a universal definition of child neglect or child physical abuse becomes even more complex when one takes into account religious and cultural considerations. Although some child needs are almost universally agreed upon (e.g., food and shelter), many aspects of parenting have grounding in the culture in which the child (or the parent) grew up. When cultures intermingle, the differences in parenting approaches

often lead to misunderstanding and conflict. It is crucial not only to learn about cultural differences in child rearing but also to assess the consequences of these cultural practices within the current cultural context. A family who safely left an 8-year-old child as a caregiver of younger siblings in their homeland may place these children at risk in an urban environment where the crime rate and lack of involved neighbors pose greater threats to the children.

As Korbin and Spilsbury (1999) point out, one must not only consider issues of cultural variability but also avoid excusing every parental behavior on the basis of cultural differences. They state:

> Cultural competence avoids both unmoderated ethnocentrism and unmoderated relativism. Ethnocentrism is the belief that one's own cultural beliefs and practices are not only preferable but also superior to all others. In contrast, cultural relativism is the belief that each and every culture must be viewed in its own right as equal to all others, and that culturally sanctioned behaviors cannot be judged by the standards of another culture. (p. 71)

Thus, although both religious and cultural considerations have important roles in a child's upbringing, such considerations do not excuse every parenting behavior.

The concept of *clear or probable harm* can help to clarify whether certain cultural or religious practices constitute maltreatment. For instance, in the case of child neglect, one should assess whether denial of a child's basic needs has occurred before initiating intervention by agencies charged with protecting children. Religious exemption laws exist in most states allowing parents to refuse some forms of conventional medical care (e.g., routine vaccinations) or conventional schooling. With regard to medical practices, courts generally do not intervene with religious practices unless the child has the potential to suffer serious harm, such as from life-threatening infection or cancer.

Consideration of culture must also take into account the other factors that often define the life of ethnic minorities in the United States. Immigrants are frequently marginalized in our society and live in poverty. Although most underprivileged families do not intentionally neglect their children, many studies have shown that the rate of neglect is higher among the poor who have fewer resources. One must differentiate whether maltreatment results from cultural differences, whether the family does not have adequate financial or social supports to parent properly, or both. An approach sensitive to these issues will facilitate more successful interventions in most situations. An excellent discussion of competing variables that come into play when cultures collide can be found in Anne Fadiman's (1998) book *The Spirit Catches You and You Fall Down*.

Terao, Borrego, and Urquiza (2001), address several lapses in the field of child maltreatment, noting that clinicians continue to differ in how they decide which practices constitute child maltreatment. The authors also observe that decision-making processes seem vague and often unexplored systematically by research. They propose a decision-making model that accounts for the caregiver's level of acculturation as well as parenting practices, but emphasize that professionals must comply with strictures to report reasonable suspicions of child maltreatment regardless of cultural considerations. However, the authors suggest that the level of family acculturation constitutes an important factor in determining the appropriate clinical intervention, specifying that for poorly acculturated families a psychoeducational approach may be fitting. A more therapeutic approach might be indicated when families are fully aware of normative parenting practices.

ETIOLOGICAL CONSIDERATIONS

Attempting to understand the etiology of child maltreatment constitutes a critical step toward developing effective prevention and intervention strategies. This complex enterprise must take into account the form of caregiving breach, as well as family, social, cultural, religious, and psychological variables. Wolfe (1999), Kolko (1996), and Erickson and Egeland (1996) provide excellent overviews of some of the complex factors implicated in the etiology of child maltreatment. Discussions of etiology most often consider multidimensional factors, including child attributes, caregiver attributes, and the evolution of their relationship, as well as social and cultural factors. Wolfe (1999) suggests that child abuse seldom results from some extremely abnormal or pathological influence. To the contrary,

child abuse is seen as the culmination of interrelated events both within and outside of the family. This argument provides the major basis for studying abusive behavior within a multilevel context of individual, family, and societal events. These events may be extreme forms of more everyday events and stressors that all families may experience to some degree. (p. 71)

Some of the variables often associated with child maltreatment include low social support, family isolation, high levels of life stress, caregiver history of maltreatment, child temperament, negative cognitive-attributional caregiver styles, substance abuse, and dysfunctional family interactional patterns (Erickson & Egeland, 1996; Kolko, 1996). However, due to the heterogeneity of family constellations as well as types of maltreatment, none of these factors necessarily hold relevance in any particular case. Conversely, any of these factors may be of paramount importance. For instance, although parental psychosis is not commonly implicated in the evolution of maltreatment, a delusional system could, in a specific case, constitute a critical factor in the etiology of physical abuse. Poverty or cultural misconceptions can override more benign parental practices in other instances.

MEDICAL CONSULTATIONS AS PART OF THE FORENSIC EVALUATION PROCESS

The evaluation of child abuse and neglect is a multifaceted task, and usually not only involves several disciplines but also necessitates the adoption of complex and numerous roles depending upon the form of the maltreatment and the evaluation questions. Unlike many forensic questions that may involve psychosocial input, problems of child physical abuse and neglect most often have implications for the medical as well as psychological status of the child, therefore requiring a multidimensional analysis of the issues involved and a collaborative approach. Each profession represented in the evaluation of a case may have different priorities, whereas all professionals should hold as a predominant concern the best interests of a child.

Legal definitions of child physical abuse and child neglect vary by state, although most emphasize overt, usually medical, consequences to a child and focus on caregiver intent to inflict harm or on the incapacity of a caregiver to protect a child from being harmed (Wolfe, 1999). Thus, nonaccidental injury to a child through acts of commission or omission by caregivers often takes precedence in the consideration of whether a child has fallen prey to physical abuse or neglect. The emphasis on physical harm requires the input of medical professionals, such as physicians or nurse practitioners. As children often suffer from more than one type of abuse or neglect, several medical specialists frequently become involved in a single child's case. Controversy and discord may arise at the initial medical diagnostic stage of evaluation, with physicians more or less conservative in their inclination to suspect child maltreatment and varying in their comfort interfacing with child protection systems. It will often prove helpful to have a medical expert in child protection matters available for consultation to physicians in other specialty areas, and many hospitals have formed multidisciplinary child protection teams to aid in the identification of child abuse and neglect.

MULTIDISCIPLINARY METHODS FOR CHILD ABUSE EVALUATION

Aside from medical professionals, many other disciplines are represented in the investigation and evaluation of child protection cases. In a national survey of multidisciplinary team approaches to the investigation and resolution of child abuse and neglect, Kolbo and Strong (1997) found that teams usually included CPS workers, law enforcement officers, and representatives of the legal system. Hospital child protection teams most likely include medical and mental health professionals, including physicians, nurses, social workers, psychologists, and psychiatrists.

In order to understand the process of evaluation, in a general sense, one must realize that evaluation questions vary widely and that a single child might become the focus of multiple evaluations, each requiring the input and coordination of various professionals. Barnum (1997) summarized the types of evaluation questions commonly raised in a case of alleged child abuse and neglect as including questions of *fact* (determining with a degree of certainty what has happened to a child), *harm*,

parental capacity, and *prognosis*. Barnum has encapsulated these questions as what happened? what harm did it cause? what help can the parents provide now? and what hope is there for the future?

Melton et al. (1997) provide an excellent discussion of the diverse means by which a clinician may become involved in the legal system in child maltreatment cases. They highlight investigation, emergency decisions, adjudication (including competency and credibility determinations and proving child injury and abuse), and disposition and postdispositional review. Kuehnle et al. (2000) postulate that the primary goal of the mental health evaluator is to "assess the best fit between the child's needs and the parents' abilities, and to make recommendations that assist the court and participants in meeting the best interests of the child" (p. 368). Toward this end, they propose a four-factor model to guide evaluations, which involves evaluation of (1) parent factors (e.g., stability, parent history, previous child maltreatment reports, parenting skills, implementation of structures for safety, willingness for services, availability of services), (2) environmental factors (e.g., socioeconomic status, social support, physical living conditions, other family violence), (3) child factors (child development, disabilities affecting needs, history of injuries), and (4) parent–child relationship (parent-to-child factors, child's attachment to surrogates).

Kuehnle et al. (2000) direct the mental health professional's attention toward forensic evaluation questions that arise following the initial allegations of child abuse and neglect. However, the initial investigation phase in child protection, before notification goes to child protection agencies, constitutes a critical, yet controversial phase of assessment. Melton et al. (1997) observe that historically clinicians infrequently became involved with child protection cases before adjudication but have over time become increasingly involved in the initial investigation stage. During the investigation period, avoiding role confusion can sometimes become difficult. Most literature specifies that mental health workers should maintain clarity regarding their role status in a case, and clearly differentiates between the roles of clinical versus forensic evaluators. But, as noted by Tishelman, McLeod, and Meyer (2000), these roles sometimes vary in an unpredictably fluid manner. For instance, a neutral evaluator has a legal obligation to report a suspicion of maltreatment to a child protection agency due to immediate concerns regarding a child's safety. This may or may not have any relationship to the original evaluation question. In this case, the clinician's neutrality becomes questionable even before completion of the initial evaluation. The evaluator may have to testify in court at a subsequent point.

Documentation is an important consideration, and relevant to all facets of child maltreatment assessment, including the medical and psychosocial realms. All salient aspects of interviews should be recorded in some form as well as steps taken to diagnose medical conditions and test alternative hypotheses as to the cause of a child's disturbing presentation. The American Psychological Association (1998) cautions psychologists to retain and store all records "with the understanding that they may be reviewed by other psychologists, the court or the client" (p. 8).

MEDICAL EVALUATION OF CHILD ABUSE AND NEGLECT

The same ambiguity of roles experienced by mental health professionals can complicate medical evaluation of child physical abuse. Medical personnel are extensively trained to attend to the medical well-being of a child. In child maltreatment, their role expands to include forensic issues. Physicians are mandated to contact CPS in cases of suspected maltreatment, and may ultimately be asked to appear in court to testify in forensic matters. If the hospital or clinic to which the child presents has a mental health worker, the two professionals can collaborate in the assessment of the injury and psychosocial risk factors in the case.

Evaluation of physical abuse involves obtaining a detailed history and conducting a thorough medical examination because the many different mechanisms of injury can result in significantly varied presentations. The following variables constitute important components in the evaluation of physical abuse: historical factors related to the means of injury, timing of the presentation for medical evaluation, type of injury and its consistency with the history given, and the child's general medical status. Careful attention should be given to the

child's developmental milestones. Occasionally, the suspicion of possible inflicted injury arises because the reported mechanism of injury is impossible given the motor skill development of the child victim (e.g., femur fractures in nonambulatory infants). In addition, an experienced medical professional will usually take note of a child's demeanor during the physical examination, including unusual affect and anxiety reactions. It is important that the clinician consider alternative explanations for the apparent injuries, especially the possibility of disease processes that predispose the child to injury with trivial insult. Several excellent references exist that provide useful atlases of various types of physical abuse injury and helpful advice regarding the work-up of children for possible child abuse (e.g., American Academy of Pediatrics, 1998; Kleinman, 1998; Reece & Ludwig, 2001).

Sometimes a suspicion of abuse arises when the medical history is obtained (prior to the physical examination). An inconsistency in the narration of events leading up to and causing the injury can cause initial concern. Different family members may give variable accounts or caregivers may relate different versions of the same events. Often inconsistencies become apparent later when the child is examined and the injuries observed are not medically consistent with the story given. This discrepancy may provide the first (and even the only) indication that the medical clinician has encountered a case of physical abuse. Patterns of injury can provide important evidence that the injury is nonaccidental. Bruises, lacerations, burns, petechiae, and scars must all be noted. Bruises in a semicircular pattern, for example, can indicate the presence of a bite injury. Burn patterns, such as lesions corresponding to an iron or radiator, can also suggest nonaccidental injury. Extremity burns may appear in a so-called stocking-glove distribution, which can result from deliberate immersion of extremities in scalding bath water (Jenny, 2001). Examining every body area is important, including behind the ears, between the fingers and toes, and in the genital and perianal regions. In addition to noting the presence of various injuries, the clinician must also determine whether the age of the injury appears consistent with the history provided by the caregiver. Injuries of different ages may indicate repeated inflicted injury.

Concerns about possible physical abuse may also arise due to a child's presentation with certain medical symptoms highly correlated with physical abuse. A history of apnea (temporary cessation of breathing), seizure activity, or altered mental status in an otherwise healthy infant constitute a symptom cluster seen commonly in a baby who has experienced violent shaking or other serious physical trauma. Such alarming symptoms would almost always lead to immediate transport to a hospital for assessment and treatment of potentially life-threatening conditions. Because many possible causes for such symptoms exist, inflicted injury may not readily become apparent until evaluation and treatment are substantially under way. Caregivers in cases of inflicted injury typically give misleading or entirely fabricated histories, which may delay accurate diagnosis.

Cutaneous Injury

Direct force applied to the skin may result in bruising, laceration, abrasion, or scarring after healing. Possible mechanisms of injury include actions such as hitting or striking the child (whether with a human hand or with inanimate objects, e.g., belts, electric cords, sticks, or lead pipes), biting, pinching, cutting, and ligature restraint. This type of physical abuse can occur in the course of corporal punishment or discipline, which can complicate deciding whether abuse has, in fact, occurred. Cultural factors may be relevant and complicate an appraisal of whether the injury comports with abusive practices. For instance, alternative customs, such as coining and cupping (cultural healing practices of abrading the skin with a coin or creating a vacuum with a cup, leading to bruising) can cause quite dramatic but medically inconsequential skin findings.

Certain medical conditions can predispose children to bruising or bleeding with little or no trauma. The list of these conditions is quite long; the most commonly investigated include hemophilia, leukemia, and disorders of platelet function. Physicians should consider and rule out such conditions, if a child presents with bleeding or bruising and no history of significant trauma. Burns constitute another example of potentially inflicted injury in children. The mechanisms for burns include dry contact with hot objects (e.g., radiators, hot irons, or cigarettes), contact with hot liquid (including splattering, pouring, and immersion),

and contact with caustic chemicals. Apparent inflicted burns in the diaper area should be differentiated from diaper rash.

Head and Visceral Injury

Abusive head trauma is the most common cause of child abuse fatality (Alexander, Levitt, & Smith, 2001). Such injury often results from blunt trauma to the head (as might occur due to a fall or blow to the head). The brain itself may show signs of injury, or the vessels around the brain may bleed, causing hematomas (collections of blood) around the brain. Evaluating such injuries typically involves radiography via computerized tomography scan (CT), magnetic resonance imaging (MRI), or ultrasound.

Shaken baby syndrome (SBS) is a constellation of signs and symptoms that includes brain injury caused by the effects of whiplash forces on the intracranial structures (Alexander et al., 2001). The ensuing damage to the brain (subdural hemorrhage and cerebral edema) and eyes (especially retinal hemorrhage) provides physical findings that aid clinicians in making this diagnosis. Fractures such as rib and long bone fractures can occur in SBS, as can cutaneous and other soft tissue injury; however, these other injuries are not always present. The bleeding and brain swelling often progress after the initial insult. Many of the symptoms of SBS are nonspecific and can be suggestive of other medical causes. These symptoms range from mild to severe and include vomiting, fussiness, apnea, cyanosis, and seizure. Although children may recover from a mild episode of SBS, a more significant insult may cause neurological devastation or death.

Abdominal injury poses a difficult diagnostic problem in abused children because external signs of injury are seldom evident. The abdomen can absorb a significant amount of force without developing superficial bruising or other skin injury. For this reason, even minimal abnormalities on abdominal examination warrant further evaluation with blood tests or radiologic studies. For further discussion of visceral injuries, see Ludwig (2001).

Fractures

Fractures can occur accidentally in normally active children. Because there are no fractures considered absolutely pathognomonic for inflicted injury, the circumstances surrounding the fracture incident are of paramount importance when identifying physical abuse. Some of the factors that need to be considered include the amount and type of force necessary to produce a given fracture, the region of the body (whether well protected or more vulnerable), and the feasibility (whether the developmental stage of the child or the description of the injury matches the observed injury). Furthermore, the physician must evaluate whether a child is presenting with a condition that could render the bones more fragile than usual. Prematurity can be associated with osteopenic (poorly mineralized) bones, particularly in a baby with a complicated neonatal course. The appearance of the bones on an X-ray can be a clue to the presence of osteopenia because mineralization affects the density of bones on film. Osteogenesis imperfecta (brittle bone disease) refers to a group of inherited conditions that will cause the bones to be fragile and susceptible to injury. The disease has a wide variety of presentations and can range from very severe with multiple fractures occurring before the first year of life to a more mild form that is difficult to detect. Differentiating true inflicted injury from conditions mimicking child physical abuse is occasionally difficult, but always vital, and is a core contribution of the medical clinician to the multidisciplinary evaluation of child physical abuse (Bays, 2001).

Munchausen Syndrome by Proxy

Munchausen syndrome by proxy (MBP) is defined as "the deliberate creation of actual or apparent illness or the false reporting of illness in a child or other dependent" (Levin & Sheridan, 1995, p. ix). The extent of parental pathology in this syndrome is quite varied and can range from reports of symptoms that the child is not experiencing (resulting in medical testing and medical intervention) to actually inducing symptoms (including smothering, giving oral medication, and injecting medication). It can be quite difficult to diagnose MBP before the child has been medically or surgically treated for factitious illness. Diagnosis is typically the result of careful review of the medical record, review of the testing results, and careful observation of the caretaker's behavior with the health care team. Some patients are admitted to the hospital to afford closer scrutiny of both the symptoms and the interactions between caregiver and child. Although videotape cameras can provide invaluable information, their use is limited by state-to-state variation in the legality of videotaping while in the hospital. Refer to Levin and Sheridan (1995) and Rosenberg (2001) for a more in-depth review of the relevant issues.

In summary, when evaluating a physically abused child, several tools are available to the physician, and unfortunately, no specific algorithm exists with regard to assessment. A child's medical history, the narrative account of the mechanism of injury, physical examination, laboratory studies, knowledge of diagnostic indicators and differential diagnoses, and the ability to collaborate with professionals in other disciplines are each important to the cogent identification of child physical abuse.

MEDICAL EVALUATION OF CHILD NEGLECT

The definition of neglect is evolving as greater understanding has developed regarding the causes and consequences of neglect for children and families. There is still no uniform agreement regarding what constitutes neglect, despite the fact that neglect is the most prevalent type of maltreatment. Additionally, there is no agreement on whether there should be consistency between clinical and research definitions of neglect. As Zuravin (1999) notes in her extensive discussion on this topic, "It is probable that more effort has been spent discussing the shortcomings of existing definitions and providing guidance for the development of new ones than on the formulation of standardized and well-operationalized definitions and on measurement research" (p. 26).

This lack of consistency is evidenced by the widely varying approach taken by CPS agencies across the United States when addressing possible causes of medical, physical, or emotional neglect. Definitions vary from vague descriptions that do not consider environmental variables to specific definitions that list various subtypes of neglect and the context within which they occur. Terminology almost uniformly focuses on caregiver *acts of omission* or *failure to provide resources* that meet children's basic needs. This narrow approach does not take into consideration the family, community, and societal factors that contribute to the situation. Many states also require evidence of actual harm and do not include the concept of potential harm, a consequence of neglect that is often harder to measure empirically.

For practical purposes, child neglect is often divided into various categories. The most common subtypes are discussed below. However, it is important to note that these categories are not mutually exclusive, and many circumstances of neglect may be consistent with a number of categories. For example, the child of a substance-abusing parent might be subject to physical neglect due to the parent's inability to provide adequate supervision. This same child may also experience *emotional abuse or neglect* due to the substance-abusing parent's inability to nurture the child, and *medical neglect* when the parent is unable to comply with routine medical care for their child. See Table 11.1 for a summary of common forms of child neglect.

Physical Neglect

This category often constitutes the most tangible, and therefore the most common, form of neglect recognized by state CPS agencies. It includes the failure to provide adequate food, clothing, or shelter to meet a child's basic needs. The consequences can often be measured objectively, as in a child who is failing to grow or who is homeless or without adequate clothing for the prevailing environmental conditions.

Physical neglect can also include failure to provide adequate supervision. Again, failure to supervise often results in tangible consequences. A child may be found home alone or left in the care of a person not able to care for the child properly. Poor supervision can also result in accidents, injuries, or ingestions that require medical attention. A child may be poorly cared for, leading to hygienic conditions that may have medical consequences.

Medical Neglect

Although at first glance the concept of medical neglect seems easy to define, this category is complicated by cultural and religious factors that often influence the definition of *proper medical care.*

Table 11.1   Possible indicators of child neglect

Physical neglect

Lack of shelter or adequate clothing

Inadequate hygiene, which may contribute to medical problems

Lack of adequate nutrition
  Repeated hunger
  Failure to thrive

Failure to provide adequate supervision or protection
  Children left home alone or in care of inadequate caregiver
  Drug or poison ingestions
  Accidental injuries
  Failure to provide proper safety equipment (car seat, seat belt, bike helmet)
  Exposure to domestic violence

Drug exposure
  In utero
  Direct and indirect (passive) exposure to drugs

Medical neglect

Failure to seek medical care
  Missed appointments for routine health care maintenance
  Lack of attention to illness or chronic medical conditions (noncompliance)

Failure to provide proper medicines

Poor dental hygiene/multiple caries

Educational neglect

Children not enrolled in school

Chronic school truancy

Failure to attend to special educational needs

Emotional neglect

Lack of affection, nurturance, or love

Repeated negative or abusive statements made toward child

Constant rejection of child

Exposure to constant drug use, violence, pornography, or criminal acts

Unfair expectations that cannot be met, leading to stress and poor self-esteem

Fatal child neglect

Failure to provide for a child's elemental needs

Failure of supervision leading to fatal injury or ingestion

Neglect of medical condition that proves fatal to the child

Additionally, one must take into account the accessibility and affordability of health care. Dubowitz (1999) notes that severe limits exist in access to health insurance and health care for many children in the United States, and this factor may impede the ability of caregivers to provide adequately for the children even when they have adequate motivation.

In practical terms, a definition of medical neglect involves failure to provide and follow-up with medical care, resulting in actual or potential severe harm. Medical neglect can include failure or refusal to seek care for illness such as asthma, diabetes, or other chronic conditions or failure to give medicines to treat these conditions. Additionally, failure to seek care in medical emergencies such as accident or severe illness can lead to a diagnosis of neglect. Dental neglect also falls into this category, although only rarely will CPS intervene in cases of dental neglect. The American Academy of Pediatric Dentistry (1997) defines such neglect as "the willful failure of parent or guardian to seek and follow through with treatment necessary to ensure a level of oral health essential for adequate function and freedom from pain and infection" (p. 3).

Educational Neglect

This subtype of neglect includes children not enrolled in school, not allowed to attend school, or allowed to be chronically truant from school. Again, culture and religion should enter into consideration of possible neglect, as a family may choose to home-school their child or may be from a culture where children stop attending school as soon as they can work and contribute to family income. Occasionally, an older child may have to care for younger children so that an adult caregiver can work, resulting in absence from school.

Emotional Neglect

McGee and Wolfe (1991) indicate that psychological maltreatment constitutes an extremely prevalent and destructive subtype of child maltreatment. Despite this conclusion, the definition of emotional neglect remains inconsistent and difficult to tackle legally. McGee and Wolfe (1991) discuss the complex interaction between parental behaviors and child outcome, pointing out that the consequences of parental behavior relate to the particular vulnerability of the child. This child vulnerability depends on multiple factors, including developmental stage, family support, and individual resilience.

On a practical level for both research and clinical applications, the definition of psychological maltreatment often focuses on parental behavior. The American Psychological Association (1998) defines emotional abuse as "a repeated pattern of behavior that conveys to children that they are worthless, unwanted, or only of value in meeting another's needs: [This] may include serious threats of physical or psychological violence" (p. 9).

Fatal Child Neglect

When considering child fatalities, child welfare professionals have focused on deaths due to physical abuse. Abusive deaths are conceptually easier to define than deaths due to neglect, as there are often clear and dramatic physical findings that confirm the cause of death. This leads to more ease in investigating and prosecuting these child fatalities. The concept of death due to abuse is also stronger in public awareness, as these cases often receive wide publicity and the sense of community outrage is high. Fatalities due to neglect are often difficult to recognize, define, and prosecute. They are frequently seen as the result of a single episode of neglect, although thorough investigation may reveal a wider pattern of neglect. Grieving caregivers may generate sympathetic emotions in professionals that can interfere in investigation and prosecution of fatal child neglect. Additionally, these deaths may be complicated by cultural or religious factors, with debate about what constitutes acceptable and intentionally neglectful parenting practice.

Bonner, Crow, and Logue (1999) base their definition of fatal child neglect on Rosenberg's (1994) concept of three main parental responsibilities:

> Fatal child neglect is usually defined as the death of a child due to parental failure to provide for a child's needs adequately, supervise a child, or intervene to protect a child from harm. The responsibility to meet these needs falls primarily on parents, although other caregivers, community members, and society as a whole share in this responsibility. (p. 159)

Identification of Child Physical Abuse and Neglect

Mental health practitioners in interdisciplinary clinical settings (e.g., hospitals or community health centers), as opposed to forensic settings, are commonly asked to evaluate a child to determine whether concerns regarding possible maltreatment are warranted, as a precursor to notifying a child protection agency. Although forensic and clinical evaluation roles are partly distinguished by the identity of the client (the court vs. the individual, child, or family, respectively), ultimately forensic and clinical methods of evaluation should be sufficiently supported by the data. In either instance, case formulations and conclusions need to be credible in order to proceed toward a disposition that will enhance the child's best interests (Tishelman et al., 2000).

The identification of child physical abuse and neglect, unlike child sexual abuse, commonly relies heavily on medical data, and medical findings often inspire initial decisions to report concerns to child protection agencies, regardless of accompanying psychosocial data. Nevertheless, circumstances and context are often of critical importance in the initial appraisal of child maltreatment concerns, especially when medical findings are suggestive of abuse or neglect but not diagnostic, or when original suspicions emanate from psychosocial data (e.g., caregiver report inconsistent with a child's presentation). Additionally, family factors can be of paramount concern when trying to formulate an understanding of a child's emotional status and safety. For instance, a child may fear retribution from a caregiver if maltreatment is uncovered, or a caregiver prone to violence may be incited to increase threatening behaviors in response to reports of maltreatment. It is crucial to plan for a child's safety by informing child protection agencies of relevant concerns in order to prevent potential endangerment of vulnerable children and adults.

Some authors eschew the role of investigative interviewer for a mental health professional. Melton et al. (1997) note that "the most controversial use of clinicians' testimony in child maltreatment cases relate to the questions, 'What happened?' and 'Who did it?'" (p. 461). Concerns about the methodology used to determine possible abuse or neglect of a child have skyrocketed in the past decade. Some of this type of concern was inspired by a series of controversial and highly visible cases involving allegations of sexual abuse in which investigative interviews were performed in a manner that called into question the accuracy of the initial allegations of sexual abuse. Even when a child's presentation is medically consistent with neglect or physical abuse, conclusions about causation can be exceedingly difficult, and often additional data are needed, such as that obtained through psychosocial evaluation (for an extensive discussion of cases involving questionable allegations of child sexual abuse, see Ceci & Bruck, 1995; Kuehnle, 1996).

Consulting a mental health professional may help in determining whether to alert a child protection agency due to concerns of child maltreatment. In the absence of personnel experienced and trained in the assessment of child maltreatment, social workers lacking special expertise may be asked to provide psychosocial information to the medical staff, including information related to risk factors for abuse and the credibility of parental report. Interviews should be conducted separately with a child, when such an interview is appropriate, as well as with each legal caregiver. Milner, Murphy, Valle, and Tolliver (1998) cite a variety of factors that may influence the interview process, including evaluator gender, evaluator profession, and personal history of maltreatment. Evaluators should remain aware of possible biases and make very attempt to maintain an objective and neutral stance.

Caregiver Evaluation

Clinicians must review confidentiality at the outset of a caregiver interview, as it is possible that the information obtained may be scrutinized by a variety of professionals in a number of venues if the case proceeds to a child protection agency for further investigation. Psychosocial information obtained from a caregiver interview usually includes data pertaining to the child's developmental history, special needs, psychiatric and medical history, social and school functioning, and behavioral adjustment. In addition, each caregiver, interviewed individually, is often asked to describe the nature of the current problem and his or her understanding of how it developed or occurred, with particular attention given to the consistency of this report with the medical data obtained and the reliability of multiple caregivers' reports. In addition to questions about physical/medical injuries, it is crucial that screening questions be asked related to other forms of child maltreatment and family violence, including those related to domestic violence. An attempt should be made to understand the child's psychosocial history, family environment, sources of particular stress and vulnerability, and life stability. Areas of inquiry include family structure (historically and currently), household composition, psychiatric history, substance abuse, chronic stress factors (e.g., occupational, financial, psychosocial), and acute stressors (e.g., death, divorce). It is extremely important to attempt an understanding of the cultural vantage point of the child and caregiver and to acquire a sense of the caregiver's assumptions related to a child's needs, appropriate caregiving, and possible environmental constraints on appropriate caregiving. For instance, cultural factors can carry enormous weight in a caregiver's appraisal of the presenting problem. Caregiver perspectives toward corporal punishment and societal norms regarding discipline very widely around the globe and are reflected in diverse caregiver practices. External constraints (e.g., financial, time, transportation limitations) or internal limitations (medical or cognitive disabilities) may impair a caregiver's ability to provide adequate care for a child in one or more realm, regardless of intent, ultimately leading to concerns of child neglect.

Finally, aside from the factual information obtained, a clinician should assess the mental status of a caregiver and the manner in which the information is conveyed. The clinician can then generate hypotheses concerning psychiatric stability, cognitive status, and judgment. The clinician should also consider situational factors because affective lability may be consistent with a situation in which a child's medical well-being is compromised. Corroborative data about the caregiver's mental status and situational factors affecting family functioning can provide a sense of a caregiver's baseline functioning (for a review of areas of caregiver inquiry, see Giardino, Christian, Giardino, & Ingris,

1997; for additional interview guidelines, see American Academy of Child and Adolescent Psychiatry, 1997).

Child Interview

Children are often interviewed in an attempt to obtain information related to concerns regarding possible maltreatment. Outpatient evaluations provide greater flexibility for assessment, allowing the use of a comprehensive evaluation model. When the child is an inpatient or presents in an emergency department, staff often feel compelled to formulate a more immediate opinion regarding the etiology of a child's problems and to develop a plan for discharge that takes into account a child's safety. Unfortunately, clinical experience suggests that a number of factors may inhibit or distort a child's disclosure of maltreatment under such time pressure, including the ambiguity of postdischarge placement, fear of perpetrator retribution, fear of betraying a caregiver, fear of abandonment, shame, and self-blame. Additionally, many children are too young or too sick to be adequate sources of information. However, in all cases, if a child feels compelled to disclose, the information provided may be susceptible to undue influence by the demand characteristics of the evaluation process and may be both clinically and forensically unreliable. Mental health evaluators need to be sensitive to the safety concerns and comfort level of a child, as well as the child's developmental abilities and special needs. It is often helpful to conduct caregiver interviews and collect collateral data before a child is interviewed, especially if a child requires special considerations, such as a child with documented difficulties in receptive or expressive language or with medical conditions that can inhibit communicative abilities. The clinician should be cautious about conducting an evaluation of a child in an acute emotional crisis, as disclosure of maltreatment may intensify the child's distress and further jeopardize his or her mental health, safety, or both.

Literature, drawn from many different bodies of research as well as clinical experience, suggests several factors to consider when evaluating the veracity of information obtained from a child. Kuehnle (1996) outlined a number of guidelines to consider in assessing the credibility of a child's sexual abuse allegations, which can be extrapolated to child maltreatment assessment in general (see Kuehnle, 1996). Numerous authors suggest that the most credible information is obtained from children when the evaluator attempts to reduce the demand characteristics of the evaluation session, is neutral in approach to the child, entertains alternative hypotheses to avoid selectively reinforcing information consistent with preconceived notions of what has taken place, and maintains a nonauthoritarian stance. An evaluator must attempt to screen the child initially to determine communicative capacities, and to use language appropriate to the child's developmental level. In addition, more general, open-ended questions yield the most credible information (e.g., "What happened?"), whereas leading questions in which the answer is embedded in the question (e.g., "Your father poured hot oil on you, didn't he?") should always be avoided. Unfortunately, research indicates that younger children are least able to provide coherent, sequenced narratives and are less responsive to general questions than are their older cohorts, and the practitioner may need to balance the desire to obtain forensically and clinically relevant data with apprehensions regarding a child's welfare (for extensive discussion of the methodology of the child interview, see Ceci & Bruck, 1995; Kuehnle, 1996; Poole & Lamb, 1998; Saywitz & Goodman, 1996).

Due to concerns regarding the complexity of accurate identification of child maltreatment, attempts have been made to develop structured protocols to enhance the credibility of a child's report (e.g., Orbach et al., 2000). However, these attempts have generally been applied to suspected child sexual abuse rather than other forms of maltreatment, most likely because the former type of abuse is least likely to be identified on the basis of medical evidence. Many other researchers have proposed structured models of interviewing children to enhance the believability of their report, and numerous reviews and books have been published outlining strategies for promoting optimal comfort for a child while maintaining the integrity of data obtained (e.g., Ceci & Bruck, 1995; Davies et al., 1996; Goodman & Bottoms, 1993; Hewitt, 1999; Hoorwitz, 1992; Kuehnle, 1996; Orbach et al., 2000; Orbach & Lamb, 2000; Poole & Lamb, 1998; Saywitz & Comparo, 1996; Saywitz & Goodman, 1996).

In summary, clinicians must apply considerable background experience and knowledge to each case in which they suspect child maltreatment. Generally, it is important that psychosocial evaluators have a sophisticated understanding of child development, a strong background in general child mental health, specialized training in child maltreatment and family violence, and a sensitivity to cultural, socioeconomic, and minority issues. A multidisciplinary team approach to initial assessment should facilitate the understanding of a child's presentation along a number of dimensions (e.g., medical and psychosocial), and respectful debate can aid review of the data from multiple perspectives.

References

Alexander, R. C. Levitt, C. J., & Smith, W. L. (2001). Abusive head trauma. In R. M. Reece & S. Ludwig (Eds.), *Child abuse: Medical diagnosis and management* (pp. 47–80). Philadelphia: Lippincott Williams & Wilkins.

American Academy of Child and Adolescent Psychiatry. (1997). Practice parameters for the forensic evaluation of children and adolescents who may have been physically or sexually abused. *Journal of the American Academy of Child & Adolescent Psychiatry, 36,* 423–444.

American Academy of Pediatric Dentistry. (1997). Pediatric dentistry: Reference manual 1997–1998. *Pediatric Dentistry, 19,* 24.

American Academy of Pediatrics. (1998). *A guide to references and resources in child abuse and neglect* (2nd ed.). Elk Grove Village, IL: Author.

American Professional Society on the Abuse of Children. (1995). *Psychosocial evaluation of suspected psychological maltreatment in children and adolescents.* Chicago: Author.

American Psychological Association, Committee on Professional Practice and Standards. (1998). *Guidelines for psychological evaluations in child protection matters.* Washington, DC: American Psychological Association.

Ammerman, R. T. (1998). Methodological issues in child maltreatment research. In J. R. Lutzker (Ed.), *Handbook of child abuse research and treatment* (pp. 117–132). New York: Plenum.

Barnum, R. (1997). A suggested framework for forensic consultation in cases of child abuse and neglect. *Journal of the American Academy of Psychiatry & the Law, 23*(4), 581–593.

Bays, J. (2001). Conditions mistaken for child physical abuse. In R. M. Reece & S. Ludwig (Eds.), *Child abuse: Medical diagnosis and management* (pp. 177–206). Philadelphia: Lippincott Williams & Wilkins.

Bonner, B. L., Crow, S. M., & Logue, M. B. (1999). Fatal child neglect. In H. Dubowitz (Ed.), *Neglected children: Research, practice and policy* (pp. 69–88). Thousand Oaks, CA: Sage.

Ceci, S. J., & Bruck, M. (1995). *Jeopardy in the courtroom: A scientific analysis of children's testimony.* Washington, DC: American Psychological Association.

Davies, D., Cole, J., Albertella, G., McCulloch, L., Allen, K., & Kekevian, H. (1996). A model for conducting forensic interviews with child victims of abuse. *Child Maltreatment, 1,* 189–199.

Dubowitz, H. (1999). Neglect of children's health care. In H. Dubowitz (Ed.), *Neglected children: Research, practice and policy* (pp. 109–131). Thousand Oaks, CA: Sage.

Erickson, M. F., & Egeland, B. (1996). Child neglect. In J. Briere, L. Berliner, J. A. Bulkley, C. Jenny, & T. Reid (Eds.), *The APSAC handbook on child maltreatment* (pp. 4–20). Thousand Oaks, CA: Sage.

Fadiman, A. (1998). *The spirit catches you and you fall down.* New York: Farrar, Straus & Giroux.

Giardino, A. P., Christian, C. W., Giardino, E. R., & Ingris, J. D. (1997). Psychosocial assessment. In A. P. Giardino, C. W. Christian, & E. R. Giardino (Eds.), *A practical guide to the evaluation of child physical abuse and neglect* (pp. 233–246). Thousand Oaks, CA: Sage.

Goodman, G. S., & Bottoms, B. L. (Eds.). (1993). *Child victims, child witnesses: Understanding and improving testimony.* New York: Guilford.

Hewitt, S. K. (1999). *Assessing allegations of sexual abuse in preschool children: Understanding small voices.* Thousand Oaks, CA: Sage.

Hoorwitz, A. N. (1992). *The clinical detective: techniques in the evaluation of sexual abuse.* New York: W. W. Norton.

Jenny, C. (2001). Cutaneous manifestations of child abuse. In R. M. Reece & S. Ludwig (Eds.), *Child abuse: Medical diagnosis and management* (pp. 47–80). Philadelphia: Lippincott Williams & Wilkins.

Kaplan, S. J., Pelkovitz, D., & Labruna, V. (1999). Child and adolescent abuse and neglect research: A review of the past 10 years. Part I: Physical and emotional abuse and neglect. *Journal of the American Academy of Child & Adolescent Psychiatry, 38* (10), 1214–1222.

Kleinman, P. K. (1998). *Diagnostic imaging of child abuse* (2nd ed.). Saint Louis: Mosby.

Kolbo, J. R., & Strong, E. (1997). Multidisciplinary team approaches to the investigation and resolution of child abuse and neglect: A national survey. *Child Maltreatment, 2,* 61–72.

Kolko, D. J. (1996). Child physical abuse. In J. Briere, L. Berliner, J. A. Bulkley, C. Jenny, & T. Reid (Eds.), *The APSAC handbook on child maltreatment* (pp. 4–20). Thousand Oaks: CA: Sage.

Korbin, J. E., & Spilsbury, J. C. (1999). Cultural competence and child neglect. In H. Dubowitz (Ed.), *Neglected children: Research, practice and policy* (pp. 69–88). Thousand Oaks, CA: Sage.

Kuehnle, K. (1996). *Assessing allegations of child sexual abuse.* Sarasota, FL: Professional Resource Press.

Kuehnle, K., Coulter, M., & Firestone, G. (2000). Child protection evaluations: The forensic stepchild. *Family & Conciliation Court Reviews, 38*(3), 368–391.

Levin, A. V., & Sheridan, M. S. (1995). *Munchausen syndrome by proxy: Issues in diagnosis and assessment.* New York: Lexington Books.

Ludwig, S. (2001). Visceral injury manifestations of child abuse. In R. M. Reece & S. Ludwig (Eds.), *Child abuse: Medical diagnosis and management* (pp. 157–176). Philadelphia: Lippincott Williams & Wilkins.

McGee, R. A., & Wolfe, D. A. (1991). Psychological maltreatment: Toward an operational definition. *Development & Psychopathology, 3,* 3–18.

Melton, G. B., Petrila, J., Poythress, N. G., & Slobogin, C. (1997). *Psychological evaluations for the courts: A handbook for mental health professionals and lawyers.* New York: Guilford.

Milner, J. S., Murphy, W. D., Valle, L. A., & Tolliver, R. M. (1998). Assessment issues in child abuse evaluations. In J. R. Lutzker (Ed.), *Handbook of child abuse research and treatment* (pp. 75–116). New York: Plenum.

Orbach, Y., Hershkowitz, I., Lamb, M. E., Sternberg, K. J., Esplin, P. W., & Horowitz, D. (2000). Assessing the value of structured protocols for forensic interviews of alleged child abuse victims. *Child Abuse & Neglect, 24,* 733–752.

Orbach, Y., & Lamb, M. E. (2000). Enhancing children's narratives in investigative interviews. *Child Abuse & Neglect, 24,* 1631–1648.

Poole, D. A., & Lamb, M. E. (1998). *Investigative interviews of children.* Washington, DC: American Psychological Association.

Reece, R. M., & Ludwig, S. (Eds.). (2001). *Child abuse: Medical diagnosis and management* (2nd ed.). Philadelphia: Lippincott Williams & Wilkins.

Rosenberg, D. A. (1994). Fatal neglect. *APSAC Advisor*, 7(4), 38–40.

Rosenberg, D. A. (2001). Munchausen syndrome by proxy. In R. M. Reece & S. Ludwig (Eds.), *Child abuse: Medical diagnosis and management* (pp. 363–384). Philadelphia: Lippincott Williams & Wilkins.

Saywitz, K., & Camparo, L. (1998). Interviewing child witnesses: A developmental perspective. *Child Abuse & Neglect, 22*, 825–843.

Saywitz, K. J., & Goodman, G. S. (1996). Interviewing children in and out of court: Current research and practice implications. In J. Briere, L. Berliner, J. A. Bulkley, C. Jenny, & T. Teid (Eds.), *The APSAC handbook on child maltreatment* (pp. 297–318). Thousand Oaks, CA: Sage.

Terao, S. Y., Borrego, J., & Urquiza, A. J. (2001). A reporting and response model for culture and child maltreatment. *Child Maltreatment, 6*, 158–168.

Tishelman, A. C., McLeod, S. K., & Meyer, S. K. (2000, November). *Clinical versus forensic sexual abuse evaluations: Distinct models or points along a continuum.* Paper presented at the Northeast Child Maltreatment Conference, Providence, RI.

U.S. Department of Health and Human Services, Children's Bureau. (2004). *Child maltreatment 2002.* Washington, DC: U.S. Government Printing Office.

Wang, C. T., & Harding, K. (1999). *Current trends in child abuse reporting and fatalities: The results of the 1998 annual fifty state survey* (Working Paper No. 808). Chicago: Prevent Child Abuse America.

Wolfe, D. A. (1999). *Child abuse: Implications for child development and psychopathology.* Thousand Oaks, CA: Sage.

Zuravin, S. J. (1999). Child neglect: A Review of definitions and measurement research. In H. Dubowitz (Ed.), *Neglected children: Research, practice and policy* (pp. 24–46). Thousand Oaks, CA: Sage.

12

Assessing Risk for Violence Among Juvenile Offenders

Randy Borum

TRENDS IN YOUTH VIOLENCE

Since the mid-1980s, youth violence has increasingly gained recognition as a significant public health problem (Hamburg, 1998; U.S. Department of Health and Human Services, 2001; Zimring, 1998). Beginning around 1985, reported rates of violence committed by juveniles began a sharp and substantial increase. The trend became consistently observed in prevalence estimates derived from official arrest records, youth self-reports, and victimization surveys (Snyder & Sickmund, 1999). Between 1987 and 1992, the number of offenses against persons handled by juvenile courts increased by 56% (Snyder & Sickmund, 1999). Although most of these cases (76%) involved assault, between 1985 and 1992, the number of homicides committed by youths and the number they committed with guns doubled (Blumstein, 1995).

Since about 1993, these alarming rates of juvenile homicide and most forms of juvenile violence have declined significantly (Snyder & Sickmund, 1999); however, the level of public concern remains very high, and the absolute frequency of these risky behaviors in youths continues to be quite troublesome. Although, in 1999, the juvenile murder rate reached its lowest point since 1966, authorities still arrested approximately 1,400 juveniles for murder or nonnegligent manslaughter. Moreover, juvenile arrests for aggravated assault and self-reports of serious violence by adolescents have not shown a marked decline since the peak in 1993 (U.S. Department of Health and Human Services, 2001). Consequently, assessing violence risk and reducing violent behavior among children and adolescents have emerged as high-priority objectives in forensic mental health services and in juvenile justice (Hamburg, 1998; Zimring, 1998). Although the contexts and applications of these assessments vary, determining a youth's risk for future violence has uniformly become a critical factor in prevention and intervention efforts.

TRENDS IN JUVENILE JUSTICE AND CONTEXTS FOR RISK ASSESSMENT

In the juvenile justice context, violence risk has become a focal issue in decisions to "transfer" juveniles to the jurisdiction of adult court and in decisions about the supervision and release of juvenile offenders under the purview of the criminal and/or juvenile justice system (Snyder, Sickmund, & Poe-Yamagata, 2000). Why has this issue become more prominent now in the past? Subsequent to the rise in youth violence and public fear of youths, there emerged a significant and pervasive shift in juvenile justice policy, with movement away from a focus on rehabilitation and toward a more punitive philosophy (Grisso, 1996, 1998). Two major consequences of this trend include increases in (a) the number of juveniles—particularly those who commit violent offenses—transferred to adult court and (b) the number of juveniles incarcerated or placed under community correctional supervision in the adult criminal justice system (Snyder et al., 2000). In the 5-year period between 1992 and 1997, 44 states modified their statutes to make it easier to try juveniles as adults (Snyder et al., 2000).

The laws and policies in most states regarding the applicable criteria for juvenile transfer follow from the U.S. Supreme Court decision in *Kent v. United States* (1966), in which the Court delineated the following "criteria and principles concerning waiver of jurisdiction":

An offense falling within the statutory limitations . . . will be waived if it has prosecutive merit and if it is heinous or of an aggravated character, or—even though less serious—if it represents a pattern of repeated offenses which indicate that the juvenile may be beyond rehabilitation under Juvenile Court procedures, or if the public needs the protection afforded by such action.

The determinative factors which will be considered by the Judge in deciding whether the Juvenile Court's jurisdiction over such offenses will be waived are the following:

1. The seriousness of the alleged offense to the community and whether the protection of the community requires waiver.
2. Whether the alleged offense was committed in an aggressive, violent, premeditated or willful manner.
3. Whether the alleged offense was against persons or against property, greater weight being given to offenses against persons especially if personal injury resulted.
4. The prosecutive merit of the complaint, i.e., whether there is evidence upon which a Grand Jury may be expected to return an indictment (to be determined by consultation with the [prosecuting attorney]).
5. The desirability of trial and disposition of the entire offense in one court when the juvenile's associates in the alleged offense are adults who will be charged with a crime in [criminal court].
6. The sophistication and maturity of the juvenile as determined by consideration of his home, environmental situation, emotional attitude, and pattern of living.
7. The record and previous history of the juvenile, including previous contacts with [social service agencies], other law enforcement agencies, juvenile courts and other jurisdictions, prior periods of probation to [the court], or prior commitments to juvenile institutions.
8. The prospects for adequate protection of the public and the likelihood of reasonable rehabilitation of the juvenile (if he is found to have committed the alleged offense) by the use of procedures, services and facilities currently available to the Juvenile Court.

Clearly, most of these factors relate either directly or indirectly to the juvenile's degree of dangerousness or violence risk. Given that waiver of jurisdiction can have serious consequences for the juvenile's disposition, ensuring the accuracy of risk-related information—particularly that which is informed by an understanding of adolescent development—is essential.

UNDERSTANDING VIOLENT BEHAVIOR IN JUVENILES

It is critical for evaluators conducting forensic risk assessments of young offenders to understand the developmental context of aggressive behavior. Faulty assumptions and presuppositions about the nature and prevalence of violence in youths can easily lead to faulty conclusions about risk.

Developmental Issues

First, the evaluator should know that delinquent behavior in adolescence occurs with remarkable frequency, and that most youthful offender behavior does not persist into adulthood. Criminal/delinquent activity during adolescence occurs so frequently that, at least in some subgroups, it seems statistically normative (Elliott, Ageton, Huizinga, Knowles, & Canter, 1983; Hirschi, 1969). For example, the Centers for Disease Control and Prevention (CDC) Youth Risk Behavior Survey examined a national sample of more than 12,000 high school students—not a particularly high-risk group—and found that approximately 37% reported involvement in a physical fight one or more times in the prior 12 months (46% of boys and 26% of girls) (Kann et al., 2000). Most of those who act out with episodic violence in adolescence, however, do not continue to offend later in life. After age 17, violence participation rates drop dramatically, and about 80% of those who evidence violent behavior during adolescence will stop engaging in such behavior by age 21 (Elliott, Huizinga, & Morse, 1986). Thus, the occurrence of a violent act during adolescence does not necessarily imply that the youth stands at risk of being a long-term or serious offender.

Second, the evaluator should consider that one cannot gauge a youth's developmental capacities based solely on his or her chronological age. Different youths develop different cognitive and social skills at different rates. Moreover, estimates of "normal" or average age ranges for certain abilities derive largely from research conducted with Caucasian, middle-class children enrolled in school. The applicability of these normative estimates to minority youths living in poverty—disproportionately represented in the justice system—may prove somewhat limited since research has demonstrated that economic disadvantage may delay or inhibit certain developmental capacities.

In addition, different physical, cognitive, and social developmental markers emerge at very different rates—and one does not necessarily follow from the other. People can easily, yet mistakenly, assume that a young person who seems physically well developed and looks older that his age (e.g., tall, mature features, facial hair) must have all the concomitant cognitive and social capacities that one would expect of an older person. Physical maturity does not necessarily relate to cognitive, social, and emotional maturity.

Third, those conducting forensic assessments of juveniles must appreciate the instability and inconsistency inherent in child and adolescent development. Adolescence constitutes a time of major changes, and the trajectory of those changes and emerging markers does not always follow a linear or consistent path. Grisso (1998) has aptly characterized youth in the developmental period as "moving targets." A cross-sectional "snapshot" of the personality, thinking, emotion, and behavioral functioning of a child—as opposed to an adult—has less predictive power and less likelihood of reflecting the child's typical patterns.

Adolescence is a critical period for forming one's identity. During this time, children often "try on" different roles, styles, or traits to see how they feel or fit with one's emerging sense of self. As a result, personality traits—and behavioral manifestations of those traits—evidence less stability and less consistency in juveniles than in adults. One will more likely see a greater range of variability in styles and behaviors across different contexts in this population.

Adolescence also constitutes a period in which social influence becomes increasingly critical in development. During early childhood, most significant developmental changes result primarily as a function of biological processes. In later adolescence, however, the focus of influence becomes more environmental than biological. As young people mature and become increasingly self-reliant, parental influence shows a progressive decline. In early adolescence, peers become a major source of influence, yet their dominance typically peaks around 14 years of age and starts to decline in later high school years (Steinberg & Schwartz, 2000).

Fourth, one must recognize that physical, intellectual, emotional, and social developmental processes often do not progress at steady, linear, uniform rates. Quite commonly, one sees "spurts" (periods of rapid advance), "delays" (periods where advances are not occurring at the expected rate), and "regressions" (periods where developmental progress is lost or returns to an earlier state) in different areas of development. Not uncommonly, certain capacities will become evident in one context or circumstance but not in others.

Type and Severity of Violence and Aggression

Two critical conclusions from the empirical research should guide an evaluator's appraisal of the nature and severity of future violence: (a) that the severity of the instant offense does not necessarily predict the likelihood or severity of future offenses, and (b) that youths manifest different forms of aggressive behavior, each involving different psychological processes.

On the first point, despite the inference from *Kent*, the severity of the instant offense does not necessarily predict the likelihood or severity of future violence or criminal activity. This issue frequently emerges in cases where a juvenile has committed a homicide and thus confronts a presumption that the youth's offense per se reveals him to be a severe and persistent offender. Several studies have compared youths who commit murder to nonviolent delinquent offenders and have found somewhat surprising differences (Cornell, 1990; Cornell, Benedek, & Benedek, 1987). A study by Cornell and colleagues compared two groups of juveniles referred for evaluation—those who had committed homicide and those who had committed larceny. Those who committed homicide proved *less likely* than their nonviolent counterparts to have a history of prior arrests or placement in a juvenile facility, psychiatric problems, or problems with school adjustment. Youths convicted of homicide also proved *less likely* to have a known history of prior violent behavior than juveniles convicted on assault charges (Cornell, 1990; Cornell et al., 1987).

On the second point, numerous studies have identified at least two distinct subtypes of aggressive behavior in youths, most commonly referred to as *reactive* and *proactive* aggression. Each type has different cognitive, affective, and behavioral mediators and a different mechanism for development. Reactive aggression, usually characterized by an angry retaliatory response to a perceived provocation or threat, constitutes the most common type in youths. The contributing cognitive factor often involves a hypersensitivity to—or even a tendency to misperceive—hostile or aggressive social cues from others. The actor usually experiences physiologic arousal and anger, and the act itself often seems rather impulsive. In contrast,

proactive aggression often seems more overtly instrumental (i.e., used as a tactic to gain a desired outcome). It does not typically appear retaliatory, nor does it occur in response to perceived provocation. The contributing cognitive factors include beliefs in the legitimacy of aggression to attain a goal and positive expectations for success by using aggression. The actor typically does not experience intense arousal or anger at the time, and the act usually seems more deliberate than impulsive.

Given the distinctive mechanisms involved, the precipitants, and contexts, the optimal interventions for reactive and proactive aggression will likely take quite different forms. For example, it may prove less effective to prescribe anger management training to reduce violence risk in a youngster with an exclusive pattern of proactive aggression. Likewise, interventions to enhance empathy or diminish antisocial attitudes may meet with less success in an impulsive youngster whose only acts of aggression seem angry and reactive.

Finally, with regard to differing forms of aggression—for purposes of assessment—it will often prove helpful to distinguish between assessing risk for general violence and risk of targeted violence. One can conceptualize the risk for "general violence" as the likelihood that a given youth will commit any serious violent or aggressive act to any other person over a given period of time. In contrast, the term "targeted violence" as developed by Fein and Vossekuil (1999) to refer to situations in which a person has come to official attention because of some communication or behavior of concern, suggesting that he or she may pose a risk of harm to an identified or identifiable target.

This distinction becomes important because the factors considered and the assessment approach may differ (Borum & Reddy, 2001; Reddy et al., 2001). For example, in the wake of several high-profile school shootings around the nation, some psychologists find themselves asked to conduct a "risk assessment" on students who have reportedly made some threatening remark or written some disturbing material. These assessment should arguably rely on a fact-based assessment approach, and may—for a variety of reasons—not rely primarily on base rates or a tally of empirically based risk factors for *general* violence (for additional information on a fact-based model of assessment, see Borum, Fein, Vossekuil, & Berglund, 1999;

Borum & Reddy, 2001; Fein et al., 2002; Fein & Vossekuil, 1998; Fein, Vossekuil, & Holden, 1995; Reddy et al., 2001) .

Patterns of Juvenile Offending

Just as varying types of aggression exist, distinctive patterns of violent and delinquent offending in juveniles also lend themselves to classification. Moffitt (1993, 1997) has identified two primary types of delinquent patterns—life course persistent and adolescence limited—each of which tends to differ somewhat in the timing and duration of their offending careers. The life-course-persistent group is relatively small (approximately 5–9%) and consists of offenders who engage in antisocial behavior at every developmental stage, usually beginning prior to age 13. They appear at both ends of the age–crime curve. They frequently have co-occurring disorders (e.g., oppositional defiant disorder, attention deficit hyperactivity disorder), may characteristically engage in predatory (proactive) violence, and tend to have poor/superficial attachments to others.

The adolescence-limited offenders present much more commonly. They typically manifest violent and delinquent behavior only between the ages of 14 and 18, and largely account for the "peak" observed in the age–crime curve. By definition, offenders with this pattern typically have better childhood premorbid histories (e.g., fewer behavior problems and less likelihood of co-occurring disorder). The first emergence of antisocial behavior typically occurs not in childhood but in adolescence (after 13). Their pattern of offending seems less consistent, and any predatory (proactive) violence tends not to be stable or characteristic of their behavior. Adolescence-limited offenders most often form and maintain developmentally appropriate attachments to others.

RISK FACTORS FOR YOUTH VIOLENCE

An extensive scientific and professional literature documents the factors that may increase (risk factors) or decrease (protective factors) the risk of violence and aggression in children and adolescence (Cottle, Lee, & Heilbrun, 2001; Derzon,

2001; Hawkins et al., 1998; Howard & Jenson, 1999; Howell, 1997; Lipsey & Derzon, 1998; Loeber & Stouthamer-Loeber, 1998). Most of the published research on risk factors for youth violence has used general violence as its criterion of interest (i.e., it has examined that factors may be associated with any type of violent or aggressive act to any other person over a given period of time).

The U.S. Surgeon General's report on youth violence reviewed the literature on risk factors for serious violent offenses in late adolescence (ages 15–18), including those risk factors that emerge early (ages 6–11) and those that emerge later (ages 12–14) (U.S. Department of Health and Human Services, 2001). The early risk factors that showed a "large" effect in predicting adolescent violence included general offenses and substance use. Those with a "moderate effect" included male gender, low socioeconomic status/poverty, antisocial parents, and aggression (for males). Those showing a small, but significant, effect included psychological condition; hyperactivity; poor parent–child relations; harsh, lax, or inconsistent discipline; weak social ties; problem (antisocial) behavior; exposure to television violence; poor attitude toward or poor performance in school; medical, physical issues; low IQ; other family conditions; broken home/ separation for parents; antisocial attitudes and beliefs (i.e., dishonesty for males only); abusive or neglectful parents; and antisocial peers (U.S. Department of Health and Human Services, 2001).

The picture for late risk factors differed somewhat. Three late risk factors showed a "large" effect in predicting adolescent violence: weak social ties; antisocial, delinquent peers; and gang membership. The only factor to show a "moderate effect" was general offenses. Those factors showing a small but significant effect included psychological condition; restlessness; difficulty concentrating (for males); risk taking; poor parent–child relations; harsh, lax, or inconsistent discipline/poor monitoring and supervision; aggression (males only); male gender; poor attitude toward or poor performance in school; academic failure; physical violence; neighborhood crime, drugs; neighborhood disorganization; antisocial parents; antisocial attitudes and beliefs; crimes against persons; problem (antisocial) behavior; low IQ; broken home; low socioeconomic status/poverty; abusive parents; other family conditions; family conflict (for males); and substance use (U.S. Department of Health and Human Services, 2001).

ASSESSING RISK FOR GENERAL AGGRESSION IN JUVENILES

Some psychologists remember the intense pessimism that pervaded the field of "violence prediction" in the 1980s. At that time, a review of the best available research suggested that mental health professionals erred more often than they accurately predicted when an individual would subsequently engage in violent behavior (Monahan, 1981). Since then, considerable advances in research and practice have occurred with respect to assessing violence potential, supplanting that early pessimism with a more cautious, pragmatic optimism suggesting that mental health professionals may have the ability to distinguish violent from nonviolent individuals with a "modest, but better than chance, degree of accuracy" (Mossman, 1994). Notably, however, most of these advances have focused on adult psychiatric patients and criminal offenders (Borum, 1996, 2000; Borum, Swartz, & Swanson, 1996; Douglas, Cox, & Webster, 1999; Monahan & Steadman, 1994; Otto, 2000). The integration of science and practice specifically related to youth violence has developed more slowly; however, some conceptual and technological advances can assist in improving violence risk assessments for children and adolescents.

Risk Assessment Versus Violence Prediction

Over the past two decades, the conceptual bases and assumptions underlying assessments of violence potential have evolved from a violence prediction model to a more clinically relevant risk assessment/management model (Borum et al., 1996; Heilbrun, 1997; Litwack, Kirschner, & Wack, 1993; Melton, Petrila, Poythress, & Slobogin, 1997; Monahan, 1996; Monahan & Steadman, 1994; Webster, Douglas, Eaves, & Hart, 1997). In practice, the fundamental purpose or objective of a risk assessment involves *preventing* violent behavior, not simply *predicting* its occurrence (Heilbrun, 1997). Accordingly, the field has moved away

from language and approaches that focus on primarily on violence prediction to those that focus more on prevention and management. As applied to assessment practice, this shift has led assessors away from an exclusive focus on the individual as the subject of the assessment and toward a broader appraisal and weighing of situational factors. It has also led to an understanding of the concept of dangerousness or risk that seems more contextual (highly dependent on situations and circumstances), dynamic (subject to change), and continuous (varying along a continuum of probability) (National Research Council, 1989). This view seems particularly appropriate for appraising violence potential in juveniles since, as noted above, personality traits and dispositional characteristics tend to show much less stability in children and adolescents than in adults, therefore inherently limiting their predictive power. Given the dominance of social influence during adolescence, clinicians must use careful examination of situational and contextual factors to appraise accurately the nature and degree of violence risk that a youth may pose.

Risk Assessment Approaches

As evidence mounted in the mid-1980s suggesting that unstructured and purely "clinical" risk assessment approaches were not highly effective (Monahan, 1981), researchers and practitioners began to search for alternatives that could lead to better predictive accuracy and better practice. Some moved toward the development of statistical (actuarial) formulas as a method of assessing violence risk (Dawes, Faust, & Meehl, 1989; Grove & Meehl, 1996; Melton et al., 1997; Miller & Morris, 1988; Quinsey, Harris, Rice, & Cormier, 1998), although no such formulas exist for use with children and adolescents. Others worked to improve clinical judgments, leading ultimately to the development of the *structured professional judgment* or *guided clinical assessment* approach. In this approach, an evaluator conducts a risk assessment by referring to a checklist of items that have been drawn from the existing professional literature, and selected based on their demonstrated relationship to violence in the population of interest. Each item is operationally defined and typically divided into two (present/absent) or three levels, so that it may be scored or coded. This strategy encourages the evaluator to gather and focus on information that has a demonstrated relationship to violent behavior in youths and to make a judgment about risk that is informed by a systematic analysis of those factors. Preliminary empirical studies attest to the promise of this approach showing that judgments made using these tools have greater accuracy than those made without the benefit of a guided protocol and have as much or more accuracy than actuarial formulas (Dempster, 1998; Kropp, Hart, Webster, & Eaves, 1999; Hanson, 1998).

Despite its promise, the application of structured professional judgment protocols to children and adolescents remains in a very nascent stage of development. Although at least one instrument has demonstrated validation to assist in making judgments about general delinquent recidivism in young offenders (Hoge & Andrews, 2001), only two designed and available specifically to assist in making judgments about violence risk currently exist. One focuses on children, and the other on adolescents.

The Early Assessment Risk List for Boys (Augimeri, Webster, Koegl, & Levene, 2001) was designed to aid evaluators in making judgments about future violence and antisocial behavior among boys under the age of 12, particularly those who exhibit behavioral problems and are considered at high risk. The protocol contains 20 items, each of which is assigned a score of 0, 1, or 2 depending on the certainty and severity of the characteristic in a given case. This blending of "certainty" (i.e., characteristic is definitely present in the case) and "severity" (e.g., academic deficits 1 year vs. 2 years below grade level) is not uncommon in guided assessment protocols, although it certainly can create some conceptual confusion. The 20 items fall into three categories: 6 "family" items (household circumstances, caregiver continuity, supports, stressors, parenting style, antisocial values and conduct), 12 "child" items (developmental problems, onset of behavioral difficulties, abuse/neglect/trauma, hyperactivity/impulsivity/attention deficits, likeability, peer socialization, academic performance, neighborhood, authority contact, antisocial attitudes, antisocial behavior, and coping ability), and 2 "responsivity" items (family responsivity and child responsivity).

In the manual, the authors describe a preliminary retrospective study of 378 boys and 69 girls, all of whom were under 12 when they attended a court-based intervention program for young offenders. On a subsample of 120 cases, evidence of good interrater reliability among three independent raters existed, with an intraclass correlation coefficient of .82 for single measure and .93 for average measure. Furthermore, using the full sample, an analysis of the relationship between total scores and subsequent criminal convictions after age 12 found that those with scores designated "high" (21–36) were significantly more likely to have had a conviction than were those with scores designated "low" (3–21) (chi-squared = 5.1, df = 1, P = .02).

The Structured Assessment of Violence Risk in Youth (SAVRY; Borum, Bartel, & Forth, 2000) is designed to focus specifically on violence risk in adolescents. The SAVRY protocol includes 24 "risk" items, divided into three categories (historical, individual, and social/contextual) and six "protective" items. The risk items each have a three-level coding structure (i.e., high, moderate, and low), and the protective items have a two-level structure (i.e., present or absent). Specific coding guidelines are provided for each level.

The SAVRY combines risk factors from the Surgeon General's report with other empirically based risk factors for youth violence in an applied framework, broadly categorized as historical, individual, and social/contextual. These factors have undergone review, analysis, and careful documentation in the professional literature (Borum, 2000; Borum et al., 2001; Hawkins et al., 1998; Howard & Jenson, 1999; U.S. Department of Health and Human Services, 2001).

Historical Risk Factors

Historical risk factors focus on past behavior or experiences, such as prior episodes of violence. Many of these factors have shown strong empirical associations with general violence risk recidivism in juveniles; however, because they are static and not amenable to change, they may prove less helpful than the others for needs assessment and intervention planning. The SAVRY includes the following historical factors:

- History of violence
- History of nonviolent offending

- Early initiation of violence
- Past supervision/intervention failures
- History of self-harm or suicide attempts
- Exposure to violence in the home
- Childhood history of maltreatment
- Parental/caregiver criminality
- Early caregiver disruption
- Poor school achievement

Individual Risk Factors

Other significant risk factors for violent offending in youths focus on the young person's attitudes and key aspects of psychological and behavioral functioning. Some of these items may seem somewhat "clinical" in nature, containing aspects that relate to symptoms or disorders generally recognized as "clinical syndromes" in child and adolescent populations. Nevertheless, it is noteworthy that many of these "features" associate to increased risk of violence and aggression, independent of whether the diagnosis or syndrome itself accurately describes the child. The individual risk factors in the SAVRY include:

- Negative attitudes (e.g., particularly antisocial attitudes or attitudes that endorse violence)
- Risk taking/impulsivity
- Substance use difficulties
- Anger management problems
- Attention deficit/hyperactivity difficulties
- Low empathy/remorse
- Poor compliance
- Low interest/commitment to school

Social/Contextual Risk Factors

The final grouping of risk factors focuses upon the influence of interpersonal relationships (peer and family), connection to social institutions, and environment. Most violent behavior is largely determined by situational and transactional factors. This is particularly true with juveniles, since in adolescence the strongest influence of others shifts primarily from parents/caregivers to one's peer group. Youths in early adolescence seem particularly susceptible to pressures to conform their behavior to gain acceptance by others—a phenomenon that usually peaks around the age of 14 and then declines as a young person develops increasing behav-

ioral autonomy and independence. Even in later adolescence, however, the contribution of social and contextual factors to violence and aggression becomes substantial. SAVRY items in this domain include:

- Peer delinquency
- Peer rejection
- Stress and poor coping
- Poor parental management
- Lack of personal/social support
- Community disorganization

Protective Factors

The presence of one or more important risk factors does not mean that violence will certainly occur. Just as some risk factors increase the likelihood of violence, individual and contextual protective factors that can reduce the negative impact of a risk factor or otherwise act to diminish the probability of a violent outcome. In addition to assessing risk factors, professional risk assessments should include a careful assessment of protective and mitigating factors. While the absence of a risk factor may, in some sense, be considered "protective" and used accordingly in formulating a risk appraisal, research has identified numerous examples of positive protective factors (i.e., those that are notable for their presence, not their absence), as opposed to negative protective factors (i.e., those notable for the absence of a risk factor). Those in the SAVRY include:

- Prosocial involvement
- Strong social support
- Strong attachments and bonds
- Positive attitude toward intervention and authority
- Strong commitment to school
- Resilient temperament and personality traits

The first SAVRY validation study involved a retrospective analysis of a sample of 104 incarcerated male delinquents with relatively serious criminal histories, ranging from 15 to 19 years of age (mean = 17.53; standard deviation = 0.89) (Bartel, Forth, & Borum, 2004). This study compared the SAVRY to two measures that associated with violence and recidivism in adolescent offenders—the Psychopathy Checklist: Youth Version (PCL:YV;

Forth, Kosson, & Hare, 2003) and the Youth Level of Supervision Inventory (YLSI; Hoge & Andrews, 2001). In univariate analyses, the SAVRY total score, individual component scale, and YLSI total score produced the largest correlations with indices of past violent behavior. Multivariate analyses showed that institutional aggressive behavior was predicted only by the SAVRY Individual/Clinical scale ($R^2 = .18$), and violent versatility was predicted only by the SAVRY Total Risk scale ($R^2 = .21$).

We also conducted a series of hierarchical regression analyses to examine the whether the SAVRY had any incremental validity beyond the other measures in predicting violence. Three of the violence indices were chosen as dependent variables: institution aggressive behavior, frequency of violence, and number of aggressive conduct disorder symptoms. Results were as follows:

- Institutional aggressive behaviors: Adding the SAVRY improved the predictive power of the YLSI, although this gain was small (multiple regression from .38 to .43). Once both scales were in the model the SAVRY accounted for a slightly larger portion of the variance than did the YLSI. Adding the PCL:YV did not improve the performance of the SAVRY, whereas the SAVRY added to the predictive power of the PCL:YV in predicting institutional aggressive behaviors.
- Frequency of aggressive behaviors: The addition of the SAVRY only marginally improved the predictive power of the YLSI (from .35 to .37). Once both scales were in the model the YLSI accounted for a slightly larger portion of the variance than did the SAVRY. The SAVRY and PCL:YV performed equally well in predicting the frequency of aggressive behaviors.
- Number of aggressive conduct disorder symptoms: Adding the SAVRY significantly improved to the predictive power of the YLSI (multiple regression from .40 to .52) in predicting the number of conduct disorder symptoms. With both scales included in the model, the SAVRY accounted for a substantially larger portion of the variance than did the YLSI (betas .47 vs. .07). In addition, the SAVRY added to the predictive power of the PCL:YV and accounted for a larger proportion of the variance than did the PCL:YV in predicting conduct disorder symptoms.

A second study consisted of a retrospective follow-up on 108 young male offenders evaluated at a youth forensic service (McEachran, 2001). The dependent variable consisted of official crimes committed after reaching adulthood (generally around 3-year follow-up). The sample included violent recidivists, nonviolent recidivists, and nonrecidivists (36 in each group). Interrater reliabilities were relatively high (.83) for the SAVRY total score and moderate (.72) for the summary risk rating.

One cautionary note is necessary for interpreting some of these findings. The author of this study used a scoring strategy in which calculating the "SAVRY total" score involved adding the converted codes for the 24 risk factors, then subtracting from that the sum of the converted codes for the protective factors. This deviates somewhat from the intended protocol where the SAVRY total score simply represents the sum of the risk factor items. The protective factors are considered separately and not subtracted. The effect that this scoring variation may have had on the study results remains unknown. Results were as follows:

- The PCL:YV scores tended to show somewhat larger correlations (.46 for total) with officially recorded violent recidivism than the SAVRY scores (.32 for total), however, the SAVRY summary risk ratings correlated very highly with violence (.67).
- A similar pattern was seen using receiver operating characteristic analysis where the area under the curve (AUC) for the PCL:YV total score was .79, and the SAVRY total score was .70, but the AUC for the summary risk rating was .89.

These preliminary data support the validity of the SAVRY in assessing violence risk in adolescents. In particular, they suggest that SAVRY-informed risk ratings may have a strong association with violent behavior. Additional studies can be found on the SAVRY Web site (www.fmhi.usf.edu/mhlp/savry/statement.htm).

Estimating Risk

Regardless of the approach one chooses to gather and organize risk-related information, the evaluator must ultimately make a decision and appraisal concerning violence risk in the instant case. Even the structured assessment instruments are not designed to provide a numerical meter of risk (e.g., score of 1–10 is low) because the facts of the case might make a simple tally of risk factors or scores relatively meaningless. For example, a teen known to have a gun in his possession, expressing homicidal intent toward a particular target, and talking about knowing where to find the target at any given point in the day would seem imprudently rated as "low risk" without requiring action based solely on the absence of other significant risk factors in the case (e.g., past history of violence, substance abuse, childhood victimization). How, then, should an evaluator estimate violence risk?

I suggest using an approach that anchors the estimate of risk in factors that have a strong relationship to adolescent violence based on known research studies, and titrating that with information from dynamic and case-specific factors. The ultimate appraisal of risk should be individualized and developmentally informed. The evaluator should consider risk factors derived from research, as well as from the youth's own history or recent behaviors, and all risk-related information should be weighed in light of the developmental issues discussed above. Of particular interest to the evaluator who conducts assessments both for children and adolescents is that—in predicting violence in late adolescence—different risk factors may operate in early versus later years (see U.S. Department of Health and Human Services, 2001). For example, having delinquent peers in childhood (e.g., ages 6–11) does increase the risk for serious adolescent violence, but only modestly. In adolescents (e.g., ages 12–14), however, having antisocial/delinquent peers constitutes one of the strongest predictors of subsequent violence: its effect approximates a ninefold increase at this stage compared with the early stage. Indeed, most interventions for reducing violence in adolescents will prove ineffective if the delinquent peer factor remains unaddressed and unmitigated.

A heuristic that I have used to anchor estimates relative risk in adolescents involves using a visual flow chart to guide my iterative consideration of key risk factors (for a similar guide for adults, see Melton et al., 1997, p. 291). This chart is rationally derived based roughly on the strength of the empirical relationship between the risk factor and violence, with more static factors considered in the first phase and more dynamic factors in the latter phase. This does not constitute a regression tree and has no basis in a specific actuarial or statistical formula or model. It simply constitutes a heuristic device for guiding a risk estimate.

In the first step, one determines whether the youth has engaged in serious violence (e.g., violence sufficiently severe to cause injury or committed with a weapon) during childhood (before age 13). As noted above, early onset of violent offending links strongly to the likelihood and severity of future violence. Next, one could consider whether the youth has a co-occurring disruptive behavior disorder (or serious problems related to such a disorder), such as conduct disorder or attention deficit hyperactivity disorder. Conduct disorder will reflect a history of multiple antisocial behaviors, and hyperactivity forms a notable risk factor for violence in adolescents, creating a risk of arrest that is 5–25 times greater than if hyperactivity does not exist. The third step gives attention to whether the youth has engaged in serious violence during adolescence (at or after age 13), since past violent behavior associates with risk of future violent behavior.

The next phase of the flow chart is composed of three "dynamic" risk areas. The first of these considers the presence of delinquent peers/associates. Because I use this chart for estimating risk in adolescents, this factor weighs more heavily to account for the strong relationship between it and subsequent violence specifically found in the older age group. Then, one may consider the presence of antisocial attitudes, particularly those that would condone or support the use of violence as a legitimate strategy to solve problems or achieve a goal. Youths who possess more of these attitudes and beliefs and possess them more strongly would place at higher risk. Finally, the evaluator might consider the presence of serious problems at home and/or at school. Prior reviews of risk factors for youth violence have highlighted how poor achievement, disregard for school, and school-related problem behaviors associate to risk for future violence. Similar research-based associations exist for a range of home-based problems, including antisocial parents, poor parental management/supervision, and maltreatment. Again, youths with more problems and more serious problems have in past studies linked to a higher risk for violence.

The estimate derived from systematic consideration of key factors can serve as an anchor point for the overall likelihood of general (and typically serious) violence. In communicating an estimate of relative risk (e.g., low, moderate, high), a question often arises about the basis for comparison (i.e., "relative to what?"). One potential strategy involves calculating a base rate estimate of the prevalence/probability of serious violence among youths of a similar age. In addition to official arrest statistics, several large-scale, longitudinal studies of youths can provide relevant data on this point, including the National Youth Survey (Elliott, 1994); the Rochester Youth Development Study, the Pittsburgh Youth Study, and the Denver Youth Study (Huizinga, Loeber, & Thornberry, 1995); the CDC's Youth Risk Behavior Survey (Kann et al., 2000); and the Monitoring the Future Survey (Maguire & Pastore, 1999). The evaluator can then identify the comparison rate and source (e.g., in a large-scale, long-term follow-up study of more than XXXX youths in the community, and average of XX% had engaged in at least one act of serious violence by age 18) and state the estimate in the current case, relative to that rate (e.g., in my opinion, based on an appraisal of the following factors [listing empirical and individual risk and protective factors], without further intervention, Johnny Smith currently poses a moderate risk of serious violence).

CONCLUSION

As youth violence has become a prominent point of public concern, psychologists and other professionals have often been called upon to assess the risk of future violence in juveniles. Evaluators who conduct such assessments must understand the distinction between general violence and targeted violence, and the focus of the referral question, before beginning an examination. Assessments of violence risk in children and adolescents should also be developmentally informed and guided by an understanding of violent and aggressive behavior in youths and by an understanding of how key principles of human development apply to the appraisal of risk. Using these tools, perhaps with the assistance of a structured assessment tool, psychologists can systematically examine factors that

have a demonstrated relationship to violence risk in juveniles and refine the risk judgment based on a comprehensive analysis of the examinee's history. These procedures should lead to more effective risk assessments, to better intervention plans, and ultimately to enhanced violence prevention.

References

Augimeri, L., Webster, C., Koegl, C., & Levene, K. (2001). *Early Assessment Risk List for Boys: EARL-20B, version 2—consultation edition.* Toronto: Earlscourt Child & Family Centre.

Bartel, P., Forth, A., & Borum, R. (2004). *Development and validation of the Structured Assessment for Violence Risk in Youth (SAVRY).* Manuscript submitted for publication.

Blumstein, A. (1995). Youth violence, guns, and the illicit drug industry. *Journal of Criminal Law & Criminology, 86,* 10–36.

Borum, R. (1996). Improving the clinical practice of violence risk assessment: Technology, guidelines and training. *American Psychologist, 51,* 945–956.

Borum, R. (2000). Assessing violence risk among youth. *Journal of Clinical Psychology, 56,* 1263–1288.

Borum, R., Bartel, P., & Forth, A. (2000). *Manual for the Structured Assessment for Violence Risk in Youth (SAVRY): consultation edition.* Tampa: Louis de la Parte Florida Mental Health Institute, University of South Florida.

Borum, R., Fein, R., Vossekuil, B., & Berglund, J. (1999). Threat assessment: Defining an approach for evaluating risk of targeted violence. *Behavioral Sciences & the Law, 17,* 323–337.

Borum, R., & Reddy, M. (2001). Assessing violence risk in Tarasoff situations: A fact-based model of inquiry. *Behavioral Sciences & the Law, 19,* 375–385.

Borum, R., Swartz, M., & Swanson, J. (1996). Assessing and managing violence risk in clinical practice. *Journal of Practical Psychiatry & Behavioral Health, 2*(4), 205–215.

Cornell, D. G. 1990. Prior adjustment of violent juvenile offenders. *Law & Human Behavior* 14:569–577.

Cornell, D., Benedek, E., & Benedek, D. (1987). Juvenile homicide: Prior adjustment and a proposed typology. *American Journal of Orthopsychiatry, 57,* 383–393.

Cottle, C., Lee, R., & Heilbrun, K. (2001). The prediction of criminal recidivism in juveniles: A meta-analysis. *Criminal Justice & Behavior, 28,* 367–394.

Dawes, R., Faust, D., & Meehl, P. (1989). Clinical versus actuarial judgment. *Science, 243,* 1668–1674.

Dempster, R. (1998). *Prediction of sexually violent recidivism: A comparison of risk assessment instruments.* Unpublished master's thesis, Simon Fraser University, Burnaby, BC.

Derzon, J. (2001). Antisocial behavior and the prediction of violence: A meta-analysis. *Psychology in the Schools, 38,* 93–106.

Douglas, K., Cox, D., & Webster, C. (1999, September). Violence risk assessment: Science and practice. *Legal & Criminological Psychology,* 4(Pt. 2), 149–184.

Elliott, D. S. (1994). Serious violent offenders: Onset, developmental course, and termination The American Society of Criminology 1993 presidential address. *Criminology, 32,* 1–21.

Elliott, D., Ageton, S., Huizinga, D., Knowles, B., & Canter, R. (1983). *The prevalence and incidence of delinquent behavior: 1976–1980* (National Youth Survey Report No. 26). Boulder, CO: Behavioral Research Institute.

Elliott, D. S., Huizinga, D., & Morse, B. J. (1986). Self-reported violent offending: A descriptive analysis of juvenile violent offenders and their offending careers. *Journal of Interpersonal Violence,* 1, 472–514.

Fein, R. A., & Vossekuil, B. (1998). *Protective intelligence & threat assessment investigations: A guide for state and local law enforcement officials* (NIJ/OJP/DOJ Publication No. NCJ 170612). Washington, DC: U.S. Department of Justice.

Fein, R. A., & Vossekuil, B. (1999). Assassination in the United States: An operational study of recent assassins, attackers, and near-lethal approachers. *Journal of Forensic Sciences, 50,* 321–333.

Fein, R. A., Vossekuil, B., & Holden, G. A. (1995, September). Threat assessment: An approach to prevent targeted violence. *National Institute of Justice: Research in Action,* 1–7.

Fein, R. A., Vossekuil, F., Pollack, W. S., Borum, R., Modzeleski, W., & Reddy, M. (2002). *Threat assessment in schools: A guide to managing threatening situations and to creating safe school climates.* Washington, DC: U.S. Secret Service & U.S. Department of Education.

Forth, A. E., Kosson, D. S., & Hare, R. D. (2003). *The psychopathy checklist: Youth version.* Toronto, Ontario: Multi-Health Systems.

Grisso, T. (1996). Society's retributive response to juvenile violence: A developmental perspective. *Law & Human Behavior, 20,* 229–247.

Grisso, T. (1998). *Forensic evaluation of juveniles.* Sarasota, FL: Professional Resource Press.

Grove, W., & Meehl, P. (1996). Comparative efficiency of informal (subjective, impressionistic) and formal (mechanical, algorithmic) prediction procedures: The clinical-statistical controversy. *Psychology, Public Policy & Law, 2,* 293–323.

Hamburg, M. A. (1998). Youth violence is a public health concern. In D. S. Elliott, B. A. Hamburg, & K. R. Williams (Eds.), *Violence in American schools: A new perspective* (pp. 31–54). Cambridge, UK: Cambridge University Press.

Hanson, K. (1998). What we know about sex offender risk assessment. *Psychology, Public Policy & Law, 4,* 50–72.

Hawkins, J., Herrenkohl, T., Farrington, D., Brewer, D., Catalano, R., & Harachi, T. (1998). A review of predictors of youth violence. In R. Loeber & D. Farrington (Eds.), *Serious and violent juvenile offenders: Risk factors and successful interventions* (pp. 106–146). Thousand Oaks, CA: Sage.

Heilbrun, K. (1997). Prediction vs. management models relevant to risk assessment: The importance of legal decision-making context. *Law & Human Behavior, 21,* 347–359.

Hirschi, T. (1969). *Causes of delinquency.* Berkeley, CA: University of California Press.

Hoge, R., & Andrews, D. (2001). *The Youth Level of Service/Case Management Inventory (YLS/CMI).* Ottawa, ON: Carleton University.

Howard, M., & Jenson, J. (1999). Causes of youth violence. In J. Jenson & M. Howard (Eds.), *Youth violence: Current research and recent practice innovations* (pp. 19–42). Washington, DC: National Association of Social Workers Press.

Howell, J. C. (1997). *Juvenile justice and juvenile violence.* Thousand Oaks, CA: Sage.

Huizinga, D., Loeber, R., & Thornberry, T. P. (1995). *Recent findings from the Program of Research on the Causes and Correlates of Delinquency.* Washington, DC: U.S. Department of Justice, Office of Justice Programs, Office of Juvenile Justice and Delinquency Prevention.

Kann, L., Kinchen, S. A., Williams, B. I., Ross, J. G., Lowry, R., Grunbaum, J. A., Kolbe, L. J., & State and Local YRBSS Coordinators. (2000). Youth risk behavior surveillance; United States, 1999. *Morbidity & Mortality Weekly Report CDC Surveillance Summary, 49,* 1–96.

Kent v. United States, 383 U.S. 541 (1966).

Kropp, P., Hart, S., Webster, C., & Eaves D. (1999). *Manual for the Spousal Assault Risk Assessment Guide* (3rd ed.). Toronto: Multi-Health Systems.

Lipsey, M., & Derzon, J. (1998). Predictors of violent or serious delinquency in adolescence and early adulthood: A synthesis of longitudinal research. In R. Loeber & D. Farrington (Eds.), *Serious & violent juvenile offenders: Risk factors and successful interventions* (pp. 86–105). Thousand Oaks, CA: Sage.

Litwack, T., Kirschner, S., & Wack, R. (1993). The assessment of dangerousness and prediction of violence: Recent research and future prospects. *Psychiatric Quarterly, 64,* 245–255.

Loeber, R., & Stouthamer-Loeber, M. (1998). Juvenile aggression at home and at school. In D. S. Elliott, B. A. Hamburg, & K. R. Williams (Eds.), *Violence in American schools* (pp. 95–126). New York: Cambridge University Press.

Maguire, K., & Pastore, A. L. (1999). *Sourcebook of criminal justice statistics, 1998* (U.S. Department of Justice, Office of Justice Programs, Bureau of Justice Statistics, NCJ 176356). Washington, DC: U.S. Government Printing Office. (Also available on the World Wide Web at www.albany.edu/sourcebook/)

McEachran, A. (2001). *The predictive validity of the PCL-YV and the SAVRY in a population of adolescent offenders.* Unpublished master's thesis, Simon Fraser University, Burnaby, BC.

Melton, G., Petrila, J., Poythress, N., & Slobogin, C. (1997). *Psychological evaluations for the courts: A handbook for mental health professionals and lawyers* (2nd ed.). New York: Guilford.

Miller, M., & Morris, N. (1988). Predictions of dangerousness: An argument for limited use. *Violence & Victims, 3,* 263–270.

Moffitt, T. E. (1993). Adolescence-limited and life-course-persistent antisocial behavior: A developmental taxonomy. *Psychological Review, 100,* 674–701.

Moffitt, T. (1997). Adolescence-limited and life-course-persistent offending: A complementary pair of developmental theories. In T. Thornberry (Ed.), *Developmental theories of crime and delinquency* (pp. 11–54). New Brunswick, NJ: Transaction.

Monahan, J. (1981). *Predicting violent behavior: An assessment of clinical techniques.* Beverly Hills, CA: Sage.

Monahan, J. (1996). Violence prediction: The last 20 years and the next 20 years. *Criminal Justice & Behavior, 23,* 107–120.

Monahan, J., & Steadman, H. (1994). *Violence and mental disorder: Developments in risk assessment.* Chicago: University of Chicago Press.

Mossman, D. (1994). Assessing predictions of violence: Being accurate about accuracy. *Journal of Consulting & Clinical Psychology, 62,* 783–792.

National Research Council. (1989). *Improving risk communication.* Washington, DC: National Academy Press.

Otto, R. (2000). Assessing and managing violence risk in outpatient settings. *Journal of Clinical Psychology, 56*(10), 1239–1262.

Quinsey, V., Harris, G., Rice, M., & Cormier, C. (1998). *Violent offenders: Appraising and managing risk.* Washington, DC: American Psychological Association.

Reddy, M., Borum, R., Vossekuil, B., Fein, R., Berglund, J., & Modzeleski, W. (2001). Evaluating risk for targeted violence in schools: Comparing risk assessment, threat assessment, and other approaches. *Psychology in the Schools, 38*(2), 157–172.

Snyder, H. N., & Sickmund, M. (1999). *Juvenile offenders and victims: 1999 national report* (NCJ 178257). Washington, DC: U.S. Department of Justice, Office of Justice Programs, Office of Juvenile Justice and Delinquency Prevention. (Also available on the World Wide Web at www.ncjrs.org/html/ojjdp/nationalreport99/toc.html)

Snyder, H. N., Sickmund, M., & Poe-Yamagata, E. (2000). *Juvenile transfers to criminal court in the 1990s: Lessons learned from four studies.* Washington, DC: U.S. Department of Justice, Office of Justice Programs, Office of Juvenile Justice and Delinquency Prevention.

Steinberg, L., & Schwartz, R. (2000). Developmental psychology goes to court. In T. Grisso & R. Schwartz (Eds.), *Youth on trial: A developmental perspective on juvenile justice* (pp. 9–31). Chicago: University of Chicago Press.

U.S. Department of Health and Human Services. (2001). *Youth violence: A report of the Surgeon General.* Rockville, MD: U.S. Department of Health and Human Services, Substance Abuse and Mental Health Services Administration, Center for Mental Health Services, National Institutes of Health, National Institute of Mental Health. (Also available on the World Wide Web at www.surgeongeneral.gov/library/youthviolence)

Webster, C. D., Douglas, K., Eaves, D., & Hart, S. (1997). *HCR-20: Assessing risk for violence, version 2.* Burnaby, BC: Simon Fraser University & Forensic Psychiatric Services Commission of British Columbia.

Zimring, F. (1998). *American youth violence.* New York: Oxford University Press.

13

Psychological Evaluation for Child Custody

Steven N. Sparta
Philip M. Stahl

GENERAL ORIENTATION

Even the most experienced forensic psychologists recognize that child custody evaluations constitute the most difficult and challenging of all types of psychological evaluations (Otto, 2003). Factors that contribute to this difficulty include, but are not limited to, the needs to assess children at different stages of development, to accurately assess a wide range of potential psychopathology, to recognize the limitations in available psychological tests for assessing parental competence, and to determine whether observed dysfunctions represent enduring personality traits or products of situational factors likely to remit over time; the need for the evaluator to attempt to retain professional objectivity despite frequent challenges by parents and/or attorneys; and the likelihood that one or both parties will feel dissatisfied with the outcome. Those considering such work must also determine whether they have the temperament and/or commitment to conduct very comprehensive exams and to be frequently subjected to a highly adversarial experience with both parents and their attorneys. Not uncommonly, the evaluator may become the

subject of distorted representations or accusations. Evaluators have great ethical responsibility because recommendations can have particularly significant ramifications for children's futures.

Various relevant laws, ethical standards, professional practice guidelines, and relevant research findings can guide child custody evaluations. Examples of professional practice guidelines include the "Guidelines for Child Custody Evaluations in Divorce Proceedings" (American Psychological Association [APA] Committee on Professional Practice and Standards, 1994), *Model Standards for Child Custody Evaluations* (Association of Family and Conciliation Courts, 1994), and the "Practice Parameters for Child Custody Evaluation" (American Academy of Child and Adolescent Psychiatry, 1997). Such documents represent a starting point. Evaluators should strive for ethically sensitive interactions with participants while producing clearly understood reports that reflect sound methodology and purpose and that provide psychologically appropriate suggestions for resolving the dispute (Stahl, 1994).

The "Guidelines for Child Custody" (APA Committee on Professional Practice and Standards,

1994) state that the primary purpose of the evaluation involves assessing the best psychological interests of the child and that "the focus of the evaluation is on parenting capacity, the psychological and developmental needs of the child and the resulting fit." Recognizing the forensic nature of such evaluations, other documents may also provide guidance, such as the "Specialty Guidelines for Forensic Psychologists" (Committee on Ethical Guidelines for Forensic Psychologists, 1991). Martindale and Gould (2004) have cautioned practitioners against misapplying their training as clinicians when performing a forensic evaluation for child custody and discuss the appropriateness of using some psychodiagnostic assessment instruments. Kirkpatrick (2004) has argued for 26 minimum standards of practice that go beyond the aspirational nature of guidelines. Some jurisdictions have made attempts to establish minimal and consistently applied criteria for consideration in *every* child custody evaluation. For example, the Judicial Council of California (California Rules of Court, 2003a) addresses the responsibility of the evaluator, the scope of the evaluation, ethical issues, the manner of cooperation with professionals in other jurisdictions, requirements for training and qualifications of examiners, and cost-effective procedures.

Child custody evaluations ideally take place pursuant to an advance stipulation of the attorneys for each parent that then becomes incorporated in a court order or, in the alternative, by the motion of the court. The court order can help to minimize potential controversies by explicitly setting forth which parent has responsibility for what portion of payment, the scope and focus of the evaluation, and whether special issues such as a waiver of privilege regarding the psychotherapy records will apply. Depending on the jurisdiction, court appointment may also confer quasi-judicial immunity against lawsuits. Before proceeding, evaluators should determine whether any reasonably foreseeable conflicts exist that should disqualify them from performing the evaluation.

After the order is issued, the evaluator still needs to obtain a fully informed consent from the parents regarding the nature and purpose of the evaluation. Evaluators should strive at all times to approach participants with respect, to carefully explain and document informed consent prior to

the start of assessment, and to adhere to relevant protocols or procedures. Evaluators should not accept assignments beyond the limits of their training and experience and should always exercise care to avoid not only actual conflicts of interest but also any appearance of conflict. Informed consent requires sufficient detail to explain financial costs, limits of confidentiality, anticipated procedures, and the reasonably foreseeable involvement of the evaluator in the future process, such as possible court testimony about allegations or custody recommendations. Optional sections can include the evaluator's right to withdraw from the case if, in the opinion of the evaluator, any party makes it impossible for the evaluator to perform the customary evaluation procedures.

In most jurisdictions, the evaluator sends a detailed report to the court and the attorneys, with an understanding that, unless there is a significant risk of harm to one of the family members, the parents will review all or part of the report. After the parents review the report and consult with their attorneys, it may become possible for both parents to reach a mutual agreement regarding a child-sharing plan or to decide whether they will proceed to a contested court hearing. Such reports will yield best results when written with an anticipation of possible reconciliation of differing views and with an explanation of findings or recommendations in terms of the child's best interests. The evaluator should always complete the report with an understanding that court testimony may occur. In anticipation of such testimony, the evaluator fully explains in the report the sources and limitations of data and provides an analysis of the underlying rationale for the opinions given in the report.

ETHICAL CONSIDERATIONS

The demanding nature and complexity of child custody evaluations has resulted in a significant number of complaints to ethics committees and licensing boards. For example, when one of us (SNS) chaired the APA Ethics Committee in 2002, child custody–related problems represented the largest percentage of complaints as a primary factor underlying allegations made within the category of inappropriate professional practice (APA, 2003), although a greater number of cases occurred in the category of dual relationship (e.g., sexual misconduct) and loss of license. Kirkland and Kirkland (2001) noted that in the 1999 report of the ethics committee, child custody complaints constituted the only area of forensic practice that warranted a singular, separate entity. These same authors surveyed 61 member boards of the Association of State and Provincial Psychology Boards and found that child custody evaluations can disproportionately result in license-board complaints, although the overall rate remains low.

At a minimum, evaluators always provide objective, informed, relevant, and comparative psychological information to the court about different family members, whether or not they provide specific recommendations for child custody. Legal criteria for awarding custody address issues broader than psychological best interests. Evaluators also recognize their ethical responsibility to state when a given question posed goes beyond the available methods or data to permit an opinion by the evaluator. Often conscious and unconscious pressures push evaluators to exceed the limits of their data. Differences of opinion exist concerning the advisability of psychologists' providing recommendations regarding custody because of concerns about addressing ultimate legal issues without a sufficient professional basis for doing so (e.g., Melton, Petrila, Poythress, & Slobogin, 1997; Woody, 2000). Recent reviews of psychologists' practices and procedures show an overwhelming willingness to make explicit recommendations about child custody, with 94% of evaluators responding "yes" to making specific custody recommendations and only 3% responding "no" (Bow & Quinnell, 2002).

Because the frequency of a given practice among practitioners does not necessarily indicate ethical appropriateness, the evaluator should continually question him- or herself about the reasonableness of the underlying support for the conclusion. Martindale and Gould (2004) advocate a forensically informed approach that goes beyond simply meeting a standard of care criterion with an understanding of how ethics and methodology are intimately related.

A related ultimate issue in child custody recommendations involves allegations of domestic violence, physical and sexual abuse, and other forms of child maltreatment. The child custody evaluator must always remain objective and offer an opinion only when reasonably supported by the data. In many cases involving conflicting serious allegations of abuse, the evaluator may provide the court with valuable findings about the parents and child while stopping short of making an ultimate conclusion about whether a specific individual committed abuse. Melton and Limber (1989) cautioned psychologists against overstating the conclusions that could be drawn from their data, making an important distinction between professional involvement *after* a dispositional finding of abuse has been issued from the court and the situation of a professional in a child custody conflict who has accepted appointment *before* any conclusion exists. Some treatment settings accept the allegation of child sexual abuse as true for purposes of providing protective treatment, and in those types of settings, an allegation about a parent involved in a custody dispute will be regarded as true. In the context of a child custody evaluation, harm can result to a child who is unprotected from abuse, and harm can also result to a child and/or a parent who falls victim to a false allegation. The custody evaluator must always consider the child's welfare as paramount while always remaining cognizant of the rights and psychological welfare of other family members. At a minimum, the evaluation can inform the court about each participant's preferences and the underlying reasons for such, can provide comparative data about each of the parents, and can serve as a basis for recommendations designed to address psychological issues that affect the child's best psychological interests.

An ethical question may arise if an attorney asks an experienced child custody evaluator to consult with a family-law client in another context. For example, sometimes attorneys wish to prepare anxious clients for future mental health assessments or to obtain advance information on their clients to better advise them regarding their legal interests. Professionals should remain aware of the potential for distortion of future evaluation processes as a result of possible practice effects from repeated testing, of coaching parents about the evaluation process, or of providing other information that risks contaminating the future evaluation.

Many jurisdictions have seen an increase in the number of parents who legally represent themselves in divorce proceedings, designated as being in *propria persona*, or *pro per* or *pro se*. In states that permit such self-representation in divorce proceedings, the child custody evaluator should attend to the fact that the self-represented parent may not understand the rules of court and other procedural matters. Extra time may prove necessary to explain and document adherence to child custody evaluation procedures without the examiner crossing a boundary and becoming an advocate or permitting manipulation by a parent feigning ignorance of the procedures. Experienced evaluators will pay particular attention to such details in order to avoid compromising the evaluation process or the risk of having the evaluation invalidated by the court.

DIFFERENCES BETWEEN CLINICAL AND FORENSIC SERVICES

Psychologists may have many potential roles in child custody matters. These roles may include:

- Mediator, including both confidential and nonconfidential mediation
- Psychological evaluator when the custody evaluator does not do his or her own psychological testing
- Psychotherapist, either for mother, father, children, or the family
- Consultant, usually for one attorney
- Special master or parent coordinator
- Reviewer of another evaluator's child custody evaluation, perhaps hired by one attorney or perhaps ordered by the court to conduct a reevaluation

Psychologists must remain aware of the purpose and methods associated with their role and should avoid combining tasks or switching among different roles under most circumstances. At a minimum, one should never agree to serve as a child custody evaluator in a case in which one has previously functioned as a mediator, consultant, or therapist.

A significant difference between clinical and forensic services relates to the conclusions and recommendations one can offer. This distinction becomes most relevant to psychotherapists. Whereas the child custody evaluator can clearly make recommendations about the best psychological interests of the child and about the custody and

visitation needs of the child, a psychotherapist cannot. Such recommendations would exceed the scope of the psychotherapist's engagement, because the clinical role does not include making legally related recommendations. Making a recommendation about the child's best interests from a clinical role is ill advised for several reasons. A child's therapist may not have interviewed one of the parents or may not possess information from other relevant collateral sources. APA ethical guidelines (APA, 2002) prohibit a psychologist from making findings and recommendations about people not seen, and making custody recommendations requires a psychologist to see all the relevant family members. Making recommendations related to visitation or custody may also disrupt the therapeutic alliance with the client or other close family members, making it impossible to continue functioning in a therapeutic role. In addition, these different roles require different models, as the clinician uses clinical judgment and the custody evaluator uses scientific judgment. In essence, there are a number of critical differences between the clinical and forensic roles. See Greenberg and Shuman (1997) and Shuman and Sales (1998) for a more detailed identification of the differences between a clinical/therapeutic role and that of forensic examiner.

LEGAL CONSTRUCTS RELATED TO A CHILD'S "BEST INTERESTS"

What the law recognizes as best for children regarding their custodial placements has varied considerably in historical context. English common law treated children as chattel whose ownership rested with the father and paternal lineage. During the late 1800s, the "tender years" doctrine viewed mothers as uniquely appropriate to assume custody of young children after divorce. Under this doctrine, only a showing of maternal unfitness in some manner would preclude the mother's custody. The current standard in the United States is the focus on the "best interests of the child," developed in part from rejection of sexist presumptions about parental capability and a shift to "no fault" divorce statutes. Other variants on this principle include the "presumption of equality" and the "least detrimental alternative" when evaluating parents for custody. Although different levels of specificity exist among the states as to how to define best interests, all 50 states have adopted this standard (Rohman, Sales, & Lou, 1987).

Evaluators find themselves asked to address different aspects of the child custody decision. One type of custody decision refers to the authority of a parent to make decisions on behalf of the child (i.e., legal custody), whereas the other type of custody decision refers to the actual placement of the child relative to both parents (i.e., physical custody). In some states, judges make the decision about child custody. In other states (e.g., Texas) juries make the decision. The vast majority of divorces involving children result in custody decisions made by the parents without the need for psychological assessment or contested court hearings. One reason flows from the practice in some states that mandates mediation of a child custody dispute before the parents may proceed toward a contested court hearing. Another factor relates to simple economics—litigating custody adds considerable costs to a divorce.

Psychologists must remain aware of both the psychological and the legal constructs that relate to a child's best interests. Each state may define psychological best interests in a different manner, although similarities were found in a review by Schutz, Dixon, Lindenberger, and Ruther (1989). Many potential psychological best-interest concepts deserve consideration, including:

- The degree to which one parent can facilitate a relationship with the other parent
- The presence or absence of domestic violence or other forms of abuse within the family
- The quality and style of parenting, including, for example, whether or not a parent uses an authoritarian style, a disorganized style, or an authoritative style
- The ability of the parent to shield the child from conflict or other psychologically detrimental influences
- The presence or absence of significant psychological and/or behavioral disturbance that might affect one's parenting, for example, mental health or substance abuse
- The child's wishes or desires regarding placement

At the same time, laws in every jurisdiction not only focus on definitions of best interests but also address possible legal presumptions regarding custody. Some states presume that best interests are served when children reside in the primary residence of one parent, whereas another state may presume that sharing of parental time will yield the best outcome. Evaluators should remain aware of whether the applicable jurisdiction has any legal presumptions of this sort and what constitutes adequate rebuttal of such a presumption in the child's best interests. Many states have presumptions that a parent who perpetrates domestic violence shall not have sole or joint custody of a child. Other presumptions in some states pertain to relocation or removal from the state, in which the parent who wants to move has a greater or lesser burden than the other parent when the court considers the relocation request. These presumptions can flow from either statute or case law.

In addition to the basic statutes and case law related to child custody, evaluators should also remain aware of any special rules of court. For example, California has specific rules setting out uniform standards for what every child custody evaluation must include (Rule of Court 5.220; California Rules of Court, 2003a) and for the training and continuing education requirements for all child custody evaluators (Rule of Court 5.225; California Rules of Court, 2003b). Readers are referred to the laws in their own state to fully understand the requirements of the court.

THE EFFECTS OF DIVORCE ON CHILDREN

The scope of this chapter does not include describing the history of divorce research. We urge custody evaluators to remain up-to-date on all of the relevant research, not only in the area of divorce but also on the relevant developmental research and relevant research in the areas of domestic violence, alienated children, sexual abuse, and others germane to child custody. Some of the developmental literature describes how childhood functioning evolves as the by-product of varied and complicated factors, including but not limited to genetic, peer-group, parental, and other socialization influences (Harris, 1995). The complexity of these findings from the developmental psychology literature should caution evaluators against making hasty judgments about the presumed causation of problems or the role of a particular parent.

When the evaluator obtains relevant parent–child findings, it may prove difficult to determine the relative importance of each factor relative to the child's best psychological interest. The evaluation can potentially inform the court about the nature of the parent–child relationship, the psychological functioning of each family member, the child's preference, information relevant to child-protection allegations, and other factors likely to improve or worsen the psychological functioning of each family member.

- The psychological literature in the past several years has described certain principles that appear to yield clear guidance. Children from divorced families have a greater risk for psychological difficulties than children from intact families, especially in the first 2 years after divorce. Over time, however, resilience rather than risk becomes the normative outcome of a parent's divorce (Amato, 1993).
- Children seem to benefit from regular contact with both parents, assuming that both parents show "good-enough" parenting qualities and do not behave in ways detrimental to the child (Kelly & Lamb, 2000).
- Children of divorce seem to experience more psychological pain than children not experiencing divorce, but psychological pain and psychopathology seem different (Kelly & Emery, 2003).
- Very young children need sufficient time with each parent in order to form adequate emotional attachments with both parents (Kelly & Lamb, 2000; Warshak, 2000).
- Children generally benefit when both parents have consistent involvement in a wide array of day-to-day experiences (Kelly & Lamb, 2000).
- Children's experiences and needs link, in part, to developmental needs.
- Children's reactions to the divorce will relate to their functioning during the marriage. Children who experienced significant psychological problems in the marriage seem more likely to be experiencing significant psychological problems in the early stages of the divorce (Kelly, 2000).
- Children exposed to and brought into the middle of parental conflict have a greater likelihood of negative outcomes than children shielded from the parental conflict (Kelly, 2000).

- Ultimately, long-term adjustment appears affected by predivorce adjustment, by the child's temperament and coping abilities, by the degree of conflict and presence or absence of domestic violence, by each parent's support of the child's relationship with the other parent, by the involvement and support of both parents, and by other social supports (Kelly, 2000; Hetherington & Kelly, 2002).

Divorce constitutes a longitudinal process that is affected by a host of preseparation and postseparation factors. Children's postdivorce problems show a significant relationship to parental and family influences that long predate the divorce (Kelly, 2000). For example, prior problems in family interpersonal intimacy among parents and children can have an effect on children's adjustment (Sun, 2001). This situation can have implications for helping families to avoid fatalistic conclusions solely based on the fact that a divorce has occurred. On the other hand, divorce factors can include economic loss, lessened emotional availability from the parents, and relocations from school or home environments (Lamb, Sternberg, & Thompson, 1997), all well recognized as risk factors for children's subsequent adjustment.

GETTING STARTED

The first step in undertaking an evaluation involves obtaining a copy of the court order appointing you as the evaluator. It is generally unwise to accept a referral for child custody evaluation without having at least a stipulated agreement of the parties filed with the court, because court appointment often conveys at least limited immunity from subsequent suit. Any questions, controversies, or concerns should be addressed *before* agreeing to meet with the parents. Try to have the attorneys and the court clarify the scope of the evaluation and any particular evaluation questions before initiating the evaluation. If you feel unclear about the request in hand, or if you do not feel comfortable with the scope or nature of the referral, do not proceed without sufficient clarification or resolution.

The next step for the evaluator involves obtaining adequate informed written consent prior to beginning the evaluation. The court order specifies the legal authority to conduct the evaluation, but ethical standards require an informed consent of the parties pertaining to a number of issues, preferably in writing. We suggest including the following in an informed consent obtained from all adult participants:

- A statement of the purpose of the evaluation and of the fact that the evaluation role does *not* involve therapeutic services
- Descriptions of the evaluation procedures, including the possible use of psychological testing, interview data, home visits, collateral information, and similar issues, to the extent that you will use these procedures
- A description of the limits of confidentiality, in particular a clear acknowledgment that the family or probate court will have access to all data and reports
- A complete description of the financial arrangements, including retainer fees, hourly charges, dates payments must become due, and any restrictions on completion or release of the report prior to final payment
- A statement that you will be reporting findings about any allegations to the extent appropriate and that you may make recommendations about many things, including a child-sharing arrangement, possible therapeutic needs, and some type of postdivorce parenting relationship
- A statement that the findings and recommendations will flow from the totality of the data and may or may not seem consistent with the views of either parent
- An explanation of the examiner's policy regarding withdrawal from a case if, in the opinion and sole discretion of the examiner, either parent's actions make it impossible for the examiner to conduct the customary evaluation procedures. This is necessary for addressing cases in which one or both parties attempt to threaten or harass the evaluator, refuse to complete required evaluation tasks, or engage in other action that prevents the evaluator from rendering an ethical and sufficiently informed opinion
- A statement that the evaluator will follow all legally mandated reporting responsibilities, including applicable child abuse reporting or "duty to protect" situations

After obtaining an informed consent, the evaluator can obtain from the parent or can record in evaluation notes the parent's responses to a variety of criteria related to parental functioning. The evaluator can formulate an assessment protocol to follow in all child custody evaluations. Doing so enhances the consistency and standardization for evaluation methods. Evaluators should consider addressing the following:

- Whether either parent has a history of criminal behavior, domestic violence, substance use and abuse, or child abuse; consider requesting or recommending that a criminal record check be completed on each party
- Each parent's beliefs about the child, the child's functioning, and the child's needs, including special needs
- Each parent's view of his or her relationship with the child, discipline techniques, and involvement in daily life, and each parent's view of his or her strengths and weaknesses as a parent
- Each parent's view of the other parent's relationship with the child, discipline techniques, involvement in daily life, and strengths and weaknesses as a parent
- What each parent expects that the other parent will say
- Each parent's perception of the coparental communication and the typical source of the problems
- Any other relevant information that a parent wants the evaluator to know at the commencement of the evaluation

When conducting the evaluation, do not engage in substantive *ex parte* communication with one attorney. Good practice suggests documenting telephone communications, because sometimes parents may reveal highly significant information through indirect or covert methods. This includes memorializing the date and content of telephone voice-mail messages, as well as preserving any electronic messages received.

CONDUCTING THE EVALUATION: THE RANGE OF DATA SOURCES

Based on local statute, professional practice guidelines, relevant case law, and ethical considerations, a number of evaluation components must make up virtually every custody evaluation.

These components include ample interviews with and assessment of each parent, ample interviews with and assessment of each child, conjoint sessions of parents and children for comparable lengths of time, review of available records, and interviews with agreed-on sources of collateral information. Gould (2004) offered a guide for evaluating the probative value of child custody evaluations, in part by explaining scientifically informed methods and procedures in the context of a child custody evaluation. One example would include the concept of convergent validity, a forensic methodology that always includes data from a variety of sources and then determines the degree to which independent sources of information converge on the same conclusion.

Despite the existence of guidelines that recommend multiple assessment protocols for evaluating parents, a recent survey examined 60% of custody evaluations completed in one circuit court over a 2-year period and found substantial variety in the techniques employed and a lack of consistency with the available guidelines (Horvath, Logan, & Walker, 2002). These authors emphasized the importance of using standardized interview and testing procedures in child custody evaluations when allegations of child abuse exist.

Shear (2004) describes the evaluation process as one that gathers and integrates particular information about the family with general information that includes group data from the professional literature. The protocol reflects a scientifically informed process in data collection and analysis while pragmatically focusing on a parenting plan. Evaluators should not aspire to adhere rigidly to presumed protocol standards to the exclusion of careful analysis of the risks and benefits of alternative parenting plans.

In approaching the adult interviews, one should consider convergent styles of presentation. On the one hand, parents must have the opportunity to "tell their story" and describe their perceptions about their children and the other parent. This open-ended dialogue can prove quite useful in understanding each parent's feelings, perceptions, and objectives regarding contested issues. At the same time, one should also establish a semi-structured set of questions to consider in all child custody evaluations. For the sake of relevance and reliability, it helps if the child custody evaluator

employs a protocol designed to gather particular data necessary to understand the family, the child, and the child's needs. Developing a balanced style that allows for both of these objectives will likely give the evaluator the highest quality set of interview data.

In the adult interviews, the evaluator will gather data on the following:

- The history of the marital relationship and problems
- The reasons for separation
- The history of conflict between the parents, pre- and postseparation
- The history of caring for the children and the tasks and roles of each parent in the history of the family; each parent's perception of the child's needs and that parent's custodial preferences, including the rationale for that custodial preference
- The parent's current life situation, including work, work hours, living arrangements, stability, and planned changes
- Each parent's life history, including the history of family relationships, school history, abuse or neglect in the parent's home, history of antisocial behaviors, substance use, and violence
- Each parent's perceptions of parenting style
- Each parent's developmental history of each child, with inquiry about the degree of involvement, attachment, knowledge about the child, and interest which that parent has experienced with the child
- Each parent's report of his or her own respective strengths and weaknesses and the report of the other parent's strengths and weaknesses

In order to demonstrate comparability of evaluation procedures between parents and to assist the evaluator in standardizing data collection not just within cases but also among all child custody cases, the evaluator should use uniform interview formats. Such forms or procedures can include history forms, interview questions for adults or children, and the criteria used for recording and rating observational interactions between parent and child.

A similar approach should apply to the child interviews. First, establish some rapport with the child and help the child feel comfortable in communicating in general and in particular about the family. Speak to the child in developmentally appropriate terms. Clarify the limits of confidentiality at the child's level of understanding, explaining that there are no "secrets" and that the child's parents, as well as the court, "may learn what we talk about here." In addition to the interview data, note the child's temperament and level of developmental functioning and the child's affect and emotional functioning concerning specific and general issues. During the child interviews, the evaluator may gather data on the following:

- The child's psychological and emotional functioning and the presence or absence of any special needs
- An understanding of the child's "complete life," including information concerning friends, relationships with siblings, school functioning, and extracurricular interests
- The child's perception of each parent, including the child's descriptions of likes and dislikes, discipline issues, support or nonsupport, and the routines in each home; with older children and adolescents, data about how the parents support their age-appropriate autonomy and facilitate future goals

Evaluators might also consider conducting home visits to gather additional information about the family's relationships. Home visits can help the evaluator observe the parent–child interactions in a natural setting for the child. In such circumstances one should attempt to unobtrusively observe parent–child interactions to the extent feasible. Collateral sources of information provide valuable information about parent–child relationships in different contexts and at different times in the family's life.

Ultimately, the evaluator will want to consider the child's feelings about his or her relationship with each parent and his or her feelings about the divorce. Without asking the child to choose between the parents, the evaluator will want to remain sensitive to the child's preferences about where he or she lives or how the child wants to spend his or her time with each parent. Knowing the reasons for the preference, including information about the child's motives, the anticipated consequences of the preference, and how the child expects the stated preference to affect the relationship with each parent will prove useful (Sparta, 1998).

When possible, evaluators will want to speak to relevant collateral contacts. Data from collateral contacts may prove essential in cases involving allegations of abuse, and such sources must understand informed consent regarding the limits of confidentiality. Sources must understand that the data they provide may become known to all parties and the court. Professional collateral sources can include former or current psychotherapists, teachers, day-care professionals, pediatricians, police, or child protection investigators. Evaluators may also consider speaking with nonprofessional collateral sources, sometimes requested by the parent. Grandparents, recreational coaches, music teachers, neighbors, day care providers, and others may potentially provide valuable information that can be verified in subsequent interviews with the appropriate parent. The information obtained from these sources represents a potentially useful basis for follow-up interviewing. Evaluators should maintain comparability of procedures for each parent throughout the evaluation unless a specific reason related to the evaluation findings justifies a deviation. Along with comparable evaluation attention, one should also balance the focus on strengths and weaknesses and on health and pathology in the family. Evaluators need to provide enough information to help parents and the court understand the nature of relevant problems and how they affect the best psychological interests of the child or the implications they have for one type of child sharing plan versus another. Focusing only on negative attributes may foster further conflict. The art of writing child custody evaluations includes providing the court with comprehensive and relevant information on strengths and weaknesses of parents, while recognizing the need for parents to maintain dignity and hope following completion of the process.

The evaluator must also consider the involvement of parental companions and the extent to which they warrant formal evaluation. For example, if a parent requesting primary custody is cohabiting with a partner who has significant access to the children, the partner will most likely need to be involved in the evaluation process in some fashion. If child protection allegations against the companion exist, a more formal evaluation will be necessary. The evaluator must secure a clear agreement among the appropriate parties and ensure that every participant has given informed consent. In the event that the "significant other" does not wish to participate, the court may have to resolve the potential conflict generated by not having sufficient information due to the lack of that person's participation. Ethical codes and professional practice guidelines may prohibit the evaluator from rendering professional opinions about individuals who have not been evaluated. When other parties, such as companions of either parent, will not participate in an evaluation, evaluators should take care about their statements involving such individuals.

Some situations may warrant a focused evaluation of only one parent for a specific purpose. Although related to a child custody determination, such assessments differ from child custody evaluations. In other cases, the court may order an individual evaluation of only one parent for suspected alcohol or drug abuse. Psychologists conducting such evaluations would limit their findings and opinions to the available data and then defer ultimate recommendations about the child custody schedule to the court. One must always consider deception, exaggeration, misperception, and other forms of distortion and attempt to control for such behavior through cross-validation of the data among family members, through examining test-taking tendencies as reflected in psychological test subscales, and through careful evaluation against credible sources of collateral information. Base-rate estimates of parental psychological characteristics must take into consideration the highly unusual circumstances surrounding the child custody conflict, which may exaggerate negative judgments about parental functioning.

PSYCHOLOGICAL TESTING

Grisso (2003) has examined how psychological constructs should be related to the specific psycholegal issues presented by a particular legal proceeding. The decision whether to administer a particular test or perform an assessment procedure should depend on the degree to which the data accurately inform the court in making a best-interests decision. Tests developed for a wide range of traditional clinical purposes do not meet the definition of forensically formulated assessment instruments, and thus one must weigh any conclusions drawn in the context of a child custody matter carefully and report the findings with limitations where appropriate. For example, the MMPI-2 (Butcher, Dahlstrom, Graham, Tellegen, & Kaemmer, 1989) is the most frequently used assessment tool among psychologists for conducting child custody evaluations (Ackerman & Ackerman, 1996), but this instrument was originally developed for routine diagnostic assessment of patients in a treatment context. Although use of the MMPI-2 may be very useful in many child custody evaluations, the instrument was not developed to yield best child custody determinations for individual families. Evaluators should be cautioned against overinterpreting test data, always being clear why the test is being employed and accurately interpreting results in the context of all other data. Data may help to clarify specific parental functions or attitudes, to evaluate alleged diagnostic formulations, to assess response tendencies, or to screen for unidentified psychological characteristics. Although test scores per se cannot serve as dispositive factors in any child custody recommendation, carefully considered data integrated within a multivaried assessment can provide important independent anchors against which to compare interview data (Horvath et al., 2002).

Gould (2004) cautions that tests used in a forensic context should have a clearly stated underlying theory and science, established reliability and validity, normative data, and other measurement-related criteria. Conclusions drawn from such instruments have only as much validity as the quality of the instruments used to formulate opinions. The response style of the parent represents another important factor in determining the usefulness of the test results.

Case law regarding expert testimony has increased attention to the questions of whether forensic assessment procedures have relevance and sufficient validity for their purpose (for example, *Daubert v. Merrell Dow Pharmaceuticals, Inc.*, 1993; *Kumho Tire Co. v. Carmichael*, 1999). Although the judge in a child custody matter may permit an evaluator to render an opinion regarding a range of different types of opinions, the professional must carefully consider whether a reasonable basis exists to support his or her opinion.

Studies on the use of psychological tests in child custody proceedings, including those that provide more accurate empirical normative data for participants who are undergoing child custody evaluations, have increasingly appeared in print. For example, custody litigants tend to exhibit defensive reporting and/or exaggeration of socially desirable traits on some MMPI-2 subscales (Bathurst, Gottfried, & Gottfried, 1997; Posthuma & Harper, 1998). The absence of validity scale elevations usually associated with defensive responding can prove helpful to the evaluator in understanding the response tendencies of the parent. Whether a parent denies legitimate symptoms of psychopathology, responds in a relatively forthright manner, or inflates socially desirable traits constitutes an important distinction in understanding the parent. The evaluator recognizes that there may not be any easy way to distinguish among the alternatives without a careful analysis of a broad range of comprehensive data. Bagby, Nicholson, Buis, Radovanovic, and Fidler (1999) also found underreporting of symptoms, with the Wiggins Social Desirability scale and the Superlative scales more sensitive than the traditionally relied on L and K scales. More recent research has also examined whether male and female custody litigants score differently (Gottfried, Bathurst, & Gottfried, 2003).

The Millon Clinical Multiaxial Inventory-III (MCMI-III; Millon, 1994) also finds occasional use as an assessment tool for adults in child custody proceedings. The MCMI-III uses "base rate" scales associated with various categories of psychological disorder. Otto and Butcher (1995) cautioned that the instrument might overpathologize individuals. McCann et al. (1998) did not reach the same conclusion, but they noted possible inflation of the strength of scores in female participants on the Histrionic and Compulsive Personality scales.

Otto (2000) noted that although authors and publishers of a number of child custody instruments currently available claim that their instruments can be used to assess constructs relevant to the child custody decision, such instruments have become the subject of criticism, and no general agreement exists regarding the utility of their inclusion in an assessment. Often, psychologists receive requests to review the methods utilized in another assessment. When conducting such reviews, evaluators should not be overly critical of other professionals' failure to use a particular instrument, nor should evaluators rely excessively on

any particular instrument. A more recent reanalysis of Ackerman's 1996 survey data by Hagen and Castagna (2001) indicated that except for the use of the MMPI for adults, hardly any consensus exists for practice, let alone a standard for practice involving particular testing instruments used in child custody evaluations. Heinze and Grisso (1996) and Otto, Edens, and Barcus (2000) have also published cautionary reviews of child custody instruments.

We take it as an encouraging sign that the range of tests used by child custody evaluators has broadened from those noted in an initial survey in 1986 (Keilin & Bloom, 1986) to Ackerman's 10 years later. For example, more focused assessment instruments such as the Children's Depression Inventory (Kovacs, 1992) or the Michigan Alcohol Screening Test (Selzer, 1971) now exist. Such test selection can reflect a more appropriate choice of instrument to assess a specific issue contested between the parents. In the case of a childhood depression inventory, such data are important for identifying not only childhood mood disorders but also valuable parent–child relationship factors that may worsen or ameliorate the child's suffering. To the extent that test data are instrumental in highlighting such problems, the valuable information provided can advance the child's best psychological interests. Similarly, in cases in which allegations of parental alcohol abuse occur, a focused assessment designed for that purpose can provide more relevant and normative-based assessment of a given parent's functioning while permitting follow-up interviewing with each parent. The follow-up interview can reference specific alcohol-related behaviors occurring at specific time periods, important for potentially uncovering alcohol problems, or, conversely, for identifying exaggerated, distorted, or baseless reports by the other parent. Compounding the complexity in interpretation of assessment data within the context of a child custody dispute, alleged substance abuse may have occurred in the past but may no longer constitute a pertinent factor at the time of the evaluation.

At the first joint ABA and APA conference, which concerned marital and child custody problems, Sparta (1997) noted the importance of not overinterpreting testing data and how the assessment of the relationship between parent and child often seemed obscured by parents' assumptions that evaluation would simply reflect a measure of psychopathology between two parents. Carefully explaining to the parents that the evaluation focus involved the child's best interests, as reflected in the relative strengths and weaknesses of each parent's relationship with him or her, helped to minimize the risk that parents would misunderstand the meaning of the results (e.g., excessively focus on the importance of testing data or causing a parent who was not recommended for primary custody to erroneously believe he or she was considered psychologically unfit).

Parents may request that testing take place at home. Some evaluators may delegate administrative assistants to instruct parents how to complete testing (e.g., the MMPI-2). Because child custody evaluators serve the court, they must carefully monitor the conditions under which test data collection occurs. Failure to do so may violate the standardized test administration instructions, because the examiner has no way of ensuring that the parent did not speak with others, refer to extrinsic materials, or even ask a different person to complete the task. For example, Caldwell (1997) finds it highly problematic and hard to imagine that a forensic evaluation circumstance in which a participant is allowed to take home the MMPI-2 would prove acceptable. Pope, Butcher, and Seelen (1993) have also noted that such a practice violates a published opinion of the APA's Committee on Professional Standards (1984): that, whenever a psychologist does not have direct, first-hand information as to the condition under which the test data collection occurred, no assurance regarding the authenticity of the responses exists, and the entire test can be summarily dismissed as hearsay evidence.

COLLATERAL SOURCES OF INFORMATION

The available professional practice guidelines for conducting child custody evaluations recommend obtaining collateral sources of information. Such information often proves invaluable for corroborating hypotheses generated by testing or other evaluation data, as well as identifying previously unidentified but relevant considerations. Parental relationship factors become very important in determining the child's best psychological interests,

and collateral information can provide an ecological context for judging the nature of the relationship within different situations and across different time periods. Often, the evaluator must persist in making the requests necessary to accomplish this goal, as participants may unconsciously avoid or purposefully mislead in order to conceal potentially damaging information. Possible sources of information can include past and current teachers, day-care providers, mental health professionals, child protection investigators, neighbors, pediatricians, visitation supervisors, other family members, neighbors, members of law enforcement agencies, and motor vehicle records. Before making such inquiries, first obtain from the evaluated parties signed authorizations that explicitly state that a potential exchange of information is occurring, along with a reconfirmation that no confidentiality or privilege will exist and that the obtained information in the report may be used freely by the evaluator. When contacting a collateral resource, the evaluator should make clear that there is no confidentiality regarding any information provided and that such information will potentially become available to the parties, their attorneys, and/or the court. Although some evaluators require a signed authorization, at a minimum the evaluator should document in the file that such a notice was provided to the person contacted and that his or her understanding was agreed on.

INTERIM RECOMMENDATIONS

The evaluator may encounter requests to provide opinions or recommendations prior to final report completion. Such requests may appear deceptively simple but may involve several complex evaluation issues. An evaluator has an obligation not to provide an opinion without an adequate professional basis to support the opinion, necessitating that the evaluator decline the request, defer to the court, or suggest the use of a different professional to address the immediate question. In other situations, the evaluator may have already obtained reasonably compelling information, and the child's best interests could likely suffer if a decision were made without the benefit of what the evaluator knows. In such appropriate circumstances, when the child's safety and welfare requires, a carefully examined and *conditional* recommendation may be warranted, but such actions should be reserved only for special circumstances.

THE CHILD CUSTODY REPORT

Because the court, attorney, and parents will use the evaluation report, presenting findings and opinions in clear, nontechnical language becomes critically important. The report should include major findings about each participant, along with an understanding of the underlying rationale for the major recommendations. The report provides a starting point for the detailed inquiry about the methods, adequacy, relevance, and persuasive logic underlying the opinions within the report. Interpretation of findings should accord with relevant legal standards and specific evaluation questions. It may be misleading to include DSM diagnoses and certain other professional mental health concepts or jargon, as it may imply exaggerated impairment in general or erroneously imply that specific parenting capacity impairment exists solely because of the existence of a DSM diagnosis. Martindale and Otto (2000) suggest that the report should explain the examiner's conceptualization of the parents and child, the uniqueness of the family situation, and how the examiner reached his or her opinions. Evaluators should consider including the following in all reports:

- The purpose of the evaluation, including specific questions or issues contained in the court order or stipulated agreement between the parties for evaluation
- Dates of evaluation, who was seen, and the date of the report
- Relevant history, including the history regarding the marital relationship, separation, allegations, custody preferences of the parents, and past history of different custodial arrangements
- Assessment procedures, including listing all tests; a listing of reviewed records or other data relied on in the formulation of opinions
- Confirmation that each party was evaluated individually and that the children were assessed conjointly with each parent
- All significant psychological findings
- An understanding of the strengths and limitations of the data

- Expressed preferences of the child
- Discussion of factors which exacerbate or ameliorate conflict between the parents
- A discussion of findings in terms of the child's best psychological interests should always be provided

Whenever possible, discussion of findings and recommendations can occur in terms of common interests or preferences between the parents, attempting to maximize the prospects of parental agreement and settlement. Analysis of specific custodial arrangements should occur in context of the evaluation findings, accompanied by an explanation of why one type of plan is more likely to serve the child's best interests.

Kelly (1994) reminded evaluators that, given the increasingly more diverse styles, values, and traditions in our culture, child custody decisions should involve a high degree of individualization, always reflecting the child's best interests in terms of data from the evaluation regarding the parent–child relationship and/or an individual parent's functioning. Particularly in highly contested proceedings, parties may attempt to influence the child custody decision process with strongly held beliefs about what constitutes an "appropriate" family. Evaluators exercise great care not to substitute their own values for scientific opinion and to give consideration to and respect for the preferences and practices of each family.

Bow and Quinnell (2002) examined child custody reports from across the United States and found that almost all included a description of parental strengths and weaknesses, summarized findings, and made general recommendations for helping the family's adjustment, along with recommendations for specific child custody arrangements. They also found that in three quarters of the reports participants listed the documents reviewed but that only two thirds specifically referenced those documents in the report. It may be helpful to make clear when certain data do *not* cause concern or corroborate certain allegations, because making no mention of them in the report raises unanswered questions about whether they were ever considered.

Child protection or domestic violence concerns demand careful consideration from those with the requisite training and experience to assess such issues. The evaluator may feel compelled to make a mandated report of child abuse, but more often the case will show that an investigation by the appropriately authorized agency has occurred and been closed as inconclusive. The evaluation report should explain all reasons why the allegations lack persuasive validity and should outline possible interventions or services tailored to the specific circumstances of the family, such as supervised visitation and exchanges; focused treatment recommendations, such as anger management or domestic violence treatment programs; substance abuse treatment; and methods to monitor potential flight risk, along with ways to monitor compliance with orders. Reports may also include whether the child requires assessment for special education services or tutoring and how each parent can better facilitate the child's growth. Some developmental disorders require substantial parental ability and commitment; the report can describe how each parent addresses these needs. Evaluators should describe factors that may enhance or interfere with each parent's ability to profit from future mediation services and give reasons that the appointment of legal counsel for children would prove beneficial. Consideration of whether child–parent interactions should require any form of monitoring or supervision warrants discussion. If necessary, exchanges can occur in public settings, at school with only one parent present, or in other alternate protective circumstances.

The parent's ability to provide child access to, and foster a positive relationship with, the other parent always constitutes a "best interest" consideration that the report should address. This factor relates to any discussion of the advantages and disadvantages of a shared custody arrangement or why a primary custodial arrangement has greater potential benefit to the child. The ability of two parents to maintain high-quality relationships with children usually rests on sufficient opportunity to share important experiences across the week (e.g., Kelly & Lamb, 2000), and this fact may argue for sufficient weekday and weekend custodial arrangements each week. Other literature describes the risks to children from assuming joint physical custody arrangements when a high degree of expressed parental hostility exists (e.g., Lamb et al., 1997). The report should provide a clear rationale for recommendations.

Every evaluation report can potentially be the subject of future deposition or court testimony. Prudence dictates that evaluators write their reports with consideration of this possibility, striving to provide clear, honest, adequately supported professional conclusions. Anticipating and addressing possible rival hypotheses and explaining how these findings and conclusions were considered and why they were accepted or rejected will enhance the findings or conclusions.

CHILDREN'S EXPRESSED PREFERENCE

Although state laws vary, most follow the Uniform Marriage and Divorce Act model code that a child's best interests include a consideration of "the wishes of the child as to his/her custodian" (National Conference of Commissioners on Uniform State Laws, 1971). Some statutes specify an age by which children's preferences should be given significantly greater weight, but the preference is not automatic. When interviewing the child, the evaluator should take care not to place the child into a guilt-inducing choice by asking and/or coercing the child to choose between his or her parents. The child's ability to divulge emotionally sensitive material may depend on having more extended time than 1–hour appointments will allow, and the evaluator may wish to allow for an extended interview when exploring the child's preference. Careful attention is paid to nonverbal deviations from characteristic behavior or mood, as well as to the content of the child's reports. Rather than simply eliciting a preference from the child, the evaluator can allow the child opportunities to explain the reasons for his or her feelings or preferences. The evaluator can pose questions in terms of actual or hypothetical situations involving each parent to determine how each would address the child's needs.

When the child volunteers a custodial preference, the evaluator should take cognizance of how much weight the child's preference contributes to the overall conclusions. Sparta (1998) cites reasons for respecting the child's preference, including the recognition that the child has intimate knowledge about both parents over extended periods of time across a wide variety of situations. Grisso et al. (2002)

noted that the law generally denies minors the right to make decisions independent from parents, but legal precedents exist that allow children to make independent decisions under certain conditions for some matters, including mental health treatment, medical care, and privacy protections. Arguably, without a compelling argument for the need to protect or enhance the child's welfare, the child's carefully considered and mature preference should have considerable weight. Warshak (2003) provided rationales for giving children's voices a hearing but cautions against some children having the final say.

However, the child's expressed preference may not reflect the child's best interests when the child has formulated a protective identification with an aggressive family member or feels a need to "take care of" a parent perceived as vulnerable or troubled and the child is coerced into making a choice consistent with the anticipated preference of the feared parent. Other motives include the child's belief that the choice will reduce the risk of conflict between the parents or desire to protect one parent from the feared retaliation of the other. Domestic violence and child abuse cases represent more obvious examples in which this potential might be realized. Because the emotional pressure in domestic conflict cases can be enormous, the evaluator should remain vigilant to signs of such pressure.

SPECIAL CONSIDERATIONS IN CHILD CUSTODY EVALUATION

The court may order a psychological evaluation because of serious concerns about a variety of issues, including but not limited to allegations of specific forms of mental illness, domestic violence, physical or sexual abuse of a child, or substance abuse. Evaluators should have the appropriate education, training, or experience in the relevant areas before accepting such a case. This chapter cannot provide the reader with the required core knowledge but only highlight necessary considerations for these types of cases.

Mental Illness

Mere existence of a mental illness does not resolve questions of the child's best psychological interests.

The presence or absence of a mental disorder becomes one factor for consideration within the context of all evaluation data with reference to the child's best interests. Greenwald (1997) notes that one parent may use allegations of mental illness as a weapon against the other, and the evaluator must discern whether any validity exists to the allegation or carefully examine whether the disorder impairs the parent–child relationship. Greenwald also suggests that the custody evaluator determine the degree and nature of the impairment, how it interferes with parenting capacities or the child's relationship with the parent, the available resources for the impaired parent, to what degree the other parent assumed compensatory caretaking responsibilities, and a consideration of the strengths, weaknesses, or resiliencies of the child. Evaluators need to consider particularly symptoms of untreated bipolar disorder, schizophrenia, and other psychoses or of recurring major depressive disorder. Symptom evaluation must consider the consequences with and without the benefit of medication and psychotherapy. The parent's future ability to adequately care for a child may also depend partly on the level of insight he or she has regarding his or her own problems and on the parent's motivation for treatment.

Independent of mental illness, evaluators always consider the functional ramification of a parent's personality traits and judgments with reference to the impact on the child. For example, when symptoms involve hypervigilant protectiveness by a parent that impairs the child's autonomy and self-confidence, there are psychological "best interest" considerations whether or not the parent meets threshold criteria for a psychiatric diagnosis.

Domestic Violence

Domestic violence has attracted special recognition in recent years. Although older court decisions focused more heavily on the mistaken assumption that only direct abuse to the child constituted a relevant consideration, laws in many states changed in recognition of the fact that substantial detrimental effects on children could result from witnessing or living in a home replete with domestic violence. Research began to show that children who witnessed violence could experience just as much trauma as children who directly experienced abuse (Fantuzzo & Moore, 1999). In 1994, the National Council of Juvenile and Family Court Judges (1994) recommended model legislation that presumed that granting custody to a parent who abused his or her spouse would not serve the best interests of children. By 1996, states began to rewrite custody laws and to include domestic violence as a consideration for judges in making custody determinations. The California Family Code Section 3044 (California Rules of Court, 2003a) includes a "rebuttable presumption" against a perpetrator of domestic violence having joint or sole custody of the children. The presumption is rebuttable by certain factors listed in the statute, including whether or not the perpetrator has completed a domestic violence intervention program, whether or not continued abusive actions have occurred, and whether or not granting custody to the perpetrator advances the children's best interests. Child custody evaluators must have a thorough understanding of domestic violence legislation in their state, as well as of the current psychological research findings.

Child custody evaluators must understand the different types of violence and the way violence manifests itself in different families. In many families, the perpetrator is male, and the violence typically occurs intermittently or episodically and unpredictably. In such families, the violence serves to allow the perpetrator to maintain power and control over his partner, and a heightened risk of lethality may occur at the time of separation. In some families, the violence is less likely associated with power and control and more typically associated with major mental illness or substance abuse. In other families, the mother may initiate the violent behavior. In families in which domestic violence exists between the parents, other types of child abuse may also occur. Conflicts may follow an ongoing or occasional pattern of violence, triggered by either male or female partners. Such families experience "common couples' violence." Finally, in many families, no violence occurs except around separation. Some research suggests that in as many as 50% of divorcing families one to three episodes of violence will occur around the time of separation and divorce. This "separation-engendered" violence constitutes a distinct category because it can be either male or female initiated and because it may result in PTSD symptoms in the children.

Evaluators must also understand the impact of domestic violence on children. An excellent resource for understanding this impact is "Domestic Violence and Children," an issue of *The Future of Children* (1999), available at the Web site (www.futureofchildren.org). Several articles outline the impact of domestic violence on children, whether the child is the direct victim or a witness to the violence in the home. In general, the impact can be significant and can include internalizing (i.e., anxiety, insecurity, depression, hypervigilance, withdrawal), externalizing (i.e., bullying, fighting, acting out), or mixed symptoms in children. Very young children often show significant regression, nightmares, and attachment difficulties, whereas school-age children may exhibit school problems and difficulties in peer relationships. Adolescents who live in violent homes seem to have a particular risk for developing gang affiliations, substance abuse problems, suicidal ideation, and emotional numbness.

Cases that involve domestic violence allegations require a different set of goals than cases in which parents are in conflict and cannot agree. Where families are in conflict without domestic violence, the goals for the family include cooperative, shared parenting and reasonable communication so that the child's life between homes is seamless. For those families who experience domestic violence, safety is the most important factor. Shared, cooperative parenting will not be the goal, because domestic violence victims remain at risk for future violence and control by the violent partner when there is ongoing communication and contact. Friendly-parent provisions of most state laws, although relevant to the family without domestic violence, create risk for domestic violence victims. It is critical for child custody evaluators to consider safety first when evaluating these families.

The child custody evaluator should conduct a domestic-violence-sensitive evaluation and consider the following when conducting the evaluation:

- The history of violence in the family and the form it has taken, keeping in mind that violence can take physical, emotional, economic, or sexual forms
- The current risk of violence and the need for a safety plan
- The degree of direct violence to the children

- The quality of the relationships with each parent and the children and the history of the attachments
- The emotional functioning of the children, especially the child's underlying insecurities and any emotional constriction
- Whether the children are at any risk of abuse

Once the evaluator has considered these factors, it is important to do a risk analysis related to the custody and access recommendations. If the evaluator determines that the risk of renewed violence remains low, if the children have a healthy relationship with the parent who has a history of violence, and if effective treatment and monitoring mechanisms exist, the full range of access and custody options can be considered. If, on the other hand, the evaluator determines that the risk of violence remains high but observes that each parent has some responsibility for the eruptions, the evaluator will want to make recommendations that ensure everyone's safety but that support both parents' relationships with the children. In such circumstances, for example, the evaluator will, at a minimum, expect all child transfers to occur in a safe place or with only one parent present. Finally, if the evaluator determines that ongoing risk exists for one parent and the children and that one parent has a history of domestic violence against the other, custody and access options would be limited. In these circumstances, one must recognize that the abuser will likely try to undermine the other's parenting, so access to the abuser should occur only in ways that limit such opportunities.

We reiterate that this chapter cannot provide a beginning evaluator with sufficient information to fully assess domestic violence custody issues, but rather serves only as an introduction to the issue. We urge novice evaluators to read and absorb the references, to take specialized training, and to obtain consultation, especially when working in this or other complex areas.

Alienation

As with domestic violence, one cannot in a few pages describe the comprehensive and complex issue that was originally referred to as "parental alienation syndrome" and that has more recently been described as "the alienated child." In 1980,

Wallerstein and Kelly provided the first glimpses of children who refused visitation with their fathers. In 1987, Gardner first published his book on the parental alienation syndrome (Gardner, 1987), and over the next 15 years, numerous articles theorizing on the subject and focusing on the behaviors and emotions of the parents and the children have appeared. Considerable controversy abounds over whether or not the phenomenon even exists. Limited research data and differing philosophies on the topic complicate efforts at clarification. Some concerns focused on the term *syndrome* as unjustifiably implying a level of scientific support that does not exist and the subsequent use of the concept inappropriately to marginalize parents who expressed legitimate abuse concerns. The most recent debate on this topic has occurred between those who describe alienation from the viewpoint of the child and those who view it as a dynamic situation (see a series of articles in the July 2001 *Family Court Review*). This latter viewpoint stands in sharp contrast to the views described by the late Richard Gardner in his writings (Gardner, 1987). Bruch (2002) describes a lack of rigorous analysis that endangers children. Warshak (2001a) acknowledges the position of the Kelly group (e.g., Kelly, 2000; Kelly & Johnston, 2001) but continues to support the syndrome position first discussed by Gardner. In his book *Divorce Poison*, Warshak (2001b) describes his comprehensive view of the problem and what parents, courts, and psychologists can do to help.

We believe that, within this context, custody evaluators should review certain items. First, one must take a broad view of the family dynamics. This view should include:

- Getting a good history of the relationships and exploring the history of family conflicts
- Considering the dynamics during the marriage, especially the intensity and chronicity of conflict, as well as the strength of attachments with each parent during the marriage
- Assessing the behaviors of both the "alienating" and the "rejected" parents and evaluating how the emotional pressures and behaviors of each parent contribute to the dynamics of the alienation; look for signs of overreactions or a lack of empathy in either parent

Second, it becomes especially important to consider various dynamics within the child. Questions to consider include the following:

- What are the forces on the child that are contributing to the rejection? Pressure can come from each parent, relatives, siblings, the litigation itself, and even therapists.
- Does the child feel intense loyalty conflict, and how does the child manage such conflict?
- Does the child have insecure attachments with either or both parents? If so, how does this manifest itself and contribute to the rejection of one parent?
- Is the child feeling a need to take care of an emotionally fragile parent by rejecting the other parent?
- How do parents and teachers define the child's temperament? Does the child show signs of positive self-esteem or does the child exhibit strong feelings of insecurity?
- Does the child have long-standing legitimate fears of or anger toward a parent, with the estrangement coming from the history of a poor relationship?

Third, the evaluator should look at the behaviors exhibited by the child:

- Does the child exhibit very strong and intense rejection, or show signs of ambivalence, especially evident when the child spends time with the rejected parent?
- Does the child feel encouraged by one or both parents to keep secrets from the other parent or act as a spy on the other parent?
- Does the child act fearful, angry, or both, and what dynamics contribute to such emotions?
- How does the child function in the rest of his or her life? Do school problems, difficulties with authority figures, substance abuse problems, and so forth, appear, or does the child function well with peers, at school, and in extracurricular activities?

Fourth, the evaluator needs to consider whether the alienation dynamics appear:

- Mild, that is, the child does go with the rejected parent, albeit with some protests
- Moderate, that is, the child puts up major protests in going with the other parent, but still maintains some contact with the rejected parent

- Severe, that is, the child absolutely refuses to go with one parent, or maintains a hostile attitude and acting-out behaviors when forced to spend time with that parent

Finally, the evaluator needs to consider all of these dynamics and not just the actions of the parents when recommending interventions for these families. In the more unitary approach advocated by Gardner (1987), if one parent appears to promote alienation and if the child's rejection appears severe, a single response is recommended (i.e., a change of custody into the home of the rejected parent). In this approach, the dynamic of alienation is given great weight in the consideration of a change of custody, sometimes with tragic consequences. In the more complex approach advocated by Kelly and Johnston (2001), no simple solution applies to all families. Rather, this approach recognizes that multiple interventions might be needed. The evaluator will certainly need to consider all contributing factors and all possible remedies, including equal custody and a change of custody. Alienation has no more or less weight as a factor in making recommendations. If the alienation reaches severe intensity, and if the child has significant problems in other aspects of his or her life, a change of custody would seem worth implementing if the attachment with the rejected parent had previously seemed positive and secure. On the other hand, if the attachment has historically been insecure, or if the child has a legitimate reason for the estrangement, a change of custody would not seem indicated, particularly if other very significant problems exist.

In addition to the consideration of a change of custody, one must also consider other recommendations. Some cases become so polarized that pressure to radically alter the proportion of custody in one direction or another builds, although such a plan may not fit consistently with the child's needs. In the mild-to-moderate family situations, parent education and specialized educational programs for children will likely prove successful interventions. The evaluator will consider various treatment options, including treatment for each parent and for the child, or possibly family interventions. If multiple therapists are working simultaneously with such a family, it becomes important to ensure that the therapists talk with one another and avoid becoming participants in the polarization of the family. It is also important to have the judge or a judicial designate (such as a special master or parenting coordinator) in place to ensure that all participants follow court orders, especially any orders that ensure some contact between the child and the rejected parent.

Finally, it is important to be careful when evaluating allegations of alienation to recognize that victims of domestic violence are often accused of alienating the children from the other parent. In this way, the evaluator will be sensitive to those situations in which the parent is not alienating the children from the other parent but rather in which there is a clear pattern of abuse that has led to the child's estrangement from the abusive parent. Differentiating between the alienating parent and the victim of domestic abuse is perhaps one of the most difficult tasks for the child custody evaluator and requires the evaluator to be sensitive to all of these complex issues.

PARENTING PLANS FOR YOUNG CHILDREN

Prior to the 1990s, a common perception in the mental health community held that children had one primary attachment early in life and that children needed to spend all of their overnight time with their primary parent, whether the parents were either divorced or never married. Custody evaluators have been challenged when asked to make overnight recommendations for young children, with no consensus among professionals. For example, Hodges (1991) advocated against overnights with the non-custodial parent until children were at least 5, and Stahl (1999) advocated against overnights until children were at least 3. Warshak (personal communication, 2004) suggested that those ideas were not legitimately based on research. Newer research (Warshak, 2000; Kelly & Lamb, 2001; Pruett, Ebling, & Insabella, 2004) suggested that children develop multiple attachments and that, although there may be differences in the attachments between the child and each of his or her parents, there was no research basis for suggesting that overnights might be harmful to very young children.

The first articles suggesting that overnights should be a reasonable consideration for infants and toddlers appeared in 2000 and 2001 (Kelly & Lamb, 2000); Warshak, 2000; Lamb & Kelly, 2001). Their articles suggested that children benefit from effective parenting and that the relationships with both parents have emotional significance, helping to shape the child's overall development. An empirical study by Pruett et al. (2004) examined young children's adjustment to overnights and concluded that it was more important to ask whether overnights occurred on a regular unchanging schedule. Although potential risks do exist for children of divorce, the majority of children do not experience serious negative effects, which seem to be modulated by the healthy quality and positive involvement of both parents in a wide range of the children's life experiences and activities, including overnights. Kelly and Lamb (2000) suggested that parenting plans for very young children should include short separations from both parents and regular interactions in diverse contacts, including overnights. They believe that the continuity with both parents has extreme importance and warrants preservation and that routines also have great importance for young children. They stated that parents who are responsive to the psychological needs of their children should develop schedules for children under ages 2 or 3 that include more transitions rather than fewer to ensure the continuity of both relationships and of the child's sense of security and comfort during the time of great change.

Warshak (2000) suggested that "blanket restrictions," although based on a desire to help children, were based on myth rather than research. He concluded that:

> blanket restrictions requiring young children to spend every night with the same parent after divorce run counter to current knowledge about the needs and capacities of young children and their parents. In particular, the opinion that children can tolerate sleeping during the day in their father's presence, and in the presence of hired attendants in day care centers, but not at night with their fathers does not represent a scientific judgment. It reveals a bias often rooted in inaccurate assumptions about early child development. (Warshak, 2000, p. 440)

Kelly and Lamb (2000) and Warshak (2002) all suggest that overnights for infants and toddlers should be routinely considered unless significant problems exist that would argue against such a plan.

At the same time, other articles suggested caution (Solomon & George, 1999; Solomon & Biringen, 2001), asserting that a significant risk of disorganized attachments may occur in infants and toddlers who have overnights with a noncustodial parent. In particular, they expressed concern that, when significant conflict exists between the parents and when children have difficult temperaments, children run a greater risk of harm through moving between caregivers than they do when they spend all of their overnights with one primary custodial parent. These authors caution against a shift in public policy that would encourage routine overnights without more research to confirm that no harm will accrue to the children.

In response to these concerns, Warshak (2002) stood by his earlier statements and suggested that the best approach for undertaking any particular course of action will involve a combination of humility and ambition. He suggested that evaluators need humility to recognize the specific limitations of any one study, as well as the general limitations of social science research and theory. He suggested that evaluators need ambition to draw on the widest range of information, to deal with inconsistent results from different studies by determining which findings have stronger support, and to identify and challenge beliefs that, although commonly held, have poor empirical or theoretical support. Warshak (2002) concluded that overnights with both parents are not necessarily best for all children but that overnights should not routinely be excluded as a consideration in formulating a child-sharing plan.

In response to this debate, Gould and Stahl (2001) suggested a number of factors that the custody evaluator should consider to aid in understanding the particular parenting plan that might prove best for a given child and family. They stated:

> whether one believes that very young children are able to have overnight parenting time with each parent . . . or need to have a stable, single night placement . . . , there is no substitute for researching the particular parenting history of the family being evaluated. (p. 373)

They argue that by doing this evaluators can avoid a bias in either direction and reach a more accurate prediction of what will actually serve the child's best interests. The factors evaluators will want to consider include:

- Whether or not the child has had a history of joint caretaking and whether he or she has shown little, if any, difficulty in being parented and cared for by each parent while the family was intact; if the child has not shown any such difficulty, then one might look closely at continuing the parenting arrangement that existed prior to the separation
- The attachment history between the infant and each parent
- The relative strengths and weaknesses of both parents and the ability of the parents to complement each other and fulfill the responsibilities of both parents during the time that the child is in their care
- The complementary fit between the parents and any potential significant differences in parenting competence
- The temperament of the child
- The communication between the parents
- The care being given to the child by someone other than the parents when neither parent is available

As with the other special issues in this chapter, we recommend that custody evaluators learn as much as they can about this complex issue and strive to understand each particular family under evaluation rather than hold onto preconceived notions about which type of parenting plan will prove best for all children.

FLIGHT RISK/PARENTAL ABDUCTION

Little in the psychological literature addresses flight risks and the relevant issues for child custody evaluators. However, at a recent California Judicial Education program, Johnston (2004) described the factors that courts might consider in determining whether or not a significant risk for child abduction by a parent existed. After making it clear that assessing risk for parental abduction constitutes a very difficult challenge, she described a number of factors that courts may wish to consider when assessing the particular risk of abduction in any given case. These risk factors include:

- Younger age of children
- Concerns about child neglect or exposure to violence/crime
- Unsubstantiated sex abuse allegations
- Parent's disrespect for law, including sociopathic, narcissistic, paranoid traits
- Low socioeconomic status
- Cultural ethnic minorities or sects
- Unmarried relationships
- Less emotional support and practical help from kin, friends

Johnston (2004) also described a variety of risk factors that might distinguish abducting families from nonabducting families. These profile factors include the following:

- Behavioral indicators common to all abducting families:
  - Parent dismisses the value of the other parent for child
  - The child is very young or vulnerable to influence
- Prior threat or actual abduction
- The abducting parent is suspicious or distrustful of social support
- The abducting parent has paranoid or delusional features
- The abducting parent has a sociopathic personality
- The abducting parent is a foreign national with ties to his or her homeland
- The abducting parent feels disenfranchised and has social support in another locale

Finally, Johnston (2004) described a variety of behaviors that the court may consider when assessing the risk. These behavioral indicators of risk may include the following:

- The abducting parent has spoken a threat to take the child or has a history of hiding the child, refusing visits, or snatching the child back and forth
- The abducting parent has no financial or emotional ties to the area
- The abducting parent has resources to survive in hiding or help from others to do so and/or has liquidated assets or made a significant withdrawal of cash

Although the specific custody assignment accepted may not allow an evaluator to become involved in the assessment of such risks, we believe that evaluators may be called on in some cases, especially in a limited or brief assessment, to assist the court in identification of such risks. We believe that the preceding lists will assist an evaluator in considering the relevant factors and advising the court if called on in these matters.

RELOCATION OR REMOVAL EVALUATIONS

In a recent survey of statutory and case law among the states, it appears that there are four different presumptions related to parental relocation or removal of the child in a parent's custody from the state in which the other parent resides. In some states, the presumption holds that a custodial parent has the right to move unless such a relocation is shown to likely have detrimental effects on the child or appears designed to interfere with the child's access to the other parent. In 1996, for example, the California Supreme Court recognized such a presumption in its decision in *In re Marriage of Burgess*. Many states have followed the Burgess decision to continue this trend. Another presumption in some states holds that the relocating parent must show that such a move is in the child's best interest prior to the court's allowing it. Before the Burgess decision, this was the tendency in California, and it has remained viable under statutory or case law in other states after *Burgess* was decided. The third possible presumption holds that a request for relocation triggers a change of circumstance in which the court must determine which parent's custody is in the child's best interests. This de novo review requirement applies in many states in which joint physical custody exists. Finally, some states have no presumption or any guidance in relocation cases in either statutory or case law. In addition, presumptions of this sort change frequently as a function of both statute and case law, underscoring the need for custody evaluators to stay abreast of local law and court rules.

Little psychological research has addressed relocation cases in divorce until quite recently. Research on attachment and separation suggest that children are capable of forming strong attachments to multiple caretakers and that older children, at least by the age of 5, have the ability to maintain those attachments at greater distance and time between connections. Although all custody evaluations require the evaluator to make a prediction about a child's adjustment when parents divorce, relocation cases require a more difficult prediction, because few options exist and because children will not have access to both parents on a regular and frequent basis. The literature clearly suggests that children benefit from frequent and continuing access to both parents. In many relocation cases, no good solution exists. Nonetheless, courts must make a decision as to whether or not children may move with a relocating parent, and evaluators are asked to provide input into this decision.

Stahl (1999) outlined a number of factors that the evaluator might want to consider in assisting the court in making this difficult decision. Child and family factors to consider include:

- The nature of the child's relationship with each parent both before and after separation
- What the *actual* custodial arrangement is now
  - How well it works
  - What the problems are
  - Why someone has primary custody
- The developmental stage of the child and the capacities of the child to maintain a relationship at a distance (i.e., effect of the move on normal developmental tasks)
- Gender, temperament, and fit between each parent and child
- The potential meaning of the loss to the child; that is, what the child will *truly* experience if the proposed move does or does not take place
- The mental health of the moving parent and whether he or she will facilitate a positive relationship with other parent over time
- The history of the moving parent in facilitating or interfering with the other parent's access
- The child's special needs and whether there are siblings, friends, or activities that will be lost to the child and the impact a move would have on such relationships, needs, or activities
- Given the child's age and ability to express himself or herself, what his or her wishes are

More related questions to consider include the following:

- How can we expect the child to deal with issues of instability and change?
- How will the child deal with losses that may reemerge with the move?
- What realities will affect visitation if the move proceeds (e.g. money, geography, flexibilities of parents)?
- What are the reasons for the move, both stated *and* hidden?
- Is the move representative of patterns of stability or instability on the part of the moving parent?
- Are there any alternatives less disruptive than a move away?
- Given the circumstances, are there any alternative parenting plans that might be suggested?

When the evaluator has the answer to all of those questions, he or she will have greater ability to put the move into perspective and potentially make an appropriate mother-custody or father-custody recommendation. In addition, the court, aided by the judicial presumptions, will have the ability to make a better decision if all of these factors have become well understood. We must remember that the evaluator makes a recommendation to the court and uses psychological issues in reaching conclusions and recommendations. The court needs to interpret the data and apply state law to those data in order to reach a conclusion about the relocation.

Austin (2000) suggested that a custody evaluator should perform a risk-benefit analysis, paying close attention to the following factors:

- History of involvement by the noncustodial parent, including postseparation involvement
- Geographical distance
- Cognitive and emotional status of the child
- Psychological health of both parents
- History of child or spousal maltreatment
- Age of child
- Economic considerations
- Visitation and transportation schedules
- Changing needs and wishes of the child

Austin (2000) believes that the greatest danger for evaluators involves overpredicting harm in allowing for a move and thereby clouding interpretation. For example, many evaluators believe that children need both parents when that cannot constitute a realistic consideration in a relocation case. Ultimately, Austin believes that the most constructive role for an evaluator involves identifying relevant variables, assessing the risk both with and without a move, and making clear the limitations of the evaluator's ability to predict and reach conclusions.

Kelly and Lamb (2003) proposed that the courts consider a number of factors before deciding on any request to move. These factors include:

- Psychological adjustment and parenting capacities of relocating parents
- Psychological adjustment and parenting skills of nonrelocating parents
- Extent and focus of conflict
- Economic realities following relocation
- The distance between the two homes

They also address ways that relationships of nonmoving parents with relocating children can be maintained, including:

- Using mediation to facilitate agreements
- Modifying schedules to accommodate changing developmental needs
- Communication via various means to maintain relationships between children and parents.

Kelly and Lamb's (2003) considerations are important factors for evaluators to pay attention to in any given case. In recent years, two significant state Supreme Court decisions (*Baures v. Lewis*, 2001, and *Marriage of LaMusga*, 2004) have also outlined the task for judges in relocation cases. *Baures* directs the court to determine first whether or not the moving parent has a good-faith reason for moving. If the parent's proposed relocation arises primarily out of bad faith—in other words, primarily to thwart the child's relationship with the other parent—the move will be disallowed. Once the moving parent establishes such a good-faith reason to move, the nonmoving parent must make a prima facie showing that the move will cause the child some detriment; otherwise, the move is allowed. If detriment is found, the New Jersey Supreme Court directed judges to consider 12 factors in a best-interests analysis related to custody by the mother or by the father in the event of the move. These *Baures* factors include:

- Length of relationships (parent to parent and parent to child)
- Whether parents were married
- Parents' time-sharing agreement
- Quality of parenting time
- Quantity of parenting time
- Age of child
- Reason for move; whether it is for a fresh start
- Advantages to the moving parent and the child
- Parents' personal relationship
- Travel time and cost of travel
- Demands of second marriage
- Feasibility of parallel move

LaMusga recognized that issues of good faith and bad faith are quite complex, so the court declined to apply the *Baures* test first. This decision requires the noncustodial parent to show that a relocation would prove detrimental to the child if the child were to move with the custodial parent. If the showing of detriment cannot be met, the child will move with the custodial parent. If the trial court makes a finding of detriment, then the judge is to make a best-interests analysis related to parental custody considering the following eight factors:

- The children's interest in stability and continuity of the custodial arrangement
- The distance of the move
- The age of the children
- The children's relationships with both parents
- The relationship between the parents, including but not limited to:
  - Their ability to communicate and cooperate effectively
  - Their willingness to put the interests of the children above their individual interests
- The wishes of the children, if they are mature enough for such an inquiry to be appropriate
- The reasons for the proposed move
- The extent to which the parents are currently sharing custody

In most states, if parents significantly share custody, the court must perform the delicate best-interests analysis of mother custody versus father custody and whether or not the child should remain in the current jurisdiction or go to the new, proposed jurisdiction. Thus, given all of the preceding, it seems clear that evaluators may be called on to help the court identify and address issues of good faith versus bad faith, sources of potential detriment (or lack thereof), and answers to the particular questions relevant in any given case. The particular questions will vary from state to state and from case to case. However, it appears that, more and more, courts seem to be looking to guidance and direction from child custody evaluators in relocation matters.

Ultimately, Stahl (2004) suggests that it is important for the evaluator to provide specific answers to the questions noted previously and also to provide the court with a multiple set of recommendations, depending on how the court may weigh the factors involved. Because courts weigh the various factors in different ways than the evaluator might, evaluators might want to outline the various factors that would lean in favor of the move and those that lean against it. By encouraging the court to weigh those factors, the evaluator helps to ensure that the evaluation is advisory only and keeps the decision making in the hands of the court. An example of such an advisory recommendation for a 12-year-old child might read as follows:

> If we exclude Michael's expressed desire to move with his mother to Omaha, the evidence addressed in this evaluation would suggest that it is in his best interest to remain in Denver during the school year. Some benefits include his ability to maintain consistency and routine in his day-to-day care, to continue to benefit from his relationship with his father, and to avoid further losses or changes in his life.
>
> However, we cannot exclude Michael's wishes in this matter. As mentioned above, Michael is clear regarding his choice to move with his mother and to be with his father during the majority of non-school time, and it is both this examiner's and his therapist's opinion that he has made an excellent and thoughtful analysis of the issues facing him before making this decision that will affect him. Given his age (12) and his thoughtful and thorough consideration, it is this examiner's opinion that his preference should carry significant weight. Thus, the court will need to determine how much weight to give Michael's preference and integrate that with the rest of the factors noted above.
>
> If the court determines that Michael's preference should have greater weight than the stability and continuity offered by remaining in Denver, then I would recommend that he move

with his mother during the school year and that Michael be with his father during significant portions of non-school time (to be followed by suggested child-sharing plans reflecting a different potential court decision).

Many judges and evaluators have a particularly difficult time dealing with relocation requests, because there are often no "good" answers. We urge custody evaluators to pay close attention to statutory and case law in their jurisdiction and to do a careful analysis of each family using the factors noted herein.

SUMMARY

Evaluators should strive to perform objective, scientifically informed evaluations that incorporate the minimum standards detailed in the available literature. Ethical considerations are inseparable from professional practice parameters. Nowhere is the need for care and caution more evident than in highly charged child custody conflicts. This chapter describes basic considerations for those conducting such evaluations, along with discussion of the more complex referral questions, which include child abuse, domestic violence, move-away cases, parent alienation, and flight risk/parental abduction. We urge all child custody evaluators to gain specialized training in performing child custody evaluations, especially in those complex issues. Families suffer harm when child custody evaluators do not help the court understand issues, including those times when family violence or other forms of abuse are confused to represent all forms of mutual high conflict. Instead, it is critical that child custody evaluators do a thorough assessment of all relevant factors to ensure safety for all family members while making recommendations that serve in the best interests of children.

References

Ackerman, M. J., & Ackerman, M. C. (1996). Child custody evaluation practices: A 1996 survey of psychologists. *Family Law Quarterly, 30,* 565–586.

Amato, P. R. (1993). Children's adjustment to divorce: Theories, hypotheses, and empirical support. *Journal of Marriage and Family, 55,* 23.

American Academy of Child and Adolescent Psychiatry. (1997). Practice parameters for child custody evaluation. *Journal of the American Academy of Child and Adolescent Psychiatry, 36,* 57S–68S.

American Psychological Association. (2002). Ethical principles of psychologists and code of conduct. *American Psychologist, 57,* 1060–1073.

American Psychological Association. (2003). Report of the Ethics Committee 2002. *American Psychologist, 58,* 650–657.

American Psychological Association Committee on Professional Practice and Standards. (1994). Guidelines for child custody evaluations in divorce proceedings. *American Psychologist, 49,* 677–682.

American Psychological Association Committee on Professional Standards. (1984). Casebook for providers of psychological services. *American Psychologist, 39,* 663–668.

Association of Family and Conciliation Courts. (1994). *Model standards for child custody evaluations.* Madison, WI: Author.

Austin, W. (2000). A forensic psychology model of risk assessment for child custody relocation law: Psycho-legal dilemmas in relocation. *Family Court Review, 38*(2), 192–207.

Bagby, R. M., Nicholson, R. A., Buis, T., Radovanovic, H., & Fidler, B. J. (1999). Defensive responding on the MMPI-2 in family custody and access evaluations. *Psychological Assessment, 11,* 24–28.

Bathurst, K., Gottfried, A., & Gottfried, A. (1997). A normative data for the MMPI-2 in child custody litigation. *Psychological Assessment, 9,* 205–211.

Baures v. Lewis, 770 A.2d 214 (N.J. 2001).

Bow, J. N., & Quinnell, F. A. (2002). A critical review of child custody evaluation reports. *Family Court Review, 40,* 164–176.

Bruch, C. S. (2002). Parent alienation syndrome and alienated children—getting it wrong in child custody cases. *Child and Family Law Quarterly, 14,* 381–400.

Butcher, J. N., Dahlstrom, W. G., Graham, J. R., Tellegen, A., & Kaemmer, B. (1989). *Minnesota Multiphasic Personality Inventory-2 (MMPI-2): Manual for administration and scoring.* Minneapolis: University of Minnesota Press.

Caldwell, A. (1997). *Forensic questions and answers on the MMPI and MMPI-2.* (Report available from the author, P.O. Box 24624, Los Angeles, CA 90024)

California Rules of Court. (2003a). Rule 5.220: Uniform standards for practice for court-ordered child custody evaluations. Retrieved August 15, 2004, from www.courtinfo.ca.gov/rules/titlefive/title5-1-284.htm#TopOfPage

California Rules of Court. (2003b). Rule 5.225. Education, training, and experience standards for court-appointed child custody investigators and evaluators. Retrieved August 15, 2004, from www.courtinfo.ca.gov/rules/titlefive/title5-1-285.htm#TopOfPage

Committee on Ethical Guidelines for Forensic Psychologists. (1991). Specialty guidelines for forensic psychologists. *Law and Human Behavior, 15,* 655–665.

Daubert v. Merrell Dow Pharmaceuticals, Inc., 509 U.S. 579, 113 S.Ct. 2786 (1993).

Domestic violence and children. (1999). *The Future of Children, 9*(3). Retrieved January 14, 2005, from www.futureofchildren.org

Family Court Review (2001) 39, 243–343.

Fantuzzo, J. W., & Moore, W. K. (1999). Prevalence and effects of child exposure to domestic violence. *The Future of Children, 9,* 21–32.

Gardner, R. A. (1987). *The parent alienation syndrome and the differentiation between fabricated and genuine child sexual abuse.* Cresskill, NJ: Creative Therapeutics.

Gottfried, A. W., Bathurst, K., & Gottfried, A. E. (2003). What judicial officers should know about psychological testing in child custody matters. *California Family Law News, 25,* 9–16.

Gould, J. W. (2004). Evaluating the probative value of child custody evaluations: A guide for forensic mental health professionals. *Journal of Child Custody, 1,* 77–96.

Gould, J. W., & Stahl, P. M. (2001). Never paint by the numbers: A response to Kelly & Lamb (2000), Solomon (2001), & Lamb & Kelly (2001). *Family Court Review, 39,* 372–376.

Greenberg, S. A., & Shuman, D. W. (1997). Irreconcilable conflict between therapeutic and forensic roles. *Professional Psychology: Research and Practice, 28,* 50–57.

Greenwald, J. (1997, April). *The impact of parental mental or physical health, domestic abuse and substance abuse on parenting capacity: How parental background factors affect children and recommendations in custody evaluations.* Paper presented at the meeting on Children, Divorce and Custody of the American Bar Association and the American Psychological Association, Los Angeles.

Grisso, T. (2003). *Evaluating competencies: Forensic assessments and instruments.* Perspectives in Law and Psychology (2nd ed., pp. 461–480). New York: Kluwer Academic/Plenum.

Hagen, M. A., & Castagna, N. (2001). The real numbers: Psychological testing in child custody valuations. *Professional Psychology: Research and Practice, 32,* 269–271.

Harris, J. (1995). Where is the child's environment? A group socialization theory of development. *Psychological Review, 102,* 458–489.

Heinze, M. C., & Grisso, T. (1996). Review of instruments assessing parental competencies used in child custody evaluations. *Behavioral Sciences and the Law, 14,* 293–313.

Hetherington, E. M., & Kelly, J. B. (2002). *For better or worse: Divorce reconsidered.* New York: W. W. Norton.

Hodges, W. F. (1991). *Interventions for children of divorce: Custody, access, and psychotherapy.* New York: Wiley-Interscience.

Horvath, L., Logan, T., & Walker, R. (2002). Child custody cases: A content analysis of evaluations in practice. *Professional Psychology: Research and Practice, 33,* 552–565.

In re Marriage of Burgess, 913 P.2d 473 Cal. (1996).

Johnston, J. (2004, April). *Parental abduction of children.* Paper presented at the annual meeting of the California Judicial Education and Research (CJER).

Keilin, W. G., & Bloom, L. J. (1986). Child custody evaluation practices: A survey of experienced professionals. *Professional Psychology: Research and Practice, 17,* 338–346.

Kelly, J. B. (1994). The determination of child custody. In *The Future of Children: Children and Divorce* (pp. 121–142). Los Altos, CA: David and Lucille Packard Foundation.

Kelly, J. B. (2000). Children's adjustment in conflicted marriage and divorce: A decade review of research. *Journal of the American Academy of Child and Adolescent Psychiatry, 39,* 963–973.

Kelly, J. B., & Emery, R. (2003). Children's adjustments following divorce: Risk and resilience perspectives. *Family Relations: Interdisciplinary Journal of Applied Family Studies, 52,* 352–362.

Kelly, J. B., & Johnston, J. R. (2001). The alienated child: A reformulation of parental alienation syndrome. *Family Court Review, 39,* 249– 266.

Kelly, J. B., & Lamb, M. E. (2000). Using child development research to make appropriate child custody access decisions for young children. *Family and Conciliation Courts Review, 38,* 297–311.

Kelly, J. B., & Lamb, M. E. (2003). Developmental issues in relocation cases involving young children: When, whether, and how? *Journal of Family Psychology, 17,* 193–205.

Kirkland, K., & Kirkland, K. L. (2001). Frequency of child custody evaluation complaints and related disciplinary action: A survey of the Association of State and Provincial Psychology Boards. *Professional Psychology: Research and Practice, 32,* 171–174.

Kirkpatrick, H. D. (2004). A floor, not a ceiling: Beyond guidelines: An argument for minimum standards of practice in conducting child custody and visitation evaluations. *Journal of Child Custody, 1,* 61–75.

Kovacs, M. (1992). *Manual for the Children's Depression Inventory.* New York: Mental Health Systems.

Kumho Tire Co. v. Carmichael, 526 U.S. 137 (1999).

Lamb, M., Sternberg, K., & Thompson, R. (1997). The effects of divorce and custody arrangements on children's behavior, development and adjustment. *Family and Conciliation Courts Review, 35,* 393–404.

Lamb, M. E., & Kelly, J. B. (2001). Using the empirical literature to guide the development of parenting plans for young children: A rejoinder to Solomon and Biringen. *Family Courts Review, 39,* 365–371.

Marriage of LaMusga. (2004). 32 Cal.4th 1072, 12 Cal.Rptr.3d 356, 88 P.3d 81, 2004 CFLR 9617, FIRST ALERT #F-2004-1143.

Martindale, D. A., & Gould, J. W. (2004). The forensic model: Ethics and scientific methodology applied to custody evaluations. *Journal of Child Custody, 1,* 1–22.

Martindale, D. A., & Otto, R. K. (2000). Communicating with the custody evaluator. *Family Advocate, 23,* 30–33.

McCann, J., Flens, J., Campagna, V., Collman, P., Lazzaro, T., & Connor, E. (1998, October). *The MCMI-III in child custody evaluations.* Paper presented at the Millon Clinical Inventories Conference on Personology and Psychopathology, Chicago.

Melton, G. B., & Limber, S. (1989). Psychologists' involvement in cases of child maltreatment: Limits of role and expertise. *American Psychologist, 44,* 1225–1233.

Melton, G. B., Petrila, J., Poythress, N. G., & Slobogin, C. (1997). *Psychological evaluations for the court: A handbook for mental health professionals and lawyers* (2nd ed.). New York: Guilford.

Millon, T. (1994). *Manual for the Million Clinical Multiaxial Inventory—III (MCMI-III).* Minneapolis, MN: National Computer Systems.

National Conference of Commissioners on Uniform State Laws. (1971). Uniform Marriage and

Divorce Act. *Family Law Quarterly, 6,* 106–111.

National Council of Juvenile and Family Court Judges. (1994). *Model code on domestic and family violence.* Reno, NV: Author.

Otto, R. K. (2000). *Child custody evaluation: Law, ethics, and practice.* Tampa, FL: Louis de la Parte Florida Mental Health Institute.

Otto, R. K. (2003). Child custody evaluation. In A. Goldstein (Ed.), *Handbook of psychology: Vol. 11. Forensic psychology* (pp. 179–208). Hoboken, NJ: Wiley.

Otto, R. K., & Butcher, J. N. (1995). Computer assisted psychological assessment in child custody evaluations. *Family Law Quarterly, 29,* 79–96.

Otto, R. K., Edens, J. F., & Barcus, E. (2000). The use of psychological testing in child custody evaluations. *Family and Conciliation Courts Review, 38,* 312–340.

Pope, K., Butcher, J., & Seelen, J. (1993). *The MMPI, MMPI-2, and MMPI-A in Court.* Washington, DC: American Psychological Association.

Posthuma, A., & Harper, J. (1998). Comparison of MMPI-2 responses of child custody and personal injury litigants. *Professional Psychology: Research and Practice, 29,* 437–443.

Pruett, M. K., Ebling, R., & Insabella, G. (2004). Critical aspects of parenting plans for young children: Introducing data into the debate about overnights. *Family Court Review, 42,* 39–59.

Rohman, L., Sales, B., & Lou, M. (1987). The best interests of the child in custody disputes. In L. Weithorn (Ed.) *Psychology and child custody determinations.* Lincoln: University of Nebraska Press.

Schutz, B., Dixon, E., Lindenberger, J., & Ruther, N. (1989). *Solomon's sword: A practical guide to conducting child custody evaluations.* San Francisco: Jossey-Bass.

Selzer, M. L. (1971). The Michigan Alcohol Screening Test: The quest for a new diagnostic instrument. *American Journal of Psychiatry, 127,* 1653–1658.

Shear, L. E. (2004). When form fails to follow function: Benjamin and Gollan's *Family Evaluation in Custody Litigation* [Book review]. *Journal of Child Custody, 1,* 127–141.

Shuman, D., & Sales, B. (1998). The admissibility of expert testimony based upon clinical judgment and scientific research. *Psychology, Public Policy and Law, 4,* 1226–1252.

Solomon, J., & Biringen, Z. (2001). Another look at the developmental research: Commentary on Kelly and Lamb's "Using child development research to make appropriate child custody access decisions for young children." *Family Court Review, 39,* 355–364.

Solomon, J., & George, C. (1999). The development of attachment in separated and divorced families: Effects of overnight visitation, parent and couple variables. *Attachment and Human Development, 1,* 2–33.

Sparta, S. (1997, April). *The American Psychological Association guidelines for child custody evaluations: Three years after implementation.* Paper presented at the meeting of the American Bar Association and the American Psychological Association, Los Angeles.

Sparta, S. (1998, Fall). Evaluating children's expressed preferences in divorce proceedings. *Family Law News, State Bar of California Family Law Section, 21,* 5–7.

Stahl, P. M. (1994). *Conducting child custody evaluations: A comprehensive guide.* Newbury Park, CA: Sage.

Stahl, P. M. (1999). *Complex issues in child custody evaluations.* Thousand Oaks, CA: Sage.

Stahl, P. M. (2004, February). *To move or not to move in a post-LaMusga environment.* Paper presented at the annual conference of the California Chapter of the Association of Family and Conciliation Courts, Los Angeles

Sun, Y. (2001). Family environment and adolescents' well being before and after parents' marital disruption: A longitudinal analysis. *Journal of Marriage and Family, 63,* 697–713.

Wallerstein, J., & Kelly, J. B. (1980). *Surviving the breakup: How children and parents cope with divorce.* New York: Basic Books.

Warshak, R. A. (2000). Blanket restrictions: Overnight contact between parents and young children. *Family and Conciliation Courts Review, 38,* 422–445.

Warshak, R. A. (2001a). Current controversies regarding parent alienation syndrome. *American Journal of Forensic Psychology, 19*(3), 29–59.

Warshak, R. A. (2001b). *Divorce poison: Protecting the parent–child bond from a vindictive ex.* New York: Regan Books.

Warshak, R. A. (2002). Who will be there when I cry in the night? *Family Court Review, 40,* 208–219.

Warshak, R. A. (2003). Payoffs and pitfalls of listening to children. *Family Relations, 54*(4), 373–384.

Woody, R. H. (2000). *Child custody: Practice standards, ethical issues, and legal safeguards for mental health practitioners.* Sarasota, FL: Professional Resource.

14

Assessing Eligibility for and Appropriateness of Special Education Services

Stephen T. DeMers
Leah Nellis

Since initial passage of landmark federal legislation the Education for All Handicapped Children Act of 1975, psychologists have played a central role in the determination of a student's eligibility for special education services. Although this federal law and its subsequent amendments do not specifically require a psychologist's involvement, the law does mandate a comprehensive evaluation by a qualified examiner. Consequently, most state special education plans and local school district procedures call for employing school psychologists or making contractual arrangements with licensed psychologists to meet this assessment mandate. The federal special education legislation also authorizes other roles for psychologists, such as providing child or family counseling when such a service becomes necessary in order to provide an appropriate education; providing an evaluation independent of the school district at the parent's request; or participating in the placement and planning meetings for special education services when the psychologist has information that the parents or the school feel is essential to proper decision making.

This chapter focuses on the latter roles, that is, serving as an independent evaluator or participat-

ing in school decision making. Such requests for outside participation by a psychologist from the community most often arise in the context of a dispute between the parents or legal guardians of a student and the school over whether or how best to serve the student. Federal and state special education law and regulations have evolved over the years such that parents and legal guardians have acquired extensive and specific procedural and due process rights to challenge decisions made by school officials. Parents and legal guardians often seek help from community-based psychologists who have no affiliation with or allegiance to the schools. Although such psychologists clearly meet the standard of independence, they often lack full awareness of the requirements under special education law as to what constitutes a comprehensive and defensible psychological assessment that can survive the challenges inherent in any dispute between the parents and the school.

School psychologists or other psychologists employed regularly by the public schools develop, in the course of their training and experience, an extensive knowledge of the special education statutes and other federal and state legislation and case law that affect psychological practice in the schools. Psychologists regularly employed by the schools also learn the particular ethical issues that arise when one practices in a large and complex social institution such as the public schools. However, many child, family, applied developmental, or other psychologists could find themselves involved in special education decision making or other forms of school practice (either willingly or unwillingly) without a clear appreciation of the legalities and complexities of such practice. This chapter provides a basic introduction to the major pieces of federal legislation, as well as the common ethical dilemmas that affect the delivery of psychological services in public schools. We also offer a description of the required components and characteristics of a comprehensive special education assessment as mandated by federal special education law and regulations. The chapter concludes with a review of the legal and ethical complexities associated with two controversial topics related to special education assessment. First, we discuss the controversy surrounding the use of discrepancy formulas in the identification of learning disabilities; second, we review the provisions in IDEA that deal with the suspension or expulsion from school of students with emotional disabilities because of violent, threatening, or physically harmful behavior.

MAJOR FEDERAL LEGISLATION AFFECTING PSYCHOLOGICAL ASSESSMENT IN SPECIAL EDUCATION

Three pieces of federal legislation have provided the majority of the mandates that affect psychological assessment: the Individuals with Disabilities Education Act (i.e., IDEA, formerly the Education for All Handicapped Children Act), Section 504 of the Rehabilitation Act of 1973, and the Family Educational Rights and Privacy Act of 1974 (FERPA). Significant litigation preceded and followed each of these federal laws , both initially prompting the legislation and then leading to refinements of the legally imposed mandates. We summarize major aspects of each of these federal laws and their impact on psychological assessment in separate sections. Also, we review the standards

in the APA *Ethical Principles and Code of Conduct* (2002) that are most salient to special education determination cases and disputes in schools.

IDEA: The Individuals with Disabilities Education Act

Public education in the United States is funded and regulated primarily by the states and state law and not by the federal government. The U.S. Constitution does not guarantee public education (*San Antonio Independent School District v. Rodriguez*, 1973). However, because of the disparity in how states dealt with such educational issues as access to schooling for children with disabilities and freedom-of-speech rights of students in schools, federal intervention into educational practices in the states has occurred in order to protect the Constitutional rights of students and parents (Jacob & Hartshorne, 2003; Reschly & Bersoff, 1999). The passage of federal special education legislation resulted from several high-profile court cases that pointed out the disparities in how states responded to the educational needs of students with disabilities. In *Pennsylvania Association of Retarded Citizens (PARC) v. Commonwealth of Pennsylvania* (1971, 1972), parents of mentally retarded children sued the state for access to special education programs for all mentally retarded children. Not only did the federal court that heard this case side with the parents, but the court also ordered the state to locate all students previously excluded from the public schools and to provide them with a free and appropriate education designed to help them achieve self-sufficiency. In a similar case on behalf of students with emotional, behavioral, and learning impairments (*Mills v. Board of Education of the District of Columbia*, 1972), the court again ruled in favor of the plaintiffs and ordered the schools to develop an apropriate educational plan and to curtail the use of suspension and discipline for students with disabilities. As similar cases evolved in numerous other states (Martin, 1979), the federal government passed the Education for All Handicapped Children Act (EHA, also known as Public Law 94-142) in 1975 to bring some uniformity across the states in services provided to students with disabilities.

EHA was amended in 1990 and renamed the Individuals with Disabilities Education Act (IDEA) to reflect the shift in terminology from use of the term *handicap* to *disability*. In 1997, IDEA was again amended and expanded to focus more on the provision of appropriate services, as well as the appropriate identification and placement of students with disabilities (Yell, Drasgow, & Ford, 2000). In December 2004, IDEA was reauthorized again and signed into law. Most provisions of the 2004 reauthorization took effect in July 2005, although the Department of Education is still developing implementing regulations, and this process often takes years to complete (see www.nasponline .org for updates on IDEA 2004 provisions and implementing regulations). Since its original passage and throughout its various ammendments, IDEA has had a profound influence on state and local special education services and on the conduct of psychologists who work with school-age children suspected of having disabilities. EHA and IDEA have mostly served to empower parents (and their advocates) in their attempts to secure appropriate educational services by requiring school districts to provide students the following:

(a) A free, appropriate education in the least restrictive environment necessary to assist the child to progress academically

(b) Development of an individual educational plan (IEP) based on academic strengths and weaknesses identified through a comprehensive multidisciplinary assessment

(c) Parental informed consent for assessment, initial placement, or denial of placement and any change in placement in special education

(d) Parental rights to participate in decision making, to appeal decisions they disagree with, to obtain independent evaluation of their children, and to seek an impartial hearing of disputes

The 2004 reauthorization of IDEA added new provisions for ensuring special education services for children who are homeless or otherwise highly mobile and also the addition of a required resolution session prior to a due process hearing in order to increase possibility of an amicable resolution to disputes between parents and school officials. These new procedural rights of parents could be important vehicles for psychologists serving as independent evaluators or advocates for their clients involved in such disputes.

In order to qualify for services under IDEA, a student must meet a two-pronged test of eligibility. First, in most states, he or she must be evaluated and determined to qualify as having one or more of the following disabilities recognized by IDEA: mental retardation; specific learning disability, serious emotional disturbance, autism, traumatic brain injury, hearing impairments (including deafness), visual impairments (including blindness), orthopedic impairments, and other health impairments. Second, it must be determined that this disability prevents the student from progressing academically in the regular instructional program commensurate with his or her potential. Reschly (2000) has argued that the 1997 amendments to IDEA empower the states to develop a noncategorical approach to identifying and serving students that would avoid many of the dilemmas faced by school-based decision makers when students with educational needs do not fit neatly into predetermined diagnostic categories. However, the 2004 amendments to IDEA still emphasize a predominately categorical approach to identifying students with disabilities under IDEA.

Because access to an appropriate education under IDEA depends on a student's qualifying as eligible for special education services, the parents' right to an independent evaluation in situations in which they question the actions of the school system becomes crucial to the parents' ability to participate fully in the decision-making process concerning their child's education. Such independent evaluations must occur in a manner that will address the required components for a special education eligibility assessment under IDEA, or the parents' ability to challenge a school system placement decision could be seriously compromised. A later section of this chapter describes these required components so that psychologists who have less familiarity with IDEA can help parents be effective advocates for their children.

The Rehabilitation Act of 1973

Although it was originally considered primarily an antidiscrimination law aimed at protecting individuals with disabilities in employment settings, the courts and the U.S. Department of Education have interpreted Section 504 of the Rehabilitation Act of 1973 as extending similar protections to students in public schools (Martin, 1992). For public school students and their parents, Section 504 offers another avenue for students to assert a legal right to appropriate instructional accommodations.

The main impact of the Rehabilitation Act on public schools is a broadening of the category of potentially eligible individuals recognized as disabled. Section 504 has no proscribed list of recognized disabilities; thus anyone with a documented physical or mental impairment can assert a right to specialized educational services if he or she can show an adverse educational impact resulting from this exceptionality. Furthermore, unlike the IDEA focus on "serious emotional disturbance," the Section 504 definition of handicapped includes "any mental or psychological disorder, such as mental retardation, organic brain syndrome, emotional or mental illness and specific learning disabilities," making any diagnosis recognized in the *Diagnostic and Statistical Manual of the American Psychiatric Association* (APA, 2000) a potential basis for a claim for educational accommodations. According to Jacob and Hartshorne (2003), diagnoses not typically or specifically addressed under IDEA that would constitute a handicapping condition under Section 504 include attention-deficit/hyperactivity disorder (ADHD), learning disabilities in individuals without a severe discrepancy between ability and achievement, social maladjustment and emotional impairment, demonstrable drug and alcohol dependencies, and health impairments, including communicable diseases.

The protections afforded to students and their parents under IDEA with regard to the timelines and conduct of the assessment and participation in the placement-and-planning decision making are much less explicit under Section 504. However, Jacob and Hartshorne (2003) summarize the court cases and legal opinions that have upheld the parents' right to obtain reasonable educational accommodations for their child's disabling conditions even though the child did not qualify under IDEA. And the courts have used the protections afforded under IDEA to gauge the reasonableness and appropriateness of the school district's conduct in meeting their obligations under Section 504 (Zirkel & Kincaid, 1993).

Family Educational Rights and Privacy Act

In 1974 the Family Educational Rights and Privacy Act (FERPA) was passed, giving parents and students dramatically increased access to and control over their educational records. Although this law has its greatest impact on psychologists employed by the public schools, many features of FERPA are relevant to psychologists who conduct independent evaluations or serve as advocates for children and parents who seek appropriate educational services.

According to a study conducted in the late 1960s (Russell Sage Foundation, 1970), parental access to the child's school records was seriously impaired by the record-keeping practices of most public schools. Some of the more flagrant abuses cited included the release of school records to third parties (e.g., potential employers) without the parent's or student's knowledge or consent and making it difficult for parents to discover the contents of their children's school records or to challenge any inaccuracies the records might contain.

Under FERPA, educational records are defined as any records maintained by the schools and identified as containing information about a particular student. Exceptions to this definition include records of physicians, psychologists, or related personnel who provide treatment to students that is not considered part of their instructional program and also the private notes of school personnel (including teachers, counselors, and psychologists) as long as these notes are used only by their maker and not shared with other school personnel. Some school psychologists and special education directors have maintained that raw test data and test protocols should be considered private notes of the psychologist and thus not accessible under FERPA. This issue of access to test protocols has been debated extensively in the professional literature (see Jacob & Hartshorne, 2003; Reschley & Bersoff, 1999), but suffice it to say that various legal opinions and at least one court case have concluded that parents and their advocates have a right to inspect the raw data that schools use to make decisions about special education eligibility.

FERPA addressed directly the abuses of parental access and control of school records identified by the Russell Sage Foundation (1970). Under

FERPA parents or students over 18 years of age have a right to inspect, review, copy, and request a change in the student's school record (Jacob & Hartshorne, 2003). Interestingly, the law specifies that divorced or separated parents still have access to the minor child's school records regardless of custody unless the court has acted to specifically bar one parent's access to these records (*Fay v. South Colonie Central School District*, 1986). A parent or student of majority age may request that the school amend its records based on a claim that it contains inaccurate information, misleads, or violates the right to privacy of the student (Jacob & Hartshorne, 2003). The school can agree to amend the record or disagree and apprise the student and parent of their rights to an impartial hearing. The parent or student has a right to introduce any information he or she chooses to refute the school record, including data and reports from independent psychological assessment or treatment. Even if the hearing officer rules in favor of the school district, the parent or student may enter into the record a statement of their disagreement with the record.

FERPA has resulted in a dramatic shift in the balance of power between school district employees and parents and students in their control over the content and release of school records. Because of FERPA requirements, psychologists working with students and their parents outside the school will have much greater access to the information that the schools relied on in making its decisions about special education.

APA ETHICAL STANDARDS AND PRACTICE GUIDELINES AFFECTING SPECIAL EDUCATION ASSESSMENT

We assume that most psychologists have some familiarity with the ethical standards and practice guidelines of the American Psychological Association. However, certain aspects of both types of professional regulation are particularly relevant in special education assessment practice and deserve special attention. APA's *Ethical Principles of Psychologists and Code of Conduct* (American Psychological Association, 2002) contain provisions that both reinforce legal requirements imposed by the federal laws described previously and also create ethical obligations with the potential to conflict with these requirements.

Several sections of the APA ethical standards contain ethical obligations that bear on special education assessment work by psychologists. First, Standard 2.01 notes that psychologists only provide services within their defined boundaries of competence, based on their education, training, and supervised experience. Although only the strictest interpretation of this standard would require one to be trained as a school psychologist or, specifically, in special education assessment to be competent to conduct such an assessment, this standard does suggest that the practitioner must have the ability to demonstrate some specific knowledge, skills, or abilities that adequately prepared him or her to conduct such assessments in a competent manner. Public schools serve a diverse population of students, and cultural competence is an essential component of clinical competence in such a multicultural environment. Section 2.01b requires that psychologists obtain the training and experience necessary to competently provide services to individuals from diverse backgrounds when such diversity may affect the results of the psychologist's work with that individual. Psychologists who contract with schools to provide assessment services should be mindful of Sections 3.07, Third Party Requests for Services, and 3.11, Psychological Services Delivered to or through Organizations, of APA's code. Clarifying the nature of the professional role with all parties (i.e., the school, the parents, and the student) and deciding who will have access to what information resulting from the professional relationship are crucial issues to be negotiated before services are rendered. School officials are not necessarily aware of psychologists' ethical obligations, so the psychologist is obligated to ensure that all parties understand the professional role and allegiances in such circumstances. Section 3.10(b), dealing with informed consent, notes that psychologists dealing with minors or others incapable of giving informed consent still seek the agreement or assent of the recipient of services. Whereas the parents of a child being considered for special education may desire a comprehensive independent evaluation, the child, particularly an adolescent, may not be a willing participant. Issues of rapport and adequate motivation to ensure validity and accuracy of the results obtained are all related to the child's willing participation.

Section 9 of the APA ethical standards contains most of the relevant ethical obligations in performing special education eligibility determinations. Standard 9.01(a) states that assessments, recommendations, reports, and evaluative statements by psychologists are based on information and techniques that are sufficient to substantiate their conclusions. This obligates the psychologist to be knowledgeable about the determination of special education eligibility prior to concluding that a child he or she has worked with is or is not eligible. Standard 9.02 requires that psychologists use psychological assessment techniques appropriate in light of research or evidence of the usefulness and proper application of the techniques and that they use assessment techniques with established reliability and validity for the client being assessed or that they describe the limitations of their conclusions where such evidence of developmental, linguistic, or cultural appropriateness is not available. Standard 9.08 cautions against the use of obsolete tests or test results, and Standard 9.11 obligates the psychologist to maintain test security consistent with law and contractual obligations.

Section 4 of the APA ethical standards deals with issues of privacy and confidentiality. In general, the ethical standards on confidentiality should not present any special complications in special education assessments as long as the psychologist discusses the limits of confidentiality with the client and recognizes that in the legal arena no right to confidentiality resides with the child separate from the parent or legal guardian (see Jacob & Hartshorne, 2003, and Reschly & Bersoff, 1999) .

Psychologists who wish to engage in special education assessments should also take time to review at least two of the many practice guidelines issued by APA as aspirational statements about how psychologists should conduct their practices. APA's guidelines on record keeping (1993) contain recommendations about the content, retention, and release of client records that may conflict with the requirements of IDEA or FERPA outlined earlier. These record-keeping guidelines are currently being expanded and revised and are likely to be adopted by APA in 2005. APA also has developed guidelines describing appropriate test-user qualifications for competent test use (Turner, DeMers, Fox, & Reed, 2001) that also have relevance to special education assessments. The test-user guidelines include sections describing the psychometric knowledge and sensitivity to cultural, ethnic, and racial characteristics of test takers necessary for proper test use. These guidelines also describe the specific knowledges and skills required to conduct competent assessments in the school setting, including special education eligibility. Finally, the American Educational Research Association (AERA), the American Psychological Association (APA), and the National Council on Measurement in Education (NCME; 1999) have published the second edition of their jointly approved *Standards for Educational and Psychological Testing*, which contain a wealth of information and guidance about the proper content and conduct of assessments, including chapters on assessing persons with disabilities and those with diverse cultural and linguistic backgrounds.

In summary, APA ethical standards and practice guidelines offer some guidance to psychologists interested in the conduct of special education elibility assessments. Most of these standards and guidelines support the legal requirements of federal special education legislation, but psychologists are cautioned to be aware of possible conflicts between their legal and ethical requirements, especially in such complex areas as confidentiality, using psychometrically and culturally valid assessment procedures, and releasing copyrighted test materials.

CHARACTERISTICS OF SPECIAL EDUCATION ASSESSMENT REQUIRED BY IDEA

Assessment activities within special education remain largely unchanged in IDEA 2004 from the provisions described within IDEA 1997 as the "Procedures for Evaluation and Determination of Eligibility" (IDEA, 1997, §§300.530–300.543). Initial special education evaluations are conducted in concordance with such regulations to determine whether a child has a disability under IDEA (1997, §300.7) and to identify his or her educational needs. When a disability is identified, evaluation results are utilized to develop content of a child's individualized education program (IEP) that allows for participation and progress within the general curriculum. Reevaluations of eligibility are required when requested by either the school or the parents as a result of changes in the student's educational performance. Previous versions of IDEA required that reevaluations occur at least every 3 years; however, IDEA (2004) allows parents and schools to override this requirement if they agree that a reevaluation is not necessary.

For psychologists, assessment practices must manifest four required characteristics to meet IDEA regulations. Under IDEA, assessments of individuals to determine eligibility for special education must be multifaceted and comprehensive, technically adequate, nondiscriminatory and fair, and functionally relevant.

Multifaceted and Comprehensive Evaluation

Under regulations promulgated with IDEA (1997) and unlikely to change under the new regulations, a "full and individual initial evaluation" (IDEA, 1997, §300.531) must take place to determine eligibility and educational needs prior to the receipt of special education and related services. Further, current regulations speak to the comprehensive and multifaceted nature of the assessment (§300.532). Evaluations must address all areas related to a suspected disability, including health, vision, hearing, motor abilities, communication, intelligence, academic skill, and social/emotional functioning. Additionally, the evaluation must be "sufficiently comprehensive to identify all of the child's special education and related services needs, whether or not commonly linked to the disability category in which the child has been classified" (§300.532[h]). Such regulations clearly require that evaluations be thorough so that decisions are based on multiple sources of information as opposed to a single piece of data. Moreover, evaluations must entail a variety of tools, including not only standardized tests such as measures of cognitive ability and academic achievement but also interviews, behavioral observations, and curriculum-based performance and authentic assessment procedures (Shinn, 2002).

The preceding regulations require consideration of all domains but do not necessarily require direct assessment of all within an initial evaluation (Reschly, 2000). Professionals responsible for conducting evaluations, often school psychologists, must utilize professional judgment directed by ethical considerations and professional best practice to develop individualized assessment practices based on the reason for referral and the child's individual needs. Best practices emphasize a problem-solving approach wherein assessment practices and instruments are selected in response to presenting concerns within the context of a developmental and educational history specific to a given student and designed to facilitate intervention development (Reschly & Grimes, 2002). An appropriate evaluation battery, selected based on child characteristics such as age, language background, communicative status, strengths, and educational needs, should follow. Thus professionals will have the ability to consider all domains of functioning and assess within each area as appropriate.

Although ethical considerations guide psychologists in designing an assessment battery, IDEA also speaks to the process for determining what assessment data are necessary. For both initial evaluations and reevaluations, the determination of needed assessment data comes from a group of individuals based on a review of existing information, including that obtained from parent and teacher reports, observations, classroom assessments, and prior evaluations, when appropriate. Data necessary to address issues such as whether a disabilitiy exists, the present level of performance, educational needs, and modifications needed for progress in the general curriculum or toward IEP goals are identified and guide the remainder of the evaluation process. If no additional data are needed, the public agency is not required to evaluate unless requested by the parents. This has allowed school personnel to conduct reevaluations that prove more functional or vocational in nature as opposed to "retesting" with standardized measures used in initial eligibility determination.

Some schools use the decisions from such reviews to form an evaluation plan that serves as a component of informed parental consent by articulating the domains for assessment. Although this approach facilitates the development of individualized evaluations, professionals must retain the opportunity to modify the plan based on information obtained during the evaluation process, when appropriate. This becomes particularly important for initial evaluations and in settings in which the evaluation plan evolved without input from a psychologist. Psychologists should remain cognizant of such evaluation plans but continue to select assessment domains and tools based on the child's needs and characteristics, seeking additional consent if necessary.

Psychologists unfamiliar with IDEA and special education eligibility determination practices may be surprised to learn that the elements included in the typical psychological assessment report are insufficient to address all mandated areas under IDEA. According to IDEA (1997) regulations, the evaluation must be sufficiently comprehensive to identify all of the child's special education needs and the need for any related services, whether or not these areas of need are commonly linked to the suspected disability category being considered. In an independent evaluation, the nature and extent of the assessment are determined solely by the provider, but the school still needs to consider all relevant areas of concern. The independent evaluator should be aware of the comprehensive nature of the typical special education assessment in order to address as many of the areas of interest as possible within the limits of his or her competence.

In addition to the necessary identifying information and a description of the behaviors or deficits that led to the child being referred for evaluation, a comprehensive special education evaluation typically includes the following components, if they are suspected to be relevant to the child's educational performance:

(a) Developmental history
(b) Health and physical status (including vision, hearing, or other sensory or neurological factors)
(c) Cognitive functioning (including verbal and nonverbal reasoning, processing speed, perceptual organization, etc.)
(d) Academic functioning (including reading skills, reading comprehension, math reasoning and skills, spelling, and written expression)
(e) Communication skills (including speech and language skills and receptive and expressive communication)
(f) Social competence
(g) Emotional adjustment and functioning

(h) Vocational skills and functioning (especially for adolescents)
(i) Behavior observations in multiple settings (e.g. structured and unstructured classroom periods, lunch room, playground, hallways, and assemblies)

Details about conducting such a comprehensive assessment can be found in sources such as Thomas and Grimes (2002) and Merrell (1999).

Technically Adequate
Assessment Procedures

Section 300.532 of IDEA (1997) states that instruments utilized to assess the relative contribution of cognitive and behavioral factors, in addition to physical or developmental factors, stand as technically sound and that any standardized tests given to a child must have validity for the specific purpose for which they are used. Psychologists practicing in public schools, like those working in other settings, look to the *Standards for Educational and Psychological Testing* (AERA, APA, & NCME, 1999) for guidelines in evaluating the technical properties of tests and assessment procedures. Although specific criteria are not delineated, individual test users are responsible for selecting and utilizing technically adequate procedures based on test reliability, validity, and adequacy of test norms (Turner, DeMers, Fox, & Reed, 2002).

Reliability refers to the consistency of measurement or the degree to which test results and scores remain free from random and unsystematic error (AERA, APA, & NCME, 1999). Test manuals should include test stability and internal consistency reliability estimates for total scores, index scores, and subtest scores. Salvia and Ysseldyke (1995) recommend that tests should have a minimum reliability of .90 with respect to high-stakes decisions such as special education placement.

A fundamental consideration in test evaluation and selection is validity, or "the degree to which evidence and theory support the interpretations of test scores entailed by proposed uses of tests" (AERA, APA, & NCME, 1999, p. 9). The issue of validity pertains to a particular usage of an instrument, not to the test instrument in general. Evidence of test validity flows from empirical studies of test content, internal structure, and test-criterion relationships and should be considered collectively in determining test validation. Although test publishers remain responsible for providing empirical validity evidence, test users have ultimate responsiblity for selecting test instruments validated for the specific purpose or population to which the test will apply (Turner et al., 2002).

An additional psychometric consideration in norm-referenced assessment concerns the adequacy of the norms. The adequacy of test norms varies as a function of the size and representativeness of the norm sample and the relevance of the norms to the purpose of evaluation (Salvia & Ysseldyke, 1995). Demographic variables such as age, gender, geographic location, ethnicity, and education level warrant consideration in selection of the norm group. Norm samples should be large enough so that subgroups in the population have adequate representation and test scores hold stable. Salvia and Ysseldyke (1995) recommend that a minimum of 100 participants per age or grade group be represented in the sample. Relevancy refers to whether interpretations based on a norm-group comparison cogently relate to the purpose of the evaluation. For example, national norms may become appropriate when an assessment aims at determining how an individual compares with national peers in intellectual, physical, or communication development. In some instances, a more meaningful comparison of an individual's performance might focus on local peers who are similar in characteristics such as geographic area, cultural background, disability, and educational curriculum. Test users retain responsibility for selecting tests developed and normed for an appropriate population for each individual under evaluation, and the appropriateness of the norm group should have major consideration in test interpretation.

Nondiscriminatory and Fair Assessment

Regulations in IDEA (1997) that are likely to be retained in the new regulations to come specifically address the assessment of individuals with limited English proficiency or disabilities and those from culturally diverse backgrounds. In general, selection and administration of tests and other assessment procedures must not discriminate against children from racial and cultural minority groups.

Further, administration of tests and assessment procedures must take place in the child's native language or other mode of communication unless it is not feasible to do so (IDEA, 1997, §300.532(1)). This requires that assessment of a child occur in the language which he or she normally uses and includes communication through methods such as sign language and braille.

Additionally, regulations state that for students having limited proficiency with the English language or having sensory, motor, or speech impairments, assessment and administration must proceed in such a manner that disability determination and the child's need for special education are emphasized and the impact of the child's English-language skills or disability are minimized. Thus assessments should be administered and interpreted to provide a valid measure of a child's cognitive, academic, or behavioral skills, without penalty for failure associated with a disability or English proficiency. The regulations further state that if modification of standardized procedures occurs to better meet the needs of the child, the evaluation report must include a description of any adaptations or accommodations.

Issues of bias in psychological assessment have generated fervent debate in the research literature and most often focus on the use of intelligence tests with ethnic minorities (Reynolds, Lowe, & Saenz, 1999). In the context of psychological testing, the term *bias* refers to systematic error related to construct-irrelevant variance that results in higher or lower scores for members of an identifiable group, such as an ethnic minority (AERA, APA, & NCME, 1999; Reynolds et al., 1999). Test bias can result from psychometric features of a test, such as the content of test items, representativeness of standardization samples, construct validity, or differential test-criterion relationships, as well as testing atmosphere, approach toward interpretation, and inequitable outcomes and consequences such as special education placement (AERA, APA, & NCME, 1999; Reynolds et al., 1999). Reynolds et al. (1999) provide a comprehensive summary of the past research investigating test bias and conclude that evidence does not support the contention that tests show cultural bias. However, one can reduce bias in the assessment process itself by examining possible bias in the referral of children for assessment and by using multiple methods to assess abilities in more culturally and linguistically appropriate ways. Although test instruments may not have inherent bias, the issue of fairness refers to the use of test results and the appropriateness of outcomes based on test results (Cohen & Swerdlik, 1999). Minority overrepresentation in special education and underrepresentation in programs for gifted and talented education have received attention as an illustrative unfair consequence of assessment practices and eligibility determination. Regulations that require schools to address disproportional representation of minority children in special education and needed procedural review (Reschly, 2000) have been expanded and codified in IDEA (2004) with a provision that the school officials must make the public aware of the efforts being made to reduce the racial imbalance.

The goal of fair and nondiscriminatory assessment practices certainly lies at the heart of IDEA, as well as of professional standards and ethical guidelines for psychologists. Addressing all aspects of competent assessment for individuals from culturally diverse backgrounds or with disabilities falls well beyond the scope of this chapter; however, interested readers are referred to chapters such as Ortiz (2002), Lukomski (2002), Bradley-Johnson & Morgan (2002), Scribner (2002), and the January 2005 issue of the *American Psychologist*, which focuses on genes, race, and psychology. Psychologists will need to seek continuing professional development opportunities to acquire the complex and ever-evolving skills and competencies necessary for effective assessment of individuals with diverse backgrounds.

Functional Relevance

IDEA (1997) introduced an emphasis on assessments that provide information that is functional and relevant to the identification of a student's educational needs. The 2004 amendments to IDEA maintain this emphasis. Evaluators will find such information obtainable from multiple methods of assessment, including review of work samples, direct assessment of academic and behavioral skills, observation, functional analysis, and assessment of the instructional environment. Further, the information must have relevance to the student's involvement and progress in the general curriculum

and development of the IEP. This regulation makes it clear that evaluations should link to the natural environment and to procedures such as functional behavioral assessment and curriculum-based assessment (Reschly, 2000). This emphasis on functionally relevant assessment data will require those working in school settings or with school-age children and adolescents to focus increasingly on a child's skills and difficulties within the context of a given instructional environment and with a focus on educational needs and instructional, as well as behavioral, intervention. Although such a focus may direct assessment strategies away from eligibility determination issues and thereby be regarded as more fair and valid, access to the instructional material and environment assumed by such an approach will be a considerable challenge for psychologists functioning outside the schools as independent evaluators.

CONTROVERSIAL ISSUES RELATED TO SPECIAL EDUCATION ELIGIBILITY

Use of IQ-Achievement Discrepancy in Learning Disability Determination

Learning disabilities (LD) constitute the most frequently identified disabilities under IDEA and also the most controversial in terms of definition and eligibility criteria. Kavale and Forness (2000) discuss the differences and similarities among numerous definitions of LDs, including the most frequently cited definition embodied in IDEA. IDEA defines a specific learning disability as:

> a disorder in one or more of the basic psychological processes involved in understanding or in using language, spoken or written, that may manifest itself in an imperfect ability to listen, think, speak, read, write, spell, or to do mathematical calculations, including conditions such as perceptual disabilities, brain injury, minimal brain dysfunction, dyslexia, and developmental aphasia. The term does not include learning problems that are primarily the result of visual, hearing, or motor disabilities, of mental retardation, of emotional disturbance, or of environmental, cultural, or economic disadvantage. (IDEA, 1997, §300.7)

Like the definition, many regard the diagnostic criteria used in the identification of LD as problematic and potentially harmful to some children (Lyon et al., 2001). Under IDEA (1997) regulations, a child can qualify as having an LD if he or she "does not achieve commensurate with his or her age and ability levels in one or more of the above areas, if provided with appropriate learning experiences; and has a severe discrepancy between achievement and intellectual ability in one or more of the following areas: oral expression, listening comprehension, written expression, basic reading skill, reading comprehension, mathematics calculation, and mathematics reasoning" (§300.541). The discrepancy provision, originally added in 1975, provides specific criteria for eligibility determination.

In practice, the presence of a discrepancy is addressed through the use of norm-referenced instruments of intelligence and academic achievement and has become associated with the concept of "expected underachievement" (Lyon et al., 2001). Although multiple methods for calculating ability-achievement discrepanies exist, the two most commonly used approaches involve simple difference and predicted-achievement methods (Flanagan, Andrews, & Genshaft, 1997). Some psychologists have expressed concern regarding the use of various discrepancy methods due to psychometric and statistical issues (Reynolds, 1984) and encourage practitioners to use procedures based on conormed instruments that consider regression toward the mean and the meaningfulness of a statistical discrepancy (Flanagan et al., 1997). Inconsistency across school districts can complicate the use of the discrepancy criterion. For example, a child determined eligible in one state may not qualify in another (Reschley, 2000). Further, the existence or absence of an ability-achievement discrepancy should not stand as the sole criterion in the identification of a learning disability (IDEA, 1997, §300.532; Dumont, Willis, & McBride, 2001; Kavale & Forness, 2000) but serve as one component in the decision-making process.

The ability-achievement discrepancy criterion also creates concern regarding conceptual implications for the field of learning disabilities, especially reading disabilities (RD). By definition, learning disabilities constitute a heterogeneous class of disabilities; however, the preponderance of the literature regarding the appropriateness of the discrepancy criterion becomes central to RD. Lyon et al. (2001) address the conceptual issues complicated by the utililization of IQ-achievement discrepancy for identifying children with LD, especially RD. Articulated concerns include: (a) that IQ is often viewed as a predictor of one's potential, or ability to learn, as opposed to a current measure of cognitive functioning; (b) that requiring children to demonstrate a discrepancy often results in delayed identification and failure following a significant period of academic struggling; and (c) that often an inequitable provision of services results, based on the absence or presence of a discrepancy. Additionally, disagreement continues regarding whether an ability-achievement discrepancy significantly contributes to the differentiation between low-achieving readers who have a discrepancy and low-achieving readers who do not have a discrepancy (Fuchs, Fuchs, Mathes, & Lipsey, 2000; Lyon et al., 2001) and whether the presence of a discrepancy reflects intrinsic processing differences between such groups (Francis, Shaywitz, Stuebing, Shaywitz, & Fletcher, 1996).

Proposed modifications to the use of an ability-achievement discrepancy range from maintaining the discrepancy as one criterion in a larger framework (Kavale, 2001) to eliminating the measurement of intelligence in favor of direct assessment of academic skills (Fletcher et al., 1998). Lyon and others support providing early reading interventions as a component of regular education in an effort to prevent reading failure that may otherwise occur for some children, thus reducing the number of children at risk and subsequently in need of remediation. The provision of appropriate instruction and early intervention allows for the identification of children who do not respond to well-implemented, validated interventions and instead need more intensive services and programs. Indeed, the concept of "responsiveness to intervention" has received attention as a potential identifying characteristic of children with learning disabilities (Gresham, 2001). In addition, a dual-discrepancy identification model that involves both academic performance and learning rate below the level of classroom peers has earned empirical support (Fuchs, Fuchs, & Speech, 2002).

With passage of the 2004 amendment to IDEA, Congress responded to the concerns raised about the use of discrepancy formulas in identification of learning disabilities when it authorized school districts to use nondiscrepancy approaches. Specifically, the new law states that in determining the presence of a learning disability, a local education agency may use the response-to-intervention approach as part of the process (IDEA, 2004, §614(a), 2 & 3). Although the language is permissive, the intent of Congress is clear from the reports of both House and Senate committtees that considered IDEA (2004). Regulations being drafted are likely to articulate much more emphatically the preference for evidence of a processing deficit and response to instructional interventions over simple differences in scores on standardized tests.

Zero-Tolerance Policies and Exclusion of Students With Disabilities From School

School administrators have historically used suspension and expulsion, or removal of the student from school, as a frequent disciplinary procedure to deal with unruly behavior. However, in a 1988 landmark case called *Honig v. Doe*, the U.S. Supreme Court ruled that an emotionally disturbed student could not suffer removal from school for more than 10 consecutive days, even for dangerous behavior, because such removal constituted a change in his or her educational placement. This decision led to great concern among school officials that the inability to suspend or expel violent or dangerous students, even those determined to have an emotional disability, prevented them from trying to keep schools safe and secure places for all students (Osbourne, 1998). With the recent eruption of high-profile episodes of school violence such as the one at Columbine High School in Colorado, school boards across the country have implemented so-called zero tolerance policies, whereby a student who brings a weapon to school or makes a credible threat of violence faces automatic suspension or other removal from school. The *Honig v. Doe* decision has prompted challenges to these zero-tolerance policies in cases in which the student is identified as having a disability.

The 1997 amendments to IDEA addressed this concern by creating a set of rules and procedures that school districts must follow in determining whether or not the student's behavior constitutes a manifestation of his or her disability. If a school district can conclude that the student's behavior does not result from or or stands unrelated to his or her disability, then the district has the freedom to use its normal procedures for discipline or removal from school. If, however, the student's behavior has a relationship to the disability, then the student may not be suspended or expelled from the school for more than 10 days except under special circumstances that involve carrying a weapon to school, inflicting serious bodily harm, or drug use (Zirkel, 1999). Even under these special circumstances, the school district may remove the student for a maximum of 45 days, during which time the system must provide an interim alternative educational setting (IAES) and develop strategies for modifying and implementing the student's educational service plan (Telzrow & Naidu, 2000).

IDEA (1997) introduced the notion of a manifestation determination to address the problem of disciplining students with disabilities. The 2004 amendments maintain this requirement, with added leeway for schools to remove a student temporarily (up to 45 school days) when the student's behavior involves weapons, bodily harm, or drug use. A manifestation determination evaluation is a legally mandated individualized review of the causal relationship between a student's inappropriate, violent, or dangerous behavior and his or her disability or suspected disability (see Kubrick, Bard, & Perry, 2000). Before considering removing a student from school, the school system has responsibility for conducting the manifestation determination according to proper procedures and concluding that the critical behavioral incident that prompted the review does not relate to the student's disability. A manifestation determination must include a review of the adequacy and appropriateness of the student's current placement, consideration of whether a change in placement would likely address the student's misbehavior, and also a determination of whether a relationship exists between the student's misbehavior and the disability.

The manifestation determination is formally conducted similarly to the school-based decision-making process used to decide eligibility for special education (Kubrick, Bard, & Perry, 2000). The student's teachers (including special education), administrators, and an assessment specialist capable of interpreting assessment data must participate, and their parents must be invited; attempts to involve the parents must be documented if the parents choose not to attend. Of key relevance to psychologists who work with emotionally impaired students outside the schools is the provision in the law for parents to supply evaluative data from outside the schools (e.g., private psychological evaluations). Parents have a right to introduce information from professionals who work outside the school that may influence the conclusions from the manifestation determination or that may provide a basis for the parents to appeal an adverse decision by the school system (Kubrick, Bard, & Perry, 2000). Importantly, IDEA extends the rights of students with disabilities to those who have not yet formally acquired classification as disabled but who seem likely to have disabilities (Zirkel, 1999). Thus any student of concern to teachers or school administrators for inappropriate behavior or who has come to the attention of school officials (i.e., the school has notice of a suspected disability) qualifies as entitled to an expedited evaluation to determine eligibility under IDEA.

Parents of students with emotional and behavioral disorders who have received services from outside professionals will likely seek the involvement of these professionals in any school district action to conduct a manifestation determination. Therefore, psychologists who work with school-age children and adolescents with emotional and behavioral disorders should become familiar with the requirements and procedures outlined in IDEA for the proper handling of discipline and school removal decisions for such students.

CONCLUSIONS

Federal special education law recognizes and welcomes the participation of independent evaluators in the conduct of assessments for determination of special education eligibility. As part of the procedures empowering parents to be active and essential participants in the decision-making process that surrounds the appropriate educational placement and programming of their child, the IDEA requires schools to accept and consider (and sometimes even pay for) assessments conducted by qualified person-

nel selected by the parents and independent of the school system. Psychologists wishing to serve in such a capacity may be unfamiliar with the specific legal requirements and special ethical considerations related to conducting such evaluations. This chapter has provided a brief introduction to the major laws and ethical obligations that influence the proper conduct of such assessments. The reader is encouraged to seek additional guidance and knowledge of the unique challenges encountered when conducting psychological assessments as part of special education deliberations.

References

American Educational Research Association, American Psychological Association, & National Council on Measurement in Education. (1999). *Standards for educational and psychological testing.* Washington, DC: Author.

American Psychological Association. (1993). Record-keeping guidelines. *American Psychologist, 48*(9), 984–986.

American Psychological Association. (2000). *Diagnostic and statistical manual of mental disorders* (4th ed., text rev.). Washington, DC: Author.

American Psychological Association. (2002). *Ethical principles of psychologists and code of conduct.* Washington, DC: Author.

Americans with Disabilities Education Act of 1990 (ADA), Pub L. No. 101-336, 42 U.S.C. Sec. 12101.

Bradley-Johnson, S., & Morgan, S. K. (2002). *Best practices in planning effective instruction for students who are visually impaired or blind.* In A. Thomas & J. Grimes (Eds.), *Best practices in school psychology: IV* (Vol. 2, pp. 1405–1418). Bethesda, MD: National Association of School Psychologists.

Cohen, R. J., & Swerdlik, M. E. (1999). *Psychological testing and assessment: An introduction to tests and measurement.* Mountain View, CA: Mayfield.

Dumont, R., Willis, J., & McBride, G. (2001). Yes, Virginia, there is a severe discrepancy clause, but is it too much ado about something? *School Psychologist, 55*(1), 1–15.

Education of All Handicapped Children Act of 1975, Pub. L. No. 994-142, renamed the Individuals With Disabilities Education Act in 1990, 20 U.S.C., Chapter 33.

Family Educational Rights and Privacy Act of 1974, part of Pub. L. 93-380, commonly called the

FERPA or the Buckley Amendment, 20 U.S.C. Sec. 1232g. Regulations appear at 34 C.F.R. Sec. Part 99.

Fay v. South Colonie Central School District, 802 F. 2d. 21 (2nd Cir. 1986).

Flanagan, D. P., Andrews, T. J., & Genshaft, J. L. (1997). The functional utility of intelligence tests with special education populations. In D. Flanagan, J. Genshaft, & P. Harrison (Eds.), *Contemporary intellectual assessment: Theories, tests, and issues* (pp. 457–483). New York: Guilford.

Fletcher, J. M., Francis, D. J., Shaywitz, S. E., Lyon, G. R., Foorman, B. R., Stuebing, K. K., & Shaywitz, B. A. (1998). Intelligent testing and the discrepancy model for children with learning disabilities. *Learning Disabilities Research and Practice, 13,* 186–203.

Francis, D. J., Shaywitz, S. E., Stuebing, K. K., Shaywitz, B. A., & Fletcher, J. M. (1996). Developmental lag versus deficit models of reading disability: A longitudinal, individual growth curves analysis. *Journal of Educational Psychology, 88,* 3–17.

Fuchs, D., Fuchs, L. S., Mathes, P. G., & Lipsey, M. W. (2000). Reading differences between low-achieving students with and without learning disabilities: A meta-analysis. In R. Gersten, E. P. Schiller, & S. Vaughn (Eds.), *Contemporary special education research* (pp. 81–104). Mahwah, NJ: Lawrence Erlbaum.

Fuchs, L. S., Fuchs, D., & Speech, D. L. (2002). Treatment validity as a unifying construct for identifying learning disabilities. *Learning Disabilities Quarterly, 25*(1), 33–45.

Gresham, F. (2001, April). *Responsiveness to intervention: An alternative approach to the identification of learning disabilities.* Paper presented at the Learning Disabilities Summit: Building a Foundation for the Future, Washington, DC.

Honig v. Doe, 484 U.S., 98 L. Ed. 2nd 686, 108 S.Ct. 592.

Individuals with Disabilities Education Act of 1990, Pub. L. 101-476, 20 U.S.C. Chapter 33.

Individuals with Disabilities Education Act Amendments of 1997, Pub. L. No. 105-17, 34 C.F.R §300, 20 U.S.C. 1400 et seq.

Individuals with Disabilities Education Act Amendments of 2004, Pub. L. No. 108-446.

Jacob, S., & Hartshorne, T. S. (2003). *Ethics and law for school psychologists* (4th ed.). New York: John Wiley.

Kavale, K. A. (2001, April). *Discrepancy models in the identification of learning disability.* Paper presented at the Learning Disabilities Summit: Building a Foundation for the Future, Washington, DC.

Kavale, K. A., & Forness, S. R. (2000). What definitions of learning disability say and don't say: A critical analysis. *Journal of Learning Disabilities, 33*(3), 239–256.

Kubrick, R .J., Bard, E. M., & Perry, J. D. (2000). Manifestation determinations: Discipline guidelines for children with disabilities. In C. F. Telzrow & M. Tankersley (Eds.), *IDEA Amendments of 1997: Practice guidelines for school-based teams* (pp. 65–104). Bethesda, MD: National Association of School Psychologists.

Lukomski, J. A. (2002). *Best practices in program planning for children who are deaf and hard-of-hearing.* In A. Thomas & J. Grimes (Eds.). *Best practices in school psychology: IV* (Vol. 2, pp. 1393–1404). Bethesda, MD: National Association of School Psychologists.

Lyon, G. R., Fletcher, J. M., Shaywitz, S. E., Shaywitz, B. A., Torgesen, J. K., Wood, F. B., et al. (2001). Rethinking learning disabilities. In C. E. Finn, Jr., R. J. Rotherham, & C. R. Hokanson, Jr. (Eds.), *Rethinking special education for a new century* (pp. 259–287). Washington, DC: Thomas B. Fordham Foundation and Progressive Policy Institute.

Martin, R. (1979). *Continuing challenges in special education law.* Urbana, IL: Carle Media.

Martin, R. (1992). *Continuing challenges in special education law* (rev. ed.). Urbana, IL: Carle Media.

Merrell, K. W. (1999). *Behavioral, social and emotional assessment of children and adolescents.* Mahwah, NJ: Lawrence Erlbaum.

Mills v. Board of Education of District of Columbia, 348 F. Supp. 866 (1972); contempt proceedings, 551 Educ. of the Handicapped, L. Rep. 643 (D.D.C. 1980).

Ortiz, S. O. (2002). Best practices in nondiscriminatory assessment. In A. Thomas & J. Grimes (Eds.), *Best practices in school psychology: IV* (Vol. 2, pp. 1321–1336). Bethesda, MD: National Association of School Psychologists.

Osbourne, A. G. (1998). Governing discipline under 1997 IDEA. *School Business Affairs, 64*(8), 21–24.

Pennsylvania Association for Retarded Citizens (PARC) v. Commonwealth of Pennsylvania, 334 F. Supp. 1257 (D.C.E.D. Pa. 1971), 334 F. Supp. 279 (D.C.E.D. Pa. 1972).

Rehabilitation Act of 1973, Pub. L. No. 93-112, 29 U.S.C. Sec. 794. Regulations implementing

Section 504 appear at 34 C.F.R. Part 104 (1996).

Reschly, D. J. (2000). Assessment and eligibility determination in the Individuals with Disabilities Education Act of 1997. In C. F. Telzrow & M. Tankersley (Eds.), *IDEA Amendments of 1997: Practice guidelines for school-based teams* (pp. 65–104). Bethesda, MD: National Association of School Psychologists.

Reschly, D. J., & Bersoff, D. N. (1999). Law and school psychology. In C. R. Reynolds & T. B. Gutkin (Eds.), *Handbook of school psychology* (3rd ed., pp. 1077–1112). New York: John Wiley.

Reschly, D. J., & Grimes, J. P. (2002). Best practices in intellectual assessment. In A. Thomas & J. Grimes (Eds.), *Best practices in school psychology: IV* (Vol. 2, pp. 1337–1350). Bethesda, MD: National Association of School Psychologists.

Reynolds, C. R. (1984). Critical measurement issues in learning disabilities. *Journal of Special Education, 18*, 451–476.

Reynolds, C. R., Lowe, P. A., & Saenz, A. L. (1999). The problem of bias in psychological assessment. In C. R. Reynolds & T. B. Gutkin (Eds.), *Handbook of school psychology* (3rd ed., pp. 549–595). New York: John Wiley.

Russell Sage Foundation. (1970). *Guidelines for the collection, maintenance, and dissemination of pupil records.* Hartford, CT: Connecticut Printers.

Salvia, J., & Ysseldyke, J. E. (1995). *Assessment* (6th ed.). Boston: Houghton Mifflin.

San Antonio Independent School District v. Rodriguez, 411 U.S. 1, 93 S.Ct. 1278 (1973).

Scribner, A. P. (2002). *Best practices and intervention practices with second language learners.* In

A. Thomas & J. Grimes (Eds.), *Best practices in school psychology: IV* (Vol. 2, pp. 1485–1500). Bethesda, MD: National Association of School Psychologists.

Shinn, M. R. (2002). Best practices in using curriculum based assessment in problem solving. In A. Thomas & J. Grimes (Eds.), *Best practices in school psychology: IV* (pp. 671–697). Bethesda, MD: National Association of School Psychologists.

Telzrow, C. F., & Naidu, K. (2000). Interim alternative educational settings: Guidelines for prevention and intervention. In C. F. Telzrow & M. Tankersley (Eds.), *IDEA Amendments of 1997: Practice guidelines for school-based teams* (pp. 65–104). Bethesda, MD: National Association of School Psychologists.

Thomas, A., & Grimes, J. (2002). *Best practices in school psychology: IV.* Bethesda, MD: National Association of School Psychologists.

Turner, S., DeMers, S., Fox, H., & Read, G. (2001). APA's guidelines for test user qualifications. *American Psychologist, 56*(12), 1009–1113.

Yell, M. J., Drasgow, E., & Ford, L. (2000). The Individuals with Disabilities Education Act of 1997: Implications for school-based teams. In C. F. Telzrow & M. Tankersley (Eds.), *IDEA Amendments of 1997: Practice guidelines for school-based teams* (pp. 65–104). Bethesda, MD: National Association of School Psychologists.

Zirkel, P. A. (1999). The IDEA's suspension/expulsion requirements: A practical picture. *West's Education Law Reporter, 134*, 19–23.

Zirkel, P. A., & Kincaid, J. M. (1993). *Section 504, the ADA and the schools* [pamphlet]. Horsham, PA: LRP.

15

Examining Children in Personal Injury Claims

Michael A. Goldberg

Two significant changes in the legal system have paved the way for the greatly increased role of psychologists in personal injury lawsuits. First, a recent significant trend in American laws has seen shifts from allowing claims only for physical injury to allowing claims for recovery of damages for emotional injury associated with physical injury and, most recently, to allowing claims for emotional injury independent of physical injury. Second, the Federal Rules of Civil Procedure (2003), which form the basic legal models for personal injury claims in most states, now allow mental "examinations" explicitly by psychologists. Although the demand for psychologists to conduct personal injury evaluations has grown tremendously, training and scholarship in the area remain limited for psychologists. The emphasis in forensic psychological training and scholarship continues to focus chiefly on the areas of criminal and family law.

This chapter seeks to provide a starting point for psychologists who are contemplating conducting evaluations of children whose guardians are seeking compensation for injuries through the courts. This chapter focuses on providing a com-

prehensive overview of the relevant legal issues and highlighting several of the important practice issues commonly faced when psychologists complete evaluations in personal injury cases. Reading this chapter will not replace the need for thorough training (e.g., workshops offered by the American Academy of Forensic Psychology and postdoctoral fellowships), supervised practice, and legal/collegial consultation that should underlie all forensic examiners' foundation for practice.

LEGAL ISSUES IN EVALUATING PERSONAL INJURY CLAIMS

Torts is the area of law under which a victim seeks monetary compensation for legally defined civil "wrongs" imposed on him or her. A "tort" constitutes a wrongful or illegal act committed by one person against another. Negligence forms the primary type of tort under which a child may seek compensation in a personal injury case. In all tort cases, the plaintiff (i.e., the allegedly injured child) bears the burden of proving the legally mandated elements.

Many psychologists avoid taking on personal injury cases because they mistakenly believe that they might have to draw conclusions to a degree of certainty that their data will not necessarily be able to support as valid. However, an understanding of the legal standards enables psychologists to provide evaluations in personal injury cases without compromising ethical obligations. As psychologists, our understanding of the scientific method and issues of reliability and validity uniquely equip us to provide evaluations in personal injury cases that both meet the needs of the courts and comport fully with our ethical standards. Psychologists can accomplish this by approaching personal injury evaluations similarly to research studies: by defining the hypotheses, deciding on the data necessary to support those hypotheses, collecting and analyzing the data, ruling out alternative hypotheses, and making valid conclusions supported by the data, with an analysis of the validity.

We must recognize that the level of certainty for psychologists' conclusions that is required by courts in such cases lies at a legally defined level that is lower than that required by our dissertation committees and journal editors. The legal concept of "standard of proof" corresponds to our research probability of error. Our legal system sets the degree of likelihood necessary to ensure the correctness of the conclusion. The standard of proof that the plaintiff must meet in most tort matters lies at the "preponderance of the evidence" level. Under this standard, the majority (i.e., at least 51%) of the evidence must support the necessary conclusion, a considerably lower threshold than the "beyond a reasonable doubt" standard typical in criminal law and the $p < .05$ confidence interval often necessary to have one's research published. For example, a child mauled by a neighbor's dog must prove that his or her psychological damage (e.g., persistent fears, avoidance of situations and relationships involving the potential to encounter a dog, etc.) more likely than not resulted from, or became exacerbated by, the attack and is not likely attributable to another factor.

Legal Criteria

In order to define the relevant hypotheses and to design appropriate data collection procedures for the evaluation, the clinician must have a good understanding of the legal criteria necessary to prove a personal injury case. Personal injury cases fall conceptually into two phases, liability and compensation. To prevail, a plaintiff must first prove that the defendant (e.g., the dog owner) had legal liability. Once the plaintiff has proven the presence of all legal elements of liability by a preponderance of the evidence, the compensation phase of the case proceeds. The psychologist must have a good understanding of the legal elements of both phases, while noting with caution that these criteria may lack precise definition. It is also important for the evaluator to understand and maintain clear and proper role definition throughout his or her involvement in the case.

Liability Phase

Most torts involve five legal requirements for a personal injury claim to prove liability. These requirements stand in sharp contrast to other types of forensic mental health cases, such as child custody cases, in which the "best interest of the child(ren)" typically constitutes the sole legal criteria. These five requirements include (1) legal duty, (2) breach or dereliction of that duty, (3) proximate cause, (4) actual damage, and (5) compensability. If the plaintiff fails to prove any one element, his or her claim fails. Discussion of the five elements follows.

Legal Duty

Legal duty refers to an obligation that requires one person to conform to a particular standard with respect to another person. Duties may arise explicitly under law or from inference on the part of judges and juries who apply a general understanding of what they believe is "how reasonable people would conduct themselves." Town ordinances requiring dogs to be leashed constitute an example of a legally explicit duty that most reasonable people have to prevent their dogs from trespassing on their neighbor's property, where a dog could cause harm to a child. Applying the usual "reasonably prudent person" standard, a jury may infer that a dog owner whose dog had a history of attacking others had a duty to protect a neighbor child from an attack by his or her dog, even if the attack occurred on the dog owner's property. Psychologists may find that they are asked to address the issue of duty in some legal applications, for example, malpractice cases involving other psychologists; however, they rarely have to address this issue in most personal injury cases.

Breach or Dereliction of Duty

Having determined that a defendant owed the plaintiff a legal duty, the plaintiff must prove that the defendant failed to meet that duty by act or omission. A neighbor who allows his dog to run free in the neighborhood may have breached his duty by this act. Likewise, a child may claim dereliction of duty if he or she was psychologically damaged as the result of seeing his or her sibling drown in their neighbor's pool if the neighbor failed (i.e., omission) to fence in the pool, assuming that city ordinances mandate such barriers or that a typically "reasonably prudent" person would take such steps.

Whether based on an alleged act or on an omission, tort claims may also proceed for "negligent" or "intentional" infliction of emotional distress. One often thinks of negligence as a careless error or omission (e.g., failing to fence a pool) made without intention or by accident. Intentional infliction of emotional distress differs from psychologists' typical view of the concept of intent. An act planned with the desired goal of causing harm (e.g., ordering a dog to attack) clearly qualifies as "intentional." However, an act may also qualify as "intentional" if the defendant knew, or should have known, that reasonably foreseeable harm could occur. The "reasonable person" standard typically applies when determining whether the defendant should have known about the risk of harm. If the jury determines that a "reasonable person" should have known that harm could likely occur, the defendant has violated the duty. However, the court often considers how the specific defendant is constituted when applying the "reasonable person" standard. Thus psychologists may find themselves asked to evaluate the defendant's ability to foresee harm, given his or her emotional and cognitive functioning at the time of the incident in question.

When a plaintiff makes a claim under a tort of intentional infliction of emotional distress, he or she must typically also prove that the breach or dereliction of duty reached an "extreme" or "outrageous" level. The plaintiff must prove that the act violated, greatly offended, and went beyond all possible bounds of the community's sense of decency. This determination rarely comes to psychological evaluators for a response.

Proximate Cause

The issue of causation often comes to psychological evaluators for expert opinions. As others have noted (e.g., Melton, Petrila, Poythress, & Slobogin, 1987), a "clash" often seems evident between the definitions of causation held in tort law and by the behavioral sciences. Although the two perspectives clearly differ, psychologists can cope effectively with this "clash" by understanding the legal concept of causation, by applying the scientific approach to conducting the examinations, and by making conclusions that the data suggest as more likely accurate than not.

In tort law the "proximate cause" involves determining a cause and linking that cause as "proximate" to the injury. Determining causation often involves the "but for" test. That requires determining that "but for" the defendant's conduct, the damage would not have happened. The next determination involves whether the defendant's conduct stood "proximate" to the injury. The conduct must occur near to the injury and be seen as "the straw that broke the camel's back." Thus a pet owner's negligence may not rise into consideration as the proximate cause of injuries related to a dog bite if two teenagers pushed a child into a fenced-in area in which the dog was contained. In such a case, "but for" the actions of the teenagers the child would not have been bitten. Thus the court may determine that having a vicious dog securely fenced in on one's property does not constitute "proximate" cause in such a case.

Actual Damage

If a neighbor allows his pit bulldog to roam the neighborhood, and if that dog attacks a child but the child sustains no injury beyond initial fright, that neighbor has no legal liability in a personal injury case. The law does not allow compensation for negligent behavior unless someone has truly suffered an injury. According to the law, if no harm occurred, then no foul exists.

The determination of "actual damage," along with proximate cause, forms the part of the case that psychologists most often become involved in assessing. The law requires that "real and significant" damage exist. Thus the psychologist must determine whether psychological injury exists and describe the severity of the damage.

The law generally applies the "egg shell plaintiff" standard, which implies that some plaintiffs have particular vulnerability to the effects of certain stresses that might prove insignificant for others. In addition, the law requires consideration of the plaintiff's damages relative to his or her functioning before the negligence. Thus a defendant has liability for the injury, even if he or she is unaware of the plaintiff's preexisting special vulnerability. The court, with the assistance of the psychological examiner, attempts to determine the degree of injury relative to the plaintiff's condition at the time of the injury. For example, a child diagnosed with posttraumatic stress disorder and under treatment for symptoms related to a mauling by a dog would still warrant compensation if attacked by a second dog, as long as the court believes that the child's functioning had, more likely than not, deteriorated subsequent to the second attack. The mere fact that the child previously had difficulty sleeping, avoided dogs, and reported intrusive flashbacks before the second incident does not preclude damages for additional symptoms or for an increase in the frequency and severity of those symptoms subsequent to the second attack. The psychologist's role in such a case involves describing the child's preincident functioning and how it changed relative to the incident in question.

Compensability

The fifth criteria required to prove liability involves a determination that the complaint constitutes a type that the law views as compensable. Four models generally describe how the states determine compensability of a psychological injury. Although psychologists rarely become involved in directly determining compensability, their examinations may prove useful indirectly in making that determination. For example, economic experts are often retained to examine the psychologist's expert report and give an opinion about compensability. In this context, understanding the particular model in play in the specific jurisdiction when completing a psychological examination in a personal injury case becomes very important. The United States Court of Appeals, in the case of *Plaisance vs. Texaco, Inc., et al.* (1992), neatly described the four models, in decreasing order of difficulty, for a plaintiff to establish as:

Physical injury or impact rule: allows compensation for emotional injury as long as some physical contact occurred. In a jurisdiction employing this rule, a child traumatized by a dog that ferociously chased but never caught him or her would not qualify for compensation, regardless of the severity of psychological distress.

Zone of danger rule: allows compensation for emotional injuries without physical contact that result "from witnessing peril or harm to another if the plaintiff is also threatened with physical harm as a consequence of the defendant's negligence." A child watching her brother mauled by the neighbor's dog would not qualify for compensation under this rule if she had watched from a window inside her home. However, if the dog had chased both her and her brother and caught and mauled the brother while she watched from an arm's length, she would likely qualify for compensation if witnessing this event resulted in severe psychological injury.

Bystander proximity rule: allows compensation even if the plaintiff did not stand in the zone of danger so long as the plaintiff: (a) stood physically near the incident that caused harm; (b) personally observed the incident; and (c) has a close relationship to the victim. Under this rule, a child observing her brother under attack by the dog on their front lawn may qualify for compensation for her psychological injury even if she observed the incident from a window inside the home. The issue of how closely related the plaintiff is to the victim is not usually very explicit in the law. It is possible that psychologists may be asked to provide information about the relationship between the plaintiff and the victim. For example, it may be ambiguous whether a nonadopted stepchild is considered "close" to his or her stepparent, whom he or she may have observed becoming injured. In such cases a solid understanding of research on attachment is often necessary.

Full recovery rule: allows for compensation when "a reasonable person, normally constituted, would not be able to cope adequately with the mental distress occasioned by the circumstances." If this rule comes into play, the plaintiff can recover compensation if the jury determines that the typical person would have experienced psychological injury as a result of the negligence. Once again, the psychologist may be asked to assist the court in understanding normative psychological functioning and how the plaintiff's response seems similar or different.

Compensation Phase

Once a determination that a defendant has liability occurs, having met all five elements of liability, the damages phase of the case proceeds to determine the amount of compensation due the plaintiff. The law permits compensation for several types of damages. Compensatory damages address the actual losses suffered by the plaintiff. For example, the plaintiff may recover compensation for the actual pain and suffering caused by the injury. Psychologists, however, do not usually have the training to translate emotional suffering into economic terms. The role of the psychologist involves simply describing the pain and suffering so that those charged with determining the amount of compensation (e.g., other experts or the jury) can best do their job.

Types of Damages

Two specific types of general compensatory damages include loss of consortium and hedonic damages. Loss of consortium refers to compensation for losing the love and companionship of a close relative. Hedonic damages consist of compensation for one's decreased enjoyment in life. With regard to the latter type, the task of the psychologist involves simply describing for the court how the injury, more likely than not, will affect the individual's ability to enjoy life.

Juries may also award special compensatory damages. This involves compensation for actual damage to the plaintiff, but these damages are not necessarily the direct result of the injury. These may include the costs of medical or psychological treatment, loss of income to the family, property damage, and so forth. Juries can also award future damages, such as those related to diminished working capacity.

Lastly, a jury may also award punitive or exemplary damages. These types of damages constitute compensation to the plaintiff in excess of the actual damage. Such damages enable punishment of the defendant for outrageous conduct and aim to deter similar future conduct.

Defensive Responses to Claims for Damages

Once the plaintiff bears the burden of proving liability and makes his or her case for damages, the defendant has a chance to argue that the amount of compensation should be limited by particular types of mitigating circumstances. Three types of defensive responses include contributory negligence, last clear chance, and failure to mitigate.

Contributory negligence involves the argument that although the defendant has some liability, the negligence of the plaintiff also contributed to the injury. For example, a child who trespasses on a neighbor's property and thereby incurs an attack by a vicious dog restrained on the property may have contributed to the injury. Thus, although the jury may find the dog owner liable for failing to take reasonable measures to prevent the trespass or attack of the animal he knew to be dangerous, the compensation may decrease if the jury believes the child's negligence contributed to the injury.

A defendant may also argue that the compensation should decrease because the plaintiff failed to take advantage of an opportunity to avoid injury. In this case the jury must determine that a reasonable person, constituted in a manner similar to the plaintiff, would likely have had and have taken the opportunity to avoid the injury. Attorneys commonly refer to this situation as the *last clear chance* argument.

Failure to mitigate the results of the injury is the third common defensive response to claims for damage. Once injury has occurred, the plaintiff has a legal obligation to attempt to ameliorate the harm. For example, the plaintiff must seek and participate in appropriate treatment. A jury may decrease the compensation for a dog-bite victim if the defendant effectively argues that the child had access to treatment with a strong likelihood of benefit but the plaintiff failed or refused to participate. Thus knowledge of the empirical research on treatment effectiveness and its applicability to a particular case becomes particularly important in such cases.

ADMISSIBILITY OF EXPERT OPINIONS

Even as changes in the laws allowing claims for emotional injury and changes in the Federal Rules of Civil Procedure have created a greater demand for psychologists to conduct evaluations in personal injury cases, recent Supreme Court decisions have changed the requirements for admissibility of expert testimony. It is critical that psychologists understand these standards, conduct their evaluations with them in mind, and are prepared to respond to scrutiny in their context.

From 1923 to 1993 the Frye standard (*Frye v. United States*, 1923) required basing scientific expert testimony on "generally accepted" practice in the relevant "field." No requirement for scientific soundness of a theory or assessment method used by an expert witness existed. This standard allowed psychologists and other mental health "experts" to testify regarding many controversial theories and methods. In 1993 the Supreme Court ruled in *Daubert v. Merrell Dow Pharmaceuticals, Inc.*, limiting admissible scientific expert testimony only to relevant and reliable content. This decision also held that the trial judge must ensure that the expert's testimony rests on a reliable foundation and has relevance for the question at hand. To assist the judges in this gatekeeping role, the Supreme Court provided six specific questions that are useful in determining the reliability of a scientific theory or technique:

1. Is the proposed therapy on which the testimony is based testable (falsifiable)?
2. Has the proposed theory been tested using valid and reliable procedures and with positive results?
3. Has the theory been subjected to peer review and publication?
4. What is the known or potential error rate of the scientific theory or technique?
5. What standards controlling the technique's operation maximize its validity?

6. Has the theory been generally accepted as valid in the relevant scientific community?

The responsibility of the trial judge to exclude unreliable testimony became further clarified in the subsequent Supreme Court decision in *General Electric Co. v. Joiner* (1997). The Joiner case also added a seventh factor necessary for admissibility of expert testimony: The trial judge was now also required to ensure that the expert's conclusions reasonably follow from the theory to the case. Thus it is not sufficient that the theory and methodology meet the minimal scientific standards set out in *Daubert*; the conclusions must also clearly link to the theory or methods.

In *Kumho Tire Co., Ltd., et al. v. Carmichael et al.* (1999), the Supreme Court reversed an Appeals Court decision that held that *Daubert* factors did not apply to the expert's testimony when the expert claimed skill or experience as the basis for his or her expertise rather than a scientific basis. The *Kumho* case held that the *Daubert* criteria apply to all experts. Thus, to qualify as admissible, all expert testimony must satisfy the seven standards put forth in both *Daubert* and *Joiner*. All psychologists should prepare to demonstrate the reliability of their methods and procedures and that their conclusions follow from acceptable scientific theories.

PRACTICE ISSUES

A comprehensive understanding of the practical and ethical issues involved in conducting evaluations of children in personal injury cases is impossible within the bounds of a single chapter. Other chapters in this book address many issues in the forensic evaluation of children directly related to personal injury examinations. Readers should have an exceptionally strong understanding of the "Specialty Guidelines for Forensic Psychologists" (Committee on Ethical Issues for Forensic Psychologists, 1991) and use them, along with the current *Ethical Principles of Psychologists and Code of Conduct* (American Psychological Association, 2002), as a constant guide for decision making. The remaining portion of this chapter attempts to provide a brief overview of several of the issues most relevant to conducting examinations of children in personal injury cases, including role conflicts, conducting the examination (i.e., defining the client, determining the assessment questions, collecting data), and the proper use of traditional psychiatric diagnoses in forensic personal injury evaluations of children.

Role Conflicts

Personal injury cases can become a fertile breeding ground for potential violations of the ethical principles and/or the forensic guidelines with respect to potential conflicts of interest inherent in multiple-role relationships. By virtue of the fact that claimants are seeking compensation for injuries, personal injury plaintiffs are more likely than criminal defendants and subjects of custody evaluations to be seeking treatment. Lawyers and their clients will often pressure psychologists to combine the roles of clinician and forensic examiner. Lawyers typically want their clients to seek treatment. Failure to seek treatment may be perceived as a lack of injury and as a failure of the obligation to ameliorate the harm that can be used as a defensive maneuver to minimize the amount of damages. However, as others have noted (e.g., Mart, 1997), lawyers commonly attempt to use therapists' opinions in lieu of a comprehensive and unbiased "expert" forensic evaluation. Motivation for these "stealth" evaluations may include lawyers' attempts to avoid the costs of a true expert evaluation for which they may have financial responsibility if they fail to win their case. In this context they may attempt to use the treating clinician as a legal expert to give opinion about cause, harm, prognosis, and so forth. Likewise, a psychological examiner who has formed a relationship with the plaintiff, has become familiar with the details of the case, and has developed an understanding of the pain and suffering of the individual may be asked to provide treatment during the examination. Understanding and avoiding the inherent conflicts in both of these situations demands careful attention. Although the legal system may permit these mixings of roles, they often clearly violate forensic guidelines, ethical standards, and licensing regulations.

Greenberg and Shuman (1997) provide one of the most comprehensive analyses of the conflict between these roles and the reasons for avoiding them. The strongest argument for avoiding these two roles together involves the foreseeable risk of alienating the patient by providing thorough, fair, and unbiased opinion, thus jeopardizing the psychotherapeutic alliance and the continuation of treatment. The role of the forensic examiner involves conducting a thorough and unbiased evaluation that assists the court in answering certain questions dictated by the laws. The role of a psychotherapist involves forming and maintaining a relationship with the explicit purpose of alleviating the pain and suffering of the patient. A clinician cannot give a fair and unbiased opinion without the risk of alienating his or her patient by providing information potentially detrimental to the patient's legal claim for compensation. As expert witnesses, in an adversarial forum, psychologists will find themselves subject to attempts to impeach their conclusions. The opposing side will likely argue that the clinician has an inherent bias toward not providing an opinion that upsets his or her patient and increases the risk that that patient will lose trust in the clinician as a therapist and terminate treatment. Furthermore, the risk of ethical, licensing, or malpractice claims against the therapist for failing to meet appropriate obligations to avoid harmful multiple-role relationships increases significantly when mixing these roles.

Although the mention of such potential complaints should increase anxiety sufficiently so that one will avoid such multiple-role relationships, the treating clinician may not be able to avoid providing testimony at deposition or in court. Providing testimony as a clinician violates no ethical code or practice guideline per se. The therapist who becomes involved in the litigation must have a clear understanding of the difference between a "fact witness" and an "expert witness."

As the treating professional, it may be appropriate to comply with a patient's request to provide information in the context of the litigation. However, the psychotherapist should remain in the role as fact witness and avoid pressure to act as an expert witness. The treating clinician should provide only facts, observations, and perceptions that he or she has come to know firsthand through the clinician's role and should avoid forming opinions relevant to the legal matters at hand (Shapiro, 1991). It may be professionally appropriate and ethical as a fact witness to testify that, in the context of one's clinical evaluation, an opinion was formed and to disclose that opinion. This testimony is to the fact that one has formed the opinion. However, the clinician must take care not to imply or suggest that he or she has collected, analyzed, and based his or her opinion on those data necessary to form valid conclusions.

The evaluation typically conducted by treating psychologists differs considerably from that conducted by a forensic examiner. The treating clinician typically does not have the opportunity, nor generally the need, to perform the functions of a forensic evaluator in order to provide appropriate treatment, nor to collect all of the data necessary to thoroughly weigh the theories proposed by both sides. For example, a child psychotherapist typically bases his or her evaluation and clinical impressions on information provided by the child and the child's guardians without any attempt to validate or disprove these reports. Clinicians must take care to avoid leading lawyers and courts to believe that an opinion based on a preponderance of the clinical evidence constitutes one based on a preponderance of all of the evidence. Similarly, when testifying as a treating clinician, the treating clinician must exercise care to maintain a clear understanding of the legal implication of being an expert and object to being qualified as an expert witness, regardless of his or her expertise in the area.

Competence

Forensic evaluators are ethically mandated to conduct evaluations only in areas of psychology in which they have specialized knowledge, skill, experience, and education (Committee on Ethical Issues for Forensic Psychologists, 1991). Personal injury evaluations of children require documented knowledge, skill, experience, and education in child development, child assessment, child psychopathology, childhood trauma reactions, and child treatment, in addition to the typical areas of competence for all forensic evaluators. Although it may appear obvious to state, the foregoing warrants emphasis. It is worth stating clearly herein, given the frequency with which I have observed generally competent psychologists conducting forensic evaluations of children without sufficient training and demonstrated competence in some relevant areas. Attorneys wishing to impeach an evaluator's

credibility have often read the *Specialty Guidelines for Forensic Psychologists* (Committee on Ethical Issues for Forensic Psychologists, 1991) and volumes such as this current book, and may be effectively prepared to impeach the psychologist's qualifications as an expert in a given child case. Even if qualified by the court as an expert, a psychologist's credibility in the eyes of the jury may diminish greatly if it is shown that he or she lacks appropriate demonstrated competence. One should also anticipate the potential reaction and response of the attorney who has hired and paid for the psychologist's services if his or her competence to conduct the evaluation has been impeached in open court. Likewise, courts in states such as Massachusetts have allowed malpractice suits against expert witnesses. It is advised that psychologists familiarize themselves with the laws in their particular states regarding potential liability or immunity when serving as expert witnesses.

Conducting the Examination

Conducting psychological examinations affords a wonderful forum for the many psychologists who have a strong foundation in and appreciation for the scientific method but have chosen not to pursue predominately research-oriented careers. Psychologists who conceptualize examination as an individual research study are best suited to meet the goal of providing the most valid conclusions that will best withstand the attempts of the opposing side to impeach the psychological expert. Although the natural circumstances in which these evaluations are conducted prohibit the control of internal validity issues in the manner usually required for dissertation committees and peer-reviewed journals, the understanding of threats to validity and attempts to control variables uniquely prepares psychologists to collect data and form opinions that meet the legal standard of proof in personal injury cases: a preponderance of the evidence.

Defining Client

In conducting personal examinations, the client is the attorney who retains the expert. It is very important to understand that the role of psychological examiner in these cases is to assist the attorney in the ongoing litigation and not to alleviate the pain and suffering of any party or to take on any other role. Understanding that the attorney stands as the client has several important implications. First, once the attorney is clearly defined as the client, all of the assessment will generally qualify as being legally privileged as an "attorney work product." The work will have protection from discovery by the opposing side until the attorney who hired the expert places that expert on the witness list or directs the expert to testify. Thus the psychological examiner who is committed to conducting a comprehensive and fair examination can put forth conclusions that are detrimental to the case being made by the attorney who retained him or her, knowing that the attorney who has hired him or her can choose not to use the examination without providing it to other side. Although some lawyers may be shopping for an expert to testify the way they want, many or most want a competent and thorough examination of their clients. Such an examination provides them with the opportunity to gain a good understanding of the merits of their case and plan their strategy accordingly, thus avoiding the risk of investing many hours into a case in which they ultimately recover minimal or no compensation.

Although the client should always be the attorney by whom the examiner is retained, the goal of good psychological evaluation in a personal injury case is to conduct an independent, thorough, and optimally valid evaluation. Ultimately, the psychologist's role consists of serving as an unbiased expert who assists the court in making decisions in accordance with the laws. Making this understanding clear to the retaining attorney at the outset of the relationship, as part of a written informed consent, provides the added benefit of enhancing the perception of the expert's credibility during later testimony. Likewise, attorneys who are truly shopping for an expert to say whatever they wish will decide not to use the psychologist, thus protecting his or her reputation in the community.

Defining the Assessment Questions

The starting point in planning the examination is to develop clear evaluation questions related to the legal criteria discussed previously. The psycholo-

gist should ask the retaining attorney which legal issues to examine, what theory applies to each issue, what he or she expects the opposing theory to be, what evidence he or she has to support or refute the opposing theories, and what evidence he or she believes the other side has to support or refute the psychologist's theories. An outline (see the appendix to this chapter) is provided to assist the evaluator in working with retaining attorneys to define the evaluation.

Once the desires of the retaining attorney become clear, the psychologist should evaluate whether he or she has the particular expertise necessary to assess the specific questions and should communicate this to the attorney early in the process. Evaluating whether psychological harm has actually occurred typically falls within the psychologist's domain of competence. However, a plaintiff's attorney may request the psychologist to give a conclusion as to whether the defendant should have known that his or her act had a reasonable certainty of causing harm. For example, if the defendant's culture may have implications that are germane to determining this issue, any given evaluator may lack the ability to adequately assess this issue. In this situation, it is important to recall that most courts consider the "reasonably prudent person" as being constituted in a similar manner to the defendant. Thus the psychological examiner must have the competence to understand normative behavior of the population from which the defendant comes.

Collecting Data

Within the context of the legal criteria discussed earlier, psychological examinations in personal injury cases typically focus on determining whether injury has occurred, the role of the defendant's action or negligence in that injury, and the prognosis for rehabilitation and future functioning. As such, the examination can best be conceptualized as a pre-post single-case study in which one typically needs to develop a retrospective understanding of the plaintiff's functioning prior to the incident in question, of the changes or lack of changes subsequent to that incident, of the role of the incident in causing the changes relative to other possible factors, and of the likelihood of future functioning. In order to form an opinion that is supported by a "preponderance of the evidence," the psychologist must make a reasonable attempt to collect all of the readily apparent relevant data that might support or refute each hypothesis. In setting up the initial agreement with the retaining attorney, it is imperative for the psychologist to ensure time and resources to collect the data necessary to give an informed opinion. Psychologists should avoid attempts by attorneys to persuade them to neglect certain data that they deem necessary for a comprehensive and unbiased evaluation.

Most psychologists understand that they lack the scientific ability to evaluate the types of hypotheses put forth in a personal injury case in such naturalistic settings and to make conclusions with a probability of error of less than 5%. However, using the constructs of convergent validity, it is typically possible to make conclusions that "more likely than not" are accurate. That is, by collecting different sources and types of data, using various methods of data collection, and analyzing the degree to which the data converge or diverge in supporting a particular hypothesis, a psychologist can conclude, with a reasonable degree of certainty, that a preponderance of evidence supports or does not support a particular hypothesis.

The three primary types of data used are interviews, collateral data (i.e., documents, records, and interviews), and psychological tests. A good starting point involves creation of a table that charts (1) the specific legal criteria being assessed, (2) the plaintiff's and the defendant's respective conclusions for each element, and (3) the specific data believed necessary in order to provide a comprehensive evaluation of that issue. As data are collected, the examiner often learns of new data that he or she will want to add to the list. This matrix serves as an excellent organizational strategy with which to prepare the final work product.

An excellent review of forensic interviewing of children is contained elsewhere in this volume (see Gudas & Sattler, chapter 8). Most of the principles and procedures discussed in that chapter are generalizable to the interviews of parties in personal injury cases. However, the use of collateral documents and records and of psychological testing in personal injury cases warrants a more specific discussion herein.

COLLATERAL DATA   The use of collateral data is an integral part of the personal injury evaluation of children. The reliance on these data differentiates forensic personal injury examinations from nonforensic clinical assessments. It is well known that psychologists have very limited ability to detect deception from interviews alone (e.g., Ekman & O'Sullivan, 1991). Collateral data can be used very effectively to support or refute conclusions based only on interview data.

Collateral data also permit an examination of a child's functioning at different time periods correlated with different life events. For example, if a plaintiff is claiming that a child's functioning has greatly decompensated as the result of a traumatic auto accident, it is important to collect any data that address the child's actual functioning before and after the accident. Besides interviewing teachers, coaches, and others who have directly observed the child, it may be useful to collect other documents and records that speak to the legal issues being evaluated. For example, a review of the parents' day planners, checkbooks, and credit card statements may provide data about significant changes, or lack of changes, in the child's life secondary to the accident. Educational and medical records usually must be reviewed. If a child has been observed having nightmares or reenacting trauma scenes in his or her play while sleeping at a friend's house or by a babysitter, these data more likely support a parent's claims regarding presence of symptoms that exist within the home.

Psychologists should always consider the possibility that other observers or sources of data may have information that refutes or supports a plaintiff's claim. An evaluator must examine every hypothesis and ask him- or herself and the parties involved what data and what people will have information that supports or refutes the hypothesis. Although these data might not speak directly to proximate cause, they may help to establish or refute whether actual damage has occurred. In essence, a thorough forensic evaluator must think as a criminal investigator would and collect and analyze any data that support or refute conclusions made by both parties. Furthermore, it is well recognized in the professional field and in court decisions that consulting a variety of collateral sources and using those data as the basis of one's opinion has become essential for competent forensic practice (Shapiro, 1991). In that the *Daubert* decision still requires that the methodology be widely accepted in the field, failing to collect and analyze data from collateral sources may result in an effective challenge of admissibility.

PSYCHOLOGICAL TESTING   Reviews of the role of psychological testing in forensic evaluations (e.g., Ewing, 1996; Heilbrun, 1992) and personal injury evaluations in general exist (e.g., Greenberg, 2003) and may be useful for the reader. With regard to evaluating children in personal injury cases, there is no single psychological test that reliably assesses the proximate cause of most complaints or whether a child plaintiff is malingering or exaggerating injury. Likewise, there is no agreed-on battery of tests that exists for psychological evaluations of children in personal injury cases. However, a well-trained child examiner can choose and implement many of the existing psychological tests to assist in the assessment of specifically defined questions of law. Likewise, it may prove useful to determine whether psychological testing data were collected before an alleged injury that may be helpful in establishing preinjury functioning by providing a comparison point. In general, psychological tests may be useful as data that assist in confirming or disconfirming hypotheses already generated and in generating new hypotheses.

The requirement for proving "actual damage" usually requires demonstration that the damage is "real and significant." Psychometric tests that attempt to quantify mental states and conditions and that allow for comparison with normative data and possibly preinjury data may be particularly useful in personal injury evaluations of children.

It is important to discuss and integrate test results as one particular type of data, with specific strengths and limitations, and to base conclusions on the convergence and divergence of all available data from other data available. *The Ethical Principles of Psychologists and Code of Conduct* (APA, 2002) and *Specialty Guidelines for Forensic Psychologists* (Committee on Ethical Issues for Forensic Psychologists, 1991) recommend that psychologists indicate any significant limitations in the interpretation of testing results. Greenberg (2003) provides an excellent example of a statement that may be used as a preface for interpretation of psychological testing results that may help examiners meet the ethical standards.

Several instruments have been developed in the past 20 years that attempt to measure trauma-related responses in children. This group includes the Trauma Symptom Checklist for Children, the Clinician-Administered PTSD Scale for Children, the Child Dissociative Checklist, the Child Posttraumatic Stress Reaction Index, the Children's Impact of Traumatic Events Scale, Child Rating Scales of Exposure to Interpersonal Abuse, When Bad Things Happen Scale, and the Child's Reaction to Traumatic Events Scale (as cited in Sparta, 2003). Sparta (2003) provides an excellent description and overview of these scales that may serve as a good starting point for further investigation of their potential usefulness in a particular case.

It is also important to keep the *Daubert* and *Kumho* admissibility criteria in mind when choosing a test battery and to be prepared to defend the battery according to these legal criteria. One specific psychometric measure of child functioning that may have particular utility in assessing children who claim psychological injuries is the Behavior Assessment System for Children (BASC; Reynolds & Kamphaus, 1992). The BASC is a multidimensional measure of adaptive and problem behaviors, with versions for preschool (ages 4–5), child (ages 6–11), and adolescent (ages 12–18) levels. The demonstrated reliability and validity of the measure and the growing body of literature that supports it suggest that it will likely withstand *Daubert/Kumho* scrutiny. Also, the BASC's growing popularity among educators may result in the existence of preinjury comparison data. The BASC allows systematic collection and analyses of data from parents, teachers, and the child that permit psychometric comparison between data sources and against a normative sample.

The BASC shares much clinical utility with the Achenbach System of Empirically Based Assessment (ASEBA) (Achenbach, 2005). One important aspect that differentiates the BASC and makes it particularly useful in child tort cases involves the presence of validity scales similar to those found in the Minnesota Multiphasic Personality Inventory-2 (MMPI-2). The BASC (Reynolds

& Kamphaus, 1992) parent and teacher report versions include a measure of the respondent's tendency to respond in an excessively negative manner about the child's behaviors or self-perceptions and emotions. The MMPI-2 is routinely accepted as one of the best self-report measures to assess malingering and other forms of response distortion. The effectiveness of the MMPI-2 has been recognized in courts throughout the country. Given the presence of validity scales on the BASC similar to those on the MMPI-2 and its strong reliability and validity, it is likely that the BASC will gain similar use and acceptance in the courts as a measure of children's adaptive and problematic behaviors. However, unlike the MMPI-2, no data currently exist that examine the efficacy of the BASC in tort cases.

Other, more traditional child assessment instruments such as the Children's Depression Inventory (CDI) (Kovacs, 1992) and the Revised Children's Manifest Anxiety Scale (RCMAS) (Reynolds & Richmond, 1985) are also often useful in measuring a range of distressing symptoms related to anxiety and depression. The RCMAS has the added utility in a forensic setting of providing a validity scale that measures the degree to which the reporter is denying negative items that most other children will acknowledge. Thus it may be useful in describing the child's tendency to minimize problems in cases in which the child's self-report indicates significantly less distress than indicated by other observers and data sources.

Diagnosis

The decision as to whether the forensic examiner should use clinical diagnoses in personal injury examinations is controversial and discussed frequently in the literature (e.g., Grisso, 1986; Grove & Barden, 1999; Slovenko, 1994; Sparr & Boehnlein, 1990; Stone, 1993). The psychological examiner should become well versed in the arguments for and against the use of formal diagnostic categories that are likely to form the basis of cross-examinations and depositions. Further, examiners are strongly encouraged to familiarize themselves with the preface of the *Diagnostic and Statistical Manual of Mental Disorders* (*DSM-IV*; American Psychiatric Association, 1994), which explicitly cautions that clinical diagnosis is insufficient to establish mental defect for legal purposes. The *DSM-IV* (1994) also explicitly states "it is precisely because impairment, abilities, and disabilities vary widely within each diagnostic category that assignment of a particular diagnosis does not imply a specific level of impairment or disability" (p. xxiii).

Diagnoses are often considered prejudicial. The absence of a diagnosis may benefit the defendant, whereas the presence of a diagnosis may benefit the plaintiff. However, it is important that the examiner understands that no known section anywhere in tort law—for the plaintiff or for the defendant—requires offering proof regarding the presence or absence of any formal diagnosis. Diagnoses are not dispositive in proving most tort law standards. The court seeks a comprehensive understanding of the change in the plaintiff's functioning relative to the incident in question. As Grisso (1986) argues, forensic examinations should be based more on competency than on clinical diagnosis. The court needs to know what the plaintiff actually can do or not do, combined with an understanding of his or her actual functional experience, more than whether the individual meets particular diagnostic criteria. The objective and informed forensic assessment can assist the court in making appropriate determinations regardless of diagnosis. The diagnosis alone usually will prove insufficient in personal injury cases.

In spite of arguments against the need for diagnosis, avoiding the issue of diagnoses in these cases is nearly impossible. Careful understanding of the various diagnoses that often coexist with PTSD and share similar presentations with PTSD is imperative. In attempting to impeach arguments for proximal cause of a particular act, attorneys often attempt to use preexisting psychological disorders to explain the condition of the plaintiff after the alleged trauma.

For example, one attorney attempted to argue that, because the plaintiff had a history of depressive symptoms before the alleged negligent act, the preexisting depression was the cause of the plaintiff's difficulties rather than the defendant's action. However, a careful analysis of the developmental history demonstrated that the plaintiff had not been experiencing major depression immediately before the negligent acts. The diagnosis of major depressive episode was made in addition to, not instead of, that of posttraumatic stress disorder. Studies (e.g., Maes, Mylle, Delmeire, &

Altamura, 2000) that showed that more than 25% of individuals diagnosed with PTSD also have major depression. The studies demonstrated that approximately half of those with PTSD who were diagnosed with comorbid major depression were experiencing it for the first time and that half were experiencing a recurrent major depressive episode. Thus it is not unusual for somebody who either has had or has never had major depression to experience these symptoms along with posttraumatic stress disorder. As this example demonstrates, helping the court understand how diagnoses are not mutually exclusive and can coexist is a common component of completing forensic examinations of children in personal injury cases. Particularly when one of the diagnoses under consideration is generally accepted as having a strong genetic/biological etiology (e.g., bipolar disorder), attorneys may attempt to argue that the actions of the defendant cannot have caused the claimed problems However, it is clear that PTSD and bipolar illness commonly coexist. Kessler, Sonnega, Bromet, Hughes, and Nelson (1995) found elevated lifetime rates of mania among adults and adolescents with PTSD. Hezler, Robins, and McEvoy (1987) reported strong association between manic-depressive illness and PTSD. A growing body of evidence suggests that stressful life events influence the onset and course of bipolar disorder (e.g., Reilly-Harrington, Alloy, Fresco, & Whitehouse, 1999). Several studies have documented higher rates of stressful and traumatic life events preceding the onset of bipolar episodes. Studies have found that as many as 50% of bipolar patients recall a major stressful life event preceding the initial episode of bipolar disorder. There are at least four research studies that indicate that patients who have bipolar disorder and are functioning well have had higher than normal rates of stressful life events that preceded the relapse of the illness. Experts (e.g., Hlastala et al., 2000) believe that it is a common misconception that bipolar disorder is a completely biological process. Thus, although bipolar disorder appears to have a biological/genetic base, negative life events play a role in its onset and course. Stress and trauma are believed to affect the frequency and timing of episodes of bipolar disorder. Thus, armed with the scientific literature about diagnosis and developmental psychopathology, psychological examiners often help the court understand the role that trauma can play in triggering or exacerbating psychological functioning in the context of many diagnoses besides PTSD.

To counter the defendant's attempts to use the plaintiff's preexisting psychiatric diagnoses to account for his or her condition following the alleged negligent act, knowledge of the developmental psychopathology literature can be useful in explaining why a particular defendant may have developed his or her condition in response to the traumatic event. Recall that, as discussed earlier, the court generally applies the "egg shell plaintiff" standard. That is, the court considers the damage relative to how the plaintiff was constituted at the time of the injury. Thus it may be important to help the court understand how and why a plaintiff with a preexisting diagnosis or psychological condition may be more likely to have been hurt by the act in question than a normally constituted individual would be. For example, Schurr, Friedman, and Rosenberg (1993) found a longitudinal relationship among a variety of personality traits that were associated with the emergence of PTSD. These include dissatisfaction, gloominess, and irritability. Likewise, King, King, Gudanowski, and Vreven (1995), studying combat soldiers, found that the perception of threat was a stronger predictor of PTSD than the intensity of actual combat trauma experienced. Thus, if a plaintiff's pretrauma functioning was characterized by a tendency toward dissatisfaction, gloominess, and irritability and if these tendencies could explain why he or she may have perceived a trauma more intensely than most others, this information may be useful in explaining why a particular plaintiff was hurt more by a specific event or events than most people might be.

APPENDIX

Defining the Personal Injury Evaluation

- Liability
  - Legal duty
  - Breach or dereliction of duty
  - Proximate cause
  - Actual damage
  - Compensability
    - Which model applies? Physical injury, zone of danger, bystander proximity, or full recovery?

- Damages
  - Loss of consortium
  - Hedonistic damages
  - Compensatory damages
  - Defensive responses to claims for damages
    - Contributory negligence
    - Last clear chance
    - Failure to mitigate

References

Achenbach, T. M. (2005). *The Achenbach system of empirically based assessment.* Burlington: University of Vermont Research Center for Children, Youth, and Families.

American Psychiatric Association. (1994). *Diagnostic and statistical manual of mental disorders* (4th ed.). Washington, DC: Author.

American Psychological Association. (2002). *Ethical principles of psychologists and code of conduct.* Washington, DC: Author.

Committee on Ethical Issues for Forensic Psychologists. (1991). Specialty guidelines for forensic psychologists. *Law and Human Behavior, 15,* 655–665.

Daubert v. Merrell Dow Pharmaceuticals, Inc., 509 U.S. 579, 113 S.Ct. 2786 (1993).

Ekman, P., & O'Sullivan, M. (1991). Who can catch a liar? *American Psychologist, 46,* 913–920.

Ewing, C. P. (1996). Introduction to psychological testing and the law. *Behavioral Sciences & Law, 14,* 269–270.

Federal Rules of Evidence. (2003). Washington, DC: U.S. Government Printing Office.

Frye v. United States, 54 App. D.C. 46,47, 293 F. 1013-14 (D.C. Cir. 1923).

General Electric Co. v. Joiner, 118 S. Ct. 512 (1997).

Greenberg, S. (2003). Personal injury examinations in torts for emotional distress. In A. M. Goldstein & I. B. Weiner (Eds.), *Handbook of psychology. Vol. II: Forensic psychology.* Hoboken, NJ: John Wiley.

Greenberg, S., & Shuman, D. (1997). Irreconcilable conflict between therapeutic and forensic roles. *Professional Psychology: Research and Practice, 29,* 50–55.

Grisso, T. (1986). *Evaluating competencies: Forensic assessment and instruments.* New York: Plenum.

Grove, W. M., & Barden, R. C. (1999). Protecting the integrity of the legal system: The admissibility of testimony from mental health experts under Daubert/Kumho analyses. *Psychology, Public Policy, and Law, 5,* 224–242.

Heilbrun, K. (1992). The role of psychological testing in forensic assessment. *Law and Human Behavior, 16,* 257–272.

Hezler, J. E., Robins, L. N., & McEvoy, L. (1987). Post-traumatic stress disorder in the general population: Findings of the epidemiologic catchment area survey. *New England Journal of Medicine, 317,* 1630–1634.

Hlastala, S., Frank, E., Kowalski, J., Sherrill, J. T., Tu, X. M., Anderson, B., & Kupfer, D. (2000). Stressful life events, bipolar disorder, and the "kindling model." *Journal of Abnormal Psychology, 109*(4), 777–786.

Kessler, R. C., Sonnega, A., Bromet, E., Hughes, M., & Nelson, C. B. (1995). Posttraumatic stress disorder in the National Comorbidity Survey. Archives of General Psychiatry, 52(12), 1048–1060.

King, D. W., King, L. A., Gudanowski, D. M., & Vreven, D. L. (1995). Alternative representations of war zone stressors: Relationships to posttraumatic stress disorder in male and female Vietnam veterans. *Journal of Abnormal Psychology, 104*(1), 184–196.

Kovacs, M. (1992). *The Children's Depression Inventory.* New York: MultiHealth Systems.

Kumho Tire Co., Ltd., et al. v. Carmichael, et al., 119 S. Ct. 1167 (1999).

Maes, M., Mylle, J., Delmeire, L., & Altamura, C., (2000). Psychiatric morbidity and comorbidity following accidental man-made traumatic events: Incidence and risk factors. *European Archives of Psychiatry and Clinical Neuroscience, 250,* 156–162.

Mart, E. G. (1997, March). Psychotherapist testimony in PI cases: Coping with the stealth evaluation. *Massachusetts Bar Association Lawyers Journal, 3,* 10.

Melton, G. B., Petrila, J., Poythress, N. G., & Slobogin, C. (1987). *Psychological evaluations for the courts: A handbook for mental health professionals and lawyers.* New York: Guilford.

Plaisance v. Texaco, Inc., et al., 966 F.2d 166 (5th Cir. 1992).

Reilly-Harrington, N. A., Alloy, L. B., Fresco, D. M., & Whitehouse, W. G. (1999). Cognitive styles and life events interact to predict bipolar and unipolar symptomatology. *Journal of Abnormal Psychology, 108*(4), 567–578.

Reynolds, C. R., & Kamphaus, R. W. (1992). *The Behavioral Assessment System for Children (BASC).* Circle Pines, MN: American Guidance Service.

Reynolds, C. R., & Richmond, B. O. (1985). *The Revised Children's Manifest Anxiety Scale.* Los Angeles: Western Psychological Services.

Schurr, P. P., Friedman, M. J., & Rosenberg, S. D. (1993). Preliminary MMPI scores as predictors of combat-related PTSD symptoms. *American Journal of Psychiatry, 150,* 479–483.

Shapiro, D. L. (1991). *Forensic psychological assessment: An integrative approach.* Needham Heights, MA: Allyn & Bacon.

Slovenko, R. (1994). Legal aspects of post-traumatic stress disorder. *Psychiatric Clinics of North America, 17,* 439–446.

Sparr, L. F., & Boehnlein, J. K. (1990). Posttraumatic stress disorder in tort actions: Forensic minefield. *Bulletin of the American Academy of Psychiatry and Law, 18,* 283–302.

Sparta, S. N. (2003). Assessment of childhood trauma. In A. M. Goldstein (Ed.), *Handbook of psychology: Vol. 11. Forensic psychology.* New York: John Wiley.

Stone, A. (1993). Post-traumatic stress disorder and the law: Critical review of the new frontier. *Bulletin of the American Academy of Psychiatry and Law, 21,* 23–36.

16

Neuropsychological Considerations in Forensic Child Assessment

Karen E. Wills
Jerry J. Sweet

WHAT IS A PEDIATRIC NEUROPSYCHOLOGICAL EVALUATION?

Pediatric neuropsychologists evaluate children's cognitive, behavioral, and emotional functioning in light of knowledge regarding the developing brain and brain-behavior relationships. That body of knowledge, which is rapidly increasing, comes from research in developmental neuroscience, developmental psychology, pediatrics, and child psychopathology. Research in these related fields informs the development and selection of clinical tests, as well as the interpretation of test findings.

Many formal psychological tests used in other contexts also have utility in neuropsychological assessment. These include intelligence tests, such as the Wechsler or Stanford-Binet scales; achievement tests, such as the Woodcock-Johnson; and adaptive behavior measures, such as the Vineland Social Maturity Scale. Neuropsychologists also utilize additional tests of children's attention, memory, motor skills, social-emotional status, and executive function. Neuropsychologists analyze the pattern of results on these and other tests, to-

gether with information derived from parent and teacher interviews, reviews of medical and school records, and direct observation of the child's behavior. All of this information regarding the child's history and present status is considered in the context of the child's social, educational, and medical history, in an effort to understand how various factors may have contributed to the child's current functioning.

WHAT IS A PEDIATRIC NEUROPSYCHOLOGIST?

The title *neuropsychologist* remains largely unregulated in the United States (except in Louisiana), despite laws controlling use of the title *psychologist*. Neuropsychologists who specialize in working with children should have had training in child development and pediatric psychology, in addition to appropriate training in neuropsychology (Adams, 1988). Some psychologists call themselves neuropsychologists without having adequate training. In the absence of professional regulation, it may prove helpful to locate neuropsychologists who have attained board certification by a widely accepted professional group that employs rigorous credential review and examination procedures or to work with those who are recommended by a board-certified senior colleague. For example, the American Board of Professional Psychology awards the diplomate in clinical neuropsychology (i.e., ABCN) to both pediatric and adult-focused neuropsychologists. Pediatric neuropsychologists with ABCN certification have both relevant experience and solid training. Although the number of board-certified neuropsychologists continues to grow rapidly, there remain many excellent clinicians who have not undertaken the expensive, time-consuming, and voluntary board-certification process. On the other hand, several "vanity boards" bestow titles in neuropsychology or forensic psychology for a fee; such ersatz credentials do not provide reliable guidance regarding an individual's quality of training or experience.

The match between the neuropsychology expert's skills and the particular case has considerable importance. The neuropsychologist should possess or acquire relevant cultural and linguistic competencies for working with the child and knowledge regarding the particular type of injury or diagnosis (e.g., head trauma, neurotoxins, mental retardation, or hearing loss). In addition, one must take care to avoid any conflict of interest or "dual relationships." For example, neuropsychologists should not serve as experts on cases that involve their immediate employers, colleagues, family or friends, or current or former patients.

WHEN CAN PEDIATRIC NEUROPSYCHOLOGISTS BEST ASSIST IN FORENSIC ASSESSMENT?

Pediatric neuropsychologists often find themselves consulted in forensic contexts when someone has allegedly caused brain injury to a child. For example, attorneys may consult a neuropsychologist while handling lawsuits involving alleged malpractice during delivery or neonatal care; motor vehicle accidents that injured a child; alleged negligence by adult supervisors, such as when a child has fallen from an upstairs window or sustained a near-drowning incident; or alleged housing-code viola-

tions by a landlord after a child ingests lead paint chips (see chapters on civil litigation, chapter 15, and pediatric lead exposure, chapter 17, this volume). In such cases, the neuropsychologist's role is to evaluate the child's status, diagnosis, and prognosis and to give an opinion as to whether the event at issue caused or significantly contributed to a neuropsychological disorder. The neuropsychologist should function as an impartial evaluator, not an advocate. A detailed discussion of the role of pediatric neuropsychologists in personal injury litigation (Dennis, 1989) provides an excellent overview and guide.

Neuropsychological concerns may arise in the context of forensic evaluations that do not initially involve questions about brain injury. For example, neuropsychological evidence may have relevance in custody determination or termination of parental rights, particularly in cases of alleged severe neglect or abuse. Child abuse investigations sometimes give rise to questions regarding whether serious physical abuse, such as shaking or beating, has caused brain damage (Miller, 1999). Even in the absence of physical trauma, prolonged severe neglect can result in brain dysfunction, manifested in behavior problems or developmental delay (Buchanan & Oliver, 1977; Glaser, 2000). Neuropsychological evidence of brain dysfunction consequent to abuse or neglect may imply a need for court-ordered special interventions in custody cases, such as further medical work-up, parental guidance and caregiver training in cases of family reunification or adoption, or funding for rehabilitative therapies and special education for adoptees.

Neuropsychologists may also become involved with arbitration or due process hearings in special education cases when a child's learning or behavior problems may reflect brain dysfunction (Lorber & Yurk, 1999). Knowledge of neuropsychological research can help in understanding the educational and rehabilitation needs of children who have well-documented neurological conditions, such as cerebral palsy, spina bifida, leukemia, autism, epilepsy, meningitis, or head injury.

Juvenile delinquency proceedings may become complicated by questions about whether a brain injury, epilepsy, or other medical or neurodevelopmental condition compromised a child's capacity to know right from wrong. Some neuropsychologists also assess child witnesses or victims who have known neurological disorders to determine competence to testify in formal court proceedings. For example, a hydrocephalic adolescent with mild mental retardation alleged sexual abuse. A neuropsychologist concluded, based on her mental age, language skills, and verbal memory abilities, that the girl had sufficient mental competence to discriminate truth from falsehood and could accurately remember and recount events she had experienced.

IS A FORENSIC NEUROPSYCHOLOGICAL EVALUATION NECESSARY AND APPROPRIATE?

The first step in a forensic neuropsychological evaluation involves determining whether neuropsychological testing is necessary and appropriate. Which, if any, of the forensic questions can be answered using neuropsychological assessment? In the preceding example, for instance, testing the child's cognitive functioning would not prove useful in determining whether or not sexual abuse had occurred. However, it proved valuable in determining that she could accurately remember and describe personal experiences and tell truth from falsehood.

Clear, precisely formulated questions, identified prior to testing, can help to focus a neuropsychological evaluation and thereby ensure that attorneys and/or the court have realistic expectations about how test findings can prove useful in a legal proceeding. Some forensic referral questions are similar to those of routine clinical cases: Does this child have any neuropsychological impairment? If so, what is the nature and severity of the neuropsychological impairment? What factors have caused, or significantly contributed to, the neuropsychological impairment? Is the neuropsychological impairment permanent? What will be the long-term impact of the neuropsychological impairment on the child's educational, social, and vocational attainment?

In addition to referral questions common to both clinical and forensic cases, questions not common in clinical contexts often arise in forensic assessments. In child clinical cases, the assessment nearly always focuses on *what is wrong* (whether a problem exists), *what strengths and resources are apparent*, and *what should be done* to improve the child's functioning, at home and in school, within the subsequent few years. In forensic cases, the emphasis typically shifts to *what is wrong* (whether a problem exists), *what caused the problem, what the long-term (lifetime) outcome will be*, and *what should be done* to improve adult vocational productivity and quality of life. These questions have relevance because forensic cases typically require decisions pertaining to who, or what, caused the problem, if indeed any problem exists. Sometimes attorneys ask neuropsychologists to "fractionate" or "apportion" observed impairment; for example, "Which portion of Johnny's impairment reflects his documented, preexisting learning disability, and what portion reflects his brain injury of two years ago?" or "Was it the first well-documented injury or the second well-documented injury, six months later, that caused Susie to be failing in college today?"

The "lifetime" focus becomes important because financial settlement in a forensic case may reflect the loss of adult "earning power" due to childhood injury, as well as the more immediate costs of raising and rehabilitating an injured child. Questions related to long-range prognosis may include, Will the brain injury Jason sustained at birth shorten his life span, and if so, by how much? Will the mercury poisoning Jane suffered at age 6 years affect her ability to go to college, marry, be a good mother, or hold down a well-paying job? What educational, therapeutic, financial, or psychological counseling services will Joan, who nearly drowned as a 2-year-old, require throughout her life?

WHO IS THE CLIENT?

Before commencing a forensic evaluation, the neuropsychologist clarifies the relationships among the people involved and the procedures to be followed when gathering and disclosing information about the child. Who is the legal guardian? Who will provide information about the child's history, and who will have access to that information? Who will receive the report of neuropsychological findings at what time? Will the report be oral, written, or both? What information will the report contain, and how will that information be used? Who will pay for the evaluation, and in what form or schedule will payment occur?

For both ethical and practical reasons, neuropsychologists typically prepare a written letter or "service agreement" summarizing the client-provider relationships, confidentiality issues, a general outline or plan of the evaluation (e.g., stating that interviews and individual testing will be conducted, records reviewed, etc.), and an outline regarding the payment agreement. This written statement helps to ensure that all those concerned are clearly informed of expectations regarding their respective roles. Any confusion or disagreement can be resolved more easily at the start of an evaluation than after it is completed. It is particularly important to ensure at the outset that children and parents are informed and that they consent to waive their usual clinical confidentiality privileges because the child is being evaluated in a forensic context. Children, their parents, and their attorneys should receive a statement in easy-to-read language that all information obtained during the evaluation may be disclosed in court. Materials potentially subject to disclosure in court include questionnaires, interviews, and test data obtained from the child, as well as from parents, teachers, or other sources. Their attorney may or may not have clearly explained this to the family when referring the child for testing; in any case, except when the assessment is court-ordered, parents have a right to opt out of an evaluation at any time or to talk further with their attorney before proceeding.

In some cases, an attorney will make the initial contact, request the evaluation, and arrange to pay for the neuropsychologist's time, work, and expertise. In this situation, the attorney, not the child or family, is the neuropsychologist's client. One must emphasize that the attorney does *not* pay "for an opinion," as the neuropsychologist will provide an honest opinion based on the results of the evaluation, regardless of whether or not those results support the attorney's attempt to advocate for his or her client. Clearly, the expert should still receive compensation for the time required to do the evaluation; problems in this regard have led many neuropsychologists to request partial or full payment in advance of undertaking the assessment. After the child is tested, the attorney may request

an oral report of findings prior to the preparation of any written report. If the findings do not support the client's case, the attorney may ask the neuropsychologist *not* to write a report, as the results may not become part of the legal proceeding or discovery process.

Guidelines for forensic neuropsychologists recommend that the role of the forensic expert, retained by an attorney to evaluate a child and answer forensic questions, not mix with the clinical role of treating a child's impairment. For example, an expert witness generally would not conduct a feedback and treatment-planning conference with the parents or caregivers, as this may confuse the expert role with the clinician role. The main concern here holds that establishing a clinical relationship with the child and family may bias the expert's conclusions in the direction of advocating for the child in a manner inappropriate to the role of an expert witness. The goal of an expert witness involves educating the trier of fact by presenting unbiased opinions, based on relevant scientific and clinical evidence, about specific questions pertaining to the case.

In some cases, the neuropsychological evaluation will detect problems and indicate a need for immediate intervention to avoid harming the child by educational or medical neglect, even though the neuropsychological report might not find use in litigation until years later, if ever. For example, in the case of a teenager deafened by meningitis, a neuropsychologist recognized that the child might benefit significantly from a cochlear implant, which should be provided as soon as possible after onset of acquired deafness in order to maximize the child's potential for developing functional hearing. The family lived in a rural area and had not yet had any contact with professionals knowledgeable about deafness except for physicians at the hospital they were suing, whose advice they did not trust. A local teacher of the deaf had misinformed them that cochlear implants would *not* benefit a teenager. In this case, the attorney agreed to share the expert's neuropsychological report with the family immediately, including the recommendation to pursue a cochlear implant evaluation and supporting patient education documents that explained the scientific basis for that opinion. The attorney perceived sharing this information as compatible with her primary goal of advocating for her client in the legal proceedings.

Sometimes attorneys will convey such information verbally to the child's family. Sometimes the retaining attorney will consent to provide recommendations by conveying the neuropsychological report, or a letter stating particular recommendations, to the parents or to a psychologist, therapist, educator, or rehabilitation specialist who is already involved in providing treatment. In any case, a neuropsychologist in the role of expert must avoid providing treatment directly to the child and family and must obtain the retaining attorney's consent to release copies of the report to others, including the child's parents or guardians. The expert witness cannot follow through with the family in order to encourage them to carry out recommended interventions, to recommend or help them access specific providers or agencies, to provide interventions directly, or to assess and fine-tune the effects of interventions.

In other cases, parents may request an evaluation of their child for clinical reasons, pay for it using their health insurance, and only later decide to use that report in a legal proceeding. In this situation, the child and family hold primary client status, and the neuropsychologist may address the specific concerns discussed in the original report. He or she would not offer an expert opinion about issues not addressed in that report (e.g., the forensic question as to whether or not the child's neuropsychological impairment preexisted a head injury). Just as an expert does not serve as a clinician, so should the clinician treating a particular case decline to "switch hats" if asked, at some later date, to serve in the role of an expert regarding that case.

Finally, sometimes an attorney, a clinical child psychologist, or a forensic child psychologist may wish to consult a neuropsychologist to discuss a question about a forensic case. The neuropsychologist may be asked to review and comment on the findings and interpretation of testing by some other neuropsychologist. When the neuropsychologist does not test the child directly but has access only to a review of someone else's testing records and written report, the resulting opinion may be limited to a critique of that report. For example, the neuropsychologist might offer opinions as to whether the tests administered appropriately addressed the questions asked and adequately considered the child's developmental level; whether the tests were scored, and scores reported, accurately; whether the reported findings adequately support the conclusions and recommendations; and whether alternative conclusions may follow from those findings. In such cases, one cannot usually determine the accuracy of test administration procedures or the quality of rapport between the child and examiner. In some cases, the neuropsychologist would not be able to provide an independent opinion as to the child's diagnosis or prognosis except to agree or disagree that the other examiner has adequately supported his or her conclusions, assuming adequate rapport, standardized test administration, and veridical test data.

This situation poses some particularly complex ethical dilemmas for neuropsychologists. For example, imagine that a child's family sues their ex-landlord for failure to abate lead paint. The landlord's attorney retains a neuropsychologist to review someone else's evaluation of the child. There seems a reasonable likelihood that the child has impairments, based on reported high lead levels and relevant medical reports of demonstrable lead effects, but the plaintiff's neuropsychological evaluation seems poorly done and inconclusive. That evaluation by the plaintiff's expert revealed no impairment, so it tends to support the landlord's case more than it does the child plaintiff's, and the landlord's attorney will happily accept it. Normally, in a clinical scenario, the ethical response would involve advising the child's parents to seek a second neuropsychological opinion to clarify the diagnosis and promote the child's welfare. However, in this case, the neuropsychologist's client, the landlord's attorney, may choose to accept the existing report and look no further because it helps the landlord's case.

The defense attorney's first responsibility focuses on defending the landlord, not protecting or assisting the child nor even discovering whether or not the child has any impairment or any treatment needs. Nevertheless, in cases that involve children's health and welfare, some defense attorneys have shown a willingness to communicate a neuropsychologist's recommendations to the family or their attorney after settlement or adjudication of the case so that the child can get a better evaluation and obtain treatment, if needed. The defense attorney has no legal obligation to do so.

HAS THE CHILD ALREADY BEEN EVALUATED?

Optimal validity of most neuropsychological tests occurs when the child is unfamiliar with the test materials, items, or questions. Test norms assume that the child has not seen a test item previously. Prior exposure to a test may alter a child's performance and the meaning of test results. Therefore, knowing the context for a particular evaluation is important. Has the child undergone evaluation recently through the school system or by an independent psychologist? If so, what findings resulted? Who else will participate in evaluating the child for forensic purposes, and how will that evaluation occur? In most cases, a review of previous evaluators' findings is essential in order to prevent needless repetition of the tests and to ensure that results remain uncontaminated by practice and familiarity effects—or, at least, that interpretation of results takes into account such effects when they cannot be avoided. For these reasons, evaluators who insist on "blind" evaluation (i.e., testing a child without knowing the child's history, previous testing, etc.) and those who rigidly adhere to a "fixed battery" approach may sometimes do a disservice to the child and the court.

MEDICAL HISTORY, NEUROIMAGING, AND NEUROPSYCHOLOGY

Clinically significant brain dysfunction can result from microscopic lesions too small to show up on conventional CT or MRI scans. Scalp EEG readings may fail to detect abnormalities in brain electrical activity that occur deep below the skull surface. Neuropsychological testing provides the most sensitive and accurate measure of the brain's functional status and, therefore, of the brain's physiological integrity. For this reason, courts typically have ruled that neuropsychologists are qualified to testify to the presence, nature, and severity of brain damage or dysfunction.

Interview and History-Taking

An initial interview will often prove helpful in understanding the developmental, social, family/ cultural, and medical history and background of presenting problems. Such interviews also help in evaluating the parents' understanding about what is "wrong with" the child, if anything; and in understanding their goals with respect to the litigation. Parents in this situation often seem to feel torn between presenting their child as positively as possible and emphasizing the child's need for therapeutic or educational services or his or her right to compensation for perceived injuries. When a child has suffered an injury, some parents insist, "there's nothing wrong with my kid," when in fact a serious neuropsychological impairment has resulted. Others exaggerate the severity of the child's disabilities, either inadvertently (e.g., overreacting to the emotional trauma of having an injured child) or deliberately (e.g., attempting to gain greater financial compensation). Because parents and some older children or adolescents have a range of motives for participating in a forensic neuropsychological evaluation, their self-reports may reflect bias or exaggeration (Lu & Boone, 2002). Therefore, corroborating information gleaned from parent interviews with data obtained from teachers, therapists, medical records (including birth records), school records, and historical records such as "baby books" or home videos will often prove helpful. Collecting this type of data may prove challenging but worth the substantial effort required. The expert witness should therefore advise the attorney to expend the resources needed to obtain such corroborating information.

Reviewing and Releasing Test Records

In considering the findings of previous evaluations, it may prove helpful to review the child's actual responses to test questions and stimuli, the "raw data," as well as the formal written report. Specific legal and ethical rules govern the release of test data to psychologists and nonpsychologists. Psychologists are bound by the American Psychological Association's (APA, 2002) code of ethics, and by law in some states, to make a distinction between "test materials" (such as the test manuals, questions, or stimuli) and "test data" (a particular client's responses and scores). Ethical standards, as well as copyright laws, direct psychologists to limit the public exposure of test materials so that the public will remain "naïve" about those stimuli and, therefore, the tests will remain valid. In some states (e.g., Illinois), laws require psychologists to release test materials only to another psychologist or in response to a court order.

"Test data," on the other hand, are the individual's particular *responses* to test questions and stimuli. Under current APA guidelines, these data are to be released only with client/patient consent or a court order or statute. Note that a subpoena is not a court order; generally, psychologists will need to obtain client consent or a court order before releasing data in response to a subpoena (Behnke, 2003; see also Koocher, chapter 3, this volume).

In general, the current ethical guidelines presume that test data *should* be released, with the client's consent, unless there is compelling reason to withhold it. Such reasons may exist in special cases; the ethical code notes that "psychologists may refrain from releasing test data to protect a client/patient or others from substantial harm or misuse or misrepresentation of the data or the test" (Standard 9.04; see also Standard 9.11; APA, 2002). The federal Health Insurance Portability and Accountability Act (HIPAA) regulations, as well as state, provincial, or local laws, supersede the ethical code as a guide to psychologists' legal obligations, yet they may conflict with ethical or moral judgment, in which case psychologists may need to seek legal and ethical consultation to resolve dilemmas.

Testing

Standardized tests are useful tools for eliciting specific behaviors and for comparing those observed behaviors with the responses of hundreds, or thousands, of "typically developing" children. Test standardization enables us to know that a particular pattern of responding is characteristic of 4-year-olds, or of 10-year-olds, or of children with specific atypical symptoms. Quantitative or "objective" test results may indicate that an individual responded more slowly, less accurately, or less consistently than most people of his or her age group. Qualitative observations are essential to describe *how* that individual's responses differed from "the norm." Analysis and integration of both quantitative and qualitative test-based observations, combined with informal behavioral observations, history, inter-

views, collateral informants, and review of records, contribute to the neuropsychologists' conclusions about *why* an individual's test responses form a particular pattern. It is analyzing test data and associated information as a coherent pattern, in conjunction with knowing how various patterns tend to be associated with particular types of atypical brain development or brain injury, that distinguishes the expert neuropsychologist from other specialists, such as clinical and school psychologists, who conduct psychological or psychoeducational evaluations.

Neuropsychologists, especially those who are board-certified, may employ psychometrists or "technicians" to administer all or part of the standardized tests (Sweet, Moberg, & Suchy, 2000). Psychometrists should be well trained not only in administering and scoring tests in a standardized manner but also in making qualitative behavioral observations. The National Association of Psychometrists provides useful guidelines pertaining to the qualifications and ethics of psychometrists (see www.napnet.org). The neuropsychologist supervises test selection and administration, integrates the findings of tests and interviews, makes diagnostic and prognostic conclusions based on an analysis of those data together with his or her knowledge of brain-behavior relationships, and prepares the oral or written reports. (For more information, see the official statement of the National Academy of Neuropsychology, 2000, on the use of neuropsychology test technicians in clinical practice and the report of the Division 40 Task Force on Education, Accreditation, and Credentialing, 1991, on recommendations for education and training of nondoctoral personnel in clinical neuropsychology).

Test Selection

The selection of neuropsychological tests depends on the developmental level, sensory and physical capabilities, language and culture, and educational background of the child. Culturally and developmentally competent neuropsychologists will have an array of tests to choose among and do not simply apply one test or test battery to all clients.

Modifying standardized test procedures to accommodate children who have linguistic, cultural, sensory, or other physical differences from test standardization groups; skillfully using interpreters and/or translated tests; and drawing valid inferences from nonstandardized test administrations based on awareness and consideration of relevant individual and cultural differences that may influence test performance are essential competencies for neuropsychologists who examine "special populations." In some cases, there may be no standardized test for which scores can provide a valid estimate of a particular child's mental abilities. Sometimes it may be better not to test a child at all than to risk harm by making invalid inferences based on tests not normed for someone with that child's physical condition, language background, or life experience. On the other hand, because failure to estimate a child's mental abilities also can result in harm to the child, one may sometimes rely on clinical observation, modified administration, and description of the child's performance in comparison with observed behaviors of same-age peers who have similar physical, cultural, linguistic, or other characteristics that differ from the demographics of the test standardization sample. Such comparison may be done informally (i.e., based on the clinician's anecdotal experience) or, rarely, in a formal way (i.e., by recruiting and testing a sample of children from the community or by testing siblings of an injured child).

The brain functions assessed in a typical neuropsychological evaluation include those abilities shown to be dissociable through research and clinical experience. *Dissociable* means that a client may excel at Task X yet fail at Task Y, or vice versa. Major categories of dissociable neuropsychological abilities include language or verbal abilities; spatial or visuospatial abilities; attention and concentration; verbal and visual memory; motor function; mood and affect; academic achievement in reading, writing, and mathematics; and executive function (which includes abilities to plan, organize, monitor, and appraise one's ongoing goal-directed behavior).

All neuropsychological tests are multidetermined. No test measures one, and only one, brain function. For example, a "simple" test of receptive vocabulary (pointing to a picture named by the examiner) may incidentally reflect the client's willingness to cooperate; ability to perceive and comprehend detailed line drawings; understanding that these drawings can illustrate words and that only one of them best illustrates the word

spoken by the examiner; ability to pay attention to several things at once, scan all the options, and select the one best answer; ability to point accurately to the chosen response; and ability to "shift gears" (i.e., letting go of the response that was just made in order to move on to the next stimulus word).

The association of a particular test with a particular brain-based ability is rather arbitrary, therefore. Test names or descriptions reflect the test developers' intentions, not what the client actually does with the test. For example, some so-called visual memory tests (e.g., Stanford-Binet Memory for Objects) can involve either forming visual images of the stimuli or remembering the names of the stimuli; the latter strategy invokes *verbal* memory, but not necessarily visual memory.

"IQ" or other composite scores from "intelligence tests" are so significantly multidetermined that they can sensitively reveal brain injury in some cases (Salmon & Meyer, 1986), but not in others. From a neuropsychological standpoint, IQ is one of the least interesting scores, because so many different factors can contribute to lowering it. The bulk of the evaluation often involves untangling all the factors that may have lowered the IQ score, such as effort, cultural or language differences, family and educational environment, and preexisting conditions. On the other hand, marked deficits in attention, memory, or executive function may not be reflected in a significantly impaired IQ score after a brain injury. Therefore, the neuropsychological evaluation includes specifically targeted assessments of various abilities, not simply an IQ test.

Assessment of language or verbal abilities can include tests designed to assess receptive (comprehension) and expressive (production) abilities involving word sounds and word structure (articulation, phonological and morphemic awareness); words and their meanings (vocabulary, semantic awareness); sentence structure (syntax); story structure (narrative or discourse awareness); conversational competence (turn taking, topic maintenance, etc.); pragmatics (using phrases appropriate to the social and linguistic situation); and gesture, posture, and prosody (the movements, "body language," voice "melody" and intonations).

Assessment of visuospatial abilities can include perception, memory (reproduction or recognition), and construction of abstract or meaningful images (e.g., lines or angles, faces, pictured objects, or abstract drawings). Clients may respond by naming, copying, completing, or matching the visual stimulus, either immediately (in which case it is a perceptual or naming test) or after a delay (in which case it becomes a visual memory test). Drawing and copying tasks, as well as three-dimensional construction tasks, introduce a fine motor component and are often described as "visual-motor" tests. Printing and handwriting may be included among visual-motor tests, but they also involve language and organizational or planning ability (written expression).

Motor abilities include control and coordination of limbs on the two sides of the body; posture, balance, and locomotion; strength; ability to modulate energy and activity level to fit the situation; ability to carry out smooth, rhythmic, continuous action patterns; and oral/verbal agility (articulatory and other mouth movements).

Evaluating attentional abilities usually involves observing behavior throughout testing and sometimes also giving specific tests that assess various aspects of attention. Attentional abilities include getting started (focusing or initiating attention); sustaining concentration, vigilance, and alertness; ignoring or "screening out" distractions; shifting attention flexibly when a cue or plan demands refocusing; and dividing attention or "multitasking" (keeping track of more than one thing at a time). A particular test or behavioral characteristic may be characterized as an example of "attention" by one neuropsychologist and as an example of "executive function" by another, because no clear consensus exists on the distinction between attention and executive function.

Executive function refers to the ability to regulate one's ongoing, goal-oriented behavior in accordance with situational demands. This includes the ability to formulate, plan, carry out, self-monitor, and flexibly self-correct one's own goal-directed behavior, based on self-awareness in relation to the social and environmental context. Someone with executive dysfunction may seem very effective and capable when observed in a structured situation but may have trouble applying his or her knowledge, skills, and attitudes in "the right way at the right time." This often becomes most obvious in social situations, and it can also manifest itself in ambiguous or complex work and school situations, as well. He or she may have trouble making a decision or plan about what to do or when to do it; carrying out the steps of a plan in an effective sequence; varying the pace, tempo, or intensity of an activity in keeping with situational demands; keeping track of what has been done already and what remains to be accomplished; keeping track of and correcting errors; ignoring distractions and inhibiting irrelevant or habitual responses in order to accomplish the plan; and "shifting gears" (flexibly changing his or her ideas or actions) in order to deal with changing situational demands.

Social-emotional and adaptive abilities include establishing and maintaining relationships with parents, siblings, teachers, peers of same and opposite gender, intimate or marital partners; expressing and interpreting nonverbal signs of emotion (facial expression, body language); "sizing up" a social situation; feelings and attitudes about oneself, the present situation, and future prospects; specific worries and concerns; and daily living skills (independence, responsibility, self-care skills).

Assessment of academic and vocational achievement includes reading (real and nonsense words, sentences, passages; oral fluency vs. silent comprehension); writing (fluency, punctuation, grammar, thematic content, organization); mastery of quantitative concepts (numeracy), computation, and fluent recall of math facts; and the ability to solve math word problems and multistep operations.

Clearly, not every neuropsychological evaluation can address every area of functioning listed. Depending on the specific concerns and referral questions, the examiner will select a subset of tests. In most cases, however, a comprehensive evaluation will include measures that at least screen for serious problems in the following areas: general intelligence, adaptive behavior, social-emotional functioning, language, visuospatial perception and construction, verbal and visual memory, attention, executive function, and motor skills.

Neuropsychological Report Writing

The report should answer the questions asked truthfully and as thoroughly as possible. If no evidence of any neuropsychological impairment exists, the report can state this very briefly. If evidence of impairment exists, a lengthy report may result. In some cases, as mentioned earlier, the retaining attorney may specifically request no report writing. Most attorneys will ask the neuropsychologist to provide some oral feedback, usually by telephone, before writing any report.

The written report should clearly identify the dates, duration, and location of assessment procedures. It should specify who was interviewed or tested and by whom (e.g., which parts of the evaluation involved direct contact with the neuropsychologist, which were conducted by a psychometrist or technician, and which by questionnaire or computer-administered tests or by telephone). Include a complete list of all evaluation procedures, tests, questionnaires, interviews, and records reviewed. Specify the reason for referral and the referral source. State the evaluation findings, conclusions, and recommendations as precisely and clearly as possible. The following several sections of this chapter pertain to formulating the findings, conclusions, and recommendations of a written report, with a focus on specific forensic questions.

Does the Child Have a Neuropsychological Impairment?

Tests yield false positive and false negative scores, as well as valid scores. An important aspect of a neuropsychologist's forensic expertise involves the ability to explain psychometric principles and information that guide test interpretation (Berent & Swartz, 1999; Dennis, 1989). Interpreted knowledgeably and conscientiously, psychological tests can yield results as valid as medical tests, such as X-rays (Matarazzo, 1990; Meyer et al., 2001).

A growing emphasis, in medical and legal as well as in neuropsychological arenas, focuses on "evidence-based" interpretation of test findings (Sackett, Straus, Richardson, Rosenberg, & Haynes, 2000). For example, consider the predictive value of test findings; that is, the probability that a brain abnormality exists, given a specific test score. This predictive value relates both to the "base rate" of low test scores within the general population of uninjured children and to test score reliability (Gouvier, 1999).

Did the Injury Cause This Child's Neuropsychological Impairment?

Determining whether or not the child has any identifiable neuropsychological impairment constitutes a clinical endeavor faced every day by practicing neuropsychologists. Forensic evaluations place far more emphasis on the question of *etiology* (i.e., underlying cause of identified abnormalities) than one usually encounters in the everyday clinical practice of pediatric neuropsychology. Neuropsychologists always remain alert to the possibility of uncovering treatable conditions in children presenting with learning or behavior problems of unknown etiology. For example, for some epilepsies or genetic-metabolic disorders, early detection and intervention can prevent further progressive impairment. Most of the time, however, pediatric neuropsychologists see children who have already been diagnosed by a neurologist or other physician. Therefore, the clinician's energy will more likely focus on analyzing the child's needs and capabilities and recommending interventions to facilitate development than on analyzing the extent to which various risk factors have contributed to his or her problems.

In forensic cases, providing an opinion about the "probable" cause of an impairment may require considering and discussing relevant social, psychological, educational, and physiological factors, including but not limited to the specific injury or issue under litigation (see Table 16.1 and the following discussion). Remember that "probable," the term of legal significance in a forensic context, usually means "better than 51% odds" (i.e., as opposed to the context of psychological science, in which the important threshold of "significance" usually means "better than 95% odds").

Determining the etiology of neuropsychological impairment in children often involves more complicated factors than it does in adults. First, information about premorbid functioning typically is limited, or the functions tested at the time of the assessment may not have been developmentally possible at an earlier time. Second, the effects of an injury often become more difficult to predict and measure when combined with the dynamic changes occurring normally in the developing brain. Third, because their brains are still developing

Table 16.1 Factors that affect brain-behavior development

Factor	Example
Genetic characteristics	DNA or chromosome anomaly (Down and Fragile X syndromes)
Intrauterine environment	Maternal PKU, maternal diabetes, stress hormones
Prenatal nutrition and malnutrition	Folate deficiency associated with spina bifida
Malformations	Neuronal dysmigration; craniofacial syndromes
Prenatal toxins	Prenatal drug or alcohol or other chemical exposure
Prenatal infections	TORCH syndromes (rubella and other viruses)
Prenatal injury	Amniotic band syndrome; ruptured amniotic sac
Perinatal injury (birth trauma)	Anoxia/hypoxia; intraventricular hemorrhage
Postnatal nutrition/malnutrition	Vitamin and protein deficiencies; malabsorption
Postnatal toxins	Postnatal lead or mercury toxicity
Postnatal injury	Falls, car crashes, gunshot wounds, near-drowning
Postnatal neglect and abuse	Failure to thrive; reactive attachment disorder
Access to quality medical care	Rural location; insurance restrictions
Family stress and resources	Level of income, conflict, support systems
Rehabilitation and education	Agency and school-based therapies

rapidly, children have particular vulnerabilities to the effects of a wide range of physical and social factors in the environment, which can either ameliorate or exacerbate the impact of an injury on brain development and brain function. Fourth, pediatric neuropsychologists need to consider the possibility of insufficient effort, including possible malingering by parents or even by children (Faust, Hart, & Guilmette, 1988; Faust, Hart, Guilmette, & Arkes, 1988; Lu & Boone, 2002; but see also critiques of the Faust papers, e.g., Bigler, 1990). We discuss each of these four issues next.

ESTIMATING PREMORBID FUNCTION   In a nonforensic clinical context, a neuropsychologist typically can rely on parents to describe their child's developmental history. In a forensic context, parental report rarely constitutes sufficient data, because parents may exaggerate or minimize the extent of disability following an injury and may be biased toward attributing problems to the injury rather than to preexisting conditions. Therefore, it becomes particularly important to seek corroborating information about the child's premorbid history and pre- and postinjury functioning. Relevant information can include standardized psychological or educational testing from school or other agencies, including group-administered achieve-

ment tests, which provide some information about scholastic intelligence and achievement; report card grades and teacher's comments over the years, which provide information about attention and activity, work habits, conduct and social skills, and achievement; and samples of schoolwork, which provide information about achievement, visual-motor control and coordination in drawing and handwriting, and use of language and organizational skills for written expression. Teachers' rating scales of academic skills and social-emotional functioning, such as the Achenbach Child Behavior Checklist (Achenbach & Rescorla, 2001) or the Behavior Assessment System for Children (Reynolds & Kamphaus, 1992) may be obtained from teachers who knew the child prior to the injury, as well as from the current teacher, if the injury was recent enough. Coaches, scout leaders, music or dance teachers, day-care providers, and religious school teachers may also prove to be useful informants regarding children's social-emotional behaviors and learning abilities.

Written consent of the parents and of the retaining attorney should be obtained before contacting teachers to gather information about the child's functioning. Teachers and other collateral informants deserve to know, before they fill out a questionnaire or cooperate with an interview about their student, that the information they provide may be used by the court or attorneys. Even though this knowledge may affect what the teacher says, it is unethical to imply to the teacher that the information gathered will remain confidential, when, in fact, it will not.

Comparing the child's functioning with parents' or siblings' IQ scores or with scores predicted on the basis of demographic factors usually is not helpful. The confidence range for predicting IQ from these factors varies so widely that a difference of 21 points or more is needed to demonstrate that a child's IQ differs significantly from parents' IQs or from expectations based on demographic variables. Such a comparison may be useful if the child shows significant mental retardation or if the parents have very high intellectual abilities; but for most people, who score somewhere within the average range, it will not prove helpful (Redfield, 2001).

A large and growing body of literature can assist forensic neuropsychologists in avoiding logical pitfalls, such as "affirming the consequent," ignoring population base rates of diagnosable conditions, and other sources of error (Lees-Haley & Cohen, 1999). When a child allegedly sustained prenatal or perinatal injuries involving brain impairment, or when the child is very young, there may be no reasonable way to estimate premorbid function and compare it with postmorbid status. There may be cases in which one *cannot* conclude "with a reasonable degree of neuropsychological certainty" whether or not an observed impairment was caused or exacerbated by the specific injury in question. In those cases, the neuropsychologist should not hesitate to state the opinion that no conclusion can be drawn with reasonable certainty. In other cases that have little or no documentation of premorbid status, the neuropsychologist may be able to conclude, nevertheless, that a particular injury has "possibly" or "probably" contributed to the child's observed impairment. The logic is to exclude other possible or probable causes:

(a) This child has impairment Y based on neuropsychological or other test findings.
(b) This child sustained injury X based on medical or other documents.
(c) Injury X commonly causes impairment Y, based on research literature.

(d) Injury is *not* commonly followed by normal, unimpaired, development, based on research literature.
(e) This child has not been exposed to any of the other common causes of impairment Y, based on medical or other documents, neuropsychological testing, and review of research literature about the various possible and probable etiologies of impairment Y.
(f) The occurrence of injury X was probably not the *result* of this child's impairment Y (for example, a child with a chromosomal defect might have problems with prenatal motor development that could lead to a difficult delivery and to subsequent developmental motor delays; in this case, the chromosomal defect and not the delivery problems might be the root cause of the child's developmental impairment).

When all of these conditions, 1 through 6, are carefully considered and researched, the neuropsychologist may be able to make a clear and convincing argument that "injury X caused or contributed to impairment Y." The degree of certainty—whether this causal connection is deemed "more probable than not" or merely "possible"—will depend on the specifics of the case. Often, having completed the analysis previously outlined, the neuropsychologist may state, "I know of no other causes of impairment in this case," which allows the attorney to ask the obvious question, "Is it possible that there are causes that you do not know about?" Neuropsychologists are not omniscient, so, of course, one generally would answer, "Yes, that is possible."

The plaintiff's attorney typically will want to argue that the injury "probably" (with odds of 51% or better) caused the child's impairment. The defendant's attorney usually will ask the neuropsychologist, "Could this impairment have occurred if the child had never sustained the documented injury?" and will want to argue that the odds are 51% or better that the injury is *not* the cause of the child's impairment. The neuropsychologist should anticipate both questions and be prepared to give an opinion or to state that he or she "has no opinion as to cause." When asked to "give a simple yes or no answer" to certain questions, neuropsychologists may sometimes reply that such an answer is not supported by the evidence. For example, sometimes a neuropsychologist might state that an injury is a "substantial contributing factor" in causing impairment (see the next section) but that the evidence is insufficient to determine whether or not that injury is the "main or proximate cause" of impairment.

In some cases, the neuropsychologists' assessment of the child's current functional status may be important and relevant to settling the case, even when the neuropsychologist cannot form an opinion as to the cause of the impairment. Sometimes, the question of cause is specifically excluded, by the retaining attorney, the judge, or by the neuropsychologist, from the list of questions to be addressed in the neuropsychological evaluation and report. In those cases, attorneys may choose to have medical experts testify about the cause of impairments, including functional impairments identified by the neuropsychologist.

CONTRIBUTING FACTORS   In many forensic cases, if a child who sustained an injury shows neuropsychological impairment, one party will claim that the impairment was caused or worsened by the injury, whereas another may claim that the child's problems predated the injury and/or were caused by unrelated factors. A child's medical and social history may include several different risk factors, any or all of which could affect brain development and behavior (see Table 16.1 for examples). In such a case, how can one possibly reach any conclusion about whether the specific injury in question contributed significantly to the child's impairment? The likelihood that a specific injury has exacerbated the child's problems may be deduced from the relevant research literature on outcomes in children who do not have premorbid problems. This underscores the importance of the neuropsychologist becoming conversant with current research literature about the specific type of injury under consideration and with any associated medical treatments or conditions.

In the following case, the child's problems are embedded within the context of multiple medical, social, and parenting difficulties. Rather than ignoring or denying these "unrelated" factors, a forensic expert should identify and discuss the contribution of each potentially important factor. This example comes from a case in which parents sued an obstetrician for alleged failure to diagnose and properly treat their child's complex birth defects and subsequent cognitive and emotional problems, which were associated with prolonged oxygen deprivation.

Mike's (a pseudonym) stored knowledge systems, indexed by his IQ and academic achievement test scores, are normal to superior compared with the average child of his age. However, compared with a normal child of his age, Mike demonstrates three very serious problems:

1. Mental disorganization, or deficits in "executive function," characterized by problems with planning, selecting, organizing, and arranging relevant responses in a systematic, step-by-step fashion; hyperverbal behavior and haphazard visual-spatial problem solving; and extremely poor retrieval of memorized information.
2. Emotional dysregulation, characterized by inability to modulate the intensity, duration, context, or timing of displays of emotional behavior in an age-appropriate manner.
3. Motor dyscoordination, particularly on rapid, voluntary finger sequences and eye-hand coordination, dexterity, and speed.

Mike has an extremely complicated birth history in which several related complications might have contributed to his current impairment of executive function. First, a long period of perinatal anoxia very likely contributed significantly to his current problems. Research has shown consistently that the probability of neuropsychological impairment in children with prolonged anoxia is very high (Gluckman, Pinal, & Gunn, 2001; Nyakas, Buwalda, & Luiten, 1996; Painter, 1995; Roland & Hill, 1995; Scher, 2001).

Some or all of the associated, well-documented medical complications, including umbilical cord malformation and possible associated prenatal hypoxia, transient renal failure, transient but prolonged acidosis and liver dysfunction, prophylactic treatment with phenobarbitol, and ongoing allergies and asthma, also may have contributed to Mike's present difficulties.

He has been evaluated by a pediatric medical geneticist who did not identify any specific genetic or metabolic condition that might have contributed to the occurrence of Mike's perinatal problems and his subsequent neuropsychological problems. Although the family history is significant for mild learning difficulty in his father, this is not likely to be related to the severe impairments that Mike currently demonstrates.

A final factor that must be considered in interpreting Mike's neuropsychological profile is the stress his family has experienced as a consequence of his traumatic birth and subsequent illnesses. There has been a disruption of Mike's attachment with his mother, and sufficient stress on the parents' marital relationship to result in a temporary separation, about 1 year before this evaluation was conducted. Inconsistencies in parental discipline, with his father and grandmother being relatively lax and permissive, in contrast to his mother being more strict and enforcing rules, probably contributed to Mike's oppositional, defiant, and hostile behavior, particularly toward his mother, as well as to his whining and manipulativeness with his father and grandmother. However, the fact that such behaviors have not carried over into the school environment or the testing situation indicates that Mike has not been seriously "damaged" by being overindulged. On the contrary, he appears to have benefited from a very loving, consistent, nurturing, and supportive relationship with his father and grandmother, as well as from the conscientious care of his mother. He also has had excellent exposure to preschool and early childhood learning opportunities, almost since birth.

Mike's deficits in motor and executive function probably were caused by traumatic birth and subsequent medical complications. His emotional dysregulation probably is caused by the combination of executive dysfunction with some overindulgence and stress at home. The executive dysfunction probably contributes to Mike's emotional lability, difficulty in coping with frustration and managing his feelings in an age-appropriate way, and overdependence on external supervision, rules, and reminders rather than self-directed initiation and completion of tasks. If, in addition to these cognitive problems, caregivers' discipline and expectations are inconsistent, then Mike would be expected to have particular difficulty at home in terms of managing his temper and complying with chores or homework that require sustained concentration and effort.

Is the Problem Permanent?
What Is the Prognosis?

The long-term outcome of acquired childhood brain injury is influenced by many factors (Baron, Fennell, & Voeller, 1997; Bernstein, 2000; Dennis, 2000; Farmer, 1997; Yeates, 2000). Some of the most important factors include:

(a) The nature of the injury
(b) The quality of acute medical care and rehabilitation
(c) The age at which the child is injured
(d) The age of initial evaluation
(e) The age at which outcome is assessed
(f) The time intervals between dates of injury, initial testing, and assessed or predicted outcome (e.g., a 5-year interval between ages 1 and 5 is not equivalent to the 5-year interval from ages 20 to 25)
(g) The criteria, developmental phase, or context within which "outcome" is defined (e.g., survival, categories of neurological "recovery," neuropsychological test scores, school grades, or adult income; Fletcher, Ewing-Cobbs, Francis, & Levin, 1995); and the context within which "outcome" is measured (e.g., school learning vs. job performance; Bernstein, 2000)
(h) The child's preinjury status, including any preexisting cognitive, social, emotional, or behavioral problems, and history of prior injuries
(i) The resources and stressors within the child's family, community, and educational environments

NATURE OF THE INJURY AND OF MEDICAL CARE
Brain injuries may be diffuse, affecting all or most of the brain tissue, or focal, affecting a specific brain location. Closed head injuries, from falls or motor vehicle accidents, may involve both focal injuries (specific areas of bleeding or bruising) and diffuse injuries (diffuse axonal injury to a wide area of brain tissue; see Baron et al., 1997). Toxic (poisons), anoxic (suffocation), or infectious (meningitis, encephalitis) injuries typically are diffuse, though some infections may target specific brain areas, causing focal injury. Gunshot wounds, brain tumors, and abscesses typically cause focal injuries.

The physical severity of a head injury, assessed by measures such as duration of unconsciousness, neurological status, skull fracture, and posttraumatic seizures, is a powerful predictor of long-term functioning even over a period of more than 20 years (Klonoff, Clark, & Klonoff, 1993). Nevertheless, there can be considerable variation in individual responses to head injuries of the same severity (Yeates, 2000).

The location, size, and rate of expansion of a focal injury can all affect its behavioral manifestations. For example, there is strong evidence of species-specific, hemispheric specialization of language abilities at all ages. Focal lesions of the left hemisphere typically are associated with impaired language functions in children, as well as in adults (Vargha-Khadem, Isaacs, & Muter, 1994). Larger lesions and those that have more rapid onset (such as a gunshot wound as opposed to a slow-growing tumor) typically are associated with more extensive or severe impairment (e.g., Levin, Ewing-Cobbs, & Eisenberg, 1995). However, these generalizations may not apply to every individual. For example, language difficulties can be seen in children with right-hemisphere, as well as those with left-hemisphere, lesions (Reilly, Bates, & Marchman, 1998; Thal et al., 1991). In other children, right-hemisphere language development may substantially compensate for left-hemisphere damage, particularly in cases of congenital brain damage (Bates et al., 2001; Blanchette & Smith, 2002; Boatman et al., 1999; Hertz-Pannier et al., 2002; Vargha-Khadem & Polkey, 1992).

The availability and quality of acute care and rehabilitation services may be another source of variance in outcome, and it covaries with demographic factors (McCarthy, Serpi, Kufera, Demeter, & Paidas, 2002; National Institutes of Health Consensus Development Panel on Rehabilitation of Persons with Traumatic Brain Injury, 1999). Insurance coverage and policies regarding care of indigent patients may be other sources of variance in quality of care.

AGE AT INJURY AND TIME OF TESTING Much of the neuropsychological literature about the effects of acquired brain injury is based on studies of adults who have war wounds or strokes, causing focal impairment. That literature is not very helpful in predicting outcomes of injuries in children. The age at which brain injury occurs significantly affects both the physical characteristics of the injury (Ommaya, Goldsmith, & Thibault, 2002; Yeates, 2000) and functional outcomes.

Children are more likely to have diffuse than focal brain injuries. Younger age typically is associated with more long-lasting and severe neuropsychological effects, as well as a slower recovery rate, among children with various sorts of *diffuse* injuries, including brain injuries associated with meningitis, head trauma, or radiation therapy (Taylor & Alden, 1997; Yeates, 2000). Prior to the 1980s, children often were considered more likely than adults to show full recovery from brain injuries. Different measures of outcome yield different views of a child's prognosis, however. Children are more likely than adults to survive severe head injury without permanent severe neurological deficit, as assessed, for example, by the modified Glasgow Coma Scale; however, children typically show poorer outcomes than adults on neuropsychological tests of cognition and adaptive behavior (Fletcher et al., 1995).

The age at which the child is tested and the time lag between the brain injury and evaluation date influence test findings. Acute posttraumatic symptoms may resolve within hours, days, or months, whereas other symptoms may not emerge until months or years following an injury (Fletcher et al., 1995; Yeates, 2000).

Children may "grow out of" certain symptoms of acute impairment as the brain heals and matures. For example, aphasia (impaired language production and comprehension) associated with focal left hemisphere brain injury tends to resolve more quickly and more completely in children younger than about 6 years than in older children or adults. This finding appears related to normal developmental changes in brain plasticity (Hertz-Pannier et al., 2002). Similarly, visuospatial and social impairment associated with right-hemisphere stroke can resolve substantially over time, although other neuropsychological deficits may increase (Eslinger & Biddle, 2000).

On the other hand, children who initially show minimal or no impairment may "grow into" certain types of long-term impairment, as brain systems that were damaged in early childhood become increasingly important to mature thinking and behavior (Bernstein, 2000; Dennis, 2000; Taylor, Schatschneider, & Minich, 2000). The classic example involves damage to frontal brain systems considered critically important for mature abstract reasoning and social judgment. These brain systems and their white matter connections to other brain regions are among the latest to mature fully in the normal course of brain development (see Kolb, Gibb, & Gorney, 2000). Damage to the immature system early in childhood may not yield immediately observable changes in behavior because that system is not yet being utilized in a mature fashion (analogous to the difficulty of observing a sprained ankle if a baby is only crawling and not yet walking). If there is long-lasting damage to frontal neurons and their connections, however, the consequent behavioral differences may manifest later in development, at the stage when most other youngsters can demonstrate the adultlike reasoning and judgment attributed, in part, to normal functional maturation of frontal brain systems. It is at that later developmental stage, typically beginning around puberty, that the brain-damaged youngster may stand out as immature, inflexible, or limited in abstract and social reasoning when compared with uninjured peers.

The nature of the neuropsychological impairment, as well as its severity, may vary with the age at which the injury occurs. This certainly is the case for congenital disorders caused by prenatal toxins (teratogens; see Rodier, 1995). Postnatal head injury or poisoning might cause more serious problems with attention than with language skills at one age, whereas at an earlier age, this pattern of deficits might be reversed (Dennis, Guger, Roncadin, Barnes, & Schachar, 2001; Levin et al., 1995; Shaheen, 1984). Brain development continues throughout childhood and adolescence, with different brain systems maturing at different rates. It has been suggested that diffuse brain injuries may have greatest adverse impact on brain systems in the process of rapid development, with lesser impact on systems more fully mature and those most immature (Kolb, 1999; Levin et al., 1995; Rodier, 1995). This hypothesis is difficult to prove, but if it is true, a diffuse brain injury might function somewhat like a flood that wrecks new gravel roads (brain systems under development) but has relatively little impact on paved highways (more established, mature systems).

The nature of the functional problem can change over time, even while the underlying damage or dysfunction persists (Bernstein, 2000). For example, children with dyslexia (developmental reading and writing disorders) may have difficulty naming different colors in preschool. Later on, they may easily name colors but have difficulty naming letters or numerals. The underlying problem with "rapid naming" is the same, but the manifest symptom shifts with age and experience. Pediatric neuropsychologists need to know about developmental "warning signs" and how they may evolve into other problems in later childhood and adult life, particularly as the environmental context or performance demands shift.

OUTCOME CRITERIA   Assessment tools in pediatric neuropsychology are becoming more sensitive to variations among different skills and abilities, individual differences, and changes in functioning over time. This increased sensitivity, accuracy, and range of available testing tools makes it possible to measure deficits and to track improvement in brain-injured children. Different measures may yield different conceptualizations about the outcome of brain injury, however. In general, the more "gross" measures are less likely to show significant relationships with age, premorbid status, or other individual differences (e.g., measures of survival, clinical ratings of "full" versus "partial" neurological recovery; or ratings of "mute" versus "verbal" language ability). Measures of specific abilities are more likely to reveal variance in outcome that is related to individual differences in lesion severity, age, and so forth (Fletcher et al., 1995). For example, Dennis and colleagues (Dennis et al., 2001) report marked differences in how brain-injured children comprehend social uses of language, such as deceptive or ironic speech, as a function of lesion location and severity. These studies show that a brain-injured child may have trouble comprehending figurative or metaphorical speech despite normal vocabulary and grammar. That child's scores on most standardized tests of "language ability" would most likely be normal because few such tests measure figurative or metaphorical speech. "Absence of evidence is not evidence of absence" of deficits to which available tests are insensitive (in the adage attributed to Carl

Sagan). Yet it can be problematic in a forensic context to use experimental measures that have been shown to differentiate brain-injured from uninjured children because these measures generally do not have well-demonstrated psychometric properties or standardized norms.

Finally, neuropsychologists may differ in their theoretical conceptualization of what is meant by terms such as *disability* or *intelligence*. Bernstein (2000) emphasizes the importance of considering the context, or environmental demands, within which a brain-injured child must function. The severity of the child's "disability" varies not only with the extent to which the child is unable to meet environmental demands but also with the extent to which the environment fails to accommodate, or compensate for, the child's deficits. Sternberg and associates (e.g., Sternberg & Grigorenko, 1999) go one step further, arguing that "there is more to intelligence than IQ." In their view, intelligence includes the ability to select or to modify one's environment so as to function successfully, as well as to adapt to one's environment. This ability to select one's optimal "niche" may be related to creative or practical reasoning abilities not measured well by traditional, analytical intelligence tests. There is very little information about how brain-injured children fare with regard to creative and practical reasoning, because most studies tend to focus on how well children perform in school or on analytical reasoning tests. Some measures of "executive function" on which head-injured children score particularly poorly seem to reflect creative and practical reasoning abilities, as well as working memory and attention (Mangeot, Armstrong, Colvin, Yeates, & Taylor, 2002). Untangling these various aspects of cognition and behavior is a major task for future studies of brain injury and its outcomes. Current data about brain injury and about what makes for successful adult functioning suggest that it is important to consider environmental demands, social and behavioral functioning, creativity, and practical intelligence, as well as IQ, when describing current status and estimating prognosis for recovery in a brain-injured child.

LONG-RANGE PROGNOSIS A major theoretical and practical problem is that, when talking about the outcome of an injury, attorneys usually mean "what sort of job can he do, and how much money can he make, as an adult." Neuropsychological studies of brain-injured children have rarely followed them long enough to assess adult vocational and economic outcomes. Neuropsychological tests for children typically are measured against the "outcome" of school grades or achievement test scores up to and during college. However, IQ scores typically predict school grades and achievement, but they are comparatively poor predictors of childhood behavioral adaptation (Mangeot, Armstrong, Colvin, Yeates, & Taylor, 2002). Factors other than IQ contribute strongly to adult vocational and economic success among people who are intellectually gifted (Reis, 1987) or limited (Kerns, Don, Mateer, & Streissguth, 1997). Therefore, pediatric neuropsychologists often have to extrapolate from various studies in the developmental and clinical psychology literature about long-term prediction of adult functioning as it is related to relevant childhood characteristics, such as intelligence, attention, and behavior problems (e.g., Hechtman, 1999; Offord & Bennett, 1994). Some longitudinal outcome studies of brain-injured children exist (for example, Dennis, Spiegler, & Hetherington, 2000; Dietrich, 2000; Klonoff et al., 1993; Lidsky & Schneider, 2003; Robertson & Finer, 1993; Stancin et al., 2002; Yeates, 2000), but more are needed that span the child-adolescent-adult continuum. Furthermore, most of the long-term studies of outcomes of childhood brain injury are concerned with lead toxicity (e.g., Feldman & White, 1992; Hartman, 1995; Needleman, 1991) or traumatic brain injury (head injuries due to passenger or pedestrian motor vehicle collisions or to falls; e.g., Yeates, 2000; Klonoff et al., 1993). There are few studies of long-term effects of less common types of childhood injuries that might give rise to lawsuits (e.g., suffocation, mercury poisoning, blows to the head from an assault, gunshot wounds, etc.). Therefore, an expert neuropsychologist should be prepared not only to apply and explain existing research data relevant to a particular case but also to identify explicitly cases or questions for which relevant empirical data are lacking.

PREMORBID STATUS When a child's premorbid neuropsychological status is impaired, it can be much more difficult to detect the effects of an injury, unless those effects are severe. For example, it can be difficult to establish that a child with Down syndrome has more trouble memorizing information after a severe head injury if the memory impairment already was marked prior to the injury. Not surprisingly, children with premorbid learning disabilities score more poorly than non-learning-disabled children on attention and memory tests after traumatic brain injury (Farmer et al., 2002). It is not known whether children with *high* premorbid IQ scores recover faster or more completely from injury than those with average scores (as may be the case for adults with brain injury, consistent with a theory of cognitive reserve; Kessler, Adams, Blasey, & Bigler, 2003).

Gender and handedness may affect response to brain injury in children, as in adults. For example, Frith and Vargha-Khadem (2001) found that boys with early unilateral left-hemisphere brain injury had impaired reading and spelling performance, whereas no significant impairment of reading and spelling skills was seen in boys with right-hemisphere injury, nor in girls.

Premorbid status also includes any previous history of brain injury; such an individual is often referred to by attorneys as the "egg shell plaintiff," who by nature of a preexisting dysfunction is more vulnerable and more impaired by subsequent injury than would normally be the case. A person who already had a diffuse head injury may sustain more serious functional impairment following a second injury, compared with someone injured only once (Carlsson, Svardsudd, & Welin, 1987; Collins et al., 2002). In the field of sports medicine, active debate exists about the "second impact syndrome," an occasional and lethal result of repeated concussion (Collins et al., 2002) that some attribute to effects of posttraumatic cerebral swelling (McCrory, 2001). The impact of repeated concussion appears to be greater in children and high school athletes than in college-age athletes (McCrory, 2001).

Premorbid status may be associated with individual differences in "accident proneness" or injury risk. For example, Light and colleagues (1998) reported that children with very mild head injuries fared worse than uninjured controls on postinjury neuropsychological tests, but outcomes for the head-injured children did not differ from those for children with orthopedic injuries that did not involve the brain. As it seems unlikely that a broken leg would lower one's scores for memory or IQ tests, these findings suggest that children who get injured may tend to have some preexisting neuropsychological impairment compared with those who are not injured. Indeed, injured children (both head-injured and those with other injuries) had higher preinjury behavior problem scores than uninjured children on the Child Behavior Checklist.

Alternatively, these findings may be viewed as evidence that suffering an injury that does not affect the brain may, nevertheless, have an adverse impact on children's neuropsychological test performance, perhaps due to emotional trauma, pain, school absence, or other unidentified factors. Evidence from adult studies indicates that the severity of injuries to other, nonbrain, systems can influence neuropsychological (cognitive) outcomes, as well as having very significant impact on emotional, behavioral, and psychological adjustment (Dacey et al., 1991).

ENVIRONMENTAL INFLUENCES   Finally, children's adaptive and behavioral functioning recovers better from brain injury when their families have more resources and less stress (Yeates et al., 2002). Neuropsychological (cognitive) test scores are not as strongly influenced by family functioning as are measures of social, emotional, and adaptive behavior, particularly behavior problems (Schwartz et al., 2003). However, environmental factors may directly influence brain systems associated with learning and memory, as well as influencing social behavior, presumably via social learning opportunities (Duncan, Brooks-Gunn, & Klebanov, 1994; Kolb, 1999). One study (Yeates et al., 1997) has demonstrated significant influence of family functioning on the severity of children's verbal memory deficits following brain injury.

Unfortunately, certain kinds of brain injury may be nonrandomly associated with differences in children's sociodemographic status and family functioning. For example, much of the controversy about adverse effects of lead toxicity is related to the difficulties of untangling effects due to lead exposure from effects of other factors associated with poverty (Dietrich, 2000; Wasserman & Factor-Litvak, 2001). Family stress contributes to increased risk of childhood pedestrian injury, even when other sociodemographic factors are controlled (Christoffel, Donovan, Schofer, Wills, & Lavigne, 1996). Because sociodemographic and family factors often are associated with differences in neuropsychological test performance, research studies must be designed and interpreted carefully to ensure that injured and uninjured groups are comparable with respect to sociodemographic variables. In studying children with head injuries, it is ideal to include a group who sustained injuries not involving the brain (Yeates, 2000). Neuropsychologists should be able to assist attorneys and the court in identifying and critiquing neurobehavioral research findings that are well designed and relevant to the case.

Malingering

As noted earlier, the possibility of bias or deliberate misinformation in parental reports is best managed by obtaining information about the child from other sources, such as day-care providers, teachers, and pediatricians, and from consulting documents such as the child's school records, "baby book," and pediatric medical records.

It is possible for children to be coached or trained to "malinger," or deliberately score poorly, on neuropsychological tests (Faust, Hart, & Guilmette, 1988; Faust, Hart, Guilmette, & Arkes, 1988; Lu & Boone, 2002; McKinzey, Prieler, & Raven, 2003). Detection of malingering is a major concern in adult neuropsychology, in which the plaintiff usually is the person being tested and usually knows full well that "impaired" scores may yield a higher monetary settlement of his or her lawsuit (Sweet, 1999).

Pediatric neuropsychologists generally assume that children, especially younger children, are not very good at faking test results in a way that is plausible, consistent, or difficult to detect. Prior to the 1980s, neuropsychologists tended to make the same assumption about adult litigants, but subsequent research has demonstrated that "symptom validity" tests and related procedures can reveal clear evidence of malingering in adults that is not obvious to a neuropsychologist in the absence of such procedures (Sweet, 1999). It is theoretically possible that children could fake symptoms or, at least, could put forth insufficient effort during testing in a way that even an expert neuropsycholo-

gist might overlook, although research studies have yet to demonstrate this possibility convincingly. Certainly, there are children, and especially adolescents, whose apparently poor attitude, motivation, and effort lead the expert to question the validity of test scores based on behavioral observations and clinical experience. Further research on symptom validity measures for children, and more generally on validity indicators embedded within neuropsychological tests, appears warranted in order to provide more objective information about effort, in general, and about the possibility of child malingering, in particular.

Until more evidence is available, it may be useful to administer more than one test of abilities that tend to be particularly sensitive to brain injury (such as memory, word retrieval, or processing speed, for example), as well as multiple tests of abilities less likely to change (such as vocabulary knowledge or reading recognition). Where there is evidence of impairment, consider whether the nature and level of severity of the impairment is consistent across tests and whether the pattern of impaired versus unimpaired performance is consistent with research evidence about expected effects of brain injury. Finally, consider whether the child seems sufficiently sophisticated to have "malingered" a consistent, plausible pattern of test results. Even this approach may be difficult to apply, however, because there is less information for children than for adults about which specific tests, or types of tests, are likely to show changes as a consequence of particular types of brain injury. Appraising the congruence between test data and collateral information (such as teacher's reports), which is probably more accessible and more extensive for children than for adults, is at least a face-valid way to check for malingering in children or adolescents and their parents.

RECOMMENDING INTERVENTIONS

An expert does not provide or direct treatment for a child under evaluation in relation to legal proceedings. In addressing the question of whether the child will need special educational, medical, psychotherapeutic, or other interventions, however, the pediatric neuropsychological report will commonly include general recommendations. For example, the neuropsychologist might state an opinion that the child will need speech therapy, a medical genetics workup, or behavior management to treat specific problems, but he or she would not make a specific referral to any particular provider.

Little empirical evidence exists about the efficacy of various strategies for rehabilitation of children with brain injuries or how to tailor specific strategies for specific needs, although there is some evidence that supports efficacy of brain injury rehabilitation in general (Beaulieu, 2002; NIH Consensus Development Panel, 1999). Though children cannot show "loss of earnings" resulting from injury, childhood brain injury may have a considerable adverse impact on parents' work and family finances (Osberg et al., 1997). Although some rehabilitation centers provide acute care for children with severe brain injuries, most children are sent back to school, and into families' care, as soon as they can walk and speak. School-based programming may be supplemented by outpatient speech therapy, physical therapy, and occupational therapy appointments and occasionally by outpatient "cognitive rehabilitation," but rarely are these therapies coordinated or integrated with one another in order to optimize long-range vocational and economic goals.

Schools may limit services related to rehabilitation of skills not clearly germane to "educational needs," for example, occupational therapy to facilitate independent bathing or dressing. Moreover, when the schools do provide services, the level of knowledge and skill regarding children with brain injuries, who are a low-incidence population, may be limited (NIH Consensus Development Panel, 1999). Traumatic-brain-injury special education services often apply only to children who have suffered a blow to the head (from falls, motor vehicle accidents, assaults, or sports-related injuries). The category of physical and other health impairments may be used to provide school-based services to other brain-injured children (such as those who sustained birth trauma or toxic exposure). This "category" of educational needs is so broadly defined that case managers (often physical or occupational therapists) may lack essential information about cognitive and emotional functioning in brain-injured children. Therefore, pediatric neuropsychologists often play a critical role in taking a holistic, integrative view of the child's needs and strengths and in consulting to the school system and other therapists about a "game plan" for comprehensive assessment, rehabilitation, and follow-up.

A forensic expert will lack direct feedback and follow-through with family and schools but, via written opinions, may characterize the child's needs and available resources, clarify the prognosis, and identify interventions reasonably expected to ameliorate the short-range and long-range adverse impact of injury. When there is no evidence of neuropsychological impairment, reading the expert's written opinion may relieve parents' unnecessary worry about their child's future. Therefore, well-written expert opinions relevant and appropriate to legal proceedings can also, incidentally, fulfill a therapeutic function for injured children and their families.

ETHICAL ISSUES IN FORENSIC NEUROPSYCHOLOGY

Although surveys have shown that involvement in forensic activities has become a common part of professional practice for clinical neuropsychologists (e.g., Sweet, Peck, Abramowitz, & Etzweiler, 2003; Koocher, chapter 3, this volume), examination of publication content of the sizeable forensic neuropsychology literature from 1990 through 2000 identified relatively few publications concerning ethics (Sweet, King, Malina, Bergman, & Simmons, 2002). Attorneys and psychologists may disagree regarding whether ethics are aspirational (cf. *Black's Law Dictionary*, Garner, 1999) or mandatory. Psychologists generally view the standards promulgated by the American Psychological Association as a necessary context for acceptable clinical practice. Ethical standards can be difficult to understand and apply in an increasingly complex real world of clinical practice; ethical standards can be even more enigmatic within a context of forensic practice. In part, the reason is that relatively unique situations can arise in the course of rendering an opinion in a forensic case to which clinicians may have no prior exposure. For example, the following examples would not be expected to occur in the conduct of routine clinical practice: (a) being asked by a plaintiff's attorney to delete mention of unsavory history information revealed in the interview of the plaintiff, (b) being asked by defense attorneys to assure the trier of fact that the plaintiff was not malingering during the neuropsychological testing, and (c) being informed by the examinee that an attorney or a parent had coached their responses to a personality test or test of ability contained within the battery of tests being administered.

When acting as a neuropsychological expert witness, numerous issues pertaining to ethics can arise with relatively high frequency, including: limitations or absence of confidentiality; awareness of inappropriate billing mechanisms potentially requested by plaintiff attorneys (e.g., liens, letters of protection or assignation, or use of health insurance); a need to maintain test security and control release of records; practicing within limits of competency and within scope of practice; undermining of objectivity due to influence of multiple pressures; truthfulness; and resolution of conflict between forensic expectations, legal rules, and ethical responsibilities (Sweet, Grote, & van Gorp, 2002). The most recent changes in the *Ethical Principles of Psychologists and Code of Conduct* (APA, 2002) resulted in the dispersal of a number of specific issues formerly contained within a section titled "Forensic Activities" into more general sections. Nevertheless, very few primary ethical standards have been changed substantively as applied to forensic neuropsychology. The two most important changes pertaining to forensic activities from the prior to the current ethical standards were to: (1) remove the implication that psychologists always try to personally evaluate forensic referrals, rather than perform only records review, when they offer opinions, and (2) revise the definition of the information referred to as test data that should be released on court order, while retaining security of test materials.

In addition to the APA *Ethical Principles*, the guidelines for specialty practice in forensic psychology (Committee on Ethical Guidelines for Forensic Psychologists, 1991) can be informative and helpful to forensic neuropsychologists. However, the specific issues that arise for neuropsychologists involved in forensic activities can be unique and challenging. In this regard, the writings on ethics for clinical neuropsychologists by Binder and Thompson (1995), Bush (2005), and Bush and Drexler (2002) are good resources. More

particularly with regard to forensic neuropsychology, the writings of Bush (2005); Grote, Lewin, Sweet, and van Gorp (2000); Guilmette and Hagan (1997); Johnson-Greene and Bechtold (2002); Johnson-Greene, Hardy-Morais, Adams, Hardy, and Bergloff (1997); and Sweet, Grote, and van Gorp (2002) are very relevant. Additionally, some forensic neuropsychology authors have explored the potential for bias or lack of objectivity in reporting findings within adversarial proceedings (Sweet & Moulthrop, 1999; van Gorp & McMullen, 1997), which is thought to be a common problem for all expert witnesses, not just neuropsychologists.

References

Achenbach, T. M., & Rescorla, L. A. (2001). *Manual for the ASEBA: School-Age Forms and Profiles*. Burlington: University of Vermont Research Center for Children, Youth, and Families.

Adams, K. (1988). Neuropsychology is not just in the eye of the provider. *Professional Psychology: Research and Practice, 19,* 488–489.

American Psychological Association. (2002). Ethical principles of psychologists and code of conduct. *American Psychologist, 57,* 1060–1073.

Baron, I. S., Fennell, E., & Voeller, K. (1997). Head trauma. In I. S. Baron, E. Fennell, & K. Voeller, *Pediatric neuropsychology in the medical setting* (pp. 292–315). New York: Oxford University Press.

Bates, E., Reilly, J., Wulfeck, B., Dronkers, N., Opie, M., Fenson, J., et al. (2001). Differential effects of unilateral lesions on language production in children and adults. *Brain and Language, 79,* 223–265.

Beaulieu, C. (2002). Rehabilitation and outcome following pediatric traumatic brain injury. *Surgical Clinics of North America, 82,* 393–408.

Behnke, S. (2003, July/August). Release of test data and APA's new Ethics Code. *Monitor on Psychology,* 70–72.

Berent, S., & Swartz, C. (1999). Essential psychometrics. In J. Sweet (Ed.), *Forensic neuropsychology: Fundamentals and practice* (pp. 1–26). Lisse, Netherlands: Swets & Zeitlinger.

Bernstein, J. H. (2000). Developmental neuropsychological assessment. In K. Yeates, M. D. Ris, & H. G. Taylor (Eds.), *Pediatric neuropsychology: Research, theory, and practice* (pp. 405–438). New York: Guilford.

Bigler, E. (1990). Neuropsychology and malingering: Comment on Faust, Hart, and Guilmette

(1988). *Journal of Consulting and Clinical Psychology, 58,* 244–247.

Binder, L., & Thompson, L. (1995). The ethics code and neuropsychological assessment practices. *Archives of Clinical Neuropsychology, 10,* 27–46.

Blanchette, N., & Smith, M. (2002). Language after temporal or frontal lobe surgery in children with epilepsy. *Brain and Cognition, 48,* 280–284.

Boatman, D., Freeman, J., Vining, E., Pulsifer, M., Miglioretti, D., Minahan, R., et al. (1999). Language recovery after left hemispherectomy in children with late-onset seizures. *Annals of Neurology, 46,* 579–586.

Buchanan, A., & Oliver, J. (1977). Abuse and neglect as a cause of mental retardation: A study of 140 children admitted to subnormality hospitals in Wiltshire. *British Journal of Psychiatry, 131,* 458–467.

Bush, S. (Ed.). (2005). *Ethics casebook for neuropsychologists.* London: Psychology Press.

Bush, S., & Drexler, M. (Eds.). (2002). *Ethical issues in clinical neuropsychology.* Lisse, Netherlands: Swets & Zeitlinger.

Carlsson, G., Svardsudd, K., & Welin, L. (1987). Long-term effects of head injuries sustained during life in three male populations. *Journal of Neurosurgery, 67,* 197–205.

Christoffel, K., Donovan, M., Schofer, J., Wills, K., & Lavigne, J. (1996). Psychosocial factors in childhood pedestrian injury: A matched case-control study. *Pediatrics, 97,* 33–42.

Collins, M., Lovell, M., Iverson, G., Cantu, R., Maroon, J., & Field, M. (2002). Cumulative effects of concussion in high school athletes. *Neurosurgery, 51,* 1175–1179.

Committee on Ethical Guidelines for Forensic Psychologists. (1991). Specialty guidelines for forensic psychologists. *Law and Human Behavior, 15,* 655–665.

Dacey, R., Dikmen, S., Temkin, N., McLean, A., Armsden, G., & Winn, H. (1991). Relative effects of brain and non-brain injuries on neuropsychological and psychosocial outcome. *Journal of Trauma, 31,* 217–222.

Dennis, M. (1989). Assessing the neuropsychological abilities of children and adolescents for personal injury litigation. *Clinical Neuropsychologist, 3,* 203–229.

Dennis, M. (2000). Childhood medical disorders and cognitive impairment: Biological risk, time, development, and reserve. In K. Yeates, M. D. Ris, & H. G. Taylor (Eds.), *Pediatric neuropsychology: Research, theory, and practice* (pp. 3–24). New York: Guilford.

Dennis, M., Guger, S., Roncadin, C., Barnes, M., & Schachar, R. (2001). Attentional-inhibitory control and social-behavioral regulation after childhood close head injury: Do biological, developmental, and recovery variables predict outcome? *Journal of the International Neuropsychological Society, 7,* 683–692.

Dennis, M., Spiegler, B., & Hetherington, R. (2000). New survivors for the new millennium: Cognitive risk and reserve in adults with childhood brain insults. *Brain and Cognition, 42,* 102–105.

Dietrich, K. (2000). Environmental neurotoxicants and psychological development. In K. Yeates, M. D. Ris, & H. G. Taylor (Eds.), *Pediatric neuropsychology: Research, theory, and practice* (pp. 206–234). New York: Guilford.

Division 40 Task Force on Education, Accreditation, and Credentialing. (1991). Recommendations for education and training of nondoctoral personnel in clinical neuropsychology. *Clinical Neuropsychologist, 5,* 20–23.

Duncan, G., Brooks-Gunn, J., & Klebanov, P. (1994). Economic deprivation and early childhood development. *Child Development, 65,* 296–318.

Eslinger, P., & Biddle, K. (2000). Adolescent neuropsychological development after early right prefrontal cortex damage. *Developmental Neuropsychology, 18,* 297–329.

Farmer, J. (1997). An ecological systems approach to childhood traumatic brain injury. In E. D. Bigler, E. Clark, & J. Farmer (Eds.), *Childhood traumatic brain injury: Diagnosis, assessment, and intervention* (pp. 261–275). Austin, TX: Pro-Ed.

Farmer, J., Kanne, S., Haut, J., Williams, J., Johnstone, B., & Kirk, K. (2002). Memory functioning following traumatic brain injury in children with premorbid learning problems. *Developmental Neuropsychology, 22,* 455–469.

Faust, D., Hart, K., & Guilmette, T. (1988). Pediatric malingering: The capacity of children to fake believable deficits on neuropsychological testing. *Journal of Consulting and Clinical Psychology, 56,* 578–582.

Faust, D., Hart, K., Guilmette, T., & Arkes, H. (1988). Neuropsychologists' capacity to detect adolescent malingerers. *Professional Psychology: Research and Practice, 19,* 508–515.

Feldman, R., & White, R. (1992). Lead neurotoxicity and disorders of learning. *Journal of Child Neurology, 7,* 354–359.

Fletcher, J., Ewing-Cobbs, L., Francis, D., & Levin, H. (1995). Variability in outcomes after traumatic brain injury in children: A developmental perspective. In S. Broman, M. Michel, & M. Broman (Eds.), *Traumatic head injury in children* (pp. 3–21). New York: Oxford University Press.

Frith, U., & Vargha-Khadem, F. (2001). Are there sex differences in the brain basis of literacy related skills? Evidence from reading and spelling impairments after early unilateral brain damage. *Neuropsychologia, 39*, 1485–1488.

Garner, B. (Ed.). (1999). *Black's law dictionary.* (7th ed.). St. Paul, MN: West Group.

Glaser, D. (2000). Child abuse and neglect and the brain: A review. *Journal of Child Psychology and Psychiatry, 41*, 97–116.

Gluckman, P., Pinal, C., & Gunn, A. (2001). Hypoxic-ischemic brain injury in the newborn: Pathophysiology and potential strategies for intervention. *Seminars in Neonatology, 6*, 109–120.

Gouvier, D. (1999). Base rates and clinical decision-making in neuropsychology. In J. Sweet (Ed.), *Forensic neuropsychology: Fundamentals and practice* (pp. 27–28). Lisse, Netherlands: Swets & Zeitlinger.

Grote, C., Lewin, J., Sweet, J., & van Gorp, W. (2000). Responses to perceived unethical practices in clinical neuropsychology: Ethical and legal considerations. *Clinical Neuropsychologist, 14*, 119–134.

Guilmette, T., & Hagan, L. (1997). Ethical considerations in forensic neuropsychological evaluations. *Clinical Neuropsychologist, 11*, 180–187.

Hartman, D. (1995). *Neuropsychological toxicity* (2nd ed.). New York: Plenum.

Hechtman, L. (1999). Predictors of long-term outcome in children with attention-deficit/hyperactivity disorder. *Pediatric Clinics of North America, 46*, 1039–1052.

Hertz-Pannier, L., Chiron, C., Jambaque, I., Renaux-Kieffer, V., Van de Moortele, P., Delalande, O., et al. (2002). Late plasticity for language in a child's non-dominant hemisphere: A pre- and post-surgery fMRI study. *Brain, 125* (part 2), 361–372.

Johnson-Greene, D., & Bechtold, K. (2002). Ethical considerations for peer review in forensic neuropsychology. *Clinical Neuropsychologist, 16*, 97–104.

Johnson-Greene, D., Hardy-Morais, C., Adams, K., Hardy, C., & Bergloff, P. (1997). Informed consent and neuropsychological assessment: Ethical considerations and proposed guidelines. *Clinical Neuropsychologist, 11*, 454–460.

Kerns, K., Don, A., Mateer, C., & Streissguth, A.

(1997). Cognitive deficits in nonretarded adults with fetal alcohol syndrome. *Journal of Learning Disabilities, 30*, 685–693.

Kessler, S., Adams, H., Blasey, C., & Bigler, E. (2003). Premorbid intellectual functioning, education, and brain size in traumatic brain injury: An investigation of the cognitive reserve hypothesis. *Applied Neuropsychology, 10*, 153–162.

Klonoff, H., Clark, C., & Klonoff, P. (1993). Long-term outcome of head injuries: A 23-year follow-up study of children with head injuries. *Journal of Neurology, Neurosurgery, and Psychiatry, 56*, 410–415.

Kolb, B. (1999). Synaptic plasticity and the organization of behaviour after early and late brain injury. *Canadian Journal of Experimental Psychology, 53*, 62–76.

Kolb, B., Gibb, R., & Gorney, G. (2000). Cortical plasticity and the development of behavior after early frontal cortical injury. *Developmental Neuropsychology, 18*, 423–444.

Lees-Haley, P., & Cohen, L. (1999). The neuropsychologist as expert witness: Toward credible science in the courtroom. In J. Sweet (Ed.), *Forensic neuropsychology: Fundamentals and practice* (pp. 443–468). Lisse, Netherlands: Swets & Zeitlinger.

Levin, H. S., Ewing-Cobbs, L., & Eisenberg, H. (1995). Neurobehavioral outcome of pediatric closed head injury. In S. Broman, M. Michel, & M. Broman (Eds.), *Traumatic head injury in children* (pp. 70–94). New York: Oxford University Press.

Lidsky, T., & Schneider, J. (2003). Lead neurotoxicity in children: Basic mechanisms and clinical correlates. *Brain, 126* (Part 1), 5–19.

Light, R., Asarnow, R., Satz, P., Zaucha, K., McCleary, C., & Lewis, R. (1998). Mild closed-head injury in children and adolescents: Behavior problems and academic outcomes. *Journal of Consulting and Clinical Psychology, 66*, 1023–1029.

Lorber, R., & Yurk, H. (1999). Neuropsychological applications and consultations in schools. In J. Sweet (Ed.), *Forensic neuropsychology: Fundamentals and practice* (pp. 369–417). Lisse, Netherlands: Swets & Zeitlinger.

Lu, P., & Boone, K. (2002). Suspect cognitive symptoms in a 9-year-old child: Malingering by proxy? *Clinical Neuropsychologist, 16*, 90–96.

Mangeot, S., Armstrong, K., Colvin, A., Yeates, K., & Taylor, H. G. (2002). Long-term executive function deficits in children with traumatic brain injuries: Assessment using the Behavior Rating Inventory of Executive Function (BRIEF). *Child Neuropsychology*, *8*, 271–284.

Matarazzo, J. (1990). Psychological assessment versus psychological testing: Validation from Binet to the school, clinic, and courtroom. *American Psychologist*, *45*, 999–1017.

McCarthy, M., Serpi, T., Kufera, J., Demeter, L., & Paidas, C. (2002). Factors influencing admission among children with a traumatic brain injury. *Academic Emergency Medicine*, *9*, 684–693.

McCrory, P. (2001). Does second impact syndrome exist? *Clinical Journal of Sports Medicine*, *11*, 144–149.

McKinzey, R., Prieler, J., & Raven, J. (2003). Detection of children's malingering on Raven's Standard Progressive Matrices. *British Journal of Clinical Psychology*, *42* (Part 1), 95–99.

Meyer, G., Finn, S., Eyde, L., Kay, G., Moreland, K., Dies, R., et al. (2001). Psychological testing and psychological assessment: A review of evidence and issues. *American Psychologist*, *56*, 128–165.

Miller, L. (1999). Child abuse brain injury. *Journal of Cognitive Rehabilitation*, *17*, 10–19.

National Academy of Neuropsychology. (2000). Use of neuropsychology test technicians in clinical practice. *Archives of Clinical Neuropsychology*, *15*, 381–382.

National Institutes of Health Consensus Development Panel on Rehabilitation of Persons with Traumatic Brain Injury. (1999). Rehabilitation of persons with traumatic brain injury. *Journal of the American Medical Association*, *282*, 974–983.

Needleman, H. (1991). *Human lead poisoning.* Boca Raton, FL: CRC Press.

Nyakas, C., Buwalda, B., & Luiten, P. (1996). Hypoxia and brain development. *Progress in Neurobiology*, *49*, 1–51.

Offord, D., & Bennett, K. (1994). Conduct disorder: Long-term outcomes and intervention effectiveness. *Journal of the American Academy of Child and Adolescent Psychiatry*, *33*, 1069–1078.

Ommaya, A., Goldsmith, W., & Thibault, L. (2002). Biomechanics and neuropathology of adult and paediatric head injury. *British Journal of Neurosurgery*, *16*, 220–242.

Osberg, J., Brooke, M., Baryza, M., Rowe, K., Lash, M., & Kahn, P. (1997). Impact of childhood brain injury on work and family finances. *Brain Injury*, *11*, 11–24.

Painter, M. (1995). Animal models of perinatal asphyxia: Contributions, contradictions, clinical relevance. *Seminars in Pediatric Neurology*, *2*, 37–56.

Redfield, J. (2001). Familial intelligence as an estimate of expected ability in children. *Clinical Neuropsychologist*, *15*, 446–460.

Reilly, J., Bates, E., & Marchman, V. (1998). Narrative discourse in children with early focal brain injury. *Brain and Language*, *61*, 335–375.

Reis, S. (1987). We can't change what we don't recognize: Understanding the special needs of gifted females. *Gifted Child Quarterly*, *31*, 83–89.

Reynolds, C. R., & Kamphaus, R. W. (1992). *BASC: Behavior Assessment System for Children: Manual.* Minneapolis, MN: American Guidance Service.

Robertson, C., & Finer, N. (1993). Long-term follow-up of term neonates with perinatal asphyxia. *Clinical Perinatology*, *20*, 483–500.

Rodier, P. (1995). Developing brain as a target of toxicity. *Environmental Health Perspectives*, *103* (Suppl. 6), 73–76.

Roland, E., & Hill, A. (1995). Clinical aspects of perinatal hypoxic-ischemic brain injury. *Seminars in Pediatric Neurology*, *2*, 57–71.

Sackett, D., Straus, S., Richardson, W., Rosenberg, W., & Haynes, R. (2000). *Evidence-based medicine: How to practice and teach EBM.* Edinburgh, UK: Churchill Livingstone.

Salmon, P. G., & Meyer, R. G. (1986). Neuropsychology and its implications for personal injury assessment: Children. In M. I. Kurke & R. G. Meyer (Eds.), *Psychology in product liability and personal injury litigation* (pp. 133–155). Washington, DC: Hemisphere.

Scher, M. (2001). Perinatal asphyxia: Timing and mechanisms of injury in neonatal encephalopathy. *Current Neurology and Neuroscience Reports*, *1*, 175–184.

Schwartz, L., Taylor, H. G., Drotar, D., Yeates, K., Wade, S., & Stancin, T. (2003). Long-term behavior problems following pediatric traumatic brain injury: Prevalence, predictors, and correlates. *Journal of Pediatric Psychology*, *28*, 251–263.

Shaheen, S. (1984). Neuromaturation and behavior development: The case of childhood lead poisoning. *Developmental Psychology*, *20*, 542–550.

Stancin, T., Drotar, D., Taylor, H. G., Yeates, K., Wade, S., & Minich, N. (2002). Health-related quality of life of children and adolescents after traumatic brain injury. *Pediatrics*, *109*, E34.

Sternberg, R., & Grigorenko, E. (1999). Genetics

of childhood disorders: I. Genetics and intelligence. *Journal of the American Academy of Child and Adolescent Psychiatry, 38,* 487–488.

Sweet, J. (1999). Malingering: Differential diagnosis. In J. Sweet (Ed.), *Forensic neuropsychology: Fundamentals and practice* (pp. 255–286). Exton, PA: Swets & Zeitlinger.

Sweet, J., & Moulthrop, M. (1999). Self-examination questions as a means of identifying bias in adversarial cases. *Journal of Forensic Neuropsychology, 1,* 73–88.

Sweet, J., Grote, C., & Van Gorp, W. (2002). Ethical issues in forensic neuropsychology. In S. Bush & M. Drexler (Eds.), *Ethical issues in clinical neuropsychology* (pp. 103–133). Lisse, Netherlands: Swets & Zeitlinger.

Sweet, J., King, J., Malina, A., Bergman, M., & Simmons, A. (2002). Documenting the prominence of forensic neuropsychology at national meetings and in relevant professional journals from 1990–2000. *Clinical Neuropsychologist, 16,* 481–494.

Sweet, J., Moberg, P., & Suchy, Y. (2000). Ten-year follow-up survey of clinical neuropsychologists: Part I. Practices and beliefs. *Clinical Neuropsychologist, 14,* 18–37.

Sweet, J., Peck, E., Abramowitz, C., & Etzweiler, S. (2003). National Academy of Neuropsychology/ Division 40 (American Psychological Association) practice survey of clinical neuropsychology in the United States: Part II. Reimbursement experiences, practice economics, billing practices, and incomes. *Archives of Clinical Neuropsychology, 18,* 109–127.

Taylor, G., & Alden, J. (1997). Age-related differences in outcomes following childhood brain insults: An introduction and overview. *Journal of the International Neuropsychological Society, 3,* 555–567.

Taylor, G., Schatschneider, C., & Minich, N. (2000). Longitudinal outcomes of *Haemophilus influenzae* meningitis in school-age children. *Neuropsychology, 14,* 509–518.

Thal, D., Marchman, V., Stiles, J., Aram, D., Trauner, D., Nass, R., & Bates, E. (1991). Early lexical development in children with focal brain injury. *Brain and Language, 40,* 491–527.

van Gorp, W., & McMullen, W. (1997). Potential sources of bias in forensic neuropsychological consultation. *Clinical Neuropsychologist, 11,* 287–290.

Vargha-Khadem, F., Isaacs, E., & Muter, V. (1994). A review of cognitive outcome after unilateral lesions sustained during childhood. *Journal of Child Neurology, 9* (Suppl.), 2S67–2S73.

Vargha-Khadem, F., & Polkey, C. (1992). A review of cognitive outcome after hemidecortication in humans. *Advances in Experimental Medicine and Biology, 325,* 137–151.

Wasserman, G. & Factor-Litvak, P. (2001). Methodology, inference, and causation: Environmental lead exposure and childhood intelligence. *Archives of Clinical Neuropsychology, 16,* 343–352.

Yeates, K. (2000). Closed-head injury. In K. Yeates, M. D. Ris, & H. G. Taylor (Eds.), *Pediatric neuropsychology: Research, theory, and practice* (pp. 92–116). New York: Guilford.

Yeates, K., Taylor, H. G., Drotar, D., Wade, S., Klein, S., & Stancin, T. (1997). Premorbid family environment as a predictor of neurobehavioral outcomes following pediatric traumatic brain injury. *Journal of the International Neuropsychological Society, 3,* 617–630.

Yeates, K., Taylor, H. G., Wade, S., Drotar, D., Stancin, T., & Minich, N. (2002). A prospective study of short- and long-term neuropsychological outcomes after traumatic brain injury in children. *Neuropsychology, 16,* 514–523.

17

A Pediatric Lead Litigation Primer: Foundations for Mental Health Assessment

Steven B. Bisbing

NATURE OF THE PROBLEM

There is no question that the United States has made huge strides toward reducing lead exposure in the past 25 years. Widespread use of leaded gasoline once sent millions of tons of lead into the atmosphere that was absorbed by plants, foods, soil, and, eventually, children. Leaded gasoline is now banned in the United States. House paints once contained up to 50% lead. The paint industry reduced lead levels in interior paint in 1955, and federal legislation banned lead from all paints in 1978. As a result of these and other measures, average childhood blood lead levels have dropped 80% since the late 1970s (Mahoney, 1990).

Unfortunately, various government surveys estimate that in the year 2000 up to 38 million homes had some amount of lead paint and another 25 million had hazardous conditions involving lead. Interestingly, approximately two thirds of those with hazardous conditions were owned or rented by middle- or upper-income families. Sadly, a projected 5.6 million homes with hazardous levels of lead were occupied by at least one child

under the age of 6 (Centers for Disease Control and Prevention [CDC], 2000).

LITIGATION

It has been reported that a body lead burden of 25 micrograms per deciliter of blood (µg/dl) can produce significant and lasting neurological damage and learning problems in children (CDC, 1985). Consequently, in the past 20 years the CDC has steadily lowered the minimum blood-lead levels that it considered a potential health threat and has recommended nationwide testing of children for lead poisoning. During the ensuing time, the news media has made the public more acutely aware of the potential hazards associated with lead exposure. In addition, federal, state, and local municipalities have enacted statutes and regulations pertaining to the treatment and testing of lead-based sources (President's Task Force on Environmental Health Risks and Safety Risks to Children, 2000). This increased awareness has resulted in a relatively significant body of case law that involves the liability of a variety of defendants for injuries to children caused by lead exposure. The significance of these claims cannot be overestimated, as an estimated 75% of all private houses built before 1980 contain lead-based paint (Nadakavukaren, 2000). Further, there are some who consider lead poisoning in children to be one of the most significant environmental and public health problems facing the United States (Schettler, 2001).

FORENSIC IMPLICATIONS

This chapter provides essential information regarding the nature of pediatric lead exposure and its associated effects. Forensic experts who conduct evaluations of children suspected of lead exposure need to understand the mechanisms of such exposure, the potential biopsychosocial impact on child development, and some of the most common factors that can skew the validity of evaluation results. Please note that a thorough discussion of various assessment methods—including pediatric neuropsychological evaluation of cognitive deficits and the forensic assessment of developmental, social, and psychological functioning of children—can be found in other chapters in this volume. It is, therefore, omitted in this chapter.

LEAD EXPOSURE

Description

Lead is a ubiquitous soft, heavy, blue-gray metal that forms approximately 0.002% of the Earth's crust. From a chemical perspective, lead occurs in inorganic form, namely as lead salts of widely varying water solubility, as well as in organic form. Easily smeltable from galena ore, it became one of the earliest metals used by humans. Nonetheless, like other nonessential heavy metals, it has no known biological benefits (National Institute for Occupational Safety and Health [NIOSH], 1997).

Sources

All humans have some amount of lead in their bodies, primarily due to exposure to man-made causes. There are numerous sources of lead in the environment (see Appendix A of this chapter). Common contact often occurs if a person resides or works near a building that contains deteriorated lead-based paint, lives close to a hazardous waste site, or is involved in employment or an activity in which lead is used (CDC, 2000). Moreover, food cans that have been improperly soldered, folk medications or remedies (CDC, 1993), some imported candy (CDC, 2002), lead glazes used in coloring pottery and ceramic ware (CDC, 1993), and water passing through aged leaded pipes all constitute potential sources of lead exposure. Factory and manufacturing plant workers, as well as miners, may also bring lead dust home on their skin and clothes and unwittingly expose their families (Baker et al., 1977).

Exposure

Both children and adults are susceptible to health effects from lead exposure. However, the most common modes of exposure and resulting impact are somewhat different. Generally, exposure to lead can occur through breathing air, eating food, drinking water, or touching dirt or dust that contains lead. Due to their behavior and more vulnerable physiology, children are far more sensitive than adults to lead exposure (CDC, 1985). For example, because of more frequent hand-to-mouth behavior, children generally come in contact with and ingest soil granules, house dust, and paint flakes at a much higher rate than adults. More specifically, infants and toddlers are closer to and spend more time on the ground or floor, where they may come in contact with lead-contaminated dust, soil, or particles. For children, therefore, the most common routes of exposure involve the ingestion of lead paint chips and inhalation of lead paint dust (Haynes, Lanphear, Tohn, Farr, & Wioads, 2002). To a lesser extent, lead can also be absorbed from dust that settles on the skin (Sayre, Charney, Vostal, & Pless, 1974).

Houses and apartments built before 1978, the year that a federal ban on lead paint took effect, remain a leading source of exposure for children (Binder, Matte, Kresnow, Houston, & Sacks, 1996). This is especially true of dwellings built prior to 1950, when lead-based paint was routinely used. Economically deprived children generally have increased risk for exposure because their families can often afford to live only in older buildings, which have a greater likelihood of not having undergone rehabilitation to current health code standards. However, children from more affluent backgrounds, including those living in the suburbs, can also be at risk if, for example, they live in homeowner-renovated houses (Clickner, Albright & Weitz, 1995).

Residential exposure of children largely results from one of two sources. The first, and typically most common, is the flaking of lead-based paint in older, typically run-down, houses and apartments. The second source involves renovation or remodeling activities that disturb lead-based paint, which results in significant amounts of lead residue and dust deposited in the air and surrounding surfaces (CDC, 1997).

Biology

Absorption of lead can cause a variety of problems ranging from neurotoxic effects, such as hyperactivity and diminished intelligence, to severe effects that include cerebral edema and coma. The human body absorbs lead primarily through the gastrointestinal tract or the lungs. Whereas adults normally inhale lead dust particles, children commonly are exposed through oral ingestion. Once lead enters the body, it is generally stored in bone, soft tissue, and the blood. The amount of lead in the body is measured by blood-lead levels (micrograms of lead per deciliter of blood, or g/dL PbB) or by the concentration of lead in bone or teeth.

Excessive amounts of lead in the body can damage a child's essential body functions. For example, a child who has blood-lead levels of 40 g/dL may suffer from impaired hemoglobin synthesis, whereas a child with a reading of 70 g/dL may develop anemia. Blood levels in excess of 80 g/dL can result in chronic lead nephropathy, a degenerative process of the renal tissue and function. The most serious effects of acute lead poisoning are to the central nervous system. Convulsions, coma, and coronary failure can occur. Moreover, problems in the peripheral nervous system can produce motor dysfunction, muscle weakness, and lack of coordination. Decreased fertility can also be caused by increased lead levels in the body.

Asymptomatic children with significant lead levels may exhibit adverse effects involving intel-ligence, educational achievement, motor skills, attention, and behavior (Rummo, Routh, Rummo, & Brown, 1979), The effects of lead, especially in these areas of functioning, are not always easy to detect. The reason is that they could be related to a number of nonlead factors, including the child's age, gender, genetic factors, parental care, and social and/or cultural factors.

Physiology and Pathology

Like all nonessential heavy metals, lead poses hazards to living matter. Societies dating back centuries have long understood the detrimental heath effects of lead. As a result, it is one of the most frequently and best studied neurotoxic elements. Comprehensive reviews of the chemical, environmental, and biological aspects of lead are readily available from a variety of sources and should be consulted for more in-depth and up-to-date information (Agency for Toxic Substances and Disease Registry [ATSDR], 1999; Environmental Protection Agency [EPA], 2005).

The physiological changes in the body following the introduction of lead are relatively complex and long acting (Lidsky & Schneider, 2003). The following is a bare overview and is intended only as a simplified introduction. Shortly after lead enters the body, it becomes absorbed into the blood and travels through soft tissue to the organs (e.g., brain, heart, kidneys, liver, lungs, muscles, and spleen). Lead in blood has an estimated half-life of 35 days; in soft tissue, 40 days; and in bone, 20 to 30 years (Kaufman, Burt, & Silverstein, 1994). After several weeks, most of the lead becomes absorbed into the bones and teeth. Approximately three quarters of the lead in a child's body becomes stored in their bones. When it becomes deposited in the bones, it is referred to as an individual's "body burden" of lead. The body does not naturally convert lead into any other form. Once absorbed within the organs, the lead not stored in the teeth and bones becomes excreted in urine or feces. Approximately one third of the lead entering a child's body will leave as waste. Interestingly, even persons with a significant or increasing body burden of lead will not necessarily be aware of its existence for some time or only under certain conditions. For example, children who have been exposed to lead are most commonly identified under three circumstances: (1) they are observed ingesting lead paint chips or being exposed to lead dust, (2) a significant lead level is detected from a blood test, or (3) there are visible signs of toxicity. Pediatric lead toxicity is typically noticeable on hot, sunny days. On such occasions classic symptoms of lead poisoning are generally exhibited, including unexplained lethargy, as well as complaints of weakness, fatigue, nausea, vomiting, and/or occasional seizures. In these situations exposure to sunlight triggers vitamin D (calcium pathway of bone change) in the body, which subsequently releases large amounts of lead into the blood. At the cellular level, lead interferes with normal calcium metabolism, producing an intracellular buildup of calcium by binding to most calcium-activated proteins. Once bound, lead interferes with the normal action of these proteins. Moreover, lead can block the normal activities of enzymes in brain cells. This can result in neuronal damage and, in extreme cases, death. This possibility is of particular concern during early child development, when brain cells have particular susceptibility to such trauma (Rodier, 1995). Consequently, the fetus and the young child have the greatest potential for experiencing nonfatal levels of lead poisoning, which includes permanent brain damage (Bellinger, Leviton, Waternaux, Needleman, & Rabinowitz, 1987).

Lead exposure can result in a variety of detrimental health effects. Injury especially occurs in at least three organ systems: the blood-forming organs, the peripheral and central nervous systems, and the kidneys. Lead exposure is also highly toxic to reproductive processes (Rom, 1976).

Over the past two decades, science has uncovered evidence of neurological and other deficits at levels once thought to be safe (Canfield et al., 2003; Needleman & Landrigar, 2004). Presently, no precise threshold for anatomical harm exists (Schwartz, 1994). However, some studies report damage to the central nervous system (CNS) as a result of seemingly modest lead exposure (i.e., 10–15 micrograms per deciliter of whole blood or *mcg/dL*) at age 2 (Kaufman, Clouse, Olson, & Matte, 2000), with continued impairment in neurological development affecting intellectual functioning at age 5 (Lanphear, Dietrich, Auinger, & Cox, 2000). Sustained lead toxicity, especially at levels exceeding 50 mcg/dL, has been linked to a rela-

tively broad range of neurological, physiological, and behavioral effects (Ruff, Bijur, Markowitz, Ma, & Rosen, 1993).

It is notable that the absence of direct contact to environmental lead does not necessarily preclude potential harm. If, for example, a nonpregnant woman has been exposed to sufficient quantities of lead, it can accumulate in the bones. During pregnancy metabolic changes can cause the stored lead to be released into the blood. Lead readily crosses the placenta, placing the fetus at risk. Fetal exposure can potentially produce adverse neurological consequences in utero and during postnatal development. Reported developmental consequences of prenatal exposure to low to moderate levels of lead include low birth weight and premature birth (Winder, 1993). Because the unborn child is extremely sensitive to any environmental toxins, the potential for damage is even greater than that of exposing a child or an adult to the same amount of lead (Dietrich et al., 1987).

Assessment and Diagnosis

The evaluation of suspected lead exposure generally involves taking a clinical history and conducting a physical examination and laboratory testing, regardless of whether the individual is a child (Cory-Slechta et al., 2001) or an adult (Department of Labor, 2005). Signs of potential exposure may often be revealed through careful interviewing regarding the patient's background and daily routine. When assessing a child, gathering relevant data from significant others, including parents, caretakers, relatives, and/or schoolteachers, is usually essential.

The physical examination should generally focus on the neurological, hematological, gastrointestinal, cardiovascular, and renal systems. With children, carefully gathering accurate information regarding speech, hearing, and other developmental milestones is especially important. Iron deficiency commonly occurs among children ages 9 to 24 months. Because iron and calcium deficiencies exacerbate the absorption of lead, an evaluation of a young child's diet and nutritional status becomes essential. In the event that there is evidence of pica (i.e., consumption of nonfood items such as paint chips), an X-ray of the stomach is often conducted. On long-bone radiographs, opacities may be observed after 4 to 8 weeks of lead exposure. Dense zones of calcium, inappropriately referred to as "lead lines," typically become visible in larger bones (e.g., tibia, radius). Lead lines observed in smaller bones (e.g., fibula or ulna) may indicate longer lead exposure, usually of several months' duration. It is notable that X-rays prove useful only for ruling in the presence of lead, generally long-term exposure. A negative X-ray does *not* rule out lead toxicity.

Laboratory tests constitute the most common diagnostic technique for lead exposure. These include urinalysis, erythrocyte protoporphyrin (EP) level, and blood lead level (BLL). The most useful screening and diagnostic test for lead toxicity is a blood lead level. It responds relatively rapidly to abrupt or intermittent changes in lead consumption and, within a limited range, produces a linear response to lead intake levels. For lead levels below 25 mcg/dL, a serum ferritin level and/or other iron studies can help assess whether anemia exists. For chronic exposures, however, blood lead levels tend to *underrepresent* the total body burden. Notably, up until the mid-1990s, the test of choice for screening asymptomatic and suspected populations at risk was EP (DeBaun & Sox, 1991). Erythrocyte protoporphyrin is the red blood cell component known to increase in response to high amounts of lead in the blood. However, this test does not show sufficient sensitivity at lower levels of exposure (e.g., under 35 mcg/dL). Accordingly, false negative results occur frequently in children exposed to lead at lower levels (Parsons, Reilly, & Hussain, 1991).

The potential variance in accuracy that can exist regarding a child's reported exposure to lead can be a major source of contention between parties in a civil lawsuit. Generally, a successful claimant must establish lead exposure that is both associated with the defendant's property and at levels sufficient in quantity and duration to likely produce known neurobehavioral consequences. Accordingly, it behooves litigation parties to examine the probable accuracy of the lead burden value that is assigned to a child. This can usually be accomplished by a forensic expert independently assessing various factors that are known to correlate with the determination of body lead burden and its probable effects. These factors include:

(a) The existence of an environmental lead source
(b) The nature and extent of ingestion (total body lead burden), if any
(c) The age of the child
(d) The pre- and postexposure health status of the child
(e) The method(s) used to determine the existence and amount of lead in the body

This latter factor may require several examinations, as more than one lab may be providing lead burden values. Data relevant to all of these factors can usually be found in the medical records of the exposed child and in environmental survey records associated with the property in question. The absence of this information should prompt the examining forensic expert to urge the legal counsel who engaged him or her to timely seek their discovery.

Treatment

The intervention needed will generally depend on a patient's blood lead level (see Appendix B of this chapter). Asymptomatic patients with blood lead levels below 25–30 mcg/dL typically require only a cessation of contact with the lead source. For such patients, follow-up to confirm decreasing blood lead levels is customary. Sound clinical practice also dictates identification and correction of any dietary deficiencies, especially iron and calcium, as well as educating home occupants on the preventable hazards of lead (American Academy of Pediatrics Committee on Drugs, 1995). Some experts report that the adverse effects of lead exposure are reversible in whole or in part with early and aggressive intervention and consistent follow-up (Glotzer & Bauchner, 1992).

The CDC generally recommends that children with blood lead levels of 45 mcg/dL or above promptly undertake chelation treatment (CDC, 1991). Children with levels between 25 and 45 mcg/dL may undergo chelation depending on the examining practitioner's experience and preference (Chisholm, 1990).

Children with toxic levels of lead (> 69 mcg/ dL) commonly require inpatient hospitalization for a 5- to 7-day course of chelation. Treatment involves a series of injections of calcium disodium ethylenediaminetetraaceate acid (CaNa2EDTA), a chelating agent. The EDTA molecule has a high attraction for lead. Consequently, lead in major organs will bond to EDTA in a form that the body can excrete in the urine. Typically, a 1-week regimen of daily injections of EDTA significantly reduces the total body lead burden. However, sometimes extended chelation treatment becomes necessary because of unusually high initial lead levels, requiring additional injections of EDTA to reduce the measurable lead to an acceptable level (e.g., at or around current CDC limits).

When a forensic assessment occurs after chelation treatment, the forensic expert must consider the potential for "secondary adversities" (Sparta, 2003). A common secondary adversity associated with chelation treatment is a range of transient emotional problems experienced by children, such as separation effects, fear, confusion, and pain or discomfort. The psychological problems resulting from medical treatment would not have existed but for the lead exposure, and thus they may constitute a relevant litigation consideration. However, the seriousness of these problems is typically short term and, therefore, is generally not a reliable source of lasting compensable damages.

An unusual phenomenon commonly occurring during the process of reducing lead exposure (e.g., removal from the lead source) or ridding of lead from the body (e.g., chelation treatment) is an unexpected *increase* in blood lead level values. This is sometimes referred to as a "rebound phenomenon" (Goyer, Cherian, Jones, & Reigart, 1995). It can occur when blood lead levels begin to drop due to normal excretion or treatment and the body replaces the lost lead through a mobilization of lead stored in bones and teeth. This physiological process actually compensates for the lead that is initially lost; thereby temporarily producing an unexpected elevated lead level. Therefore, it is a sound clinical practice to have relatively frequent lead levels taken to obtain a reliable and accurate measurement. Conversely, not all posttreatment elevations in lead levels reflect an internal rebound effect. Before making such a diagnosis, reexposure to the same or another lead source should be ruled out. For example, it is not uncommon for a child to become reexposed to lead in the same or similar manner as before treatment due to inadequate supervision and/or insufficient safeguards at known or foreseeable locations where lead is likely present (e.g., poor cleanup, lack of protective barriers). As a result, the child's lead levels are generally maintained or even elevated over time despite appropriate medical intervention. This becomes not only a significant clinical issue but also a potentially divisive matter if a lawsuit is brought on the basis of negligence.

LITIGATION

Although disagreement continues regarding the incidence of lead-exposed children in the United States, it is generally undisputed that it remains a serious public health problem—especially among families that reside in older, deteriorating homes and apartments. As a result, state and federal legislation enacted since the 1970s has repeatedly focused on reducing the risk of exposure. Unfortunately, such laws have had mixed success at best and oftentimes with isolated effects limited to particular circumstances or jurisdictions. Not surprisingly, injured parties have not always obtained needed relief from individuals or institutions perceived responsible. As a result, a relatively substantial number of lawsuits have been filed against property owners and landlords (Wriggins, 1997).

It is extremely difficult to determine the exact number of lead exposure cases. The reason, in large part, is that a significant number are rarely, if ever, reported due to dismissal or pretrial settlement. However, verdicts and settlements that are published typically indicate that they are costly to litigate. For example, in *Viarruel v. O'Malley* (1991) the litigation costs for the defense alone were in excess of $300,000. However, successful plaintiffs have obtained high six- and even seven-figure judgments (e.g., *Griffin v. Krup*, 2002) and settlements (e.g., *Cadena v. Aquaeduct Realty et al.*, 2001).

Theories of Liability

There are generally a circumscribed number of potential theories of liability, depending on the defendant and the jurisdiction. The possible defendants in a lead exposure case will be dictated by several factors, including the nature and date of exposure, age and possible injuries of the exposed child, and prevailing law. In general, defendants may vary and can include landowners and landlords of single-family homes and multiple dwellings, local and state agencies and governments, deleading contractors, and paint manufacturers.

Where a suit is brought is frequently critical to determining the applicable theory or theories of liability. For example, several jurisdictions have legislation involving lead paint poisoning prevention requirements that results in the imposition of strict liability on owners if a resident is poisoned by lead on their property (e.g., *Bencosme v. Kokoras*, 1997). This theory essentially imposes on a property owner the affirmative responsibility to inspect a property, identify the existence of any lead (e.g., lead-based paint), and properly abate it. This responsibility is typically irrespective of whether or not the owner is aware of the presence of lead on his or her property.

Other states, such as New York, however, reject strict or absolute liability in favor of a negligence-oriented claim. According to general negligence law a landlord or property owner must have *actual or constructive notice* of a potential lead paint hazard. On such knowledge, an owner then has a legal duty to make reasonable efforts to abate the hazard so to prevent endangering any residents.

Jurisdictions in which lead litigation is most active include California, Illinois, Maryland, Massachusetts, Michigan, Mississippi, New Jersey, New York, Ohio, Pennsylvania, Rhode Island, Texas, West Virginia, and Wisconsin (Kaminski, Bottari, & Boulhosa, 1998). This reason in large part is that there is either an abundance of older public housing in which lead paint was likely used at one time, but remains unabated, and/or that established paint manufacturers are located within the state.

PERSONAL INJURY

The area of liability in which forensic expertise, especially in psychology and neuropsychology, is most likely to be needed involves personal injury to a child from lead exposure due to negligence. In order to recover damages as the result of negligence, the plaintiff must generally establish by a preponderance of evidence (1) the presence of lead on the defendant's property, (2) that a child has been exposed to the lead, and (3) that the exposure caused recognizable injuries.

In pediatric lead litigation in which common-law negligence is applied, a critical threshold that must initially be established is whether the defendant knew or should have known that there was lead on the property and that children would be at risk of exposure. Notice of this dangerous condition will generally trigger a duty of the defendant to reasonably and in a timely fashion ameliorate the lead hazard. If a defendant breaches this duty and a child is damaged as a direct result of being exposed to lead on the property, then a prima facie case for negligence will generally have been made.

CAUSATION

Oftentimes the most difficult element of proof in a pediatric lead exposure case, legally and scientifically, is proving causation. Medical causation refers to scientific and medical evidence that exposure to lead caused a child's injuries. In contrast, legal causation is proof that the defendant is responsible for being aware of the lead, for safeguarding potentially affected tenants, and/or for safely disposing of the lead to which the plaintiff child was exposed and which allegedly caused the claimed injuries.

One fundamental reason that causation can be so difficult to establish in a toxic exposure case is the radically different ways that science and law approach it. Legal causation is basically a policy question about when responsibility attaches because of the connection between a defendant's conduct and a plaintiff's injury. In reality, there can be scores of possible causes of a given result, but the law addresses only a limited number of them, to the exclusion of all of the others. Legal causation is based on a standard of "preponderance of the evidence." In other words, the plaintiff must establish that causation is "more probable than not." Courts have generally quantified this standard as meaning a probability of greater than 50%. Theoretically, this mathematically reduced probability is all or nothing. If the plaintiff establishes that the requisite causal link between exposure and injury is at least 51 percent likely, then he or she is entitled to recover all of the damages that can be demonstrated. However, if the probability of causation is only 49 percent, then, generally, there is no recovery.

Science takes a very different position regarding causation. Based on terms of "etiology" rather than social policy, scientists develop theories or hypotheses about a cause-and-effect relationship and then rigorously test these theories to see whether a particular relationship exists or not. In statistical analysis, the term *cause* is used only when a particular association or relationship between variables (e.g., exposure and injury) approaches certainty. It is important to distinguish between the two "certainties": scientific (e.g., statistical certainty) and legal (e.g., reasonable medical certainty). The latter refers to the legal standard of preponderance of the evidence. The former refers to a 1% (.01 significance level) or 5% (.05 significance level) probability that the hypothesis being tested (e.g., a causal relationship between exposure and injury) will occur. Obviously, the scientific standard is much more rigorously applied and thus projects a greater level of actual likelihood of occurrence or connection.

To establish each of the required elements in a negligence action, especially causation, expert testimony is generally necessary. Although both parties have equal discretion in utilizing forensic expertise, it is the plaintiff who bears the responsibility of establishing or proving each element pursuant to the requisite legal standard. In pediatric lead exposure cases, there can be enormous problems with proof of causation, especially if long-term exposure is reported. At the very least, plaintiffs, especially their experts, will commonly encounter a variety of factors that potentially influence the legal determination of causation. These include the lack of adequate exposure data; the latency period between exposure and the first signs of a cognizable injury; evidence of injury causes irrespective of lead exposure; multiple sources of lead exposure, including the defendant's property; the lack of unique or signature effects of lead; medical and scientific uncertainty and dispute regarding lead-related injuries; difficulty identifying the "guilty" defendant; and the enormous expenditures of time and resources commonly associated with complex litigation.

Despite what seem to be insurmountable barriers to proving causation, it can be done if available technology and knowledge are properly and timely employed. Legally, the minimum that must be established is that lead is present on the defendant's property (e.g., flaking paint), that there is a plausible route of exposure (e.g., lead dust in the air or paint chips on the floor), and that there is a probable and direct relationship between exposure and injury (e.g., child ingestion of lead paint chips coupled with unexplained symptoms and/or adverse changes in daily functioning). In essence, to establish each of the fundamental links in causation, there must be a timely and thorough gathering of relevant data (e.g., exposure; the child's medical and life history) that is then rigorously analyzed by a competent forensic expert (Provder, 1993). The failure of either litigation party to engage in this process will likely result in weaknesses in their respective positions that can later prove detrimental, if not fatal, to accomplishing their desired outcome.

Alternative Causes

The general legal requirement that there be a probable and direct relationship between a child's reported exposure to lead from the defendant's property and recognizable injuries can be especially vexing. Generally, numerous factors may affect a child's susceptibility to eventually developing a given condition (Anthony, 1987). Host factors—such as age, gender, race, culture and specific health immunity, genetic factors, environmental factors (e.g., heat, altitude, bacteria, viruses, other chemical exposures), other medical conditions, and prior exposure to a toxicant—can all contribute to the development of an organic disease, cognitive dysfunction, or psychological condition (Hartman, 1989). Accordingly, clinicians and forensic experts must gather a variety of data regarding the child and his or her history, his or her typical environment, and the reported exposure and then carefully analyze or differentiate it. "Differential diagnosis" involves the systematic process of distinguishing between diseases or complaints that have similar symptoms in order to narrow them down to one "probable" diagnosis or cause. This type of diagnosis is an essential element in establishing medical causation and is commonly critical in any toxic tort litigation. The reason is that most physical and psychological injuries allegedly connected to toxic exposure will have the potential of a multifactorial etiology. In other words, chronic diseases and symptoms, including psychological disorders, are often the result of a variety of factors that have combined and interacted over a period of time. An example of this problem is the determination of the cause of cancer. It is thought that the carcinogenic process is multifactorial in etiology and multistage in development.

In pediatric lead litigation, the plaintiffs' experts should be able to distinguish or account for the potential plethora of environmental and host factors that provide alternative explanations for any complaints that are being attributed to lead exposure. In essence, then, in order to meet the causation requirement, plaintiffs must prove that exposure to lead from the defendant's property or product was the most probable cause of their injuries, to the exclusion of all other reasonable causal sources. It is similarly incumbent on the defense's forensic experts to identify the nature and range of all potential alternative causes, their degree of likelihood of causing or contributing to the plaintiff's complaints, and their lack of relationship with the reported exposure to lead.

An axiomatic aspect of an effective forensic evaluation of damages is the ruling out of the most common sources or causes that can produce injuries similar to those generally associated with the reported cause of action (e.g., lead exposure). This would seem especially essential in claims involving children, as they are generally likely to be susceptible to a broader range of harms than most adults. Appendix C of this chapter provides a sample list of alternative causes of injuries that generally correspond with at least some of the major consequences commonly associated with extended lead exposure. The failure of either party to carefully evaluate the history of the child plaintiff, including significant third parties (e.g., parents, siblings), and to account for any potential alternative causes of his or her injury complaints will likely undermine their position.

Damages

Compensable damages recoverable in pediatric lead exposure suits are similar to those found in other types of personal injury litigation. They generally include pain and suffering, economic loss, and applicable medical expenses. In cases of especially egregious negligence, some jurisdictions may permit recovery for punitive damages, which are in addition to any compensatory award (Massachusetts General Laws, 1994).

Generally, the type of damages in which the largest awards are typically made involve economic or vocational injury. This usually refers to some impairment (short term, partial, complete, and/or permanent) in the ability to earn wages in the future (Bruce, 1984). A common injury claim is that lead exposure has significantly impaired a child's intellectual or cognitive functioning. As a consequence, this impairment is projected to have an adverse impact on the plaintiff's earning capacity as an adult (*Anderson v. Litzenberg*, 1997). Not surprisingly, if the plaintiff's claim is successfully established, the monetarial award for related economic or vocational damages can be substantial. For example, in the case *Powell v. City of New York* (1999), an 8-year-old plaintiff was exposed to lead for nearly 6 years, with measured blood lead levels between 14 and 18 mg/dcL. Based on neuropsychological expert testimony, the plaintiff established that as a result of the lead exposure from the defendant's property (city housing), he suffered various cognitive and behavioral problems. It was further alleged by the plaintiff's expert that the lead-related cognitive impairment was the reason that he had repeated the first grade three times. The neuropsychological expert also concluded that the plaintiff's lead-based cognitive impairment would make it unlikely that he would graduate from high school. Based on these findings, a forensic economist testified that the child's earning potential as an adult had been severely compromised. After only 4 hours of deliberation, a jury awarded $3,850,000, of which $3,000,000 was for "future lost earnings."

In an attempt to mitigate or rebut a claim of loss of earning capacity, there are a number of arguments that the defendant may raise provided supporting data exist. For example, a forensic psychological or neuropsychological expert may present evidence that the parents possess modest or below-average intelligence, a history of poor academic achievement, or some form of cognitive dysfunction. This information, coupled with supporting evidence that the home environment is rife with distractions, lacks parental supervision, has limited or no positive stimulation, and/or places little value on academic achievement, may make a compelling counterargument regarding the plaintiff's lack of current and, likely, future success in school. The significance of these data may then be buttressed by citing published research regarding the influence of parental intelligence and the home environment on a child's intelligence (Bochard & McGue, 1981). Similarly, a non-lead-exposed sibling who is doing poorly in school may also provide the defense an additional counterargument based on genetics to consider (Paul, 1980).

After a child is diagnosed with high levels of lead, the child may undergo a number of treatments and incur substantial medical bills. The usual treatment is some form of chelation, which may require hospitalization. If the initial lead level is unusually high or if the child is reexposed to lead following an initial deleading intervention, then extended and multiple hospitalizations may be required. The cost of current and ongoing medical expenses, as well as money for foreseeable health care costs in the future, may be awarded to a successful plaintiff as part of a total compensatory judgment.

In most cases, a child does not experience pain from lead exposure, with a few exceptions. If blood-lead levels are in the toxic range, there is long-term exposure, which can result in illness or gastrointestinal distress; or if the child undergoes multiple series of chelation injections, then there may be a factual basis for a pain-and-suffering claim. Nonetheless, this area of damages is typically limited and does not usually account for a significant percentage of a successful monetarial award.

Regardless of the nature of the plaintiff's reported injuries, generally the most effective means of proving or, in the case of the defense, countering a claim of damages will be through expert testimony. Common areas of forensic expertise that are utilized include clinical psychology, neuropsychology, and vocational counseling (Provder, 1993). The effectiveness of these forensic experts in a pediatric lead exposure case will, in large part, depend on the thoroughness and accuracy of their data gathering, the rigor of their analysis, and the extent of their knowledge of the effects of lead on the developing child. Other chapters in this volume provide an excellent overview of several approaches to the assessment of children in different forensic contexts. Accordingly, I direct attention to Appendix D of this chapter, which summarizes

suggested topics about which a forensic examiner should consider gathering data when evaluating causation, as well as the claim of damages, in a pediatric lead case.

Defenses

The typical, and often successful, defense strategy is to argue that the plaintiff's injury claims are caused by factors other than reported exposure to lead on the defendant's property. As reflected in Appendix C of this chapter, a number of factors can produce or significantly contribute to the development of problems that are commonly associated with lead exposure. The successful defense is typically one that factually establishes several of these "alternative causes" as relevant to the plaintiff's history and current life functioning. Forensic psychological testimony is often an effective means not only of introducing this information but also of explaining the role it likely plays in creating or worsening the plaintiff's injury complaints. For example, supported data about a single adult household that is occupied by several other children and a parent who is frequently away can create a reasonable impression that the plaintiff resides in a chaotic home environment in which there is little, if any, quality stimulation or favorable adult–child interaction. Expert testimony regarding the relationship between a child's home environment and his or her performance in school can then be used to buttress the defense argument that factors other than lead exposure are the likely cause of any cognitive deficits or poor academic achievement. Moreover, if the plaintiff has moved during or following the period in which exposure to lead is supposed to have taken place, the case against any one landlord becomes more complex to make. The more such possibilities the defendant can raise, the greater the likelihood that aspects of the plaintiff's case will be compromised, if not outright rebutted.

Other defenses that will likely rely on the testimony of at least one, if not several, forensic experts, including psychologists, include (a) the amount of exposure is too slight to cause the alleged injuries or any significant impairment; (b) there is insufficient scientific evidence establishing lead as the cause of the injuries claimed by the plaintiff; (c) continuing elevated levels of lead after timely lead abatement or effective treatment intervention indicates that the plaintiff's continued exposure is likely from sources other than the defendant's product or property; (d) elevated levels of lead following notice of a lead hazard in the home or during lead abatement raises the likelihood that the parents are contributing to their child's exposure by not providing appropriate supervision; (e) there is little evidence of any significant lead-related injury; and (f) lead treatment intervention is being negligently provided, unnecessarily extending exposure, increasing blood lead levels, and delaying the identification of a source of lead so it can be timely abated.

Experts

Experts play a critical role in pediatric lead litigation. Each element of a negligence suit will typically be established and/or countered through expert testimony. Due to the amount of science and medicine that may be involved, a variety of experts may be utilized. For example, to address the initial matter of lead exposure and its probable source, a toxicologist, industrial hygienist, and/or environmental engineer may be called to testify. The critical issue of linking lead exposure to a particular injury or causation typically requires the expertise of a pediatric neurologist or occupational physician. To explain damages, either party might rely on a child clinical psychologist or neuropsychologist. In terms of future medical expenses and potential economic loss, the services of a vocational counselor and/or forensic economist are frequently relied on.

SUMMARY

The effects that chemical agents, particularly industrial substances, might have on the fetus and the behavior of the developing child have become an area of increasing scientific interest and research. Depending on the substance, the extent of exposure, and other factors, the potential for toxic tort litigation becomes significant. Lead has attracted by far the most study in terms of pollutant exposure and child development. Past studies by the National Center for Health Statistics report that at least 4% of American children of all races

and social positions have excess lead in their bodies (Agency for Toxic Substances and Disease Registry, 2000). For children who live at or below the poverty level, the prevalence is significantly higher.

Despite the statistics on lead exposure, there remain a significant number of equivocal studies regarding the extent of potential adverse health effects. Serious methodological flaws and experimental design limitations continue to significantly affect the validity and reliability of many lead studies (Bellinger, 1995). Notwithstanding these reservations, lead has been implicated in producing a variety of cognitive, psychological, and developmental effects, especially at elevated levels. These effects include behavioral difficulties in school-age children, intelligence deficits, hyperactivity, neuropsychological deficits, and various psychological deficits.

Unfortunately, despite the known health consequences associated with lead exposure and the thousands of children who remain at risk, state and federal efforts to eradicate this public health problem remain inadequate. Although not intended as a solution, civil litigation provides at least a limited means for some exposed children to obtain some degree of recompense against negligent property owners and product makers. Although the tort litigation literature involving pediatric lead claims is relatively small, it would be a grave mistake for plaintiffs and defendants to overlook this group of "quiet claimants." Novel claims of injury, as well as varying theories of liability against a wide range of individual, corporate, and governmental defendants, continue to slowly elevate these cases to an increasingly greater level of significance. The historical scientific question, Does lead exposure cause problems in children? has largely been replaced in the civil legal system by the more ominous inquiry, What is the extent of the problems likely to be produced by lead exposure over an appreciable period of time? Notwithstanding mounting evidence that significant lead exposure will likely produce some cognizable injury to a child, this relationship must still be established by competent evidence on a case-by-case basis. The forensic expert plays a critical role in this complex litigation, addressing essential issues that include exposure, causation, treatment, and damages. To be most effective in communicating to the court, it behooves the forensic expert to possess a sound understanding of the fundamental medical and legal aspects of this area of civil litigation (Koger, Schettler, & Weiss, 2005).

AUTHOR NOTE

This chapter is solely intended to introduce the reader to many of the basic clinical, legal, and forensic aspects of this topic. It is not to be construed as advice or authority of any type. Moreover, some of the legal principles and/or theories may not be applicable in all jurisdictions. Accordingly, readers should consult appropriate medical, mental health, and/or legal authorities for current and accurate information relating to any particular set of facts.

Due to editorial restrictions, considerable citations to supporting references have deliberately been omitted. Fortunately, lead has been and continues to be a well-studied substance, and information is easily accessed electronically (see generally http://www.cdc.gov/nceh/lead/).

APPENDIX A:
COMMON WORLDWIDE
SOURCES OF LEAD

Environmental

- Ceramics
- Leaded gasoline
- Paint containing lead
- Plumbing apparatus
- Soil/dust near lead industries and/or lead-painted homes

Hobbies and Similar Activities

- Car and boat repair
- Glazed pottery firing
- Home remodeling
- Lead-based soldering (e.g., electronics)
- Painting
- Preparing fishing equipment (e.g., lead weights, sinkers)
- Stained-glass production

Occupational

- Auto repair
- Battery manufacturing
- Construction
- Bridge construction and repair
- Glass manufacturing
- Lead smelting and refining
- Lead mining
- Plumbers, pipe fitters
- Printers
- Police
- Rubber manufacturing
- Steel welding and cutting

Substance Consumption

- Cosmetics
- Folk remedies
- Gasoline "huffing"

Source: Agency for Toxic Substances and Disease Registry. (1988). *The nature and extent of lead poisoning in children in the United States: A report to Congress*. Atlanta, GA: Author.

APPENDIX B: GUIDELINES FOR
BLOOD LEAD LEVEL
(BLL) SCREENING

Screening BLL ($\mu g/dL$) <10

- Follow-Up Testing: None
- Follow-Up Intervention: Reassess or rescreen in 1 year

Screening BLL ($\mu g/dL$) 10–14

- Follow-Up Testing: 3 mos.
- Follow-Up Intervention: Obtain confirmatory venous BLL within 1 mo.; family lead education

Screening BLL ($\mu g/dL$) 15–19

- Follow-Up Testing: 2 mos.
- Follow-Up Intervention: Obtain confirmatory venous BLL within 1 wk.; family lead education; if BLL in this range persists, conduct careful environmental history

Screening BLL ($\mu g/dL$) 20–44

- Follow-Up Testing: 1–4 wks.
- Follow-Up Intervention: Obtain confirmatory venous BLL within 1 wk.; family lead education and case management; conduct environmental investigation; refer patient for support services

Screening BLL (μg/dL) 45–69

- Follow-Up Testing: 48 hrs.
- Follow-Up Intervention: Obtain confirmatory venous BLL w/in 2 days; initiate case and clinical management (including comprehensive family lead education); initiate environmental investigation and lead hazard control; initiate chelation therapy; refer patient for support services

Screening BLL (μg/dL) >69

- Follow-Up Testing: Immediately
- Follow-Up Intervention: Hospitalize and initiate medical care (e.g., chelation treatment); obtain immediate confirmatory venous BLL; follow guidelines for levels between 45–69

Source: Lane, W. G., & Kemper, A. R. (2001). American College of Preventive Medicine Practice Policy Statement. Screening for elevated blood lead levels in children. *American Journal of Preventive Medicine, 20,* 78–82.

APPENDIX C: SAMPLE INJURY SOURCES THAT MAY MIMIC COMPLAINTS ASSOCIATED WITH LEAD EXPOSURE

Diminished School Performance

- Absenteeism
- Low birth weight
- Nutritional status
- Parental discord/divorce
- Individual or family member illnesses
- Single parent
- Substance abuse in the family
- Exposure to violence

IQ/Intellectual Functioning

- Anemia
- Child abuse and neglect
- Congenital defects
- Cultural factors, deprivation
- Emotional problems; hyperactivity
- Examiner effect
- Mother-child interactions (nature and quality)
- Parental intelligence

- Maternal substance use during pregnancy (e.g., illicit drugs, smoking, alcohol)
- Toxic exposure (e.g., household products)

Behavior/Attention Deficit

- Child of alcoholic caretaker
- Food allergy, dietary issues
- Head injury
- Infantile transient folic acid deficiency
- Infantile respiratory distress syndrome
- Maternal substance use during pregnancy
- Premature and/or traumatic birth
- Exposure to violence
- Genetics

Source: National Research Council, Board on Environmental Studies and Toxicology. (1993). *Measuring lead exposure in infants, children, and other sensitive populations* Washington, DC: National Academy Press.

APPENDIX D: SUGGESTED FORENSIC EXAMINATION TOPICS

Child Variables

- Developmental milestones since birth
- Nutritional status and diet
- Speech and hearing capacity
- Neurobehavioral problems affecting classroom behavior and/or socialization
- Proclivity to mouth reachable objects or from the ground
- Home and neighborhood environment

Home Occupants

- Occupational history of all home occupants
- Interpersonal relations of occupants— especially with suspected exposed child
- Family history, including the use of atypical medicines and remedies
- Hobbies of all home occupants
- Household pets and their health condition

Residence

- Age, location, and physical condition of residence
- Home remodeling and/or repair activity
- Presence of imported or glazed ceramics
- Source of drinking water and type of pipe

- Presence and accessibility of household cleaners
- Proximity to industrial and hazardous waste sites

Alternative Sources of Potential Lead Exposure

Age, location, and physical condition of:
- School
- Day care center
- Play areas (indoor and outdoor)
- Residential buildings (e.g., occupied and abandoned)
- Abandoned cars
- Former residence(s)

Source: Centers for Disease Control (1991).

References

Agency for Toxic Substances and Disease Registry. (2000). *Lead toxicity*. Atlanta, GA: Department of Health and Human Services.

American Academy of Pediatrics, Committee on Drugs. (1995) Treatment guidelines for lead exposure in children. *Pediatrics, 96,* 155–160.

Anderson v. Litzenberg, 694 A.2d 150, 161 (Md. Ct. Spec. App. 1997).

Anthony, E. J. (1987). Risk, vulnerability, and resilience: An overview. In E. J. Anthony & B. J. Choler (Eds.), *The invulnerable child* (pp. 3, 10–11). New York: Guilford.

Baker, E. L., Folland, D. S., Taylor, T. A., Frank, M., Peterson, W., Lovejoy, G., et al. (1977). Lead poisoning in children of lead workers: Home contamination with industrial dust. *New England Journal of Medicine, 296,* 260–261.

Bellinger, D. (1995) Interpreting the literature on lead and child development: The neglected role of the "experimental system." *Neurotoxicological Teratology, 17,* 201–212.

Bellinger, D., Leviton, A., Waternaux, C., Needleman, H., & Rabinowitz, M. (1987). Longitudinal analyses of prenatal and postnatal lead exposure and early cognitive development. *New England Journal of Medicine, 316,* 1037–1043.

Bencosme v. Kokoras, 400 Mass. 40, 507 N.E.2d 748 (1987)

Binder, S., Matte, T. D., Kresnow, M., Houston, B., & Sacks, J. J. (1996). Lead testing of children and homes: Results of a national telephone survey. *Public Health Reports, 111,* 343–346.

Bochard, J. M., & McGue, M. (1981). *Familial studies of intelligence: A review*. St. Paul: University of Minnesota.

Bruce, C. J. (1984). The calculation of an infant's lost earnings. *Alberta Law Review, 22,* 292–293.

Cadena v. Aquaeduct Realty et al., No. 14634/97 (N.Y. [Bronx] Sup. Ct. Sept. 24, 2001)

Canfield, R. L., Henderson C. R., Cory-Slechta, D. A., Cox, C., Jusko, T. A., & Lanphear, B. P. (2003). Intellectual impairment in children with blood lead concentrations below 10 μg per deciliter. *New England Journal of Medicine, 348,* 1517–1526.

Centers for Disease Control and Prevention. (1985, January). *Preventing lead poisoning in young children*. Atlanta, GA: Author.

Centers for Disease Control and Prevention. (1991, October). *Preventing lead poisoning in children: A statement by the Centers for Disease Control.* Atlanta, GA: Author.

Centers for Disease Control and Prevention. (1993). Lead poisoning associated with the use of traditional ethnic remedies: California, 1991–1992. *Morbidity and Mortality Weekly Report, 42,* 521–524.

Centers for Disease Control and Prevention. (1997). Children with elevated blood lead levels attributed to home renovation and remodeling activities: New York, 1993–1994. *Morbidity and Mortality Weekly Report, 45,* 1120–1123.

Centers for Disease Control and Prevention. (2000). Blood lead levels in young children: United States and selected states, 1996–1999. *Morbidity and Mortality Weekly Report, 49,* 1133–1137.

Centers for Disease Control and Prevention. (2002). Childhood lead poisoning associated with tamarind candy and folk remedies: California, 1999–2000. *Morbidity and Mortality Weekly Report, 53,* 27–29.

Chisholm, J. J., Jr. (1990). Evaluation of the potential role of chelation therapy in treatment of low to moderate lead exposures. *Environmental Health Perspectives, 89,* 67–74.

Clickner, R. P., Albright, V. A., & Weitz, S. (1995). The prevalence of lead-based paint in housing: Findings from the national survey. In J. Breen & C. Stroup (Eds.), *Lead poisoning: Exposure, abatement, regulation* (pp. 3–12). Boca Raton, FL: CRC Press.

Cory-Slechta, D. A., Crofton, K. M., Foran, J. A., Sheets, L. P., Weiss, B., & Mileson, B. (2001). Methods to identify and characterize developmental neurotoxicity for human health risk assessment: I. Behavioral effects. *Environmental Health Perspectives, 109*(Suppl. 1), 79–91.

DeBaun, M. R., & Sox, H. C., Jr. (1991). Setting the optimal erythrocyte protoporphyrin screening decision threshold for lead poisoning: A decision analytic approach. *Pediatrics, 88,* 121–131.

Department of Labor. (July 1, 2005). *Occupational safety and health standards,* 29, C.F.R. 1910. 1025 para. (j) (3) (A)–(F).

Dietrich, K., Krafft, K., Bornschein, R., Hammond, P., Berger, O., Succop, P., & Bier, M. (1987). Low-level fetal lead exposure effect on neurobehavioral developmental in early infancy. *Pediatrics, 80,* 721–730.

Environmental Protection Agency. (2005). *Lead in paint, dust, and soil.* Retrieved May 24, 2005, from www.epa.gov/lead/leadpbed.htm

Glotzer, D. E., & Bauchner, H. (1992). Management of childhood lead poisoning: A survey. *Pediatrics, 89,* 614–618.

Goyer, R. A., Cherian, G. M., Jones, M., & J. R. Reigart. (1995). Role of chelating agents for prevention, intervention, and treatment of exposures to toxic metals. *Environmental Health Perspectives, 103,* 1048–1052.

Griffin v. Krup, No. 108083/97 (N.Y. [Manhattan] Sup. Ct. Jan. 17, 2002).

Hartman, D. E. (1989). *Neuropsychological toxicology (identification and assessment of human neurotoxic syndromes).* New York: Pergamon.

Haynes, E., Lanphear, B. P., Tohn, E., Farr, N., & Wioads, G. G. (2002). The effect of interior lead hazard controls on children's blood lead concentrations: A systematic evaluation. *Environmental Health Perspectives, 110,* 103–107.

Kaminsky, A., Bottari, P. J., & Boulhosa, M. L. (1998). *A complete guide to lead paint poisoning litigation.* Washington, DC: American Bar Association.

Kaufman, J. D., Burt, J., & Silverstein, B. (1994). Occupational lead poisoning: Can it be eliminated? *American Journal of Industrial Medicine, 26,* 703–712.

Kaufman, R. B., Clouse, T. L., Olson, D. R., & Matte, T. D. (2000). Elevated blood lead levels and blood lead screening among US children aged one to five years: 1999–1994. *Pediatrics, 106,* E79.

Koger, S. M., Schettler, T., & Weiss, B. (2005). Environmental toxicants and developmental disabilities. *American Psychologist, 60,* 243–255.

Lanphear, B. P., Dietrich, K., Auinger, P., & Cox, C. (2000). Cognitive deficits associated with blood lead concentrations < 10 µg/dL in U.S. children and adolescents. *Public Health Reports, 115,* 521–529.

Lidsky, T. I., & Schneider, J. S. (2003). Lead neurotoxicity in children: Basic mechanisms and clinical correlates. *Brain, 126,* 5–19.

Mahoney, M. (1990). Four million children at risk: Lead paint poisoning victims and the law. *Stanford Environmental Law Journal, 9,* 46–51.

Massachusetts General Laws, ch. 111, §199(b) (1994).

Nadakavukaren, A. (2000). *Our global environment: A health perspective* (5th ed.). Prospect Heights, IL: Wineland.

National Institute for Occupational Safety and Health. (1997). *Registry of toxic effects of chemical substances (RTECS).* Washington, DC: Author.

Needleman, H. L., & Landrigar, P. J. (2004). What level of lead in blood is toxic for a child? *American Journal of Public Health, 94,* 8.

Parsons, P. J., Reilly, A. A., & Hussein, A. (1991). Observational study of erythrocyte protoporphyrin screening test for detecting low lead exposure in children: Impact of lowering the blood lead action threshold. *Clinical Chemistry, 37,* 216–225.

Paul, S. M. (1980). Sibling resemblance in mental ability: A review. *Behavioral Genetics, 10,* 277–290.

Powell v. City of New York, No. 10080/95 (Kings Cty. [N.Y.] Sup. Ct., Nov. 17, 1999).

President's Task Force on Environmental Health Risks and Safety Risks to Children. (2000). *Eliminating childhood lead poisoning: A federal strategy targeting lead paint hazards.* Washington, DC: U.S. Department of Housing and Urban Development.

Provder, E. (1993). Using vocational experts in cases involving injured children. *Trial, 29,* 39–40.

Rodier, P. M. (1995). Developing brain as a target for neurotoxicity. *Environmental Health Perspectives, 103,* 73–76.

Rom, W. N. (1976). Effects of lead on the female and reproduction: A review. *Mt. Sinai Journal of Medicine, 58,* 542–552.

Ruff, H., Bijur, P., Markowitz, M., Ma, Y. C., & Rosen, J. F. (1993). Declining blood lead levels and cognitive changes in moderately exposed lead-poisoned children. *Journal of American Medical Association, 269,* 1641–1646.

Rummo, J., Routh, D., Rummo, N., & Brown, J. F. (1979). Behavioral and neurological effects of symptomatic and asymptomatic lead exposure in children. *Archives of Environmental Health, 34,* 120–124.

Sayre, J. W., Charney, E., Vostal, J., & Pless, D. (1974). House and hand dust as potential sources of childhood lead exposure. *American Journal of the Disabled Child, 127,* 167–170.

Schwartz, J. (1994). Low-level lead exposure and children's IQ: A meta-analysis and search for a threshold. *Environmental Research, 65,* 42–55.

Schettler, T. (2001). Toxic threats to neurologic development of children. *Environmental Health Perspectives, 109*(Suppl. 6), 813–816.

Sparta, S. (2003). Assessment of childhood trauma. In A. M. Goldstein (Ed.), *Handbook of forensic psychology: Vol. 11.* New York: John Wiley.

Viarruel v. O'Malley, CA No. 90–1227 (Suffolk [MA.] Super. Ct., Apr. 2, 1991).

Winder, C. (1993). Lead, reproduction and development. *Neurotoxicology, 14,* 303–317.

Wriggins, J. (1997). Genetics, IQ, determinism, and torts: The example of discovery in lead exposure litigation. *Boston University Law Review 77,* 1026–1028.

18

Bullying and Stalking in Children and Adolescents: Assessing Obsessional Harassment

Joseph T. McCann

Peer relationships play a critical role in shaping personality and social behavior during childhood and adolescence, and the behavioral sciences have focused considerable attention on ways young people interact with one another. Various forms of asocial behavior, such as bullying, group exclusion, teasing, name calling, and peer rejection, have long been recognized as problems among young people. Although discrete episodes of negative behavior among peers often occur, repetitive forms of social exclusion and harassment have increasingly become the focus of clinical and research attention (Schuster, 1996). Olweus (1993) has noted that bullying among schoolchildren that involves systematic and repetitive harassment has existed for quite some time, but no systematic attempts to study this phenomenon occurred until the late 1970s.

Bullying and other forms of obsessional harassment are highly relevant to the work of forensic psychologists; for instance, increasing attention has focused on the need for assessing risk for violence in young people, particularly in the wake of several highly publicized school shootings. In 1999 the United States Secret Service began an intensive study of 37 school shooting incidents involving 41 attackers in an effort to obtain useful information for school officials and other professionals responsible for preventing targeted violence in schools (Vossekuil, Reddy, Fein, Borum, & Modzeleski, 2000). This study found that in over two thirds of school shooting cases, attackers felt bullied, threatened, or persecuted prior to the shooting incident and that a number of attackers had experienced severe, chronic bullying. Vossekuil and his colleagues concluded that bullying appeared to play an important role in motivating school shootings and that efforts to deal with the problem of bullying in schools should continue.

Stalking constitutes another form of obsessional harassment related to bullying. Meloy and Gothard (1995) define stalking as "the willful, malicious, and repeated following and harassing of another person that threatens his or her safety" (p. 258). Recently, evidence has emerged that stalking can occur in late childhood and adolescence (McCann, 1998, 2000, 2001). Other prevalent forms of obsessional harassment among young people related to stalking include dating and courtship violence (O'Keefe, Brockopp, & Chew, 1986, Roscoe &

Callahan, 1985), sexual harassment (American Association of University Women Educational Foundation, 1993) and sexual aggression (Araji, 1997).

Forensic psychologists working with children and adolescents will likely find an increase in requests for services in cases that involve obsessional forms of harassment. Such services will likely include assessments of a youth's risk for violence, treatment planning, or specific psychological factors raised at sentencing (see Medoff & Kinscherff, chapter 21, this volume). The two common forms of obsessional harassment selected for review in this chapter, bullying and stalking, have conceptual similarities and reflect many of the challenging psychological issues that practitioners may face in cases in which young people encounter persistent and repetitive harassment.

BULLYING

Definitions and Prevalence

According to Olweus (1993), bullying occurs when a student "is exposed, repeatedly over time, to negative actions on the part of one or more other students" (p. 9), with *negative action* being defined as attempted or actual infliction of injury or discomfort on another person. Hazler (1996) has defined bullying as "repeatedly (not just once or twice) harming others" through "physical attack or by hurting others' feelings through words, actions, or social exclusion" (p. 6). These definitions reflect the notion of bullying as a social phenomenon in which one or more students engage in aggressive behavior directed at a specific victim and repeated over time. Moreover, some researchers have suggested that bullying involves an imbalance of power in which a physically stronger peer harasses or harms another smaller or physically weaker person (Olweus, 1993; Hazler, 1996). In addition, an important distinction exists between bullying, which involves a single student harassing a single victim, and mobbing, which involves a group of students harassing or acting aggressively toward an individual victim (Schuster, 1996).

Considerable variability exists in the prevalence rate of bullying reported in various studies. Many factors have hampered efforts at identifying accurate incidence figures, including how researchers define bullying, the specific frequency (e.g., "always," "occasionally") of bullying adopted, and varying levels of attention given to studying bullying in various countries. In a large-scale study in Norway, Olweus (1993) found that 15% of students reported feeling bullied "now and then," although only 3% reported feeling bullied once a week. Kumpulainen, Rasanen, and Henttonen (1999) studied 1,268 students in Finland longitudinally and initially found that 8.5% engaged in bullying and 6.8% were both bullies and victims of bullying. In a follow-up study 4 years later, these researchers found that 79% of students behaved as bullies and 10.3% as both bullies and victims. Collins and Bell (1996) found that 24% of their sample of schoolchildren from Northern Ireland were identified as bullies. Data from more than 38,000 children in Australian schools revealed that about one child out of six (17%) felt bullied by a peer or group of peers on a weekly basis (Peterson & Rigby, 1999).

In the United States, bullying also ranks as a significant problem, although survey data do not provide consistent prevalence rates. According to data cited by Oliver, Hoover, and Hazler (1994) about three out of four students (81% of males and 82% of females) report feeling bullied. However, these prevalence rates seem much higher than incidences cited in studies on bullying from other countries, and no clear basis exists to show why Oliver and colleagues cited such a high rate. Duncan (1999) studied a sample of 375 children in the United States and found that 25% reported feeling victimized by a bully and 28% acknowledged engaging in bullying behavior overall. Studies on bullying from various countries suggest that the prevalence of bullying among schoolchildren hovers around 15–25%, which supports the conclusion that this repetitive form of aggressive harassment constitutes a pervasive social problem among young people.

Descriptive Features

Considerable variability exists as to the specific behaviors that constitute bullying, although Olweus (1993) argues that the accurate use of the term *bullying* requires some imbalance of strength between perpetrator and victim. The various forms of harassment used to define the term *bullying* include teasing, name calling (Crozier & Dimmock, 1999), kicking, threats (Schuster, 1996), obscene gestures, social or group exclusion (Olweus, 1993), and similar forms of intimidation.

Age and gender effects also vary in bullying research. Schuster (1996) reviewed the data on age effects and noted contradictory findings, with some studies finding a decrease in bullying with increasing age, others showing no age effects, one study showing an increase in bullying with increasing age, and another showing a curvilinear relationship. Sourander, Helstela, Helenius, and Piha (2000) found that victimization occurred more persistently than bullying over an 8-year period in that victims of bullying at age 16 had typically also experienced the phenomenon at 8 years of age. Although a majority of students reporting victimization at age 8 did not engage in bullying at age 16, the presence of emotional and behavioral problems at age 8 appeared to be associated with bullying 8 years later. These findings support the notion that early identification of and intervention for emotional and behavioral problems in children constitutes an important component of preventive efforts for dealing with bullying behavior.

Research generally reveals significant gender effects in bullying, with boys showing more involvement in bullying as both perpetrators and victims (Olweus, 1993; Schuster, 1996). Salmivalli, Lagerspetz, Bjorkqvist, Osterman, and Kaukiainen (1996) found that boys' roles in bullying most likely involve acting as the primary bully, as someone who assisted in the bullying, or as someone who reinforced and supported a bully's harassment of the victim. Girls seemed more likely to participate in bullying as defenders of the victim or peripheral outsiders to bullying, although girls also participated as bullies and reinforced or assisted other bullies occasionally, but to a lesser degree than males.

Although bullying typically seems characterized by a pattern of aggressive behavior directed at peers, some research has focused on personality characteristics of children who bully others. Olweus (1996) noted, for example, that research does not support the view that inner feelings of anxiety and insecurity motivate bullies to engage in aggressive behavior. Rather, most perpetrators of bullying show a pattern of dominance and aggression associated with little or no anxiety,

whereas others seem more passive and insecure. In addition, bullies tend to appear physically stronger than their peers, have strong needs to dominate others and assert themselves, become angry easily, and display greater oppositional behavior (Olweus, 1993). Other personality characteristics of bullies include a lack of empathy, antisocial tendencies, general conduct disturbances, and egocentricity (Olweus, 1993, 1996; Schuster, 1996).

Research also indicates that victimization by bullies can have long-term consequences on social and emotional development of children. Although many bullying victims function well in adulthood, others show persistent problems with depression, low self-esteem, and a lack of assertiveness (Olweus, 1993; Schuster, 1996). Other studies have found that children who were victimized by bullies have significant behavioral difficulties later in life, including an increased propensity to act out, inattention, excessive dependency, and hypersensitivity (Duncan, 1999; Schwartz, McFadyen-Ketchum, Dodge, Pettit, & Bates, 1998). The greatest levels of psychological disturbance occur in children who both bullied others and experienced victimization by bullying (Duncan 1999; Kumpulainen et al., 1998). Children who acted as both victims and perpetrators of bullying seem at higher risk for continuing to engage in bullying over longer periods of time (Kumpulainen et al., 1999).

Forensic Assessment Issues

Clarifying the purpose of the evaluation constitutes the first step in any forensic examination, along with formulation of clear referral questions reflecting the needs of the court, attorney, or agency referring the youth for assessment. In some cases, the issue of bullying may constitute a primary focus of concern because the youth has exhibited a persistent and repetitive pattern of aggressive behavior toward peers, resulting in the need for a mental health evaluation. Other cases may involve different referral questions, such as a youth referred for treatment and disposition planning, sex-offender risk assessment, or other referral questions that are not directly linked to bullying. However, even if bullying does not form a primary focus of the referral question, bullying-related issues provide a very useful source of information in many evaluations.

Forensic evaluations that focus on issues related specifically to bullying, aggression, or violence potential require an assessment of the development of aggressive reaction patterns in the youth (Olweus, 1996). Bullies tend to display aggressive behavior in many different settings and contexts, and therefore it becomes important to identify specific triggers that precipitate aggressive behavior, as well as the settings and contexts in which such behavior occurs. Particular victim characteristics, verbal interactions, peer influences, or other factors that contribute to bullying behavior may exist and vary across perpetrators. In addition, one must determine whether the youth shows aggressive behavior in one type of setting (e.g., only with peers present) or whether the aggression becomes manifest in a variety of contexts (e.g., aggression toward adults or vandalism).

Other factors important to evaluate in children and adolescents who bully include the nature of early relationships with primary caretakers and family dynamics. Olweus (1996) noted a greater likelihood of a child becoming aggressive toward others later in life if the parent or caretaker expresses a negative emotional attitude toward the child. Similarly, overly permissive parents or those who utilize extremely harsh or power-assertive child-rearing methods increase the likelihood that their child will be aggressive later in life (Olweus, 1996). Therefore, when taking a psychosocial history from the child and collateral informants, one should evaluate the emotional tone of the parent-child relationship, the methods used by parents for disciplining the child, and family attitudes about aggression and violence that may affirm or condemn the use of violence as a means for solving problems.

Peer relationships constitute another area that provides a rich source of data on the patterns and dynamics of bullying. Children and adolescents show a higher risk of aggressive and violent behavior if they belong to a youth gang or have peers who endorse violence as a means of solving problems (Hawkins et al., 1998). If a child or adolescent who engages in bullying behavior has such peer-group influences, the bullying may arise as part of a generalized pattern of aggressive acting out.

Another factor related to peer relationships that warrants evaluative attention involves the extent to which a child has a history of being a victim of bullying. Some bullying victims "experience chronic and intense maltreatment from peers, causing reduced opportunities for adaptive friendship or other appropriate outlets such as the development of specific competencies" (McCann, 2001, pp. 132–133). The unavailability of adaptive outlets, such as sports, music, dating relationships, and supportive friendships, can lead to highly conflicted and ambivalent emotions that result in provocative behaviors, such as the teasing and bullying of younger or physically weaker peers. Given the poorer long-term adjustment of children who both act as perpetrators and have experienced victimization by bullying, the evaluator must examine these issues as part of the assessment process. In addition to a child's bullying and victimization experiences, the availability of social supports and other resources for coping with the highly conflicted emotions generated by bullying requires attention.

The issue of bullying in the forensic psychological examination has significance for several reasons. In those cases in which referral of the child or adolescent followed aggressive behavior, an assessment of the severity and the dynamics surrounding bullying behavior can help to establish whether the child's aggression is isolated to specific circumstances or is part of a more pervasive conduct disorder. The dynamics of bullying behavior can also help in making prognostic statements about a particular child or adolescent, as research indicates that bully-victims have poorer adjustment and long-term outcome than children who only bully or who have experienced only victimization. Of course, persistent and severe bullying behavior that is associated with a lack of empathy and antisocial or psychopathic personality traits also suggests a poorer prognosis (Frick, Barry, & Bodin, 2000).

STALKING

Definition and Prevalence

Although stalking has long been observed throughout history as a pathological form of romantic attachment (Meloy, 1999), it did not attain formal definition as a crime until California passed the nation's first antistalking law in 1990 (Saunders, 1998). The significance of stalking as a social problem resulted in a rapid proliferation of antistalking legislation (National Institute of Justice, 1993). Stalking now carries criminal penalties in all state and federal jurisdictions in the United States, as well as national and provincial jurisdictions in Canada, Great Britain, and Australia (Bradfield, 1998; McCann, 2001; Meloy, 1999).

The legal definition of stalking refers to repetitive threatening or harassing behavior that creates a credible threat of harm for the victim (Thomas, 1993). Moreover, a course of conduct in which more than one instance of harassing or threatening behavior that would make a reasonable person fear for his or her safety must occur (National Institute of Justice, 1993). Common forms of stalking include physically following the person, repeated telephone calls, threatening letters, repetitive trespassing or vandalism, and constant surveillance of the victim (McCann, 2001; Meloy, 1996, 1998). Other operational definitions of stalking have been used in social science research to facilitate study of such behavior. Meloy (1996), for example, used the term *obsessional following* to describe an abnormal or long-term pattern of threat or harassment directed toward a specific individual that includes "more than one overt act of unwanted pursuit of the victim that is perceived by the victim as being harassing" (p. 148). A related term, *obsessive relational intrusion*, is defined as "repeated and unwanted pursuit and invasion of one's sense of physical or symbolic privacy by another person, either stranger or acquaintance, who desires and/or presumes an intimate relationship" (Cupach & Spitzberg, 1998, pp. 234–235).

Recent data indicate that stalking constitutes a pervasive social problem. In one survey, 8% of women and 2% of men in the United States reported having felt stalked at some time in their lives (Tjaden, 1997). Although scholarly attention on stalking has focused predominantly on adults, evidence shows that this form of obsessional harassment occurs in younger populations. Cases of stalking behavior in children and adolescents exist in the professional literature (McCann, 1998; Urbach, Khalily, & Mitchell, 1992); however, stalking research has focused primarily on adult samples, with few formal studies on the phenomenon of stalking in children and adolescents.

Research on college students provides some indication of the extent of the problem, as the college years represent a transitional period between late adolescence and adulthood. Fremouw, Westrup, and Pennypacker (1997) studied two samples of college students and found a self-reported rate of stalking victimization of 24.2% among 593 students, with 30.7% of college women and 16.7% of college men reporting having felt stalked. McCreedy and Dennis (1996) found in a sample of 760 college students that 6.1% reported having felt stalked at some time in their lives. In a study of chief student affairs officers at 2- and 3-year colleges, Gallagher, Harmon, and Lingenfelter (1994) found that 34.5% of 590 officers surveyed reported having to intervene in one or more stalking cases within the previous year. These findings suggest that stalking is a pervasive problem on college campuses in the United States.

McCann (2001) has reviewed anecdotal evidence of stalking and related forms of obsessional harassment in children and adolescents, a study that provides evidence that stalking constitutes a significant problem in school-age children and adolescents. A study of restraining orders issued in Massachusetts against teenagers for threatening, abusive, and stalking behavior revealed that 757 such orders issued from courts over a 10-month period. Similarly, data on related forms of violence in school-age children, such as dating and courtship violence, sexual harassment, and sexual aggression, reveal that stalking may constitute a severe subtype of these problems. For example, a large national study of American schools revealed that of those children (81%) who experienced some form of sexual harassment, 32% received unwanted pictures or notes, 7% reported being spied on, 23% avoided familiar places as a result of harassment, 10% stopped attending activities, and 10% changed the route they traveled to and from school (American Association of University Women Educational Foundation, 1993). These findings reveal that a significant subset of victims experience harassment as intrusive and that it severely affects their daily routines.

Descriptive Features

The clinical and behavioral characteristics of children and adolescents who engage in stalking parallel many of those characteristics observed among adult stalking offenders, although some differences do appear to exist. McCann (1998) presented a series of case reports that showed that subtypes of stalking in adolescents matched the widely cited typology outlined by Zona, Sharma, and Lane (1993). More specifically, Zona and his colleagues identified three different types of stalking: erotomanic, love obsessional, and simple obsessional. Erotomanic stalking refers to repetitive following and approach behavior motivated by the perpetrator's belief that he or she is loved by the victim (American Psychiatric Association, 1994). Love-obsessional stalking is characterized by individuals who maintain a fanatical love of the victim associated with delusional beliefs and serious mental illness. Simple obsessional stalking characterizes those cases in which the perpetrator and victim had a prior relationship with one another, usually of an intimate nature. Adolescents have exhibited each of these forms of stalking behaviors (McCann, 1998; Urbach et al., 1992).

McCann (2000) studied a small sample of child and adolescent stalkers and identified some trends in the stalking behavior of young perpetrators, although the small sample size limits generalizations of his findings. The sample had a mean age of 14 years, with a range of 9 to 18 years. Most perpetrators were male, whereas most victims were female. For victims, the age groups were about evenly divided between same-age peers and adults. Additionally, just over half of young stalking perpetrators in the sample threatened the victim, and 31% of the cases involved violence. These findings seem consistent with those in the adult stalking literature in respect to the fact that half of adult stalkers threaten their victims and about 25–33% of adult stalkers become violent (Meloy, 1996). McCann also noted that the most common forms of pursuit and harassment in the sample of child and adolescent perpetrators involved physical approach, telephoning, and letter writing, which also parallel the more common forms of harassment in adult stalking cases. Based on a review of extensive research on stalking in younger populations, McCann (2001) concluded that late latency or early adolescence seems the prime developmental period in which stalking first becomes feasible.

Despite similarities between juvenile and adult stalking patterns, some differences have become evident in preliminary data. McCann (2000, 2001) noted that young stalking offenders appear to more commonly target casual acquaintances, whereas the most common perpetrator–victim pattern in adult cases occurs between prior intimate partners (Meloy, 1998). One reason posited for this finding involves differences in psychosexual development between adolescents and adults. McCann notes, "Because adolescents are experiencing greater uncertainty about their identity and expanding their sexual exploration, their capacity or opportunity for intimacy is less than it is in adults. Therefore, the young obsessional follower may develop fixations that involve sexual feelings that are directed more at casual acquaintances rather than prior intimate partners" (McCann, 2001, p. 62).

Other stalking patterns have been identified in children and adolescents. One form of stalking-related behavior involves fixation on a public figure. Although the idealization of media figures occurs commonly in young people, these fixations can indicate psychological disturbance in some cases. Various factors differentiate pathological and benign fixation, such as the youth's capacity for distinguishing fantasy-based from reality-based expectations (e.g.., the likelihood of an actual relationship with the media figure). The presence of suicidal ideation or gestures related to the public figure's activities, unsanctioned approach behavior (e.g., attempts to visit the public figure that have a low probability of success), and comorbid delusions or other forms of severe psychopathology may also occur. Another form of stalking behavior observed in isolated cases of juvenile stalking involves intrafamilial stalking (McCann, 2000, 2001), in which adolescents either obsessionally harass or find themselves harassed by a parent or other primary caretaker. This unusual pattern of stalking may occur in cases in which the parent–child relationship has deteriorated to the point at which a pattern of harassment develops. Such patterns appear similar to those seen in cases in which a prior intimate partner harasses and stalks an estranged lover. Intrafamilial stalking in child and adolescent cases is identified when there is a pattern of behavior that meets the formal legal definition of stalking and when the victim (i.e., either parent or child) has taken some legal action against the behavior (e.g., seeking a protective order) and perpetrator and victim are living apart (McCann, 2001).

Forensic Assessment Issues

The particular issues addressed in forensic evaluations of juvenile stalking offenders depend largely on context. Referring questions that courts or agencies may pose include the perpetrator's level of risk for violence, his or her amenability to treatment, and recommendations for intervention or case management. The dearth of research on juvenile stalking hampers the formulation of empirically based conclusions and recommendations. However, McCann (2001) has noted that general principles of juvenile risk assessment, treatment planning, and case management strategies found in the adult stalking literature can prove useful when evaluating young stalking offenders.

Because stalking involves some implicit or explicit threat to the victim, a major concern in stalking cases involves determination of whether or not the perpetrator will become violent. According to Grisso (1998), several general factors become important considerations when evaluating the potential for violence in children and adolescents. These include (1) substance abuse; (2) peer influences and supports; (3) family conflict and aggression; (4) social stressors; (5) personality variables such as impulsivity, psychopathy, and anger that increase the risk for violence; (6) specific mental conditions (e.g., psychosis, attention-deficit/hyperactivity disorder) that can influence behavior; (7) a history of abuse or trauma; (8) neurological factors; (9) prior responses to treatment; and (10) situational factors (e.g., weapon access, formulation of plans for violence).

In addition, some factors cited in the literature may reduce the risk for violence by serving as protective factors (Witt & Dyer, 1997). These factors include (1) adequate and stable self-esteem, (2) resilient temperament, (3) positive social attitudes, (4) a healthy capacity for attachment and bonding, (5) stable and accessible social supports, (6) good academic achievement, and (7) healthy attachment to parents. Although such general factors apply to most risk assessments of violent behavior, a few seem relevant to stalking. Conceptualizing stalking as a disturbance in attachment (Kienlen, 1998; Meloy, 1996) and identity (McCann, 2001) suggests a need to focus on factors such as attachment capacity, the stability of self-esteem, social supports, positive social influences, and resiliency in dealing with loss or abandonment as particularly relevant when evaluating risk for violence in juvenile stalking cases.

As the underlying pathology of adult and juvenile stalking offenders appears to be similar in some ways (McCann, 2001), the literature on risk factors for violence in adult stalking cases may provide guidance for conducting violence risk assessments in juvenile cases. For example, one variable shown to increase the risk for violence in adult stalking cases links to the presence of a prior intimate relationship between the perpetrator and victim (Meloy, 1996, 1998; Meloy, Davis, & Lovette, 2001; Zona et al., 1993). This risk factor remains unexamined in juvenile stalking cases, although intimate partner and dating violence seems to occur at similar rates among adults and adolescents (McCann, 2001). Additionally, Menzies, Fedoroff, Green, and Isaacson (1995) identify multiple object fixations as a factor associated with an increased risk for violence in adults with erotomania. McCann (1998, 2001) speculated that multiple object fixations may occur more commonly in adolescent stalking cases, representing diffuse identity formation that could result in a greater risk for violence in some cases. This hypothesis requires further testing; however, it also remains a viable hypothesis to consider in juvenile stalking cases in which a youth has shown a pattern of obsessive preoccupations with several victims.

Many stalking cases have some involvement with the legal system (Meloy, 1997), usually because the victim has taken out an order of protection or formal legal charges have been issued against the perpetrator. Another factor that may arise in forensic evaluations of children or adolescents who have engaged in stalking behavior involves whether to adjudicate the youth as an adult or to retain jurisdiction in juvenile or family court. The decision to either maintain youthful offender status or transfer the juvenile to adult status depends on a number of factors, including the amenability of the youth to treatment, the seriousness of the criminal charges, the history of prior offenses, and the potential for harm to others in the community (Grisso, 1998). McCann (2001) has argued that absent some egregious or violent offense (e.g., murder or serial sexual offending), most juvenile stalking offenders seem best served by maintaining youthful offender status. The juvenile justice system generally has a stronger treatment orientation than the adult system and provides opportunities for monitoring the offender's behavior through probation, mandated mental health treatment, and residential placement if the youth presents an increased risk to others in the community.

Finally, Meloy (1997) has noted that the mental health treatment of adult stalking offenders primarily follows from the Axis I and Axis II diagnoses. This approach seems appropriate for juvenile stalking offenders as well (McCann, 2001). Individual psychotherapy seems warranted for personality disturbances such as impulsivity, attachment problems, and other factors that play a role in maintaining stalking behavior. Group treatment for juvenile sex offenders may prove appropriate for youths whose stalking behavior involves sexual assault. Specific treatments for depression, anxiety, and other clinical syndromes (e.g., cognitive-behavioral therapy) also seems indicated when these factors play a part in the stalking. The use of medication will often prove helpful for the treatment of psychosis, depression, attention-deficit/hyperactivity disorder, and other conditions that respond to pharmacological agents.

The issues that arise when providing forensic assessment and treatment services to young stalking victims have similarities to those in cases that involve related forms of relationship aggression. Some studies of stalking victims originated on samples that included adolescents. These studies indicate that stalking victims experience a range of adverse psychological problems as a result of the stalking, including symptoms of posttraumatic stress disorder (Westrup, Fremouw, & Thompson, 1999), greater cautiousness and less comfort in social situations (Hall, 1998), higher levels of anxiety and suspiciousness, and fears of being a victim of crime (McCreedy & Dennis, 1996) or physical injury (Gallagher et al., 1994). Assessment of young stalking victims should include standardized assessment of presenting symptoms such as anxiety, depression, traumatic stress, and concerns about personal safety. Assessment of social supports, including family and peer relationships, and school functioning also becomes important. Supportive treatment of young stalking victims should also focus directly on alleviating symptoms attributable to the stalking.

Advising young stalking victims and their families about useful strategies for dealing with stalking behaviors will also help. Among the various recommendations to consider are (a) installing adequate lighting around the home; (b) maintaining an unlisted telephone number; (c) using a caller identification device; (d) reporting all threats to parents, school officials, and law enforcement authorities; (e) providing school personnel with identifying information about a stalking perpetrator not enrolled in the school; (f) providing notice of any court orders of protection to appropriate personnel; (g) varying travel routes to and from school; (h) developing contingency plans for transportation; (i) enlisting peers to serve as supports and escorts at times of greatest vulnerability (e.g., late hours or at school); (j) keeping emergency numbers on hand; and (k) maintaining an open and supportive relationship with parents and school officials (McCann, 2001; National Victim Center, 1997). Evaluate any decision to obtain a personal order of protection on a case-by-case basis. Seeking a protective order risks exacerbating the stalking offender's anger, and such orders prove ineffective in some cases. However, restraining orders generally seem more effective than not (McCann, 2001; Meloy, Cowett, Parker, Hofland, & Friedland, 1997).

CONCLUSION

Many forms of interpersonal violence that occur in adult relationships also occur with some frequency in children and adolescents, including sexual aggression, dating violence, and sexual harassment. Some forms of aggression in harassing and threatening behaviors evoke fear in victims and occur repeatedly over time. This chapter provided an overview of bullying and stalking, two common forms of obsessional harassment among children and adolescents. Bullying and stalking have conceptual similarities in that they involve more than one instance of threatening or harassing behavior directed at a specific victim.

The problem of obsessional harassment among children and adolescents has only recently become the focus of empirical study. Within the past two decades bullying behavior has attracted systematic study (Olweus, 1993). Stalking behavior in young people has also found recognition as a significant problem only within the past few years (McCann, 1998, 2001). However, legal trends suggest that obsessional harassment will continue as a pressing concern for schools, as recent U. S. Supreme Court opinions have held that schools may potentially be liable for sexual harassment of their students by teachers (*Gebser v. Lago Vista Independent School District*, 1998) and by other students (*Davis v. Monroe County Board of Education*, 1999). School officials may be in the best position from which to observe obsessional harassment among students and to make referrals for intervention and treatment (McCann, 1998, 2001). These trends also suggest that forensic mental health professionals who provide assessment and treatment services to courts, agencies, schools, families, and students will find themselves increasingly called on to consult in cases involving obsessional forms of harassment.

References

American Association of University Women Educational Foundation. (1993). *Hostile hallways: The AAUW survey on sexual harassment in America's schools*. Washington, DC: Author.

American Psychiatric Association. (1994). *Diagnostic and statistical manual of mental disorders* (4th ed.).Washington, DC: Author.

Araji, S. K. (1997). *Sexually aggressive children: Coming to understand them*. Thousand Oaks, CA: Sage.

Bradfield, J. L. (1998). Anti-stalking laws: Do they adequately protect stalking victims? *Harvard Women's Law Journal, 21*, 229–266.

Collins, K., & Bell, F. (1996). Peer perceptions of aggression and bullying behavior in primary schools in Northern Ireland. In C. F. Ferris & T. Grisso (Eds.), *Understanding aggressive behavior in children* (pp. 336–338). New York: New York Academy of Sciences.

Crozier, W. R., & Dimmock, P. S. (1999). Name-calling and nicknames in a sample of primary school children. *British Journal of Educational Psychology, 69*, 505–516.

Cupach, W. R., & Spitzberg, B. H. (1998). Obsessive relational intrusions and stalking. In B. H. Spitzberg & W. R. Cupach (Eds.), *The dark side of close relationships* (pp. 233–263). Mahwah, NJ: Lawrence Erlbaum.

Davis v. Monroe County Board of Education, 526 U.S. 629 (1999).

Duncan, R. D. (1999). Peer and sibling aggression: An investigation of intra- and extrafamilial bullying. *Journal of Interpersonal Violence, 14*, 871–886.

Fremouw, W. J., Westrup, D., & Pennypacker, J. (1997). Stalking on campus: The prevalence and strategies for coping with stalking. *Journal of Forensic Sciences, 42*, 666–669.

Frick, P. J., Barry, C. I., & Bodin, S. D. (2000). Applying the concept of psychopathy to children: Implications for the assessment of antisocial youth. In C. B. Gacono (Ed.), *The clinical and forensic assessment of psychopathy: A practitioner's guide* (pp. 3–24). Mahwah, NJ: Lawrence Erlbaum.

Gallagher, R. P., Harmon, W. W. , & Lingenfelter, C. O. (1994). CSAO's perception of the changing incidence of problematic college student behavior. *NASPA Journal, 32*(1), 37–45.

Gebser v. Lago Vista Independent School District, 524 U.S. 274 (1998).

Grisso, T. (1998). *Forensic evaluation of juveniles*. Sarasota, FL: Professional Resource Press.

Hall, D. M. (1998). The victims of stalking. In J. R. Meloy (Ed.), *The psychology of stalking: Clinical and forensic perspectives* (pp. 113–137). San Diego, CA: Academic Press.

Hawkins, J. D., Herrenkohl, T., Farrington, D. P., Brewer, D., Catalano, R. F., & Harachi, U. W. (1998). A review of predictors of youth violence. In R. Loeber & D. P. Farrington (Eds.), *Serious and violent juvenile offenders: Risk factors and successful interventions* (pp. 106–146). Thousand Oaks, CA: Sage.

Hazler, R. J. (1996). *Breaking the cycle of violence: Interventions for bullying and victimization*. Washington, DC: Accelerated Development.

Kienlen, K. K. (1998). Developmental and social antecedents of stalking. In J. R. Meloy (Ed.), *The psychology of stalking: Clinical and forensic perspectives* (pp. 51–67). San Diego, CA: Academic Press.

Kumpulainen, K., Rasanen, E., Henttonen, I., Almqvist, F., Kresanov, K., Linna, S. L., et al. (1998). Bullying and psychiatric symptoms among elementary school-age children. *Child Abuse and Neglect, 22*, 705–717.

Kumpulainen, K., Rasanen, E., & Henttonen, I. (1999). Children involved in bullying: Psychological disturbance and the persistence of the involvement. *Child Abuse and Neglect, 23*, 1253–1262.

McCann, J. T. (1998). Subtypes of stalking/obsessional following in adolescents *Journal of Adolescence, 21*, 667–675.

McCann, J. T. (2000). A descriptive study of child and adolescent obsessional followers. *Journal of Forensic Sciences, 45*, 195–199.

McCann, J. T. (2001). *Stalking in children and adolescents: The primitive bond.* Washington, DC: American Psychological Association.

McCreedy, K. R., & Dennis, B. (1996). Sex-related offenses and fear of crime on campus. *Journal of Contemporary Criminal Justice, 12,* 69–80.

Meloy, J. R. (1996). Stalking (obsessional following): A review of some preliminary studies. *Aggression and Violent Behavior, 1,* 147—162.

Meloy, J. R. (1997). The clinical risk management of stalking: "Someone is watching over me." *American Journal of Psychotherapy, 51,* 174–184.

Meloy, J. R. (1998). The psychology of stalking. In J. R. Meloy (Ed.), *The psychology of stalking: Clinical and forensic perspectives* (pp. 1–23). San Diego, CA: Academic Press.

Meloy, J. R. (1999). Stalking: An old behavior, a new crime. *Psychiatric Clinics of North America, 22,* 85–99.

Meloy J. R., Cowett, P. Y., Parker, S. B., Hofland, B., & Friedland, A. (1997). Domestic protection orders and the prediction of subsequent criminality and violence toward protectors. *Psychotherapy, 34,* 447–458.

Meloy, J. R., Davis, B., & Lovette, J. (2001). Risk factors for violence among stalkers. *Journal of Threat Assessment, 1(1),* 3–16.

Meloy, J. R., & Gothard, S. (1995). A demographic and clinical comparison of obsessional followers and offenders with mental disorders. *American Journal of Psychiatry, 152,* 258–263.

Menzies, R., Fedoroff, J. P., Green, C., & Isaacson, K. (1995). Prediction of dangerous behavior in male erotomania. *British Journal of Psychiatry, 166,* 529–536.

National Institute of Justice. (1993). *Project to develop a model anti-stalking code for states* (NIJ Publication No. NCJ 144477). Washington, DC: U.S. Government Printing Office.

National Victim Center. (1997). *Stalking: Safety plan guidelines.* Arlington VA: Author.

O'Keefe, N. K., Brockopp, K., & Chew, E. (1986). Teen dating violence. *Social Work, 31,* 465–468.

Oliver, R., Hoover, J. H., & Hazler, R. (1994). The perceived roles of bullying in small-town midwestern schools. *Journal of Counseling and Development, 72,* 416–420.

Olweus, D. (1993). *Bullying at school: What we know and what we can do.* Oxford, UK: Blackwell.

Olweus, D. (1996). Bullying at school: Knowledge base and an effective intervention program. In C. F. Ferris & T. Grisso (Eds.), *Understanding aggressive behavior in children* (pp. 265–276). New York: New York Academy of Sciences.

Peterson, L., & Rigby, K. (1999). Countering bullying at an Australian secondary school with students as helpers. *Journal of Adolescence, 22,* 481–492.

Roscoe, B., & Callahan, J. F. (1985) Adolescents' self-report of violence in families and dating relations. *Adolescence, 20,* 545–553.

Salmivalli, C., Lagerspetz, K., Bjordqvist, K., Osterman, K., & Kaukiainen, A. (1996). Bullying as a group process: Participant roles and the relations to social status within the group. *Aggressive Behavior, 22,* 1–15.

Saunders, R. (1998), The legal perspective on stalking. In J. R. Meloy (Ed.), *The psychology of stalking: Clinical and forensic perspectives* (pp. 25–49). San Diego, CA: Academic Press.

Schuster, B. (1996). Rejection, exclusion, and harassment at work and in schools. *European Psychologist, 1,* 293–317.

Schwartz, D., McFadyen-Ketchum, S. A., Dodge, K. A., Pettit, G. S., & Bates, J. E. (1998). Peer group victimization as a predictor of children's behavior problems at home and in school. *Development and Psychopathology, 10,* 87–99.

Sourander, A., Helstela, L., Helenius, H., & Piha, J. (2000). Persistence of bullying from childhood to adolescence: A longitudinal 8-year follow-up study. *Child Abuse and Neglect, 24,* 873–881.

Thomas, K. R. (1993). How to stop the stalker: State antistalking laws. *Criminal Law Bulletin, 29,* 124–136.

Tjaden, P. (1997). *The crime of stalking: How big is the problem?* (NIJ Research in Brief No. TNCJ 16392). Washington, DC: U.S. Department of Justice.

Urbach, J. T., Khalily, C., & Mitchell, P. P. (1992). Erotomania in an adolescent: Clinical and theoretical considerations. *Journal of Adolescence, 15,* 231–240.

Vossekuil, B., Reddy, M., Fein, R., Borum, R., & Modzeleski, W. (2000). *U.S.S.S. safe school initiative: An interim report on the prevention of targeted violence in schools.* Washington, DC: U.S. Secret Service, National Threat Assessment Center.

Westrup, D., Fremouw, W. J., & Thompson, N. (1999). The psychological impact of stalking on female undergraduates. *Journal of Forensic Sciences, 44,* 554–557.

Witt, P. H., & Dyer, F. J. (1997). Juvenile transfer cases: Risk assessment and risk management. *Journal of Psychiatry and Law, 25,* 581–614.

Zona, M. A., Sharma, K. K., & Lane, J. (1993). A comparative study of erotomanic and obsessional subjects in a forensic sample. *Journal of Forensic Sciences, 38,* 894–903.

19

Forensic Assessment of Amenability to Rehabilitation in Juvenile Delinquency

Robert Kinscherff

The first juvenile court in the United States was established in 1899. By 1925, all but two states had established separate courts or probation services for juveniles guided by a vision of rehabilitation through individualized justice. The lower and upper ages at which juveniles are subject to the jurisdiction of the juvenile court vary according to state law, as do the kinds of offenses within the jurisdiction of the court. Not all states have a court department specifically called "juvenile court," but this term applies to other courts that sit in "juvenile session" or otherwise have juvenile jurisdiction in delinquency matters.

Under the model evolved for adjudication of juveniles accused of "delinquent" conduct that would constitute "criminal" acts if committed by an adult, attention to the individual circumstances of each juvenile should result in both the protection of society and the improved functioning of the juvenile through targeted interventions. Only under unusual circumstances and for the most serious crimes would a juvenile court waive its jurisdiction to permit trial and sentencing of a juvenile in adult courts.

During the 1950s and 1960s, the ability of the juvenile justice system to rehabilitate juveniles came into question. Rehabilitative efforts administered through state "training" or "reform" schools proved ineffective, and juveniles often experienced deprivation of their liberty without basic legal due process. A series of U.S. Supreme Court decisions imposed more legal formality on juvenile court proceedings, and some states attempted to implement a continuum-of-care model to replace routine institutionalization of young offenders in juvenile justice facilities.

During the 1980s the American public perceived a significant increase in serious juvenile crime and that the juvenile courts were too lenient. Ironically, just as rates of serious violent crime by juveniles decreased significantly during the 1990s, legislatures in 47 states and the District of Columbia enacted laws that made the juvenile courts substantially more punitive. States began to emphasize community protection and offender accountability to a greater degree. Steps included relaxing the confidentiality of juvenile delinquency proceedings, automatic transfer for trial and sentencing in adult court for specific serious crimes, provisions making it easier to transfer a juvenile for trial in adult court, and expansion of the sentencing authority available to juvenile courts, such as imposition of terms of incarceration to adult prisons (Snyder & Sickmund, 1999).

The forensic assessment of a juvenile's amenability to rehabilitation often plays a critical role in a juvenile delinquency matter. This is especially true since recent reforms have exposed juveniles to increasingly punitive options. Except for cases in which juveniles are automatically transferred for trial on charges that carry mandatory sentences if convicted, the question of whether a juvenile is amenable to rehabilitation may determine whether a juvenile stands trial as an adult or a juvenile, undergoes sentencing as an adult or a juvenile, or faces commitment to state juvenile justice authorities, assignment to community probation, or diversion out of a delinquency case before juvenile court for more appropriate servicing through mental health, child protection, or educational systems.

Stakes can run high, even in apparently minor or "first offense" cases. For example, a juvenile assigned to improper or inadequate intervention may find any failure to respond to those interventions cited later as a reason why he should be treated more harshly or even tried as an adult for subsequent offenses, as it may seem that he failed to respond to intervention. In other cases the stakes may involve whether a juvenile remains in the community, is committed to the custody of state juvenile justice authorities, or faces trial or sentencing as a juvenile or an adult. The issue of amenability to rehabilitation has long played a critical role during the capital sentencing phases of persons sentenced to death for crimes committed under age 18, particularly given the neuropsychiatric impairments and psychosocial circumstances commonly exhibited by juveniles convicted of capital crimes and sentenced to death (see Lewis et al., 1988).

Clinical professionals must appreciate that the concept of "rehabilitation" is broader than the concept of clinical "treatment." Medication or psychotherapeutic interventions are often elements in the rehabilitation of a juvenile delinquent, but rehabilitation efforts encompass all domains, permitting a juvenile to live in the community without criminal misconduct. Attention to the "rehabilitation" of a juvenile ordinarily includes assessment of educational, vocational, social, and other needs associated with reducing risk of recidivism.

The following important implications arise from the differences between "rehabilitation" and "treatment":

- Assessments of amenability to rehabilitation involve a broader scope than many "clinical" assessments. Recommended services or interventions must *specifically* link to factors that give rise to the delinquent misconduct and to factors that would reduce recidivism risks.
- The recommended services or interventions must actually be available. Rehabilitation cannot occur if the recommended services remain inaccessible; the law in some states further specifies that the services or interventions must be accessible through the juvenile justice system.
- General clinical training will not ordinarily sufficiently prepare a mental health professional for forensic assessment of a juvenile's amenability to rehabilitation. Although solid clinical skills are essential, evaluators must also have intimate familiarity with relevant law, resources accessible through the juvenile justice system, research regarding delinquent misconduct and the range of impairment found among delinquents, and interventions among various kinds of delinquent populations.

ESTABLISHING THE FORENSIC CONTEXT OF THE EVALUATION

Establishing the Referral Question

The first step in any given case involves establishing whether "amenability to rehabilitation" forms an explicit legal factor in the case presented for evaluation. Particularly in "transfer" or "waiver" cases (i.e., moving the trial and punishment to adult jurisdiction and criminal standards), "youthful offender" cases (trial as a juvenile, but possible punishment under either adult or juvenile standards), or cases involving possible extension of a commitment to juvenile justice authorities, the term *amenability to rehabilitation* may constitute an explicit factor for consideration by the court as a matter of law. If so, the evaluator should appreciate that case law may apply in the jurisdiction that further refines that concept for the court and with which the evaluator should become familiar so that the evaluation can attend to specific features or factors required by law.

More commonly, "amenability to rehabilitation" constitutes an unarticulated concern that accompanies referral in cases prior to adjudication or when the court requests evaluation to assist in imposing a disposition following adjudication. The background question in many cases may actually be, what needs to be done so that this youth does not reoffend, and how likely is it that these steps will work? Clarifying referral questions is a valuable skill that helps clinicians focus evaluations to the specific information, opinions, or recommendations required by the court. Clinicians may have to inquire about who made the recommendation for evaluation to the court, what concerns or information gave rise to the referral, and what kinds of information the court would find useful.

Referral questions that implicitly involve assessments of amenability to rehabilitation may seem vague ("psychosocial evaluation of defendant"), focused on potentially helpful interventions (Does the defendant need drug treatment?), requests for suggestions (What treatment should be part of the defendant's conditions of probation?), or broad and potentially outside of the expertise of clinicians (Should the defendant be committed to the juvenile justice authorities?). Clinicians should ascertain that the evaluation answers the concerns on the part of the forensic *client* that prompted referral for evaluation.

Assessment of "amenability to rehabilitation" implies assessment of risk of reoffense. Particularly in cases that involve physical or sexual violence against persons, the risk assessment of potential violence becomes an explicit or implicit referral question that evaluators must adequately address as part of the broader assessment of amenability to rehabilitation. Other chapters in this book provide information regarding risk assessment and management in cases involving physically and sexually aggressive offenses (see Medoff & Kinscherff, chapter 21, this volume).

Establishing the Client of the Evaluation

Establishing the "client" for purposes of the evaluation must occur before beginning the assessment. The professional relationship with the identified client will ordinarily dictate what concerns prompted the referral, what kind of evaluation would prove most useful to the client, the rules of confidentiality or privilege that apply, the purpose and focus of the evaluation, and the proper informed consent required.

If the evaluation originates from a court order, then the court stands as the client unless specific other orders have been issued. Any psychotherapist–client privilege ordinarily becomes waived, and the juvenile and the attorney must have explicit notice of this prior to conducting the evaluation. The evaluation itself is the work product of the court, and dissemination may not occur without the prior authorization of the court unless local practices or rules clearly provide to the contrary. Probation officers are often considered officers of the court, and therefore the rules governing court-ordered evaluations apply to evaluations requested or secured by them. Some jurisdictions may require consent of the parents before proceeding even if the evaluation originates with a court order. As a result, clinicians must familiarize themselves with relevant law and practices for their jurisdiction.

When defense counsel initiates the evaluation, that attorney becomes the client, and attorney–client privilege prevails. Defense counsel may seek evaluations prior to adjudication on the charges or after adjudication but prior to disposition. Defense counsel may also seek evaluations involving amenability to rehabilitation at postdispositional proceedings, such as violation of probation or proceedings to determine whether circumstances warrant an extension of a juvenile's commitment to state juvenile justice authorities. In each case, the attorney–client privilege prevails, and the evaluator may not release or discuss the results of the evaluation without prior approval by defense counsel.

The law regarding how licensed clinicians should proceed in the event of a conflict between attorney–client privilege and mandated reporting requirements remains unclear in many jurisdictions. For example, a licensed mental health professional may incur a mandated reporting requirement on learning of circumstances of child abuse during the evaluation that would not require a defense attorney to make such a report. Best practice suggests that forensic evaluators should familiarize themselves with the relevant law in the jurisdiction in which the evaluation will take place and to advise the attorney prior to conducting the evaluation on how they would proceed in the event such a conflict arose.

If the prosecution secures the evaluation, then the prosecutor stands as the client. The duty of prosecutors to divulge relevant information (especially if it is exculpatory) means that no attorney–client privilege exists for the forensic evaluation. Obviously, the juvenile defendants and their defense counsel must have notice that the prosecution has arranged for the evaluation, as well as any relevant information regarding the focus, scope, and procedures planned.

Juvenile justice authorities may also retain forensic evaluations of amenability to rehabilitation. These may occur during a period of assessment or "classification" on the commitment of the juvenile, during the period of commitment to assess progress or identify needs, or in anticipation of a potential request for an extension of commitment. Evaluators retained by juvenile justice authorities to conduct these evaluations essentially become agents of those authorities and must precisely clarify to the juvenile, to an attorney representing the juvenile, and to the parents or other legal guardians of the juvenile the purpose of the evaluation, the planned uses of the information obtained from the evaluation, and the likelihood that the evaluation may become part of court proceedings. If any likelihood exists that the evaluation may find introduction into court proceedings, the juvenile and his or her defense counsel must have notice of this prior to proceeding with the evaluation.

Similarly, clinicians working in residential facilities or other programs that provide contracted work to juvenile justice authorities must clarify the purposes and likely use of their clinical work. For example, some residential facilities have contracts with state juvenile justice authorities to provide institutional care for delinquent youths. Outpatient mental health facilities may service juveniles committed to the juvenile justice system but placed in the community or juveniles not committed to the juvenile justice system but who are on probation from the Juvenile Court. Clinicians in these programs must clarify in advance of providing clinical services or evaluations what rules of confidentiality or privilege may apply and the likelihood that their clinical work will become part of

future court proceedings. These understandings must become an explicit element of the informed consent process of the case, especially when the clinician may be asked to formally assess issues of amenability to rehabilitation.

Clinicians retained by a juvenile's parents or legal guardians to conduct evaluations of amenability to rehabilitation should proceed with caution. Depending on the jurisdiction, parents may or may not have the right to assert privilege on behalf of their minor child. Parents may lack access to court documents or other key information that is accessible to the court or defense counsel. The clinician may unwittingly create a discoverable report that is deemed damaging by defense counsel, thus creating a conflict among the juvenile, his or her family, and the defense counsel. The best practice, if approached by a juvenile's parents or legal guardians for this kind of evaluation, involves requiring that retention originate with defense counsel so that it becomes the attorney's work product even if the parents still pay the costs of the evaluation.

ESTABLISHING THE FORENSIC CONTEXT OF THE EVALUATION: PREADJUDICATION EVALUATIONS

As suggested previously, evaluation of a juvenile's amenability to rehabilitation may occur at multiple points in a given case. Clinicians who provide these kinds of evaluations must have intimate familiarity with factors that govern these cases, such as the legal rules and practices that prevail at different points in the proceedings, the ultimate issues that the court must decide at the point of seeking the evaluation, and the kinds of factors that a court must legally consider in making a determination.

Although an evaluation of amenability to rehabilitation may arise at any one of several points, such evaluations generally occur at two distinct phases: preadjudication and postadjudication.

Preadjudication evaluations occur prior to a juvenile's admission to the allegations or a finding of delinquency by a court. The most common kind of preadjudication evaluation occurs in anticipation of further proceedings within juvenile court. Less common, but involving extremely high stakes, are evaluations for "transfer" or "waiver" proceedings to determine whether or not a juvenile would stand trial as an adult.

Preadjudication evaluations of delinquency cases that will remain within the jurisdiction of the juvenile court are barred in a few states due to concerns regarding self-incrimination and due process, but they commonly occur in most states. Local practices typically determine whether or not the alleged offenses are specifically discussed as part of the evaluation. However, defense counsel should always have ample notice prior to conducting such a preadjudication evaluation to determine whether the attorney will permit discussion of the alleged offenses and address any other issues regarding potential self-incrimination.

Barnum (1990) holds that clinicians should ordinarily be extremely reluctant to draw any conclusions regarding intervention needs or amenability if these conclusions are based primarily on a juvenile's denial of the alleged offenses prior to adjudication. Denial of alleged offenses prior to adjudication may mean different things with vastly different clinical significance. The possibilities include calculated lying about the charges simply to avoid consequences, anxious avoidance of acknowledging the allegations out of shame or fear, compliance with instructions from defense counsel or others to offer no admissions, or actual innocence of the alleged offenses. No research data suggest that clinicians can reliably distinguish among these possibilities prior to adjudication when a juvenile denies alleged offenses, and efforts by the clinician to rely on victim statements or other evidence risk improperly rendering the clinician an arbiter of the evidence and judge of the case.

General evaluations that do not involve any discussion of the alleged offenses may still yield information of value to the court when considering disposition should adjudication find that the juvenile is delinquent; for example, when the evaluation yields information about cognitive abilities or limitations, psychiatric or substance abuse intervention needs, or special educational needs. If the specific nature of the alleged offenses has significant implications for understanding the juvenile's intervention needs or amenability to rehabilitation, the best practices suggest further evaluation of these issues *after* adjudication, should the court still need information to assist in disposition.

"Transfer" or "waiver" hearings determine whether a juvenile will stand trial and face sentencing as an adult. In some jurisdictions, these hearings occur before any legal finding of facts, whereas in other jurisdictions the issue of a possible adult criminal sentence arises only after a finding that the juvenile has committed the alleged offenses. In the latter instance, the evaluator can rely on the facts as found by the court, and the evaluation becomes essentially an aid in disposition.

However, when transfer or waiver hearings occur *before* adjudication, they pose complex challenges to evaluators, as it will *not* yet have been legally established that the juvenile actually committed the alleged offenses. Under these circumstances, juveniles still have the right against self-incrimination, and therefore denial of the alleged offenses may have a range of different clinical meanings or may simply reflect the advice of counsel.

Judges must typically consider multiple factors in making waiver decisions, including the seriousness of the alleged offense, history of the juvenile's response to prior interventions, and amenability of the juvenile to rehabilitation through interventions available through the juvenile justice system and within the time frame available by law. Evaluators must be familiar in detail with the relevant law governing waiver proceedings in the applicable jurisdiction, as well as with the kinds of resources accessible through that court or that state's juvenile justice authorities.

In some cases, defense counsel will permit the juvenile to acknowledge the alleged conduct or some variant of the allegations, and the evaluator will have the ability to discuss the acknowledged misconduct in some detail. In other cases, defense counsel will not permit discussion of the allegations, or the juvenile simply asserts innocence of the charges. The denial of the charges prior to adjudication raises the same difficulties described earlier when juveniles deny charges before adjudication outside of the waiver context.

The more that the assessment of amenability to rehabilitation relies on whether or not the youth committed the alleged offense, the more the evaluator must exercise caution in clarifying the limits of the evaluation for the court. Consider, for example, a transfer case in which a juvenile charged with homicide presented with very little in the way of a history of deviant socialization or delinquent misconduct, no history of identified psychiatric disorder, and apparently adequate adjustment to family, school, and peers. However, the murder involved a victim well known to the defendant, multiple stabbings and ritualized mutilation of the body, postmortem handling of the body, and evidence of a sexual motivation for the killing. He denied committing the offense and offered an alternative account in which he reported coming on the crime scene after the victim's death, allegedly at the hands of an intruder.

In this case, knowing whether or not the juvenile committed the crime became essential for understanding his prospects for rehabilitation. If he had not committed the offense, little, if any, need for "rehabilitation" as a juvenile delinquent would exist. His denial would reflect his innocence of the crime.

On the other hand, if he had committed the offense, with characteristics indicating that it involved premeditation and reflected sexual sadism, very different implications could be drawn. No reliable psychotherapeutic treatment exists for sexual sadism. The specialized juvenile justice treatment unit to which he would have been assigned if found delinquent as a homicide perpetrator had no capacity for treating sexual offenses; the unit had no capacity for treatment of sexual sadism, because this motivation for homicide is such a rare event among juveniles. At the very least, the juvenile justice authority would have had to alter their policies and practices and place him in another secure unit with a sexual offender treatment program and expend resources to access specialized consultation and interventions for the sexual sadism.

If he committed the murder, his denial of the charges prior to adjudication may have reflected compliance with advice of counsel, simple prevarication to avoid consequences, or one of several other possibilities. If he committed the murder and the assessment of the offense characteristics were accurate, then no intervention available through that state's juvenile justice system could reliably result in a likelihood of "rehabilitation" for sexual sadism that had already motivated a premeditated sexual homicide by mid-adolescence. A court might reasonably consider this (along with other developmental, functional, and clinical character-istics of the defendant) in making a decision about whether or not to try and sentence the defendant as an adult.

A responsible forensic opinion regarding amenability to rehabilitation would rely heavily on something that did not yet exist: a legal determination of whether or not the juvenile had committed the murder. In the absence of this determination, responsible forensic opinion could only outline the difference that such a determination would make, characterize the unremarkable developmental course of the juvenile prior to his arrest, describe the clinical concerns raised by evidence of sexually sadistic motivation for the homicide, and describe the lack of effective treatments for sexual sadism generally and through the resources of the juvenile justice system.

Contrast this case with another one in which the specifics of the allegations contribute less to an assessment of amenability to rehabilitation. This second case involved charges of armed robbery against a juvenile already committed to the custody of juvenile justice authorities. This juvenile had a history of severe and repeated physical aggression toward persons dating to preschool, multiple arrests for assault and robbery prior to age 14, failure due to assaults in two residential schools, and an escape from a secure juvenile justice facility. During the escape he allegedly used a gun to rob two elderly persons. He had an IQ of 75 and, at age 16, still read at a second-grade level. All of his adult male relatives except his maternal grandfather were serving lengthy prison terms for crimes against persons. His mother had refused to accept custody of him, as his father had been imprisoned when the boy was 8. He had lived with his paternal grandmother until his first residential placement at age 12, but she became terrified of him, and he frequently threatened and hit her. He had a strong affiliation with a violent street gang dating back to age 9. He had repeatedly failed earlier community probations due to lack of compliance and had strongly resisted treatment in all settings.

Obviously, one must assess and consider many more facts before forming an opinion regarding his amenability to rehabilitation. Just as clearly, an evaluator can say more about this case whether or not the juvenile actually committed the alleged offense. His long-standing history of family criminality, violent conduct, gang affiliation, and intervention failures alone distinguish him from the first case. Even if he denied the current offense, an evaluator would have multiple historical factors that—at least at first blush—would argue against his likelihood of rehabilitation. However, as discussed later, an evaluation of this second case would require more information about this youth's history and functioning before offering an opinion regarding amenability to rehabilitation to a court. Other important facts to know include whether prior interventions properly took his cognitive limitations into consideration, what kinds of resources exist for him through his state's juvenile justice system, and the kinds of success that system has with youths with similar histories.

ESTABLISHING THE FORENSIC CONTEXT OF THE EVALUATION: POSTADJUDICATION EVALUATIONS

The most common kind of postadjudication evaluations provide data used by courts to help make decisions after a finding of delinquency. Such evaluations, sometimes called aid in disposition or aid in sentencing evaluations, ideally occur *after* a finding of facts in the delinquency case has occurred. In reality, courts may refer a juvenile for evaluation prior to adjudication with the idea of having a report ready for use for plea negotiations or in the event that a delinquency finding occurs. When conducting an evaluation in anticipation of legal findings not yet rendered, such "aid in disposition" evaluations pose the same clinical and ethical challenges as do the preadjudication evaluations described earlier.

Ideally, courts delay imposing a disposition or accepting plea agreements until a completed evaluation occurs, although in many cases the court will have already made a threshold disposition decision. For example, courts sometimes refer a defendant for an evaluation after having made a decision to place the youth on probation; in those cases, the court has made a determination that the youth will remain in the community, and the evaluation typically asks for recommendations regarding services needed as a condition of probation. In those cases in which the evaluation ultimately yields findings and opinions that the youth cannot safely or ap-

propriately obtain services in the community while on probation, the evaluator has the unenviable role of conveying that information to the court. When reasonable to do so, the evaluator might also recommend conditions of probation, along with suggestions about how to make these less than optimal interventions more effective or how to protect public safety while the interventions have a chance to take effect.

When the court has adjudicated the case and made findings of legal fact, the evaluator may be entitled to rely on those findings as facts for purposes of the evaluation. Clarifying the referral issue will help the clinician focus the evaluation. Courts may have an interest in a variety of different issues, including assessment of which system will most likely prove effective in reducing recidivism risk (e.g., juvenile justice, mental health, child welfare, educational), recommendations or prognostic assessments regarding specific services, intensity of probation supervision, or assessments of previously unidentified concerns or needs identified during the adjudication process (e.g., psychiatric impairment, educational needs, substance abuse, family dysfunction).

Allegations of violations of probation may arise following adjudication and initial disposition. Courts that find juveniles in violation of conditions of probation typically retain authority to commit youths to juvenile justice authorities or make other orders. Courts in these cases may request assessments of reasons for the juvenile's failure to comply with probation conditions, identification of potential targets of intervention that may assist the juvenile to successfully complete probation (e.g., simplifying probation conditions for cognitively limited juveniles, substance abuse or mental health treatment for juveniles whose ability to comply with probation are compromised by impairments associated with those problems), or suggestions about what further conditions of probation may be warranted (e.g., assignment to intensive probation programs with greater supervision).

Postadjudication evaluation may occur in proceedings in which the youth stands trial by a juvenile or adult criminal court but disposition may involve juvenile justice, adult corrections, or "split sentence" options. "Split sentence" options permit commitment of the delinquent to the juvenile justice system to a particular age, followed by a period of actual or suspended adult correctional time. Unlike "transfer" or "waiver" hearings, the facts of the case will have full adjudication *before* the court accepts forensic evaluation reports regarding these disposition options, and the evaluator can then rely on the court's findings of fact. As with "waiver" or "transfer" hearings, the juvenile's "amenability to rehabilitation" commonly constitutes an explicit factor that the court must consider as a requirement of law.

Assessment of amenability to rehabilitation may also occur following commitment to juvenile justice authorities. Most states presumptively commit juvenile offenders to juvenile justice authorities up to a certain age (most commonly 17 to 21 years of age), but they may extend that term of commitment (in some states up to age 24 in certain circumstances). The legal test for extending commitments will vary by state, and evaluators should familiarize themselves with the specific test to be used in each case. Some states require only a showing that the juvenile remains "dangerous," whereas other states have a different threshold.

In such cases, juveniles have already experienced interventions through the juvenile justice system. The evaluator should become intimately familiar with the nature and quality of those specific interventions, with the juvenile's progress or lack of progress and how juvenile justice authorities assessed it, and with existing options for intervention in the event that extension of the juvenile's term of commitment occurs.

STRUCTURE FOR EVALUATION OF AMENABILITY TO REHABILITATION

Thomas Grisso (1998) has offered a useful framework for structuring evaluations of amenability to rehabilitation. His framework involves answering four key assessment questions:

1. What are the youth's important characteristics?
2. What must change?
3. What modes of intervention could accomplish the rehabilitation objective?
4. What is the likelihood of change, given the relevant interventions?

Grisso also rightly observes that the amount of information that may be developed for each of these questions will vary for different kinds of amenability to rehabilitation evaluations.

Evaluators should recognize that an adequate assessment of rehabilitative potential requires multiple sources of information and ordinarily cannot be adequately completed simply by interviewing the juvenile and/or the juvenile's parents or caregivers. The higher the stakes of the evaluation are, the more care one must take to collect sufficient information and the more steps must be taken to independently corroborate key facts.

Sources of information may include (1) interviews with the juvenile and key family members; (2) interviews with probation officers, school officials, therapists, or others who have relevant information; (3) review of relevant police reports, crime scene reports, autopsy reports, victim or witness statements, or other information relevant to understanding the circumstances of the offense; (3) review of relevant educational, social service, medical, child protection, or other records; (4) documentation or visits to intervention programs accessible through probation or the juvenile justice authorities that may potentially be recommended in the case; and (5) informational contacts with defense counsel and prosecuting attorney.

It is *essential* that evaluators consistently attend to the specific links among (1) the youth's characteristics and functioning, (2) the charged offenses and possibly misconduct that has not resulted in formal charges, and (3) the specific modalities and prognoses of interventions that may prove effective and available. Evaluators must recognize that the primary concern of the court is reducing recidivism and not necessarily the treatment of clinical conditions. At each point at which an intervention is assessed or recommended, the evaluator must take pains to establish the link between the intervention and the reduction of risk of reoffense.

For example, an evaluator may establish that a juvenile adjudicated to be a delinquent because of auto theft meets criteria for attention-deficit/hyperactivity disorder (ADHD). Although clearly *clinically* indicated to recommend treatment for ADHD, the *forensic* impact that effective treatment of the

ADHD may have on the juvenile's auto theft remains unclear.

Effective treatment of the ADHD may reduce his risk of stealing cars if the factors triggering the theft relate to factors such as marked impulsivity or difficulty with anticipating or responding to likely consequences of his actions. In this situation, effective treatment of ADHD could result in reduction or elimination of misconduct. On the other hand, effective treatment of ADHD in a socialized delinquent for whom car theft constitutes acceptable behavior might simply render him more focused and more able to avoid making mistakes that might lead to his arrest while continuing to steal cars. Or the untreated ADHD may act as an impediment to other interventions that target the delinquent misconduct, such as interfering with an ability to benefit from counseling that challenges his beliefs that car theft is acceptable. If so, effective treatment of ADHD becomes a necessary precondition so that the other recommended interventions can yield the best outcome.

Similarly, one must consider links between the youth's characteristics and the available intervention resources. For example, concerns regarding community protection may argue for placement in a juvenile justice facility. However, for a juvenile whose cognitive capacities fall significantly above or below the cognitive capacities assumed by programming available within the facility, the likely effectiveness of the programming declines. Juveniles whose psychiatric impairments lie beyond the capacity of the facility to manage most likely will not benefit from programming to which other youths might respond and may even be disciplined for conduct that is best understood as the expression of psychiatric illness rather than defiance or rule breaking.

The point is that effective *clinical* intervention may not always result in effective *forensic* intervention, and clinical evaluators must remain mindful of how interventions actually bear on the behavior that has brought the juvenile before the court. Indeed, in some unusual cases, effective clinical interventions that target specific psychiatric impairments may actually increase the risk of reoffense by making the juvenile more capable of planning and implementing criminal behavior with less chance of being caught.

CONDUCTING EVALUATIONS OF AMENABILITY TO REHABILITATION

The goal of the evaluation involves (1) identifying the kinds of historical (static) factors that have contributed to the evolution of any trajectory of persisting delinquent misconduct, (2) identifying any dynamic (contextual, clinical, attitudinal, environmental, social) factors that contributed to specific incidents of delinquent misconduct that constitute targets of rehabilitative intervention, (3) identifying any protective factors or strengths useful in encouraging rehabilitation, and (4) describing the prospects for successful intervention and recommending those interventions that are necessary to rehabilitation.

Although the amount of information gathered will vary depending on the circumstances, on any factors that the court must specifically consider as a matter of law, and on the kind and stakes of the evaluation, the following kinds of information routinely warrant consideration in assessing amenability to rehabilitation. Most of the relevant research and practice in conducting these assessments has evolved with male adolescents, and they may require adjustments before making use of these evaluation dimensions for cases involving females or preadolescents. For research on delinquency and conduct disorder in girls, see Keenan and Shaw (1997), Research Forum (2000), and Pajer (1998).

Developmental History (Medical, Mental Health, and Intervention History)

Information elicited from the juvenile, parents, or other caregivers and collateral contacts regarding the juvenile can help to create a developmental history. Whenever possible, evaluators should obtain and review medical and mental health records in detail. Collateral contacts with current and former care providers also often prove highly useful. When gathering information from current and former care providers, it is important to focus on gathering data that form the basis of opinions. For example, in conducting an evaluation of a youth who had committed a second sexual offense, I contacted a former therapist and his current sexual offender treatment clinician. The former described the youth as "psychopathic" and "refractory to any treatment" and recommended incarceration. The latter described the same youth as "anything but psychopathic" and "showing significant progress in treatment" despite the relatively minor reoffense. This disparity of clinical opinion illustrates why an evaluator should press for the specific data that form the basis for clinical and prognostic opinions in order to make an independent judgment.

Particular attention should focus on the developmental evolution of disruptive or antisocial behaviors. This includes consideration of temperament, early developmental experiences and evolution of attachment capacities, the familial and social environment in which the problem behavior emerges, and the ways in which misconduct becomes reinforced for the juvenile. The goal is to offer a clinical developmental narrative that describes the emergence and/or persistence of misconduct.

One of the best predictors of persisting antisocial behaviors in male adolescents is early childhood onset of these behaviors. Characteristics of delinquents at higher risk for a diversity of antisocial conduct and violence compared to persons who have lower remission rates of problem behaviors include: preschool onset of behavior problems; evolution of both overt (e.g., fighting) and covert (e.g., lying, stealing) conduct problems; greater impairment by problems with impulsivity and hyperactivity; lower academic achievement; greater affiliation with delinquent peers and limited prosocial skills; and greater innovation and diversity of misconduct. Research (Loeber et al., 1993) demonstrates that preadolescent youths known to the juvenile courts are responsible for a disproportionate share of serious and violent delinquent careers and have a higher likelihood of becoming chronic offenders.

Developmental characteristics of delinquents with lower risk of violence to persons but still at risk for drug offenses and crimes against property include: onset of conduct disturbance from late childhood to early adolescence; primarily non-aggressive misconduct; capacities for social skills and satisfying interpersonal attachments; limited innovation and diversity of misconduct; and misconduct that typically occurs with peers rather than alone. Youths with this developmental pathway typically demonstrate significant remission of misconduct spontaneously or with standard inter-

ventions that target delinquency. This pattern is reflected in the jump in delinquent conduct as youths enter middle school, the higher prevalence of crimes against property than against persons, and the spontaneous remission of delinquency of all kinds in mid-adolescence to early young adulthood.

Cote, Zoccolillo, Tremblay, Nagin, and Vitaro (2001) have described a similar form of early-onset developmental trajectory toward conduct disorder for girls, although girls as a group have less likelihood than boys of manifesting conduct disorder in adolescence. Serious delinquency among female adolescents has increased even as it has decreased among male adolescents, creating difficulties for juvenile justice systems designed primarily to serve adolescent male offenders and often lacking the resources to address the needs of female offenders.

Medical events (e.g., head injury, anoxia or low weight at birth, intrauterine alcohol or drug exposure), developmental conditions (e.g., pervasive developmental disorders, mental retardation) or medical conditions (e.g., brain injury, genetic syndromes, epilepsy, diabetes) should be described in relevant detail if they have clinical significance for understanding the emergence or persistence of misconduct, ongoing treatment needs, or prognosis for intervention. This specifically includes characterization of the juvenile's cognitive capacities, the functional impact of any cognitive difficulties, any implications of cognitive difficulties for the emergence or persistence of misconduct, and any implications of such difficulties for intervention. Because previously undetected cognitive limitations or specific verbal or nonverbal learning disabilities commonly occur in juvenile delinquents, evaluators should remain sensitive to evidence that possibly suggests below-average cognitive abilities or learning disabilities.

Mental health diagnoses and interventions, including medications, should also be documented. Evaluators should check to determine that any past *Diagnostic and Statistical Manual of Mental Disorders* (DSM; American Psychiatric Association, 1994) diagnosis of conduct disorder is actually warranted based on rigorous application of the diagnostic criteria; clinicians do not always exercise meticulous care in awarding this diagnosis, and juveniles who do not warrant the diagnosis typically have a better prognosis than those who meet full DSM criteria for conduct disorder.

Evaluators should also remain alert to the fact that the DSM diagnosis of conduct disorder constitutes primarily a list of serious behaviors, many of which could lead to a felony charge for delinquent misconduct, and which often reflects serious and versatile misconduct. Because the diagnosis itself constitutes only a behavioral description, evaluators must look beyond the diagnosis for etiology, social context of misconduct, and significantly important and treatable comorbid conditions. Indeed, judges feel predictably frustrated and unimpressed when a delinquent youth sent for an evaluation acquires only a diagnosis of conduct disorder and little more information that proves useful for the court.

The impressive prevalence of traumatic experiences among delinquents (see Spaccarelli, Coatsworth, & Bowden, 1995; Massa & Reynolds, 1999; Song, Singer, & Anglin, 1998; Cauffman, Feldman, Waterman, & Steiner, 1998) requires that clinicians take a history of trauma and its developmental and functional consequences as a standard part of the evaluation. Also, conduct disorders, mood disorders, anxiety disorders, substance abuse disorders, impulse control disorders, cognitive limitations and learning difficulties warrant specific assessment. This point has particular importance given research that indicates that the prognosis for treatment of conduct disorders becomes more guarded in the presence of these comorbid conditions. Such conditions may complicate rehabilitation interventions and require specific interventions prior to, or along with, other interventions.

As indicated previously, it is essential that the evaluator specifically characterize what, if any, effect developmental, cognitive, diagnostic, or other factors have on (1) the emergence and/or persistence of the juvenile's delinquent conduct and (2) facilitating or complicating any rehabilitative interventions that might be attempted. An adequate characterization of these can help the courts immensely, as well as future service providers who will have responsibility for any rehabilitative interventions.

Key factors for assessment in this dimension include (currently or by history):

- Preschool onset of persisting aggression
- Pattern, if any, of previous rule breaking, overt/covert misconduct

- Attention-deficit/hyperactivity disorder plus persisting aggression
- Childhood onset of DSM diagnosis of conduct disorder
- Impulsivity, impaired mood, or anger modulation
- Substance abuse (and contribution to any delinquent acts)
- Cognitive impairments or impairing learning disabilities
- Intense sense of alienation
- Current mood symptoms (e.g., lack of motivation, irritability)
- Current psychotic symptoms that impair judgment or reality testing
- Trauma-related symptoms and links to misconduct or interventions

Family History and Functioning

An assessment of family history should address historical factors, including: child maltreatment of the juvenile, including neglect; exposure of the child to domestic violence; parental substance abuse, criminality, or mental illness; disruptions of attachment that may include parental loss from death, incarceration, divorce, separation, or substitute care placements; juvenile's intimidation or aggression against siblings or other family members; and parental support for interventions. A history of family events and family-related stresses may reveal whether or not the delinquent misconduct links to family functioning, intrafamilial victimization by the juvenile or others, or the willingness or ability of the family to support community-based rehabilitation interventions.

Some juveniles show markedly different functioning depending on the adults with whom they reside. For example, a juvenile characterized as aggressive and "out of control" at home and at school while residing with a parent may present entirely differently during a period in which he is residing with a grandparent or in foster care. Evaluators should document and assess these kinds of variations for what appears to make the difference in the juvenile's conduct and functioning.

Evaluators should assess family functioning for current capacities to address the misconduct of the juvenile, especially if community disposition options will include probation. Perhaps the single most important question involves the demonstrated ability of the parents or other caregivers to consistently provide effective supervision of the juvenile in the community. Other important factors include: demonstrated capacity of the parents or caregiver to support interventions and/or become involved in the interventions themselves, demonstrated capacity of the parents to impose appropriate and effective limits on the juvenile, and current resources or sources of strength available to the family.

Key variables for assessment of this dimension include (currently and by history):

- Adequacy of parental or other adult supervision
- Adequacy of parental involvement in educational and other activities
- History of family stresses, transitions, or conflicts
- Childhood abuse, especially neglect or exposure to domestic violence
- Poor child management practices
- Any history of victimizing siblings or other family members
- Parental criminality or substance dependence

Social and Peer Functioning

Evaluators should develop a history of the juvenile's functioning outside of the family, particularly with other adults in the community (e.g., coaches, ministers, employers) and with peers. Evaluators should investigate the ability of the juvenile to make and maintain satisfying and mutually respectful relationships with adults in the community. Similarly, one should address the ability of the juvenile to make and maintain satisfying and mutually respectful relationships with peers. Focusing particular attention on the developmental role of "best friends," the selection of these friends, any diversity among groups of friends (e.g. some delinquent friends, some nondelinquent friends), and methods of negotiating conflicts among these friends will help clarify peer functioning. Exploring the tensions that might arise between these friendships and the expectations of family, school, or others has considerable value. Paying attention to the evolution of early teen affiliations, especially if the juvenile has affiliated with deviant youth groups or gangs that may have contributed to the evolu-

tion of delinquent misconduct, will also prove valuable.

Most serious delinquent offenses, particularly crimes against persons, occur in the context of other delinquent activity (e.g., drug use or trafficking) and involve other peers. These situations also often involve escalation of conflict between groups of juveniles. Assessment of the social context in which delinquent conduct occurs often becomes critical to understanding the dynamics, motives, and characteristics of delinquent offenses.

Gang membership poses special challenges for assessment. Groups of youths that adults sometimes refer to as "gangs" range from highly organized and violent criminal groups to unstable groupings of marginally functioning and alienated youths primarily engaged in substance use and/or property crimes. Gang membership may reflect anything from an embrace of an explicitly criminal lifestyle to a simple effort to avoid victimization by unenthusiastic affiliation with a local group of delinquents. Individual gang members range from hardened violent delinquents to immature, inexperienced youths who playact at being tough as a way of creating peer affiliations. Evaluators who assess juveniles involved with gangs should acquaint themselves with literature regarding gangs and gang rehabilitation and investigate the motivation for, and the degree of, gang involvement of the juvenile being evaluated. References to "gangs" in forensic reports should include concrete descriptions of the structure and organization of the gang, the type of affiliation displayed by the juvenile being evaluated, and the function that gang affiliation serves for the juvenile.

Evaluators must take into account the role that affiliation with delinquent peers may play in rehabilitation efforts. For example, although there are benefits to interventions implemented in residential or juvenile justice settings, there are also potential risks. Juveniles served in institutional settings will encounter a range of antisocial orientation among the youths within these settings, and evaluators should consider the risks of a juvenile affiliating with delinquent or criminal peer groups while institutionalized. On the other hand, a juvenile who has an extensive network of delinquent or criminal peers in the community may not have the ability to jettison the influence of those relationships while remaining in the community.

Key factors in assessing for this dimension include (currently and by history):

- Affiliation with delinquent peers
- Involvement in delinquent acts alone and with peers
- Affiliation with nondelinquent peers and prosocial activities
- Attitudes regarding adults and authority figures
- History of frequent conflicts with peers, especially if violent
- Presence of supportive, prosocial adults and activities
- Peer attitudes that justify illegal acts or violent acts

Cognitive and Educational Functioning

Evaluation must include information regarding the juvenile's general cognitive functioning and specific abilities, educational needs and achievement, and potential vocational and other strengths. Most juveniles in juvenile justice facilities function in the low-average to borderline range of cognitive capacities and have significant educational needs. However, some delinquent youths will present with mental retardation, major learning disabilities or other neurocognitive impairments, significant psychiatric impairment, or higher intellectual capacities and educational attainment. In many of these circumstances, the juvenile might not fit well with the available programming, and the capacity of the facility to provide adequate services will require assessment.

Routinely gathering educational and guidance records from school authorities will also prove helpful. These records should include any special educational assessments, disciplinary records, and descriptions of the youth's strengths, as well as weaknesses. Elementary and preschool records often yield information regarding cognitive functioning and academic potential that predate the onset of conduct problems, lower motivation to perform well in school, substance abuse or other factors that may obscure cognitive capacity, or educational potential at the time of evaluation.

When current information about cognitive functioning and academic functioning is not available, best practice is to secure cognitive and academic testing to supplement the forensic evaluation and provide independent corroboration of functioning in these domains.

Factors to assess within this dimension include (currently or by history):

- History of early elementary school maladjustment
- History of school suspensions and expulsions
- History and basis for special educational placement
- Effectiveness of remediation of learning disabilities
- History of school functioning, achievement, and truancy
- Current placement in school characterized by high delinquency
- Attitudes towards school, school achievement, vocational success

Delinquent Misconduct and Legal History

Evaluation must include assessment of the juvenile's history of delinquent misconduct and legal history. Sources of information obviously include arrest and court records, probation and juvenile justice records, and other records that will offer an "official" history, but they should also include parents or other caregivers, school officials and other persons who knew the youth in the community, medical and mental health service providers, any institutional care providers, and the juvenile him- or herself. These sources often provide information regarding delinquent misconduct not otherwise available in the "official" record of arrests and dispositions.

Familiarity with police and other investigation reports permit the evaluator to see whether the juvenile's accounts fit consistently with physical evidence or other information regarding the characteristics of the offense. Assuming that it is appropriate to directly interview the juvenile about the details of an offense, best practice requires that the evaluator have familiarity in detail with information regarding the alleged offense prior to interviewing the juvenile. If the juvenile offers accounts inconsistent with physical evidence or other accounts of the offense, the evaluator should take a detailed version from the juvenile's account before attempting to confront the juvenile with the inconsistencies.

Although one cannot take the accounts of juveniles at face value, gathering this information from them and others offers opportunities for corroborating these explanations, as well as assessing the juveniles' cognitive and emotional manner of accounting for their misconduct and coping with perceived threats or stresses. Evaluators may discover alternative explanations for what motivated misconduct or more fully appreciate the specific cognitive distortions relied on by a juvenile to justify his or her conduct.

Sometimes challenging situations arise in which a plea bargain results in dismissing key elements of a crime or the evaluator suspects that a court may have been in error when making a finding of fact. For example, I was once asked to conduct an evaluation of a case that had originally been charged as an aggravated rape with use of a weapon; because of the vulnerability of the victim, the prosecutor plea-bargained the case to a simple assault. The court wanted me to assess the defendant's amenability to rehabilitation without discussing or taking into consideration the sexual nature of the assault, the use of a gun to pistol whip and threaten the victim, and other important features of the incident. I had to decline, explaining to the court that if the plea bargain represented a legal fiction due to difficulties in prosecuting the case, then an evaluation that could not consider the actual motive for and nature of the assault was likely to be unhelpful, potentially dangerously misleading to the court, and likely outside of the boundaries of permissible professional and ethical practice.

Evaluators should focus on the concrete characteristics of the concerning behavior when considering past histories of misconduct. For example, some juveniles will have experienced discipline during elementary school or will have been referred to outpatient mental health services for exactly the same behavior (e.g., assaulting a person, stealing) that resulted in delinquency arrests in early adolescence. The younger the child, the less likely it is that a delinquency charge will exist on file for precisely the same conduct that would later result in arrest. Evaluators may have to try to inquire of parents or professional service providers what actually occurred when records do not detail the misconduct or refer only vaguely to some sort of "acting out" that warrants concern.

The evaluator's focus should place the juvenile's misconduct in a developmental and social context, including situational and dynamic risk variables and the juvenile's own perception of what motivated his or her misconduct. Evaluators should remain alert to information that may prove valuable in understanding the youth's misconduct but that may not be included in "official" records. For example, some youths charged with weapons possession may have carried the weapon out of a realistic need for self-defense against delinquent youths. Some youths who have faced suspension for fighting in school live in youth cultures in which failure to respond with fighting to particular taunts or challenges simply sets them up for further victimization. Schools may not always document instances in which disruptive conduct by a student occurred in response to genuinely belittling remarks or persisting harassment by a teacher or a peer. Police reports may not reflect the context in which misconduct occurred. Therefore, it very often proves helpful, when particular incidents seem to hold great weight in a case with high stakes, to interview collaterals who may have had firsthand knowledge of the incident or who may have information regarding the social context in which the incident occurred.

Discussion of past misconduct may provide an opportunity for the juvenile to express remorse for misconduct. Courts may take into consideration a juvenile's expression of remorse, and clinicians have traditionally held that remorse suggests a better potential for rehabilitation. However, no empirical research establishes a link between expressions of remorse during a juvenile forensic evaluation and improved potential for rehabilitation; neither does the ability of clinicians to detect the presence or absence of felt remorse or to reliably distinguish between sincere or insincere expressions of remorse. Indeed, some youths will manifest emotional numbing due to the stresses associated with their offenses or their prosecution, and this numbing may be confused with a lack of victim empathy or of remorse (Kinscherff & Toby, 1996). Others will express remorse simply in an effort to avoid consequences. Evaluators may note evidence for the presence or absence of remorse and its motivation, endurance, and sincerity, but they must exercise caution against relying on such evidence as a significant factor in assessing amenability to rehabilitation.

Factors for assessment along this dimension include (currently or by history):

- First arrest occurs prior to age 13
- First crime-against-person arrest occurs prior to age 15
- History of prior probation or other juvenile justice intervention
- Effectiveness of prior interventions in reducing delinquent misconduct
- History of carrying firearm, currently ready access to firearm
- History of any serious misconduct not resulting in formal arrest
- Presence of attitudes, values, or beliefs that justify delinquent conduct
- Specific links between delinquent misconduct and other dimensions

Characterization of Personality Development and Functioning

Assessment of adolescent personality development constitutes an essential and challenging aspect of evaluation, at least in part because personality formation remains malleable during the adolescent years. Emerging personality functioning may have important implications for understanding the circumstances under which misconduct will most likely occur, the vulnerability of the youth to stress, and the nature of his or her interpersonal interactions.

Personality functioning may also have important implications for intervention strategies. One aspect of personality functioning does have vulnerability to acute or cumulative stresses. For example, youths with disturbances of attachment and vulnerabilities to stress that reflect emerging "borderline" personality functioning or posttraumatic features may respond better to interventions that focus on their instability of mood, reactivity under stress, and attachment difficulties. Targeting interventions in this way will be helpful, particularly if their misconduct occurs during periods of acute stress and reactivity.

Youths whose misconduct relates to heightened stresses and emotional reactivity, is limited to those periods of acute reactivity, and is not justified by pervasively antisocial attitudes may show greater amenability to interventions that target anxiety or irritability (e.g., medication) and that rely on interpersonal relationships (e.g., counseling, relationship with a probation officer or facility staff). Youths with pervasive impairments in empathy and attachment, malignant narcissism, and predatory misconduct that reflect emerging psychopathic features will require substantial external monitoring, more pervasive imposed and potentially coercive structure, and a more intensive therapeutically confrontational approach.

Psychological testing may also prove helpful in characterizing the personality functioning of juveniles. Objective and empirically based tests, such as the Minnesota Multiphasic Personality Inventory—Adolescent (MMPI-A), have better forensic standing than projective tests without norms or systematic methods of interpretation. Assessment of emerging psychopathy in adolescence can now be facilitated by instruments designed for this purpose (e.g., the Psychopathy Checklist—Youth Version, developed by Forth, Kossen, and Hare, 1996) and is of particular interest because psychopathy in adulthood has proven a robust factor associated with criminal recidivism in adult males with or without mental illness. Although research in juvenile psychopathy is still developing, the factors associated with psychopathy in adulthood may overlap significantly with factors believed to work against rehabilitation as a juvenile, such as persisting antisocial attitudes and conduct, emergence of malevolent narcissism, interpersonal difficulties, and failures of juvenile justice and other interventions.

Factors typically assessed for this dimension include (currently or by history):

- Evidence of emerging psychopathy
- Antisocial, narcissistic, paranoid, or borderline personality features
- Immaturity resulting in dependence on delinquent peers or others
- Evidence of sensitivity and reactivity to situational stress
- Evidence of dissociation, emotional numbing, or other trauma features
- Any mood/anxiety symptoms and any interaction in misconduct
- Trait anger

Responses to Past Interventions

Specific attention should also be paid to the details of past attempted interventions that targeted misconduct and antisocial attitudes. These can include psychotherapeutic, educational, medication, environmental, juvenile justice, or other kinds of interventions. The clinician should gather enough history to assess (1) whether or not each intervention was successful in reducing the concerning behavior or attitudes, (2) why each seemed to be successful or unsuccessful over time, and (3) whether similar interventions seem likely to prove effective now and why this likely occurred if they have not been effective in the past.

Evaluators must exercise caution because some juveniles have experienced interventions that one would not necessarily reasonably expect to prove particularly effective with misconduct. For example, little evidence exists to suggest that play therapy or generic weekly counseling will prove particularly effective for youths who have histories of aggression and defiance dating to preschool years. If a juvenile has participated in a predictably ineffective intervention, one may want to consider the juvenile as having had essentially "no treatment" rather than having "failed" the intervention.

Additionally, evaluators should determine whether a juvenile has actually complied with recommended interventions. For example, has the youth taken prescribed medication or actually attended psychotherapy sessions or probation meetings? If compliance has presented problems, determining the factors contributing to the lack of compliance becomes important. For example, not appearing for probation meetings or counseling sessions may reflect indifference to perceived consequences, defiance of imposed expectations, difficulties with organizing and adhering to a schedule, transportation problems, immobilization by severe depression, or a host of other factors. Identifying factors that contribute to compliance problems allows better assessment of the likelihood of future compliance or of problems that are in need of solution to improve the likelihood of compliance.

Assessing the quality of the services provided to the juvenile and the "match" of the juvenile and the specific service will also have considerable value. For example, involvement in psychotherapy may have suffered due to high therapist turnover or use of an ineffective modality. Enrollment in special education services may have lacked effectiveness if the special education system was overwhelmed and underfunded. Problems of "match" between the juvenile and a specific service that otherwise seems perfectly adequate can take many forms. For example, youths with cognitive limitations or language-based learning disabilities may not benefit from a treatment group, counseling, or other interventions that rely heavily on verbal communications.

Gathering data of this sort can assist in determining whether the youth has "failed" to respond to appropriate and adequate services or whether the apparent lack of response may have as much or more to do with the quality or appropriateness of the interventions themselves. When weighing potential targets of intervention, an important consideration involves the kinds of interventions most likely to result in rehabilitation and factors that may compromise those interventions.

Factors typically assessed within this dimension include (currently or by history):

- Past interventions and their relationship to misconduct
- Compliance with interventions and reasons for compliance failures
- Complications to intervention (e.g., low IQ, impairing symptoms)
- Assessment of why past interventions succeeded or failed
- Responses to usual deterrents to misconduct (e.g., arrest, witnesses)
- Past attitudes toward any successful or failed interventions
- Current attitudes toward most likely interventions

Risks of Harm to Self or Others

Juveniles with significant disturbances of conduct have elevated risk for self-harming or suicidal behavior, particularly if they also suffer from depression and/or substance abuse. Evaluators should take a history of self-harming or suicidal thoughts and behavior, as well as high-risk conduct that places the juvenile at risk of harm. In the event that a concerning history of past self-harming conduct exists, evaluators should take into account the stressful nature of involvement in juvenile justice proceedings and take appropriate steps. Evaluators should also consider whether the delinquent behavior that puts the juvenile at physical risk represents parasuicidal conduct. For example, suicidal adolescents may engage in conduct intended to provoke a potentially lethal response from police or the targets of their misconduct (e.g., local drug dealers).

Evaluators should obtain a history of conduct that creates risks of harm to others, even if the offense that triggers evaluation amounts to a nonviolent property offense. Particular attention should focus on information relevant to (1) degree of predation or planning for violent and nonviolent misconduct, (2) potential risks to others (e.g., threatened or actual use of a weapon, firesetting), (3) most serious harm actually inflicted on another person, (4) method by which victim selection occurred and assessment of the vulnerability of potential victims, and (5) motivation for the misconduct and the intent of threatened or actual violent conduct.

Other chapters in this volume address violence risk assessment and management. Violence risk assessments, juvenile sexual offender evaluations, juvenile firesetter evaluations, or evaluations involving homicides of parents require highly specialized skills for which general clinical training and experience affords inadequate preparation.

Many high-stakes cases involve serious crimes of violence against persons. In these cases, specific assessment of violence risk is essential. For purposes of assessing amenability to rehabilitation, it is important to identify (1) the most important static and dynamic risk factors that have contributed to past episodes of violence, (2) what interventions seem optimally targeted to the most important dynamic risk factors, (3) what interventions might ideally focus on the most important strengths or protective factors with which the juvenile presents, and (4) the prognosis for those interventions and the time frame and intensity required to substantially reduce violence risk.

Containment Required During Attempts at Rehabilitation

Risks of harm to self or others drive the need to evaluate the level and kind of containment re-

quired during attempts at rehabilitation. The concept of containment includes, but is not limited to, consideration of the "opportunities" for further misconduct while rehabilitation interventions are implemented. One can limit "opportunity" for misconduct by options that range from increased supervision by family and/or probation in the community to a locked juvenile justice setting.

Assessment of containment involves the following kinds of dimensions: (1) the severity and frequency of the juvenile's conduct that harms others (public safety) and the risk that the juvenile will reoffend during attempted interventions, (2) the severity and frequency of the juvenile's self-harming conduct (protection of the juvenile) and its risk of recurrence, (3) the level of structure or coercion required to enforce compliance with rehabilitation, (4) the intensity of rehabilitative interventions required for addressing specific factors linked to the prospects for rehabilitation, and (5) the number of interventions put in place simultaneously and the likelihood that successful coordination will occur at various levels of community or institutional structure.

Assessment of these dimensions in recommending a level of containment must occur against the background of (1) high rates of self-desistence of delinquent conduct as adolescents grow older, (2) the risk of institutionalization and inadequate preparation for adulthood if placed out of the community for prolonged periods of time, (3) the generally better outcomes for delinquents who remain in the community than for those institutionalized and thereby removed from the community for treatment, and (4) the risk that institutional placement prevents developmentally normalizing experiences and creates a primary peer group of similarly delinquent youths.

Availability and Quality of Interventions

In some cases, evaluation may result in the opinion that the juvenile lacks amenability to rehabilitation, no matter what interventions become available through the juvenile justice system, whether in the community or an institutional setting. Obviously, in such a case the evaluator must carefully articulate the reasoning for this assessment, any limitations on that opinion, and appropriate comment about the limitations of the ability of mental health professionals to offer long-term prognostications of any kind.

In other cases, the evaluator may conclude that the juvenile lacks amenability to rehabilitation as a juvenile with the services actually available through the juvenile justice system in that state. However, lack of the appropriate rehabilitative services in a particular jurisdiction does *not* constitute a basis for concluding that the juvenile cannot be rehabilitated. Rather, one should advise the court that the juvenile *is amenable to rehabilitation if the proper services were accessed*; if possible, the evaluator should describe where the recommended rehabilitation services exist and how they might be accessed.

In such cases, one should also advise the court of information that bears on outcomes in the event that the youth is handled as an adult. For example, Redding (1999) found that punitively handling youths as adults may not result in outcomes favored by proponents of this approach. Youths handled as adults rather than as juveniles are often given less correctional time than they would be if handled as juveniles and find themselves in adult facilities without adequate educational and other rehabilitative programming; furthermore, juveniles charged with crimes against persons and transferred to adult courts have higher recidivism rates than those handled in juvenile justice systems. The evaluator might remind the court of the risks both the juvenile and to the public safety of placing a juvenile in adult correctional systems characterized by high levels of physical and sexual brutality and of gang activity and recruitment and high rates of recidivism.

In other cases, evaluators may offer an opinion that the juvenile seems amenable to rehabilitation and may recommend readily accessible interventions intended to accomplish that goal. Evaluators should characterize the relative risks and benefits of the recommended interventions if those may be relevant to the court's decision. Evaluators should also offer their best assessment of the likelihood that each intervention will succeed and how long it would reasonably take to determine whether the interventions demonstrate effectiveness.

In making recommendations, the evaluator must also answer the following questions and determine whether the answers make a pragmatic difference in the assessment of potential for rehabilitation:

1. Are the recommended interventions available anywhere?
2. If so, are the recommended interventions available through the juvenile justice system? If not, are there any scenarios under which these services could be accessed for this juvenile (e.g., out-of-state placement in a highly specialized program)?
3. What is the quality of the available services? If they are of inadequate quality, are there realistic alternative services that could meet the same need?
4. Can the available services adequately address conditions or circumstances that may complicate efforts at rehabilitation (e.g., psychiatric impairment, cognitive limitations, family hostility)?

Obviously, answering these critical questions requires that the evaluator have reasonable, and in some cases very detailed, information about services and service providers or sites. However, answering these questions to the greatest extent possible becomes essential because, although some juveniles may show likelihood of amenability to rehabilitation theoretically, the lack of available services of adequate quality substantially lowers the likelihood of successful rehabilitation pragmatically. This unfortunate circumstance has relevance for the court's determination in cases in which it arises, and evaluators should clearly describe the difficulty to the court, along with any options worthy of reasonable consideration.

Reporting the Results of Evaluations of Amenability to Rehabilitation

The written report of the evaluation to the court should include a listing of all sources of information relied on in the report and sufficient information for the court to assess the adequacy of the foundation for any clinical and forensic opinions. It may prove useful to report clinical and forensic opinions in separate sections in order to distinguish between these opinions for the court.

Perhaps the four most important features of a well-written evaluation report are: (1) reporting information in a way that consistently distinguishes among data, inferences drawn from those data, and clinical or forensic opinions offered with those data or inferences as their foundation; (2) remaining solidly within both the database of the evaluation and the very real limits on clinical prognostication in these kinds of cases; (3) meticulously describing risk and mediating/dynamic variables and linking any recommended interventions to those variables; and (4) remaining focused on the broader forensic issue of rehabilitation rather than solely on the clinical issue of mental health intervention.

Where relevant, the evaluator should offer a prognosis regarding specific interventions and a time frame characterizing how long it should take for the intervention to show effectiveness. Similarly, the evaluator in some cases may need to articulate a hierarchy of interventions; for example, a juvenile severely impaired by substance abuse or psychiatric symptoms may need effective treatment as a preliminary step before other interventions can prove effective. In cases in which preferred recommended interventions are not available or are of insufficient quality, the evaluator should still describe the preferred interventions and the likelihood of success of any interventions recommended as alternatives.

References

American Psychiatric Association. (1994). *Diagnostic and statistical manual of mental disorders* (4th ed.). Washington, DC: Author.

Barnum, R. (1990). Self-incrimination and denial in the juvenile transfer evaluation. *Bulletin of the American Academy of Psychiatry and Law, 18*, 413–428.

Cauffman, E., Feldman, S., Waterman, J., & Steiner, H. (1998). Posttraumatic stress disorder among female juvenile offenders. *Journal of the American Academy of Child and Adolescent Psychiatry, 37*, 1209–1216.

Cote, S., Zoccolillo, M., Tremblay, R. E., Nagin, D., & Vitaro, F. (2001). Predicting girls' conduct disorder in adolescence from childhood trajectories of disruptive behaviors. *Journal of the American Academy of Child and Adolescent Psychiatry, 40*, 678–684.

Forth, A., Kossen, D., & Hare, R. (1996). *Psychopathy Checklist—Youth Version*. Toronto, Ontario, Canada: Multi-Health Systems.

Grisso, T. J. (1998). *Forensic evaluations of juveniles*. Sarasota, FL: Professional Resource Press.

Keenan, K., & Shaw, D. (1997). Conduct disorder in girls: A review of the literature. *Clinical Child and Family Psychology Review, 2*, 3–19.

Kinscherff, R., & Toby, A. (1996, Spring). Forensic assessment in juvenile transfer proceedings: Effects of traumatic stress and chronic violence. *Expert Opinion (Law and Psychiatry Program, University of Massachusetts Medical School), 4*, 3–6.

Lewis, D., Pincus, J., Richardson, E., Prichep, L., Feldman, M., & Yaeger, C. (1988). Neuropsychiatric, psychoeducational and family circumstances of 14 juveniles condemned to death in the United States. *American Journal of Psychiatry, 145*, 584–589.

Loeber, R., Wung, P., Keenan, K., Giroux, B., Stouthamer-Loeber, M., Van Kammen, W. B., et al. (1993). Developmental pathways in disruptive child behavior. *Developmental Psychopathology, 4*, 103–133.

Massa, J., & Reynolds, W. (1999). Exposure to violence in young inner-city adolescents: Relationships with suicidal ideation, depression and PTSD symptomatology. *Journal of Abnormal Child Psychology, 27*, 203–213.

Pajer, K. (1998). What happens to "bad" girls? A review of the outcomes of antisocial adolescent girls. *American Journal of Psychiatry, 155*, 862–870.

Redding, R. E. (1999, Winter). Juvenile offenders in criminal court and adult prison: Legal, psychological and behavioral outcomes. *Juvenile and Family Court Journal, 50*, 1–20.

Research Forum (2000). *Research on women and girls in the justice system: Plenary papers of the 1999 conference on criminal justice research and evaluation–enhancing policy and practice through research* (Vol. 3). Washington, DC: U.S. Department of Justice, Office of Justice Programs, National Institute of Justice.

Snyder, H., & Sickmund, E. (1999). *Juvenile offender and victims: 1999 National Report*. Pittsburgh, PA: National Center for Juvenile Justice.

Song, L., Singer, M., & Anglin, T. (1998). Violence exposure and emotional trauma as contributors to adolescents' violent behaviors. *Archives of Pediatric and Adolescent Medicine, 152*, 521–536.

Spaccarelli, C., Coatsworth, J., & Bowden, B. (1995). Exposure to family violence among incarcerated boys: Its association with violent offending and potential mediating variables. *Violence and Victims, 10*, 163–182.

20

Forensic Assessment of Parenting in Child Abuse and Neglect Cases

Catherine Ayoub
Robert Kinscherff

Forensic mental health assessment of parenting in cases of known or alleged child abuse or neglect focuses on producing forensically defensible evidence for legal proceedings. Forensic assessments typically also yield information or recommendations relevant to child protection case management or clinical intervention. However, the primary purpose is to give judges and other legal decision makers information and opinions of sufficient scientific validity to rely on in making legal decisions regarding the protective and parenting needs of children before the courts. This chapter summarizes the law that shapes forensic assessment in cases involving child maltreatment and describes an evaluation process that is both clinically sound and forensically defensible in light of evolving rules of evidence regarding expert testimony.

Forensic evaluations are focused on the legal issues before the court and are intended to assist the court in resolving those issues. Although it is ordinarily critical to fully understand and articulate the clinical dimensions of a case, the clinical dimension alone will not usually prove sufficient to resolve legal issues. For example, a clinical assessment does not normally address legal issues

such as "the best interests of the child" or "parental fitness" currently or over the long term. A clinical determination that an episode of child maltreatment has occurred does not directly address the issue of how to balance the child's protective and developmental needs against parental rights.

STRUCTURING THE FORENSIC EVALUATION

The forensic evaluator must resolve the following questions before initiating activity in the case:

What is the legal posture of the case? Does this case already fall under a court's jurisdiction or has the request for forensic evaluation arrived prior to formal filing of a legal case? In either situation, one must carefully attend to issues of informed consent, confidentiality and privilege, and the reliability and adequacy of the clinical foundation for any forensic opinions and recommendations offered.

What kind of legal case is it? Courts may serve two functions in resolving disputes that pertain to child maltreatment. Courts may adjudicate *child protection* cases in which the state seeks to intervene in a family's life to protect the child from alleged abuse or neglect. Courts might also provide *private dispute settlement*, such as adjudicating custody disputes in which two parents struggle over what constitutes the best interests of their child as the divorce restructures the legal relationship between the parents (Mnookin, 1975).

Who is the legal client in the case? If the forensic evaluation originated with a court order, the court is the client, and any work by the evaluator becomes a work product belonging to the court. Unless local law or local practice clearly indicates the contrary, the report resulting from the forensic evaluation should go only to the court; copies should not go to attorneys or others without express authorization by the court.

If the forensic evaluation originated at the request of an attorney who represents a parent or a state agency, then the evaluation becomes the work product of the attorney and governed by attorney–client privilege. Clarification of one's potential role should take place prior to initiating the evaluation. For example, licensed mental health professionals should clarify whether they believe that their mandated duty to report child abuse overcomes attorney–client privilege that ordinarily does not require reporting past incidents of child maltreatment to child protection authorities.

Although some parents may seek to retain forensic evaluations directly, particularly in divorce custody cases, clinicians should generally not agree to do so because of concerns about forensic reliability and professional liability. In cases already before a court, best practice would involve securing a court order authorizing the forensic evaluation that indicates the legal issue requiring resolution, describes the scope of the evaluator's role, and identifies the authority of the evaluator to access information (e.g., collateral contacts, child protection records, medical and educational records, etc.).

What is the legal issue? The forensic evaluator must clearly understand the legal context of the specific case. For example, if the allegations of child maltreatment arise in the context of a divorce custody dispute, the key legal standard focuses on the "best interests" of the child as the postdivorce relationships of the family are structured. The concept of "best interests" governs the court's decisions regarding legal or physical custody, visitation, or removal of the child by a parent to another jurisdiction. In child protection proceedings, the "best interests" of the child must be balanced against parental rights and whether a parent is considered "unfit." Additionally, the evaluator should be aware of legally imposed timelines that may limit recommendations regarding possible courses of clinical intervention or that may transform the case from one focused on reunification to focus on termination of parental rights. In short, forensic evaluators must be familiar with relevant law.

What is the kind of forensic question most relevant to the legal issues at stake? Barnum (2001) observes that four separate kinds of evaluation questions may arise in child maltreatment cases. Evaluators must carefully consider which one or more of the following questions are implicitly or explicitly at the core of the referral for forensic evaluation:

1. *What happened?* This question prompts *investigation* of allegations of child maltreatment in cases in which what has happened to the child is unresolved or in dispute. The goal involves a determination of whether or how child maltreatment occurred and may involve highly specialized assessments, such as sexual abuse evaluations of preschool children. Information relevant to the alleged *facts* of the maltreatment becomes central (i.e., medical reports, child protection investigations, police reports, witness statements, and interviews with the child and parents).

2. *What harm occurred?* This question prompts inquiry into whether the conduct of the perpetrator *caused or allowed* harm to the child. This includes a description of the functioning of the child before and after the onset of maltreatment. Forensic assessment must go beyond clinical assessment to specifically link the maltreatment to specific clinical and functional problems suffered by the child as a result of the maltreatment.

Evaluators must take particular care to consider potential confounding variables when linking the clinical presentation of a maltreated child to conduct of a perpetrating parent. For example, a child who has been in one or more foster homes following removal due to alleged child abuse but prior to forensic assessment may also have been exposed to maltreatment in the foster care setting or may be distressed by the multiple transitions. A description of vulnerabilities and developmental needs of the child currently and by history constitutes a critical component in assessing continuing needs for protection.

3. *What can the parent(s) do to help?* This question focuses on current *parental fitness* and the *match* between parenting capacities and the needs of the child. Even when there has been past maltreatment, the evaluation must reflect the need of the courts to find *current* or *continuing* inadequacies in parenting. This includes assessment of a parent's ability to address any special needs or vulnerabilities of the child that arise from earlier maltreatment, as well as to support the general developmental needs of the child. It also includes assessment of the likelihood that the parent will not maltreat the child in the future. Specific parenting strengths and weaknesses relevant to the individual child must be characterized. If there is more than one child or parent involved in the forensic assessment, an analysis must be made of the parenting capacity of each parent and the effectiveness of the sum "parenting unit" for each child.

Obstacles to adequate parenting should be described and specifically linked to the needs of each child. Obstacles may involve individual factors (e.g., impairment of parenting due to limited cognition, mental illness, or substance abuse), interactive issues (e.g., one parent might be adequate but for the violence or negative influence of the other parent), or systemic problems (e.g., the resources or interventions that might otherwise prove helpful are not available). *It is critical that obstacles to adequate parenting be explicitly linked to risks to the child or the needs of the child.* For example, clinical findings of parental alcohol abuse alone may not be sufficient for a court to find an impairment of parenting. Rather, the alcohol abuse should be linked to specific parenting problems, such as neglect due to intoxication, dissipation of family funds, or physical abuse related to disinhibition or irritability due to alcohol consumption.

If interventions are recommended, the evaluator should also explicitly link the intervention to specific parenting deficits. For example, recommendations for the treatment of a parent's depression should be described in terms of how the untreated depression has impaired parenting. A recommendation for psychotherapy for a maltreated child should not only describe how successful treatment would remediate individual needs within the child

but also, when possible, improve the ability of the parent to care for the child. Whenever possible, information should be provided regarding how to access the recommended intervention, the likelihood of success, and the time required to determine whether the recommended intervention is actually effective.

The court may need to limit or structure, at least temporarily, access by the parent(s) to the child. This necessity may result in placing the child in temporary custody or issuing visitation orders pending further evaluation or litigation. In child protection cases, the court may issue orders regarding state custody of the child and contacts between the child and parent pending efforts to "reunify" the family or further evaluation or litigation.

4. *What hope is there for the future?* This question focuses attention on the *longer-term disposition* of the case. The ability of one or both parents to adequately parent the child over time is of central concern. In divorce custody cases, this involves findings on the "best interests" of the child and enduring orders governing legal and physical custody and visitation issued as part of the final divorce order. In child protection cases, the legal standard concerns the child's need for protection and whether "parental unfitness" bears on ultimate reunification of the family or termination of parental rights.

Forensic evaluation at this stage again assesses *current* or *continuing* impairments, as well as *prognosis* for parental ability to provide adequate care and protection, given the specific clinical and developmental needs of the individual child. It includes assessment of the likelihood that a parent would respond to interventions, and if so, over what time frame.

STANDARDS FOR FORENSIC ASSESSMENT

A number of professional organizations have produced guidelines or practice parameters for evaluations of children and their parents in the context of child protection matters. Among the organizations with published guidelines are the American Psychological Association (Committee on Professional Practice and Standards of the American Psychological Association, 1999), the American

Academy of Child and Adolescent Psychiatry (1997) and the American Professional Society on the Abuse of Children (1995, 1997b). Organizations have published guidelines directed at assessments in child protection matters, as well as standards for more specific forms of maltreatment, including parameters for conducting assessments of sexually abused (American Professional Society on the Abuse of Children, 1997b) or emotionally maltreated (American Professional Society on the Abuse of Children, 1995) children and adolescents.

A review across practice guidelines reveals the following key similarities in the statements of purpose. The evaluation is undertaken to provide relevant and professionally sound information and to render scientifically supported opinions with the well-being of the child as paramount. The evaluator should aim to maintain a professional and unbiased stance. The burden placed on the evaluator is great due to the potentially serious consequences of the evaluation for both the child and the parents.

A systematic approach to the process is clearly advocated, and multiple methods of data gathering are strongly recommended. Central among the recommended methods are (a) careful history taking; (b) review of all relevant and available documentation of health, mental health, and parenting practices, child protective documentation, family and marital assessments; (c) interviews and observation; and (d) psychological testing. The evaluation must produce sufficient substantiation for the findings and opinions offered to the court.

It is essential that record keeping is sufficient to allow the court and authorized others an adequate ability to review the bases for the report conclusions. Informed consents must include discussions about confidentiality, with special attention to informing participants about the absence of confidentiality for court-ordered evaluations. For example, it is important to inform clients that, because the evaluator is working for the court under appointment, the report will be sent directly to the court (unless ordered otherwise) and will become the property of the court. It will be available for release only as ordered by the court. Financial arrangements and other relevant issues as part of an informed consent should be clarified and agreed on before beginning the assessment.

Special care is recommended in reporting results and offering opinions, as the over- or underinter-

pretation of findings has the potential for serious consequences. The evaluator should be careful to not exceed the limits of his or her expertise.

CLINICAL DIMENSIONS OF A FORENSIC PARENTING ASSESSMENT

Before undertaking an evaluation of parenting capacity, an evaluator must consider the developmental and conceptual underpinnings of the assessment. In reality, the evaluator will be observing just a fraction of the child's interaction with his parents and significant others. The same is true of the information-gathering process with the parent(s) and the interaction with them over several assessment contexts.

Several authors have suggested theoretical frameworks for understanding parenting. Thomas Grisso (1986) published one of the first forensic papers that offered constructs for considering parenting capacity. He described seven areas of focus: (1) nurturing and physical care; (2) training and channeling of psychological needs (for example, those required in toilet training, weaning, provision of solid foods); (3) teaching and skill training to facilitate care and ensure safety (in areas such as language, perceptual skills, physical skills, self-care); (4) orienting the child to the immediate world of kin, neighborhood, community, and society; (5) transmitting cultural and subcultural goals and values and motivating the child to accept them for his or her own; (6) promoting interpersonal skills, motives, and modes of feeling and behaving in relation to others; and (7) guiding, correcting, and helping the child to formulate his or her own goals and plan his or her own activities.

In a 2001 article, Richard Barnum builds on Grisso's (1986) model to enumerate parenting capacities that he divides into two major categories: protection and care. Intervention on the part of the state occurs only when the minimal standards for protection and/or care for a child are not met.

Protection encompasses the parent's attention to safety as well as his or her role as advocate for the child. In terms of safety, parents are responsible for making reasonable efforts to keep their children safe from foreseeable harm. Parents are expected not only to protect their children from others but also to model positive and caring roles in the context of protection. Issues of discipline and conflict resolution fall under this heading. Although models of both correction and support may vary culturally, the child should be protected from hurt or "harm." Such harm includes both physical and emotional injury, as well as educational and social mistreatment. From the strength perspective, the parent serves not only as a safe base from which the child can explore and learn but also as an active and supportive spokesperson for the child's interests in the world.

In order to fulfill these criteria of "protection," parents are expected to have some understanding of their children's individual needs and habits and to make reasonable and consistent efforts to provide for these needs. For example, if a child has a mental or physical handicap or disability, the parent is expected to recognize the difficulty and to provide assistance to the child directly and through support from others in the community. It is important to document patterns of care, as well as critical incidents that might illustrate inadequate parenting, in the context of this interplay between the child's needs and the parent's anticipatory assessment and response.

The second domain of parenting capacity described by Barnum (2001) is that of care, which he defines as "the complex processes of socialization." These are processes that are essential to the nurturing and teaching functions of parents, aimed at promoting the child's growth and development. Included in this category are cognitive development and skill building, supervision and discipline, and emotional support, nurturance, and direction. Cognitive development and skill building involve exchanges between parent and child that include teaching, modeling, supporting independent learning, and reinforcing the learning process. At the core of the skill-building relationship is the parent–child interaction that allows for the balance between age-appropriate autonomy and support. The assessment of the child's individual needs and capacities and the fit between parent and child are critical.

Another parental skill is the ability to find or take advantage of existing opportunities for the child to learn. These skills include support and encouragement in the areas of language, self-care skills, and school and vocational functioning. Problem-solving

skills across domains are enhanced through assistance and an understanding of the child's ongoing learning process. Over- or underinvolvement can be problematic.

Supervision and discipline serve not only to protect but also to teach. Parents have a responsibility to promote good habits and ways of living by teaching, modeling, and shaping the child's environment through their supervision and their selection of others to supervise the child when they are unavailable.

An important component of supervision and discipline skills is parental awareness of the child's behavior and emotions, capabilities, and routines. Consistent and appropriate responses to these characteristics build the foundation for supervision and limit setting that systematically reinforce positive behavior and offer negative sanctions for unwanted behavior.

Emotional support, nurturance, and direction are the most important parenting skills. The parents' own emotional and social coping, as well as the ability to meet their own needs, will have a considerable impact on their ability to provide for their children.

Parental mood, frustration tolerance, and anxiety will also be important to assess, especially in the context of the parent–child relationship. If parental coping is dominated by anger and conflict or by serious sadness and lethargy, this can affect even the very youngest child in negative ways (Lyons-Ruth & Jacobvitz, 1999; Shonkoff & Phillips, 2000). Overly critical or rejecting parents, as well as uninterested and emotionally distant parents, fail to establish and maintain critically important attachment relationships with their children that serve as working models for the child's future relationships. Positive emotional interchanges between parent and child represent the most constructive interactions and promote secure attachment in the child that serves as a foundation for positive identity development.

COMPONENTS OF THE PARENTING EVALUATION

All comprehensive parenting assessments should contain a focus on the parent's individual functioning in the context of the family, evaluation of the needs and abilities of each child, and documentation of interactions between the parent and child, as well as between other caregivers and the child (see Table 20.1). Attention to sibling relationships and relationships with other significant adults may be considered as well. If the request is for assessment of parent–child interactions or attachment, this evaluation must also include assessment of the parent and the child as individuals. In assessing each component, strengths and weaknesses should be outlined by the evaluator. Historical information, as well as current data, should be gathered in each of the three areas.

In assessing the parent individually, the evaluator should consider the parent's role within the family and his or her adult relationships outside the family, functioning at work, and relationship with the child's siblings. The capacity to care for oneself is a precursor to the capacity to care for the child. Therefore, this capacity should be carefully explored prior to assessment of the parent with the child. The assets and vulnerabilities of the parent are analyzed independently from interactions with the child and then as they interact with the child's own assets and vulnerabilities. Areas of focus include cognitive, social, and emotional functioning of the parent. Information on physical health and life experience is also important. Mental illness; cognitive difficulties; educational attainment; work history; history of psychological trauma, including abuse and violence in families of origin; history of substance abuse; adult relationship history; and independent living skills are domains for investigation. For example, it is important to include information about the parent's cognitive capacities, reliability and organizational skills, social supports and adult interactions, family structure and role,

marital relationships, and capacity for nurturing. Some of the more salient deficits include mental limitation or disability, depression or other emotional difficulties, substance abuse, involvement in illegal activities, and an inability to maintain stable and positive relationships within the nuclear family, the extended family, or the community.

Assessment of the Child as an Individual

The child's biological, physical, social, and emotional development and functioning are the focus of this component of the assessment. With younger children, the evaluator can assess developmental milestones, cognitive functioning, and social development. With older children, the evaluator can assess school adjustment and performance, peer interactions, emotional health, and peer relationships. With teenagers, the evaluator can assess school and family relationships, peer relationships with attention to issues of risk-taking behaviors, mental illness, substance abuse, violence, and risky sexual behavior. The strengths and vulnerabilities of each assessment category can be summarized.

Assessment of Parent–Child Relationships

Once summary information about individual functioning of the parent and the child is completed, parent–child relationships are explored. This may be done in a number of different ways. Direct naturalistic observation of parents with their children engaged in routine activities at routine times is the most ecologically sound way to obtain information about parent–child interaction. For example, if

Table 20.1 Parenting capacity/best interests assessment process

Parent functioning	Child functioning	Parent–child interaction
1. Social	1. Social	1. Primary attachments
2. Emotional/personality	2. Emotional/trauma	2. Contact frequency
3. Cognitive	3. Cognitive	3. Interaction quality
4. Physical health	4. Physical health	focused parent–child
5. Life experience/trauma	5. Family role	parent–child–sibling
6. Marital role	6. School role	other family members
7. Family role	7. Peer role	other caregivers
8. Parenting role		
9. Community role		

parents routinely visit with their child in foster care, it may be most appropriate for the evaluator to observe, as unobtrusively as possible, one of these routine visits. The use of two-way mirrors is very helpful in this regard but is not imperative to good observational data. If children are not in the primary care of their parents, comparative observations of children with primary caregivers are helpful. Such observations can be augmented by visits in the clinician's office. Office observations are less indicative of the actual routine encounters between parent and child. However, office observations can be helpful, particularly if specific separation, reunion, and interaction behaviors are observed across caregivers in a uniform setting. Some clinicians will ask parents to engage the child in a particular teaching task. This also augments the more naturalistic observations that should precede any specific directed activity request.

Evaluators are cautious to note that observations of supervised encounters between parent and child may not represent the ongoing interaction patterns that are present when parents and children interact privately. Patterns of interaction can be supported by reviewing records of regularly documented encounters in visitation centers or in other supervised settings. The evaluator should always consider the risk of overgeneralization in regard to parenting skills, and conclusions should be offered with caution.

Children's reactions before and after visitation are important to assess, as are each parent's impressions about visitation. Patterns of emotional distress that surround visits should be noted but interpreted with care. Patterns in parenting behavior can be partly determined by comparisons between the similarities or differences in the observed behavior of parents during visits that routinely occur over time. The most robust data are those that are gathered over time through a combination of record review, directed and naturalistic observation, and comparative assessment of the child's interactions with multiple caregivers.

STRUCTURE AND METHODS OF ASSESSMENT

The suggested format of the evaluation is outlined in Table 20.2 using the principles described in the

Table 20.2 Structure of the forensic assessment

1. Identification of information used for assessment —interviews, structured assessments, observations, records reviewed, collateral contacts
2. Process of evaluation and confidentiality limits
3. Purpose of evaluation
4. Summary of history and current issues
5. Individual evaluation of parent
   a. History
      i. Family of origin
      ii. Educational history
      iii. Relational history
      iv. Mental health and substance abuse history
      v. Marital history
      vi. Work history
      vii. Criminal history
      viii. History of parenting
   b. Interviews and observations
   c. Mental status
   d. Psychological testing
   e. Summary of individual functioning
6. Individual evaluation of child
   a. Birth and developmental history
   b. Emotional and social health
   c. Physical health
   d. School history
   e. Placement history
   f. History of maltreatment and exposure to violence
   g. Peer relationships
   h. Substance abuse history
   i. Family relationships
   j. Summary of child's individual functioning
7. Parent–child interactions
   a. History of interaction and contact
   b. Observations—parent–child, caregiver–child, sibling–child
   c. Summary of parent–child interactions in the context of the child's attachment relationships
8. Summary and Conclusions
   a. Parenting fitness/capacity
      i. Cognitive support and problem solving
      ii. Supervision and discipline
      iii. Emotional support and nurturance
      iv. Protection and advocacy
   b. Child's best interests
      i. Child's functioning, including special needs
      ii. Child's maltreatment history and impact
      iii. Child's placements and options for continuity of positive attachments
   c. Risks and benefits of reunification compared with most likely alternatives

three components of the evaluation. Each report should contain sections on data gathering, record review, and collateral contacts; on interviews and observations; and on standardized psychological testing or assessment and a summary of these findings in the context of the parent's individual functioning, the child's individual functioning, and the nature and quality of the parent–child interaction. Finally, the components of parenting capacity may be used to summarize this process for the court. Paragraphs that address protection and care, including sections on cognitive support and problem solving, supervision and discipline, emotional support and nurturance, and protection and advocacy can help organize the summary of assets and vulnerabilities of each parent. Summaries of how the cognitive, social, emotional, and relational needs of the child are met over time provide a clear picture of the potential to impede the child's development in the future. In this context, continuity of attachments, relationships with family and siblings, and the child's individual special needs should be summarized to support the opinions of the evaluator.

Issues to Consider in Developing the Evaluation

An accurate and detailed history of the child's maltreatment is the foundation for the evaluation. Documentation of the facts at the time of the juvenile court involvement and augmentation of this information with additional history since the allegations should include information about duration and chronicity of the child's maltreatment, the continuity and episodic nature of its occurrence, and the interventions, past and present, that address the impact of the particular trauma on the child.

It is important to gather documentation about the child's victimization from the primary sources if at all possible. For example, consider the 5-month-old infant with a broken arm. The father states that while picking up the child, he accidentally hurt her. The Department of Social Services describes the young parents as pleasant and cooperative. The worker understands that the injury was accidental based on the father's story. The forensic evaluator requests the medical records that describe the child's injury as a transverse frac-

ture of the humerus. The medical record indicates that the description of the injury is not compatible with the father's story. The forensic evaluator calls the physician and asks directly about the force needed to cause this fracture. The physician understands that considerable force was necessary to cause the injury and that the father's account of lifting the baby from the bed is quite unlikely to have caused the child's fracture. The evaluator, at this point, is in a position to ask the father for further details about the child's injury. When confronted with the incompatibility of his story, the father admits that he was angry and intoxicated. He admits more involvement than simply lifting the child.

Knowing the child's risk and protective factors at the time of victimization is also helpful in determining impact and context that may assist in assessing future risk to the child (Cicchetti & Lynch, 1993). Domestic violence, history of past maltreatment of this child or siblings, parental history of maltreatment, serious mental illness, substance abuse, significant trauma experiences and losses, and criminal activity are essential risk factors to consider.

Of equal importance are parental strengths and supports. Information about the parents' families, in particular their stability and willingness to help, is crucial in considering the risk to the child. The parents' individual resilience represents an important assessment factor, including the ability to admit mistakes, to work with professionals, to maintain stable housing and employment, and to engage in healthy adult relationships.

Family routines, customs, and cultural and religious beliefs should be explored in the context of the evaluation. Parents require evaluation by culturally competent professionals with knowledge of relevant language and cultural practice. Risk and protective factors for the child may be culturally determined. For example, in a case of a Puerto Rican extended family, parents and paternal grandparents wanted their grandchild raised in Puerto Rico and were willing to engage in long-term integrated therapy. Therefore, the grandparents were given guardianship, with the stipulation that they would participate with their daughter-in-law and son in the treatment process and would remain a part of the monitoring system for the child when he returned home. This commitment included participating in family therapy, writing detailed reports of progress for the courts, and undertaking training to supervise visitation. Without these grandparents, reunification would have been impossible. Because of the cultural values within this family, the process seemed natural and quite acceptable to all.

In thinking about children's needs, it is valuable to also consider the history of services they have received, both in their biological homes and in alternative placements. The evaluator should request in writing documentation about focused treatment services for parents with mental health, cognitive, or substance abuse problems. Conversations with key providers are also helpful. In addition, it is often advisable to ask whether services have been coordinated and whether case management has taken place. The parent's history of response to services is often very telling. At times parents may have difficulty staying in treatment, and it is necessary to determine whether this is due to parental or agency issues.

Service plans for the family developed by departments of social services are required in almost every state. The goals of the service plan should be considered in terms of the evaluation findings in order to ensure that the elements of the service plan are consistent with the intervention needs identified in the evaluation. The compliance of each parent should be documented, as should extenuating circumstances when goals in a plan are not reached. The degree of success or failure in response to services should be noted in the report, along with an explanation of the underlying factors responsible for each type of outcome.

In assessing the child's best interests, the evaluator should consider the findings in the context of whether or not there is a proposed permanent plan or an alternative to reunification. There are a number of choices for the child, depending on his or her age and circumstances, including the following:

1. Adoption, guardianship, substitute care, or independent living. In a number of cases, some of these options have been explored by the mandated agency. At times the child may be placed in a preadoptive home. In order to comment on the child's best interests, it is necessary to know about possible alternative placements.

2. Continuing, tapering, or ending contact with parents. If adoption or guardianship is being considered, will this be an open or closed adoption? What are the guidelines for such arrangements? What about sibling or extended family contact? Issues of culture are also raised if the potential adoptive family does not share the child's ethnic heritage. The answers to these questions will allow the evaluator to explore realistic options and their impact on the child.

Table 20.2 outlines general sections of the individual parent assessment. This assessment should include information about the parent's own upbringing, with attention to his or her family life during childhood, exposure to violence or other abuse, and stability or discontinuity of care during childhood and adolescence. Current relationships with family, friends, and intimate partner should also be explored. Exploring these relationships helps the evaluator to determine the extent of the parent's social support system and to identify any disruption in the parent's current interactions. Ultimately, the issues are about each parent's ability to meet basic needs for self and the child and his or her parenting capabilities.

In talking to parents it is important to ask them to elaborate on their parenting experience. What is their understanding of the child? Are there specific developmental needs of the child in the areas of safety and socialization? How does the parent recognize these? How can they be addressed? A second set of questions relates to parenting style and discipline. What are the parent's attitude and beliefs about discipline? Does the parent have alternatives? Are the parent's practices age-appropriate? In addition to discipline, it is helpful to know about ways in which parent and child enjoy each other. Do they have favorite times or activities?

In some cases, standardized psychological testing may be helpful to further delineate a parent's cognitive, learning, and personality functioning. Cognitive testing typically consists of a screening or diagnostic measure that reflects a range of the individual's cognitive abilities. For example, the Wechsler Adult Intelligence Scale-III (WAIS-III; Wechsler, 1997) is one of the most commonly used structured tests of cognitive ability. It contains a variety of subtests that assess verbal and nonverbal cognitive functioning and compares each individual's performance with those of a group of age-matched peers. Achievement tests and specific tests that address neuropsychological functioning may be helpful if there are specific questions about the individual's learning or neuropsychological functioning (see Wills & Sweet, chapter 16, this volume, on neuropsychological assessment). Tests in the cognitive domain are often helpful in differentiating cognitive deficits from psychological difficulties. Cognitive assessment in parents with specific learning difficulties may identify specific deficits and lead to suggestions for more effective strategies for intervention. Cognitive testing may also clarify why strategies for intervention are not working or indicate the potential for change in self-care and parenting domains.

Standardized personality assessment is thought to reflect an individual's current stress management and coping style, approach to problem solving, thought content or thought process, affective features or other symptoms, perceptions of the world, and overall personality structure. Objective testing, such as the Minnesota Multiphasic Personality Inventory—2 (Regents of the University of Minnesota, 1989) is one of a group of a paper-and-pencil, forced-choice tests that provides an objective assessment of major personality characteristics that affect personality and social adjustment. A person's scores are compared with those of a normative sample to evaluate the degree to which the person shares a given set of characteristics. Objective personality assessment is generally considered more accurate than subjective methods of assessment to the extent that the individual responds in an honest and straightforward manner.

Projective testing is a method whereby ambiguous stimuli are presented to the test taker and he or she is asked to respond to the stimuli. Responses are thought to reflect the above-mentioned features of personality functioning. One such test, the Rorschach, is scored and interpreted using an empirically based system (Exner, 1991). Thus it provides normative information about all elements of the individual's responses.

Standardized testing can significantly enhance a forensic assessment but should never be used except in conjunction with the other components of the individual evaluation. It can be particularly helpful in elucidating questions that relate to the parent, including cognitive abilities, personality organization, and attitudes relevant to parenting. It can also help in the detection of serious mental illness. All of these areas of assessment may help the evaluator understand the parent's functioning in connection with his or her parenting capacity.

The individual assessment of the child includes attention to development, emotional status, relationships with adults or peers, and school performance. The evaluator should explore the child's experiences of family life in his or her biological home and/or alternative placements, including relationships with siblings and peers. Attention should be given to the child's placement history, continuity of care, and any disruptions to care. Some assessment of the past and current attachments between child and parent should be included, with attention to any special needs. The specific nature of the child's maltreatment or other trauma or victimization should also be evaluated.

In considering the child's relationships, extended family may be interviewed, especially if they are currently acting as caregivers or if they have been proposed as caregivers. The extent of the investigatory function of the forensic evaluator in this regard will depend on the court's request and the status of the child in the dependency process. If family members are being considered as possible permanent guardians, the assessment of the parents should be applied to them.

When applicable, another source of primary information about the child can be obtained from the current custodians, who may be relatives, a foster family, or a putative adoptive family. Current caregivers should be assessed for their basic capacities to care for and nurture the child, their ability to deal with a child who has experienced abuse trauma, and the synchrony or nonsynchrony of their ethnic and cultural values with those of the parent.

Another critical component of the evaluation is a focus on interactions between each parent and each child, as well as comparisons of these relationships with any other relationships the child has with current or potential alternative caregivers. This component is often executed through a series of observations of the child in a variety of contexts. To avoid directing the process, it is usually advisable to move from the least structured observations to those that are more structured. Observations of routine encounters between parent and child are usually the place to begin. Evaluators often observe parents during their scheduled visits. Parents and children may be seen in school settings, engaged together in after-school activities, or in the evaluator's office. Seasoned evaluators use both structured and unstructured observations. Some evaluators opt to include a structured teaching task so that they can compare the child's interactions across caregivers in the same context. Some evaluators will use a two-way mirror, and some will videotape the encounter for review. These decisions are often made after considering issues such as intrusiveness and rapport.

The final portion of the report is reserved for conclusions. The issues to be considered include the risks and benefits of reunification compared with other likely alternatives. In reviewing the factual basis of the opinions, the evaluator should consider the nature and etiology of the child's maltreatment, including attention to possible recidivism, the adequacy of the parent's capacity to meet the child's current needs, the prognosis for remediating parental deficits if declared "unfit," interventions and resources required for restoration, and the time frame required for safe reunification.

A second set of considerations includes the availability and adequacy of the most likely alternatives to reunification with parents. For example, the evaluator can consider substitute care, including adoption, kinship care, and residential care. The structure of the permanent plan, in regard to the child's contact with the parent (open vs. closed adoption), and reflection of the risks and advantages in the context of the child's best interests must also be considered. One way to describe the child's best interests in this final section of the report is to outline what would characterize the most likely and optimal developmental course if reunified with the parent versus the most likely and optimal developmental course if an alternative other than reunification with the parent occurs.

In writing a summary about parental fitness and/or factors associated with the child's best interests, it is important that the evaluator use caution to not overstate or understate opinions. One of the ways to check this process is to make sure that each opinion is carefully defended by the information gathered in the body of the report. A second technique that assists the author in constructing a balanced report is to use the summary section to restate the findings in the body of the report that have lead the evaluator to reach the conclusions offered.

Several additional issues are often raised in the development and execution of these evaluations. The first relates to handling ambiguities in information. It is imperative that the evaluator indicate where there may be "holes" in the data. It is advisable to consider ambiguous data with great care and to draw conclusions from clear, converging information. This does not mean that the evaluator cannot raise an issue or suggest that further investigation might be necessary to answer a given question.

A second admonition to evaluators is that they practice only within their areas of expertise. In the life of every experienced evaluator, there comes a time when he or she is faced with an area of expertise that is out of his or her knowledge base. In this case, the evaluator can seek assistance and consultation from an expert. However, if the referral question requires expertise beyond those of the evaluator, he or she may need to return the referral to the court or at least clearly state in the report that further consultation is necessary for specifically identified questions. Examples of problems that require specialized expertise include "shaken baby" or "battered child" syndromes and Munchausen-by-proxy cases. Other specialized topics include burns, head injuries, and sexual abuse cases, especially in preschool children (see other chapters in this volume).

Standards for practice typically require a period of supervision and specialized education before evaluators are able to perform forensic evaluations independently. Even the most experienced evaluators may require periodic consultation regarding difficult or complex cases. In some particularly difficult cases, several clinicians will work as a team, utilizing expertise across different professions when possible, synthesizing the information into a jointly authored report. Such multiprofessional assessments can help to reduce bias. It is also a good way to support the learning of a junior colleague in the field who is paired with a more senior partner.

References

American Academy of Child and Adolescent Psychiatry. (1997). Practice parameters for the forensic evaluation of children and adolescents who may have been physically or sexually abused. *Journal of the American Academy of Child and Adolescent Psychiatry, 36*(3), 423–442.

American Professional Society on the Abuse of Children. (1995). *Psychosocial evaluation of suspected psychological maltreatment in children and adolescents.* Chicago: Author.

American Professional Society on the Abuse of Children. (1997a). *Code of ethics.* Chicago: Author.

American Professional Society on the Abuse of Children. (1997b). *Psychosocial evaluation of suspected sexual abuse of children* (2nd ed.). Chicago: Author.

Barnum, R. (2001). Parenting assessment in cases of neglect and abuse. In D. Shetky & E. Benedek (Eds.), *Comprehensive textbook of child and adolescent forensic psychiatry* (pp. 81–96). Washington, DC: American Psychiatric Association Press.

Cicchetti, D., & Lynch, M. (1993). Toward an ecological/transactional model of community violence and child maltreatment: Consequences for children's development. *Psychiatry, 56,* 96–117.

Committee on Professional Practice and Standards of the American Psychological Association. (1999). Guidelines for psychological evaluations in child protection matters. *American Psychologist, 54*(8), 586–593.

Exner, J., Jr. (1991). *The Rorschach: A comprehensive system: Vol. 2. Interpretation.* New York: John Wiley.

Grisso, T. (1986). *Evaluating competencies.* New York: Plenum.

Lyons-Ruth, K., & Jacobvitz, D. (1999). Attachment disorganization: Unresolved loss, relational violence, and lapses in behavioral and attentional strategies. In J. Cassidy & P. Shaver (Eds.), *Handbook of attachment* (pp. 520–554). New York: Guilford.

Mnookin, R. (1975). Child-custody adjudication: Judicial functions in the face of indeterminacy. *Law and Contemporary Problems, 39,* 226–292.

Regents of the University of Minnesota. (1989). *Minnesota Multiphasic Personality Inventory—2.* Minneapolis, MN: National Computer Systems.

Shonkoff, J., & Phillips, D. (Eds.). (2000). *From neurons to neighborhoods: The science of early childhood development.* Washington, DC: National Academy Press.

Wechsler, D. (1997). *Wechsler Adult Intelligence Scale —Third Edition.* San Antonio, TX: Harcourt.

21

Forensic Evaluation of Juvenile Sexual Offenders

David Medoff
Robert Kinscherff

Forensic evaluation of juvenile sexual offenders (JSO) is primarily intended to help courts or other legal authorities to make decisions about youths whose delinquency charges arise from sexual misconduct. Such evaluations may also provide critical guidance about any containment needs required for public safety, the need for general psychotherapy or sexual-offender specific interventions, and other psychosocial or educational interventions likely to reduce the risk of recidivism. Because of the high stakes inherent in these evaluations, only persons who have had adequate training and experience or who have appropriate consultation and supervision should conduct them. The knowledge and skill base required for such evaluations qualifies them as "specialty" evaluations for which mental health professionals are not ordinarily qualified by virtue of general clinical education, training, and experience. Four components compose a complete forensic evaluation:

1. Collection of information related to risk and protective factors that are empirically related to risk of sexual and nonsexual reoffending

2. A comprehensive clinical assessment that results in a "clinical narrative" that synthesizes information about risk and protective factors; the developmental, clinical, and functional characteristics of the juvenile; and vulnerabilities and strengths that bear on reoffense risk and intervention needs

3. An assessment of sexual and nonsexual reoffense risk

4. Characterization of containment and intervention needs

The easiest part of conducting these evaluations involves collecting information about various "risk" and "protective" factors identified in the literature. However, adequate evaluation goes beyond a "cookbook" approach to include a formulation of the clinical and developmental functioning of the juvenile, the dynamics of the offense behavior and the psychological functions that it serves for the juvenile, the contexts and interactions that seem most likely to give rise to sexual misconduct, and the targets for intervention intended to reduce risk.

A multimodal model of risk assessment offers the best strategy for assessing such juvenile offenders. Part of the assessment focuses on "static" risk factors inherent in the juvenile's history and unalterable by time or intervention. Examples of "static" behaviors include preschool onset of aggressive behavior, mild mental retardation, a past history of sexual misconduct, or past failure of probation. Research may someday permit assignment of actuarial probabilities of reoffending by juveniles with particular clusters of "static" factors, but such risk prediction instruments do not yet exist. Additionally, although assessment of "static" factors anchors assessment to variables known to correlate with recidivism risk, it tells us little regarding the most effective targets for intervention.

Another part of our assessment model focuses on "dynamic" factors that can change over time or as the result of intervention. Examples of "dynamic" factors include access to a preferred victim type, cognitive distortions regarding sexual conduct, impulsivity due to a treatable disorder, or poor strategies for coping with stressful events. Such factors may also include aspects of clinical or developmental functioning, cognition, emotional functioning, mental status variables, family functioning, or contextual variables such as access to potential victims and exposure to triggering events. Attention to "dynamic" factors follows from the principle that juveniles move toward and away from incidents of sexual offense due to the interplay of risk and protective factors that are subject to change over time with effective intervention.

The third aspect of assessment involves individualized formulation of the case, specifically linking interventions to those "dynamic" factors most likely to reduce recidivism. "Cookbook" approaches that do not include integrating static and dynamic risk factors in a "clinical narrative" that addresses developmental and clinical functioning of the juvenile tend toward the simplistic, may mislead, and occasionally omit key information.

For example, simply knowing that a juvenile has sexually offended against a younger same-sex victim does not provide much useful information. That fact alone cannot distinguish among a juvenile who has selected a specific younger victim as an act of revenge against that child's parent, a cognitively limited juvenile who sought to establish both an emotional and sexual relationship with a younger child, or a juvenile who selectively prefers younger children as part of evolving pedophilia. Similarly, focusing on sexual offender "risk factors" will most likely not result in identification of a receptive language learning disability that could greatly complicate group treatment. Without taking into account a juvenile's own trauma history and methods of discharging unbearable anxiety, placement in a treatment program that relies heavily on confrontation may actually increase risk of sexual reoffense or reinforcement of maladaptive coping strategies.

The ultimate goal of forensic evaluation with JSOs demands (1) providing a holistic picture of the person's history, development, and functioning; (2) placing the sexual offense(s) within a context that takes account of the individual, interpersonal, and situational dynamics that precipitate the event; (3) describing the likelihood of reoffense in terms of static and dynamic risk and protective factors; and (4) linking containment and treatment interventions specifically to risk and protective factors most likely to result in diminished risk.

RESEARCH ON JUVENILE SEXUAL OFFENSES AND ACTUARIAL ASSESSMENT

Prevalence and Frequency Rates of Sex Offenses Committed by Juveniles

Forensic assessment of JSOs presumes an appreciation of the rates of sexual offenses, other offenses, and recidivism. Assignment of levels or types of risk always reflects comparisons against some baseline data, and forensic evaluators must be familiar with such information. Research data do *not* support the commonly held view found among uninformed clinicians who believe that juveniles who commit sexual offenses remain at very high risk for sexual recidivism. This belief creates significant challenges in identifying those juveniles who actually do have elevated risk for sexual reoffending, in identifying the most likely potential future victims, in adequately characterizing their individual clinical characteristics, and in understanding the dynamics of their offense behaviors.

The research literature contains varied estimates of the base rates for sexual offending by juveniles. Offense and recidivism rates defy easy calculation because of divergent operational definitions of what constitutes an actual sexual offense (e.g., self-report, formal charge, arrest, or adjudication) and because of the varied length of follow-up in individual research studies. Nevertheless, although prevalence and recidivism rates for juvenile sex offenders remain concerning, they clearly fall far below those of their adult counterparts (Center for Sex Offender Management, 1999; Knight & Prentky, 1993; Prentky, Harris, Frizzell, & Righthand, 2000; Rasmussen, 1999; Sipe, Jensen, & Everett, 1998; Smith & Monastersky, 1986; United States Department of Justice, Office of Juvenile Justice and Delinquency Prevention, 1999; Weinrott, 1996).

Recidivism Among Juvenile Sexual Offenders

Empirical studies have generally cited recidivism rates ranging from 2% to 14% (e.g., Hagan & Gust-Brey, 2000; Lab, Shields, & Schondel, 1993; Rasmussen, 1999; Sipe et al., 1998; Smith & Monastersky, 1986; Worling, 2001). However, the definitions of recidivism used and the methodologies of the studies vary. For example, among juveniles characterized as incarcerated violent sex offenders by Rubinstein, Yeager, Goodstein, and Lewis (1993), a sexual offense recidivism rate as high as 37% was found at 8-year follow-up. In contrast, Prentky et al. (2000) found a recidivism rate of only 3% at 2-year follow-up of 96 juvenile sex offenders previously admitted to a secure treatment facility. Rasmussen (1999) analyzed data of 170 adjudicated sex offenders and found a 14.1% recidivism rate at 5-year follow-up. Hagan and Gust-Brey (2000) found a 12% rate in their sample following a 10-year longitudinal follow-up period. Other studies have found both higher and lower rates of reoffense depending on the specific population and methodology involved (Atcheson & Williams, 1954; Hunter & Figueredo, 1999; Kahn & Chambers, 1991; Schram, Milloy, & Rowe, 1991; Worling, 2000).

Heterogeneity of Offenders, Overlap With Other Serious Delinquency

As a significant majority of JSOs will not continue to sexually reoffend following initial detection, it becomes important to consider whether some subgroups distinguish themselves by the type and likelihood of reoffense. Defining sexual offenders only by their illegal sexual behavior also mischaracterizes the broad heterogeneity of juveniles who engage in sexual misconduct. They vary widely by age, gender, evolution and pattern of sexual misconduct, cognitive and emotional functioning, presence and degree of psychiatric or other impairment, family functioning, history of prior interventions, evolution and pattern of involvement with nonsexual misconduct, and history of responses to misconduct by parents, schools, and law enforcement authorities.

Assessment of whether the sexual misconduct occurs within a broader pattern of delinquent misconduct holds particular importance. Research indicates that juveniles who are found delinquent on sexual offenses have a greater likelihood of arrest for nonsexual offenses than for new sex offenses, particularly if they have histories of long-standing aggression and nonsexual crimes (e.g., Prentky et al., 2000; Worling, 2001).

Assessment Issues: Actuarial, Clinical and Structured Clinical Methods

Until recently, the standard of practice for assessment risk of both adult and JSOs has taken a purely clinical approach, primarily due to the lack of any empirically based means of assessing such risk. However, the degree of inaccuracy associated with the historical practice of clinical assessment of adult sex offense recidivism is concerning. In their 1998 meta-analysis of sex offense recidivism studies, Hanson and Bussiere found an accuracy rate of only 0.10 for clinical assessment, as compared with a rate of .46 for actuarial measures. Smith and Monastersky (1986) also found poor rates of accuracy among clinicians estimating rates of sexual recidivism. Several actuarial scales have significantly better accuracy rates, including the Rapid Risk Assessment for Sex Offense Recidivism (RRASOR; Hanson, 1997); the Static 99 (Hanson & Thornton, 2000); and the Minnesota Sex Offender Screening Tool—Revised (MnSOST-R; Epperson et al., 2000). Actuarial measures such as these have gained wide use and acceptance in the prediction of recidivism, registration, and classification of sex offenders (e.g., Hanson, 1998; Medoff, 2000b).

Unfortunately, whereas actuarial risk assessment of adult male sex offenders has been proven a valid and reliable method (e.g., Epperson et al., 2000; Hanson, 1997; Hanson & Thornton, 2000; Quinsey, Harris, Rice, & Cormier, 1998), no such actuarial scales for the assessment of reoffense in juvenile sex offenders exist at this time (Hunter & Figueredo, 1999; Medoff, 2000a; Prentky et al., 2000; Worling & Curwen, 2001). Both a general lack of empirical research on juvenile sexual offending and problems arising from lower recidivism rates for this population account for this fact. For example, one validation study of the Juvenile Sex Offender Assessment Protocol (JSOAP) (Prentky et al., 2000) revealed only a 3% recidivism rate in the study sample of more than 96 juvenile sex offenders. This low recidivism rate prevented the validation of this tool and precluded statistical analysis of individual items for further determination of their utility as risk predictors (Prentky et al., 2000). Although the JSOAP does not qualify as an actuarial tool, it has utility as a measure for structuring clinical inquiry along four dimensions: (1) sexual drive/preoccupation, (2) impulsive/antisocial behavior, (3) clinical/treatment and (4) community stability/adjustment.

Establishing an Approach to Assessing Juvenile Sexual Offenders

Research revealing the weaknesses of unstructured clinical assessment and the lack of an empirically derived method for the risk assessment of juvenile sex offenders has generated controversy regarding the protocol that such evaluations should follow. Disagreement also exists about the best approach to combining risk or protective factors in the absence of actuarial weighting (Hanson, 2000). One important source of variability among evaluators derives from different weights being assigned to the same factor by different evaluators looking at the same case. Within this context, experimental protocols for assessment of juvenile sexual recidivism have begun to emerge. These include the JSOAP, as cited previously; the MASA (Multidimensional Assessment of Sex and Aggression; Knight, Prentky, & Cerce, 1994); and the ERASOR (Estimate of Risk of Adolescent Sexual Offense Recidivism—Version 2.0; Worling & Curwen, 2001). Although these protocols have not yet established

actuarial validity, their reliance on factors empirically associated with delinquent reoffense serves to improve risk assessment reliability by providing *structured* clinical inquiry. Use of empirically correlated risk factors anchors the clinical evaluation process to the most relevant data. The MASA, a computerized self-report inventory, includes multiple domains, such as childhood experiences, relationships with family members and peers, substance abuse, academic and occupational experiences, and behaviors and fantasies involving sex and aggression. The measure contains items associated with diverse types of offenders and includes methods for assessing response bias, prevarication, and random responding. A juvenile version of the MASA is currently being validated (R. A. Knight, personal communication, May 2001; Righthand & Welch, 2001).

The ERASOR is an empirically guided clinical assessment tool that summarizes the available literature and serves as an instrument to estimate the risk of sexual reoffense for adolescents between the ages of 12 and 18 years (Worling & Curwen, 2001). Composed of 25 risk factors, it covers five domains, including: (1) sexual interests, attitudes, and behaviors; (2) historical sexual assaults; (3) psychological functioning; (4) family/environmental functioning; and (5) treatment. Items have no numerical value assigned but instead rate as present or absent. Clinical judgment defines the overall level of risk because no empirically derived algorithm for combining risk factors to predict juvenile sexual offense recidivism exists.

How should evaluators proceed in light of the unreliability of clinical judgment in the absence of empirically established factors and the lack of rigorously established actuarial tools for the assessment of juvenile sexual reoffense? We recommend a combined approach that (1) uses existing tools for the empirically based assessment of general risk of delinquent reoffense (e.g., the Structured Assessment of Violence Risk in Youth [SAVRY]; Borum, Bartel, & Forth, 2003) and/or tools under development for juvenile sexual offenses (e.g., ERASOR, JSOAP, MASA) delinquency risk in order to establish a general risk window; and (2) supplements this information with assessment of factors that may escape capture by existing empirically based tools such as potential protective factors, potentially complicating clinical factors (e.g., limited cognitive capacities, psychiatric impairment), and factors associated with treatment readiness.

THE CLINICAL AND FORENSIC CONTEXT OF THE EVALUATION

As noted at the beginning of this chapter, competence in conducting the type of assessment we describe exceeds the usual components of preparation in professional psychology and demands specialized education and training. In addition, ethical considerations preclude conducting evaluations of this sort on patients with whom the clinician has a treatment relationship (see Koocher, chapter 3, this volume).

A history of serious delinquent misconduct constitutes a major risk factor for future reoffense, particularly if the juvenile demonstrated preschool onset of persistent interpersonal aggression. However, unlike adult sexual offenders, a significant history of nonsexual offenses in a juvenile does *not* predict future sexual reoffense, even if the juvenile committed such an offense in adolescence. Note that when an adolescent sex offender becomes involved in a subsequent juvenile complaint, it will most likely result from *nonsexual* behavior. Although it does not specifically predict sexual recidivism, understanding the specific pattern of antisocial conduct in a juvenile assessment provides information regarding general public safety risk, treatment readiness, and other relevant variables. In addition, a prior sexual offense itself represents a factor in the prediction of sexual reoffense.

An evaluation of risk of sexual reoffense will have little reliability without *both* (1) a detailed and accurate developmental/clinical history, specifically including nonsexual and sexual misconduct against persons; and (2) clarity about the nature of the sexual misconduct that gave rise to the evaluation. Because most JSOs will desist sexual offending on detection and have greater likelihood of future arrest for nonsexual offenses, a reliable clinical history will enable assessment of the juvenile's general risk of perpetrating against others (antisocial orientation) or the possible emergence of low base rate phenomena such as pedophilia.

Clarity regarding the sexual misconduct occurs chiefly when the juvenile admits to sexual misconduct that closely matches the allegations of the victim. Alternatively, the evaluator may accept findings of fact by a court for purposes of evaluation, even if the adjudicated delinquent continues to deny the allegations. Reliability problems in sexual offender evaluations arise when either (1) the juvenile denies the alleged sexual misconduct, charges are not pressed, and no other appropriate mechanism for establishing the accuracy of the allegations exists or (2) charges are pressed but the court has not yet made a determination of fact about disputed allegations. The critical difficulty for the evaluator when considering an ambiguous or disputed developmental/clinical history rests with the inability to confidently comment on historical factors empirically associated with elevated risk of nonsexual interpersonal violence or reoffense. Under such circumstances, the evaluator must characterize the ambiguities or disputes regarding the juvenile's history and explicitly limit any conclusions or opinions accordingly. Similarly, when the facts of the alleged sexual misconduct are ambiguous or disputed, the evaluator cannot confidently assess and comment on the nature or dynamics of the alleged sexual offense, nor how the alleged sexual offense fits into the broader developmental context of the juvenile's life. This serious problem carries the potential consequences of error when a juvenile is arrested for sexual misconduct and denies the allegations and the court has not yet made a determination of the facts in the case. The same problem also arises when an unwitnessed act of sexual misconduct occurs in a family, school, residential school, or other setting, the juvenile denies the alleged misconduct, and no reliable means of resolving the dispute other than subjective impressions of the credibility of the putative victim or perpetrator exist.

Few data exist to suggest that evaluators conducting assessments in the face of ambiguous or disputed allegations of sexual misconduct can reliably distinguish among defendants who are (1) innocent and telling the truth when denying the allegations; (2) guilty of some but not all of the alleged misconduct; (3) guilty of some or all of the alleged misconduct and motivated to get treatment but are deterred from admitting misconduct for some reason (e.g., fear of consequences, shame, or instruction from legal counsel); (4) guilty of some or all of the alleged misconduct, not motivated to get treatment, and simply lying when denying the allegations; or (5) guilty of some or all of the alleged misconduct and relying on the psychological defense mechanism of denial. The situation can become even more complicated when the juvenile admits to some of the alleged misconduct (e.g., admits touching the victim in the genital area) but denies other aspects that have significant implications for risk assessment (e.g., that the assaults occurred several times over a period of months and at times also involved forced intercourse at knifepoint).

Unfortunately, some professionals will conduct JSO evaluations under these circumstances for use in legal proceedings without appropriately limiting the scope of their assessments or opinions. Such evaluators tend to accept the alleged sexual misconduct as both true and accurate in all relevant detail and then infer that the defendant is either lying or manifesting the psychological defense mechanism of denial when declining to admit to some or all of the misconduct. Alternatively, the evaluator deems the juvenile's protests of innocence as "credible" and discounts or minimizes the alleged sexual offense and risk of reoffense. In each type of error, an evaluator who assumes or concludes on the basis of some personal impression what *did* occur or what *probably* occurred in the face of ambiguous or disputed evidence before an adjudication has made a *dangerously unreliable* decision, with respect to any use in legal proceedings. When the juvenile denies allegations of sexual misconduct and charges have not and will not be pressed, the evaluator may still review the evidence of sexual misconduct. Evidence might include statements by the alleged victim or witnesses or incident reports by staff in educational, residential, or other settings. However, the evaluator must consider the totality of the evidence regarding the alleged sexual misconduct. Evaluators should be very cautious and appropriately limit their findings and recommendations when the evidence of sexual misconduct essentially becomes an issue of credibility between the alleged perpetrator and the alleged victim.

Setting Up the Evaluation

The first step in conducting a forensic evaluation in JSO cases involves determining the legal context of the evaluation. This context will dictate whether and how an evaluator should proceed by *clarifying* who the "client" is for the evaluation, who owns or controls the findings of the evaluation, and what specific issues apply at the time of the evaluation. The evaluator must understand with absolute certainty the distinctions between confidentiality and privilege and what rules govern confidentiality and privilege in the jurisdiction. Next, the evaluator must obtain appropriate informed consent, making appropriate disclosure of the nature and purpose of the evaluation and providing any necessary warnings or waivers regarding confidentiality or privilege.

When Charges Are Not Pressed

Some evaluations occur without any legal involvement or immediate prospect for legal involvement. For example, assessment referrals may involve institutionalized youths in schools or other outpatient settings, where no charges are contemplated. Under these circumstances, the evaluator should secure appropriate informed consent from the legal guardian, paying specific attention to securing consent about releasing the results of the evaluation to others. The written report should specify what, if any, limitations on confidentiality or privilege apply. In addition, if the juvenile has not made admissions to the alleged sexual misconduct, the evaluator should clearly state this fact in the report, indicate any limitations this may create for the reliability of the assessment process, and clearly note the information relied on in assuming that specific forms of sexual misconduct has or has not occurred for purposes of the evaluation.

When Charges Are Pressed

Some referrals follow the filing of sexual offense charges but occur prior to any admissions to sexual misconduct by the youth or any adjudication of the facts by a court. Under these circumstances forensic evaluators may proceed with caution if retained by defense counsel, but they should ordinarily decline to conduct a JSO evaluation if the defendant is referred by a court, probation officer, family members, or others.

If retained by defense counsel, the evaluator operates under attorney-client privilege. In these circumstances, the evaluator has greater latitude to consider the potential significance of the alleged sexual misconduct even if the defendant continues to deny the allegations. Because the evaluator's role focuses on advising the attorney of the possible clinical or juvenile justice system outcomes in the event that a delinquency finding on the sexual offense charges occurs, evaluators retained by defense counsel should ascertain in advance whether counsel wants a written report and how to proceed if a conflict arises between the attorney-client privilege and a legal duty on the part of the evaluator. For example, the evaluator should clarify in advance how he or she will proceed if the defendant discloses information that would ordinarily trigger a mandated report to child protection authorities. We strongly caution evaluators to remember that such work conducted for defense counsel must not be shared with the family or other parties.

Except when evaluators have been retained by defense counsel, the evaluation should not take place without admissions to the alleged sexual misconduct by the juvenile and/or an adjudication of the facts by the court. When the juvenile makes admissions, best practice calls for the court to take these under oath as part of a guilty plea or a plea bargain. The forensic evaluation may then proceed and rely on the admissions. If the juvenile has not made partial or full admissions to the alleged sexual misconduct, the sexual offender component of evaluation should not begin until after adjudication of the disputed facts.

If the evaluator is retained by the prosecution, the evaluation will proceed according to rules governing access to defendants by such evaluators. Appropriate consent must occur, with the nature and purpose of the evaluation described, and warnings regarding confidentiality and privilege offered to the defendant. If legal minor status precludes informed consent by the juvenile, a legal counsel or guardian should also acknowledge the informing process.

When an evaluation occurs pursuant to a court order, the evaluator should clarify with all parties that the court holds primary "client" status and that the report will go directly to the court for distribution. Prior to the evaluation, appropriate warnings must be given to the juvenile regarding waiver of confidentiality and privilege and the nature and purpose of the evaluation.

Court-ordered JSO evaluations can appropriately assist the court in making dispositions. The evaluator should conduct the evaluation in a manner consistent with all legal rights and protections afforded the defendant. For example, evaluators should be familiar with local law or practice regarding any right of defense counsel to be present during interviews with the defendant or governing the legal status of potentially self-incriminating statements made during court-ordered evaluations.

FOUNDATION AND PROCEDURE FOR ADEQUATE FORENSIC ASSESSMENT

Forensic evaluations in JSO cases typically include many more sources of information than do standard clinical evaluations. Interviewing the juvenile and/or family members alone does not constitute adequate assessment of JSOs when one is seeking reliable information regarding recidivism risk, degree of containment required to effect interventions, or modality of intervention.

The evaluator should conceptualize the evaluation process as unfolding in nine phases: (1) clarification of the forensic issues in the case; (2) identification of and access to sufficient sources of reliable information; (3) clinical and functional assessment of the juvenile, including a developmental history of social relationships, aggression or rule-breaking conduct, and sexual development and experience; (4) identification and specific assessment of factors empirically linked to elevated risk of sexual and nonsexual recidivism among juveniles; (5) identification and assessment of other factors clinically relevant to risk of sexual and nonsexual recidivism in the individual case; (6) assessment of degree of containment or monitoring required to protect public safety and/or institute effective intervention; (7) access or obstacles to access of recommended interventions; (8) assessment of juvenile's likely response to the recommended interventions; and (9) identification of the most salient risk factors and proposal of a specific risk management and intervention plan that targets the most important risk variables.

In this process, the evaluator must identify the most significant historical (static) factors that are empirically associated with sexual offense recidivism risk. Some of these will be empirically supported factors, whereas others will be factors identified with reoffense risk in the evolving research on JSOs. Although such factors do not change, because they are elements of the juvenile's history, they can describe a trajectory of risk and may also identify the highest risk situations for sexual recidivism for the juvenile.

The evaluator must then identify the most significant ongoing (dynamic) variables associated with sexual offense recidivism risk in the case. These may involve *clinical* factors, such as impulsivity, poor stress tolerance, substance abuse, preoccupation with sexual fantasy, evidence of deviant sexual arousal, or early evidence of psychopathy; *family* factors, such as parental criminality, poor capacity to supervise the juvenile, easy access to pornography, or ready access to intrafamilial sexual victims; *social* factors, such as a peer group that tolerates or even values sexual or nonsexual offense behavior; *contextual* factors, such as precipitants of or opportunities for sexual misconduct; or other relevant factors. Such dynamic variables may change, and the evaluator should consider which of these constitute optimal targets for intervention in the form of containment and/or treatment.

Identification of such factors should also yield a risk management plan that identifies the conditions under which the juvenile most likely will reoffend, the degree to which the juvenile will likely participate effectively in managing reoffense risk, and the recommended steps or strategies for lowering risk in the short term and the long term.

Time pressure and access may limit the amount of information and level of detail obtained from multiple sources; therefore, evaluators should carefully consider the information necessary to adequately respond to the forensic referral questions. The higher the stakes in the case are, the more meticulous and persistent is the behavior required of the evaluator when gathering the necessary data, especially regarding factors most closely tied in the research literature to reoffense risk, intervention readiness, and containment. Evaluators may need to request assistance from the court or attorneys if critical sources are unresponsive or unavailable. Evaluators must also consider the reliability of available information regarding key risk factors (e.g., self-report of defendant only, vague information in documents or from other sources, indepen-

dent corroboration from multiple sources). Where the available information is inadequate or ambiguous, the evaluator should take care to communicate this to the court or attorney requesting the evaluation and to specifically indicate what limitations this lack of reliable information imposes on the reliability of the assessment and recommendations.

Sources of Information in Forensic Assessment of Juvenile Sexual Offenders

Useful sources of data for basic JSO assessment include:

- Information from family, school, medical and mental health, and community sources and records
- Information from state child protection, juvenile justice, mental health, or other state agency sources or records, including caseworkers and foster parents or other substitute caregivers
- Probation and court records
- Where relevant, information regarding computer access to sites or activities with sexual content, credit card purchases, and other possible evidence of sexual preoccupation
- Interview with the juvenile

Before interviewing the minor regarding the sexual offense(s), the evaluator must become familiar in detail with records, court findings, victim or witness statements, any prior admissions to the offense(s) by the juvenile, or other sources of information regarding the sexual misconduct. The evaluator must have the most complete picture possible of what was alleged, admitted, and/or adjudicated to have occurred in order to effectively interview the juvenile regarding the sexual offense(s) and, where necessary, confront prevarications (i.e., outright lies or evasion), minimization, or denial. Such sources of information might include:

- Police investigation documents, including any relevant crime scene or physical evidence reports, or law enforcement analysis of patterns of computer use or access
- Results of any medical examinations of the victims prompted by the sexual misconduct
- Victim or witness statements regarding the misconduct

- Any admissions made by the juvenile to the details of the misconduct
- Any admissions or statements made by co-defendants
- Statements made by the juvenile during the forensic interview
- Findings of fact by a court that adjudicated the sexual offense
- Where relevant, videotapes, audiotapes, computer entries, journal entries or other recordings of the offense

Interviewing the Juvenile Sexual Offender

The interview should always begin with an introduction by the evaluator, a discussion of the nature and purposes of the evaluation, and discussion of any limits on confidentiality or privilege. One advantage to not conducting the JSO evaluation until after the juvenile has made admissions and/or adjudication of the allegations involves the ability of the evaluator to rely more greatly on the "facts" of the sexual misconduct than when dispute over the facts still exists. Similarly, if he or she is retained by defense counsel, the evaluator may speculate about the possible meaning of the alleged misconduct with the attorney in a manner that does not compromise the legal rights of the juvenile or risk misleading the court. If the evaluation takes place in settings in which any admissions to misconduct solicited during the course of the interview may result in the filing of criminal charges, this fact must form part of informed consent with the juvenile and parent or legal guardian. In some cases, in which disclosures during evaluation may lead to prosecution, clarification of what happens to this kind of information must be obtained before proceeding, along with appropriate informed consent or court orders.

The initial focus of the interview with the juvenile involves assessment of empirically based historical and developmental risk factors. One should also assess more dynamic "clinical" factors such as mood disorder, degree of sexual preoccupation, or substance abuse. Assessment of the specific offense characteristics can assist in understanding the dynamics of the sexual offense (e.g., victim selection, degree of planning or predation, victim penetration) or detection of low-incidence but potentially important offense dynamics (e.g.,

sadism, evidence of early emerging pedophilia). *We strongly recommend* the use of a structured interview approach that utilizes empirically based factors to guide information gathering about risk for sexual and nonsexual reoffense.

The amount of time that should be spent conducting the evaluation will vary widely depending on factors that include the specific forensic question to be answered, how much is already known about the defendant, the clinical complexity of the case, the need for corroboration from collateral sources of information bearing on key risk and protective factors, and whether or not the juvenile can be productively interviewed. Ordinarily, however, the evaluator should anticipate spending 1 to 4 hours interviewing the juvenile regarding the sexual offense and associated risk and protective factors, in addition to the time required to complete an adequate clinical interview. This estimate does not include the time needed to gather information from other sources regarding relevant risk and protective factors.

Evaluators can utilize a variety of effective interview styles, but one must feel comfortable discussing normal and deviant sexual behavior, violent or sexualized conduct and fantasy, and child/adolescent developmental issues. Evaluators should avoid pitfalls such as failing to challenge inconsistent accounts, failing to probe for relevant data of a sexual nature, or routinely relying on an unduly confrontational style that may provoke a defensive or angry response that the evaluator then characterizes as "narcissism" or other pathologized personality feature. Excessively confrontational approaches may also result in the juvenile being characterized as "in denial" after refusing to discuss the sexual offense when the interview approach triggers shame regarding the sexual offense. A patient approach will often result in the juvenile talking about the offense in detail.

Ideally, the evaluator will create an atmosphere that facilitates the juvenile's willingness to self-report accurately. Specifically describing the process of evaluation, including the need to discuss sexuality and the sexual misconduct openly, can prove helpful. One approach might begin with relatively relaxed open-ended questioning and inquiry regarding areas of functioning unrelated to sexual development or offending. This approach affords an opportunity to create a mutually communicative relationship, as well as to observe cognitive, language, and personality functioning without too much initial intrusion by the interviewer. Greater structure can follow, if necessary, to facilitate communication or manage the interpersonal aspects of interviewing.

The discussion of the sexual offense may begin by asking the defendant to explain the incident leading to the charges. Careful review of available information regarding the offense prior to the interview allows the interviewer to assess how much the defendant discloses spontaneously and to observe the juvenile's account for cognitive distortions often associated with sexual misconduct. If the defendant offers an incomplete account, the interviewer can introduce some details and observe both the defendant's response to the fact that the interviewer has information about which the defendant was unaware and his or her ability or willingness to incorporate the newly introduced offense details.

Discussion of the sexual offense should include at least seven elements: (1) potential elements of desensitization or offense rehearsal, such as sexual fantasies, exposure to pornography or explicit sexual activity, or masturbation; (2) the manner in which the victims were selected and victim compliance elicited; (3) degree of opportunism or planning associated with the offense; (4) the social context of the offense; (5) the presence or absence of deterrent factors (e.g., nearby adults, offense in a public area) and whether and why these factors deterred or failed to deter the offense conduct during the sexual misconduct or at other times; (6) association of the sexual misconduct with any psychiatric symptoms; and (7) association of the misconduct with recent stresses such as losses, rejections, or narcissistic injuries.

Tracking the chronology of the day during which the offense occurred can prove useful, starting with the time the defendant awakened and constructing a timeline through the entire day. The evaluator should track several aspects: interpersonal contacts, including those with any codefendants and the victim; any acute stressors; ingestion of alcohol or any controlled or disinhibiting substances; exposure to any sexual material such as pornography, observing sexual activity, or engaging in sexual activity (including masturbation); onset of contemplating any offense against a person (alone or with others); onset of contemplating a sexual offense; experiences of intensified affect, such as anger, despair or desperation, or elevated mood such as in hypomania; details of offense enactment; and details of postoffense conduct. The chronology of postoffense conduct may extend beyond the date of the offense under consideration.

If the defendant does not spontaneously include the perspective of the victim or victims in the offense account, the evaluator should ask the defendant to attempt to offer an account of the activity from the victim's perspective. This contributes to assessment of the defendant's cognitive capacities (i.e., ability to adopt the perspective of another), presence of cognitive distortions, and/or capacities for empathy. Examining the general history of the defendant for evidence of capacities for empathy and mutuality in interactions other than sexual offenses often proves useful. Evaluators should exercise caution in commenting about "remorse" for the offense. Little data exist to suggest that mental health professionals have particular skill at discerning the sincerity or insincerity of expressions of remorse or the meaning of expressions of remorse either offered spontaneously, elicited by the evaluators, or absent in the assessment interview.

When the Juvenile Denies Sexual Offense After Admission or Adjudication

When a juvenile involved in legal proceedings denies the alleged offense prior to a determination of the facts by the court, clinical rigor and professional ethics require deferring the JSO evaluation until after a finding of facts occurs. Assessment of other psychiatric, medical, educational, family, or other areas of functioning is permissible, particularly when the presence or absence of a sexual offense history is not particularly relevant to the functional area being assessed. Evaluators should exercise particular caution when determining the credibility of the alleged victim and the alleged perpetrator, because making such determinations on the basis of disputed evidence risks usurping the role of the court. However, in cases in which juveniles continue to deny sexual offenses after courts have found them guilty, the evaluator may rely on the adjudicated facts in interviewing the defendant to assist the court in disposition or service providers in treatment planning and implementation. The defendant should be advised that the evaluation will presume the basic accuracy of the allegations reflected in the adjudicated offense and instructed that the more the defendant can discuss what led up to the offense, his or her conduct during and after the offense, and other sexual and nonsexual aspects of developmental history and the offense, the more likely it is that the outcome will include a recommendation for community-based placement and intervention. The evaluator should never guarantee this outcome, however, because some juveniles show early indications of psychopathy *and* a high-risk presentation that will lack any shame or anxiety that might inhibit disclosure. One can also inform the juvenile that an inability or unwillingness to discuss the adjudicated offense will more likely contribute to a recommendation for placement and intervention in residential or juvenile justice settings. If the defendant maintains denial of the adjudicated offense over the course of the JSO evaluation, the evaluator cannot confidently assess the juvenile's thinking about the offense before, during, and after it occurred. In such cases, one often cannot determine whether the denial reflects fear of consequences of admission, prevarication, or the psychological defense mechanism of denial associated with experiences of shame or anxiety. If the youth maintains denial of the adjudicated offense, the evaluator must rely almost exclusively on historical (static) risk factors and factors associated with the offense characteristics. Consistent denial makes reliable assessment of "treatment readiness" virtually impossible, and denial of an offense may make specialized interventions unworkable because they require the juvenile to discuss the offense(s) and associated risks of reoffense. When important public safety issues are at stake because of the nature of the sexual offense(s) or other crimes against persons, the evaluator must think carefully about whether the juvenile shows amenability to adequate containment, monitoring, and intervention in available community-based placement or treatment services. Ordinarily, maintaining denial following adjudication should presumptively result in a recommendation for intervention in a residential or other noncommunity setting unless the sexual offense is relatively minor and the juvenile lacks significant historical or actuarial risk factors for reoffense.

Sometimes the sexual element of a charge may have been dismissed by the court or eliminated during the course of plea bargains. Conducting JSO evaluations when the sexual elements of charges have been eliminated raises many challenging clinical and ethical issues, especially when the juvenile denies the sexual aspects of the misconduct or insists that any admissions made to secure the plea bargain were made "because my lawyer told me to admit it to get the deal, but I really did not do it." An evaluator's best practice would involve clarification for the referring court or other party that a sexual offender evaluation under these circumstances will likely prove too unreliable for use in framing specific recommendations regarding sexual offender treatment or case management. Responsible evaluators may want to decline undertaking JSO evaluations under these circumstances because of the problems with assessment reliability. Courts and other parties may require education in order to appreciate that when a JSO evaluation comes *after* a plea agreement has occurred that allows the juvenile to remain in the community, a threshold *de facto* determination has *already* taken place regarding reoffense risk and intervention needs. Deciding to place a juvenile on community-based probation and *then* referring the juvenile for a sexual offender evaluation often reduces the motivation of the juvenile to cooperate and creates potential problems for the evaluator and the court in the event that the evaluation finds a level of risk that makes community-based management risky and inappropriate.

In cases in which admissions to sexual misconduct have occurred in order to secure a plea bargain or other disposition that does not reflect the sexual elements of the charge, evaluators should insist on the following prior to the evaluation: (1) that any admissions to sexual misconduct must occur in detail and under oath as part of the plea agreement; (2) that the juvenile and defense counsel understand that any admissions made cannot later be recanted during evaluation or intervention; (3) that recanting such admissions will be treated as a violation of any terms of probation and/or prompt a return to court for review of whether the plea agreement is still in effect. Where legally permissible, these same conditions should also occur in cases that result in a "continued without a finding" *Alford* plea or other dispositions that do not result in the court adjudicating the allegations nor legally binding admissions by the juvenile to the sexual misconduct. An Alford plea is a form of guilty plea in which a defendant does not admit to the criminal act and asserts innocence, but admits that there is sufficient evidence for the prosecution to likely prove guilt to a judge or jury.

Psychological Tests and Instruments

Use of psychological tests and instruments can offer invaluable data in providing information about the juvenile's intellectual and neurological functioning, personality functioning, psychopathology and psychiatric comorbidity, behavioral functioning, and sexual deviance. Each of these domains has potentially significant implications for understanding both the evolution and dynamics of a juvenile's sexual offending and the kinds of interventions that may prove useful. For example, juveniles with poor reading and writing skills will most likely not benefit from interventions that rely heavily on written assignments; those with deficits in receptive or expressive language will have difficulties in group treatment; and those with major psychiatric impairments may require a period of treatment and stabilization before engaging in sexual-offender-specific treatment.

We recommend specific assessment of substance abuse with valid and reliable instruments due to the high rates of such behavior among juveniles with sexual and nonsexual offense histories. Similarly, specific assessment of exposure to childhood sexual or other victimization using valid and reliable tools may yield relevant data given the prevalence of serious maltreatment histories among adolescent sexual offenders, with the accompanying psychiatric vulnerabilities often resulting from such victimization. The primary purpose for such assessment involves identification of vulnerabilities in functioning that stem from victimization (e.g., PTSD symptoms) rather than to identify childhood victimization as a risk factor for sexual reoffense, as research does not generally support childhood sexual or other victimization as a risk factor for adolescent sexual offending.

However, evaluators should also remain aware of the limitations of psychological testing in JSO assessments. No unitary reliable psychological testing "profile" of JSOs exists. Some personality testing might characterize a juvenile as generally defensive, dishonest, or malingering and thus less likely to respond to interventions, but such instruments cannot detect whether or not a juvenile has told the truth when describing or denying details of a specific sexual offense. For example, a defendant may present a "defensive" protocol on psychological tests but still speak truthfully when denying a specific act of misconduct such as stealing a car or committing a sexual offense. Similarly, results of a psychological testing battery alone cannot yield a reliable assessment of risk of sexual or nonsexual reoffense.

Particularly in forensic contexts, use of projective or self-report measures that lack an adequate empirical basis or relevant norms should demand great caution because no way exists to establish the validity or reliability of any inferences drawn from them. Evaluators should avoid using such measures in forensic assessment even if they find common utility in psychological testing intended for clinical use.

Structured clinical interview instruments may assist in identifying juveniles who present with formal diagnosis of a conduct disorder. This diagnosis ordinarily signals versatile and serious patterns of rule breaking and crimes against persons and/or property. Additionally, the Structured Assessment of Violence Risk in Youth (SAVRY) may help in assessing general violence risk (Borum et al., 2003).

Psychopathy, a particularly virulent and persisting form of antisocial orientation strongly associated with greater recidivism and sexual violence among adult sexual offenders, also correlates with greater threats and more severe violence among JSOs when compared with other JSOs without a psychopathic diagnosis (Gretton et al., as cited in Forth & Burke, 1998). A juvenile version of the Psychopathy Check List is currently available (Forth, Kosson, & Hare, 2003) that will specifically assess adolescent psychopathy. Evaluators can also use instruments such as the Childhood and Adolescent Psychopathy Taxon Scale (Harris, Rice, & Quinsey, 1994) in order to assess key factors associated with adolescent psychopathy: arrest prior to age 16, fighting, diagnosis of conduct disorder, elementary school maladjustment, school suspensions, alcohol abuse, parental alcohol abuse, and failing to live with both parents until age 16 (except in the case of death of a parent).

As described previously, assessment tools specifically devised for assessment of sexual offenders may prove useful in structuring the assessment process or in supplementing the information gathered during evaluation. A variety of useful sexual knowledge and attitude self-report instruments exist. We caution evaluators to familiarize themselves with the psychometric and empirical properties of such instruments. For example, little research exists on the juvenile version of the Multiphasic Sex Inventory (MSI). Further, both the promising Estimate of Risk of Adolescent Sexual Offense Recidivism (ERASOR) and the Multidimensional Assessment of Sex and Aggression (MASA) instruments remain in validation stages as this chapter is written. Although these and other self-report measures may prove useful in assessment, they should be seen as structuring and supplementing a broader assessment process rather than relied on alone in rendering opinions and recommendations. As with any unresearched or unvalidated assessment instrument, evaluators should communicate the limits of these instruments in their reports to persons who rely on the report for judicial, probation, treatment, or other decisions.

The use of a plethysmograph for assessment of deviant sexual arousal in juveniles remains controversial (e.g., Bourke & Donohue, 1996; Cellini, 1995). Concerns regarding phallometry in adolescents range from methodological concerns about the limited research base in adolescents to ethical concerns regarding the invasive nature of the procedure and the exposure of adolescents to a range of deviant sexual material during the procedure. The Abel Assessment for Interest in Paraphilias has also received similar methodological (Smith & Fischer, 1999) and ethical criticism. Concerns regarding the use of such methods for assessing deviant sexual arousal increase when used in a forensic context without adequate scientific validation.

FACTORS FOR STRUCTURED CLINICAL ASSESSMENT

Risk Factors for Routine Inclusion in Assessment

Currently, no established *actuarial* risk factors exist for the evaluation of JSOs, as no adequately validated actuarial measures for this type of assessment

have evolved. However, although we clearly need more research, several *empirically supported* factors of risk have appeared in the peer-reviewed literature. Given the current state of research in this area, a "best practices" approach to the assessment of JSO recidivism would include the integration of empirically supported risk factors, along with *clinically supported* factors of risk that have rationally derived from the collective education, training, and experience of professionals involved in this work.

We list risk factors that have empirical support in Table 21.1. Explanations for less clearly defined factors follow. "Deviant Sexual Interest" describes juveniles who become sexually aroused by violence or by younger children. Specific aspects of deviant sexual interest that are supported by empirical research involve self-reported sexual interest in children, including sexual fantasies, grooming child victims for sexual assault, and sexual contact involving penetration with children.

Evaluators must take care to distinguish sexual offenses involving children from evidence of pedophilia. Pedophilia refers to a preference for prepubescent children as sexual partners. The involvement of a young victim in a juvenile sexual offense typically does not represent evolution of pedophilia. Rather, it more likely reflects factors associated with victim access, opportunity, targeting a child in revenge to a third party, inability of the juvenile to offend against other persons more capable of defending themselves, or other motives. This comports with research among adult male offenders that demonstrates that most who have sexual contacts with children are not pedophiles but adults who victimize children for reasons other than having a selective preference for sexual contact with prepubescent children (Douglas, Burgess, Burgess, & Ressler, 1992)

As noted in Table 21.1, mixed empirical support exists for the factor of antisocial personality features. Nevertheless, current risk prediction checklists and guidelines include a history of antisocial behavior and/or a history of delinquent conduct as risk factors. These factors do not require or presume emerging psychopathy or antisocial personality, but they include features of these diagnoses. Finally, a lack of intimate peer relationships involves an inability to create and maintain emotionally intimate relationships and does not simply refer to a lack of "social skills." An emotion-

Table 21.1 Empirically supported risk factors

Risk factor	Published studies demonstrating empirical support	Included in risk predication checklists and guidelines	Empirically supported factor in adult research
Deviant sexual interest*	Worling & Curwen, 2000; Schram, Milloy, & Rowe, 1992	Yes	Yes
Sexually assaulted two or more victims*	Rasmussen, 1999; Schram, Milloy, & Rowe, 1991; Langstrom & Grann, 2000	Yes	Yes
Sexually assaulted a child under 12 years old and victim is four years younger than offender**	Ross & Loss, 1991; Kahn & Chambers, 1991; Sipe, Jensen & Everett, 1998	Yes	Yes
Sexually assaulted a stranger*	Ross & Loss, 1991; Smith & Monastersky, 1986; Langstrom & Grann, 2000	Yes	Yes
Any male victim (for male offenders only)**	Smith & Monastersky, 1986; Langstrom & Grann, 2000	Yes	Yes
Antisocial personality features**	Langstrom & Grann, 2000; Worling & Curwen, 2000	Yes	Yes
Lack of intimate peer relationships/ social isolation**	Knight & Prentky, 1993; Langstrom & Grann, 2000; Epps, 1997; Lipsey & Wilson, 1998	Yes	Yes

*Strong support; **Mixed support.

The citations in this table can be found in Worling and Curwen (2001).

ally intimate relationship involves a relationship in which affection, warmth, self-disclosure, and dependence occurs mutually between partners. Worling and Curwen (2001) use this factor in the ERASOR; they adapted this definition from the work of Ward, McCormack & Hudson (1997).

Other factors considered in assessing sexual recidivism risk among JSOs find inclusion in the few structured tools available (e.g., JSOAP and ERASOR). These instruments provide for better reliability in assessment due to their standardized definitions and structured dimensions. Such factors include:

Behavioral/Historical

- History of nonsexual delinquent/antisocial misconduct including:
  - Early onset or persistent aggression/defiance
  - Childhood onset form of conduct disorder
  - Diversity of delinquent misconduct
  - History of school suspension/expulsion
  - Denial or obscuring of involvement in offense, especially after adjudication

- Instability of caregiver and adequacy of supervision by adult(s)
- History of parental alcoholism
- History of family transience, dislocation
- History of other factors that limit parental adequacy
- Stability of current living situation
- Affiliation with delinquent peers or social isolation from peers
- History of dropping out of sex-offender-specific treatment
- Any sexual offense following completion of sex-offender-specific treatment
- Residence in a family with a member of a specific victim class and/or unsupervised access to potential victim

Characteristics of Offender

- Impulse control deficits and/or anger control
- Evidence of emerging or established deviant sexual arousal, including:
  - Emerging or established paraphilias
  - Deviant sexual fantasy, with or without masturbation

- ○ Possession of paraphilic pornography
- ○ Evidence of sexual preoccupation beyond normal adolescent sexuality
- Severe substance abuse
- Evidence of lack of motivation for change
- Presence of cognitive distortions that maintain sexual offending
- Mentally retarded, developmentally delayed, or severely learning disabled offender with no history of specialized treatment

Characteristics of Offense

- Stranger or extrafamilial victims
- Multiple victims and/or particularly vulnerable victims (e.g., very young, mentally retarded, developmentally delayed, psychiatrically ill)
- Disproportionate methods of forcing victim compliance (e.g., use of a weapon, threat of harm, drugging victim)
- Evidence of planning and predation, sex and non-sex offenses
- Present or nearby adults or others do not deter sexual offense
- Commission of sex offense while under supervision
- Evidence of gratuitous violence (e.g., violence above and beyond that necessary to commit the offense)

Examples of Factors of Low Base Rate but of High Concern

- Evidence of ritualistic, sadistic, or stereotyped behaviors or offense characteristics
- Use of ligature as part of sexual offense
- Bizarre sexual acts, either involved in offense or not
- Thought disorder implicated in sexual offense

Controversial Risk Factors

Some factors commonly believed by many clinicians to correlate with sexual offending and sexual offense recidivism have yet to achieve validation in the peer-reviewed literature.

Denial of the Sexual Offense

Despite the common belief that denial of the sexual offense places a sexual offender at increased risk of recidivism, and despite the common presence of this factor on many risk prediction tools (e.g., Epps, 1997; Prentky et al., 2000; Ross & Loss, 1991), the research to date does not support this view. In fact, both the juvenile and adult literatures indicate that denial itself does not place a sexual offender at greater risk of recidivism (Hanson & Bussiere, 1998; Kahn & Chambers, 1991; Langstrom & Grann, 2000; Worling, 2002; Worling & Curwen, 2000; Worling & Langstrom, 2003). Denial of sexual offense may not predict recidivism, but assessing it should still specifically occur in individual cases. The motivation for denial may shed light on the personality dynamics of the offender (e.g., denial motivated out of shame for the offense or desire to avoid consequences, or true "denial" as a defense mechanism), the availability of social systems that may support or undermine interventions (e.g., denial motivated by demands by parents to keep family secrets), or possible impact on the juvenile's readiness for treatment (e.g., juveniles who steadfastly maintain denial through the course of a sex-offender-specific treatment).

Offender History of Sexual Abuse Victimization

The common belief that juveniles who have themselves been sexually abused are at greater risk to become sexual offenders has a long history. Early research appeared to support this view (e.g., Becker, Kaplan, Cunningham-Rathner, & Kavoussi, 1986; Friedrich & Luecke, 1988; Longo, 1982; Prentky & Knight, 1993; Steen & Monnette, 1989). However, refutation of this assumption has occurred more recently in both the adolescent and adult literatures, which now clearly indicate that such a history does not place either juveniles or adults at greater risk for sexual misconduct (e.g., Hagan & Cho, 1996; Hanson & Bussiere, 1998; Rasmussen, 1999; Smith & Monastersky, 1986; Spaccarelli, Bowden, Coatsworth, & Kim, 1997; Worling & Curwen, 2000; Worling & Langstrom, 2003).

Histories of sexual victimization may not specifically predict future sexual perpetration, but when juveniles who have sexually offended present with histories of sexual victimization, it becomes critical to understand the impact of those experiences on them. Experiences of sexual victimization may shape the evolution of paraphilias or deviant sexual arousal, contribute to cognitive distortions that increase sexual offense risk, or result in vulnerabilities that may greatly complicate intervention efforts. Examples of such vulnerabilities can include emotional lability and explosiveness, difficulty tolerating trauma-related material, mistrust, maladaptive responses to stress, and other features of posttraumatic adaptation to sexual victimization. Research among juveniles who have committed severe acts of sexual or physical violence demonstrates an alarming prevalence of youths with histories of profound and chronic victimization.

The specific impact of a juvenile's own victimization on his or her functioning often provides important insights for understanding the dynamics of the sexual offending and for properly matching treatment and other intervention strategies. The impairment and fragility associated with a history of trauma may require treating some youthful offenders as trauma victims before confronting them with their own offense histories. Premature confrontation as an "offender" can result in exacerbation of psychiatric impairment without any progress in the offender's treatment. Some youths will require an approach that relies heavily on interpersonal engagement and interaction, with the goal of resocialization. Still others will have evolved characterological defenses that stem from their trauma and that will require extensive external behavioral controls, carefully monitored efforts at interpersonal engagement, and consistent confrontation about their defenses and offense behaviors.

Creating an Integrated Clinical Narrative and Assessment of Risk and Needs

The information gathered during forensic evaluation demands integration in a manner that communicates the youth's developmental pathway, the dynamics and function of the offense behavior, the risks of his or her continuing to offend under certain kinds of circumstances, and the specific links between proposed interventions and specific risk or protective factors. This formulation becomes the core of the forensic evaluation.

For example, Prentky (2002) has conceptualized one developmental pathway toward sexual offending in the form of aggressive rape. This conceptualization considers the presence and relative impact in the juvenile's developmental history of sexual abuse, physical abuse, emotional abuse, and caretaker instability. Sexual abuse can contribute to the evolution of deviant sexual arousal or compulsion, as well as to emotional detachment, that in turn contributes to impersonal sex. Physical abuse, emotional abuse, and caretaker instability contribute to the evolution of deficits of empathy and attachment that give rise to antisocial orientation and juvenile delinquency, negative masculinity, and alcohol abuse; these, in turn, contribute to impulsive antisocial behavior, including sexual conduct without mutuality or even consent. The experiences of maltreatment contribute to the evolution of deviant or explicitly coercive sexual fantasies that may be intensified by virtue of increased anger or stress.

This developmental pathway could not be adequately understood or identified by a "cookbook" checklist of risk factors. However, simply describing this developmental pathway would not describe those specific precipitants ("triggers") or situations in which an act of sexual coercion will most likely reoccur. Yet without an understanding of the developmental pathway, it becomes difficult to focus interventions on the most critical targets, for example, suppression or disruption of coercive sexual fantasy; addressing empathy deficits, attachment deficits, and cognitive distortions; or taking steps to resocialize the youth away from delinquent peers. Without an appropriate functional and clinical assessment, it would not be possible to adequately focus interventions on potentially complicating factors in individual cases, for example, verbal learning disability, cognitive limitation, or mood instability due to psychiatric disorder.

It is imperative that the evaluator provide a thoughtful integration of the information obtained in the course of forensic evaluation. The conceptualizing and integrating process requires careful balancing among data (observations and information), clinical inferences based on those data (clinical formulation and "narrative"), and forensic opinions that arise from the integration of clinical inferences (level and kind of risk, needs and prognosis for containment or intervention).

FACTORS IN ASSESSING DEGREE OF CONTAINMENT REQUIRED

Public Safety Needs

Public safety constitutes a major factor to be considered in the determination of the degree of containment required. A first principle involves consideration of accessibility and vulnerability of potential victims. To the degree that a juvenile offender maintains access to the potential victims, particularly early in treatment, risk of reoffense increases. For example, juveniles with a history of intrafamilial sexual offending of siblings retain access to victims if they live at home during the course of treatment. Risk also increases with access to a vulnerable potential victim.

Another important containment factor involves available supervision. One must assess the availability and quality of supervision at any potential placement, as well as considering the circumstances that surround the prior sexual offense. This assessment includes specific consideration of factors regarding the perpetration of the prior offense despite potential risk of detection, such as: (1) the setting of the offense (offender's home, victim's home, school setting, public place); (2) the presence or absence of others during the offense; and (3) perpetration despite clear risk of detection. Such an assessment should include official and unofficial supervision, ranging from conditions of suspended sentences, continuances without findings, probation, and familial or parental supervision, as well. Consideration of these factors can provide valuable information regarding the need to adjust the consistency or intensity of supervision required to forestall reoffense while interventions work to lower risks.

The availability of sex-offender-specific treatment is another factor worthy of consideration. Quality specialized intervention programs may not exist in the community. Programs that can accommodate juveniles with cognitive or psychological impairments may not exist. Therefore, the need for specialized kinds of intervention programs may at times dictate placement. A juvenile who might otherwise have remained in the community for treatment might require placement in a residential treatment facility due to a lack of available outpatient services. Although not ideal, both the need for treatment and the potential risks posed to the public by a lack of treatment may justify the additional expense and the more restrictive environment of a residential or secure treatment program. On the other hand, institutionalization of youths should be avoided whenever possible to avoid the negative consequences of institutional care and forced interaction with other delinquent or troubled youths.

Containment Needs Required to Implement Treatment

Efficacy of treatment can interact with several factors, including the capacity for the juvenile's family or caregivers to (1) provide adequate structure and supervision, (2) support treatment, and (3) participate in interventions themselves. Simply providing transportation to and from treatment sessions does not qualify as sufficient support to assist with potential therapeutic gains. In fact, the most effective treatment to date for juvenile sex offenders involves multiple treatment interventions, including individual and group therapy, family therapy, interventions at school and at home, and the active simultaneous involvement of several systems (e.g., family, court, social services). Two specific models of treatment involving this approach are multisystemic therapy (MST; Borduin, Henggeler, Blaske, & Stein, 1990; Henggeler, Schoenwald, Borduin, Rowland, & Cunningham, 1998; Lipsey & Wilson, 1998) and multidimensional treatment foster care (MTFC; Chamberlain & Reid, 1998).

The capacity for peers to support changes from treatment is another factor related to containment needs. Shifts in attitudes, behaviors, perceptions of the self, and views of others coincide with benefits of treatment. A great need exists for toleration of these changes and support from both family and peers. Research with other forms of treatment indicates that treatment gains erode if not supported by peers.

Ready access to materials that reinforce deviance constitutes another important containment factor. Attention to the role of such materials in developing and maintaining deviant sexual interest or arousal is essential. For example, the roles of pornographic magazines, Internet pornography, and pornographic telephone services should be assessed and explored during treatment recommendation phases of an evaluation. Limiting access to many types of materials that may reinforce deviance can prove difficult, although access to such materials during treatment may undermine potential treatment outcome. The level of containment may need to increase should problems in limiting access to these materials occur.

The ability to tolerate stresses associated with treatment constitutes another factor related to containment needs. Although the quality of support from family or other caregivers will vary on a case-by-case basis, specific consideration of the juvenile's capacity to cope with stress becomes essential. Whereas the increased structure and milieu of a residential program may provide the needed additional support for some juveniles, removal from the preexisting support of family or peers may increase the level of stress for others. It therefore becomes necessary to consider stress tolerance on an individual basis and to consider placement accordingly.

FACTORS TO WEIGH IN MAKING INTERVENTION RECOMMENDATIONS

Key Factors Related to the Offender

Those offenders with extensive histories of sexual offenses and nonsexual misconduct will likely warrant more focal treatment for their sexual misconduct, in addition to more generalized treatment for their delinquent behavior. Generally speaking, sexual-offender-specific treatment involves extensive education and focus on specific variables related to the sexual assault or dysfunctional response cycle, and the treatment of more generalized delinquency includes specific interventions related to problem solving, social and interpersonal skills training, and cognitive behavior modification. Although there is clearly overlap between these modes of treatment, the structure, scope, and application of these treatment variables will vary according to need, as will the successive stages and focus of treatment.

The assessment of a juvenile's response to prior interventions becomes another crucial factor in making recommendations for future interventions. Such data yield valuable guidance by revealing

what interventions have and have not been attempted in the past, what has proven helpful, and what has failed. Such data should become integral in formulating plans that avoid replicating failures of the past while capitalizing on aspects of even partially successful interventions. This would allow consideration of alternative modes of intervention to maximize effectiveness. Consideration of options for the potential setting for treatment should occur in light of past intervention successes and failures. Consideration of placement in more structured settings with a capacity for more stringent supervision should follow prior attempts at community-based treatment that have failed.

Potential treatment complications that are linked to special needs, including developmental disabilities, mental retardation, learning disabilities, vulnerabilities stemming from offenders' own traumatic victimization, and/or psychiatric illness, also require consideration. This problem is somewhat familiar in the implementation of effective treatment for juveniles, as learning disabilities, psychiatric comorbidity, substance abuse, and lower than average intelligence occur more commonly among juvenile delinquents than among the general juvenile population.

Should any of these potentially compromising conditions exist, treatment modalities must accommodate the nature of the juvenile's potential impairment and particular level of functioning. The evaluations conducted and recommendations offered as part of the JSO evaluation should make such information readily available. For example, standard cognitive-behavioral or group treatment normally used with sex offenders would likely not prove useful for a cognitively impaired juvenile. Rather, inclusion of specialized adjustments to the treatment plans for such individuals must occur. Amenability to treatment and factors related to public safety, such as degree of dangerousness and risk of recidivism, and variables regarding the degree of containment require consideration. Please see the relevant sections in this chapter that specifically refer to these topics.

Factors in Assessing Amenability to Intervention

Developmental and clinical factors that should be considered in determining need for specialized JSO treatment, the type of intervention to be used, and the prognosis for intervention include:

- The developmental history of nonsexual and sexual misconduct
- The known or acknowledged frequency, versatility, compulsiveness, or aggression that characterize the sexual misconduct
- Evidence of evolving pedophilia, paraphilia, or other deviant sexual arousal
- The likelihood that the juvenile will desist without specialized intervention
- History of response to any prior attempted interventions that targeted misconduct and assessment of whether these prior attempted interventions were appropriate
- Treatment complications arising from limited cognition, learning disability, or other neurological factors
- Treatment complications arising from psychiatric impairments
- Evidence of emerging personality disorder, especially if psychopathy
- Capacities to tolerate stress, frustration, ambiguity
- Capacity and desire for age-appropriate and prosocial peer relationships
- Degree of support of family or other close supportive figures for intervention efforts

Assess motivation or capacity for change through investigation of factors such as:

- Capacity to acknowledge key elements of the sexual misconduct
- Capacity for victim empathy
- Capacity to recognize the impact of the sexual offense on persons other than the victim
- Demonstrated ability to comply with expectations associated with the proposed treatment
- Demonstrated ability to work with prior service providers toward goals
- Demonstrated ability to benefit the kinds of modalities of treatment available for the juvenile

Key Factors Related to Treatment Implementation

The availability of sex-offender-specific treatment at the degree of containment recommended in response to both public safety factors and the degree of structure required to implement treatment demand critical consideration. Although public safety and the implementation of treatment link directly, they deserve individual consideration. Public safety must take precedence not only for protective purposes but also because potentially successful treatment cannot occur under conditions in which risk of recidivism places public safety at risk.

The quality of sex-offender-specific treatment constitutes another important factor. Treatment programs not only differ in orientation but also vary widely in quality and sophistication. A decision to pursue poor-quality sex-offender-specific treatment may actually result in potential additional risks. These risks include: (1) the likelihood that the treatment will prove ineffective; (2) increasing risk of reoffense by creating undue levels of stress without adequate support or by placing a youth with a less established pattern of sexual misconduct in a peer group with more entrenched delinquent orientations; (3) failure to consider the impact of sex offender treatment on complicating comorbid conditions such as posttraumatic stress disorder or depression; (4) creating the illusion of having an effective intervention in place, resulting in a lowering of vigilance by those involved in the supervision of the youth. Treatment providers will most likely not acknowledge that their programs have poor track records, so detecting poor programs will prove difficult for evaluators unfamiliar with the program. However, a poor quality program jeopardizes public safety. In such cases public interests may actually dictate opting for alternatives to specialized sex offender treatment, rather than poor-quality sex offender treatment.

Consideration should also be paid to the potential risk involved in the affiliation with other offenders to a juvenile placed in a juvenile justice facility. An individualized risk-benefit analysis should focus on making an informed decision regarding this risk. The analysis should consider the individual vulnerabilities of the juvenile, the juvenile's level of naiveté versus "streetwise" sophistication, indications of past peer influence, and the juvenile's prior level of involvement with the legal system.

Public Safety Needs

Accessibility to and vulnerability of victim types is of primary concern when considering the degree of containment required for a JSO. Risk of recidivism increases as the pool of potential victims increases and as vulnerability of victims increases. For example, pure incest offenders have less recidivism risk for several reasons, including the size of the potential victim pool. If the juvenile truly offends only within his or her family, that fact limits the number of potential victims, and appropriate precautions can ensure a higher level of safety for those at risk. If, however, past victims include strangers or acquaintances, then public safety risks increase because virtually any stranger or acquaintance with certain demographic or physical features presents a risk.

Similarly, vulnerable victims such as preschool children or the mentally retarded, by definition, more easily become targeted and victimized than the general population. When sexual offenders have a history of targeting such vulnerable victims, they may take the opportunity to do so again in the future. Further, an increase in risk of reoffense may exist because the sexual offender presumes that potential detection is lessened by virtue of the victim's greater deficits in reporting.

The degree of force used in prior sexual and nonsexual offenses also constitutes a public factor. The use of coercion, threats or weaponry, gratuitous or eroticized violence, and the degree of physical damage inflicted on a victim also indicate increased risk by exemplifying the potential to which the juvenile may go during the commission of an offense. A high risk of danger to the public warrants increased confinement, even when only a single documented incident of abuse has occurred.

SPECIAL ISSUES IN REPORTING RESULTS OF JUVENILE SEXUAL OFFENDER EVALUATIONS

Several issues commonly arise related to communicating the results of JSO evaluations. Perhaps the most important reporting issue involves consistently distinguishing among data, inferences, and opinions. For example, a self-report from a juvenile that says that he becomes sexually aroused by preschoolers constitutes data from which an inference regarding development of a deviant arousal pattern follows logically. Such an inference regarding development of a deviant arousal pattern forms

part of the foundation for an opinion that the juvenile has an elevated risk for sexual reoffense. However, evaluators must clearly communicate the distinctions inherent in the findings and opinions because consumers of the reports, particularly in legal settings, should know which primary data led to the inferences and opinions. The links among data, inferences drawn from those data, and opinions based on inferences demand clear articulation. Ideally, the report should avoid clinical terminology and other jargon, but if it is used, it is important to define such terms for the nonclinician reader. In addition, evaluators must report any significant limitations inherent in their data or methods. For example, data regarding sexual misconduct that come only from the self-report of the juvenile or conclusions drawn from tools or instruments that lack empirically established norms constitute important reportable limitations. Contradictory or ambiguous data require fair presentation. Evaluators who rely on one version of events rather than another need to justify their choice without merely making a raw appeal citing "credibility."

When key facts remain ambiguous or in dispute, or when reasonable alternatives to understanding the data or drawing inferences exist, the evaluator must fairly characterize them and their implications. For example, when a juvenile acts hastily in committing a sexual offense, that behavior may mean that the juvenile acted *impulsively*, but it may also mean that he acted *opportunistically* in the context of a more deliberate effort to gain proximity to a victim. The fact that a much younger victim was selected may constitute evidence of an evolving pedophilia, or it may also represent a less discriminating effort to simply gain access to a vulnerable victim in the absence of specifically pedophilic interests.

Evaluators must use caution with the term *denial* when characterizing juveniles who do not fully endorse allegations made by others. The terms *denial* or *in denial* have a technical meaning that refers to a specific defense mechanism in which the juvenile places the recollection, experience, or sense of personal involvement in the sexual offense beyond conscious awareness. Juveniles who do not fully endorse allegations made by others may experience "denial," but they may also simply lie, or they may endorse a partial truth. Evaluators must carefully distinguish among these possibilities and justify their inferences on the basis of clinical or other data, characterizing the juvenile as "in denial" only when there is a sufficient basis that this clinical inference is justified.

Risks and benefits constitute an important consideration when making recommendations. For example, recommending that a juvenile receive treatment in a residential setting may result in more reliable attendance at treatment, greater supervision to prevent reoffense, and more attention to comorbid conditions. On the other hand, few studies suggest that residential treatment constitutes a particularly effective form of intervention for juveniles, as the juvenile's peer group during the period of institutionalization will generally consist of peers who are more impaired and delinquent than most youths in the community. Residential settings also provide no guarantee that sexual misconduct will not reoccur inside the setting. Recommending a "juvenile sex offender group" for a youth who has not clearly evolved a pattern of sexual offense may provide psychoeducation about sexuality and sexual offenses, but it also may tend to socialize participants to think of themselves as "sexual offenders" and expose them to peers with more entrenched sexual offense behaviors.

Providing specific recommendations that take into account the realities of available services is of great importance in legal settings. Making recommendations for sexual offender treatment when none is available or recommending juvenile justice management when those authorities do not have appropriate interventions or resources will not prove useful. Evaluators may describe optimal recommendations, but they should also prepare to describe what might work (although not optimal) or what might prove ineffective or of poor quality (although available).

Finally, evaluators should take care about addressing ultimate legal issues. Just as evaluators should never offer opinions about "innocence or guilt" to courts when the allegations are still in dispute, evaluators should show equal caution about recommending for or against commitment of the juvenile to juvenile justice settings. The judicial decision about whether to commit or incarcerate an adjudicated offender also requires decisions that balance the liberty of the juvenile against the needs for community safety, the need

to impose punishment against the need to provide treatment, or considerations about the adequacy or inadequacy of services in the community or in juvenile justice settings. These particular "balancing" decisions are not clinical decisions but societal and moral decisions that are properly the domain of the court, rather than of an evaluating clinician. The evaluator should simply describe the risks and benefits associated with the most likely options available to the court.

References

Atcheson, J. D., & Williams, D. C. (1954). A study of juvenile sex offenders. *American Journal of Psychiatry, 111*, 366–370.

Becker, J. V., Kaplan, M. S., Cunningham-Rathner, J., & Kavoussi, R. (1986). Characteristics of adolescent incest sexual perpetrators: Preliminary findings. *Journal of Consulting and Clinical Psychology, 1*, 85–97.

Borduin, C. M., Henggeler, S. W., Blaske, D. M., & Stein, R. J. (1990). Multisystemic treatment of adolescent sexual offenders. *International Journal of Offender Therapy and Comparative Criminology, 34*(2), 105–113.

Borum, R., Bartel, P., & Forth, A. (2003). *Manual for the Structured Assessment of Violence Risk in Youth (SAVRY)*. Tampa: University of South Florida.

Bourke, M. L., & Donohue, B. (1996). Assessment and treatment of juvenile sex offenders: An empirical review. *Journal of Child Sexual Abuse, 5*(1), 47–70.

Cellini, H. R. (1995). Assessment and treatment of the adolescent sexual offender. In B. K. Schwartz & H. R. Cellini (Eds.), *The sex offender: Vol. 1. Corrections, treatment, and legal practice* (pp. 6.1–6.12). Kingston, NJ: Civic Research Institute.

Center for Sex Offender Management. (1999). *Understanding juvenile sexual offending behavior: Emerging research, treatment approaches and management practices*. Silver Spring, MD: Author.

Chamberlain, P., & Reid, J. B. (1998). Comparison of two community alternatives to incarceration for chronic juvenile offenders. *Journal of Consulting and Clinical Psychology, 66*(4), 624–633.

Douglas, J. E., Burgess, A. W., Burgess, A. G., & Ressler, R. K. (1992). *Crime classification manual*. New York: Lexington Books.

Epperson, D. L., Kaul, J. D., Huot, S. J., Hesselton, D., Alexander, W., & Goldman, R. (2000). *The

Minnesota Sex Offender Screening Tool—Revised (MnSOST-R). St. Paul, MN: Minnesota Department of Correction.

Epps, K. J. (1997). Managing risk. In M. S. Hoghughi, S. R. Bhate, & F. Graham (Eds.), *Working with sexually abusive adolescents* (pp. 35–51). London: Sage.

Forth, A. E., & Burke, H. C. (1998). Psychopathy in adolescence: Assessment, violence, and developmental precursors. In D. Cooke, A. E. Forth, & R. D. Hare (Eds.), *Psychopathy: Theory, research, and implications for society* (pp. 205–229). Dordrecht, Netherlands: Kluwer.

Forth, A. E., Kosson, D., & Hare, R. D. (2003). *The psychopathy checklist: Youth version*. Toronto, Ontario, Canada: Multi-Health Systems.

Friedrich, W., & Luecke, W. (1988). Young school-aged sexually aggressive children. *Professional Psychology: Research and Practice, 19,* 155–164.

Hagan, M. P., & Cho, M. E. (1996). A comparison of treatment outcomes between adolescent rapists and child sexual offenders. *International Journal of Offender Therapy and Comparative Criminology, 40,* 113–122.

Hagan, M. P., & Gust-Brey, K. L. (2000). A ten-year longitudinal study of adolescent perpetrators of sexual assault against children. *Journal of Offender Rehabilitation, 31*(1/2), 117–126.

Hanson, R. K. (1997). *The development of a brief actuarial risk assessment scale for sexual offense recidivism* (User Report No. 1997–04). Ottawa, Ontario: Department of the Solicitor General of Canada.

Hanson, R. K. (1998). What do we know about sex offender risk assessment? *Psychology, Public Policy and the Law, 4*(1/2), 50–72.

Hanson, R. K. (2000). *Risk assessment*. Beaverton, OR: Association for the Treatment of Sexual Abusers.

Hanson, R. K., & Bussiere, M. T. (1998). Predicting relapse: A meta-analysis of sexual offender recidivism studies. *Journal of Consulting and Clinical Psychology, 66*(2), 348–362.

Hanson, R. K., & Thornton, D. (2000). Improving risk assessments for sexual offenders: A comparison of three actuarial scales. *Law and Human Behavior, 24*(1), 119–136.

Harris, G. T., Rice, M. E., & Quinsey, V. L. (1994). Psychopathy as a taxon: Evidence that psychopaths are a discrete class. *Journal of Consulting and Clinical Psychology, 62,* 387–397.

Henggeler, S. W., Schoenwald, S. K., Borduin, C. M., Rowland, M. D., & Cunningham, P. E. (1998).

Multisystemic treatment of antisocial behavior in children and adolescents. New York: Guilford.

Hunter, J. A., & Figueredo, A. J. (1999). Factors associated with the treatment compliance in a population of juvenile sexual offenders. *Sexual Abuse: A Journal of Research and Treatment, 11*(1), 49–67.

Kahn, T. J., & Chambers, H. J. (1991). Assessing reoffense risk with juvenile sexual offenders. *Child Welfare, 70,* 333–345.

Knight, R. A., & Prentky, R. (1993). Exploring characteristics for classifying juvenile sex offenders. In H. E. Barbaree, W. L. Marshall, & S. M. Hudson (Eds.), *The juvenile sex offender* (pp. 45–83). New York: Guilford.

Knight, R. A., Prentky, R., & Cerce, D. D. (1994). The development, reliability, and validity of an inventory for the multidimensional assessment of sex and aggression. *Criminal Justice and Behavior, 21*(1) 72–94.

Lab, S. P., Shields, G., & Schondel, C. (1993). An evaluation of juvenile sexual offender treatment. *Crime and Delinquency, 39,* 543–553.

Langstrom, N., & Grann, M. (2000). Risk for criminal recidivism among young sex offenders. *Journal of Interpersonal Violence, 15,* 855–871.

Lipsey, M. W., & Wilson, D. B. (1998). Effective intervention for serious juvenile offenders: A synthesis of research. In R. Loeber & D. P. Farrington (Eds.), *Serious and violent juvenile offenders: Risk factors and successful interventions* (pp. 313–345). Thousand Oaks, CA: Sage.

Longo, R. E. (1982). Sexual learning and experience among adolescent sexual offenders. *International Journal of Offender Therapy and Comparative Criminology, 26,* 235–241.

Medoff, D. (2000a). *Juvenile sex offenders and the role of the Massachusetts Sex Offender Registry*. Boston: Massachusetts Continuing Legal Education.

Medoff, D. (2000b). Sexual psychopaths and beyond: Massachusetts' new sex offender law and registry. *Sex Offender Law Report, 1*(6), 94.

Prentky, R. A. (2002, September). *Developments in theoretical models for coercive sexual behavior*. Paper presented at the Conference of the International Association for the Treatment of Sexual Offenders, Vienna, Austria.

Prentky, R. A., Harris, B., Frizzell, K., & Righthand, S. (2000). An actuarial procedure for assessing risk with juvenile sex offenders. *Sexual Abuse: A Journal of Research and Treatment, 12*(2), 71–93.

Prentky, R. A., & Knight, R. A. (1993). Age of onset of sexual assault: Criminal and life history correlates. In G. C. Nagayama Hall, R. Hirschman, J. R. Graham, & M. S. Zaragoza (Eds.), *Sexual aggression: Issues in etiology, assessment, and treatment* (pp. 43–62). Washington, DC: Taylor & Francis.

Quinsey, V. L., Harris, G. T., Rice, M. E., & Cormier, C. A. (1998). *Violent offenders: Appraising and managing risk.* Washington, DC: American Psychological Association.

Rasmussen, L. A. (1999). Factors related to recidivism among juvenile sexual offenders. *Sexual Abuse: A Journal of Research and Treatment, 11*(1), 69–85.

Righthand, S., & Welch, C. (2001). *Juveniles who have sexually offended: A review of the professional literature.* Washington, DC: United States Department of Justice, Office of Juvenile Justice and Delinquency Prevention.

Ross, J., & Loss, P. (1991). Assessment of the juvenile sex offender. In G. D. Ryan & S. L. Lane (Eds.), *Juvenile sexual offending: Causes, consequences, and correction* (pp. 199–251). Lexington, MA: Lexington Books.

Rubinstein, M., Yeager, C. A., Goodstein, C., & Lewis, D. O. (1993). Sexually assaultive male juveniles: A follow-up. *American Journal of Psychiatry, 150*(2), 262–265.

Schram, D. D., Milloy, C. D., & Rowe, W. E. (1991). *Juvenile sex offenders: A follow-up study of reoffense behavior.* Olympia, WA: Washington State Institute for Public Policy.

Sipe, R., Jensen, E. L., & Everett, R. S. (1998). Adolescent sexual offenders grown up: Recidivism in young adulthood. *Criminal Justice and Behavior, 25*(1), 109–124.

Smith, G., & Fischer, L. (1999). Assessment of juvenile sexual offenders: Reliability and validity of the Abel Assessment for Interest in Paraphilias. *Sexual Abuse: A Journal of Research and Treatment, 11*(3), 207–216.

Smith, W., & Monastersky, C. (1986). Assessing juvenile sex offenders' risk for reoffending. *Criminal Justice and Behavior, 13*, 115–140.

Spaccarelli, S., Bowden, B., Coatsworth, D., & Kim, S. (1997). Psychosocial correlates of male sexual aggression in a chronic delinquent sample. *Criminal Justice and Behavior, 24*(1), 71–95.

Steen, C., & Monnette, B. (1989). *Treating adolescent sex offenders in the community.* Springfield, IL: Thomas.

United States Department of Justice, Office of Juvenile Justice and Delinquency Prevention. (1999). *Juvenile arrests 1998.* Washington, DC: Author.

Ward, T., McCormack, J., & Hudson, S. M. (1997). Sexual offenders' perceptions of their intimate relationships. *Sexual Abuse: A Journal of Research and Treatment, 9*, 57–74.

Weinrott, M. R. (1996). *Juvenile sexual aggression: A critical review.* Boulder, CO: Regents of the University of Colorado, Institute of Behavioral Sciences, Center for the Study and Prevention of Violence.

Worling, J. R. (2000). *Putting practice into research: Typology of adolescent male sexual offenders with implications for etiology, risk prediction, and treatment.* Paper presented at the Annual Research and Treatment Conference of the Association for the Treatment of Sexual Abusers, San Diego, CA.

Worling, J. R. (2001). Personality-based typology of adolescent male sexual offenders: Differences in recidivism rates, victim-selection characteristics, and personal victimization histories. *Sexual Abuse: A Journal of Research and Treatment, 13*(3), 149–166.

Worling, J. R. (2002). Assessing risk of sexual assault recidivism with adolescent sexual offenders. In M. C. Calder (Ed.), *Young people who sexually abuse: Building the evidence base for your practice* (pp. 365–375). Lyme Regis, UK: Russell House.

Worling, J. R., & Curwen, T. (2000). Adolescent sexual offender recidivism: Success of specialized treatment and implications for risk prediction. *Child Abuse and Neglect, 24*, 965–982.

Worling, J. R., & Curwen, T. (2001). Estimate of Risk of Adolescent Sexual Offense Recidivism (The ERASOR—Version 2.0). In M. C. Calder (Ed.), *Juveniles and children who sexually abuse: Frameworks for assessment* (pp. 372–397). Lyme Regis, UK: Russell House.

Worling, J. R., & Langstrom, N. (2003). Assessment of criminal recidivism risk with adolescents who have offended sexually: A review. *Trauma, Violence, and Abuse, 4*(4), 341–362.

22

Assessing Childhood Trauma and Developmental Factors as Mitigation in Capital Cases

Alan M. Goldstein
Naomi E. Goldstein
Rachel Kalbeitzer

Prior chapters have considered the basis for and process of assessing the impact of physical and sexual abuse, parental neglect, domestic violence, divorce, and special educational problems on children and adolescents. This chapter addresses the role of these and other forms of childhood trauma and developmental difficulties as mitigating factors that a jury may be asked to consider when rendering a verdict in a capital case.

We first consider the relevance of the childhood history of defendants in capital murder cases to the determination of sentencing. The history of the death penalty and recent facts and figures are briefly reviewed. We discuss the roles of the psychologist, whether a child-clinical, clinical, developmental, family, neuropsychologist, or forensic psychologist; because death penalty cases allow for a consideration of many factors, such as developmental difficulties, childhood trauma, poverty, and death of a parent, the role of the expert is *not* limited solely to those psychologists with specialized forensic training. Next, we briefly review decision making in capital cases, including the relevance of both statutory and nonstatutory mitigating factors

related to the defendant's childhood history. We present relevant case law and assessment methods. This chapter concludes with a consideration of specific childhood traumas and developmental factors relevant to expert testimony in such cases.

RELEVANCE OF CHILDHOOD TRAUMA AND DEVELOPMENTAL FACTORS TO JUVENILE AND ADULT DEATH PENALTY CASES

John Doe, a somewhat intellectually limited 24-year-old man, was pressured by an older acquaintance to participate in a robbery of an armored van picking up cash from a bank. Although initially reluctant to do so (Doe had no prior criminal record), he agreed to participate. He claimed that his accomplice had threatened to kill him and members of his family if he refused to participate. In addition, Doe had undergone a recent psychiatric hospitalization, experiencing bizarre symptoms involving hallucinations, delusions, and magical thinking, and he ascribed mystical powers to his accomplice. During the commission of the crime, an armed guard and the accomplice exchanged gunfire. A bullet struck a 14-year-old girl, instantly killing her. The accomplice was shot dead as well. Doe had fired his weapon once, hitting no one. However, because he participated in a felony in which someone other than another participant was killed, he faced murder charges. The bank held federal insurance, making this a federal death penalty case. The facts of the case speak for themselves: Doe participated in the commission of a felony; a teenage girl was killed; and Doe had an opportunity to escape before any shots were fired. How does Doe's childhood history become relevant? It certainly does not alter the facts of this case.

A sentence of death constitutes a unique, irreversible punishment. In *Furman v. Georgia* (1972), the United States Supreme Court set aside the death penalty as unconstitutional; Justice Brennan, in his concurring opinion, referred to the death penalty as "the ultimate sanction" and "an awesome punishment" and stated that such cases should be treated as "a class apart." Because it is "totally irrevocable," wrote Justice Stewart, death penalty cases must be treated differently from other criminal prosecutions, in a manner that avoids capriciousness and arbitrariness. Four years later, the Supreme Court, in *Gregg v. Georgia* (1976), accepted states' rewritten death penalty statutes. The court noted that objections raised in *Furman* had been overcome because now, "The defendant is accorded substantial latitude as to the types of evidence that he may introduce [as mitigation]." The defendant could introduce a wide range of mitigating evidence to convince the jury that this ultimate punishment was not appropriate. Information relevant to the crime, as well as "the character or record of the defendant," could guide jurors in their decision making. Two years later, the Supreme Court ruled that states could not prevent capital defendants from introducing "individualized" evidence regarding mitigation (*Lockett v. Ohio*, 1978). They opined, "The limited range of mitigating circumstances which may be considered by the sentencer under the Ohio statute is incompatible with the Eighth and Fourteenth Amendments." Thus this case opened the door for the introduction of "any aspect of the defendant's char-

acter or record and any of the circumstances of the offence that the defendant proffers as a basis for a sentence less than death" (*Lockett v. Ohio*, 1978).

These cases, among others reviewed here, changed the way juries reached decisions on sentencing in capital cases. They can now consider mitigating evidence on an almost unlimited number of factors, including childhood trauma and developmental difficulties. Experts can now educate jurors about the effects of such experiences on adult intellectual, emotional, and moral development, judgment, impulse control, empathy, acquiescence to authority, suggestibility, and a wide range of other factors the jury might consider significant during deliberations. Via expert testimony, Mr. Doe was given the opportunity to explain how his background may have contributed to his role in this capital murder.

In this specific capital case, after the prosecutor reviewed the report submitted by the forensic psychologist, the defendant was offered a plea of life without the possibility of parole. Rather than risk a trial that could end with a death sentence, Mr. Doe accepted this plea bargain at the advice of his attorney.

JUVENILES AND THE DEATH PENALTY

According to Streib (2004), the first execution of a juvenile occurred in Massachusetts in 1642. Since then, over 365 individuals who were found guilty of capital murder committed when they were juveniles have been put to death in the United States. The United States Supreme Court in *Stanford v. Kentucky* (1989) ruled that the execution of juveniles age 16 or 17 did not represent a violation of the Eighth Amendment (1 year earlier, the Court had rejected Oklahoma's law permitting execution of juveniles 15 years old at the time they committed murder; *Thompson v. Oklahoma*, 1988). Until recently, each state had established its own minimum age at which the death penalty may apply. Nineteen states and the federal government had elected not to pursue the death penalty against those under the age of 18. Five states had set the threshold at age 17 (Florida, Georgia, New Hampshire, North Carolina, and Texas), whereas 14 states (including Alabama, Delaware, Kentucky, Louisiana, Michigan, Nevada, Pennsylvania, Utah, and Virginia) established age 16 as the legally sanctioned minimum age to seek execution (Streib, 2004). However, the U.S. Supreme Court recently ruled, by a 5 to 4 vote in the case of *Simmons v. Roper* (No. 03-0633, 2003) that the execution of juveniles is a violation of the Eighth Amendment, finding that such executions represent cruel and unusual punishment.

The defendant, Christopher Simmons, was 17 when he committed a capital offense. Nine months later, he was sentenced to death. However, the Missouri Supreme Court commuted his sentence, altering it to life without parole. The Missouri appeals court argued that exposing juveniles to the possibility of capital punishment was no longer viewed favorably in this country and that the execution of juveniles might offend the evolving standard of human decency, describing this standard as "fluid and evolving." The Missouri court raised questions based on juveniles' judgment, reasoning, and decision-making skills. In part, the appeals court relied on the written majority decision of the U.S. Supreme Court forbidding the use of capital punishment for those found to be mentally retarded (*Atkins v. Virginia*, 2002). In March 2005, the United States Supreme Court upheld the Missouri Supreme Court's decision in *Simmons v. Roper* (No. 03–0633). It banned the imposition of the death penalty for those under the age of 18 at the time of their crime. Writing for the majority, Justice Kennedy reasoned that the majority of states reject the concept of a juvenile death penalty and "the consistency in the trend toward abolition of the practice—provide sufficient evidence that today our society views juveniles... as 'categorically less culpable than the average criminal.'" Furthermore, he wrote, "Retribution is not proportional if the law's most severe penalty is imposed on one whose culpability or blameworthiness is diminished, to a substantial degree, by reason of youth and immaturity."

At the time of that decision, there were approximately 72 juveniles on death rows awaiting execution, most in Texas and Florida. Since 1973, states had executed 22 juvenile murderers (approximately 2% of the total number of individuals executed since 1973; Streib, 2004). It is anticipated that those juveniles awaiting execution will have their death sentences commuted.

BRIEF HISTORY OF THE DEATH PENALTY IN CAPITAL CASES

Death penalty laws developed by the American colonies originated under English common law. Some colonies rejected the death penalty outright, whereas others did not limit execution to murder but included other offenses as capital crimes, such as adultery, buggery, witchcraft, treason, and rape (Costanzo & White, 1994). Racial disparities in the application of the death penalty became readily apparent. In Virginia, for example, 5 crimes were punishable by death if committed by Whites, but 70 crimes were considered capital offenses if committed by Blacks. The first documented execution in this country occurred in 1609, in Virginia, of a man found guilty of spying for Spain (Randa, 1997).

The Eighth Amendment, ratified in 1791, stated, "Excessive bail shall not be required, nor excessive fines imposed, nor cruel and unusual punishment inflicted." According to Latzer (1998), a legal expert on the Eighth Amendment, the cruel and unusual punishment clause "was *not* intended to abolish capital punishment" (p. 2). Rather, in part, it was designed "to forbid the infliction of more pain than was necessary to extinguish life" (p. 2). He reported that it was not until 1910 that the Supreme Court ruled in a noncapital case that some punishments were disproportionate to the offense (*Weems v. United States*, 1910). This reasoning "opened the door to arguments that the death penalty was disproportionate punishment, at least for some crimes—a view ultimately adopted by the Supreme Court in the 1970's" (Latzer, 1998, p. 2).

As was previously discussed, *Furman v. Georgia* (1972) set aside the death penalty as arbitrary and capricious. *Gregg v. Georgia* (1976) upheld that state's new death penalty formula, calling for specific mitigating and aggravating factors, a bifurcated trial (i.e., separate trial and penalty phases), and the weighing of the mitigating and aggravating factors by the jury to determine the sentence. The first execution following restoration of the death penalty option occurred shortly thereafter (*Gilmore v. Utah*, 1976).

FACTS AND FIGURES

At present, 38 states and the federal government have death penalty statutes. According to the Death Penalty Information Center Web site (DPIC, 2004), at the end of 2003, over 3,400 individuals sat on death rows. Since 1976, 929 people have been put to death. At present, lethal injection is the most common means of execution, followed by electrocution, the gas chamber, hanging, and firing squad (DPIC, 2004). Of those executed, 58% were White, 34% Black, 6% Hispanic, and 2% Native American or Asian. "Almost all capital cases (81%) involve white victims, even though, nationally, only 50% of murder victims are white" (DPIC, 2004).

ROLES OF THE PSYCHOLOGIST IN DEATH PENALTY CASES

In a capital case, much like any other criminal case, a number of roles for qualified experts exist. The trial judge qualifies the expert on the *specific* topic for which testimony is to be offered. Roles include that of consultant, expert witness (i.e., on a specific topic or on the specific defendant), and expert in postconviction relief cases.

Consultant

Few attorneys have the academic background necessary to familiarize themselves, in depth, with those psychological issues and concepts likely to emerge in death penalty cases. Psychologists often possess the background, experience, skills, training, and knowledge to serve as consultants to attorneys.

A review of birth, school, mental health, and employment records by a psychological consultant may provide hypotheses for attorneys to explore with their expert witnesses, including the need to administer other tests or to interview specific third parties. Such review may suggest questions for inquiry by the attorney on both direct and cross-examinations. A consultant's review of the expert witness's (and opposing witness's) curriculum vitae, test data, interview notes, and report may significantly assist the attorney in preparing to question these experts in court. Familiarizing and providing the attorney with relevant profes-

sional literature may serve to educate him or her about significant mitigating factors in the case, thereby contributing to his or her effectiveness as counsel.

Expert Witness

As in any litigation, both sides in a case may retain psychologists as experts, with the expectation that they will ultimately testify. There are two types of expert witnesses: (1) those who educate a jury through testimony about a topic and (2) those who educate the jury about a specific defendant.

The "topic" expert has developed, through research, teaching, and/or publications, an expertise in a specific subject area (i.e., ADHD, fetal alcohol syndrome, or child sexual abuse) and will be called to the witness stand to "teach" the jury about this topic. Such testimony constitutes a guided "lecture" designed to provide information that members of the jury would not ordinarily possess and to correct misperceptions about the topic of interest (e.g., "If she were really that badly battered by her husband, she would have just left him"). When the jury must deliberate the sentence, members will need preparation with state-of-the-art information about the relevant topic.

The expert who testifies about a specific defendant will have conducted a comprehensive evaluation of that person (as described later in this chapter). The defendant and others who know the defendant will have participated in extensive interviewing and appropriate psychological testing. A record review will also have followed. Testimony will most likely consider *all* aspects of the defendant's life, from birth to the crime itself. The review will most likely focus on complications at birth (e.g., prematurity, fetal alcohol syndrome, anoxia), family background (e.g., any and all forms of abuse, poverty, exposure to domestic violence), and developmental problems (e.g., mental retardation, learning disability, undiagnosed or misdiagnosed mental disorder). When the jury begins deliberation, they will have expert information about a defendant that they otherwise most likely would have lacked. Possessing such information about a defendant's background not only satisfies the requirements of the law but also places the jury in a more knowledgeable position to decide whether a defendant's behavior and situation qualifies as "death-worthy."

Expert in Postconviction Relief Cases

In postconviction release cases, the defendant was previously found guilty of capital murder and sentenced to death. An appeal filed at the state or federal level claims either judicial error or ineffectiveness of counsel. Experts may review trial transcripts (especially previous expert testimony), test data, notes, and reports of the prior experts in the case and may also evaluate the defendant. A report is typically submitted to the court for consideration as part of its review in deciding whether to grant a new trial (or a new penalty phase of the trial). Most frequently, counsel will ask experts to evaluate and critique the work of the professional colleagues who served as experts at trial to determine the degree to which their evaluation conformed to the standard of practice in the field.

HOW A CAPITAL TRIAL IS DECIDED

Although the "ground rules" vary from state to state, a typical capital trial proceeds in bifurcated fashion; if the defendant is found guilty of capital murder, the penalty phase follows. In the penalty phase, experts may offer testimony consistent with rules of evidence in that state (or, if in federal court, with Federal Rules of Evidence) and with case law in that jurisdiction. During the penalty phase, experts may testify about the presence of *statutory* and *nonstatutory* mitigating factors.

Statutory Mitigating Factors

Statutory mitigating factors consist of a limited list of *specific* factors that appears in a state's death penalty statute, and such factors vary from state to state. Representative statutory mitigating factors include:

- Substantial impairment in the defendant's capacity to appreciate the wrongfulness of the act or to conform his or her behavior to the requirements of the law
- Finding that the defendant acted under severe mental or emotional disturbance at the time of the crime
- The defendant acted under duress at the time of the crime

- The defendant played a minor role in the commission of the crime
- The defendant has mental retardation or other significant cognitive impairment

Nonstatutory Mitigating Factors

Nonstatutory mitigating factors are frequently referred to as "Lockett factors," based on the previously cited *Lockett v. Ohio* case (1978). Because the penalty of death is irreversible, the presentation of mitigation findings must be individualized and relatively unrestricted. Consequently, the jury may hear any information regarding the defendant's background, history, characteristics, or circumstances of the offense.

Aggravating Factors

The prosecution must prove one or more aggravating factors, chosen from that state's death penalty statute. Representative aggravating factors include:

- The murder occurred during the act of committing or attempting to commit another (specified) felony
- The defendant had been under a sentence of death for a prior murder
- In committing the murder, the defendant put others at a grave risk
- The murder was heinous, cruel, or demonstrated a depraved indifference to human life
- The defendant committed the murder for pecuniary gain

The jury must decide whether the prosecution has established one or more of the claimed aggravating factors. *Typically*, the jury must agree unanimously that one or more of these factors exists beyond a reasonable doubt. If the prosecution does not prove aggravating factors, the defendant does not receive a death sentence. If established, the jurors next consider the mitigating factors presented to them. *Typically*, only one juror must find the presence of one or more mitigating factors by a preponderance of the evidence (i.e., more likely than not that it exists). If established, each juror weighs the mitigating against the aggravating factors. *Typically*, if all jurors find that the aggravating factor or factors outweigh the mitigating factor or factors, a verdict of death issues. Otherwise, the court will impose a lesser sentence. In some states, the jury must reach a unanimous decision for imposition of a death sentence. Prior to 2002, in some states, if the jury could not agree on a verdict, the trial judge would decide on the sentence. In still other states, the trial judge had the legal authority to overrule the jury's verdict. However, the U.S. Supreme Court, in *Ring v. Arizona* (2002), held that it is unconstitutional for anyone other than the jury to decide on the death penalty. If a death sentence were to be imposed by the trial judge, the Court reasoned that the defendant's right to a trial by jury, guaranteed under the Sixth Amendment, would be violated.

For a thorough discussion of how a capital trial is conducted and decided, see Cunningham and Goldstein (2003) and Eisenberg (2004).

CASE EXAMPLES

The following two cases emphasize the significance of childhood traumatic events as mitigating factors in capital cases. We have altered identifying data and provide only representative details in each case.

Case 1: Expert Testimony on a Topic

Facts of the Case

Steven Manning, age 38, had spent most of his adult life in state prison for a wide range of offenses. On the day of the crime, he entered the house of a competing drug dealer, Peter Holmes, tied up three women, and awaited Holmes's return. When Holmes entered the house, Manning pointed his gun at Holmes's head and demanded drugs and cash hidden in the house. When Holmes laughed and taunted him, Manning pulled the trigger, hitting the victim in the head from a distance of 2 feet. He ransacked the house and then drove to Boston, about 120 miles away. He abandoned his car and attempted to hijack another car, but when the driver refused to leave her vehicle, he shot her in the head, instantly killing her. Manning was captured hours later. Because the charges against Manning include running a continuous criminal enterprise (i.e., a special circumstance under federal law), Manning faces the federal death penalty.

Defendant's Background and History

Throughout his time in prison, Manning had refused to speak with any mental health professional. Facing the death penalty, he continued to refuse to meet with any mental health professional regarding mitigation. Consequently, evaluation by the traditional means of interview and testing could not take place. Despite his refusal to cooperate, however, a wealth of records existed documenting Manning's childhood background. His mother, a drug addict throughout all her pregnancies, drew on public assistance, and therefore the state department of social service maintained files on her and her family. The records documented complaints regarding child neglect and abuse, her addiction to drugs, prostitution, and domestic violence that occurred within the apartment. When Manning reached age 12, his mother developed renal disease, requiring regular hospitalization and hemodialysis, a process which generated more records that could serve as the basis for testimony.

Testimony

Based on a review of the extensive records, interviews with other family members, and a review of Manning's court testimony (offered against the advice of his attorney), expert testimony described Manning's extremely chaotic childhood. Examples provided from the records included, but were not limited to, numerous instances involving verbal and physical abuse; sexual abuse by his brother's friends; neglect; failure of the mother to provide food, clothing, and shelter (i.e., at times the family lived in abandoned buildings without heat, water, or electricity); lack of supervision or limit setting; and lack of appropriate role models. In addition, Manning was exposed to inappropriate discipline; for example, at age 5, he found his mother's hypodermic syringe taped under the bathroom sink, and when Manning showed it to her, she filled it with water and injected him with it as punishment for touching her property. Records showed that her public assistance benefits and death benefits from her husband, who died when shot by an off-duty police officer in the course of holding up a bar, were more than sufficient to support her family. However, she spent these limited funds on drugs and alcohol for herself and others, as well as engaging in sex orgies held in her apartment with Manning present. Testimony reviewed the professional literature on the implications that these numerous, severe traumatic occurrences might have had on Manning's social, intellectual, and personality development. During direct examination, limitations on testimony and opinions, consistent with *Ethical Principles of Psychologists and Code of Conduct* (American Psychological Association, 2002) and *Specialty Guidelines for Forensic Psychologists* (Committee on Ethical Guidelines for Forensic Psychologists, 1991), were explained in light of the fact that Manning had not been evaluated directly.

In this case, the jury found Manning guilty of capital murder. Testimony was offered by a number of forensic mental health experts during the penalty phase of the trial. The jury found a number of aggravating factors and the presence of a number of mitigating factors. By a vote of 11 to 1, the jury voted in favor of death. However, because unanimity is required to impose a sentence of death in federal court, Manning received a sentence of life without parole.

Case 2: Expert Testimony on a Specific Defendant

Facts of the Case

Steven Reilly, age 27, had neither a prior criminal record nor a documented substance abuse history. He had dated a 14-year-old named Joanne. Her parents had been aware of Reilly's 4-month relationship with their teenage daughter. When they thought Joanne had become pregnant by him, the parents forbade her to see him. Authorities subsequently charged him with the murder of Joanne's parents, found dead in their apartment. The defendant, accompanied by another 14-year-old girlfriend, who became involved in some aspects of this crime, killed the father by cutting his throat and striking him in the head with a baseball bat. Reilly dropped a cinder block, used as a lamp table, on the mother's head, cut her throat, and then inserted the bat into her vagina, stating, "That's for having Joanne." Reilly voluntarily surrendered to the police 12 hours after the murders. Because there was more than one victim and the murders appeared to demonstrate "a depraved indifference to human life," prosecution advanced as a capital case.

Defendant's Background and History

Only 16 years old and unmarried at Reilly's birth, his mother described herself as a victim of childhood physical and emotional abuse. Following Reilly's birth, his mother continued to live with her parents and an emotionally disturbed sister in rural South Carolina. After an altercation with her sister, Reilly's aunt took a straightedge razor and cut her 3-year-old nephew's face from temple to chin. Weeks later, after a similar argument, she placed a hot iron on the other side of Reilly's face, leaving him with severe facial disfigurement. His mother then moved to New Jersey, leaving Reilly behind. She returned for him 3 years later, having moved in with a man who served as her procurer, forcing her to work as a prostitute. She and other women used the bedrooms throughout each day and night as the location of their "business." Reilly regularly observed his mother engage in sexual acts with her customers and witnessed numerous scenes of violence between them, as well as between his mother and her common-law husband. Because of his facial scars, a severe stutter, and his Southern accent, Reilly became the object of his classmates' derision. Neighborhood boys regularly beat him, and his mother would then whip him for crying about his injuries, forcing Reilly back onto the streets to defend himself. On at least one occasion, a group of girls attacked him, painting his face with rouge and lipstick. School records describe him as "troubled, hostile to girls, and anxious." At age 12 the authorities classified him as "emotionally disturbed." Shortly before the crime, Reilly's wife, also age 27, had left him, having learned about his relationship with Joanne. She took their 1-month-old son with her. Reilly's mental state rapidly deteriorated, and his working diagnosis of severe borderline personality disorder evolved into a brief psychotic disorder. The murders were committed in an impulsive, chaotic, highly disorganized manner.

Testimony

Based on five evaluation sessions (i.e., both interviews and testing), interviews with collateral contacts, and a review of records, expert testimony was presented. It provided details of Reilly's numerous, severe childhood traumas, including his abusive, neglected, violent, and chaotic childhood, his early history of emotional disturbance, his difficulties in school, and a suicide attempt at age 13. Other testimony related these and other mitigating factors to the crime itself and as contributing factors to his rage, feelings of betrayal, loss of control, and disorganization (Cunningham & Goldstein, 2003).

In this case, the jury considered the testimony offered by experts. They found that both a number of aggravating and mitigating factors existed. In weighing these factors against each other, the jury returned a verdict of life without the possibility of parole, finding that beyond a reasonable doubt, the mitigating factors outweighed the aggravating factors.

RELEVANT CASE LAW

We now review representative United States Supreme Court decisions related to the admissibility of testimony on childhood trauma and developmental difficulties. The reader should recognize, however, that each state has its own landmark cases on the admissibility of testimony on the issues covered in this volume. The retaining attorney should provide appropriate details and explain such case law to the expert in preparation for the evaluation and testimony. For a thorough review of case law related to a wide range of issues relevant to death penalty cases, see Latzer (1998), Cunningham and Goldstein (2003), and Eisenberg (2004).

McGautha v. California (1971)

The court found that issues of trauma related to an "unhappy childhood" and having come from a "broken home" constituted relevant information for a jury to consider. This U.S. Supreme Court case is among the first to recognize that childhood trauma can be considered a mitigating factor by a jury in determining the outcome of the penalty phase of a death penalty trial.

Lockett v. Ohio (1978)

Lockett opened the door for almost any evidence regarding a capital defendant's background, his-

tory, or circumstances of the offense to serve as mitigation. Because of Lockett, few specific Supreme Court cases challenge the admissibility of mitigating evidence, such as childhood trauma and developmental difficulties. Trial court judges typically permit testimony during the penalty phase of a capital trial, granting wide latitude if the legal criteria for the admissibility of expert testimony are met (Frye v. United States, 1923; Daubert v. Merrell Dow Pharmaceuticals, Inc., 1993; Kumho Tire Co., Ltd., v. Carmichael, 1999).

Bellotti v. Baird (1979)

This case emphasizes the role of immaturity of youth as a factor to be considered by juries in their deliberations. The court found that "during the formative years of childhood and adolescence, minors often lack the experience, perspective and judgment" typical of adults. Thus, when relevant, juries in capital cases require education about child development norms and the effects of developmental disorders and delays on overall judgment and impulse control.

Eddings v. Oklahoma (1982)

Although age 16 at the time of the murder, the state tried Eddings as an adult. The trial judge considered Eddings's "youth" as a mitigating factor at sentencing but ruled, as a matter of law, that factors related to Eddings's "unhappy childhood" did *not* warrant consideration. In this very significant case, the court found that evidence of mitigation should have included: the defendant's "turbulent family history"; his "difficult [violent] family"; the fact that he was "deprived of care, concern, and parental attention"; endured "beatings by a harsh father [and] excessive punishment"; and that, as an adolescent, Eddings was "frightened and bitter." The court also stated that the sentencer should have considered that his mother raised him "without supervision" and suggested that she was an "alcoholic and possibly a prostitute."

Caldwell v. Mississippi (1985)

In this case, the court primarily addressed an issue related to closing arguments made before the jurors. However, it also refers to mitigation introduced during the penalty phase focusing on the defendant's "youth, family background, and poverty."

Skipper v. South Carolina (1986)

Although this case focused on adjustment to incarceration as a mitigating factor, it reinforces the significance of *Eddings*, as well. The court opined, "the sentencers may not refuse to consider or be precluded from considering '*any* relevant mitigating evidence' [emphasis added]."

Parker v. Dugger (1991)

The court stated that, as a nonstatutory mitigating factor, the sentencer should have heard about the defendant's "difficult childhood including an abusive alcoholic father." In *Jackson v. Herring* (1995), a case not considered by the Supreme Court but rather by the 11th Circuit Court of Appeals, the justices held that failure to inform the sentencer of the defendant's "brutal and abusive childhood at the hands of an alcoholic mother" constituted ineffectiveness of counsel.

Williams v. Taylor (2000)

The court found ineffectiveness of counsel based on failure to pursue records detailing a defendant's "nightmarish childhood." The defendant's counsel never provided information to the sentencer regarding the defendant's parents' conviction and imprisonment for criminal child neglect.

ASSESSMENT METHODOLOGIES

Capital sentencing assessments differ significantly from all other types of criminal forensic evaluation. Because of the high stakes and the *Lockett* decision, presentation of any factors considered potentially mitigating becomes essential. Consequently, psychologists must explore *all* areas of the defendant's life, from birth up to and including the crime itself. We now focus on evaluating the defendant's childhood and adolescent history as *part* of an overall assessment in a capital case. For a discussion of conducting other criminal forensic evaluations, see Grisso (1986); Melton, Petrila, Poythress, and Slobogin (1997); Golding, Skeem, Roesch, and

Zapf (1999); or Goldstein, Morse, and Shapiro (2003). The psychologist's role, in this instance, should focus on collecting data regarding the childhood, and occasionally prenatal, history of the defendant (e.g., when evaluating for fetal alcohol syndrome). The task at hand involves reconstructing the past in such a way that enables offering reliable and objective testimony, presenting psychological "snapshots" of the defendant's history. How can evaluators accomplish this task?

Interviews With the Defendant

The defendant constitutes the most important single source of information about his or her childhood; however, for numerous reasons (e.g., malingering, exaggeration, defensiveness, shame, distortion, repression), such data may be unreliable. The purposes of the interview include: (a) acquiring information; (b) assessing overall mental status; (c) identifying third-party sources of information; and (d) evaluating credibility of the defendant by exploring the accuracy of reported events. Although defendants have an identifiable reason to report or overreport childhood trauma, some also may feel embarrassed by their past, finding it difficult to reveal histories of parental physical or sexual abuse. Such feelings may necessitate multiple sessions in order to establish the degree of trust necessary to elicit reporting of such painful memories.

Psychological Testing

Psychological testing frequently provides information not readily revealed during interviews. The use of valid and reliable tests, administered properly for a valid application and interpreted correctly, adds an objective element to forensic assessments. Even the best assessment tools, however, do not provide information regarding someone's *past* behavior; they serve no purpose in documenting or providing data regarding prior childhood trauma. Some tests, however, may serve to objectively document the presence of underlying neurological disorders, establishing the validity of prior diagnoses related to ADHD, learning disabilities, and other developmental disorders. For a discussion of the role of psychological testing in forensic criminal cases, see Heilbrun (1992) and Heilbrun, Marczyk, and DeMatteo (2002).

Third-Party Information

Given that defendants may provide unreliable information regarding prior events in their lives, the need for independent corroboration becomes apparent. Accomplishing corroboration through the use of third-party information typically requires a review of records and interviews with collateral informants who were familiar with the defendant during childhood and adolescence.

A review of birth, hospital, and school records may provide verification of the defendant's self-report or indicate unreported developmental difficulties or unreported incidents. Childhood mental health records (therapy notes, psychological assessments, hospital records) frequently provide a wealth of information regarding the defendant's family background, history of abuse and neglect, and substance abuse. Such documentation may not only serve to confirm the defendant's self-report but may also convey significant credibility, as it predates the capital offense.

Interviews with third parties (e.g., parents, teachers, childhood friends, neighbors, physicians) may serve to document the reliability of the information offered by the defendant. The validity of such information requires careful assessment weighted by the relationship between informant and defendant. Heilbrun and colleagues (2002) review the literature on the use of third-party information, discussing its role in the assessment process.

Assessment of Malingering and Defensiveness

The cornerstone of any forensic assessment involves establishing the validity of the data from which expert opinions will flow. In addition to the use of third-party information, a wide range of tests and tools have been specifically developed to assess the validity of self-reports of mental illness, neuropsychological impairment, and other cognitive and memory deficits (e.g., Rogers, 1997; Rogers & Bender, 2003). However, such tests serve little purpose in verifying self-reports of childhood trauma; consequently, the reliability of such information must rely on record reviews, third-party informants, and consistency across multiple data sources.

CHILDHOOD TRAUMA AND DEVELOPMENTAL PROBLEMS AS MITIGATION

We now turn our attention to traumatic childhood experiences and developmental problems frequently cited as mitigating factors in death penalty cases. We provide representative psychological research on each mitigating factor and describe possible effects of the trauma or difficulty on crime-related behaviors. An infinite number of factors may serve as mitigation, and this list represents only a sample.

Childhood Trauma as Mitigation

Parental Abuse and Neglect

Abused and neglected children show elevated rates of adult criminality, aggression, and violent crime (Dutton & Hart, 1992; Widom, 1989). For instance, physically and sexually abused and neglected children present an increased risk of arrest for sex crimes as adults, and physically abused boys have an increased risk for violent sex crimes (Widom & Ames, 1994). Effects of abuse include loss of trust, low self-esteem, vigilance, helplessness, and self-hatred (Potter-Effron & Potter-Effron, 1989).

In addition, sexually abused children are at heightened risk for developing numerous pathological symptoms, including depression (Briere & Runtz, 1988; Paolucci, Genuis, & Violato, 2001), suicidality (Paolucci et al., 2001), anxiety (Stein et al., 1996), sexual compulsivity (Paolucci et al., 2001), and PTSD symptoms (Breslau, Davis, Andreski, & Peterson, 1991).

Although poor, inconsistent, and abusive parenting increases children's risk for violent behaviors in adulthood, the patterns of causality in such relationships defy clear documentation (Haapasalo & Pokela, 1999). Some suggest a "cultural spillover theory" in which violence in one situation breeds violence in others. Others suggest a "construct theory" in which parent discipline encourages children to focus on their own feelings, resulting in an egocentricity that overlooks the well-being of others and increasing the probability of violence toward others (Strauss & McCord, 1998). Still others propose that research fits more consistently with a "cycle of violence" hypothesis and attribute the adult violence of abused children to vicarious learning through exposure to violent models (Dutton & Hart, 1992).

Insecure Parent–Child Attachments

Research on attachment reveals that early parent–child relationships greatly affect children's behaviors, later interpersonal relationships, and overall approaches to life (Basic Behavioral Science Task Force of the National Advisory Mental Health Council, 1996). Children with insecure attachments may act hostile, distant, or overly dependent, and they may have difficulty trusting and interacting with others; thus negative and unpredictable parent–child interactions may result in social expectations and behaviors that contribute to difficult interpersonal relationships, as these children become adolescents and adults (Basic Behavioral Science Task Force of the National Advisory Mental Health Council, 1996).

Other evidence suggests that children with early attachment difficulties have an increased risk for mental health problems in adolescence and adulthood. For example, insecure attachments associated with early childhood physical or sexual abuse and neglect may constitute risk factors for borderline personality disorder (Basic Behavioral Science Task Force of the National Advisory Mental Health Council, 1996).

Loss of a Parent

Losing a parent through death, divorce, or neglect can have a lifelong impact on children's self-perception and behaviors. Leibman (1992) suggests that parental abandonment can shatter a child's sense of security, adequacy, and worth and that the trauma can disrupt normal personality development. She further suggests that an early childhood loss of this type may become a causative factor in violent offenses, such as murder, rape, and assault.

Poverty

Research has revealed that poverty puts children at increased risk for traumatic life experiences. For instance, poverty constitutes a strong predic-

tor of substantiated child maltreatment, even after controlling for other sociodemographic variables (e.g., Lee & Goerge, 1999; Wolfner & Gelles, 1993). In addition, research has suggested that children and adolescents living in impoverished neighborhoods are more likely to be involved in criminal behavior and delinquency (Simons, Johnson, Beaman, Conger, & Whitbeck, 1996), to be more aggressive (Huesmann & Guerra, 1997), and to be more violent (DuRant, Getts, Cadenhead, & Woods, 1995) compared with youths from higher socioeconomic-status households.

Witnessing Violence

Children witness violence in many forms in and out of the home. Most commonly, perhaps, children may experience repeated exposure to parents' domestic violence. Research reveals that these children tend to experience more violence in their own adult relationships (McNeal & Amato, 1998), and they tend to have more problems with psychological and social adjustment in adulthood (Henning, Leitenberg, Coffey, Turner, & Bennett, 1996). For instance, individuals who witness violence during childhood tend to display lower self-esteem and less social competence compared with others not exposed to violence (Boney-McCoy & Finkelhor, 1995). Furthermore, research has revealed a significant link between exposure to violence in childhood and antisocial behavior in adulthood (Miller, Wasserman, Neugebauer, Gorman-Smith, & Kamboukas, 1999).

Lack of Social Support

Kruttschnitt and colleagues (1987) found moderation of the link between child abuse and adult violent behavior as a result of social support systems within and outside of the home. Children who have experienced or witnessed violence tend to have better short- and long-term behavioral outcomes if they have solid support systems.

In addition, physically neglected children tend to have greater problems with social functioning, including difficulties with friends or inabilities to form strong bonds with others (Bolger, Patterson, & Kupersmidt, 1998). However, Fantuzzo and colleagues (1996) found that including socially adept peers in play sessions with neglected children resulted in diminished social deficits.

Mentally Ill Parents

Parental psychopathology can have a great and varied impact on the lifetime behaviors of children. For instance, compared with 2-year-old children of mothers with no mood disorders or with minor depression, children of mothers with major depression had higher rates of insecure attachments and more hostility to peers at age 5 (Basic Behavioral Science Task Force of the National Advisory Mental Health Council, 1996). Similarly, Pincus (1999) found that familial and maternal depression constituted one factor predictive of conduct disorder in children with attention-deficit/hyperactivity disorder. Such comorbid diagnosis becomes important because childhood conduct disorder with ADHD predicted elevated levels of adult antisocial personality disorder, psychopathy, impulsivity, substance abuse, and violence (Vitelli, 1998).

Developmental Problems as Mitigation

Fetal Alcohol Syndrome (FAS)

FAS may cause serious impairments in numerous areas of functioning, including intelligence, activity, memory, learning, language, motor, and visuo-spatial abilities (Mattson & Riley, 1998). FAS also has links to increased risk for entering the legal system. One study suggested that learning and behavioral problems associated with FAS may increase susceptibility to illegal behavior (Fast, Conry, & Loock, 1999). Another study revealed the increased substance abuse risk for individuals with fetal alcohol exposure (Yates, Cadoret, Troughton, Stewart, & Giunta, 1998).

Head Injury

After the encephalitis epidemic of 1919, organic brain damage became a documented cause of serious psychiatric disturbances. Brain damage in early childhood impairs the development of the central nervous system (Kleinpeter & Gollnitz, 1976). Furthermore, head injury and lesions to the frontal and, possibly, temporal lobes enhance the risk of violent offending (Miller, 1999).

Other Biological Factors

Numerous potential relationships exist between neuropsychological difficulties and problems with judgment, impulse control, and other executive processes related to violent behavior. For example, a lack of D_2 receptors, dopamine receptors involved in feelings of well-being and stress reduction, elevate risk for multiple behavior problems, including substance addictions, impulsive and compulsive behaviors, ADHD, sex addictions, antisocial behavior, and chronic violence (Comings & Blum, 2000).

Fishbein (2000) described how genetic and biological factors that appear in childhood as cognitive, behavioral, and psychological traits increase vulnerability to antisocial behavior and violence. She further indicated that associated physiological and biochemical responses are measurable. Other researchers have established the strong influence of genetics and neurobiology on substance abuse, personality disorders, and psychopathy (van den Bree, Svikis, & Pickens, 1998) and the impact of fetal-neonatal brain damage on cerebral dysfunctions and later psychopathy (e.g., Towbin, 1978).

In addition, recent scientific evidence examining brain development suggested that the prefrontal cortex, responsible for reasoning, does not fully develop until early adulthood (Sowell, Thompson, Holmes, Jernigan, & Toga, 1999). Therefore, adolescents may be more impulsive and have diminished capacities for reasoning and decision making, thereby increasing the risk for participating in criminal behavior.

Attention-Deficit/Hyperactivity Disorder (ADHD)

Childhood ADHD constitutes a risk factor for later hyperactivity and the development of other psychiatric diagnoses, social and peer problems, and violent and antisocial behaviors (Taylor, Chadwick, Heptinstall, & Danchaerts, 1996). Barkley (1997) explains that ADHD constitutes a disorder of undercontrol; although individuals with ADHD usually *know* how to behave, they experience difficulty inhibiting their behavior in the absence of frequent, immediate, and salient feedback. Thus, if individuals with ADHD have violent tendencies, they may find it particularly difficult to stifle that behavior.

Low IQ and Mental Retardation

Herrnstein and Murray (1994) suggest that low IQ may constitute a causal factor in delinquent behavior. However, Van Brunschot and Brannigan (1995) suggest that related factors may better account for this relationship, such as parental psychopathology, neurological and genetic abnormalities, and environmental difficulties. In *Atkins v. Virginia* (2002), the U.S. Supreme Court ruled that it is unconstitutional to execute the mentally retarded. However, the Court left it up to each state to define "mental retardation," increasing the significance of this factor as a defendant characteristic that must be assessed in capital cases. Even if a defendant does not meet the definition of "mental retardation" adopted by a specific state, a jury is nonetheless allowed to consider "low" intelligence as a mitigator against the death penalty.

Substance Abuse

Substance abuse has documented associations with an increased risk of violence (e.g., Swanson, Estroff, Swartz, & Borum, 1997). For instance, two studies of homicide offenders found that approximately half of their samples (41% and 52%, respectively) had acted under the influence of alcohol and/or drugs while committing the crimes (Beck et al., 1993; Greenfeld, 1998). Many abused substances result in lowered inhibitions, impulsiveness, restlessness, paranoia, and irritability, and they increase the probability of violence (i.e., Machiyama, 1992).

SUMMARY

Childhood trauma and developmental problems may represent powerful mitigating factors when presented during the sentencing phase of capital trials. In the legal arena, any evidence regarding the defendant's background and history becomes a valid consideration in the jury's deliberations. Child, child-clinical, clinical, developmental, fam-

ily, and forensic psychologists and neuropsychologists, because of their training and background, may qualify as experts in such cases. Testimony may focus on a review of literature regarding the effects of such traumas or the effects of developmental difficulties. Or the expert may evaluate the defendant and offer case-specific testimony regarding the effects of such events and conditions on the defendant's intelligence, judgment, or personality. Experts will have to ensure that any testimony offered has followed from multiple sources of consistent data to ensure its reliability.

References

American Psychological Association. (2002). Ethical principles of psychologists and code of conduct. *American Psychologist, 57*(12), 1060–1073.

Atkins v. Virginia, 536 U.S. 304 (2002).

Barkley, R. A. (1997). *Defiant children: A clinician's manual for assessment and parent training* (2nd ed.). New York: Guilford.

Basic Behavioral Science Task Force of the National Advisory Mental Health Council. (1996). Basic behavioral science research for mental health: Social influence and social cognition. *American Psychologist, 51*(5), 478–484.

Beck, A., Gilliard, D., Greenfield, L., Harlow, C., Hester, T., Jankowski, L., Snell, T., et al. (1993). *Survey of state prison inmates, 1991* (Bureau of Justice Statistics Publication No. NCJ-136949). Washington, DC: Department of Justice.

Bellotti v. Baird, 443 U.S. 622 (1979).

Bolger, K. E., Patterson, C. J., & Kupersmidt, J. B. (1998). Peer relationships and self-esteem among children who have been maltreated. *Child Development, 69*, 1171–1197.

Boney-McCoy, S., & Finkelhor, D. (1995). Psychosocial sequelae of violent victimization in a national youth sample. *Journal of Consulting and Clinical Psychology, 63*, 726–736.

Breslau, N., Davis, G. C., Andreski, P., & Peterson, E. (1991). Traumatic events and posttraumatic stress disorder in an urban population of young adults. *Archives of General Psychiatry, 48*(3), 216–222.

Briere, J., & Runtz, M. (1988). Symptomology associated with childhood sexual victimization in a nonclinical adult sample. *Child Abuse and Neglect, 12*(1), 51–59.

Caldwell v. Mississippi, 472 U.S. 320 (1985).

Comings, D. E., & Blum, K. (2000). Reward deficiency syndrome: Genetic aspects of behavioral disorders. *Progress in Brain Research, 126,* 325–341.

Committee on Ethical Guidelines for Forensic Psychologists. (1991). Specialty guidelines for forensic psychologists. *Law and Human Behavior, 15*(6), 655–665.

Costanzo, M., & White, L. T. (1994). An overview of the death penalty and capital trials: History, current status, legal procedures, and cost. *Journal of Social Issues, 50,* 1–18.

Cunningham, M. D., & Goldstein, A. M. (2003). Sentencing determinations in death penalty cases. In A. M. Goldstein (Ed.), *Forensic psychology* (Vol. 11, pp. 407–436). New York: Wiley.

Daubert v. Merrell Dow Pharmaceuticals, Inc., 509 U.S. 579, 113 S.Ct. 2786 (1993).

Death Penalty Information Center. (2004). *Facts about the death penalty.* Retrieved October 6, 2004, from www.deathpenaltyinfo.org/FactSheet.pdf

DuRant, R. H., Getts, A. G., Cadenhead, C., & Woods, E. R. (1995). The association between weapon-carrying and the use of violence among adolescents living in and around public housing. *Journal of Adolescence, 18,* 579–592.

Dutton, D. G., & Hart, S. D. (1992). Evidence for long-term, specific effects of childhood abuse and neglect on criminal behavior in men. *International Journal of Offender Therapy and Comparative Criminology, 36*(2), 129–137.

Eddings v. Oklahoma, 455 U.S. 104 (1982).

Eisenberg, J. R. (2004). *Law, psychology, and death penalty litigation.* Sarasota, FL: Professional Resource Press.

Fantuzzo, J., Sutton-Smith, B., Atkins, M., Meyers, R., Stevenson, H., Coolahan, K, et al. (1996). Community-based resilient peer treatment of withdrawn maltreated preschool children. *Journal of Consulting and Clinical Psychology, 64,* 1377–1386.

Fast, D. K., Conry, J., & Loock, C. A. (1999). Identifying fetal alcohol syndrome among youth in the criminal justice system. *Journal of Developmental and Behavioral Pediatrics, 20*(5), 370–372.

Fishbein, D. (2000). The importance of neurobiological research to the prevention of psychopathology. *Prevention Science, 1*(2), 89–106.

Frye v. United States, 293 F 1013 (D.C. Cir., 1923).

Furman v. Georgia, 408 U.S. 232 (1972).

Gilmore v. Utah, 429 U.S. 1012 (1976).

Golding, S. L., Skeem, J. L., Roesch, R., & Zapf, P. A. (1999). The assessment of criminal responsibility: Current controversies. In A. K. Hess & I. B. Weiner (Eds.), *The handbook of forensic psychology* (2nd ed., pp. 379–408). New York: Wiley.

Goldstein, A. M., Morse, S. J., & Shapiro, D. L. (2003). Evaluation of criminal responsibility. In A. M. Goldstein (Ed.), *Forensic psychology* (Vol. 11, pp. 381–406). New York: Wiley.

Greenfeld, L. A. (1998). *Alcohol and crime: An analysis of national data on the prevalence of alcohol involvement in crime* (Bureau of Justice Statistics Publication No. NCJ-168632). Washington, DC: U.S. Department of Justice.

Gregg v. Georgia, 428 U.S. 153 (1976).

Grisso, T. (1986). *Evaluating competencies: Forensic assessments and instruments.* New York: Plenum.

Haapasalo, J., & Pokela, E. (1999). Child-rearing and child abuse antecedents of criminality. *Aggression and Violent Behavior, 4*(1), 107–127.

Heilbrun, K. S. (1992). The role of psychological testing in forensic assessment. *Law and Human Behavior, 6*(3), 257–272.

Heilbrun, K. S., Marczyk, G. R., & DeMatteo, D. (2002). *Forensic mental health assessment: A casebook.* New York: Oxford University Press.

Henning, K., Leitenberg, H., Coffey, P., Turner, T., & Bennett, R. T. (1996). Long-term psychological and social impact of witnessing physical conflict between parents. *Journal of Interpersonal Violence, 11*(1), 35–51.

Herrnstein, R. J., & Murray, C. A. (1994). *The bell curve: Intelligence and class structure in American life.* New York: Free Press.

Huesmann, L. R., & Guerra, N. (1997). Children's normative beliefs about aggression and aggressive behavior. *Journal of Personality and Social Psychology, 72,* 408–419.Jackson v. Herring, 42 F.3d 1350, 1358 (11th Cir.1995).

Kleinpeter, U., & Gollnitz, G. (1976). Achievement and adaptation disorders in brain-damaged children. *International Journal of Mental Health, 4,* 19–35.

Kruttschnitt, C., Ward, D., & Sheble, M. A. (1987). Abuse-resistant youth: Some factors that may inhibit violent criminal behavior. *Social Forces, 66,* 501–519.

Kumho Tire Co., Ltd. v. Carmichael, 119 S.Ct. 1167 (1999).

Latzer, B. (1998). *Death penalty cases: Leading U.S. Supreme Court cases on capital punishment.* Boston: Butterworth-Heinemann.

Lee, B. J., & Goerge, R. M. (1999). Poverty, early childbearing and child maltreatment: A multinomial analysis. *Children and Youth Services Review, 21* (9–10), 755–780.

Leibman, F. H. (1992). Childhood abandonment/adult rage: The root of violent criminal acts. *American Journal of Forensic Psychology, 10*(4), 57–64.

Lockett v. Ohio, 438 U.S. 586 (1978).

Machiyama, Y. (1992). Chronic methamphetamine intoxication model of schizophrenia in animals. *Schizophrenia Bulletin, 18*(1), 107–113.

Mattson, S. N., & Riley, E. P. (1998). A review of the neurobehavioral deficits in children with fetal alcohol syndrome or prenatal exposure to alcohol. *Clinical and Experimental Research, 22,* 279–294.

McGautha v. California, 402 US 183 (1971).

McNeal, C., & Amato, P. R. (1998). Parents' marital violence: Long-term consequences for children. *Journal of Family Issues, 19,* 123–139.

Melton, G. B., Petrila, J., Poythress, N. G., & Slobogin, C. (1997). *Psychological evaluations for the courts: A handbook for mental health professionals and lawyers* (2nd ed.). New York: Guilford.

Miller, E. K. (1999). The prefrontal cortex: Complex neural properties for complex behavior. *Neuron, 22,* 15–17.

Miller, L. S., Wasserman, G. A., Neugebauer, R., Gorman-Smith, D., & Kamboukas, D. (1999). Witnessed community violence and anti-social behavior in high-risk urban boys. *Journal of Clinical Child Psychology, 28,* 2–11.

Paolucci, E. O., Genuis, M. L., & Violato, C. (2001). A meta-analysis of the published research on the effects of child sexual abuse. *Journal of Psychology, 135*(1), 17–36.

Parker v. Dugger, 498 U.S. 308 (1991).

Pincus, J. H. (1999). Aggression, criminality, and the frontal lobes. In B. L. Miller & J. L. Cummings (Eds.), *The human frontal lobes: Functions and disorders. The science and practice of neuropsychology series* (pp. 547–556). New York: Guilford.

Potter-Effron, R., & Potter-Effron, P. (1989). *Letting go of shame.* San Francisco, CA: Harper & Row.

Randa, L. (Ed.). (1997). *Society's final solution: A history and discussion of the death penalty.* Lanham, MD: University Press of America.

Ring v. Arizona, 536 U.S. 584 (2002)

Rogers, R. (1997). *Clinical assessment of malingering and deception* (2nd ed.). New York: Guilford.

Rogers, R., & Bender, S. D. (2003). Evaluation of malingering and deception. In A. M. Goldstein (Ed.), *Forensic psychology* (Vol. 11, pp. 109–132). New York: John Wiley.

Simmons v. Roper, No. 03–0633; 112 S.W.3d 397 (2003).

Simons, R. I., Johnson, C., Beaman, J. J., Conger, R. D., & Whitbeck, L. B. (1996). Parents and peer group as mediators of the effect of community structure on adolescent behavior. *American Journal of Community Psychology, 24,* 145–171.

Skipper v. South Carolina, 476 U.S. 1 (1986).

Sowell, E. R., Thompson, P. M., Holmes, C. J., Jernigan, T. L., & Toga, A. W. (1999). In vivo evidence for post-adolescent brain maturation in frontal and striatal region. *Nature Neuroscience, 2*(10), 859–861.

Stanford v. Kentucky, 492 U.S. 361 (1989).

Stein, M. B., Walker, J. R., Anderson, G., Hazan, A. L., Ross, C. A., Eldridge, G., & Forde, D. R. (1996). Childhood physical and sexual abuse in patients with anxiety disorders and in a community sample. *American Journal of Psychiatry, 153*(2), 275–277.

Strauss, M. A., & McCord, J. (1998). Do physically punished children become violent adults? In S. Nolen-Hoeksema (Ed.), *Clashing views on abnormal psychology: A taking sides custom reader* (pp. 130–155). New York: Guilford.

Streib, V. L. (2004). *The juvenile death penalty today: Death sentences and executions for juvenile crimes, January 1, 1973–June 30, 2004.* Retrieved October 6, 2004, from www.law.onu.edu/faculty/streib/documents JuvDeathJune302004 NewTables .pdf

Swanson, J., Estroff, S., Swartz, M., & Borum, R. (1997). Violence and severe mental disorder in clinical and community populations: The effects of psychotic symptoms, comorbidity, and lack of treatment. *Psychiatry: Interpersonal and Biological Processes, 60*(1), 1–22.

Taylor, E., Chadwick, O., Heptinstall, E., & Danckaerts, M. (1996). Hyperactivity and conduct problems as risk factors for adolescent development. *Journal of the American Academy of Child and Adolescent Psychiatry, 35*(9), 1213–1226.

Thompson v. Oklahoma, 487 U.S. 815 (1988).

Towbin, A. (1978). Cerebral dysfunctions related to perinatal organic damage: Clinical-neuropathologic correlations. *Journal of Abnormal Psychology, 87*(6), 617–635.

Van Brunschot, E. G., & Brannigan, A. (1995). IQ and crime: Dull behavior and/or misspecified theory? *Alberta Journal of Educational Research, 41*(3), 316–321.

van den Bree, M., Svikis, D. S., & Pickens, R. W. (1998). Genetic influences in antisocial personality and drug use disorders. *Drug and Alcohol Dependence, 49*(3), 177–187.

Vitelli, R. (1998). Childhood disruptive behavior disorders and adult psychopathy. *American Journal of Forensic Psychology, 16*, 29–37.

Weems v. United States, 217 U.S. 349 (1910).

Widom, C. S. (1989). Child abuse, neglect, and adult behavior: Research design and findings on criminality, violence, and child abuse. *American Journal of Orthopsychiatry, 59*(3), 355–367.

Widom, C. S., & Ames, M. (1994). Criminal consequences of childhood sexual victimization. *Child Abuse and Neglect, 18*(4), 303–318.

Williams v. Taylor, 529 U.S. 362 (2000).

Wolfner, G. D., & Gelles, R. J. (1993). A profile of violence toward children: A national study. *Child Abuse and Neglect, 17*(2), 197–212.

Yates, W. R., Cadoret, R. J., Troughton, E. P., Stewart, M., & Giunta, T. S. (1998). Effect of fetal alcohol exposure on adult symptoms of nicotine, alcohol, and drug dependence. *Alcoholism: Clinical and Experimental Research, 22*(4), 914.

23

Assessing Firesetting Behavior
in Children and Adolescents

David K. Wilcox

Hallmark characteristics of our most recent evolutionary ancestors, hominids, involved the use of tools and acquisition of language. The use of fire, another skill also truly unique to hominids, does not often elicit the same level of attention and interest among behavioral and social scientists. Humans stand alone among animals with respect to using fire. The use of fire, perhaps more than any other technology, has shaped the development of social groups, the control of our environment, and human interactions in countless ways.

Amid changes in human habitation that followed the Industrial Revolution, the safe control of fire became particularly important, especially as technology made it more omnipresent in both homes and workplaces. Although most industrialized countries have enjoyed a decrease in the frequency of fires and the destruction wrought by fire, some striking contrasts exist in how countries have responded to the need for increased fire safety. The United States, in particular, has lagged behind its industrialized peers in reducing the number of fires and fire-related injuries that occur each year. Compared with Western Europe and Japan, the rates of property loss and fire-related

casualties per 100,000 inhabitants in the United States are twice as high (Goudsblom, 1992). In the 1980s, Hong Kong, an area approximately twice as large as Chicago, had one third as many fire deaths. During the same period of time, Baltimore, Maryland, recorded a fire-related death rate almost 13 times as high as Amsterdam, a European urban center with a comparable population (Kolata, 1987). In 1998 the value of property directly destroyed by fires in the United States reached $8.6 billion, and the per capita death rate was 18.6 per million population—the third highest in the world, trailing only Finland and Hungary (U.S. Fire Administration, 2001).

A close look at the fire problem in the United States reveals arson as the leading cause of fires, or fires of a suspicious or incendiary origin. Although fires in the United States between 1984 and 1994 declined over 19%, a study by the National Fire Protection Association revealed that the number of arson fires declined at an average rate of only 11% (Hall, 1996), indicating that in relative terms the arson rate actually increased. The most recent study of the national arson problem attributed 28% of all the fires in the country in

1994 to arson. The resulting 548,500 suspicious or known arson fires led to 560 fire-related deaths, 3,440 injuries, and $3.6 billion in property damage (U.S. Fire Administration, 1997).

Juveniles constituted the primary culprits involved in the majority of these fires. Children and adolescents have been the primary culprits in arson fires in the United States for well over 15 years. According to the Federal Bureau of Investigation, juveniles accounted for 54% of all the arrests for arson in 1999, an increase of 9% over the course of the past decade (Federal Bureau of Investigation, 2000). A study of the actual source of ignition in fires set by juveniles and children traced 63% of the cases to a match or a lighter as the ignition source (U.S. Fire Administration, 2000).

Juvenile firesetting as a phenomenon persists even though fire departments around the country work tirelessly to promote fire safety in the public schools. Such behavior often goes unrecognized, is poorly understood, or is assumed to characterize only the most disturbed type of psychopathology in youths. Most important, such behavior can arise in almost any setting, among almost any age group and yet the dynamics that motivate firesetting seem remarkably diverse. On the one hand, a 3-year-old child can accidentally set a fire while playing with matches, resulting in the loss of scores of housing units costing hundreds of thousands of dollars, not to mention injuries or deaths. On the other hand, a depressed adolescent can set *hundreds* of fires over the course of a number of years and remain undetected, left to move on to more dangerous, aggressive behavior later in life. Clinicians, as well as other professionals who work with children and adolescents, should at least become aware of such risks and take appropriate steps to safeguard the youth and effectively stop the behavior.

AN OVERVIEW OF WHAT WE KNOW ABOUT FIRESETTING AND YOUTHS

Juvenile firesetting can be defined as a youth's involvement in burning or setting fire to any form of material, including lighting small pieces of paper or other objects or setting fire to personal property, dwellings, or structures, as well as woodlands and grasslands. Intent, as it is usually defined in legal terms, is not necessary to characterize an act of juvenile firesetting. The problem of juvenile firesetting transcends easily defined professional boundaries. Because the act results in fire, it is often considered a problem for the fire services to resolve. Because such behavior can sometimes flow from complex psychological dynamics, it often seems an issue best addressed by mental health professionals. Because setting certain types of fires constitutes criminal conduct, such behavior falls within the jurisdiction of law enforcement and the juvenile justice system. As a result of our current system of response, strategies for intervention have become fragmented and disjointed.

Whether in a court, a clinic, a juvenile justice setting, a school, a hospital, or a residential setting, clinicians will at some time hear reports of firesetting during the course of conducting assessments and working with children and adolescents. Forensic assessment referrals may involve firesetting behavior as a primary consideration, for example, in a juvenile court proceeding following a firesetting act; or the forensic referral of a juvenile may never mention firesetting, but the evaluator may wish to consider the possibility of previously unidentified problems in this area. This chapter provides an overview of the approaches that can be helpful in understanding the behavior, framing an assessment of the child or adolescent, choosing appropriate measures and interview techniques in conducting an assessment of firesetting behavior, and describing the results in a manner useful to the court or for other professionals concerned with the development of appropriate interventions.

The rather limited quality of research studies about juvenile firesetting is one reason why so much confusion exists about this behavior. Only within the past 20 years have sound empirically based studies of juvenile firesetting begun in an attempt to understand the many psychodynamics and other variables associated with this dangerous behavior. These research findings have proven useful in dispelling old clinical assumptions rooted in psychoanalytic theory, as well as inferences about the phenomenon based on case studies. The older and unsupported assumptions not only skewed our understanding of the behavior but also provided little in the way of useful data to develop meaningful interventions.

One of the benefits of the empirical research of the past 20 years has been a focus on firesetting behavior and interest in fire among nonclinical samples. These studies have effectively established a baseline for trying to understand the prevalence of this behavior in large samples of children in various communities. In the United States, several studies show that within nonclinical samples, many children display an interest in fire and a willingness to take that interest a step further in actually playing with fire. In a nonclinical sample of school-children between the first and eighth grades, 38% of children have reported actually playing with fire at least once (Grolnick, Cole, Laurenitis, & Schwartzman, 1990). In a random sample of boys ranging in age from kindergarten to fourth grade, 45% of the sampled children reported playing with fire, with some instances of fire play beginning as young as age 3 (Kafry, 1980). Recently a very large study of schoolchildren from third to eighth grades in 15 school districts throughout Oregon revealed that 32% of the students reported setting fires outside of their homes and 29% of students reported that they had set fires in their homes (Oregon Office of the State Fire Marshal, 2001b).

The studies of firesetting behavior among youths highlight the fact that firesetting or playing with matches with no intent of burning something is a behavior that occurs within a general population of children and adolescents with some degree of regularity. This does not make such behavior safe; once a match is struck or a lighter ignited, a flame simply will consume fuel. Once lit, a flame will not discriminate between burning a piece of paper, a blanket, or an entire house and taking the lives of those in the house. The significant incidence of firesetting within the general population shows that not all firesetting is pathological or indicative of complex psychological motives that may warrant psychological assessment or treatment. The strategy for intervening in these situations often necessitates services designed to educate the child about fire and how fire works, as well as to reinforce prohibitions against acting on one's curiosity by actually experimenting with fire. Why children and adolescents actually set fires, especially after they have been warned about the dangers of playing with fire or received some basic safety education, is another issue. David Kolko (1985), as well as Vaughan Hardesty and

William Gayton (2002), have written very comprehensive articles describing the history of research and treatment regarding juvenile firesetting. Jeffrey Geller (1992) has also written a very comprehensive history of the research and views on arson. Readers who wish to learn more about the history of how psychiatry and psychology have viewed these behaviors should refer to these works.

The behaviors of firesetting and pathological arson first began to draw the attention of the medical community in the middle of the 19th century. Reports began appearing in European and American journals describing a particularly disturbed type of behavior that was assumed to be pathological in nature. Described as "pyromania" or *monomanie incendiare* by Marc (1833), this behavior was seen as encompassing an intense interest in setting fires that may be driven by mental or neurological illness (Lewis & Yarnell, 1951). Sigmund Freud (1930, 1932) proposed that firesetting behavior was linked to infantile and sexual drives. These views formed the basis for later views about firesetting, which focused on psychosexual and primitive aggressive impulses as the dynamics that motivate children to set fires (Klein, 1932).

It was not until the middle of the 20th century that clinicians working with youths who set fires began to move away from the psychoanalytic views of this behavior and begin to gather descriptive data about the phenomenon. Studies by Yarnell (1940) and Lewis and Yarnell (1951) began to examine not simply the psychosexual aspects of this behavior but also the psychosocial dynamics that might motivate children and adolescents to set fires. These studies began to identify the presence of other comorbid antisocial behaviors and the impact of family dysfunction and family psychopathology as other factors associated with youths who set fires. Other studies, often relying on small samples of participants and case-review formats, attempted to identify factors that might describe and discern the elements associated with juvenile firesetting, including hyperkinesis, delinquency, limited IQ, family separation and abandonment, learning difficulties, enuresis, and social difficulties with peers (Kaufman, Heins, & Reiser, 1961; Macht & Mack, 1968; Nurcombe, 1964; Vandersall & Weiner, 1970). These more descriptive studies effectively broadened our understanding about the phenomenon of firesetting from a solely psychoanalytic focus. Comprehensive empirical research has helped delineate more relevant factors and variables about this phenomenon. The resulting data have helped professionals more accurately structure assessments and design effective treatment interventions for these youths.

Much of the current thinking about the assessment and intervention strategies for juvenile firesetting have drawn extensively from empirical studies conducted over the past 30 years. Kolko and Kazdin (1988) have found that a history of firesetting is present in 34.6% of clinical inpatient populations of youths and in 19.4% of clinical outpatient populations, thus making firesetting behavior a topic that warrants some familiarity among any clinician working with children and adolescents. Most of the studies suggest that boys clearly outnumber girls in setting fires. Kolko (1985) reviewed previous descriptive studies and found that 82% of the perpetrators were boys, and Fineman (1980) reported a ratio of nine boys to every girl who was involved in setting fires. It is interesting to note that recent findings from the Office of Juvenile Justice and Delinquency Prevention (OJJDP) reveal that in 1993, 12.5% of the juveniles arrested for arson were females, an increase of almost 53% in the number of female juveniles arrested for arson compared with findings from 1989 (OJJDP, 1996).

Although children as young as 2 and 3 years of age can be involved in firesetting, it appears that firesetting generally occurs among older children. In a variety of studies the mean age of children and adolescents who are identified as setting fires is between 9 and 10 years of age (Heath, Hardesty, Goldfine, & Walker, 1983; Kolko & Kazdin, 1990). In a larger demographic study of firesetting behavior in Massachusetts, among the 809 children and adolescents referred to intervention programs in 2001, the mean age was 11.85 years, the median age was 12 years, and the mode was 14 years, revealing an older age group involved in setting fires (Massachusetts Coalition for Juvenile Firesetter Intervention Programs, 2001). Similarly, the Oregon State Fire Marshal's Office reported that among the 997 youths seen in 2000 for firesetting and for whom age was reported, the mode was 12 years of age (Oregon Office of the State Fire Marshal, 2001a). Age alone cannot mitigate the serious effects of firesetting. It is clear that the fires

set by younger children often incur the most damage, are the most expensive in terms of dollars lost, and displace more individuals than fires set by latency age and adolescent youths (Massachusetts Coalition for Juvenile Firesetter Intervention Programs, 2002).

Perhaps one of the most important set of findings from the empirical research on juvenile firesetting has been a focus on factors in the life of the youth, the youth's behavioral functioning, and the life of the youth's family that may play a role in motivating the act of firesetting. A review of the research findings reveals a variety of factors worth noting, especially in terms of how they may provide clinical clues into the youth's firesetting, as well as other potential difficulties that may arise in the youth's life. Although many of these factors are encapsulated in items among various measures designed to assess firesetting behavior, there does not, at this time, exist a truly comprehensive model that can be used to weigh these factors in terms of judging the severity of firesetting behavior or the risk for future behavior.

In one of the first controlled studies comparing youths referred to a clinic for firesetting with youths who were also referred but did not have histories of setting fires, Heath et al. (1983) found that parents using the Child Behavior Checklist rated children who set fires as having higher scores on psychopathology dimensions, exhibiting more externalizing behavior, and having poorer interpersonal skills. These findings were confirmed by Kolko, Kazdin, and Meyer (1985), who reported that youths with firesetting behavior were not only more likely to exhibit externalizing behaviors but that they also engaged in more aggressive, cruel, and delinquent behavior and appeared to have far less social skill competency than other children and adolescents. Given these findings, it is not surprising that conduct disorder and oppositional defiant disorder are the two most prevalent diagnostic categories used to describe youths who are engaged in setting fires (Heath, Hardesty, Goldfine & Walker, 1985; Kolko et al., 1985; Kolko & Kazdin, 1988), and firesetting itself is one of the strongest predictors of continuing conduct disorder in youth (Kelso & Stewart, 1986).

Although the research does indicate that juveniles who engage in firesetting exhibit more aggressive behavior and tend to do so in an externalized fashion, it also suggests that these youths have difficulties with social interactions and problem solving in social situations (Heath et al., 1983; Kolko et al., 1985). Vreeland and Levin (1980) noted that firesetting youths had more difficulty in social interactions, particularly interactions that had the potential for conflict, and showed less capacity for solving these conflicts and problems in a socially acceptable manner. These youths have also been found to be less appropriately assertive and have lower self-esteem than youths who do not set fires (Kolko & Kazdin, 1991b). What emerges is a picture of children and adolescents who are hampered in negotiating complex social interactions, possess limited social problem-solving skills, and have low self-esteem and difficulty asserting themselves in situations. This may explain, to some degree, why there is such a high prevalence of covert antisocial behavior among juveniles who set fires. Covert behavior, although perhaps offering the opportunity to act out aggressive impulses, also helps the youth avoid the humiliation of being caught and being confronted by an authority figure in a problematic situation. This poor sense of self-esteem and the limited social skills seen in these youths may also explain why peer approval and acceptance of firesetting behavior is a significant factor that has been shown to identify youths who were 3.2 times more likely to reengage in firesetting in the future (Kolko & Kazdin, 1994). Clinically, these findings suggest that youths who set fires may have few alternatives for solving problems that arise in their lives, particularly in social situations and situations that involve conflict. For these youths, firesetting appears to provide an outlet for their anger, distress, and anxiety, feelings that represent the greatest areas of challenge in terms of their coping skills. Frequently, these youths will report that they set fires because they were bored or had nothing else to do (Kolko & Kazdin, 1986). Managing boredom, just like managing other affect states, requires a certain level of coping skills. These youths tend to act impulsively and in an externalizing fashion when confronted with situations that provoke intense reactions rather than thinking first about the consequences of their actions. In reviewing factors that contributed to recidivism on follow-up studies of youths who set fires, Kolko and Kazdin (1994) found that youths who have a significant history of setting fires

show a greater propensity to engage in externalizing behaviors, aggression, and involvement in concealed covert acts and show more curiosity about fire.

Factors associated with family dysfunction have long been targeted as characteristics coincident with firesetting in children and adolescents (Bumpass, Fagelman, & Brix, 1983; Gaynor & Hatcher, 1987; Kolko & Kazdin, 1988, 1991a, 1992; Macht & Mack, 1968; Saunders & Awad, 1991; Yarnell, 1940). The research of Kolko and Kazdin (1988, 1990, 1991a, 1992) has yielded some invaluable insights into the dysfunction in families of youths who engage in firesetting behavior. Findings reveal that parents and families of children who present with firesetting often experience greater personal and marital distress, difficulties between parents, greater exposure to stressful life events, poorer supervision, and less family affiliation. There are also indications of greater parental psychopathology (Kolko & Kazdin, 1990). Parenting styles also appear to be less consistent. These families use harsher punishment and are less likely to effectively enforce consequences for behavior (Kolko & Kazdin, 1990). Although earlier studies focused on the absence of a parent or lack of parental involvement in the life of the youth who is setting fires (Macht & Mack, 1968; Strachan, 1981), it appears that the level of disruption, poor parenting skills, and skewed emotional interactions in the family are more salient than the actual absence of a parental figure (Kolko & Kazdin, 1990).

Fineman (1980, 1995) has developed a model that explains firesetting behavior in terms of a set of interacting factors that link predisposing factors for antisocial behavior (e.g., family dysfunction and learning difficulties in school), experiences with fire (e.g., exposure in the home and with peers), and experiences that set into motion acting out behavior (e.g., stress or peer pressure) that all contribute to firesetting behavior. Fineman (1997a, 1997b, 1997c) incorporated elements of these factors into measures that had been employed by the Federal Emergency Management Agency (1979) in its firesetting interview tools for youth and families. However, a study by Slavkin (2000) has revealed that the psychometric properties of the Family Fire Risk Interview (Fineman 1997a) and the Juvenile Fire Risk Interview (Fineman, 1997b) showed low reliability and were limited in their ability to predict firesetting recidivism and psychological problems in youths.

SETTING THE STAGE FOR A FORENSIC ASSESSMENT OF FIRESETTING BEHAVIOR

Providing services in instances of juvenile firesetting invariably places the clinician in the midst of working with a behavior that can also be considered a crime. The reality of actually pressing charges, essentially recognizing that the firesetting is a criminal behavior and that the child or adolescent needs to be held accountable for this dangerous behavior, varies tremendously, and there is no consistent policy in most jurisdictions on how to address this in individual cases.

Very often the filing of charges for setting a fire and burning property can hinge on a host of factors. The firesetting incident may not be reported to the proper authorities that possess the legal authority to press charges. There may also be instances in which authorities do respond to the scene of the fire and identify the culprit as a child or adolescent but decide not to press charges because it is assumed that the youth would be "stigmatized." Unfortunately, firesetting is too often viewed as a victimless crime and therefore as not meriting the attention that other crimes do. A recent study by Ghetti and Redlich (2001) revealed that adults consider killing a victim with a gun a more serious offense than killing the same victim through an act of arson. In essence, these findings reveal that the act of arson is often thought of as demanding less accountability and a less severe sentence than a more clearly violent crime against another person. Holding children accountable for their firesetting may be stymied by the belief that firesetting is a harmless behavior and something that all children do and, as a result, does not warrant pressing charges. In other situations in which there is a willingness to hold the child accountable and press charges, state laws defining the age of culpability may limit whether the youth's behavior may be considered a crime. Even when there is a willingness to hold the child or adolescent accountable and pressing charges is an option, the reality is that fire scenes do not always offer enough forensic evidence to determine who set the fire and

to identify a culprit. This situation may lead to insufficient evidence to go forward with charges, and the district attorney may feel as though charges, even if pursued, would not be sufficient for successful prosecution.

The fact remains that a range of crimes relating to setting fires takes place in all jurisdictions in the United States, in addition to a host of lesser crimes that may not involve fire but do involve the sort of destruction and damage that result from a fire (e.g., malicious destruction of property). Pressing charges is a way of helping the child or adolescent receive the services he or she needs in order to address this behavior, as well as helping the parents and others working with the youth to place a priority on the need to take the behavior seriously and secure the necessary treatment and interventions necessary to deter him or her from setting fires in the future.

Mental health professionals need to be aware that the behavior about which they are beginning to learn more from the child or adolescent may indeed constitute a crime. How one approaches the assessment and intervention is largely governed by who refers the youth. Does the child or adolescent retain privilege, or does the context of the assessment and treatment stipulate that privilege is waived, such as in situations in which a judge has ordered an evaluation? Similarly, it is important to consider the confidentiality of information obtained in the assessment or treatment. Who will read about the findings of present or past firesetting, and what will happen to this information? Professionals need to be mindful of situations in which an active investigation of a fire that the child or adolescent has set is going on. Unless safeguards are in place and a thorough understanding of the assessment is reached with the youth and the youth's guardian, as well as with all parties involved with the youth, law enforcement officials or prosecutors may produce a subpoena to try and force the clinician to provide information about the youth's involvement in the fire in order to build a criminal case. There are other legal and ethical dilemmas that the clinician should consider before performing an assessment or treatment intervention. For instance, what would the professional do if the youth admitted to setting a fire in a dwelling in which someone was killed but previous investigations had not identified a suspect in the crime? How will the professional view a situation in which the youth admits to setting a fire that destroyed a large commercial warehouse but in which investigators were charging another individual with the fire? How will a third party (e.g., the school) who reads the assessment report react to the findings from the assessment? Will it affect whether the youth is allowed to continue to attend that school, or will the results be perceived in a manner that leads the administrators to conclude that the youth is too dangerous to remain in school?

The aforementioned represent only some of the questions and issues that may arise in a forensic assessment of firesetting. In many cases, because firesetting is often successfully conducted in a covert manner, a clinician conducting a forensic assessment for other purposes may discover that the youth has also engaged in setting fires. When firesetting is discovered, these same issues apply. Identifying firesetting as an additional issue can better ensure that the youth will receive help in remaining safe and that the safety of others in the community will be protected.

FRAMING AN ASSESSMENT: ISSUES TO CONSIDER

Sorting through the divergent strands of information and professional impressions accumulated in the course of assessing firesetting behavior requires patience and also a system of analysis that seems unfamiliar to many of those who work with other behavioral problems in children and adolescents. Firesetting incidents may not always appear to be motivated by the factors that are suggested on an initial review of the case material. The presenting incident may be the one fire that was reported, and a subsequent review of potential firesetting history may reveal numerous other fires previously unknown. Firesetting behavior does not adhere to any well-defined nosology or taxonomy. Efforts to provide classification schemes for firesetting behavior have led to a proliferation of terms and categories that have too often provided confusion rather than clarity (Geller, 1992). At best, most of the classification schemes simply provide a description of the behavior rather than a predictive pathway of how the behavior will evolve. What is needed in

the assessment of this behavior is not so much an all-encompassing taxonomy but rather a perspective on the part of the professional, as well as others involved with the youth, that is robust and comprehensive and capable of embracing the complex, interdependent variables that motivated a child or adolescent to set a fire. In essence, assessing firesetting behavior must embrace a diverse array of data to understand what led to the actual setting of the fire and to try to bring those factors together in explaining the behavior. Mental health professionals need to feel comfortable sorting through reports and clinical data that may not initially appear related but that, on further clarification, lead to a better understanding of the youth, his or her behavior, and the most appropriate types of interventions.

It is useful to keep in mind that there can be a variety of pathways that lead to this behavior. In their work on developmental psychopathology, Stephen Shirk, Ayelet Talmi, and David Olds have stated: "It is possible that individuals who develop the same disorder do so for different reasons" (2000, p. 837). Similarly, it is important for professionals not to assume that there is an easily discernible pathway that explains firesetting behavior in all youths. Psychiatry and psychology have attempted to apply a more direct, reductionistic lens to the phenomenon of firesetting behavior, but these attempts have often fallen short. These efforts have assumed that firesetting could be tied to a single factor or cluster of factors that not only define the risk for future firesetting but also identify youths who might develop firesetting tendencies. For example, research has suggested a direct link between firesetting, bedwetting, and cruelty to animals and has linked these factors with criminal behavior in adulthood (Hellman & Blackman, 1966; Wax & Haddox, 1974a, 1974b). However, the association of these factors has been shown to be more complex, making it not only more difficult to link these factors together in predicting adult criminal behavior but also somewhat ineffective in helping to understand the factors that motivate children and adolescents to set fires (Heath et al., 1983).

One aspect of assessing firesetting behavior that sometimes differs from other aspects of clinical assessment is the amount of collateral contact and information gathering needed in order to piece together a full picture of the fire itself, as well as of the youth's functioning in other areas. If the fire department responded to the fire, professionals should always consider consultation with fire department staff and request a copy of the cause and origin report that explains how the fire was actually set. Professionals also need to have a basic understanding of fire and how fire works in order to appreciate what actually occurred when the youth ignited the fire. Crossing from the clinical world into the world of fire science and arson investigation can often feel uncomfortable for clinicians, but a comprehensive assessment of the child or adolescent requires an understanding of why a fire was set.

Various states have organized juvenile firesetting efforts that are spearheaded by local fire departments to address this problem. Most of these programs appreciate the fact that clinicians are often needed to help in providing assessment and intervention services, and partnerships often develop between the arson and investigations units and clinicians interested in this behavior. These partnerships are invaluable for both the clinicians and the members of the fire service. Developing such partnerships is critical in building an effective assessment and intervention service. Within these partnerships professionals learn a great deal about fire science and fire prevention, while at the same time helping the fire service better understand the complexity of this behavior and how best to help these children and adolescents.

This multidisciplinary approach to the issue of juvenile firesetting is critical in building the services these children and adolescents need. This approach ensures that any involvement on the part of the fire department in providing fire safety education as part of an intervention will be informed by expert opinions and recommendations. Conversely, it is always helpful for professionals to have resources within the fire service for consultation about how fire works and whether or not a report of a firesetting incident obtained from the child is accurate. There are times when this behavior arises and no response or involvement comes from the fire department.

Often the reality is either that fires set by children and adolescents are covert and not witnessed by anyone or that the incident is detected or discovered by an adult such as a parent who may minimize it, not report it, or disregard it altogether. In a recent study conducted by the Massachusetts Coalition for Juvenile Firesetter Intervention Pro-

grams (2002), a substantial number of the firesetting incidents that warranted referrals of children or adolescents to intervention programs were fires that were never reported to the fire department. Out of 696 referrals in 2001, only 513 (74%) of these fires were either discovered by or reported to an adult. Among the fires that were reported to an adult, only 58 (11%) involved some sort of fire department response—either a suppression response to put out the fire or an investigation (Massachusetts Coalition for Juvenile Firesetter Intervention Programs, 2001). These statistics highlight the fact that in the majority of instances in which an incident of juvenile firesetting occurs, no one investigates the facts behind the incident. That task falls to the mental health professional in the process of conducting a firesetting assessment.

In these instances, the evaluator is the one who is in the position of uncovering and exploring the nature and history of the firesetting act. The professional needs to feel comfortable asking informed questions about the circumstances associated with the firesetting and to understand enough about fire science to know whether the answers provided by the child or adolescent are valid or meaningful in a psychological understanding of the act. Information from fire investigators or members of the fire prevention service is not only a critical asset when trying to conduct an assessment but also provides a useful resource in developing effective treatment and intervention services for children and adolescents to address their firesetting behavior. One of the most critical steps in conducting an assessment of firesetting behavior is to be absolutely clear about the referral question. Juvenile firesetting is a behavior that may occur in a variety of contexts: at school, in the neighborhood, in a home, in a juvenile court clinic, in a fire department, during the course of a hospital admission, or within a foster home or residential placement. It is important for the evaluator to be very clear with the referring party about what is expected, including the limitations of the assessment and how the assessment results will be used. When evaluators are asked about the risk for setting a fire in the future, it is imperative that they explain the many limitations on making a statement about future risk. Predicting firesetting behavior is something that even the most experienced clinicians are reluctant to do. However, mental health professionals can emphasize prevention. Most children and adolescents cannot set a fire if they cannot gain access to lighters, matches, or other sources of open flames or heat. Restricting access to fire sources, combined with adequate supervision, is perhaps the most realistic procedure for preventing future firesetting.

The assessment can provide a richer understanding of why the youth is setting fires, an identification of factors that may have contributed to the behavior, and a well-reasoned plan for addressing the behavior in a safe manner. The assessment may highlight these factors and underscore the youth's vulnerabilities and what treatment is appropriate. It would also be important to explain the strengths the child or adolescent has, as these will become critical in a successful treatment and intervention. Evaluation results can provide a foundation for the clinical team and the referring party to begin crafting a safety and intervention plan.

CONDUCTING THE ASSESSMENT

Once the parameters of the referral are clear, the clinician needs to gather information from collateral sources. Collateral sources of information are essential for properly understanding the psychodynamics of the firesetting behavior.

There is no one comprehensive psychometric instrument that can encompass all the factors that potentially explain why a child or adolescent has set fires, although instruments exist that identify risk factors that contributed to the past behavior. Unfortunately, the complex nature of firesetting behavior does not yield to easy psychometric analysis, and the clinician must choose from a variety of potential instruments or interview protocols. Critical domains must be addressed. In discussing these domains, various assessment tools will be reviewed, including those that assess aspects of emotional, social, cognitive, and family functioning. Incorporating measures into an assessment not only helps confirm hypotheses or intuitions gained during clinical interviews but also helps identify areas that may need to be addressed in addition to the firesetting behavior. The measures mentioned subsequently represent suggestions for capturing data about particularly relevant areas of functioning; they cannot be considered exhaustive for a given case.

Documenting the Youth's History With Fire and Knowledge About Fire

Most of the assessment will be similar to other types of forensic assessments of children and adolescents, concentrating on the youth's behavior with fire. Understanding the child's or adolescent's history with fire, as well as his or her knowledge about fire, is perhaps the most critical component of a firesetting assessment. Although most firesetting assessments may encompass four or five interview meetings with the youth and the family, gathering evidence about the youth's history with fire is a topic that can and should be revisited at different times over the course of these meetings. Clinicians need to complete their meetings with the youth with a very clear sense of the child's or adolescent's relationship with fire. Interview questions for the child or collateral sources of information can include: How many incidents of firesetting, reported and unreported, have there been? How directly involved is the child or adolescent in the firesetting? Does the firesetting involve the use of lighters and matches alone, or had the youth experimented with accelerants and aerosol devices to make bigger, more dangerous fires? Is the youth's curiosity and interest in fire overriding an appreciation of the danger of setting fires? How much does the youth know about fire, beyond the basic elements of fire safety learned in school, and is there an awareness of how fire works, how it can spread, and what it can burn? When and where have the firesetting incidents occurred, and what has been the context for these incidents? Is there a discernable pattern of events in the youth's life that preceded the incidents of firesetting? Does it appear that the youth associates firesetting with particular reactions to situations or as a means of coping with anger, shame, or frustration?

The preceding suggested questions are not intended to represent an exhaustive scope of inquiry regarding the nature of the firesetting act. Questions will need to be framed in simple language and often repeated or rephrased. It may be necessary to return to some questions to determine the consistency of answers or whether additional areas of inquiry are warranted.

A firesetting history and an assessment of a child's or adolescent's understanding of fire can include several very good basic screening tools in a structured and semistructured format. Although a narrative format may take additional time, it provides a chance for the youth to use his or her own language to describe his or her behavior and provides a context for the child or adolescent to take responsibility for the firesetting behavior as it is described over the course of several interviews. Ideally, using a combination of approaches offers the best approach to gaining a full understanding of the youth's history of setting fires and his or her relationship with fire and understanding of what it is he or she is doing when setting fires.

THE FIRESETTING HISTORY SCREEN

A basic measure of firesetting behavior, perhaps best suited for a clinical intake in which firesetting is not suspected but may exist, is the Firesetting History Screen (Kolko & Kazdin, 1988). This instrument contains 14 questions that ask about incidents within two time frames: the previous 12 months and longer than 12 months. The youth is asked to answer these questions, and the parents are also asked the same questions about their child's behavior. Kolko and Kazdin (1988) found relatively high agreement between parent reports and the reports of children when administering the screen in an inpatient setting (mean Kappa = .61, range = .43 to 1.00) and an outpatient setting (mean Kappa = .71, range = .55 to .91). The Firesetting History Screen can provide a very basic and useful measure in a clinical setting such as a pediatric clinic, school, court clinic, or mental health clinic or as part of a forensic interview. The screen has been used in a child and adolescent psychiatric unit and has proven helpful in identifying children and adolescents for whom firesetting is an issue but for whom firesetting had not been previously identified as a problem and was not the presenting problem for hospitalization (Wilcox, Murphy, & Goldstein, 2000).

The Firesetting Risk Inventory and Children's Firesetting Interview

Two interview tools that have received wide use in both research and clinical settings are the Firesetting Risk Inventory (Kolko & Kazdin, 1989a), which is administered to parents, and the Children's Firesetting Interview (Kolko & Kazdin, 1989b), which is administered to children and adolescents. Some of the items are similar to the questions posed in a juvenile firesetting intervention questionnaire developed by the Federal Emergency Management Administration (FEMA; 1979), as well as other early empirical research about youths and their experience with fire (Kolko, 1985, 1989).

The Firesetting Risk Interview

The Firesetting Risk Interview (FRI) is composed of 86 items that are answered by parents or caregivers, including questions specific to fire and firesetting, as well as general questions about the youth's behavior. Fifteen different subscales and scores are summed to obtain the total score for each dimension. The measure has good internal validity and construct validity. Studies have compared responses on this instrument between firesetting and nonfiresetting youths and their families. This instrument has shown that parents of children and adolescents who have a history of setting fires reveal a higher degree of exposure to fire, involvement with firesetting, and early experiences using fire. Also, parenting styles appear to incorporate greater use of harsher punishment, less effective parenting in general, and more negative behavior on the part of the child. The differences between firesetting and nonfiresetting youths, as reported by caregivers, revealed that youths with firesetting behavior showed greater curiosity about fire, more complaints about fire behavior, and less experience with more effective means of discipline and punishment. The instrument has also been shown to identify factors that have predicted recidivism for firesetting behavior (Kolko & Kazdin, 1992). Summed scores can be compared with the initial sample scores used to develop the instrument. Scores can be compared with those from the original study (Kolko & Kazdin, 1989a), or responses can be analyzed to identify areas that may need additional exploration and added attention when a treatment plan is formulated.

The Children's Firesetting Interview

The Children's Firesetting Interview (CFI) provides 46 items that encompass six factors associated with firesetting behavior in youths. In addition to answering questions, respondents are also asked to demonstrate how they would strike a book of fake matches or use the phone to report a fire, as well as demonstrating an understanding about the combustibility of tangible everyday items in the youth's life. Scores are summed and can be compared with the original results of firesetting and nonfiresetting youths from which the instrument was developed (Kolko & Kazdin, 1989b). Responses can also be used to identify areas of concern that warrant further exploration. The CFI has good internal consistency and test-retest reliability along the six factors that it measures, and studies have shown that it successfully classifies 71% of children and adolescents with firesetting histories. Two of the factors have been shown to provide predictive validity of recidivism for firesetting behavior (Kolko & Kazdin, 1992).

The FIRE Protocol

The FIRE Protocol, developed by Irene Pinsonneault and Joe Richardson (1992), has been used to establish consistent guidelines for interviewing youths who were referred to fire safety interventions following arrest for setting a fire. The protocol has been administered to more than 1,200 youths in two populations. One group has consisted of male adolescents who were referred to a firesetting group program on the basis of their conviction for arson or a similar serious crime involving the use of fire. The other group has consisted of male and female adolescents who were referred to a community firesetting intervention program following arrest for a fire-related incident. All youths were on probation and living in the community at the time of their participation in the program and completion of the protocol.

The FIRE Protocol consists of 320 questions administered in a semistructured format to the youths, as well as to the caregivers or parents. It measures 10 domains of functioning. The protocol addresses cognitive, social, emotional, and behavioral functioning; the history of the adolescent's firesetting; the youth's environment and family functioning; and how the youth both perceives and responds to the fires that were set. The protocol places an emphasis on assessing the youth's ability to take responsibility for his or her firesetting

behavior. The underpinnings of the protocol are built on research that suggests that antisocial youths often have difficulty taking responsibility for actions and that conflicts are often solved using action-oriented solutions instead of problem-solving skills (Dodge, Pettit, McClaskey, & Brown, 1986; Lochman, Lampron, & Rabiner, 1989). The interviewer administering the protocol needs to be ready to confront denial and minimization during the interview process, as well as to address the youth's tendency to avoid responsibility for the firesetting. The FIRE Protocol has not been subjected to tests for construct validity or test-retest reliability, and clearly additional research is needed to establish psychometric properties for this instrument. However, the protocol has been used successfully in juvenile-firesetting intervention programs. This instrument has also proven to be useful with adolescents who present with significant thinking distortions regarding firesetting behavior and their accountability regarding their behavior in general.

Juvenile Firesetter Needs Assessment Protocol

The Juvenile Firesetter Needs Assessment Protocol (Humphreys & Kopet, 1996) contains questions about firesetting and general behavioral functioning, while helping the clinician plan possible intervention recommendations. A semistructured interview thoroughly reviews the youth's firesetting history and additionally includes 61 questions about general mental health, family, and social functioning. The protocol guides the clinician in assigning various types of motives that may be responsible for the firesetting behavior. Possible motives include curiosity-related firesetting, crisis-driven firesetting, delinquent firesetting, and emotionally disturbed firesetting. These categories are similar to the categories initially developed in the FEMA interview guide (Federal Emergency Management Agency, 1979). The interview yields a ratio score that can be useful in determining which are the most predominate types of firesetting behavior. The protocol then lists some basic treatment and safety plan recommendations that can serve as the foundation for crafting a treatment plan for the youth and the family. This instrument is a useful tool to augment a clinical assessment of a youth who may present with firesetting, or it can be used as a screening instrument for youths already identified as requiring services for different reasons.

The Firesetting History Interview

In addition to using structured and semistructured interview tools to assess the history of firesetting behavior, evaluators should also develop some skills in interviewing youths about their experiences with fire. Many youths who may be seen for a firesetting assessment may also have learning disabilities, attentional deficits, or information processing weaknesses that produce poorly elaborated answers about the facts surrounding their firesetting behavior. When engaging these children and adolescents in an interview about their firesetting, the evaluator needs to be flexible in rephrasing questions, offering opportunities to draw diagrams and pictures of the event, or even helping the youth role-play what actually happened in a particular firesetting incident. Eliciting a history of firesetting behavior may help the youth take responsibility for his or her behavior and facilitate treatment.

Developed by Wilcox (2001) and described in detail by Wilcox and Kolko (2002), the firesetting interview includes the parent or guardian, as well as the child or adolescent. This technique employs an array of questions that begin with the most recent firesetting incident that brought the youth's firesetting to the attention of adults and precipitated a referral for assessment. Working with data obtained from collateral sources, the clinician probes for the details about the events surrounding the fire, the context of the fire, how the fire was set, and what was set on fire. Other questions are designed to determine what the youth did once the fire began and what, if anything, he or she learned from the experience. In reverse chronological order, the clinician repeats a similar set of questions about past firesetting incidents and how these events unfolded. With the parents or guardian, the evaluator obtains in a similar fashion a history of their awareness of the youth's firesetting behavior, with particular questions focusing on whether the adult had noticed any evidence of charring or debris from a small fire in various parts of the house or yard. The evaluator also elicits possible reports from other adults, such as family members or members of the youth's peer group.

A chronology of fire-related events is then transposed on a chronological time line, including those events that involve the youth's life at home, at school, and with friends. On completion of the interview, the evaluator should have a chronological record of incidents and the context in which these events transpired. This may help caregivers or treatment providers understand how firesetting behavior could represent an expression of anger, a means of coping with distress, a result of peer pressure, or a convenient way to alleviate boredom. Recognizing these patterns is important for diagnostic or treatment purposes.

Evaluating Behavioral Functioning

Firesetting is defined as a behavior, not a state of mind. However, proper assessment of the act requires a thorough understanding of as much information about the youth's spectrum of behavioral and psychological functioning as possible.

Evaluators can utilize other reliable standardized measures to gain information about the youth's functioning in other areas of his or her life. It is important to also to obtain information from adults who know the youth in a variety of other venues, for example, the school, at home, or in an after-school program. Measures to gauge the effect of treatment after the youth completes an intervention program can also be helpful. Measures that clinicians may want to consider include the Child Behavior Checklist (CBCL), including both the Teacher Report Form (TRF) and the Youth Self-Report Form, all of which provide a good measure of behavioral functioning and are helpful in identifying both internalizing and externalizing forms of behavior (Achenbach, 1991a, 1991b, 1991c). Evaluators can also use the Jesness Inventory (Jesness, 1996), which consists of 155 forced-choice (true/false) questions that had been used extensively with adjudicated youths and other youths involved in antisocial behavior. Studies have shown this measure to have good reliability and internal consistency (Lavery, Siegel, Cousins, & Rubovits, 1993). The Interview for Antisocial Behavior (Kazdin & Esveldt-Dawson, 1986) is also effective in gauging the behavioral functioning of youths who have been involved in aggressive or externalizing behavior. This measure consists of 30 items and is useful in determining the youth's involvement in antisocial behavior, as well as overt and covert aggressive behavior.

Often clinicians hear that a youth has been setting fires because he or she is "bored." It is worth examining this and gaining a sense of the youth's own threshold for arousal but not at the expense of excluding inquiry into other areas. Is there a tendency toward sensation-seeking activities, especially when boredom sets in? There is evidence to suggest that the need to seek out sensation is often associated with deviant behavior (Junger & Wiegersma, 1995). Firesetting is seen as a way to remedy the need for arousal when children and adolescents find they are feeling bored (Kolko & Kazdin, 1988). In turn, how does the youth cope with feelings of frustration or anger? What strategies are used to solve other problems that arise in social situations? Can the youth reflect on past behavior and present a reasonable account of what happened without relying on cognitive distortions? Can the youth accept responsibility for her or his past actions, or is there a pattern of blaming others, minimizing events, or denial? What does a review of the youth's history provide in terms of how the child or adolescent responds to limits, and what level of limits is needed for the youth to respond appropriately in situations? It is also important to assess the risk-taking behavior and judgment of the youth and, with older adolescents, to consider whether drug or alcohol use may be loosening inhibitions and impairing judgment. The overall picture of behavioral function should not only yield clues to why firesetting has emerged in the behavioral repertoire of the youth but also provide a sense of what sorts of behavioral interventions may be needed to craft an effective intervention plan for the child or adolescent.

Assessing Cognitive Functioning and Styles of Processing Information

It is not necessary that full psychological testing of every function be included as part of a firesetting assessment. However, evaluators need to consider the possibility of learning disabilities and cognitive deficits. In most cases, this information can be obtained from collateral sources, such as the school or other mental health providers who may have performed psychological testing. The consideration of intellectual and cognitive functioning of the child or adolescent is important for understanding how the youth makes sense of the world, solves problems in social situations, and resolves problems in situations that rely on proper judgment. Research has shown that youths who engage in aggressive behavior often have difficulty interpreting social cues because of a host of social-cognitive weaknesses (Lochman, 1992; Lochman & Dodge, 1994). In some instances these misperceptions are a function of cognitive distortions, but in other cases they may also be a function of cognitive processing deficits (Kendall, 1991). Formal testing may provide clues as to how the youth interprets social cues, as well as his or her own experience of emotional arousal. Testing may also provide information about how language is processed and whether verbal or nonverbal learning deficits exist. In addition, testing, as well as clinical interviews, may yield valuable information about how the child or adolescent interprets social cues, as well as interpersonal conflicts. These factors are important to consider in trying to understand how the child or adolescent has developed an interest in fire, why and when he or she has chosen to set fires, and what he or she is capable of understanding about what fire can do. How well the child or adolescent understands cause and effect with respect to fire, as well as to his or her own behaviors, can provide insights into how well the youth will be able to comprehend some of the basic aspects of fire science and fire safety.

Considering Family Functioning

Understanding the family context in which fire-related and other behavior takes place can lend valuable insight into the dynamics that may be motivating firesetting behavior. How fire use has been modeled for a child or adolescent within the home is very relevant to understanding perceptions of fire and how to use fire. Comprehensive interviewing, as well as careful review of collateral reports, is a critical aspect of any assessment of firesetting behavior.

Measures of family functioning can be used in assessing families of youths who set fires. The measures listed here are by no means inclusive of the various assessment measures a clinician might use. The Parenting Stress Index (Abidin, 1995) is a 101-item questionnaire that provides a useful measure of the stressors affecting the family, as well as how much stress the parents experience in their parenting role. It is designed for parents of children under 12, but there is also a version suitable for parents of adolescents up to age 19 (Sheras, Abidin, & Konold, 1998). The Beck Depression Inventory—II (Beck, Steer, & Brown, 1996), the Brief Symptom Inventory (Derogatis & Spencer, 1982), or the Symptom Checklist—90 (Derogatis, 1983) may be used, along with a review of family history, to assess overall levels of parental psychopathology. The Parent-Child Conflict Tactics Scales (Straus, 1979; Jouriles, Mehta, McDonald, & Francis, 1997) is also a useful measure to capture styles of parenting discipline, as well as the nature of conflicts between parents and youths.

Clinicians need to be aware of not only the family history—the changes in the family, separations, divorces, and other stressors that have affected the family—but also the style of functioning within the family. What ways does the family have of enforcing rules? What types of punishment are used? When rules are not obeyed, what are the typical consequences? How is the youth perceived in the family system? Is the child or adolescent described in terms of her or his shortcomings and failures, with a sense of ridicule, or is there some appreciation for the youth's strengths and talents? Do mental health or substance abuse issues affect the family? Is there a history of domestic violence in the home or documented incidents of physical or sexual trauma in the family history? How does the family perceive the firesetting behavior? Is it considered something worth the attention of the whole family in helping the youth change his or her behavior, or is it considered the youth's problem and not significant enough to warrant the parents' attention? Is there a sense that the family takes seriously the need to practice fire safety at home?

The success or failure of an intervention can hinge on whether the family system can work with the intervention team and support a change in the youth's behavior. Sometimes family system issues are so acute that additional services or treatment are needed for the whole family before the child or adolescent can be expected to change his or her own behavior. In these instances, the support and resources of a team of collateral contacts can be helpful in deciding whether the child or adolescent can safely remain in the home or whether some alternative, interim placement needs to be arranged.

Assessing Social and Emotional Functioning

The assessment of a youth's social and emotional functioning must be informed regarding what is known about firesetting behavior, not simply what is most familiar to clinicians. The assessment must produce a robust sense of how the youth is functioning in a variety of domains. Certainly, if there are clear indications of acute psychiatric symptoms, such as a mood disorder, trauma, anxiety, or attentional deficits, these need to be addressed before focusing on only the firesetting behavior. A number of measures may be useful to clinicians in assessing social and emotional functioning. Regardless of instrument choice, evaluators need to be clear of the specific purpose of the instrument and not to overgeneralize from findings. A measure of depression, such as the Children's Depression Inventory (CDI; Kovacs, 1992), can be a useful screen for depressive symptoms. The Trauma Symptom Checklist for Children (TSSC; Briere, 1996) is a useful tool in gauging the degree to which the youth may be experiencing anxiety or sequelae related to traumatic events in his or her life. The State-Trait Anger Expression Inventory (STAXI-2) is a helpful guide in gauging how the youth is responding to anger and how the youth typically copes with anger (Speilberger, 2001). In addition, it is important to attend to coping styles that the child or adolescent uses, ego defenses, the child or adolescent's fantasy life, as well as how the child or adolescent perceives relationships in her or his life. Evaluators need to consider whether the child or adolescent has experienced any form of trauma—physical abuse, domestic violence, or sexual abuse—in the past and, if so, how these experiences have affected the youth. Similarly, in assessing a child or adolescent's perceptions of relationships, it is important to attend to issues of power and aggression. How does the child or adolescent manage aggressive impulses and anger? Does the child or adolescent appear to identify more with the aggressor in situations of conflict and power or with the victim? How does the firesetting fit into these dynamics within the youth's life? Why has the youth chosen fire and setting fires as an action? What is his or her relationship with fire in the context of his or her social and emotional functioning?

The Whole Is Greater Than the Sum of Its Parts

Assessments and interventions with children and adolescents engaged in firesetting challenge many of the traditional assumptions about behavioral dysfunction and the resulting treatment recommendations. There are often a variety of interdependent factors that result in this behavior, not simply one main cause that can easily be identified and treated. Proper assessment of firesetting behavior requires a broad range of knowledge about child development, psychological functioning, family systems, service delivery options, and fire itself. In essence, firesetting behavior is greater than the sum of the various developmental domains that might be identified in the course of an assessment. Assessments must include methods sufficient to address a complex array of factors about what has been driving the firesetting behavior and what steps can be taken to ensure the child's or adolescent's safety. Developing such formulations requires patience and a willingness to carefully examine the evidence that emerges in the course of an assessment, withholding judgment until all data are carefully examined and their relationship to one another satisfactorily explained. The dynamics behind the setting of a fire sometimes seem to reside in a dimension that is obscured in a shadow. It is through the process of conducting a thorough assessment that the dimensions obscured by the shadow can become illuminated and revealed and a behavior that is dangerous can hopefully be addressed safely.

References

Abidin, R. R. (1995). *The Parenting Stress Index (PSI)* (3rd ed.). Lutz, FL: Psychological Assessment Resources.

Achenbach, T. M. (1991a). *Manual for the Child Behavior Checklist and 1991 Profile.* Burlington: University of Vermont, Department of Psychiatry.

Achenbach, T. M. (1991b). *Manual for the Teacher's Report Form and 1991 Profile.* Burlington: University of Vermont, Department of Psychiatry.

Achenbach, T. M. (1991c). *Manual for the Youth Self-Report and 1991 Profile.* Burlington: University of Vermont, Department of Psychiatry.

Beck, A. T., Steer, R. A., & Brown, G. K. (1996). *The Beck Depression Inventory—II.* San Antonio, TX: Harcourt Brace Educational Measurement.

Briere, J. (1996). *The Trauma Symptom Checklist for Children (TSCC).* Lutz, FL: Psychological Assessment Resources.

Bumpass, E. R., Fagelman, F. D., & Brix, R. J. (1983). Intervention with children who set fires. *American Journal of Psychotherapy, 37,* 328–345.

Derogatis, L. R. (1983). *The Symptom Checklist-90 Manual.* Baltimore: Johns Hopkins University School of Medicine, Clinical Psychometrics Research Unit.

Derogatis, L. R., & Spencer, M. S. (1982). *The Brief Symptom Inventory (BSI): Administration, scoring and procedures manual.* Baltimore: Johns Hopkins University School of Medicine, Clinical Psychometrics Research Unit.

Dodge, K. A., Petit, G. D., McClaskey, C. L., & Brown, M. M. (1986). Social competence in children. *Monographs of the Society for Research in Child Development, 51*(2, Serial No. 213).

Federal Bureau of Investigation. (2000). *Crime in the United States 1999.* Washington, DC: U.S. Government Printing Office.

Federal Emergency Management Agency. (1979). *Interviewing and counseling juvenile firesetters.* Washington, DC: U.S. Government Printing Office.

Fineman, K. R. (1980). Firesetting in childhood and adolescents. *Psychiatry Clinics of North America, 3,* 483–500.

Fineman, K. R. (1995). A model for the qualitative analysis of child and adult fire deviant behavior. *American Journal of Forensic Psychology, 13,* 31–60.

Fineman, K. R. (1997a). *Family Fire Risk Interview Form.* Washington, DC: Federal Emergency Management Agency.

Fineman, K. R. (1997b). *Juvenile Fire Risk Interview Form.* Washington, DC: Federal Emergency Management Agency.

Fineman, K. R. (1997c). *Parent Fire Risk Questionnaire.* Washington, DC: Federal Emergency Management Agency.

Freud, S. (1930). Civilization and its discontents. In J. Strachey (Ed.), *The standard edition of the complete psychological works of Sigmund Freud* (Vol. 21, pp. 59–145). London: Hogarth Press and the Institute of Psycho-analysis.

Freud, S. (1932). The acquisition of power over fire. In J. Strachey (Ed.), *The standard edition of the complete psychological works of Sigmund Freud* (Vol. 22, pp. 185–193). London: Hogarth Press and the Institute of Psycho-analysis.

Gaynor, J., & Hatcher, C. (1987). *The psychology of child firesetting: Detection and intervention.* New York: Brunner/Mazel.

Geller, J. L. (1992). Arson in review. *Clinical Forensic Psychiatry, 15,* 623–645.

Ghetti, S., & Redlich, A. D. (2001). Reactions to youth crime: Perceptions of accountability and competency. *Behavioral Sciences and the Law, 19,* 33–52.

Goudsblom, J. (1992). *Fire and civilization.* London: Penguin Books.

Grolnick, W. S., Cole, R. E., Laurenitis, L., & Schwartzman, P. (1990). Playing with fire: A developmental assessment of children's fire understanding and experience. *Journal of Clinical Child Psychology, 19,* 128–135.

Hall, J. R. (1996). *U.S. arson trends and patterns: 1995.* Quincy, MA: National Fire Protection Association.

Hardesty, V. A., & Gayton, W. F. (2002). The problem of children and fire. In D. Kolko (Ed.), *Handbook on firesetting in children and youth* (pp. 1–13). San Diego, CA: Academic Press.

Heath, G. A., Hardesty, V. A., & Goldfine, P. E., & Walker, A. M. (1983). Childhood firesetting: An empirical study. *Journal of the American Academy of Child Psychiatry, 22,* 370–374.

Heath, G. A., Hardesty, V. A., Goldfine, P. E. & Walker, A. M. (1985). Diagnosis and childhood firesetting. *Journal of Clinical Psychology, 41,* 571–575.

Hellman, D. S., & Blackman, N. (1966). Enuresis, fire-setting and cruelty to animals: A triad predictive of adult crime. *American Journal of Psychiatry, 122,* 1431–1435.

Humphreys, J., & Kopet, T. (1996). *The Juvenile Firesetter Needs Assessment Protocol.* Salem, OR: Oregon Department of State Police, Office of the State Fire Marshal, Juvenile Firesetter Intervention Program.

Jesness, C. F. (1996). *The Jesness Inventory.* North Tonawanda, NY: Multi-Health Systems.

Jouriles, E. N., Mehta, P., McDonald, R., & Francis, D. J. (1997). Psychometric properties of family members' reports of parental physical aggression toward clinic-referred children. *Journal of Consulting and Clinical Psychology, 65,* 309–318.

Junger, M., & Wiegersma, A. (1995). The relations between accidents, deviance and leisure time.

Criminal Behavior and Mental Health, 53, 144–174.

Kafry, D. (1980). Playing with matches: Children and fire. In D. Canter (Ed.), *Fires and human behavior* (pp. 47–61). Chichester, UK: John Wiley.

Kaufman, L., Heins, L., & Reiser, D. (1961). A re-evaluation of the psychodynamics of firesetting. *American Journal of Orthopsychiatry, 31,* 123–136.

Kazdin, A. E., & Esveldt-Dawson, K. (1986). The Interview for Antisocial Behavior: Psychometric characteristics and concurrent validity with child psychiatric inpatients. *Journal of Psychopathology and Behavioral Assessment, 8,* 289–303.

Kelso, J., & Stewart, M. A. (1986). Factors which predict the persistence of aggressive conduct disorder. *Journal of Child Psychology and Psychiatry, 27,* 77–86.

Kendall, P. C. (1991). Guiding theory for therapy with children and adolescents. In P. C. Kendall (Ed.), *Child and adolescent therapy: Cognitive-behavioral procedures* (pp. 3–22). New York: Guilford.

Klein, M. (1932). *Psycho-analysis of children.* London: Hogarth Press and the Institute of Psycho-analysis.

Kolata, G. (1987). Fire! New ways to prevent it. *Science, 235,* 281–282.

Kolko, D. J. (1985). Juvenile firesetting: A review and methodological critique. *Clinical Psychology Review, 5,* 345–376.

Kolko, D. J. (1989). Fire setting and pyromania. In C. Last & M. Hersen (Eds.), *Handbook of child psychiatric diagnosis* (pp. 443–459). New York: John Wiley.

Kolko, D. J., & Kazdin, A. E. (1986). A conceptualization of firesetting in children and adolescents. *Journal of Abnormal Child Psychology, 14,* 49–61.

Kolko, D. J., & Kazdin, A. E. (1988). Parent-child correspondence in identification of firesetting among child psychiatric patients. *Journal of Child Psychology and Psychiatry, 29,* 175–184.

Kolko, D. J., & Kazdin, A. E. (1989a). Assessment of dimensions of childhood firesetting among patients and nonpatients: The Firesetting Risk Interview. *Journal of Abnormal Child Psychology, 17,* 157–176.

Kolko, D. J., & Kazdin, A. E. (1989b). The Children's Firesetting Interview with psychiatrically referred and non-referred children. *Journal of Abnormal Child Psychology, 17,* 609–624.

Kolko, D. J., & Kazdin, A. E. (1990). Matchplay and firesetting in children: Relationship to parent, marital and family dysfunction. *Journal of Clinical Child Psychology, 19,* 229–238.

Kolko, D. J., & Kazdin, A. E. (1991a). Aggression and psychopathology in matchplaying and firesetting children: A replication and extension. *Journal of Clinical Child Psychology, 20,* 191–201.

Kolko, D. J., & Kazdin, A. E. (1991b). Motives of childhood firesetters: Firesetting characteristics and psychological correlates. *Journal of Child Psychology and Psychiatry, 32,* 535–550.

Kolko, D. J., & Kazdin, A. E. (1992). The emergence and recurrence of child firesetting: A one-year prospective study. *Journal of Abnormal Child Psychology, 20,* 17–37.

Kolko, D. J., & Kazdin, A. E. (1994). Children's descriptions of their firesetting incidents: Characteristics and relationship to recidivism. *Journal of the American Academy of Child and Adolescent Psychiatry, 33,* 114–122.

Kolko, D. J., Kazdin, A. E., & Meyer, E. C. (1985). Aggression and psychopathology in childhood firesetters: Parent and child reports. *Journal of Consulting and Clinical Psychology, 53,* 377–385.

Kovacs, M. (1992). *The Children's Depression Inventory.* North Tonawanda, NY: Multi-Health Systems.

Lavery, B., Siegel, A. W., Cousins, J. H., & Rubovits, D. S. (1993). Adolescent risk-taking: An analysis of problem behaviors in problem children. *Journal of Experimental Child Psychology, 55,* 277–294.

Lewis, N., & Yarnell, H. (1951). Pathological firesetting (pyromania). *Nervous and Mental Disease Monograph* (No. 82). New York: Coolidge Foundation.

Lochman, J. E. (1992). Cognitive-behavioral interventions with aggressive boys: Three-year follow-up and preventive effects. *Journal of Consulting and Clinical Psychology, 60,* 426–432.

Lochman, J. E., & Dodge, K. A. (1994). Social-cognitive processes of severely violent, moderately aggressive and nonaggressive boys. *Journal of Consulting and Clinical Psychology, 62,* 366–374.

Lochman, J. E., Lampron, L. B., & Rabiner, D. L. (1989). Format and salience effects in the social problem-solving of aggressive and non-aggressive boys. *Journal of Clinical Child Psychology, 18,* 230–236.

Macht, L. B., & Mack, J. E. (1968). The firesetter syndrome. *Psychiatry, 31,* 277–288.

Marc, M. (1833). Considérations médico-légales sur la monomanie et particulièrement sue la monomanie incendiaire. *Annals d'hygiène publique et de medécine légale, 10,* 367–484.

Massachusetts Coalition for Juvenile Firesetter Intervention Programs. (2001). *Kids and fire: Intervention and education, 2001.* Westport Point, MA: Author.

Massachusetts Coalition for Juvenile Firesetter Intervention Programs. (2002). *Expanding the circles of care, Datalink 2002, 6–7.* Westport Point, MA: Author.

Nurcombe, B. (1964). Children who set fires. *Medical Journal of Australia, 1,* 579–584.

Office of Juvenile Justice and Delinquency Prevention. (1996). *Female offenders in the juvenile justice system* (NCJ 160941). Washington, DC: Author.

Oregon Office of the State Fire Marshal. (2001a). *2000 juvenile firesetting: Annual report.* Salem, OR: Author.

Oregon Office of the State Fire Marshal. (2001b). *Fire interest survey: Final report.* Salem, OR: Author. •

Pinsonneault, I., & Richardson, J. (1992) *The FIRE Protocol.* Westport Point, MA: F.I.R.E. Solutions.

Saunders, E. B., & Awad, G. A. (1991). Adolescent female firesetters. *Canadian Journal of Psychiatry, 36,* 401–404.

Sheras, P. L., Abidin, R. R., & Konold, T. R. (1998). *The Stress Index for Parents of Adolescents.* Lutz, FL: Psychological Assessment Resources.

Shirk, S., Talmi, A., & Olds, D. (2000). A developmental psychopathology perspective on child and adolescent treatment policy. *Development and Psychopathology, 12,* 835–855.

Slavkin, M. L. (2000). Juvenile firesetting: An exploratory analysis. *Dissertation Abstracts International: Section B: The Sciences & Engineering, 61*(11B): 6168.

Speilberger, C. D. (2001). *The State-Trait Anger Expression Inventory—2 (STAXI-2).* Lutz, FL: Psychological Assessment Resources.

Strachan, J. C. (1981). Conspicuous firesetting in children. *British Journal of Psychiatry, 140,* 357–363.

Straus, M. A. (1979). Measuring intrafamily conflict and violence: The Conflict Tactics (CT) Scales. *Journal of Marriage and the Family, 41,* 75–88.

U.S. Fire Administration. (1997). *Arson in the United States.* Washington, DC: Author.

U.S. Fire Administration. (2000). *Children and fire in the United States: 1994–1997*. Washington, DC: Author.

U.S. Fire Administration. (2001). *Fire in the United States: 1989–1998* (12th ed.). Washington, DC: Author.

Vandersall, J. A., & Weiner, J. M. (1970). Children who set fires. *Archives of General Psychiatry, 22*, 63–71.

Vreeland, R. G., & Levin, B. M. (1980). Psychological aspects of firesetting. In D. Canter (Ed.), *Fires and human behaviour* (pp. 31–46). Chichester, UK: John Wiley.

Wax, D. E., & Haddox, V. G. (1974a). Enuresis, firesetting and animal cruelty in male adolescent delinquents: A triad predictive of violent behavior. *Journal of Psychiatry and Law, 2*, 45–71.

Wax, D. E., & Haddox, V. G. (1974b). Enuresis, firesetting and cruelty to animals: A useful danger signal in predicting vulnerability of adolescent males to assaultive behavior. *Child Psychiatry and Human Development, 4*, 151–156.

Wilcox, D. K. (2001). *The Firesetting History Interview* [Training manual]. Westport Point, MA: Massachusetts Coalition for Juvenile Firesetter Intervention Programs.

Wilcox, D. K., & Kolko, D. J. (2002). Assessing recent firesetting behavior and taking a firesetting history. In D. Kolko (Ed.), *Handbook on firesetting in children and youth* (pp. 161–175). San Diego, CA: Academic Press.

Wilcox, D. K., Murphy, L., & Goldstein, J. N. (2000, December). *Object relations and trauma in children and adolescents engaged in firesetting behavior*. Poster presented at the Center for Mental Health Services Research and Training, Cambridge Hospital Department of Psychiatry, Cambridge, Massachusetts.

Yarnell, H. (1940). Firesetting in children. *American Journal of Orthopsychiatry, 10*, 272–287.

Part III

SELECTED MEASUREMENT ISSUES

24

The MMPI-A in Forensic Assessment

James N. Butcher
Kenneth S. Pope

This chapter reviews information and issues vital to those who use the Minnesota Multiphasic Personality Inventory for Adolescents (MMPI-A) in forensic assessments, as well as to those (e.g., attorneys) who encounter its use in forensic contexts. The focus is on the MMPI-A, but the chapter also includes information relevant to conducting forensic evaluations with adolescents in order to meet the highest standards of practice and to withstand close scrutiny in the adversarial forensic system.

The first section reviews the development of the MMPI-A for those who are new to the instrument. The second section discusses essential steps for those who are considering using the MMPI-A in a forensic assessment. The third section looks at the evolving research on the MMPI-A and highlights two casebooks that provide information and case examples that illustrate case interpretation. The fourth section examines the ways in which the MMPI-A can identify invalid or misleading responses.

DEVELOPMENT OF THE MMPI-A

The original MMPI was widely used to assess adolescents. The earliest studies using the MMPI with adolescents sought to determine whether the instrument could reliably and validly identify subgroups of youths who were predisposed to delinquency. Early research by Capwell (1945a, 1945b) showed that the item pool on the MMPI provided useful clinical-personality information on delinquent girls. Monachesi (1948, 1950a, 1950b, 1953) extended Capwell's findings to boys, showing that delinquent boys and girls were significantly different from boys and girls characterized as "normal" on several MMPI scales, notably 4, 6, 7, 8, and 9, with Scale 4 being the most different. Much of the early adolescent MMPI research concentrated on identifying youths who were prone to juvenile delinquency (Hathaway & Monachesi, 1963).

The pioneering research on delinquent boys and girls led Hathaway and Monachesi (1963) to conduct a 15-year prospective study of the MMPI with normal and delinquent adolescents. A total of 15,300 ninth graders from Minnesota were administered the MMPI. Substantial demographic and biographical information on each of the participants was obtained from schools, law enforcement agencies, and social service organizations. This extensive database was then used to investigate whether delinquency and other acting-out behaviors could be predicted, as well as to describe differences in adult and adolescent personality as measured by the MMPI. Such studies on adult and adolescent differences helped in understanding how to use the MMPI with adolescents and how to take account of the actuarial differences between groups (e.g., between adults and adolescents, between adolescents who were and were not delinquent).

In developing the MMPI-A, published in 1992 (Butcher et al., 1992), the MMPI Revision Committee was aware that the MMPI test item pool needed considerable modification in order to make the instrument more effective with adolescents. For example, the original MMPI items had been written from an adult perspective and had usually been administered without modification to adolescents. In addition, the MMPI scales had been developed using adult samples and a conceptualization of psychological disorders that was oriented toward adult psychopathology. Moreover, no adolescent participants were included in the norms for the MMPI, and interpretation of the scales for adolescents was based, in part, on research with adults. It is interesting that despite these limitations, the MMPI came to be widely used with adolescents (Hathaway & Monachesi, 1963; Hathaway, Reynolds, & Monachesi, 1969).

To revise the MMPI for use with adolescents, a large representative national sample of adolescents was obtained using an experimental form for adolescents—a form made up of the original MMPI items, some new items contained on the MMPI-2, and a number of new items that address adolescent issues and behaviors such as attitudes about school and parents, peer group influence, and eating problems. These items were distributed throughout the booklet in order to make the instrument more visibly relevant to adolescents. Furthermore, items about youthful behaviors that were worded in the past tense on the MMPI and MMPI-2 were changed to the present tense for the MMPI-A.

The development of MMPI-A norms included obtaining a large, diverse, normative sample of young people from several regions of the United States, including California, Minnesota, Ohio, North Carolina, New York, Pennsylvania, Virginia, and Washington State. These various testing locations were chosen to maximize the possibility of obtaining a balanced sample of participants according to geographic region, rural–urban residence, and ethnic background.

The experimental form of the MMPI (704-item Form TX) was administered to 815 girls and 805 boys in the normative sample and was also employed in an extensive clinical evaluation study (see Williams & Butcher, 1989a, 1989b; Williams, Butcher, Ben-Porath, & Graham, 1992). The MMPI-A normative sample was composed of boys and girls, ages 14 through 18. On completion of the norms, a final MMPI-A booklet was constructed of 478 items, many of which were on the original MMPI and were also included in the MMPI-2.

In the development of MMPI-A, continuity was maintained with the MMPI-2 for several scales, including the validity scales L and K, the standard scales (the eight clinical scales and scales 5 and 0), the MacAndrew Alcoholism Scale (MAC-R), and supplementary scales A and R (Butcher et al., 1992).

A new set of adolescent-specific content scales was developed in order to capitalize on the new adolescent-specific items. In developing the MMPI-A content scales, internal-consistency statistical analyses were used with adolescent samples and verified by rational procedures (that included using a developmental perspective). Three of the MMPI-A content scales were developed using primarily the new adolescent-specific items (School Problems, Low Aspirations, and Alienation). The Family Problems Scale (A-fam) was improved with the addition of adolescent-specific content. A new scale, Conduct Problems (A-con), was substituted for the MMPI-2 Antisocial Practices (ASP) Scale on the MMPI-A when inadequate empirical validity was found for ASP with adolescents (Williams et al., 1992).

To refine content-based interpretation of the MMPI-A further, Sherwood, Ben-Porath, and Williams (1997) developed a set of content component scales for the MMPI-A content scales. These scales further break down the content included in the MMPI-A content scales; for example, the Depression Content Scale contains four component scales: Dysphoria (5 items), Self-depreciation (5 items), Lack of drive (7 items), and Suicidal ideation (4 items). Although these component scales are not long enough to provide psychometrically stable scores, they nevertheless do provide the practitioner with a means of examining the content that might influence high elevations on the parent content scale.

The assessment of substance abuse problems has been the focus of several research studies with the MMPI-A. The MAC-R scale, originally developed for detecting adult substance abuse problems, has shown effectiveness in delineating adolescent substance abuse problems as well. In addition, two new scales have been developed with MMPI-A items to describe adolescent alcohol and drug use problems: the Alcohol-Drug Problem Proneness Scale (PRO) and the Alcohol-Drug Problem Acknowledgments Scale (ACK; Weed, Butcher, & Williams, 1994). These scales have shown effectiveness in assessing adolescent substance abuse problems in cross-validation studies (Gallucci, 1997; Williams, Perry, Farbakhsh, & Veblen-Mortensen, 1999).

As with the MMPI-2, the norms for the MMPI-A were based on the uniform T-score transformation that was developed by Tellegen (1988). This transformation ensured that the percentile values were equivalent across the different MMPI scale scores (Butcher et al., 1992; Tellegen & Ben-Porath, 1992). Both the MMPI-2 and MMPI-A norms were developed using the same target distribution. This procedure ensured the percentile equivalence across the two forms of the MMPI so that if an adolescent is tested with the MMPI-A at one point and is later tested with the MMPI-2, the T scores can be meaningfully compared.

Although the recommended cutoff for clinical interpretation (i.e., a T score of 65) is used for the MMPI-2, it is slightly different for adolescents (60 to 64 T-score range) because these scores are considered to yield potentially useful personality descriptors. The MMPI-A clinical scales have been shown to have high long-term stability (Stein, McClinton, & Graham, 1998).

The United States is an ethnically diverse country in which clients from different cultural and language backgrounds might require psychological evaluation. It is important that all assessment instruments administered to an individual be adequately matched to that person's cultural and language background. For example, the MMPI-A has been translated into Spanish and normed on a Spanish-speaking U.S. adolescent population. The Spanish-language booklet (developed according to rigorous test adaptation procedures) is administered to the adolescent, and the special T scores drawn from the Hispanic norms are used to plot the profile (Butcher et al., 1998).

SOME ESSENTIAL STEPS WHEN USING THE MMPI-A IN FORENSIC CONTEXTS

When properly used, the MMPI-A provides a variety of benefits in forensic assessment of adolescents (see Table 24.1). The following steps—presented in the form of questions an examiner should ask him- or herself before conducting a forensic examination using the MMPI-A—are useful in helping to ensure that the MMPI-A is properly used and that a forensic assessment is valid and meets the highest standards.

1. *What is the MMPI-A expected to do in this assessment?*

It can be tempting to reach for a widely used assessment instrument simply because (1) it is widely used, (2) we have a copy and know how to administer it, and (3) it is one of our favorites. But no instrument can do all things in all settings. It is important to know the degree to which an assessment instrument is well matched to the assessment issue at hand. Even when certain instruments are known for their high reliability and validity, the reliability and validity have been established only for certain specific sets of criteria. Not only is it a significant responsibility to find out the established reliability and validity of the MMPI-A (and those of any other instrument under consideration) for the assessment issue at hand before conducting the assessment, but it is also much more pleasant to learn this information ahead of time instead of during cross-examination.

2. *Is the examiner qualified to conduct this assessment?*

Just as no instrument can do all things in all settings, neither can an examiner. Someone who is a leading expert in the forensic assessment of children or adults may not be qualified to perform a forensic assessment of adolescents ages 14–18. The examiner needs adequate education, training, and supervised experience not only in forensic assessment and the relevant instruments (e.g., the MMPI-A) but also in the developmental issues and other areas of competence relevant to assessing adolescents.

Table 24.1 Advantages of using the MMPI-A in forensic assessment

Some advantages of using the MMPI-A in forensic assessment include:

- Practitioners and researchers choose the MMPI over other personality measures because of its ability to assess a broad range of psychological problems using limited professional time.

- Its objective format makes it easy to administer in either individual or group settings, such as schools. Students are accustomed also to the true-false responding and are willing to disclose psychological problems by responding to MMPI-A items.

- The MMPI-A is only 478 items long (in contrast to the 567-item MMPI-2 booklet) and is readily completed by most adolescents in 1 hour.

- The MMPI-A is relatively easy to administer by computer. The computer-administered version of the test is preferred by adolescents.

- The scales for MMPI-A are easy to score—either manually or by computer. Using a computer allows many different scales, including content scales, subscales, and special scales, to be scored quickly and accurately.

- A clear advantage of the MMPI-A is that there is a parallel instrument (MMPI-2) that can be used with other family members, such as parents. This reduces the frequently occurring tendency in treatment settings to single out the referred adolescent as the only family member with problems. Adolescent clients are more willing to complete the MMPI-A knowing that their parents and/or siblings will be completing a similar instrument.

- The item-level problems assessed by the MMPI-A allow for the appropriate assessment of young people; that is, the MMPI-A has content validity for adolescent problems such as specific themes, including peer-group influences, family relations, and school issues.

- The MMPI-A contains a number of validity scales that address response distorting or invalidating conditions such as exaggerated responding, inconsistency, and faking good.

- The MMPI-A includes a number of well-researched clinical measures, content-based measures, and substance abuse measures to address a broad range of adolescent problem areas.

3. *How old is the person to be assessed?*

The MMPI-A was normed—and the reliability and validity studies focused—on people ages 14–18. However "interesting" it might be to administer the inventory to a 7-year-old child, a 57-year-old adult, or others outside the MMPI-A's age range, there is no scientific basis for interpreting the results.

4. *Is English an appropriate language?*

Even the most comprehensive forensic assessments can be undermined by assessment instruments that are poor matches for the language of the person being assessed. At present we have well-tested translations of the MMPI-A in several languages: Arabic, Chinese, Dutch, French, Greek, Italian, Hebrew, Korean, Norwegian, Russian, Spanish (U.S.), Spanish (Mexico), and Thai. For a listing of available translations and translators, see Butcher (2006).

5. *Is vision an issue?*

Some adolescents are blind or have other severe visual disabilities that prevent them from reading the standard MMPI-A test booklet and using the standard MMPI-A response sheet. The MMPI-A can be administered orally. It is better to administer the test in a standardized manner by using a tape-recorded version of the test that is available through the test distributor, Pearson Assessments, rather than by reading the items in person.

6. *Have relevant issues of informed consent and/ or assent been adequately addressed?*

Issues of informed consent and/or assent for the assessment of minors can be enormously complex, and these issues can become even more difficult in forensic contexts. It is crucial that the examiner identify everyone (the adolescent; a custodial parent or guardian; a noncustodial parent; a court or other state or federal agency) who has a right to participate in the process of authorizing or refusing the assessment and to clarify whether an assessment has been duly authorized and consented or assented to by all who have a right to involvement in the decision *before* undertaking the assessment.

7. *Have relevant issues been adequately clarified and addressed, such as privacy, confidentiality, privilege, discretionary or mandated reporting, who will receive the results (and in what form), who will have access to raw data, and how feedback will be provided to the person assessed?*

Within the complex context of a forensic assessment of a minor, it is easy to overlook the issues of what feedback is to be given to the person assessed and how and when it is to be provided. A discussion of the following 10 fundamental aspects of the feedback process is available at http://kspope.com/assess/feedabs1.php: (a) feedback as process; (b) clarification of tasks and roles; (c) responding effectively to a crisis; (d) informed consent and informed refusal; (e) framing the feedback; (f) acknowledging fallibility; (g) the misuse of feedback; (h) records, documentation, and follow-up; (i) looking toward the future; and (j) assessing and understanding important reactions.

Beyond the anticipated feedback to the person being assessed, to the court, and/or to other individuals, there is also the possibility of unanticipated requests for information. The following scenario is adapted from Pope and Vasquez (1998; see also 2005).

An attorney who is a great source of referrals for you retains you to conduct a forensic assessment on a 17-year-old boy who has been suffering from anxiety and depression and is considering filing a worker's compensation claim for his condition. He quit high school to get married about a year ago and has a 1-year-old baby. However, several months ago he moved out of the apartment he'd shared with his wife and child and had gone back to live with his parents. He works full time as an auto mechanic.

You complete the assessment and immediately begin to receive, over the course of the following year, formal requests for information from:

- The boy's physician, an internist
- The boy's parents, who are concerned about his depression
- The boy's employer, in connection with the worker's compensation claim filed by the boy
- The attorney for the insurance company that is contesting the worker's compensation claim
- The attorney for the boy's wife, who is suing for divorce and for custody of the baby
- The boy's attorney, the source of the original referral, who is considering filing a licensing and an ethics complaint against you because he does not like the assessment results and believes they are due to a faulty assessment

Each of these people asks you to send them the full formal assessment report, the raw test data, and copies of each of the tests you administered (e.g., instructions and all items for the MMPI-A).

Among the questions you face are: Do you have a legal or ethical obligation to provide any of these people all the materials they requested? Partial information? A summary? Nothing at all? Do any of the requests require the boy's written informed consent and/or his parents' consent?

There is, unfortunately, no one-size-fits-all answer to the questions in this scenario that holds across every jurisdiction. These issues tend to be influenced by constantly evolving state (or provincial) legislation and case law in the context of federal regulations. It is the responsibility of the examiner to ensure that he or she understands the relevant requirements for the specifics of the situation and the jurisdiction.

8. Is there an appropriate environment for a forensic assessment?

A room rattled by the sounds of loud construction next door and in which there are frequent intrusions and interruptions is an example of a room that is not appropriate for forensic assessment. Beyond an environment that offers reasonable quiet, privacy, and freedom from distractions is the issue of monitoring. Unless a forensic assessment using the MMPI-A and similar instruments is adequately monitored, there is no way for the examiner to know with certainty whether the examinee received "help" in filling out the form or even if he or she filled out the form. The MMPI-A and similar instruments should not be sent home, back to the ward, or to other unmonitored places with the examinee.

MMPI-A RESEARCH AND CLINICAL CASEBOOKS

Since its publication in 1992, the MMPI-A has been the subject of considerable research and a broadening of clinical use. The MMPI-A has been used extensively in the study of delinquents (Archer, Bolinskey, Morton, & Farris, 2002, 2003; Arita & Baer, 1998; Bannen, 2000; Baron, 2003; Cashel, Ovaert, & Holliman, 2000; Cashel, Rogers, Sewell, & Holliman, 1998; Glaser, Calhoun, & Petrocelli, 2002; Gomez, Johnson, Davis, & Velásquez, 2000; Green, 2000; Gumbiner, Arriaga, & Stevens, 1999; Hammel, 2001; Hunter, 2000; Losado-Paisley,

1998; Moore, Thompson-Pope, & Whited, 1996; Morton & Farris, 2002; Morton, Farris, & Brenowitz, 2002; Pena, Megargee, & Brody, 1996; Riethmiller, 2003; Stein & Graham, 1999; Toyer & Weed, 1998; Vande Streek, 2000).

Several clinical populations have also been studied: people suffering from anxiety disorders (James, Reynolds, & Dunbar, 1994), ADHD (Toyer, 1999), depression (Figuered, 2002), or eating disorders (Cumella, Wall, & Kerr-Almeida, 1999; Lilienfeld, 1994); psychiatric inpatients (Archer & Krishna-murthy, 1997; Arita & Baer, 1998; Deluca, 2003; Hilts & Moore, 2003; Janus, de Groot, & Toepfer, 1998; Janus, Tolbert, Calestro, & Toepfer, 1996; McGrath, Pogge, & Stokes, 2002; Micucci, 2002; Pogge, Stokes, McGrath, Bilginer, & DeLuca, 2002; Powis, 1999) and outpatients (Garyfallos et al., 1999); suicidal adolescents (Batigun & Sahin, 2003; Kopper, Osman, Osman, & Hoffman, 1998); sub-stance-abusing adolescents (Dimino, 2003; Gallucci, 1997; Ingersoll, 2003; Palmer, 1999; Price, 1999; Stein & Graham, 2001; Weed, Butcher, & Williams, 1994; Williams et al., 1999); sexually abused adolescents (Forbey, Ben-Porath, & Davis, 2000; Holifield, Nelson, & Hart, 2002); and those suffering from stress (Scott, Knoth, Beltran-Quiones, & Gomez, 2003). Weis, Crockett, and Vieth (2004) used the MMPI-A with effectiveness to assess adolescents being evaluated for acceptance in a "boot camp" rehabilitation program. (Additional MMPI-A research information is available at http://www1.umn.edu/mmpi.)

The use of "critical items" to detect the presence of specific psychological problems has also been explored with the MMPI-A. Although the use of critical items is somewhat controversial in forensic settings, the practitioner should be aware that a critical-item set has been developed by Forbey and Ben-Porath (1998) for use in clinical evaluations. The authors studied a sample of 419 adolescent patients from diverse clinical settings to develop their item lists. They compared the clinical samples with the adolescent normal sample to develop items that focus on specific problem areas such as aggression, conduct problems, depressed suicidal ideation, and so forth. These items have been found to be informative in providing clues to specific problem areas in clinical evaluations, but it should be kept in mind that their use in forensic evaluations has not been sufficiently explored.

Two clinical casebooks have been published on the use of the MMPI-A. The first, by Ben-Porath and Davis (1996), provides extensive case material on adolescents from a juvenile detention program. This casebook is an extremely valuable resource for teaching MMPI-A interpretation because it presents 16 detailed cases from a broad range of clinical settings and problem areas, along with a rich amount of biographical information. The second, by Butcher et al. (2000), presents a group of 14 cases from 14 other countries using translations of the MMPI-A. Psychologists in China, England, Greece, Holland, France, South Korea, Italy, Mexico, Norway, Peru, Russia, South Africa, Spain, and Thailand were asked to conduct a psychological evaluation of an adolescent and provide a detailed case history and the MMPI-A answer sheet to James Butcher in Minnesota to process the protocol on the computer-based interpretation system, the Minnesota Report. The case histories and the computer-based report are presented in the book, illustrating the considerable extent to which the computer-based MMPI-A interpretations developed for the United States fit cases of adolescents from other cultures taking the test in other languages.

INVALID AND MISLEADING PROFILES

Forensic practitioners who evaluate adolescents in preparation for a court appearance face the question: How credible is the information obtained from the adolescent? Although the issue of response credibility in self-report-based personality assessment is an important one in the clinical assessment, it is more important in forensic evaluations because of the increased motivation on the part of the adolescent to impress the examiner in a particular way, for example, to exaggerate or deny his or her problems.

It is important for the practitioner to carefully evaluate the adolescent's response attitudes in forensic testing (McCann, 1998). Yet many psychological tests used with adolescents lack a means of detecting deviant response attitudes, such as exaggerated or defensive responding, that are so prominent in forensic evaluations. There is no way for the psychologist to know whether the client has accurately presented a true picture of his or her psychological makeup unless validity scales are incorporated in the evaluation.

The MMPI-A contains several methods to assess invalidating response patterns, and these measures must be carefully addressed before clinical scale interpretation can be relied on. The first scales to assess are those that provide non-content-oriented response information. For example, it is crucial to address general "patterns" of deviant responding, such as whether the person has omitted items in the inventory, answered randomly, or responded in an "all true" or "all false" pattern. Next, it is important to determine whether he or she has responded in an inconsistent manner. Two consistency scales have been developed for this purpose, the Variable Response Inconsistency Scale (VRIN) and the True Response Inconsistency Scale (TRIN). Subsequent research has demonstrated the effectiveness of these scales in assessing inconsistency. Baer, Kroll, Rinaldo, and Ballenger (1999), for example, found VRIN to be a good predictor of random responding.

Three Infrequency scales are also used on the MMPI-A to evaluate the tendency on the part of some adolescents to exaggerate problems or to respond in a "fake-bad" direction on the test: the F scale and its component scales F1 and F2. For example, random responding has been shown to be detectable on the MMPI-A validity indicators, particularly scale F (Baer, Ballenger, Berry, & Wetter, 1997).

The F scale was originally developed for the MMPI by Hathaway and McKinley (1943) in order to assess this tendency. However, the F scale on the original MMPI never worked well with adolescents because almost all participants (even normal adolescents) tended to show high elevations on the scale. This resulted from the fact that adult responses were used to develop the scale, not those of adolescents, who tend to have a somewhat different response frequency to the items. Because of the difference between adolescents and adults, an extensive revision was required when the MMPI-A was developed to ensure that it performed as an infrequency measure for adolescents.

Three infrequency scales were developed for the MMPI-A based on adolescent response frequencies. These scales all assess the tendency for some adolescents to answer in an extreme way on the test. The F scale contains a total of 66 items; F1 comprises 33 items that occur toward the front of the booklet, and F2 comprises 33 of the later appearing items. The conjoint use of these scales gives the practitioner a picture of whether or not the adolescent has responded differently to items in the back of the booklet versus those in the front of the booklet. Empirical research has shown that the MMPI-A is highly effective at discriminating adolescents who are faking-bad on the test (Stein, Graham, & Williams, 1995). The relationship between the F scale and the K scale has also been found to be useful in assessing faking in adolescents. For example, Rogers, Hinds, and Sewell (1996) found that F-K appeared to be promising as a predictor of feigning psychopathology.

The MMPI-A has also been found to detect underreporting of symptoms in adolescent populations (Baer, Ballenger, & Kroll, 1998). Two scales on MMPI-A address the tendency on the part of some individuals to present an overly favorable or defensive response pattern on the test. The K scale, developed for adults, has also been found to be sensitive to test defensiveness in adolescents, and the L scale addresses extreme virtue claiming in adolescent samples as well (see the discussion on validity scales on the MMPI-2 in Butcher & Williams, 2000; Pope, Butcher, & Seelen, 2000). Empirical evaluations of the effectiveness of the MMPI-A in detecting fake-good response patterns have been published. Stein and Graham (1999) reported that it was possible to differentiate adolescents who were instructed to "fake good" from adolescents who took the test under standard instructions and from correctional youths who were asked to fake the test, as well as correctional youths who took the test under standard instructions.

SUMMARY

The original MMPI was used extensively to evaluate adolescents in a wide variety of settings. The earliest studies using the MMPI with adolescents sought to determine whether the instrument could reliably and validly identify subgroups of youths predisposed to delinquency. The early successes of the MMPI resulted in wide use with adolescents.

The revised instrument for adolescents, the MMPI-A, was developed using a large, representative, national sample of adolescents. The MMPI-A is made up of many of the original MMPI items, some new items developed for MMPI-2, and a number of new items that address adolescent issues and behaviors, such as attitudes about school and parents, peer group influence, and eating problems. The development of the MMPI-A norms included obtaining a large, diverse, normative sample of young people from several regions of the United States. The MMPI-A normative sample was composed of boys and girls, ages 14 through 18.

A new set of adolescent-specific content scales was developed in order to capitalize on the new adolescent-specific items. In developing the MMPI-A content scales, internal-consistency statistical analyses were used with adolescent samples and verified by rational procedures (that included using a developmental perspective). Two new scales were developed with MMPI-A items to describe adolescent alcohol and drug use problems: the Alcohol-Drug Problem Proneness Scale (PRO) and the Alcohol-Drug Problem Acknowledgments Scale (ACK).

Several well-tested translations of the MMPI-A are available: Arabic, Chinese, Dutch, French, Greek, Italian, Hebrew, Korean, Norwegian, Russian, Spanish (U.S.), Spanish (Mexico), and Thai. A standardized recorded version of the instrument is available for use with people who have severe visual difficulties that interfere with their ability to read the test items. Since its publication in 1992, the MMPI-A has been the subject of considerable research and a broadening of clinical use. The MMPI-A has been used extensively in the study of delinquents and a number of clinical populations.

This chapter also discussed specific steps that a forensic examiner can take to help ensure that a forensic evaluation using the MMPI-A is valid and meets the highest professional standards.

References

Archer, R. P., Bolinskey, P. K., Morton, T. L., & Farris, K. L. (2002). A factor structure for the MMPI-A: Replication with male delinquents. *Assessment, 9(4)*, 319–326.

Archer, R. P., Bolinskey, P. K., Morton, T. L., & Farris, K. L. (2003). MMPI-A characteristics of male adolescents in juvenile justice and clinical treatment settings. *Assessment, 10*(4), 400–410.

Archer, R. P., & Krishnamurthy, R. (1997). MMPI-A scale level factor structure: Replication in a clinical sample. *Assessment, 4*(4), 337–349.

Arita, A., & Baer, R. (1998). Validity of selected MMPI-A scales. *Psychological Assessment, 10*(1), 59–63.

Baer, R. A., Ballenger, J., Berry, D. T. R., & Wetter, M. W. (1997). Detection of random responding on the MMPI-A. *Journal of Personality Assessment, 68*(1), 139–151.

Baer, R. A., Ballenger, J., & Kroll, L. S. (1998). Detection of underreporting on the MMPI-A in clinical and community samples. *Journal of Personality Assessment, 71*(1), 98–113.

Baer, R. A., Kroll, L. S., Rinaldo, J., & Ballenger, J. (1999). Detecting and discriminating between random responding and overreporting on the MMPI-A. *Journal of Personality Assessment, 72*(2), 308–320.

Bannen, M. A. (2000). Part A. Disruptive disorders in adolescent girls: A neglected group. Part B. The clinical utility of the MMPI-A in the assessment of disruptive disordered adolescent girls. *Dissertation Abstracts International, 61*(2-B), 1070B.

Baron, A. T. (2003). Differences in psychopathology, temperament, and family/social history relative to the onset of sexual perpetration in youthful offenders. *Dissertation Abstracts International, 63*(10-B), 4889B.

Batigun, A. D., & Sahin, N. H. (2003). Can anger, impulsivity, and perceiving oneself as an inefficient problem solver be a forerunner of adolescent suicide? [Turkish]. *Turk Psikoloji Dergisi, 18*(51), 37–52.

Ben-Porath, Y. S., & Davis, D. L. (1996). *Case studies for interpreting the MMPI-A*. Minneapolis: University of Minnesota Press.

Butcher, J. N. (2006). *MMPI-2: A practitioner's guide*. Washington, DC: American Psychological Association.

Butcher, J. N., Cabiya, J., Lucio, E., Pena, L., Ruben, D. L., & Scott, R. (1998). *Hispanic version of the MMPI-A for the United States*. Minneapolis: University of Minnesota Press.

Butcher, J. N., Ellertsen, B., Ubostad, B., Bubb. E., Lucio, E., Lim, J., et al. (2000). International case studies on the MMPI-A: An objective approach. Minneapolis: MMPI-2 Workshops and Symposia.

Butcher, J. N., & Williams, C. L. (2000). *Essentials of MMPI-2 and MMPI-A interpretation* (2nd ed.). Minneapolis: University of Minnesota Press.

Butcher, J. N., Williams, C. L., Graham, J. R., Archer, R., Tellegen, A., Ben-Porath, Y. S., & Kaemmer, B. (1992). *MMPI-A manual for administration, scoring, and interpretation*. Minneapolis: University of Minnesota Press.

Capwell, D. (1945a). Personality patterns of adolescent girls: I. Girls who show no improvement in IQ. *Journal of Applied Psychology, 29,* 212–228.

Capwell, D. (1945b). Personality patterns of adolescent girls: II. Delinquents and nondelinquents. *Journal of Applied Psychology, 29,* 289–297.

Cashel, M. L., Ovaert, L., & Holliman, N. G. (2000). Evaluating PTSD in incarcerated male juveniles with the MMPI-A: An exploratory analysis. *Journal of Clinical Psychology, 56*(12), 1535–1550.

Cashel, M. L., Rogers, R., Sewell, K. W., & Holliman, N. B. (1998). Preliminary validation of the MMPI-A for a male delinquent sample: An investigation of clinical correlates and discriminant validity. *Journal of Personality Assessment, 71*(1), 49–69.

Cumella, E. J., Wall, D. A., & Kerr-Almeida, N. (1999). MMPI-A in the inpatient assessment of adolescents with eating disorders. *Journal of Personality Assessment, 73*(1), 31–44.

Deluca, V. A. (2003). The relationship of the MMPI-A and Rorschach to psychosis in adolescent psychiatric inpatients. *Dissertation Abstracts International, 64*(2-B), 959B.

Dimino, R. A. (2003). Early memories, attachment style, the role of peers, and adolescent substance use. *Dissertation Abstracts International, 63*(12-B), 6091B.

Figuered, B. V. (2002). The concurrent validity of the Minnesota Multiphasic Personality Inventory-Adolescent in the assessment of depression. *Dissertation Abstracts International, 62*(10-B), 4782B.

Forbey, J. D., & Ben-Porath, Y. S. (1998). *A critical item set for the MMPI-A*. Minneapolis: University of Minnesota Press.

Forbey, J. D., Ben-Porath, Y. S., & Davis, D. L. (2000). A comparison of sexually abused and non-sexually abused adolescents in a clinical treatment facility using the MMPI-A. *Child Abuse and Neglect, 24*(4), 557–568.

Gallucci, N. T. (1997). On the identification of patterns of substance abuse with the MMPI-A. *Psychological Assessment, 9,* 224–232.

Garyfallos, G., Adamopoulou, A., Karastergiou, A., Voikli, M., Sotiropoulou, A., Donias, S., Giouzepas, J., & Paraschos, A. (1999). Personality disorders in dysthymia and major depression. *Acta Psychiatrica Scandinavica, 99*(5), 332–340.

Glaser, B. A., Calhoun, G. B., & Petrocelli, J. V. (2002). Personality characteristics of male juvenile offenders by adjudicated offenses as indicated by the MMPI-A. *Criminal Justice and Behavior, 29*(2), 183–201.

Gomez, F. C. J., Johnson, R., Davis, Q., & Velásquez, R. J. (2000). MMPI: A performance of African and Mexican American adolescent first-time offenders. *Psychological Reports, 87*(1), 309–314.

Green, A. N. (2000). Minnesota Multiphasic Personality Inventory: Adolescent excitatory scales and demographics as predictors of male juvenile delinquent placement. *Dissertation Abstracts International, 61*(3-B), 1635B.

Gumbiner, J., Arriaga, T., & Stevens, A. (1999). Comparison of MMPI-A, Marks and Briggs, and MMPI-2 norms for juvenile delinquents. *Psychological Reports, 84,* 761–766.

Hammel, S. D. (2001). An investigation of the validity and clinical usefulness of the MMPI-A with female juvenile delinquents. *Dissertation Abstracts International, 61*(11-B), 6135B.

Hathaway, S. R., & McKinley, J. C. (1943). *Manual for administering and scoring the MMPI*. Minneapolis: University of Minnesota Press.

Hathaway, S. R., & Monachesi, E. D. (Eds.). (1963). *Adolescent personality and behavior: MMPI patterns of normal, delinquent, drop-out and other outcomes*. Minneapolis: University of Minnesota Press.

Hathaway, S. R., Reynolds, P. C., & Monachesi, E. D. (1969). Follow up of 812 girls 10 years after high school dropout. *Journal of Consulting and Clinical Psychology, 33*(4), 383–390.

Hilts, D., & Moore, J. M. (2003). Normal range MMPI-A profiles among psychiatric inpatients. *Assessment, 10(3),* 266–272.

Holifield, J. E., Nelson, W. M., III, & Hart, K. J. (2002). MMPI profiles of sexually abused and nonabused outpatient adolescents. *Journal of Adolescent Research, 17*(2), 188–195.

Hunter, L. M. (2000). Use of selected MMPI-A factors in the prediction of clinical outcomes in a community-based treatment program for juvenile sexual offenders. *Dissertation Abstracts International, 60*(11-B), 5775B.

Ingersoll, J. B. (2003). Predicting the underreporting of substance abuse symptoms in adolescent males in an outpatient substance abuse treatment program. *Dissertation Abstracts International, 63*(10-B), 4906B.

James, E. M., Reynolds, C. R., & Dunbar, J. (1994). Self-report instruments. In T. H. Ollendick & N. J. King (Eds.), *International handbook of phobic and anxiety disorders in children and adolescents* (pp. 317–329). New York: Plenum.

Janus, M. D., de Groot, C., & Toepfer, S. M. (1998). The MMPI-A and 13-year-old inpatients: How young is too young? *Assessment, 5,* 321–332.

Janus, M. D., Tolbert, H., Calestro, K., & Toepfer, S. (1996). Clinical accuracy ratings of MMPI approaches for adolescents: Adding ten years for the MMPI-A. *Journal of Personality Assessment, 67*(2), 364–383.

Kopper, B. A., Osman, A., Osman, J. R., & Hoffman, J. (1998). Clinical utility of the MMPI-A content scales and Harris-Lingoes subscales in the assessment of suicidal risk factors in psychiatric adolescents. *Journal of Clinical Psychology, 54*(2), 191–200.

Lilienfeld, L. R. (1994). *The use of the MMPI-A in the identification of risk factors for the future development of eating disorders.* Unpublished doctoral dissertation, University of Minnesota, Minneapolis.

Losado-Paisley, G. (1998). Use of the MMPI-A to assess personality of juvenile male delinquents who are sex offenders and non-sex offenders. *Psychological Reports, 83*(1), 115–122.

McCann, J. T. (1998). *Malingering and deception in adolescents.* New York: Oxford University Press.

McGrath, R. E., Pogge, D. L., & Stokes, J. M. (2002). Incremental validity of selected MMPI-A content scales in an inpatient setting. *Psychological Assessment, 14*(4), 401–409.

Micucci, J. A. (2002). Accuracy of MMPI-A scales ACK, MAC-R, and PRO in detecting comorbid substance abuse among psychiatric inpatients. *Assessment, 9*(2), 111–122.

Monachesi, E. D. (1948). Some personality characteristics of delinquents and nondelinquents. *Journal of Criminal Law and Criminology, 41,* 487–500.

Monachesi, E. D. (1950a). Personality characteristics and socioeconomic status of institutionalized and noninstitutionalized male delinquents. *Journal of Criminal Law and Criminology, 40,* 570–583.

Monachesi, E. D. (1950b). Personality characteristics of institutionalized and noninstitutionalized male delinquents. *Journal of Criminal Law and Criminology, 41,* 167–179.

Monachesi, E. D. (1953). The personality patterns of juvenile delinquents as indicated by the MMPI. In S. R. Hathaway & E. D. Monachesi (Eds.), *Analyzing and predicting delinquency* (pp. 38–53). Minneapolis: University of Minnesota Press.

Moore, J. M., Jr., Thompson-Pope, S. K., & Whited, R. M. (1996). MMPI-A profiles of adolescent boys with a history of firesetting. *Journal of Personality Assessment, 67*(1), 116–126.

Morton, T. L., & Farris, K. L. (2002). MMPI-A Structural Summary characteristics of male juvenile delinquents. *Assessment, 9*(4), 327–333.

Morton, T. L., Farris, K. L., & Brenowitz, L. H. (2002). MMPI-A scores and high points of male juvenile delinquents: Scales 4, 5, and 6 as markers of juvenile delinquency. *Psychological Assessment, 14*(3), 311–319.

Palmer, G. A. (1999). Cluster analysis of MMPI-A profiles of adolescents with substance dependence. *Dissertation Abstracts International, 59*(8-B), 4479B.

Pena, L. M., Megargee, E. I., & Brody, E. (1996). MMPI-A patterns of male juvenile delinquents. *Psychological Assessment, 8,* 388–397.

Pogge, D. L., Stokes, J. M., McGrath, R. E., Bilginer, L., & DeLuca, V. A. (2002). MMPI-A structural summary variables: Prevalence and correlates in an adolescent inpatient psychiatric sample. *Assessment, 9*(4), 334–342.

Pope, K. S., Butcher, J. N., & Seelen, J. (2000). *MMPI/MMPI-2/MMPI-A in court: Assessment, testimony, and cross-examination for expert witnesses and attorneys* (2nd ed.). Washington, DC: American Psychological Association.

Pope, K. S., & Vasquez, M. J. T. (1998). *Ethics in psychotherapy and counseling: A practical guide* (2nd ed.) San Francisco: Jossey-Bass.

Pope, K. S., & Vasquez, M. J. T. (2005) *Surviving and thriving as a therapist: Information, ideas, and resources for psychologists in practice.* Washington, DC: American Psychological Association.

Powis, D. M. (1999). Actuarial use of the MMPI-A: Generation of clinical correlate data for frequently occurring codetypes in an adolescent inpatient sample. *Dissertation Abstracts International, 59*(11-B), 6107B.

Price, B. H. (1999). Personality variables of chemically dependent adolescents as reflected in the MMPI and the Millon Adolescent Personality Inventory. *Dissertation Abstracts International, 60*(2-B), 0864B.

Riethmiller, R. J. (2003). A look at personality change among conduct disordered adolescents in residential treatment. *Dissertation Abstracts International, 63*(12-B), 6104B.

Rogers, R., Hinds, J. D, & Sewell, K. W. (1996).

Feigning psychopathology among adolescent offenders: Validation of the SIRS, MMPI-A, and SIMS. *Journal of Personality Assessment, 67*(2), 244–257.

Schopp, R. F., & Quattrocchi, M. R. (1995). Predicting the present: Expert testimony and civil commitment. *Behavioral Sciences and the Law, 13*, 159–181.

Scott, R. L., Knoth, R. L., Beltran-Quiones, M., & Gomez, N. (2003). Assessment of psychological functioning in adolescent earthquake victims in Colombia using the MMPI-A. *Journal of Traumatic Stress, 16*(1), 49–57.

Sherwood, N. E., Ben-Porath, Y. S., & Williams, C. L. (1997). *The MMPI-A Content Component Scales*. Minneapolis: University of Minnesota Press.

Stein, L. A. R., & Graham, J. R. (1999). Detecting fake-good MMPI-A profiles in a correctional setting. *Psychological Assessment, 11*(3), 386–395.

Stein, L. A. R., & Graham, J. R. (2001). Use of the MMPI-A to detect substance abuse in a juvenile correctional setting. *Journal of Personality Assessment, 77*(3), 508–523.

Stein, L. A. R., Graham, J. R., & Williams, C. R. (1995). Detecting fake-bad MMPI-A profiles. *Journal of Personality Assessment, 65*(3), 415–427.

Stein, L. A. R., McClinton, B. K., & Graham, J. R. (1998). Long-term stability of MMPI-A scales. *Journal of Personality Assessment, 70*(1), 103–108.

Tellegen, A. (1988). The analysis of consistency in personality assessment. *Journal of Personality, 56*(3), 621–663.

Tellegen, A., & Ben-Porath, Y. S. (1992). The new uniform T-scores for the MMPI-2: Rationale, derivation, and appraisal. *Psychological Assessment, 4*, 145–155.

Toyer, E. A. (1999). Development and validation of the A-ADHD: An MMPI-A scale to assess attention-deficit/hyperactivity disorder in adolescents. *Dissertation Abstracts International, 60(3-B)*, 1319B.

Toyer, E. A., & Weed, N. C. (1998). Concurrent validity of the MMPI-A in counseling program for juvenile offenders. *Journal of Clinical Psychology, 54*, 395–400.

Vande Streek, H. E. (2000). Concurrent validity of the Minnesota Multiphasic Personality Inventory, Jesness Inventory, and the Carlson Psychological Survey in a sample of juvenile delinquents. *Dissertation Abstracts International, 60*(9-B), 4951B.

Weed, N., Butcher, J. N., & Williams, C. L. (1994, May). Development of MMPI-A alcohol and drug problem scales. *Journal of Studies on Alcohol*, 196–302.

Weis, R., Crockett, T. E., & Vieth, S. (2004). Using MMPI-A profiles to predict success in a military style residential treatment program with adolescents with academic and conduct problems. *Psychology in the Schools, 4*, 563–574.

Williams, C. L., & Butcher, J. N. (1989a). An MMPI study of adolescents: I. Empirical validity of the standard scales. *Psychological Assessment: A Journal of Consulting and Clinical Psychology, 1*, 251–259.

Williams, C. L., & Butcher, J. N. (1989b). An MMPI study of adolescents: II. Verification and limitations of code type classifications. *Psychological Assessment: A Journal of Consulting and Clinical Psychology, 1*, 260–265.

Williams, C. L., Butcher, J. N., Ben-Porath, Y. S., & Graham, J. R. (1992). *MMPI-A content scales: Assessing psychopathology in adolescents*. Minneapolis: University of Minnesota Press.

Williams, C. L., Perry, C. L., Farbakhsh, K., & Veblen-Mortensen, S. (1999). Project Northland: Comprehensive alcohol use prevention for young adolescents, their parents, peers, and communities. *Journal of Studies on Alcohol, 13*, 112–124.

Measures for Evaluating Child Sexual Abuse

William N. Friedrich

Mental health assessment of a sexually abused child or teenager is made more relevant and valid by including abuse-specific measures over and above more generic tests of intelligence, behavior, and personality functioning. In addition, sexually abused children more often than not have other risk factors operative in their lives, and a careful review of prior life stressors, as well as parent–child relationships, is also necessary.

This chapter describes and reviews a number of psychometric measures that may be used as part of a comprehensive forensic assessment of a child or adolescent when sexual abuse is an issue. The criteria I used in selecting the following 18 measures included established validity and adequate reliability, abuse specificity, the use of objective report or brief interview, citation frequency, ease of access from either the author or a publisher, and my personal experience with each in forensic evaluations. In addition, the selected instruments adhere to a theoretical framework presented in Friedrich (1995) and Friedrich (2002). This framework suggests that the functioning of the sexually abused child can best be understood along the domains of attachment quality; dysregulation, such

as posttraumatic stress disorder (PTSD); sexual behavior problems; dissociation; and self-perception, particularly shame and guilt related to the abuse.

This assessment model emphasizes the need to understand the results of an evaluation of a child or teenager within the context of the parent–child relationship. Consequently, parents are vital contributors to the evaluation process, both by providing information about their children and also by informing the evaluator as to how they have been affected by their children's abuse. It is also critical that the evaluator examine current parenting practices and parental stress, particularly given the empirical literature, which suggests that the effects of sexual abuse can be understood not as a function of the child or of the abuse but as function of a "third" factor, the family environment (Rind, Tromovich, & Bauserman, 1998).

At a minimum, it is recommended that the mental health assessment of the sexually abused child also include the evaluation of his or her sexual behavior problems, PTSD symptomatology, the degree to which his or her self-perceptions have been altered by the abuse, and the impact of the abuse on the child's parents. Valid measures for each of these functions are described next.

SUGGESTED MEASURES IN THE FORENSIC EVALUATION OF THE SEXUALLY ABUSED CHILD

Parent–Child Relations—Completed by Parent

Parent–Child Conflict Tactics Scales, Form A
Parent Support Questionnaire

PTSD/Dissociation—Completed by Parent

Traumatic Events Screening Interview—Parent
Child Dissociative Checklist
Child Behavior Checklist—PTSD
Parent Emotional Response Questionnaire
Trauma Symptom Inventory
Dissociative Experiences Schedule

PTSD/Dissociation—Completed by Child

Traumatic Events Screening Interview—Child
Children's Impact of Traumatic Events Scale—Revised
Trauma Symptom Checklist for Children
Child PTSD Symptom Scale
Adolescent Dissociative Experiences Scale

Sexual Behavior Problems—Completed by Parent

Child Sexual Behavior Inventory

Sexual Behavior Problems—Completed by Child

Adolescent Sexual Behavior Inventory

Self-Perception Evaluation Techniques—Completed by Child

Children's Attributions and Perceptions Scales
My Feelings About the Abuse
Negative Appraisals of Sexual Abuse Scale

Parent–Child Conflict Tactics Scales, Form A (Straus, Hamby, Finkelhor, Moore, & Runyan, 1998)

Recommended Uses: Provides an opportunity for the parents to report both positive and negative child-rearing and discipline strategies they have used with the child who is being evaluated.

GENERAL DESCRIPTIVE INFORMATION

Symptoms Assessed: Nonviolent discipline, psychological aggression, physical assault by parent.

Number of Items; Time to Complete: 22 items; 5–10 minutes [supplemental questions assess the frequency of selected discipline strategies in the previous week, neglect, and the sexual victimization of the child].

Response Format: 8-point format, ranging from 0 = "this has never happened" to 6 = "more than 20 times in the past year"; including 7 = "not in the past year, but this happened before."

Sample Items: Swore or cursed at child; took away privileges or grounded him or her.

Type of Outcome Measure Provided: Both qualitative and quantitative information about parenting practices.

Time Frame Assessed: Past year, but the parents are also able to indicate if they have ever used that discipline strategy.

Validity Scales: None.

Forensic Utility: This is a measurement approach that has been in use for 25 years. Although this is a new version, it builds on extensive validation research and practice. Although many of the strategies are clearly negative, with proper preparation of the parents, I have found that they can provide valuable information that helps in understanding other negative (and positive) parenting the child may have experienced separate from the sexual abuse.

Psychometric Information: Internal consistency across subscales ranges from .55 on Physical Assault to .60 on Psychological Aggression to .70 on Nonviolent Discipline. The measure is sensitive to treatment improvement, documented in studies with maltreating families.

Source: Straus, Hamby, Finkelhor, Moore, & Runyan, (1998).

How to Obtain Scale: The entire scale is reproduced in the cited article.

Parent Support Questionnaire (Mannarino & Cohen, 1996)

Recommended Uses: Evaluate parents' cognitions and perceptions of their own behaviors in response to their children's sexual abuse experience.

GENERAL DESCRIPTIVE INFORMATION

Symptoms Assessed: Behaviors fall into the categories of "Support" and "Blame."

Number of Items; Time to Complete: 19 items; takes 4–8 minutes to complete.

Response Format: 5-point scale ranging from "never" to "always."

Sample Item: "Do you ever feel the sexual abuse was your child's fault?"

Type of Outcome Measure Provided: Total scores on both "Support" and "Blame."

Time Frame Assessed: Preceding 2 weeks.

Validity Scales: None.

Forensic Utility: Evaluates a very important dimension of parental response that is not addressed by any other scale. "Fake good" tendency is high. Research to date is with preteens. Although most parents in forensic settings tend to score high on Support, any critical responses to the Blame items are very illuminating and quite relevant. It is most informative when used in combination with the Parental Emotional Response Questionnaire.

Psychometric Information: The scale was developed on a pilot sample and then validated with an independent sample. Internal consistency was calculated at .73 and .70 for Support and Blame, respectively. Measures of test-retest reliability ranged from .70 to .83. Scores are not correlated with symptom level in the child, and this can be viewed as either a positive or a negative. Further research is needed to fully understand the utility of this instrument, but for the time being, it provides relevant information that can be contrasted with observed parental support for the child.

Source: Mannarino & Cohen (1996).

How to Obtain Scale: Anthony P. Mannarino, Department of Psychiatry, Allegheny General Hospital, 320 E. North Avenue, Pittsburgh, PA 15212.

Traumatic Events Screening Interview—Parent (TESI-P) (Ford et al, 2000)

Recommended Uses: Semistructured interview to determine the number of traumatic events the child or teenager has experienced, including his or her sexual abuse, as well as the child's age at the time and his or her emotional response.

GENERAL DESCRIPTIVE INFORMATION

Symptoms Assessed: Prior traumatic events and the child's emotional response to them.

Number of Items; Time to Complete: 15 potential traumas are assessed, as well as the parents' history with these same events. If the event is endorsed, then there are 11 follow-up questions, as well as the opportunity to assess multiple experiences with the event. Completion time depends on the number of possible traumatic events the child has experienced. This interview can be utilized with the TESI-P (Brief), with follow-up questions from the TESI-P for any events that are endorsed. 5–30 minutes.

Response Format: Yes/no for the events, and yes/no/unsure for the aftermath.

Sample Item: "Has your child ever been in a serious accident like a car accident, a fall, or a fire?"

Type of Outcome Measure Provided: Determination of Criterion A of PTSD diagnosis.

Time Frame Assessed: Lifetime.

Validity Scales: None.

Forensic Utility: It is essential in the diagnosis of PTSD that a valid history of Criterion A events be assessed, and this brief interview, in combination with the Child PTSD Symptom Scale (CPSS) or a similar measure, can provide valid diagnostic information on this important syndrome.

Psychometric Information: Internal consistency is .81, and test-retest reliability after 2 weeks is .84.

Source: Ford et al. (2000).

How to Obtain Scale: Kay Jankowski, National Center for PTSD (116D), VA Medical Center, 215 N. Main St., White River Junction, Vermont 05009

Child Dissociative Checklist
(Putnam, Helmers, & Trickett, 1993)

Recommended Uses: Measuring the parent or observer report of dissociation symptoms in 5- to 12-year-old children in clinical or research settings.

GENERAL DESCRIPTIVE
INFORMATION

Symptoms Assessed: Items assess the domains of dissociative amnesia, rapid shifts in demeanor, cognitive abilities or behavior, hallucinations, spontaneous trance states, identity alterations, and aggressive and sexual behaviors.

Number of Items; Time to Complete: 20 items; 4–8 minutes to complete.

Response Format: 3-point format; 0 = "not true", 1 = "somewhat true", and 2 = "very true."

Sample Item: "Child does not remember or denies traumatic or painful experiences that are known to have occurred."

Type of Outcome Measure Provided: Total scores range from 0 to 40, with scores > 11 suggestive of dissociation.

Time Frame Assessed: Preceding 12 months.

Validity Scales: None.

Forensic Utility: Recommended in those cases in which abuse and trauma levels are high, given the fact that dissociation is thought to be more likely in severe cases of trauma and maltreatment. However, the items are lengthy, often have multiple foci, and children with ADHD receive elevated scores.

Psychometric Information: Internal consistency ranges from .78 to .95, and test-retest reliability ranges from .69 to .73. Higher scores on the CDC are reported in sexually abused children relative to normal children and in individuals with a diagnosis of dissociation, with scores highest for those diagnosed with multiple personality disorder.

Sources: Friedrich, Gerber et al. (2001); Putnam, Helmers, and Trickett (1993).

How to Obtain Scale: The entire scale is included in Putnam, Helmers, and Trickett (1993).

Child Behavior Checklist (CBCL)—
PTSD (Achenbach, 1991)

Recommended Uses: Enables the evaluator to score a derived scale from the Child Behavior Checklist (4–18 years) for PTSD-related symptoms.

GENERAL DESCRIPTIVE
INFORMATION

Symptoms Assessed: Intrusive experiences, avoidance, and hyperarousal.

Number of Items; Time to Complete: 7 items in the PTSD subscale (9, 29, 45, 47, 50, 76, and 100) and 16 in the combined PTSD/Dissociation subscale (8, 9, 13, 17, 29, 40, 45, 47, 50, 66, 76, 80, 84, 87, 92, and 100); time to complete entire CBCL can be 30 minutes.

Response Format: 3-point scale: 0 = "not true", 1 = "somewhat true", and 2 = "very true or often true."

Sample Item: "Nightmares."

Type of Outcome Measure Provided: Total score.

Time Frame Assessed: 6 months.

Validity Scales: None.

Forensic Utility: Many clinicians use the CBCL to obtain parent ratings of the child, and the derived PTSD scale enables them to use this measure more fully in the assessment of PTSD. However, it is not anchored to any specific trauma, and thus it is not a direct measure of PTSD. Because the parent completes the scale, comparative data about two parents within the same family are permitted.

Psychometric Information: Internal consistency values range from .74 for the 7-item scale to .85 for the 16-item scale. Scale values for psychometric indices differ between sexually abused and nonabused children and correspond significantly to independently diagnosed PTSD. Psychometric properties are directly related to the level of trauma exposure.

Sources: Achenbach (1991); Sim et al. (in press).

How to Obtain Scale: Can only be used with the CBCL, which is available from T. M. Achenbach, Center for Children, Youth and Families, University of Vermont, 1 South Prospect St., Burlington, VT 05401.

Parent Emotional
Response Questionnaire
(Mannarino & Cohen, 1996)

Recommended Uses: Recommended for use as a rapid screen to measure parental emotional reaction to their children being sexually abused.

GENERAL DESCRIPTIVE
INFORMATION

Symptoms Assessed: Examines such reactions as fear, sadness, guilt, anger, embarrassment, shame, and emotional preoccupation.

Number of Items; Time to Complete: 15 items, 4–6 minutes.

Response Format: 5-point scale, ranging from 1 = "never" to 5 = "always."

Sample Item: "I have felt embarrassed about my child being abused."

Type of Outcome Measure Provided: The higher the total score, the more intense and severe is the parent's emotional reaction to the abuse.

Time Frame Assessed: Preceding 2 weeks.

Validity Scales: None.

Forensic Utility: Some degree of parental emotional reaction is to be expected. An excessive response may detract from the parent's ability to support his or her child or reflect difficulty associated with the parent's own prior history.

Psychometric Information: Internal consistency is .87, and test-retest reliability at 2 weeks is .90. Scores are positively correlated with both behavior problems as measured by the CBCL and sexual behavior problems as measured by the CSBI.

Source: Mannarino and Cohen (1996).

How to Obtain Scale: Anthony P. Mannarino, Department of Psychiatry, Allegheny General Hospital, 320 E. North Avenue, Pittsburgh, PA 15212.

Trauma Symptom Inventory
(Briere, 1995)

Recommended Uses: Evaluate a variety of trauma-related symptoms in adults.

GENERAL DESCRIPTIVE
INFORMATION

Symptoms Assessed: 10 clinical scales assess a variety of symptom domains that are directly related to trauma and the diagnosis of PTSD, including anxious arousal, intrusive experiences, defensive avoidance, and dissociation, as well as symptom clusters that often coexist with trauma response, such as depression, anger/irritability, sexual concerns, dysfunctional sexual behavior, impaired self reference, and tension-reduction behavior.

Number of Items; Time to Complete: 100 items, 20 minutes.

Response Format: 4-point format, 0 = "never" to 3 = "often."

Sample Item: "Sudden disturbing memories when you were not expecting them."

Time Frame Assessed: Preceding 6 months.

Validity Scales: 3 validity scales, including atypical response, response level (related to defensiveness), and inconsistent responses.

Forensic Utility: Provides an excellent, broad-based assessment of PTSD and related symptoms, but it does not generate a diagnosis. It does have the added advantage of validity scales and scales related to sexual abuse sequelae, which enhances the use of the TSI in combination with a PTSD-specific diagnostic interview.

Psychometric Information: Internal consistency for the 10 clinical scales ranges from .84 to .87. Individuals who report past trauma score higher on all 10 clinical scales than those who do not. There is a high level of sensitivity and specificity when identifying individuals with a PTSD diagnosis.

Source: Briere (1995).

How to Obtain Scale: Psychological Assessment Resources, Box 998, Odessa, FL 33556; 1-800-331-TEST.

Dissociative Experiences Schedule
(Carlson et al., 1993)

Recommended Uses: Recommended for measuring symptoms of dissociation in clinical or research settings. It is designed for use with adults and also has been translated into a number of languages.

GENERAL DESCRIPTIVE
INFORMATION

Symptoms Assessed: Items assess dissociative amnesia, derealization, depersonalization, absorption, gaps in awareness, and imaginative involvement.

Number of Items; Time to Complete: 28 items; 5–8 minutes to complete.

Response Format: 11-point scale ranging from "never" = 0 to "always" = 100.

Sample Item: "Some people have the experience of finding themselves in a place and they have no idea of how they got there. Circle a number to show what percentage of the time this happens to you."

Type of Outcome Measure Provided: Total scale scores are the average of item scores and range from 0 to 100.

Time Frame Assessed: None specified.

Validity Scales: None.

Forensic Utility: This is the most widely used and validated measure to assess dissociation in older adolescents and adults. Consequently, if dissociation is a referral issue, then it is likely that this will be the instrument of choice. Its utility with the parents of the children you are evaluating is one of its best features, because dissociation is quite common in this sample and is not well assessed by other measures.

Psychometric Information: Internal consistency for the entire measure is .95. Test-retest reliability ranges from .79 to .96. Validity studies demonstrate higher scores in participants with trauma histories, and it is effective at predicting DID diagnoses.

Source: Carlson et al. (1993).

How to Obtain Scale: Sidran Foundation, 200 E. Joppa Road, Suite 207, Towson, MD 21286, www.sidran.org.

Traumatic Events Screening Inventory—Child (Ford et al., 2000)

Recommended Uses: This protocol is a guide for both clinical and research interviewing to screen for a child's history of exposure to potentially traumatic experiences. Data from this instrument establish whether the child endorses Criterion A symptoms from the *DSM-IV*.

GENERAL DESCRIPTIVE INFORMATION

Symptoms Assessed: The interview includes 16 items that survey the domains of potential traumatic experiences.

Number of Items; Time to Complete: 16 items; 10 minutes.

Response Format: Variable.

Sample Item: "Have you ever been in a really bad accident, like a car accident, a fall or a fire?"

Type of Outcome Measure Provided: Determines whether the child reports a traumatic event and a sense of objective harm or threat in response to the event.

Time Frame Assessed: Lifetime.

Validity Scales: None.

Forensic Utility: The protocol provides hypotheses, not a definitive identification, and the findings must be corroborated by data from independent sources. However, the older the child, the more likely he or she will be able to validly report past trauma. Given that the instrument also has a question related to prior sexual abuse (age differential of 5 years, which may or may not be relevant to the child's specific situation), the child's response to the sexual abuse item can be very illuminating.

Psychometric Information: Internal consistency has been calculated at .75 and test-retest correlations are as high as .82.

Sources: Ford et al. (2000); Ribbe (1996).

How to Obtain Scale: Kay Jankowski, National Center for PTSD (116D), VA Medical Center, 215 N. Main St., White River Junction, Vermont 05009 mary.k.jankowski@dartmouth.edu.

Children's Impact of Traumatic Events Scale—Revised (Wolfe, Gentile, Michienzi, Sas, & Wolfe, 1991)

Recommended Uses: Provides a thorough assessment of a range of sexual abuse–related symptoms, including sexual issues, posttraumatic symptoms, and distortions of self and other perceptions.

GENERAL DESCRIPTIVE INFORMATION

Symptoms Assessed: Four domains are assessed with 11 subscales: PTSD, Social Reactions, Attributions about Abuse, and Eroticism. PTSD-related subscales measure intrusive thoughts, avoidance, hyperarousal, and sexual anxiety. Social reaction subscales include negative reactions by others and social support. Attributions about Abuse subscales include self-blame/guilt, personal vulnerability, dangerous world, and empowerment. The Eroticism subscale assesses the degree to which the child has a sexual focus as a result of his or her abuse. This is a somewhat common outcome and worthy of assessment.

Number of Items: 78 items.

Response Format: 3-point format; 0 = "not true," 1 = "somewhat true," 2 = "very true."

Sample Item: "Some people blame me for what happened."

Type of Outcome Measure Provided: Total scores on 11 subscales, with PTSD symptoms that generally correspond to *DSM-IV* criteria.

Time Frame Assessed: None specified, but child is expected to respond in regard to "What happened between you and (perpetrator)?"

Validity Scales: None.

Forensic Utility: Serves a similar function to the Trauma Symptom Checklist for Children, although it is longer and more comprehensive in the range of symptoms that are assessed. Although not normed, there are published reference groups that the evaluator can refer to in arriving at the level of self-reported distress.

Psychometric Information: Internal consistency of the subscales ranges from .56 to .79. This scale correlates modestly with self-report measures, but not with parent reports. It discriminates well between sexually abused and nonabused children ages 8–16.

Sources: Chaffin and Schultz (2001); Wolfe et al. (1991).

How to Obtain Scale: Vicki V. Wolfe, Child and Adolescent Center, Children's Hospital of Western Ontario, London, Ontario.

Trauma Symptom Checklist for Children (TSCC) (Briere, 1996)

Recommended Uses: Measures a variety of trauma-related symptoms in children and adolescents, with specific sensitivity to sexual abuse.

GENERAL DESCRIPTIVE INFORMATION

Symptoms Assessed: PTSD-related items include cognitive avoidance, numbing, nightmares, and intrusive thoughts. Also assesses trauma-related symptoms of anxiety, anger, depression, dissociation, and sexual concerns.

Number of Items; Time to Complete: 54 items, 10–20 minutes to complete.

Response Format: 4-point format; 0 = "never," 1 = "sometimes," 2 = "lots of times," and 3 = "almost all of the time."

Sample Item: "Can't stop thinking about something bad that happened to me."

Type of Outcome Measure Provided: T-scores are calculated for six clinical scales: anxiety, depression, anger, posttraumatic stress, dissociation (including the subscales of overt dissociation and fantasy), and sexual concerns (including the subscales of sexual preoccupation and sexual distress). Scale scores are also calculated for the two validity scales. Computer scoring is also available.

Time Frame Assessed: None specified.

Validity Scales: Hyperresponse (unusually high response level) and Underresponse (unusually low response level).

Forensic Utility: The presence of two validity scales and a very respectable volume of independent validation for its use enhance the utility of this measure. In addition, it is normed and assesses not only for PTSD-related symptoms but also for sexual concerns.

Psychometric Information: Internal consistency for each subscale ranges from .77 to .89. TSCC subscales are correlated with other self-report measures in the expected direction, and the PTSD subscale is correlated with independent assessment of intrusive thoughts, sexual abuse history, and PTSD diagnosis. Scores on the TSCC are inversely related to levels of clinician-rated parental support.

Sources: Briere (1996); Friedrich, Jaworski, Huxsahl, & Bengston (1997); Sadowski and Friedrich (2000).

How to Obtain Scale: Psychological Assessment Resources, Box 998, Odessa, FL 33556; 1-800-331-TEST.

Child PTSD Symptom Scale (Foa, Johnson, Feeny, & Treadwell, 2001)

Recommended Uses: Recommended when a diagnosis of PTSD is needed for a child or adolescent.

GENERAL DESCRIPTIVE INFORMATION

Symptoms Assessed: Reexperiencing, avoidance, arousal, as well as functional impairment.

Number of Items; Time to Complete: 17 items for PTSD, and 7 items to assess functional impairment.

Response Format: 4-point format; 0 = "Not at all or only one time," 3 = "5 or more times a week/ almost always."

Sample Item: "Having upsetting thoughts or images about the event that came into your head when you didn't want them to."

Type of Outcome Measure Provided: Scores on each symptom cluster, as well as a total score and an index of functional impairment across 7 areas of life, for example, schoolwork.

Time Frame Assessed: Preceding 2 weeks.

Validity Scales: None.

Forensic Utility: The original study examined PTSD symptoms in children after one trauma, an earthquake; further research is needed with sexual abuse. However, given its relation to the Posttraumatic Diagnostic Scale (PTDS; see next item) and its use of functional impairment items, it is an improvement over earlier child PTSD scales. PTSD symptoms must be assessed in any comprehensive evaluation of sexually abused children and teens.

Psychometric Information: This is the child version of the Posttraumatic Diagnostic Scale (PTDS), a well-validated measure for the assessment of PTSD severity and diagnosis in adults. Consequently, although the CPSS is in the early stages of validation, it has a strong heritage. Internal consistency values were excellent and ranged from .70 for arousal, .73 for avoidance, .80 for reexperiencing, and .89 for total score. Test-retest scores were moderate to excellent; that is, kappa = .55 for diagnosis and .84 for severity using the total score. Subscale scores of the CPSS correctly classified 95% of PTSD cases.

Source: Foa, Johnson, Feeny, and Treadwell (2001).

How to Obtain Scale: Edna Foa, Center for the Treatment and Study of Anxiety, University of Pennsylvania School of Medicine, Department of Psychiatry, 3535 Market Street, 6th Floor, Philadelphia, PA 19104.

Adolescent Dissociative Experiences Scale (A-DES) (Armstrong, Putnam, Carlson, Libero, & Smith, 1997)

Recommended Uses: Recommended for measuring dissociative symptoms in adolescents.

GENERAL DESCRIPTIVE INFORMATION

Symptoms Assessed: Items assess four domains of dissociation, including dissociative amnesia, absorption and imaginative involvement, passive influence, and derealization and depersonalization.

Number of Items; Time to Complete: 30 items, requires 10–15 minutes to complete.

Response Format: Teenager rates the frequency by circling a number on an 11-point scale ranging from 0 = "never" to 10 = "always."

Sample Item: "I find myself standing outside of my body, watching myself as if I were another person."

Type of Outcome Measure Provided: Total scores are the average of item scores and range from 0 to 10. Scores over 3 are more likely to be associated with a dissociation diagnosis.

Time Frame Assessed: None specified, although the patient is told to "tell how much these things happen when you *have not* had any alcohol or drugs."

Validity Scales: None.

Forensic Utility: The ability of adolescents to report dissociation symptoms accurately remains controversial, but in cases in which caregivers have reported dissociation-like symptoms or in which the sexual abuse has been severe and accompanied by other maltreatment, assessment of dissociation is necessary.

Psychometric Information: Internal consistency for total score is .93 and a test-retest correlation of .77 has been reported. A-DES scores are elevated in those experiencing a childhood history of abuse compared with those who have not. Several studies have found higher scores for patients with dissociative disorder diagnoses.

Sources: Armstrong et al. (1997); Friedrich et al. (2001).

How to Obtain Scale: Sidran Foundation, 200 E. Joppa Road, Suite 207, Towson, MD 21286 www .sidran.org.

Child Sexual Behavior Inventory (CSBI) (Friedrich, 1997)

Recommended Uses: Provides information about the child from the parent/caregiver on a wide range of sexual behaviors in 2- to 12-year-old children.

GENERAL DESCRIPTIVE INFORMATION

Symptoms Assessed: Nine domains of sexual behavior are assessed. These include boundary problems, exhibitionism, gender-role behavior, self-stimulation, sexual anxiety, sexual interest, sexual intrusiveness, sexual knowledge, and voyeuristic behavior.

Number of Items; Time to Complete: 38 items (4 additional ones are provided in the manual for children exhibiting problems with sexual intrusiveness).

Response Format: 4-point format; 0 = "never," 1 = "less than 1/month," 2 = "1–3 times/month," and 3 = "at least 1/week."

Sample Item: "Puts objects in vagina or rectum."

Type of Outcome Measure Provided: Provides a Total Score, as well as scores on Developmentally Related Sexual Behavior and Sexual Abuse-Specific Items (SASI).

Time Frame Assessed: Previous 6 months.

Validity Scales: None.

Forensic Utility: Obtaining information about sexual behavior in a sexually abused child is essential for a comprehensive evaluation. Information from multiple caregivers can be obtained and contrasted to determine the concordance of reports in multiple settings. A large percentage of sexually abused children (40–60%) will exhibit elevated scores on this measure, but there are asymptomatic children as well. Given that it is a face-valid measure, it is vulnerable to exaggeration or mini-

mization. Evaluations of sexually aggressive children should also include the sexual aggression items published in the manual.

Psychometric Information: Internal consistency ranges from .72 in normative samples to .92 in sexually abused samples. Test-retest reliability at 4 weeks is .85 and at 3 months posttherapy is .47. Consistently discriminates between sexually abused and nonabused children, as well as between sexually abused children and children with psychiatric disorders.

Sources: Friedrich (1997); Friedrich et al. (2001).

How to Obtain Scale: Contact Psychological Assessment Resources, Box 998, Odessa, FL 33556; 1-800-331-TEST.

Adolescent Sexual Behavior Inventory (ASBI): Parent and Self-Report (Friedrich, Lysne, Sim, & Shamos, 2004)

Recommended Uses: These two measures ask identical questions, allowing parent report and adolescent self-report about both positive and negative sexual behaviors.

GENERAL DESCRIPTIVE INFORMATION

Symptoms Assessed: There are five similar factors for each scale: Sexual Knowledge/Interest, Deviant Sexual Interests, Sexual Risk/Misuse, Sexual Fear, and Concerns about Appearance.

Number of Items; Time to Complete: 50 items, 7–12 minutes.

Response Format: 3-point format; 0 = "not true," 1 = "somewhat true," 2 = "very true."

Sample Item: "I run away from home to unsafe places."

Time Frame Assessed: 12 months.

Validity Scales: Response level (reveals tendency to minimize or exaggerate responses).

Forensic Utility: This measure fills an important gap in that it enables a clinician to assess a range of sexual behaviors in teenagers. Evaluations of sexual abuse victims must include an assessment of sexual behavior, and the items included in this scale allow the evaluator to screen for the empirically related behaviors, for example, sexual victimization in relationships, promiscuity, and so forth. However, psychologists who work with adolescent sex offenders report that they begin with nondisclosure and only become more open during the course of treatment.

Psychometric Information: Internal consistency ranges from .78 to .90 across subscales. Total score on ASBI-Parent significantly correlated with total score and with Delinquency and Aggression subscales on the CBCL. Parent report also correlates significantly with TSCC Sexual Concerns. ASBI-Self correlates with CBCL Aggression and also with TSCC Sexual Concerns. Sexually abused teens differ from nonabused psychiatric teens on ASBI-Parent subscales of Knowledge/Interest, Deviant Interest, Sexual Risk/Misuse, and Fear. Similar differences, except for Deviant Interest, exist for the ASBI-Self.

Sources: Friedrich et al. (2004); Friedrich (2002) (ASBI is contained in this volume).

How to Obtain Scale: The Mayo Clinic, Generose 1B, Rochester, MN 55905.

Children's Attributions and Perceptions Scales
(Mannarino & Cohen, 1994)

Recommended Uses: Recommended to interview the child regarding their attributions and perceptions related to their sexual abuse. Items are not duplicated by existing instruments.

GENERAL DESCRIPTIVE
INFORMATION

Symptoms Assessed: Feeling different from peers, responsibility for negative events, credibility with adults, and interpersonal trust.

Number of Items; Time to Complete: 18 items, 4–8 minutes.

Response Format: 5-point format, 1 = "never" to 5 = "always."

Sample Item: " Do you blame yourself when things go wrong?"

Type of Outcome Measure Provided: Yields a total score and four subscale scores: Feeling Different from Peers, Personal Attributions for Negative Events, Perceived Credibility, and Interpersonal Trust.

Time Frame Assessed: Previous 6 months.

Validity Scales: None.

Forensic Utility: It is recommended that any evaluation of a sexually abused child or adolescent include data from the patient about his or her attributions for the events and assess the degree to which the child has a more pessimistic or guilty view of him- or herself and his or her life. The data can complement information about PTSD or an affective disorder in the child.

Psychometric Information: Internal-consistency scores range from .64 to .73 across the four subscales, and 2-week test-retest reliability for the total score is .75. Total and three of four subscale scores distinguish between abused and nonabused children.

Source: Mannarino and Cohen (1994).

How to Obtain Scale: Anthony P. Mannarino, Department of Psychiatry, Allegheny General Hospital, 320 E. North Avenue, Pittsburgh, PA 15212.

My Feelings About the Abuse
(Feiring, Taska, & Lewis, 1998)

Recommended Uses: Recommended for use as a brief assessment of shame related to the sexual abuse experience.

GENERAL DESCRIPTIVE
INFORMATION

Symptom Assessed: Shame related to victimization.

Number of Items; Time to Complete: Four items, 1 minute (an eight-item version is now being used, but there are no data on psychometric features).

Response Format: 3-point format; 1 = "not true," 2 = "somewhat true," 3 = "very true."

Sample Item: "When I think about what happened, I want to go away and hide."

Type of Outcome Measure Provided: Total score.

Time Frame Assessed: Not specified.

Validity Scales: None.

Forensic Utility: This measure is most useful in understanding the impact of sexual abuse on children and adolescents, particularly in combination with objective symptom scales and with general attributional style, as well as with abuse severity. I believe it gives explanatory power to the evaluator who is trying to understand the persistently symptomatic victim.

Psychometric Information: Internal consistency has been measured at .87, and test-retest reliability after 2 weeks was .78. Two studies have found that shame appears to mediate the relation between abuse attributions and symptoms.

Sources: Feiring, Taska, and Lewis (1998); Feiring, Taska, and Chen (2002).

How to Obtain Scale: Candace Feiring, Institute for the Study of Child Development, UMDNJ-Robert Wood Johnson Medical School, 97 Paterson Street, New Brunswick, NJ 08903.

Negative Appraisals of Sexual Abuse Scale (Spaccarelli, 1995)

Recommended Uses: Determines the specific meaning of the sexual abuse events to the individual child and teenager. Scores are consistent with the cognitive coping model that emphasizes that it is the individual's perceptions of the event that best predict coping, rather than the event alone.

GENERAL DESCRIPTIVE INFORMATION

Symptoms Assessed: Eight different groups of negative appraisals, including physical pain/damage; negative self-evaluation; global, negative self-evaluation; sexuality; negative self-evaluation by others; loss of desired resources; harm to relationships/security; harm to others; and criticism of others.

Number of Items; Time to Complete: 56 items, 10–15 minutes.

Response Format: 4-point scale, ranging from "not at all" to "a lot."

Sample Item: All items begin with a root that is worded as follows: "In relation to what happened with that person, did it ever make you think or feel that…" [you were a bad person; you would get sick or catch a disease, etc.].

Type of Outcome Measure Provided: Eight subscale scores.

Time Frame Assessed: The postabuse time period.

Validity Scales: None.

Forensic Utility: Responses provide a critical link to understanding why some victims are more symptomatic and others are less so. This scale helps the evaluator understand the unique attributions that the victim made about the abuse.

Psychometric Information: The eight scales, ranging from four to nine items each, have alpha coefficients ranging from .78 to .90. Negative appraisal scores were related to victims' self-reports of depression, anxiety, and posttraumatic stress symptoms and to parent reports of child depression and total symptoms. The scores predicted unique variance after controlling for level of stressful events experienced.

Source: Spaccarelli (1995).

How to Obtain Scale: Complete measure, scoring information, and scale means and standard deviations are available in the article cited.

SUMMARY

Forensic conclusions by mental health evaluators often rely on the use of multiple methods of data collection, sometimes including specific types of psychometric measures relevant for their purpose. The assessment of the sexually abused child is always complex and requires the consideration of a number of different types of psychological processes. Carefully selected instruments that are valid for their purpose can significantly improve the potential contribution of the forensic report. The foregoing review of different measures provides the mental health professional with a choice of various types of assessment tools that should enhance the breadth, accuracy, and relevance of evaluation findings.

References

Achenbach, T. M. (1991). *Manual for the Child Behavior Checklist/4–18 and 1991 Profile*. Burlington: University of Vermont, Department of Psychiatry.

Armstrong, J., Putnam, F. W., Carlson, E., Libero, D., & Smith, S. (1997). Development and validation of a measure of adolescent dissociation: The Adolescent Dissociative Experiences Scale. *Journal of Nervous and Mental Disease, 185*, 491–497.

Briere, J. (1995). *Trauma Symptom Inventory*. Odessa, FL: Psychological Assessment Resources.

Briere, J. (1996). *Trauma Symptom Checklist—Children.* Odessa, FL: Psychological Assessment Resources.

Carlson, E. B., Putnam, F. W., Ross, C. A., Torem, M., Coons, P., Dill, D. L., et al. (1993). Validity of the Dissociative Experiences Scale in screening for multiple personality disorder: A multicenter study. *American Journal of Psychiatry, 150,* 1030–1036.

Chaffin, M., & Schultz, S. (2001). Psychometric evaluation of the Children's Impact of Traumatic Events Scale—Revised. *Child Abuse and Neglect, 25,* 401–411.

Feiring, C., Taska, L., & Chen, K. (2002). Trying to understand why horrible things happen: Attribution, shame and symptom development. *Child Maltreatment, 7,* 26–41.

Feiring, C., Taska, L., & Lewis, M. (1998). The role of shame and attributional style in children's and adolescents adaptation to sexual abuse. *Child Maltreatment, 3,* 129–142.

Foa, E. B., Johnson, K. M., Feeny, N. C., & Treadwell, K. R. H. (2001). The Child PTSD Symptom Scale: A preliminary examination of its psychometric properties. *Journal of Clinical Child Psychology, 30,* 376–384.

Ford, J., Racusin, R., Ellis, C. G., Daviss, W. B., Reiser, J., Fleischer, A., & Thomas, J. (2000). Child maltreatment, other trauma exposure, and posttraumatic symptomatology among children with oppositional defiant and attention deficit hyperactivity disorders, *Child Maltreatment, 5,* 205–218.

Friedrich, W. N. (1995). *Psychotherapy with sexually abused boys.* Newbury Park, CA: Sage.

Friedrich, W. N. (1997). *Child Sexual Behavior Inventory.* Odessa, FL: Psychological Assessment Resources.

Friedrich, W. N. (2002). *Psychological assessment of sexually abused children, adolescents, and their parents.* Newbury Park, CA: Sage.

Friedrich, W. N., Fisher, J., Dittner, C., Acton, R., Berliner, L., Butler, J., et al. (2001). Child Sexual Behavior Inventory: Normative, psychiatric and sexual abuse comparisons. *Child Maltreatment, 6,* 37–49.

Friedrich, W. N., Gerber, P. N., Koplin, B., Davis, M., Giese, J., Mykelbust, C., & Franckowiak, D. (2001). Multimodal assessment of dissociation in adolescents: Inpatients and juvenile sex offenders. *Sexual Abuse, 13,* 167–178.

Friedrich, W. N., Jaworski, T. M., Huxsahl, J., & Bengston, B. (1997). Dissociative and sexual behaviors in children and adolescents with sexual abuse and psychiatric histories. *Journal of Interpersonal Violence, 12,* 155–171.

Friedrich, W. N., Lysne, M., Sim, L. A., & Shamos, S. (2004). Assessing sexual behavior in high risk adolescents with the Adolescent Clinical Sexual Behavior Inventory (ACSBI). *Child Maltreatment, 9,* 239–250.

Mannarino, A. P., & Cohen, J. A. (1994). The Children's Attributions and Perceptions Scale: A new measure of sexual abuse related factors. *Journal of Clinical Child Psychology, 23,* 204–211.

Mannarino, A. P., & Cohen, J. A. (1996). Family related variables and psychological symptoms found in sexually abused girls. *Journal of Child Sexual Abuse, 5,* 105–120.

Putnam, F. W., Helmers, K., & Trickett, P. K. (1993). Development, reliability, and validity of a child dissociation scale. *Child Abuse and Neglect, 17,* 731–742.

Ribbe, D. (1996). Psychometric review of Traumatic Event Screening Instrument for Children (TESI-C). In B. H. Stamm (Ed.), *Measurement of stress, trauma, and adaptation* (pp. 386–387). Lutherville, MD: Sidran Press.

Rind, B., Tromovitch, P., & Bauserman, R. (1998). Meta-analysis of research with college students on the impact of sexual abuse. *Psychological Bulletin, 124,* 22–53.

Sadowski, C. M., & Friedrich, W. N. (2000). Psychometric properties of the Trauma Symptom Checklist for Children (TSCC) with psychiatrically hospitalized adolescents. *Child Maltreatment, 5,* 364–372.

Sim, L. A., Friedrich, W. N., Lengua, L., Trane, S., Fisher, J., Davies, W. H., et al. (in press). Parent report of PTSD and dissociation symptoms: Normative, psychiatric, and sexual abuse comparisons. *Journal of Traumatic Stress.*

Spaccarelli, S. (1995). Measuring abuse stress and negative cognitive appraisals in child sexual abuse: Validity data on two new scales. *Journal of Abnormal Child Psychology, 23,* 703–727.

Straus, M. A., Hamby, S. L., Finkelhor, D., Moore, D. W., & Runyan, D. (1998). Identification of child maltreatment with the Parent-Child Conflict Tactics Scales: Development and psychometric data for a national sample of American parents. *Child Abuse and Neglect, 22,* 249–270.

Wolfe, V. V., Gentile, C., Michienzi, T., Sas, L., & Wolfe, D. A. (1991). Children's Impact of Traumatic Events Scale: A measure of post-sexual-abuse PTSD symptoms. *Behavioral Assessment, 13,* 359–383.

26

Measuring Adolescent Personality and Psychopathology With the Millon Adolescent Clinical Inventory (MACI)

Joseph T. McCann

The assessment of adolescent personality and psychopathology presents unique challenges for the clinical and forensic psychologist. Adolescence is a stage of development characterized by several changes, including the onset of puberty, a shift in social attachments from the primary family to peers and intimate partners, and expanding cognitive skills. As such, adolescence varies according to chronological age, developmental and social changes, and educational status (Petersen, 1988). Moreover, adolescence typically involves strong pressures and conflicts that result in modest psychological difficulties that one can reasonably consider normative for the teenage years (Coleman, 1992).

Considerable movement in the field of psychological assessment has focused on developing tests and procedures specifically for adolescents. No longer do psychologists simply view adolescents as younger individuals who can be assessed with measures traditionally based on adult samples. A number of assessment instruments have been developed specifically to measure the problems and concerns that are unique to adolescents (McCann, 1997, 1998a, 1998b).

One such tool, the Millon Adolescent Clinical Inventory (MACI; Millon, Millon, & Davis, 1993) consists of 160 items in self-report inventory format, with 31 scales measuring various personality styles, personal concerns, and clinical syndromes frequently encountered among adolescents in clinical settings. This chapter provides a concise overview of the development, psychometric properties, scales, and interpretation of the MACI. Although a detailed analysis of these issues falls beyond the scope of the chapter, this overview provides a context for understanding applicability of the instrument in forensic evaluations of adolescents.

THEORETICAL AND PSYCHOMETRIC FOUNDATIONS

Millon's theoretical model of personality and psychopathology distinguishes the MACI from other personality assessment instruments. The MACI draws on a comprehensive theory of personality and psychopathology (Millon, 1981, 1990; Millon & Davis, 1996) that guided construction and development of the instrument and that serves as a framework to facilitate interpretation. A basic principle of Millon's theory holds that clinical syndromes often develop as extensions of personality and that an understanding of the person is necessary to fully grasp the impact specific symptoms have on functioning. Originally proposed as a social learning model (Millon, 1969) and later expanded into an evolutionary model (Millon, 1990), the theory underlying the MACI posits three basic dimensions to personality. The first dimension involves the person's orientation to life preservation through the avoidance of painful experiences and the seeking out of pleasurable experiences (i.e., pain vs. pleasure polarity). The second dimension addresses the source of the person's life-enhancing experiences, found either in one's relationships with others or by focusing on oneself (i.e., self vs. other polarity). The third dimension addresses the person's instrumental style of seeking out life-enhancing experiences, through active manipulation of the environment or passive accommodation (i.e., active vs. passive polarity).

A major principle of Millon's theory assumes that normal personality is based on flexibility between each end of the polarity. Pathology develops when a person becomes fixated on a particular source of life-enhancing experiences (e.g., self) and a particular instrumental coping style (e.g., passive). The person may become fixated on the self (independent) or on the other (dependent), or the person can become conflicted about the desirability of self- or other-oriented pursuits (ambivalent). A person may develop disturbances in the pleasure-pain polarity by an absence of pleasurable life experiences (detached) or a reversal of pleasure and pain (discordant). Each of the individual personality patterns measured by the MACI reflects disturbances in instrumental coping styles, as well as the nature or source of life-enhancing experiences.

NORMATIVE SAMPLE

Intended for use with adolescents ages 13 to 19, the MACI has separate normative conversion tables for males ages 13–15, females ages 13–15, males ages 16–19, and females ages 16–19. As such, the MACI norms take into account differences not only between males and females but also between early and late adolescence. The normative sample included 1,017 adolescents, 579 of whom made up the development sample used to assign items to scales. Two cross-validation samples with 139 and 194 adolescents in each group provided data to develop base-rate conversions for raw scores.

The predominantly White normative sample included representation of African American, Hispanic, Native American, and other racial or ethnic groups. Adolescents in the MACI normative sample represented school grades 7 through the first year of college. All adolescents in the norm groups came from clinical settings, including outpatient mental health, inpatient mental health, general hospital units, residential treatment settings, and other mental health service settings (e.g., school counseling offices). A common issue often raised regarding the Millon inventories in the context of forensic settings involves the normative sample, which consists of data obtained from clinical or treatment settings rather than forensic settings. This concern becomes relevant to norm-referenced tests, in which the primary method of interpretation focuses on how a particular adolescent's score compares with those of others of the same age and gender. However, the MACI uses a criterion-referenced rather than a norm-referenced model, in which interpretation of raw scores involves determining whether or not a particular adolescent's score falls in the range for a specific diagnosis, clinical syndrome, or concern. Therefore, the MACI may prove useful in "diverse mental health settings" in which clinicians have an interest in "identifying, predicting, and understanding a wide range of psychological difficulties that are characteristic of adolescents" (Millon et al., 1993, p. 5).

DEVELOPMENT AND SCALE COMPOSITION

Development of the MACI followed a three-stage process of test construction: (1) theoretical-substantive, (2) internal-structural, and (3) external-criterion (Millon et al., 1993). The theoretical-substantive stage of construction involved developing individual items written to reflect significant content dimensions of the specific personality patterns outlined in Millon's (1969, 1981, 1990; Millon & Davis, 1996) theory, as well as prominent psychological concerns and clinical syndromes commonly observed in adolescents. Re-evaluation of items in subsequent stages of construction led to revisions intended to further refine the content validity.

The internal-structural stage of construction consisted of examining the frequency of endorsement of individual items, as well as correlations between item responses and scores on individual scales to ensure that individual scales on the MACI had adequate internal consistency. The external-criterion stage of construction focused on individual item responses and the correlation of overall scale scores with other measures of the key constructs. These external criteria consisted of other self-report instruments, as well as clinician ratings of personality traits, expressed concerns, and clinical syndromes from adolescents in the development and cross-validation samples.

Final selection of individual scales and indices on the MACI profile drew on the prominence of various personality styles in Millon's theory, as well as the clinical significance of particular concerns and syndromes across various clinical settings (Millon et al., 1993). This process resulted in the inclusion of some scales of greater interest in assessing adolescents (e.g., eating disorders), as opposed to adult populations (e.g., psychosis or bipolar disorder).

Another significant feature of the MACI involves use of a differential item weighting scheme that calls for certain items on each scale to contribute varying raw score points to the total scale score. Because the MACI has 160 items and 31 scales or indices, and because the number of items on each scale ranges from 16 to 48 items per scale, considerable item overlap exists across the scales. Nevertheless, such item overlap fits theoretical expectations given the similarity between various personality styles and clinical syndromes (e.g., egotistic vs. unruly borderline tendencies vs. identity diffusion). Differential item weighting provides a means for enhancing discriminant validity while preserving theoretically predicted comorbidity of certain personality styles, concerns, and clinical syndromes. Each item on a MACI scale contributes either 3, 2, or 1 raw score point, depending on how well the content of the item represents the construct under consideration (i.e., theoretical-substantive validity), as well as the relative degree to which the item correlates with the overall raw score of each scale (i.e., internal-structural validity). Each item on the MACI loads as a prototypic item (i.e., contributes 3 raw score points) for only one scale on the test. If an item occurs as scorable on any other scale, it serves as either a secondary (i.e., contributes 2 raw score points) or tertiary (i.e., contributes 1 raw score point) item.

Raw scores on the MACI convert to base-rate (BR) scores on a standardized scale based on the prevalence of various disturbances or clinical syndromes in the normative sample. BR scores follow an ordinal scale of measure (McCann, 1999) anchored at four major points: 0, 75, 85, and 115. A BR score of 0 corresponds to a raw score of 0, and a BR score of 115 corresponds to the maximum possible raw score. A BR score of 75 or higher corresponds to the "presence" of the personality style, expressed concern, or clinical syndrome, and a BR score of 85 or higher corresponds to the "prominence" of the construct being measured. A more detailed discussion of the BR score concept is contained in McCann (1999). For forensic purposes one must recognize that the BR score is criterion-referenced (not norm-referenced), that the underlying distribution of scores is skewed (as is the distribution of many psychopathological constructs in clinical and forensic populations), and that the scale of measurement is ordinal rather than interval. One final issue related to producing the MACI profile involves adjusting the final BR scores based on factors affecting the overall profile. These four adjustments include (1) the raw score of Scale X, which adjusts for the adolescent's level of self-disclosure; (2) a BR score greater than 85 on Scales EE (Anxious Feelings) and FF (Depressive Affect), which adjust for the tendency to overreport certain personality traits based on acute anxiety or depression, (3) the relative BR score difference between Scales Y (Desirability) and Z (Debasement), which adjust for biased self-reporting, and (4) a denial/complaint adjustment, which adjusts for either denial or overreporting based on the adolescent's personality style. Although research has not demonstrated whether these adjustments increase diagnostic accuracy, their effects have a more direct psychometric purpose; they preserve the prevalence-rate-based BR score conversions. As a result, the percentage of elevations that occur on any one MACI scale should correspond to the prevalence rate of the personality style, expressed concern, and clinical syndrome in the normative sample. These profile adjustments preserve these rates, thus increasing the accuracy of interpretive statements on the MACI, which state that an adolescent has a BR elevation on a particular scale that corresponds to the level observed in adolescents in the normative sample who were clinically judged to have that personality style, expressed concern, or clinical syndrome rated as present (i.e., BR ≥ 75) or prominent (i.e., BR ≥ 85).

ADMINISTRATION AND SCORING

The MACI is a paper-and-pencil psychological test that can be scored either by hand or by computer. Although differential item weighting and the profile adjustments complicate scoring of the MACI, making computer scoring a desirable option, clinicians new to the instrument should hand score the MACI several times to learn the nuances of the profile. The hand scoring will make the forensic psychologist more adept at asking questions about the instrument in courtroom testimony.

Overall, the MACI can be self-administered by adolescents between the ages of 13 and 19, inclusive, who have a sixth-grade reading level. For adolescents who have adequate auditory comprehension but whose reading level falls below sixth grade, the MACI can be administered orally, either with a standard tape recording of the items (available from the test publisher, NCS Assessments) or by having the examiner read individual items to the adolescent (McCann, 1999).

LIMITATIONS OF THE MACI

McCann (1999) has outlined various advantages and disadvantages of the MACI. Among the advantages cited is the brevity of the instrument, relative to other self-report measures. Brevity is particularly relevant to the assessment of adolescents, as resistance and noncompliance frequently arise in this age group. Another advantage of the MACI derives from the fact that the scales reflect a wide array of concerns and clinical problems specific to adolescence. In addition, the instrument is grounded in a comprehensive theory of personality and psychopathology developed by a member of the DSM-IV work group on personality disorders. This advantage is particularly relevant to forensic applications of the MACI, as the DSM-IV (American Psychiatric Association, 1994) represents a major learned treatise used to judge the diagnostic conclusions of the expert witness (Dyer & McCann, 2000). Other advantages of the MACI include the broad normative age range (13–19), separate norms for both males and females and for early and late adolescents, and good internal consistency reliability.

Disadvantages of the MACI include the fact that the profile does not have scales that measure more serious forms of psychopathology, such as thought disorder, paranoid ideation, or bipolar mood disturbances (McCann, 1999). Another concern raised about the MACI focuses on the item overlap across various scales. As discussed by McCann (1999), differential item weighting addresses this concern and provides a useful way of identifying specific items that can be used for enhancing interpretation.

RELIABILITY

Internal Consistency

The internal consistency reliability of MACI scales as determined for the development sample ($N =$ 579) and the cross-validation sample ($N = 333$) used the alpha coefficient. In the development sample, internal consistency coefficients ranged from a low of 0.73 on Scale Y to a high of 0.91 on Scale B. In the cross-validation sample, alpha coefficients ranged from a low of 0.73 on Scale 3 to a high of 0.90 on Scale B. These data indicate that the MACI scales provide uniformly precise measures of the constructs. Moreover, the high level of internal consistency observed in the development sample held steady when evaluated in the cross-validation sample.

Test-Retest

The MACI manual reports test-retest reliability coefficients for 47 adolescents selected from the development and cross-validation samples. The test-retest interval ran 5–7 days, and coefficients ranged from a low of 0.63 on Scale 1 to a high of

0.92 on Scale 9. The average test-retest reliability coefficient was 0.81 for the Personality Patterns scales, 0.79 for the Expressed Concerns scales, and 0.83 for the Clinical Syndromes scales. Although these results support the stability of MACI scores over a relatively short period of time, the long-term stability of MACI scores over months or years remains unknown.

RELIABILITY AND EVIDENTIARY STANDARDS

When using the MACI in forensic settings, the admissibility of the test with respect to legal standards constitutes an important consideration. Several standards exist for evaluating the admissibility of expert testimony, including the *Frye* test (*United States v. Frye*, 1923), also known as the general acceptance test, and the *Federal Rules of Evidence* (Green & Nesson, 1992) standard affirmed by the U.S. Supreme Court in *Daubert v. Merrell Dow Pharmaceuticals* (1993). Similarly, Heilbrun (1992) has outlined several criteria to guide selection of psychological tests in forensic evaluations based on the relevance of the test to the psycholegal issue under study, on the psychometric properties of the test, and on the appropriateness of conclusions drawn from test results. Heilbrun stated that psychological tests used in forensic evaluations should have established reliability, and he recommends a coefficient of 0.80 or higher; otherwise, explicit justification should be provided for accepting lower coefficients. McCann and Dyer (1996) have discussed how internal consistency reliability constitutes an appropriate standard for evaluating reliability of a psychometric instrument, because this form of reliability pertains to the precision of the measurement.

Internal consistency coefficients for 18 of 29 MACI scales exceed the 0.80 standard outlined by Heilbrun (1992), and five of the scales have coefficients that fall within a few points of this level. The remaining six scales have internal consistency coefficients that are 0.73 or greater, above the generally accepted level of 0.70 adopted in many psychometrics texts. Moreover, the mean test-retest reliability coefficients for the MACI Personality Patterns, Expressed Concerns, and Clinical Syndromes scales meet the 0.80 standard recommended by Heilbrun, although some variability exists across various individual scales; therefore, the MACI generally meets the reliability standard for use of psychological tests in forensic assessment. Once can address challenges to forensic use of the MACI based on those few scales with reliability slightly below this level, by noting that reliability of the MACI holds up better than other widely used multiscale inventories (McCann & Dyer, 1996).

VALIDITY OF THE MACI

Empirical Findings

Two major sources of data reported in the MACI manual helped to establish validity of the scales. The first criterion involved clinician ratings of individual personality patterns, expressed concerns, and clinical syndromes measured by MACI scales. Overall, there was modest correspondence between clinician ratings and MACI BR scores for the Clinical Syndromes scales, with the highest correlations obtained for scales CC (0.34), EE (0.39), and BB (0.52). According to McCann (1999), low convergent validity between clinician ratings and BR scores for the Personality Patterns and Expressed Concerns scales reflects a general trend in personality assessment research of low correlations between self-report measures and clinician ratings of personality. Moreover, the low convergence between clinician ratings and self-reports reflects method variance in which external observations of pathology may differ from subjective self-reports that are influenced by response styles (Dyer & McCann, 2000). Several other self-report instruments were used to test criterion validity of the MACI, including the Beck Depression Inventory (Beck & Steer, 1987), the Beck Anxiety Inventory (Beck & Steer, 1990), the Beck Hopelessness Scale (Beck & Steer, 1988), the Eating Disorder Inventory—2 (Garner, 1991), and the Problem Oriented Screening Inventory for Teenagers (National Institute on Drug Abuse, 1991). Overall, correlations between MACI BR scores and these collateral self-report instruments support the criterion validity of the MACI scales (Millon et al., 1993).

Other published research has supported the validity of the MACI. For instance, Hiatt and

Cornell (1999) found that scales 28 (Doleful) and FF (Depressive Affect) proved fairly accurate for identifying depression in adolescents, with overall hit rates ranging between 46% and 89% depending on the specific cutoff score used. These researchers also found, however, that scale GG (Suicidal Tendency) had a weak association with adolescent patients' placement on suicidal precautions. In another study of adolescent suicide attempters, Velting, Rathus, and Miller (2000) found the MACI useful as a dimensional, rather than a categorical, measure of maladaptive personality styles that discriminate between adolescents with and without histories of previous suicidal behavior.

Using factor analysis, Romm, Bockian, and Harvey (1999) identified four MACI profiles that are clinically useful in identifying types of adolescents who are often encountered in residential treatment settings. These profiles included (1) Defiant/Externalizing, (2) Inadequate/Avoidant, (3) Self-Deprecating/Depressive, and (4) Reactive Abused adolescents. Murrie and Cornell (2000) investigated the ability of the MACI to identify psychopathic personality traits as defined by the Psychopath Checklist—Revised (PCL-R; Hare, 1991). Their results showed that specific MACI scales correlated with psychopathy in a direction consistent with theoretical predictions and that scale BB (Substance Abuse Proneness) correctly identified 79% of high- and low-psychopathy adolescents. Moreover, Murrie and Cornell (2000) developed a 20-item psychopathy scale for the MACI that identified 83% of high- and low-psychopathy adolescents. As such, these independent studies on MACI validity support its use as a measure of adolescent psychopathology.

VALIDITY AND EVIDENTIARY STANDARDS

The psychological constructs measured in a forensic evaluation should have some demonstrated relevance to the psycholegal issues under consideration (Heilbrun, 1992; Marlowe, 1995). With respect to legal standards, admissibility of testimony based on psychological test results depends on various factors, including the specific rules of evidence in many state court jurisdictions (McCann, Hammond, & Shindler, 2003). General

acceptance of a test has become the overriding consideration. According to a recent survey of psychological test usage with adolescents among 346 psychologists, the MACI ranked 15th in overall use and as one of the top five most important test instruments for use with adolescents (Archer & Newsom, 2000). Under a *Daubert* (1993) standard, various issues guide admissibility, including the extent to which the test has found acceptance by peer review, has an established or knowable rate or standard error, and draws on testable principles or theory. As the research previously cited shows, the MACI has undergone peer review with a focus on the rate of error (in terms of correct diagnostic classification). Moreover, the results obtained by Archer and Newsom (2000) support the general acceptance of the MACI in the psychological community. Challenges to MACI-based expert testimony will likely arise with respect to questions about the relevance of test findings to the legal issue under litigation or the manner in which test results apply in a specific case (McCann & Dyer, 1996).

ASSESSING PROFILE VALIDITY: THE MODIFYING INDICES

In forensic evaluations, strong incentives often exist for clients to distort information they provide to the evaluator. Depending on the context, motivation may exist to minimize problems, exaggerate relatively minor concerns, intentionally deceive the examiner, or attempt to feign a major mental disorder. Psychological tests find frequent use in assessing the level of openness with which people report their problems and the level of distortion that may apply (McCann, 1998b). The MACI has four scales or indices used to evaluate reliability and validity of adolescent self-reports, which satisfies another standard outlined by Heilbrun (1992): that psychological tests used in forensic evaluations have some method for evaluating the examinee's response style.

Scale VV, the Reliability Index, does not appear as a formal scale on the MACI profile, but it consists of two rarely endorsed items with bizarre content. Positive scores on this index indicate random or irrelevant responding, extreme oppositional attitudes toward taking the test, confusion, reading difficulties, or other factors that affect consistency and reliability. Scores range from 0 to 2, and the MACI manual recommends considering scores of 0 as "valid," a score of 1 as "questionable," and a score of 2 as "invalid" (Millon et al., 1993).

Scale X, Disclosure, does not constitute a true scale in that no individual items compose the score. Rather, Scale X consists of the differentially weighted raw score totals from the Personality Patterns scales (i.e., scales 1 through 8B). Although originally designed to measure an adolescent's openness or willingness to reveal personal information in a neutral manner (i.e., independent of positive or negative impression management), scale X correlates positively with negative impression management and inversely with positive impression management. High scores indicate excessive reporting of personal problems, negative impression management, distress, or overreporting of symptoms. In addition, scale X is the only MACI scale considered to function bidirectionally in that low scores (i.e., BR < 35) indicate defensiveness, denial, minimization, or a lack of insight into one's problems.

Scale Y, Desirability, consists of items often endorsed by adolescents who attempt to create an unrealistically favorable impression. Items from this scale overlap with scales 4 (Dramatizing), 5 (Egotistic), and 7 (Conforming), so that elevations on these other scales can sometimes occur along with a Scale Y elevation. High scores reflect a need to be seen as well adjusted, a lack of insight, denial or minimization of problems, and a need for approval or acceptance. Although Scale Y scores do not figure in the formal computer algorithms that determine MACI profile validity, McCann and Dyer (1996) have suggested that the MACI profile might be invalid when BR scores exceed 90, unless the resulting profile appears inconsistent with a socially desirable response set (McCann, 1999).

Scale Z, Debasement, consists of items that are frequently endorsed by adolescents who report an unusual level of negative symptoms or self-critical attitudes and that overlap with Scales 2A (Inhibited), 2B (Doleful), 8B (Self-Demeaning), A (Identity Diffusion), and B (Self-Devaluation). High scores on these scales link to negative attitudes about oneself: excessive distress or a tendency to exaggerate or complain about concerns or problems. Although elevations here may suggest negative impression management, high scores on scale Z can also occur in adolescents who have a number of problems that cause significant distress. Scale Z does not figure into the computer algorithms for determining MACI profile validity; however, McCann and Dyer (1996) have suggested that the MACI profile might become invalid when BR scores exceed 90.

PERSONALITY PATTERNS SCALES

Each of the Personality Patterns scales was designed to measure a basic personality style outlined in Millon's theory of personality (Millon, 1981, 1990; Millon & Davis, 1996). Although these scales correspond to individual personality disorders outlined in the *DSM-IV* (American Psychiatric Association, 1994), the scales are intended to reflect personality styles along a continuum, from less pronounced to more severe levels of pathology. Individual names given to each scale reflect less severe variants of formal personality disorders, which serves as a reminder that some personality disturbances in adolescents may reflect maladaptive traits that occur situationally or that are limited to a distinct developmental phase. Nevertheless, the scales can assist in making personality disorder diagnoses within the context of a comprehensive assessment.

Scale 1: Introversive

This scale measures traits associated with schizoid personality disorder, including social detachment, a lack of pleasure or vitality, restricted emotional displays, and a preference for solitary activities. A factor analytic study revealed four major content dimensions: existential aimlessness, anhedonic affect, social isolation, and sexual indifference (Davis, 1994; McCann, 1997).

Scale 2A: Inhibited

This scale measures traits associated with avoidant personality disorder, including hypersensitivity to rejection, expectations that relationships will end painfully, and feelings of inadequacy. A factor analysis of individual items revealed six major content dimensions: existential sadness, self-conscious restraint, preferred detachment, sexual aversion, feelings of rejection, and unattractive self-image (Davis, 1994; McCann, 1997).

Scale 2B: Doleful

This scale measures traits associated with depressive personality disorders, such as chronic depression, pessimism, feelings of loss or abandonment by a major attachment figure, and brooding. Four content dimensions identified through factor analysis include: brooding melancholia, social joylessness, self-destructive ideation, and abandonment fears (Davis, 1994; McCann, 1997).

Scale 3: Submissive

This scale measures traits associated with dependent personality disorder, including passive dependency, excessive compliance, a lack of assertiveness, and neediness. According to a factor analysis of individual items, six content domains are associated with this scale: deficient assertiveness, respect for authority, pacific disposition, attachment anxiety, social correctness, and seeking guidance from others (Davis, 1994; McCann, 1997).

Scale 4: Dramatizing

This scale measures traits associated with histrionic personality disorder, such as attention seeking, gregariousness, dramatic or manipulative behaviors, and excessive emotionality. A factor analytic study revealed five major content dimensions: convivial sociability, attention seeking, attractive self-image, optimistic outlook, and behavioral disinhibition (Davis, 1994; McCann, 1997). This scale is sometimes elevated in profiles with a socially desirable response set, particularly if scale 7 is also elevated (McCann, 1999).

Scale 5: Egotistic

This scale measures traits associated with narcissistic personality disorder, including grandiosity, a lack of empathy for others, feelings of entitlement, and strong needs for admiration and praise. Six content dimensions emerged in factor analysis: admirable self-image, social conceit, having a con-

fident purpose and identity, self-assured independence, empathic indifference, and feelings of superiority (Davis, 1994; McCann, 1997).

Scale 6A: Unruly

This scale measures traits associated with antisocial personality disorder, including rejection of social norms, deceitfulness and manipulative behavior, exploitation of others, and rejection of authority. A factor analysis yielded six content domains: impulsive disobedience, substance abuse, rejection of authority, unlawful activities, callous manipulation, and sexual absorption (Davis, 1994; McCann, 1997).

Scale 6B: Forceful

This scale measures personality traits associated with sadistic personality disorder as originally proposed in the *DSM-III-R* (American Psychiatric Association, 1987). These traits include aggressive control of others, intimidation, hostility, and a lack of empathy or concern for others. A factor analytic study revealed three major content dimensions: abrasive intimidation, precipitous anger, and deficient empathy (Davis, 1994; McCann, 1997).

Scale 7: Conformity

This scale is intended to measure personality characteristics associated with the obsessive-compulsive personality disorder, such as excessive conformity to external rules and expectations, rigidity, and emotional or behavioral constriction. Five content dimensions identified in a factor analysis of individual items included: interpersonal restraint, emotional rigidity, adherence to rules, social conformity, and responsible conscientiousness (Davis, 1994; McCann, 1997). This scale tends to measure positive impression management unless it is very highly elevated (i.e., BR > 85) or appears in combination with other scales that reflect negative personality traits or characteristics (e.g., scales 2A, 3, or 8B; McCann, 1999).

Scale 8A: Oppositional

This scale measures personality characteristics associated with negativistic or passive-aggressive personality disorder; despite its name, the scale should not be construed as a measure of oppositional defiant disorder (McCann, 1999). High scores link to irritability, negative attitudes toward others, vacillating self-image, and passive-aggressive behavior. Five content dimensions identified in a factor analysis included: self-punitiveness, angry dominance, resentment, inconsiderate social behavior, and defiant conduct (Davis, 1994; McCann, 1997).

Scale 8B: Self-Demeaning

This scale measures personality characteristics associated with self-defeating personality disorder as originally proposed in *DSM-III-R*, including self-effacing attitudes, internalization of negative attitudes about oneself, and low self-esteem. In a factor analysis of individual items, four content dimensions emerged: negative outlook about oneself or one's future, self-devaluation, undeserving self-image, and hopelessness (Davis, 1994; McCann, 1997).

Scale 9: Borderline Tendency

This scale measures personality traits associated with borderline personality disorder, including emotional instability, identity diffusion, and ambivalent attachments. Four content dimensions identified in a factor analysis of individual items included: empty loneliness, impulsive reactions to stress, uncertain self-image, and suicidal impulsivity (Davis, 1994; McCann, 1997).

EXPRESSED CONCERNS SCALES

Eight scales make up the Expressed Concerns section of the MACI profile. Originally developed as measures of difficulties unique to adolescents, these scales have also become viewed as a means of assessing the adolescent's perception of issues he or she finds troubling and willingly acknowledges (McCann, 1997, 1999). Some adolescents with problems in one or more of these areas, however, may not necessarily produce an elevated score on the respective scale because they lack willingness to admit or discuss the problem. For example, a teenager with a documented history of conduct problems involving manipulating and taking advantage of others may not necessarily produce an elevation on Scale F (Social Insensitivity) because he or she does not have insight into his or her callous behavior or does not view it as problematic.

Scale A: Identity Diffusion

This scale is intended to measure problems with direction in life, future goals, and self-development. Elevations reflect confusion and uncertainty about oneself, a lack of direction or focus, or poorly defined aspirations for one's career and future.

Scale B: Self-Devaluation

This scale measures adolescents' tendencies to evaluate themselves negatively. Therefore, high scores reflect feelings of inadequacy, low self-esteem, and self-criticism.

Scale C: Body Disapproval

This scale assesses problems with body image. Elevated scores indicate poor body image, dissatisfaction with one's physical appearance, and concerns over how one is maturing and developing physically.

Scale D: Sexual Discomfort

This scale evaluates an adolescent's level of discomfort or tension over issues related to sexuality and the denial of sexual feelings. Elevations are often associated with immature attitudes about sex, feelings of guilt or shame about sexual feelings, and discomfort talking about issues related to sex.

Scale E: Peer Insecurity

This scale is intended to measure problems or concerns that an adolescent has with respect to rejection by peers. High scores reflect feelings that one does not fit in well with peer groups, an inability to find secure and comfortable peer relationships, and negative self-appraisal relative to other teenagers.

Scale F: Social Insensitivity

This scale measures the extent to which an adolescent presents as indifferent to and unconcerned about the feelings and reactions of others. Elevated scores suggest callous manipulation of others, hostility, lack of empathy, and a disregard for the rights of others. In some cases in which an adolescent has a history of socially insensitive behavior, this scale may not necessarily yield elevated scores if the adolescent appears unwilling to acknowledge these behavioral propensities (McCann, 1999).

Scale G: Family Discord

This scale measures the extent to which an adolescent experiences conflict or tension in family relationships. Not surprisingly, this scale has the most frequent incidence of elevation in MACI profiles, in part because adolescents who experience problems often attribute blame to their parents. Elevations indicate strained family relationships, a feeling that parents do not understand, an unsupportive family situation, and feelings of parental rejection.

Scale H: Childhood Abuse

Intended to measure concerns about prior physical, sexual, or emotional abuse, this scale becomes elevated as a function of feelings of shame, embarrassment, or guilt over prior abuse. The fairly general item content means that elevations on this H scale do not necessarily reveal whether the abuse occurred recently or in the past, whether it consists of a particular type of abuse, or whether there are links to a particular perpetrator.

CLINICAL SYNDROMES SCALES

As a group, these seven scales measure clinical problems commonly observed in adolescent populations that usually constitute a major reason for initiating a psychological evaluation or treatment. Although some problems observed among adolescents do not link specifically to the Clinical Syndromes scales, selection of individual scales in this section of the profile evolved based on their general importance and frequency of occurrence across various settings. Some of the items on these scales overlap with particular Personality Patterns and Expressed Concerns scales, reflecting the theoretical principle that clinical syndromes often mir-

ror behavioral and emotional extensions of the adolescents' underlying personality style.

Scale A: Eating Dysfunction

This scale is intended to measure the likelihood that an adolescent suffers from an eating disorder such as anorexia nervosa or bulimia nervosa. Significant elements on this scale focus on body image disturbances and disrupted patterns of eating. Item content also reveals that secondary problems, such as depression and low self-esteem, also associate with high scores on this scale.

Scale BB: Substance Abuse Proneness

This scale measures problems related to alcohol and drug abuse in adolescents. High scores address excessive use of alcohol, social and academic problems related to substance abuse, and excessive alcohol- or drug-seeking behavior. In some cases, modest elevations may identify adolescents who may not currently actively abuse substances but who demonstrate potential hazards because of risk-taking or sensation-seeking behaviors and attitudes associated with substance abuse (McCann, 1999).

Scale CC: Delinquency Predisposition

This scale addresses the extent to which an adolescent has difficulty adhering to social norms and rules. Significant elevations correlate with defiance of authority, acting out, rule-breaking behavior, a lack of empathy toward others, or a history of legal problems.

Scale DD: Impulsive Propensity

This scale attempts to measure impulsive and reckless behavior. High scores link to sexual or aggressive acting out, excessive or dangerous risk taking, negative emotional outbursts, and a lack of concern about the consequences of one's behavior.

Scale EE: Anxious Feelings

Designed to assess general feelings of anxiety, tension, and worry, elevations on this scale indicate rumination, indecision, social fears, and hypersensitivity to rejection, as well as uneasiness about current life circumstances and worries about the future.

Scale FF: Depressive Affect

This scale measures depression, sadness, and dysphoria. Adolescents who score high on this scale report many symptoms associated with depression, including low energy, apathy, fatigue, sadness, pessimism, and hopelessness.

Scale GG: Suicidal Tendency

This scale assesses suicidal ideation, thoughts of self-harm, and a wish for death. Although no research exists on the accuracy of this scale for predicting suicide attempts (McCann, 1999), high scores typically reflect suicidal ideation, hopelessness, and a feeling that others would be better off if the adolescent were dead.

INTERPRETIVE STRATEGIES

As a multiscale inventory, the MACI measures a broad range of personality styles, clinical symptoms, and personal concerns. However, interpretation of the MACI profile requires an analysis not only of individual scales but also of patterns of scale elevations. Certain scale elevations take on different meanings depending on other scale elevations in the profile. Several factors affect the profile configuration, including the specific problems an adolescent is experiencing and psychometric properties, such as item overlap and response styles. McCann (1999) has outlined an integrated approach to MACI profile interpretation, recommending sequential consideration of certain factors. The first step involves reviewing relevant clinical and historical information about an adolescent to provide a background against which profile analysis takes place. The second involves assessing the validity of the MACI profile to determine whether the results provide an accurate picture of the adolescent's current functioning. Third, individual sections of the MACI profile are reviewed to identify prominent personality traits, expressed concerns, and clinical syndromes. In the final step, the profile is integrated in order to assess problems and concerns differently, depending on the adolescent's individual personality style. Other relevant factors to consider when integrating the MACI profile include the properties of the MACI itself (e.g., measurement issues related to items), the nature of the theoretical constructs being measured (e.g., personality styles and clinical syndromes that share common dimensions), and the individual context in which the adolescent evaluation takes place (e.g., whether a presentencing evaluation may increase the likelihood of socially desirable responding). McCann (1999) provides a more complete discussion of MACI interpretation.

FORENSIC APPLICATIONS OF THE MACI

The MACI has a number of potential applications in forensic settings (McCann & Dyer, 1996). Legal cases have illustrated some uses of the Millon inventories with adolescents. In *United States v. Dennison* (1986), for example, psychological test results provided a basis for expert testimony that informed the court of several mental health issues, leading the court to rule against transferring an adolescent charged with assault for trial in adult criminal court. Expert testimony has also addressed the emotional capacity of a juvenile victim witness to testify against an adult charged with sexually assaulting her (*In the Matter of Subpoena Issued to L.Q.*, 1988), the voluntary nature of confessions made by adolescents in criminal cases (McCann, 1998a), and various criminal issues such as mental state at the time of offense and sentencing (McCann & Dyer, 1996). Although the MACI has a wide range of applications in forensic settings, the most commonly encountered cases include child custody evaluations, personal injury cases, juvenile status offense and transfer hearings, violence risk assessment, and disputed confessions.

CIVIL APPLICATIONS

Child Custody and Parental Fitness Evaluations

In cases of divorce in which custody of the children is at issue, the primary consideration is the best interests of the child (Melton, Petrila, Poythress, & Slobogin, 1997). A different type of case in family court occurs when an allegation of chronic abuse or neglect arises and the overall fitness of a parent becomes an issue. Parental fitness evaluations differ from child custody examinations. According to Dyer (1999), the presumption in most child custody cases holds that either parent qualifies as fit—unless proven otherwise. Child custody decisions are guided by the best interests of the child standard; yet in parental fitness cases involving repeated chronic abuse or neglect, the decision to restrict or terminate parental rights must include consideration of the need for permanency planning and the likelihood that abuse or neglect will continue in the future.

Child custody and parental fitness evaluations focus largely on the psychology of the parents and the nature of their interactions with the children. Because the MACI has a lower age limit of 13, it will have limited uses in family court cases involving child custody and parental fitness. Parental fitness cases typically involve young children, and in child custody cases adolescents can usually inform examiners about their wishes and desires concerning placement. In some custody cases, there may be evidence of emotional or psychological maladjustment in younger adolescents that should be considered when making recommendations. As such, the MACI is not likely to have broad applications in parental fitness evaluations, given the normative age range of the instrument, but it has circumscribed utility in child custody evaluations in which psychological or emotional maladjustment is suspected in adolescents who are part of the evaluation process.

Personal Injury Cases

The psychological examination of adolescents who claim emotional or psychological damages in personal injury cases requires a comprehensive assessment involving careful review of the teenager's history, current clinical status, response style, and collateral information as to the adolescent's functioning both before and after the alleged injury. The potential utility of the MACI in these types of cases depends on the specific issues raised. For example, MACI is potentially useful for evaluating potential malingering or deception (McCann,

1998b), the chronicity of emotional turmoil, amenability to treatment, current emotional concerns, and personality factors that affect how an adolescent responds to stress. In one case, an adolescent claimed severe depression and suicidal ideation as a result of inadequate special education services. Although the legal claim suggested that the student had had good adjustment prior to the wrongful or negligent actions of the school district, elevations on the MACI Doleful (2B) and Depressive Affect (FF) scales not only revealed current depression but also suggested a chronic depression that had existed for several years, a finding supported by collateral records. These data alone did not provide clarification as to the cause of the depression or the degree to which school matters contributed. Rather, the data merely provided a counterargument to assertions that the student demonstrated good adjustment previously and suddenly became depressed as the result of the school system's actions.

Psychoeducational Evaluations

Numerous state and federal laws place a duty on schools that receive public funds to provide for the special education needs of students with learning disabilities, developmental disorders, and other mental conditions that adversely affect academic performance. An important source of information in psychoeducational assessment involves psychological testing related to the student's self-concept, emotional adjustment, social behavior, and other emotional factors that may become a potential focus of treatment related to the student's adjustment. Research has documented that many students with learning disabilities have negative self-perceptions, have less favorable peer ratings than other students, and often misinterpret social behaviors, which leads to interpersonal problems (Cook, 1979; Knoff & Paez, 1992). The MACI does not identify learning disabilities in students, but it can provide useful collateral information for evaluating a wide range of emotional and behavioral problems (McCann, 1999). In this context MACI data may help in the design of psychological interventions, as well as remedial programs, not only to address the student's specific educational needs but also to fit the student's personality style and individual clinical needs. Note, however, that, because of heterogeneity among personality styles and clinical concerns of learning-disabled students, no MACI profile specifically identifies learning-disabled students (McCann, 1999).

CRIMINAL APPLICATIONS

Status Offense and Juvenile Transfer

The creation of separate juvenile criminal courts in the United States came about because of the notion that young offenders require services tailored to the special needs of children and adolescents (Grisso, 1998). Juvenile criminal courts developed out of this treatment-and-rehabilitation-oriented model (Grisso, 1998; McCann, 1998b). Consequently, two legal procedures developed as a result of this philosophy for adjudicating young offenders as status offenses and for juvenile transfer (or waiver) hearings. Status offenses "criminalize" misbehavior in children and adolescents because of their legal status as minors. These offenses often follow from statutes that define the status of a Person in Need of Supervision (PINS) or Child in Need of Supervision (CHINS). Petitions for such designation permit juvenile courts to adjudicate young offenders for misbehavior such as truancy, failing to adhere to curfew, substance abuse, or associating with undesirable peers. Juvenile transfer hearings occur in certain egregious cases (e.g., violent crimes such as murder, rape, severe assault, or chronic criminal behavior) that determine whether the young offender should be transferred from the jurisdiction of juvenile court to adult court, where sentencing laws permit harsher and lengthier punishment.

Courts consider a number of factors when making the decision to transfer a juvenile offender to adult status or in adjudicating and sentencing a status offender (see Kinscherff, chapter 19, this volume). Many of these factors involve the psychological status of the youth, and the issues in status offense and juvenile transfer hearings overlap considerably. According to McCann (1998b), among the various factors that courts consider in these cases are the youth's need for or amenability to treatment (e.g., substance abuse treatment, inpatient vs. outpatient treatment); the need for criminal justice versus mental health placement; the risk

for suicide or homicide; the likelihood of recidivism; the stability and cohesiveness of the youth's family and social environment; and the youth's level of insight and capacity to make sound decisions. To the extent that the MACI provides information on these factors, it has utility in forensic psychological evaluations undertaken in status offense or juvenile transfer proceedings.

Violence Risk Assessment

A number of key variables are relevant to an adolescent's risk of harming others. The major variables to assess include: history of violent behavior (i.e., chronicity, recency, frequency, and severity or degree of harm to others), school problems, substance abuse, history of family problems (i.e., history of abuse, exposure to violence, or poor parental bonding), mental disorders, maladaptive personality traits or personality disorders (i.e., psychopathy, lack of empathy, impulsive anger), negative peer relations, lack of social supports, contextual factors (i.e., neighborhood crime, availability of drugs), and poor social supports (Borum, 2000; Grisso, 1998). The evaluation of risk for violence in adolescents should follow the principle that violent behavior has multiple determinants that encompass demographic and clinical characteristics of the youth, his or her social environment, stressors, historical factors, and contextual variables.

The MACI provides a useful measure of many relevant factors considered in violence risk assessment, although it remains important to recognize that the test does not encompass all relevant variables. Rather, the MACI provides one source of data interpretable within the context of other data sources. Relevant MACI scales that provide useful information in a violence risk assessment include measures of impulsivity (scale DD), of antisocial behavior and delinquency (scales 6A, F, and CC), of anger (scales 6A, 8A), of lack of empathy (scales 6B, F), of poor social supports and alienation (scales 1, 2A, E, and G), of psychopathy (scales BB, 6A, 6B, CC, DD; Murrie & Cornell, 2000), of substance abuse (Scale BB), of psychiatric disturbances (scales 2B, 8B, 9, A, B, EE, FF, and GG), and of history of abuse (Scale H).

The MACI does not provide measures for other relevant factors, such as thought disorder, paranoid thinking, bipolar mood disturbances, poor bonding to school, history of violent behavior, or important environmental or contextual factors such as access to weapons. Response styles can distort overall validity of the MACI profile (McCann, 1999). Therefore, evaluating the validity of individual MACI profiles requires recognition of the adolescent's tendency to deny, minimize, exaggerate, or in other ways distort his or her self-reports. This general vulnerability of self-report instruments to the influences of distorted responding requires that violence risk assessments incorporate a wide range of data from other data sources, such as mental health and legal records, as well as interviews with other individuals concerning the adolescent's risk for violence.

Disputed Confessions

In *Fare v. Michael C.* (1979), the U.S. Supreme Court held that even though a juvenile's request to have a probation officer present during police questioning did not constitute a request to have an attorney present, courts should undertake an examination of the circumstances surrounding a juvenile's waiver of Miranda rights to determine whether the waiver was knowingly and voluntarily made. As a result of these legal safeguards, there has been research into the capacity of adolescents to waive their Miranda rights and agree to police interrogation (Grisso, 1980, 1981). In addition to the capacity of juveniles to comprehend and waive Miranda rights, there has also been research on the effect of police interrogation tactics and the voluntary nature of confessions provided by juveniles in criminal cases (Gudjonsson, 1992; McCann, 1998a). Cases that involve disputed confessions also involve an array of potential issues, including the ability of an adolescent to understand verbal or written Miranda warnings, possible coercion during police interrogation, and the voluntary nature of a statement. McCann (1998b) has outlined various psychological assessment issues that arise when forensic examinations are sought for adolescents in disputed confession cases. Among the various factors to consider are the characteristics of the defendant (e.g., age, intelligence, reading level, personality factors), circumstances of arrest (e.g., timing, Miranda warnings used), the adolescent's mental state during custody (e.g., intoxication), and style of interrogation. The MACI

is likely to be of greatest use in delineating personality characteristics that increase (e g., submissiveness, self-demeaning) or decrease (e.g., oppositionality, forcefulness) the adolescent's propensity to acquiesce to external suggestion or pressure. In addition, the MACI may be useful in highlighting various aspects of the adolescent's mental state that affect his or her decision making in interpersonal situations, such as anxiety, worry, or feelings of inadequacy. It is important to remember, however, that findings from a psychological assessment in disputed confession cases provide information on how the adolescent might respond in an interrogation setting but that there are no validated psychological techniques that can determine the truthfulness or falsity of a confession (McCann, 1998a).

In one case an adolescent with a learning disability and no prior history of violence or mental health treatment provided a highly detailed confession in an attempted murder case following 10 hours of intensive police interrogation, during which it was suggested to him that he must confess if he ever hoped to receive help. His MACI revealed prominent submissive (scale 3) and conforming (scale 7) personality characteristics. The test results indicated minimal behavioral or emotional disturbance but a strong propensity to acquiesce to those in authority. No opinion was offered about the ultimate truthfulness of his confession, although several months after his conviction new evidence unequivocally demonstrated his innocence and resulted in overturning his conviction.

Limitations of Profile Evidence

One feature of multiscale psychological tests such as the MACI involves creation of a profile that is used to assess individual personality and psychological functioning. In forensic contexts, some attorneys attempt to seize on this feature by asking psychologists to offer opinions about whether or not a civil litigant or a criminal defendant "fits the profile" of someone in a given class of individuals. For example, a defense attorney may ask the expert to determine whether an adolescent accused of a sex offense fits the profile of a sex offender based on his MACI results. Counsel hopes to demonstrate that his or her adolescent client does not "fit the profile" of someone who would commit such an offense, thus creating a degree of reasonable doubt. Similarly, prosecuting attorneys may seek this type of expert testimony to prove that an adolescent "fits the profile" of a particular offender. Such profile evidence has inherent difficulties for a number of reasons outlined by McCann and Dyer (1996). One major difficulty grows out of faulty reasoning that confuses the probability of an event, given certain data, with the probability of the data, given a certain event. As a hypothetical example, suppose a forensic expert has empirical data showing that 65% of juvenile sex offenders have an elevated scale 6A (Unruly) on the MACI that exceeds a BR score of 85. Now suppose that an attorney raises this finding in a court proceeding and attempts to elicit expert testimony that the adolescent on trial also has an elevation on scale 6A that exceeds a BR score of 85. Such a presentation could readily create an incorrect presumption in the minds of jurors that a 65% probability exists that the adolescent most likely qualifies as a sex offender. Such a conclusion is both inaccurate and based on faulty reasoning. Even if one can demonstrate that only 15% of non-sex offenders have elevations on scale 6A that exceed a BR of 85, one cannot make any predictive or conclusive statements about the likelihood that the adolescent is a sex offender based on MACI results, because many non-sex offenders also have elevations on scale 6A.

Another problem with profile evidence involves attempting to use psychological test data validated for one purpose (i.e., the assessment of personality and psychopathology) to establish the validity of something for which the data have no predictive validity (i.e., guilt or innocence). As such, psychologists who use the MACI in forensic settings should be cautious when asked to use the test results for proving or disproving that an adolescent fits some categorical risk or offense profile.

References

American Psychiatric Association. (1987). *Diagnostic and statistical manual of mental disorders* (3rd rev. ed.). Washington, DC: Author.

American Psychiatric Association. (1994). *Diagnostic and statistical manual of mental disorders* (4th ed.). Washington, DC: Author.

Archer, R. P., & Newsom, C. R. (2000). Psychological test usage with adolescent clients: Survey update. *Assessment, 7,* 227–235.

Beck, A. J., & Steer, R. A. (1987). *Beck Depression Inventory manual.* San Antonio, TX: Psychological Corporation.

Beck, A. J., & Steer, R. A. (1988). *Beck Hopelessness Scale manual.* San Antonio, TX: Psychological Corporation.

Beck, A. J., & Steer, R. A. (1990). *Beck Anxiety Inventory manual.* San Antonio, TX: Psychological Corporation.

Borum, R. (2000). Assessing violence risk among youth. *Journal of Clinical Psychology, 56,* 1263–1288.

Coleman, J. C. (1992). The nature of adolescence. In J. C. Coleman & C. Warren-Adamson (Eds.), *Youth policy in the 1990s: The view forward* (pp. 8–27). London: Routledge.

Cook, L. D. (1979). The adolescent with a learning disability: A developmental perspective. *Adolescence, 14,* 697–707.

Davis, R. (1994). *The development of content scales for the Millon adolescent clinical inventory.* Unpublished master's thesis, University of Miami, FL.

Daubert v. Merrell Dow Pharmaceuticals, Inc., 509 U.S. 579, 113 S.Ct. 2786 (1993).

Dyer, F. J. (1999). *Psychological consultation in parental rights cases.* New York: Guilford.

Dyer, F. J., & McCann, J. T. (2000). Millon clinical inventories, research critical of their forensic application, and Daubert criteria. *Law and Human Behavior, 24,* 487–497.

Fare v. Michael C., 442 U.S. 707 (1979).

Garner, D. M. (1991). *Eating Disorder Inventory—2: Professional manual.* Odessa, FL: Psychological Assessment Resources.

Green, F. D., & Nesson, C. R. (1992). *Federal rules of evidence: Selected legislative history and new cases and problems.* Boston: Little, Brown.

Grisso, T. (1980). Juveniles' capacities to waive Miranda rights: An empirical analysis. *California Law Review, 68,* 1134–1166.

Grisso, T. (1981). *Juveniles' waiver of rights: Legal and psychological competence.* New York: Plenum.

Grisso, T. (1998). *Forensic evaluation of juveniles.* Sarasota, FL: Professional Resource Press.

Gudjonsson, G. (1992). *The psychology of interrogations, confessions, and testimony.* West Sussex, UK: John Wiley.

Hare, R. D. (1991). *Manual for the Hare Psychopathy Checklist—revised.* Toronto: Multi-Health Systems.

Heilbrun, K. (1992). The role of psychological testing in forensic assessment. *Law and Human Behavior, 16,* 257–272.

Hiatt, M. D., & Cornell, D. G. (1999). Concurrent validity of the Millon Adolescent Clinical Inventory as a measure of depression in hospitalized adolescents. *Journal of Personality Assessment, 73,* 64–79.

In the Matter of Subpoena Issued to L.Q., 545 A. 2d 792 (N.J. Super. A. D. 1988).

Knoff, H. M., & Paez, D. (1992). Investigating the relationship between the Millon Adolescent Personality Inventory and the personality inventory for children with a sample of learning disabled adolescents. *Psychological Reports, 70,* 775–804.

Marlowe, D. B. (1995). A hybrid decision framework for psychometric evidence. *Behavioral Sciences and the Law, 13,* 207–228.

McCann, J. T. (1997). The MACI composition and clinical applications. In T. Millon (Ed.), *The Millon inventories: Clinical and personality assessment* (pp. 363–388). New York: Guilford.

McCann, J. T. (1998a). A conceptual framework for identifying various types of confessions. *Behavioral Sciences and the Law, 16,* 441–453.

McCann, J. T. (1998b). *Malingering and deception in adolescents: Assessing credibility in clinical and forensic settings.* Washington, DC: American Psychological Association.

McCann, J. T. (1999). *Assessing adolescents with the MACI: Using the Millon adolescent clinical inventory.* New York: John Wiley.

McCann, J. T., & Dyer, F. J. (1996). *Forensic assessment with the Millon inventories.* New York: Guilford.

McCann, J. T., Hammond, T. R., & Shindler, K. L. (2003). The science and pseudoscience of expert testimony. In S. O. Lilienfeld, J. M. Lohr, & S. J. Lynn (Eds.), *Science and pseudoscience in contemporary clinical psychology* (pp. 77–108). New York: Guilford.

Melton, G. B., Petrila, J., Poythress, N. G., & Slobogin, C. (1997). *Psychological evaluations for the courts: A handbook for mental health professionals.* New York: Guilford.

Millon, T. (1969). *Modern psychopathology: A biosocial approach.* Philadelphia: Saunders.

Millon, T. (1981). *Disorders of personality: DSM-III: Axis II.* New York: John Wiley.

Millon, T. (1990). *Toward a new personology: An evolutionary model.* New York: John Wiley.

Millon, T., & Davis, R. D. (1996). *Disorders of personality: DSM-IV and beyond.* New York: John Wiley.

Millon, T., Millon, C., & Davis, R. (1993). *Millon Adolescent Clinical Inventory manual.* Minneapolis, MN: National Computer Systems.

Murrie, D. C., & Cornell, D. (2000). The Millon Adolescent Clinical Inventory and psychopathy. *Journal of Personality Assessment, 75,* 110–125.

National Institute on Drug Abuse. (1991). *The adolescent assessment/referral system manual* (DHHS Publication No. ADM 91–1735). Washington, DC: U.S. Government Printing Office.

Petersen, A. C. (1988). Adolescent development. *Annual Review of Psychology, 39,* 583–607.

Romm, S., Bockian, N., & Harvey, M. (1999). Factor-based prototypes of the Millon Adolescent Clinical Inventory in adolescents referred for residential treatment. *Journal of Personality Assessment, 72,* 125–143.

United States v. Dennison, 652 F. Supp. 211 (D.N.M., 1986).

United States v. Frye, 293 F. 1013 (D.C. Cir., 1923).

Velting, D. M., Rathus, J. H., & Miller, A. L. (2000). MACI personality scale profiles of depressed adolescent suicide attempters: A pilot study. *Journal of Clinical Psychology, 56,* 1381–1385.

Index

CPSIA information can be obtained at www.ICGtesting.com
Printed in the USA
LVOW13*1219140813

347744LV00001B/11/P